An Economic Interpretation of The Constitution of The United States

&

The History Of The United States

CHARLES A. BEARD

2015 by McAllister Editions (MCALLISTEREDITIONS@GMAIL.COM). This book is a classic, and a product of its time. It does not reflect the same views on race, gender, sexuality, ethnicity, and interpersonal relations as it would if it was written today.

CONTENTS

BOOK ONE 1

AN ECONOMIC INTERPRETATION OF THE CONSTITUTION OF 1

THE UNITED STATES 1

- Introduction to the 1935 Edition. 2
- Preface 7
- Chapter 1. 8
- Chapter 2. 16
- Chapter 3. 32
- Chapter 4. 38
- Chapter 5. 42
- Chapter 6. 85
- Chapter 7. 102
- Chapter 8. 118
- Chapter 9. 129
- Chapter 10. 137
- Chapter 11. 161
- Conclusions. 176

BOOK TWO 178

HISTORY 178

OF THE 178

UNITED STATES 178

- PREFACE 179

PART I. THE COLONIAL PERIOD 181

- CHAPTER I 181
- CHAPTER II 189
- Chapter III 196
- CHAPTER IV 204

PART II. CONFLICT AND INDEPENDENCE 214

- CHAPTER V 214
- CHAPTER VI 225

PART III. THE UNION AND NATIONAL POLITICS 243
- CHAPTER VII 243
- CHAPTER VIII 254
- CHAPTER IX 264

PART IV. THE WEST AND JACKSONIAN DEMOCRACY 278
- CHAPTER X 278
- CHAPTER XI 287
- CHAPTER XII 302

PART V. SECTIONAL CONFLICT AND RECONSTRUCTION 312
- CHAPTER XIII 312
- CHAPTER XIV 321
- CHAPTER XV 333

PART VI. NATIONAL GROWTH AND WORLD POLITICS 349
- CHAPTER XVI 349
- CHAPTER XVII 359
- CHAPTER XVIII 370
- CHAPTER XIX 381
- CHAPTER XX 393

PART VII. PROGRESSIVE DEMOCRACY AND THE WORLD WAR 407
- CHAPTER XXI 407
- CHAPTER XXII 419
- CHAPTER XXIII 427
- CHAPTER XXIV 434
- CHAPTER XXV 442
- APPENDIX 459
- POPULATION OF THE UNITED STATES, BY STATES: 1920, 1910, 1900 469
- APPENDIX 471
- POPULATION OF THE OUTLYING POSSESSIONS: 1920 AND 1910 472

BOOK ONE

AN ECONOMIC INTERPRETATION OF THE CONSTITUTION OF

THE UNITED STATES

Introduction to the 1935 Edition.

This volume was first issued in 1913 during the tumult of discussion that accompanied the advent of the Progressive party, the split in Republican ranks, and the conflict over the popular election of United States Senators, workmen's compensation, and other social legislation. At that time Theodore Roosevelt had raised fundamental questions under the head of "the New Nationalism" and proposed to make the Federal Government adequate to the exigencies created by railways, the consolidation of industries, the closure of free land on the frontier, and the new position of labour in American economy. In the course of developing his conceptions, Mr. Roosevelt drew into consideration the place of the Judiciary in the American system. While expressing high regard for that branch of government, he proposed to place limitations on its authority. He contended that "by the abuse of the power to declare laws unconstitutional the courts have become a law-making instead of a law-enforcing agency." As a check upon judicial proclivities, he proposed a scheme for the "recall of judicial decisions." This project he justified by the assertion that " when a court decides a constitutional question, when it decides what the people as a whole can or cannot do, the people should have the right to recall that decision when they think it wrong." Owing to such declarations, and to the counter-declarations, the "climate of opinion" was profoundly disturbed when *An Economic Interpretation of the Constitution* originally appeared.

Yet in no sense was the volume a work of the occasion, written with reference to immediate controversies. Doubtless I was, in common with all other students, influenced more or less by "the spirit of the times," but I had in mind no thought of forwarding the interests of the Progressive Party or of its conservative critics and opponents. I had taken up the study of the Constitution many years before the publication of my work, while a profound calm rested on the sea of constitutional opinion. In that study I had occasion to read voluminous writings by the Fathers, and I was struck by the emphasis which so many of them had placed upon economic interests as forces in politics and in the formulation of laws and constitutions. In particular I was impressed by the philosophy of politics set forth by James Madison in number X of the *Federalist* (below, page 14), which seemed to furnish a clue to practical operations connected with the formation of the Constitution - operations in which Madison himself took a leading part.

Madison's view of the Constitution seemed in flat contradiction to most of the theorising about the Constitution to which I had been accustomed in colleges, universities, and legal circles. It is true, older historians, such as Hildreth, had pointed out that there had been a sharp struggle over the formation and adoption of the Constitution, and that in the struggle an alignment of economic interests had taken place. It is true that Chief Justice Marshall, in his *Life of George Washington*, had sketched the economic conflict out of which the Constitution sprang. But during the closing years of the nineteenth century this realistic view of the Constitution had been largely submerged in abstract discussions of states' rights and national sovereignty and in formal, logical, and discriminative analyses of judicial opinions. It was admitted, of course, that there had been a bitter conflict over the formation and adoption of the Constitution; but the struggle was usually explained, if explained at all, by reference to the fact that some men cherished states' rights and others favoured a strong central government. At the time I began my enquiries the generally prevailing view was that expressed recently by Professor Theodore Clarke Smith: "Former historians had described the struggle over the formation and adoption of the document as a contest between sections ending in a victory of straight-thinking national-minded men over narrower and more local opponents." How some men got to be "national-minded" and "straight-thinking," and others became narrow and local in their ideas did not disturb the thought of scholars who presided over historical writing at the turn of the nineteenth century. Nor were those scholars at much pains to explain whether the term "section," which they freely used, meant a segment of physical geography or a set of social and economic arrangements within a geographic are, conditioned by physical circumstances.

One thing, however, my masters taught me, and that was to go behind the pages of history written by my contemporaries and read "the sources." In applying this method, I read the letters, papers, and documents pertaining to the Constitution written by the men who took part in framing and adopting it. And to my surprise

I found that many Fathers of the Republic regarded the conflict of the Constitution as springing essentially out of conflicts of economic interests, which had a certain geographical or sectional distribution. This discovery, coming at a time when such conceptions of history were neglected by writers on history, gave me "the shock of my life." And since this aspect of the Constitution had been so long disregarded, I sought to redress the balance by emphasis, "naturally" perhaps. At all events I called my volume "an economic interpretation of the Constitution." I did not call it "the" economic interpretation, or "the only" interpretation possible to thought. Nor did I pretend that it was "the history" of the formation and adoption of the Constitution. The reader was warned in advance of the theory and the emphasis. No attempt was made to take him off his guard by some plausible formula of completeness and comprehensiveness. I simply sought to bring back into the mental picture of the Constitution those realistic features of economic conflict, stress, and strain, which my masters had, for some reason, left out of it, or thrust far into the background as incidental rather than fundamental.

When my book appeared, it was roundly condemned by conservative Republicans, including ex-President Taft, and praised with about the same amount of discrimination, by Progressives and other on the left wing. Perhaps no other book on the Constitution has been more severely criticised, and so little read. Perhaps no other book on the subject has been used to justify opinions and projects so utterly beyond its necessary implications. It was employed by a socialist writer to support a plea for an entirely new constitution and by a conservative judge of the United States Supreme Court to justify an attack on a new piece of "social legislation." Some members of the New York Bar Association became so alarmed by the book that they formed a committee and summoned me to appear before it; and, when I declined on the ground that I was not engaged in legal politics or political politics, they treated my reply as a kind of contempt of court. Few took the position occupied by Justice Oliver Wendell Holmes, who once remarked to me that he had not got excited about the book, like some of his colleagues, but had supposed that it was intended to throw light on the nature of the Constitution, and, in his opinion, did so in fact.

Among my historical colleagues the reception accorded the volume varied. Professor William A. Dunning wrote me that he regarded it as the "pure milk of the word," although it would "make the heathen rage." Professor Albert Bushnell Hart declared that it was little short of indecent. Others sought to classify it by calling it "Marxian." Even as late as the year 1934, Professor Theodore Clarke smith, in an address before the American Historical Association, expressed this view of the volume, in making it illustrative of a type of historical writing, which is "doctrinaire" and "excludes anything like impartiality." He said: "This is the view that American History, like all history, can and must be explained in economic terms . . . This idea has its origin, of course, in the Marxian theories."[1] Having made this assertion, Professor Smith turned his scholarly battery upon *An Economic Interpretation of the Constitution*.

Now as a matter of fact there is no reason why an economic interpretation of the Constitution should be any more partisan than any other interpretation. It may be employed, to be sure, to condemn one interest in the conflict of another interest, but no such use of it is imposed upon an author by the nature of the interpretation. Indeed an economic analysis may be coldly neutral, and in the pages of this volume no words of condemnation are pronounced upon the men enlisted upon either side of the great controversy which accompanied the formation and adoption of the Constitution. Are the security holders who sought to collect principal and interest through the formation of a stronger government to be treated as guilty of impropriety or praised? That is a question to which the present inquiry is not addressed. An answer to that question belongs to moralists and philosophers, not to students of history as such. If partiality is taken in the customary and accepted sense, it means "leaning to one party or another." Impartiality means the opposite. Then this volume is, strictly speaking, impartial. It supports the conclusion that in the main the men who favoured the Constitution were affiliated with certain types of property and economic interest, and the men who opposed it were affiliated with other types. It does not say that the former were "straight-thinking" and that the latter were "narrow." It applies no moralistic epithets to either party.

---

[1] *American Historical Review*, April, 1935, p.447.

On the other hand Professor Smith's statement about the conflict over the Constitution in his *interpretation* of the nature of things, in that it makes the conflict over the Constitution purely psychological in character, unless some economic content is to be given to the term "section." In any event it assumes that straight-thinking and national mindedness are entities, particularities, or forces, apparently independent of all earthly considerations coming under the head of "economic." It does not say how these entities, particularities, or forces got into American heads. It does not show whether they were imported into the colonies from Europe or sprang up as the colonial epoch closed. It arbitrarily excludes the possibilities that their existence may have been conditioned if not determined by economic interpretations and conceptions. Whoever does not believe that the struggle over the Constitution was a simple contest between the straight-thinking and narrower and local men of the respective sections is to be cast into outer darkness as "Marxian" or lacking in "impartiality." Is that not a doctrinaire position?

Not only is Professor Smith's position exclusive. It is highly partial. The men who favoured the Constitution were "straight-thinking" men. Those who opposed it were "narrower men". These words certainly may be taken to mean that advocates of the Constitution were wiser men, men of a higher type of mind, than the "narrower" men who opposed it. In a strict sense, of course, straight-thinking may be interpreted as thinking logically. In that case no praise or partiality is necessarily involved. A trained burglar who applies his science to cracking a safe may be more logical than an impulsive night watchman who sacrifices his life in the performance of duty. But in common academic acceptance a logical man is supposed to be superior to the intuitional and emotional man.

Nor is there exactness in such an antithesis as "straight-thinking" and narrowness. Narrowness does not, of necessity, mean lack of straight-thinking. Straight-thinking may be done in a narrow field of thought as well as in a large domain. But there is a true opposition in national-mindedness and local-mindedness, and the student of economic history merely enquires whether the antithesis does not correspond in the main to an economic antagonism. He may accept Professor Smith's psychological antithesis and go beyond it to enquire into its origins. But in so doing he need not ascribe into its origins. But in so doing he need not ascribe any superior quality of intellect to the one party or the other. To ascribe qualities of mind - high or low - to either party is partiality, dogmatic and doctrinaire partiality. It arbitrarily introduces virtues of intellectual superiority and inferiority into an examination of matters of fact.

In the minds of some, the term "Marxian," imported into the discussion by professor Smith, means an epithet; and in the minds of others, praise. With neither of these have I the least concern. For myself I can say that I have never believed that "all history" can or must be "explained" in economic terms, or any other terms. He who really "explains" history must have the attributes ascribed by the theologians to God. It can be "explained," no doubt, to the satisfaction of certain mentalities at certain times, but such explanations are not universally accepted and approved. I confess to have hoped in my youth to find "the causes of things," but I never thought that I had found them. Yet it seems to me, and does now, that in the great transformations in society, such as was brought about by the formation and adoption of the Constitution, economic "forces" are primordial or fundamental, and come nearer "explaining" events than any other "forces." Where the configurations and pressures of economic interests are brought into an immediate relation to the event or series of events under consideration, an economic interpretation is effected. Yet as I said in 1913, on page 18, "It may be that some larger world process is working through each series of historical events; but ultimate causes lie beyond our horizon." If anywhere I have said or written that "all history" can be "explained" in economic terms, I was then suffering from an aberration of the mind.

Nor can I accept as a historical fact Professor Smith's assertion that the economic interpretation of history or my volume of the Constitution had its origin in "Marxian theories." As I point out in Chapter I of my *Economic Basis of Politics*, the germinal idea of class and group conflicts in history appeared in the writings of Aristotle, long before the Christian era, and was known to great writers on politics during the middle ages and modern times. It was expounded by James Madison, in Number X of the Federalist, written in defence of the Constitution of the United States, long before Karl Marx was born. Marx seized upon the idea, applied it with rigour, and based predictions upon it, but he did not originate it. Fathers of the American Constitution were well aware of the idea, operated on the hypothesis that it had at least a considerable validity, and expressed it in numerous writings. Whether conflicting economic interests bulk large in contemporary debates over protective tariffs, foreign trade, transportation, industry, commerce, labour, agriculture, and the nature of the Constitution itself, each of our contemporaries may decide on the basis of his experience and knowledge.

Yet at the time this volume was written, I was, in common with all students who professed even a modest competence in modern history, conversant with the theories and writings of Marx. Having read extensively among the writings of the Fathers of the Constitution of the United States and studied Aristotle, Machiavelli, Locke and other political philosophers, I became all the more interested in Marx when I discovered in his works the ideas which had been cogently expressed by outstanding thinkers and statesmen in the preceding centuries. That interest was deepened when I learned from an enquiry into his student life that he himself had been acquainted with the works of Aristotle, Montesquieu, and other writers of the positive bent before he began to work out his own historical hypothesis. By those who use his name to rally political parties or to frighten Daughters of the American Revolution, students of history concerned with the origins of theories need not be disturbed.

For the reason that this volume was not written for any particular political occasion but designed to illuminate all occasions in which discussion of the Constitution appears, I venture to re-issue it in its original form. It does not "explain" the Constitution. It does not exclude other explana- tions deemed more satisfactory to the explainers. Whatever its short-comings, the volume does, however, present some indubitable facts pertaining to that great document which will be useful to students of the Constitution and to practitioners engaged in interpreting it. The Constitution was of human origin, immediately at least, and it is now discussed and applied by human beings who find themselves engaged in certain callings, occupations, professions, and interests.

The text of this edition remains unchanged, although I should make minor modifications here and there, were I writing it anew. Two facts, however, unknown to me in 1913, should be added to the record as it stands. Both were called to my attention by Professor James O. Wettereau, who has made important contributions to the history of the period. On page 93, I state that Benjamin Franklin "does not appear to have held any public paper." Evidence to the contrary is now available. In February, 1788, Franklin wrote concerning the public indebtedness: "Such Certificates are low in Value at present, but we hope and believe they will mend, when our new Constitution of Government is established. I lent the old Congress £3000 hard money in Value, and took Certificates promising interest at 6 per cent, but I have received no Interest for several years, and if I were now to sell the principal, I could not get more than 3s 4d for the Pound which is but a sixth part."[2] This adds Franklin to the list on page 150.

The second fact pertains to the formulation of Hamilton's funding system, based on the authority of the Constitution. It was long believed that this system was largely, if not entirely, the child of Hamilton's brain. But two letters found by Professor Wettereau among the Oliver Wolcott Papers in the Connecticut Historical Society indicate an opposite view. Hamilton's First Report on the Public Credit was laid before the House of Representatives on January 9, 1790. In November of the preceding year, William Bingham, "Philadelphia merchant, capitalist, and banker," wrote a long letter to Hamilton, in which he recommended "virtually all of the essential measures subsequently proposed by the Secretary of the Treasury." During the same month of 1789, Stephen Higginson, "mariner, merchant, and broker," of Boston, also wrote a letter to Hamilton advocating measures similar to those laid before Congress by the Secretary of the Treasury, and warning him against the perils of the opposition certain to be raised. Bingham who was actively engaged in speculating in public securities, asked Hamilton to inform him "how far any of my Sentiments coincide with yours." Whether Hamilton replied is unknown at present, but Thomas Willing, Bingham's father-in-law (below, page 108) claimed to have seen Hamilton's "whole price" suggested for funding. The new historical discoveries by

---

[2] A.H. Smyth, Writings of Franklin, Vol. IX, p. 635.

professor Wettereau throw light on the spirit of Hamilton's financial system and his connection with the mercantile and banking interests.[3]

To these notes of confirmation a memorandum of correction should be added. Page 29 may be taken to imply that the "landed aristocracy" of New York was *solidly* opposed to the Constitution, leaving no room for exceptions. Seldom, if ever, is there total class-solidarity in historical conflicts, and Doctor Thomas C. Cochran is entirely right in objecting to the implied generalisation.[4] He properly calls attention to the fact that "while the 'Manor Lords' feared land taxes they also held public securities to an extent which made many of the favourable to the establishment of adequate [federal] revenue. Thus while the strength of the Anti-federalists rested on the landed classes, the most powerful of these landlords were often found in the opposition ranks." Hence, although his interpretation is economic, it corrects a generalisation too sweeping in character, and should be properly noted.

Two other *caveats* should be entered. It has been lightly assumed by superficial critics, if not readers of the volume, that I have "accused the members of the Convention of working merely for their own pockets." The falsity of this charge can be seen by reference to page 73 of the original text still standing. There I say clearly: "The only point considered here is: Did they [the members] represent distinct groups whose economic interests they understood and felt in concrete, definite form through their own personal experience with identical property rights, or were they working merely under the guidance of abstract principles of political science?"

It has been lightly assumed that this volume pretends to show that the form of government established and powers conferred were "determined" in every detail by the conflict of economic interests. Such pretension was never in my mind; nor do I think that it is explicit or implicit in the pages which follow. I have never been able to discover all pervading determinism in history. In that field of study I find, what Machiavelli found, *virtu, fortuna*, and *necessita*, although the boundaries between them cannot be sharply delimited. There is a determinism, a necessity, in the world of political affairs; and it bears a relation to economic interests; otherwise Congress might vote $25,000 a year in present values to every family in the United States, and the Soviet Government might make every Russian rich, but this is not saying that every event, every institution, every personal decision is "determined" by discoverable "causes."

Nevertheless, whoever leaves economic pressures out of history or out of the discussion of public questions is in mortal peril of substituting mythology for reality and confusing issues instead of clarifying them. It was largely by recognising the power of economic interests in the field of politics and making skilful use of them that the Fathers of the American Constitution placed themselves among the great practicing statesmen of all ages and gave instructions to succeeding generations in the art of government. By the assiduous study of their works and by displaying their courage and their insight into the economic interests underlying all constitutional formalities, men and women of our generation may guarantee the perpetuity of government under law, as distinguished from the arbitrament of force. It is for us, recipients of their heritage, to enquire constantly and persistently, when theories of national power or states' rights are propounded: "What interests are behind them and to whose advantage will changes or the maintenance of old form accrue?" By refusing to do this we become victims of history - clay in the hands of its makers.

Charles A. Beard
New Milford,
August, 1935.

---

[3] "Letters from Two Business Men to Alexander Hamilton," by James O. Wetterau, *Journal of Economic and Business History*, Vol III, August, 1931, pp. 667 ff.

[4] *New York in the Confederation*, p. 17.

Preface

The following pages are frankly fragmentary. They are designed to suggest new lines of historical research rather than to treat the subject in an exhaustive fashion. This apology is not intended as an anticipation of the criticism of reviewers, but as a confession of fact. No one can appreciate more than I do how much of the work here outlined remains to be done. The records of the Treasury Department at Washington, now used for the first time in connection with a study of the formation of the Constitution, furnish a field for many years' research, to say nothing of the other records, printed and unprinted, which throw light upon the economic conditions of the United States between 1783-1787.

If it be asked why such a fragmentary study is printed now, rather than held for the final word, my explanation is brief. I am unable to give more than an occasional period to uninterrupted studies, and I cannot expect, therefore, to complete within a reasonable time the survey which I have made here. Accordingly, I print it in the hope that a few of this generation of historical scholars may be encouraged to turn away from barren "political" history to a study of the real economic forces which condition great movements in politics.

Students already familiar with the field here surveyed will discover that I have made full use of the suggestive work already done by Professor Turner, Drs. Libby, Ambler, and Schaper.

I am indebted to Mr Merwin of the Treasury Department for his great courtesy in making available the old records under his jurisdiction; to Mr. Bishop, of the Library of Congress, for facilitating the examination of thousands of pamphlets as well as for other favours; and to Mr. Fitzpatrick, of the Manuscript Division, for keeping his good humour while bringing out hundreds of manuscripts which seemed to yield results wholly out of proportion to the labour entailed.

I am under deep obligation to two friends, nameless here, without whose generous sympathy and encouragement, this volume could not have been written.

Charles A. Beard

Washington, D.C.
February, 1918.

Chapter 1.

Historical Interpretation in the United States.

Broadly speaking, three school of interpretation have dominated American historical research and generalisation. The first of these, which may be justly associated with the name of Bancroft, explains the larger achievements in our national life by reference to the peculiar moral endowments of a people acting under divine guidance; or perhaps it would be more correct to say, it sees in the course of our development the working out of a higher will than that of man. There is to be observed in the history of the struggle for the Constitution, to use Bancroft's words, "the movement of the divine power which gives unity to the universe, and order and connection to events."[5]

Notwithstanding such statements, scattered through Bancroft's pages, it is impossible to describe in a single phrase the ideal that controlled his principles of historical construction, because he was so often swayed by his deference to the susceptibilities of the social class from which he sprang and by the exigencies of the public life in which he played a by no means inconspicuous part. Even telling the whole truth did not lie upon his conscience, for, speaking on the question of the number of Americans who were descendants from transported felons and indented servants, he said that "Having a hand full, he opened his little finger."[6]

Nevertheless , Bancroft constantly recurs in his writings to that "higher power" which is operating in human affairs, although he avoids citing specific events which may be attributed to it. It appears to him to be the whole course of history, rather than any event or set of events, which justifies his theory. "However great," he says, "may be the number of those who persuade themselves that there is in man nothing superior to himself, history interposes with evidence that tyranny and wrong lead inevitably to decay; that freedom and right, however hard may be the struggle always prove resistless. Through this assurance ancient nations learn how to renew their youth; the rising generation is incited to take a generous part in the grand drama of time; and old age, staying itself upon sweet Hope as its companion and cherisher, not bating a jot of courage, nor seeing cause to argue against the hand or the will of a higher power, stands waiting in the tranquil conviction that the path of humanity is still fresh with the dews of morning, that the Redeemer of the nations liveth."[7]

The second School of historical interpretation, which in order of time followed that of Bancroft, may be called the Teutonic, because it ascribes the wonderful achievements of the English-speaking peoples to the peculiar political genius of the Germanic race. Without distinctly repudiating the doctrine of the "higher power" in history, it finds the secret to the "free" institutional development of the Anglo-Saxon world in innate racial qualities.

The thesis of this school is, in brief, as follows. The Teutonic peoples were originally endowed with singular political talents and aptitudes; Teutonic tribes invaded England and destroyed the last vestiges of the older Roman and British culture; they then set an example to the world in the development of "free" government. Descendants of this specially gifted race settled America and fashioned their institutions after old English models. The full fruition of their political genius was reached in the creation of the Federal Constitution.

For more than a generation the Teutonic theory of our institutions deeply influenced historical research in the United States; but it was exhausted in the study of local government rather than of great epochs; and it

---

[5] *The History of the Constitution of the United States (1882 ed.),* Vol. II, P. 284.

[6] American Historical Review, Vol II, p. 13.

[7] Bancroft, op cit., Vol I. P. 6.

produced no monument of erudition comparable to Stubb's *Constitutional History of England*. Whatever may be said of this school, which has as its historical explanation and justification,[8] it served one exceedingly useful purpose; it was scrupulously careful in the documentation of its preconceptions and thus cultivated a more critical spirit that that which characterised the older historians.

The Third school of historical research is not to be characterised by any phrase. It is marked rather by an absence of hypotheses. It representatives, seeing the many pitfalls which beset the way of earlier writers, have resolutely turned aside from "interpretation" in the larger sense, and concerned themselves with critical editions of the documents and with the "impartial" presentation of related facts.

This tendency in American scholarship has been fruitful in its results, for it has produced more care in the use of historical sources and has given us many excellent and accurate surveys of outward events which are indispensable to the student who would inquire more deeply into underlying causes.[9]

Such historical writing, however, bears somewhat the same relation to scientific history which systematic botany bears to ecology; that is, it classifies and orders phenomena, but does not explain their proximate or remote causes and relations. The predominance of such a historical ideal in the United States and elsewhere is not altogether inexplicable; for interpretative schools seem always to originate in social antagonisms.[10] the monarchy, in its rise and development, was never correctly understood as long as it was regarded by all as a mystery which must not be waded into, as James I put it, by ordinary mortals. Without the old regime there would have been no Turgot and Voltaire; Metternich and Joseph de Maistre came after the Revolution.

But the origin of different schools of interpretation in controversies and the prevalence of many mere preconceptions bolstered with a show of learning should not lead us to reject without examination any new hypotheses, such as the theory of economic determinism, on the general assumption of Pascal "that the will, the imagination, the disorders of the body, the thousand concealed infirmities of the intelligence conspire to reduce our discovery of justice and truth to a process of haphazard, in which we more often miss than hit the mark." Such a doctrine of pessimism would make of equal value for the student who would understand for instance, such an important matter a s the origin of the state, Mr Edward Jenk's severely scientific *History of Politics* and Dr. Nathaniel Johnston's *The Excellency of Monarchical Government, especially the English Monarchy, wherein is largely treated of the Several Benefits of Kingly Government and the Inconvenience of Commonwealths. . . . Likewise the Duty of Subjects and the Mischief of Faction, Sedition, and Rebellion*, published in 1686.

It is not without significance, however, that almost the only work in economic interpretation which has been done in the United States seems to have been inspired at the University of Wisconsin by Professor Turner, now of Harvard. Under the direction of this original scholar and thinker, the influence of the material

---

[8] It has been left to a Russian to explain to Englishmen to origin of Teutonism in historical writing. Se the introduction to Vinogradoff, *Villainage in England*. W.J. Ashley, in his preface to the translation of Fustel de Coulanges, *Origin of Property in Land*, throws some light on the problem, but does not attempt a systematic study.

[9] What Morley has said of Macaulay is true of many eminent American historical writers" "A popular author must, in a thoroughgoing way, take the accepted maxims for granted. He must suppress any whimsical fancy for applying the Socratic elenchus; or any other engine of criticism, scepticism, or verification to those sentiments or current precepts or morals which may in truth be very equivocal and may be much neglected in practice, but which the public opinion of his time requires to be treated in theory and in literature as if they had been cherished and held *semper unique et ab omnibus*." *Miscellanies*, Vol I., p. 272.

[10] For instance, intimate connections can be shown between the vogue of Darwinism and the competitive ideals of the mid-Victorian middle-class in England. Darwin got one of his leading ideas, the struggle for existence, from Malthus, who originated it as a club to destroy the social reformers. Godwin, Condorcet, and others, and then gave it a serious scientific guise as an afterthought.

circumstances of the frontier on American politics was first clearly pointed out. Under his direction also the most important single contribution to the interpretation of the movement for the federal Constitution was made; O.G. Libby's *Geographical Distribution of the Votes of the Thirteen States on the Federal Constitution*.

In a preface to this work, Professor Turner remarks that the study was designed to contribute "to an understanding of the relations between the political history of the United States, and the physiographic, social, and economic conditions underlying this history.... It is believed that many phases of our political history have been obscured by the attention paid to State boundaries and to the sectional lines of North and South. At the same time the economic interpretation of our history has been neglected. In the study of the persistence of the struggle for state particularism in American constitutional history, it was inevitable that writers should make prominent the state as a political factor. But, from the point of view of the rise and growth of sectionalism and nationalism, it is much more important to note the existence of great social and economic areas, independent of state lines, which have acted as units in political history, and which have changed their political attitude as they changed their economic organisation and divided into new groups."[11]

Although the hypothesis that economic elements are the chief factors in the development of political institutions has thus been used in one or two serious works, and has been more or less discussed as a philosophic theory,[12] it has not been applied to the study of American history at large - certainly not with that infinite detailed analysis which it requires. Nor has it received at the hands of professed historians that attention which its significance warrants. On the contrary, there has been a tendency to treat it with scant courtesy and to dismiss it with a sharpness bordering on contempt.[13] Such summary judgement is, of course, wholly unwarranted and premature; for as Dr. William Cunningham remarks, the validity of no hypothesis can be determined until it has been worked to its utmost limits. It is easier to write a bulky volume from statutes, congressional debates,[14] memoirs, and diplomatic notes than it is to ascertain the geographical distribution and political significance of any important group of economic factors. The theory of economic determinism has not been tried out in American History, and until it is tried out, it cannot be found wanting.

Sadly as the economic factors have been ignored in historical studies, the neglect has been all the more pronounced in the field of private and public law. The reason for this is apparent. The aim of instruction in these subjects is intensely practical; there are few research professorships in law; and the "case" system of teaching discourages attempts at generalisation and surveys.[15] Not even the elementary work has been done. There has been no generous effort to describe the merely superficial aspects of the development of private law in the United States. There has been no concerted attempt to bring together and make available to students the raw materials of such a history. Most of the current views on the history of our law are derived from

---

[11] See also the valuable and suggestive writings on American history by Professor W.E. Dodd, of Chicago University; W.A. Schaper, "Sectionalism in South Carolina," *American Historical Association Report* (1900), Vol I; A. Bentley, *The Process of Government*; C.H. Ambler, *Sectionalism in Virginia*. There are three works by socialist writers that deserve study; Simons, *Social Forces in American History*; Gustavus Myers, *History of Great American Fortunes and History of the Supreme Court*.

[12] See Seligman, *The Economic Interpretaion of History*.

[13] Vincent, in his treatise on *Historical Research* (1911), dismisses the economic theory without critical examination.

[14] The *Congressional Record* requires more care in use than any other great source of information on American Politics.

[15] Attention should be drawn, however, to the good work which is being done in the translation of several European legal studies, the "Modern legal Philosophy Series", under the editorial direction of the Association of American Law Schools. Perhaps the most hopeful sign of the times is the growth of interest in comparative jurisprudence. See Borchard, "Jurisprudence in Germany," Columbia Law Review, April, 1912.

occasional disquisitions of judges which are all too frequently shot through with curious errors of fact and conception.

Nor has England advanced far beyond us in the critical interpretation of legal evolution - its explanation in terms of, or in relation to, the shifting economic processes and methods in which the law is tangled. It is true that English scholars have produced admirable histories of the law in its outward aspects, such as the monumental work of Pollock and Maitland; and they have made marvellous collections of raw materials, like the publications of the Selden society. But apart from scattered and brilliant suggestions thrown off occasionally by Maitland[16] in passing, no interpretation has been ventured, and no effort has been made to connect legal phases with economic changes.

In the absence of a critical analysis of legal evolution, all sorts of vague abstractions dominate most of the thinking that is done in the field of law. The characteristic view of the subject taken by American commentators and lawyers immersed in practical affairs is perhaps summed up as finely by Carter as by any other writer. "In Free, popular states," he says, "the law springs from and is made by the people; and as the process of building it up consists in applying, from time to time, to human actions the popular ideal of standard of justice, justice is only interest consulted in the work. . . . The law of England and America has been a pure development proceeding from a constant endeavour to apply to the civil conduct of men the ever advancing standard of justice."[17] In other words, law is made out of some abstract stuff known as "justice." What sets the standard in the beginning and why does it advance?

The devotion to deductions from "principles" exemplified in particular cases, which is such a distinguishing sign of American legal thinking, has the same effect upon correct analysis which the adherence to abstract terms had upon the advancement of learning - as pointed out by Bacon. The absence of any consideration of the social and economic elements determining the thought of the thinkers themselves is all the more marked when contrasted with the penetration shown by European savants like Jhering, Menger, and Stammler. Indeed, almost he only indication of a possible economic interpretation to be found in current American jurisprudence is implicit in the writings of a few scholars, like Professor Roscoe Pound and Professor Goodnow,[18] and in occasional opinions rendered by Mr Justice Holmes of the Supreme Court of the United States.[19]

---

[16] For examples of Maitland's suggestiveness, see the English Historical Review, Vol IX, p. 439, for a side light on the effect of money economy on the manor and consequently on feudal law. See also the closing pages of his *Constitutional History of England*, where he makes constitutional law in large part of the history of the law of real property. "If we are to learn anything about the constitution, it is necessary first and foremost that we should learn a good deal about the land law. We can make no progress whatever in the history of parliament without speaking of tenure; indeed our whole constitutional law seems at times to be but an appendix to the law of real property" (p. 538). Maitland's entire marvellous chapter on "The Definition of Constitutional Law" deserves the most careful study and reflection. He was entirely emancipated from bondage to systematists (p. 539).

[17] J.C. Carter, *the Proposed Codification of Our Common Law (1884)*, pp. 6-8.

[18] Of the newer literature on law, see the following articles by Professor Roscoe Pound: "Do we need a Philosophy of Law?" Columbia Law Review, Vol. V, p. 339; "Need of a Sociological Jurisprudence," Green Bag, Vol. XIX, p. 607; Mechanical Jurisprudence," Columbia Law Review, Vol. VIII, p. 605; "Law in Books and Law in Action," American Law Review, Vol. XLIV, p. 12; Professor Munroe Smith, "Jurisprudence" (in the Columbia Law Review University Lectures in Arts and Sciences); Goodnow, *Social Reform and the Constitution*.

[19] Consider, for example, the following remarks by this eminent Justice in his dissenting opinion in the New York Bakery case. " The case is decided upon an economic theory which a large part of the country does not entertain. . . . The Fourteenth Amendment does not enact Mr. Herbert Spencer's *Social Studies* . . . .

What here has been said about our private law may be more than repeated about our constitutional history and law. This subject, though it has long held an honourable position in the American scheme of learning, has not yet received the analytical study which its intrinsic importance merits. In the past, it has often been taught in the law schools by retired judges who treated it as a branch of natural and moral philosophy or by practical lawyers who took care for the instant need of things. Our great commentaries, Kent, Storey, Miller, are never penetrating; they are generally confined to statements of fact; and designed to inculcate the spirit of reverence rather than of understanding. And of constitutional histories, strictly speaking, we have none, except the surveys of superficial aspects by Curtis and Bancroft.

In fact, the juristic theory of the origin and nature of the Constitution is marked by the same lack of analysis of determining forces which characterised older historical writing in general. It may be stated in the following manner: The Constitution proceeds from the whole people; the people are the original source of all political authority exercised under it; it is founded on broad general principals of liberty and government entertained, for some reason, by the whole people and having no reference to the interest or advantage of any particular group or class. "By calm meditation and friendly councils," says Bancroft, "the [the people] had prepared a Constitution which, in the union of freedom with strength and order, excelled every one known before.... In the happy morning of their existence as one of the powers of the world, they had chosen justice for their guide; and while they proceeded on their way with a well-founded confidence and joy, all the friends of mankind invoked success on their endeavour as the only hope for renovating the life of the civilised world."[20]

With less exaltation, Chief Justice Marshall states the theory, in his opinion in the case of McCulloch *v.* Maryland: "The government proceeds directly from the people; is 'ordained and established' in the name of the people and is declared to be ordained 'in order to form a more perfect union, to establish justice, insure domestic tranquillity, and secure the blessings of liberty' to themselves and their posterity. The assent of the States, in their sovereign capacity, is implied in calling a convention, and thus submitting that instrument to the people. But the people were at perfect liberty to accept or reject it; and their act was final.... The government of the union, then (whatever may be the influence of this fact on the case) is emphatically and truly a government of the people. In form and in substance it emanates from them. Its powers are granted by them, and are to be exercised directly on them, and for their benefit... It is the government of all; its powers are delegated by all; it represents all, and acts for all."[21]

In the juristic view, the Constitution is not only the work of the whole people, but it also bears no traces of the party conflict from which it emerged. Take, for example, any of the traditional legal definitions of the Constitution; Miller's will suffice: "A constitution in the American sense of the word, is an instrument by which the fundamental powers of the government are established, limited, and defined, and by which these powers are distributed among the several departments for their more safe and useful exercise, for the benefit of the body politic.... It is not, however, the origin or private rights, nor the foundation of laws. It is not the cause, but the consequence of personal and political freedom. It declares those natural and fundamental rights of individuals, for the security and common enjoyment of which governments are established."[22]

Nowhere in the commentaries is there any evidence of the fact that the rules of our fundamental law are designed to protect any class in its rights, or secure the property of one group against the assaults of another. "The Constitution," declares Bancroft, "establishes nothing that interferes with equality and individuality. It

---

General propositions do not decide concrete cases. The decision will depend on a judgement or intuition more subtle than any articulate major premise. 198 U.S. 75.

[20]   *Op. cit.* Vol. II, p. 367.

[21]   4 Wheaton, p. 316. No doubt the learned Justice was here more concerned with discrediting the doctrine of State's rights than with establishing the popular basis of our government.

[22]   S.F. Miller, *Lectures on the Constitution* (1891), p. 71.

knows nothing of differences by descent, or opinions, of favoured classes, or legalised religion, or the political power of property. It leaves the individual along-side of the individual. . . . As the sea is made up of drops, American society is composed of separate, free, and constantly moving atoms, ever in reciprocal action . . . so that the institutions and laws of the country rise out of the masses of individual thought, which, like the waters of the ocean, are rolling evermore."[23]

In turning from the vague phraseology of Bancroft to an economic interpretation of constitutional history, it is necessary to realise at the outset that law is not an abstract thing, a printed page, a volume of statutes, a statement by a judge. So far as it becomes of any consequence to the observer it must take real form; it must govern actions; it must determine positive relations between men; it must prescribe processes and juxtapositions.[24] A statute may be on the books for an age, but unless, under its provisions, a determinate arrangement of human relations is brought about or maintained, it exists only in the imagination. Separated from the social and economic fabric by which it is, in part, conditioned and which, in turn, it helps to condition, it has no reality.

Now, most of the law (except the elemental law of community defence) is concerned with the property relations of men, which reduced to their simple terms mean the processes by which the ownership of concrete forms of property is determined or passes from one person to another. As society becomes more settled and industrial in character, mere defence against violence (a very considerable portion of which originates in forcible attempts to change the ownership of property) becomes of relatively less importance; and property relations increase in complexity and subtlety.

But it may be said that constitutional law is a peculiar branch of the law; that it is not concerned primarily with property or with property relations, but with organs of government, the suffrage administration. The superficiality of this view becomes apparent at a second glance. Inasmuch as the primary object of a government, beyond the mere repression of physical violence, is the making of the rules which determine the property relations of members of society, the dominant classes whose rights are thus to be determined must perforce obtain from the government such rules as are consonant with the larger interests necessary to the continuance of their economic processes, or they must themselves control the organs of government. In a stable despotism the former takes place; under any other system of government, whee political power is shared by any portion of the population, the methods and nature of this control become the problem of prime importance - in fact, the fundamental problem in constitutional law. The social structure by which one type of legislation is secured and another prevented - that it, the constitution - is a secondary or derivative feature arising from the nature of the economic groups seeking positive action and negative restraint.

In what has just been said there is nothing new to scholars who have given any attention to European writings on jurisprudence. It is based in the first instance on the doctrine advanced by Jhering that law does not "grow," but in fact is, "made" - adapted to precise interests which may be objectively determined.[25] It was

---

[23]   Op. cit. Vol. II, p. 324.

[24]   See A. Bentley, *The process of Government.*

[25]   In the preface to his first edition, Jherinng says: "Die Schrift, von der ich hiermit die erste Halfete der Offentlichkeit ubergebe, ist eine Auslauferin von meinem Werk uber den Geist des romischen Rechts. Der letze Band desselben. . . schloss ab mit einer Grundlegung der Theorie der Rechte im subjecktiven Sinn. In der ich eine von der herrschenden abweichende Begriffsbesttimmung des Rechts im subjektiven Sinn gab, indem ich an Stelle des Willens, auf den jene den Begriff desselben grundeten das Interesse setze. Dem folgenden Bande war die weitere Rechtfertigung und Verwertung dieses Gesich vorbehalten. . . . Der Begriff des Interesses notigte mich, den Zweck ins Auge zu fassen, und das Recht im subjektiven Sinn drangte mich zu dem im objektiven Sinn, und so gestaltete sich das ursprungliche Untersuchungsobjekt zu einem ungleich erweiterten, zu dem des gegenwartigen Buches: der Zweck im Recht. . . Der Grundgedanke des gegenwartigen Werkes besteht darin, dass der Zweck der Schoper des gesamten Rechts ist, dass es keinen Rechtssatz gibt, der nicht einem Zweck, d.i. einem praktischen Motiv seinen Ursprung verdankt".

not original with Jhering. Long before he worked out the concept in his epoch-making book, *Der Zweck in Recht*, Lassalle had set it forth in his elaborate *Das System der erworbenen Rechte*,[26] and long before Lassalle had thought it through, our own Madison had formulated it, after the most wide-reaching researches in history and politics.[27]

In fact, the inquiry which follows is based upon the political science of James Madison, the father of the Constitution and later President of the Union he had done so much to create. This political science runs through all of his really serious writings and is formulated in its most precise in The Federalist[28] as follows: "The diversity in the faculties of men, from which the rights of property originate, is not less an insuperable obstacle to a uniformity of interests. The protection of these faculties is the first object of government. From the protection of different and unequal faculties of acquiring property, the possession of different degrees and kinds of property immediately results; and from the influence of these on the sentiments and views of the respective proprietors, ensues a division of the society into different interests and parties... the most common and durable source of factions has been the various and unequal distribution of property. Those who hold and those who are without property have ever formed distinct interests in society. Those who are creditors, and those who are debtors, fall under a like discrimination. A landed interest, a manufacturing interest, a mercantile interest, a moneyed interest, with many lesser interests, grow up of necessity in civilized nations, and divide them into different classes, actuated by different sentiments and views. The regulation of these various and interfering interests forms the principal task of modern legislation, and involves the spirit of party and faction in the necessary and ordinary operations of the government."

Here we have a masterly statement of the theory of economic determinism in politics.[29] Different degrees and kinds of property inevitably exist in modern society; party doctrines and "principles" originate in the sentiments and views which the possession of various kinds of property creates in the minds of the possessors; class and group divisions based on property lie at the basis of modern government; and politics and constitutional law are inevitably a reflex of these contending interests. Those who are inclined to repudiate the hypothesis of economic determinism as a European importation must, therefore, revise their views, on learning that one of the earliest, and certainly one of the clearest, statements of it came from a profound student of politics who sat in the Convention that framed our fundamental law.

---

[26] Was ist es, das den innersten Grund unserer politischen und socialen Kampfe bildet? Der Begriff des erworbenen Rechts ist wieder einmal streitig gerwerworden - und diesser Streit is es, der das Herz der heutigen Welt durchsittert und die tief inwendigste Grundlage der politisch-socialen Kampfe des Jahrhunderts bildet. Im Juristichen, Politischen, Oekonomischen ist der Begriff des erworbenen Rechts der treibende Springquell all weitern Gestalung, und wo sich das Juristische als das Privatrechtliche vollig von dem Politischen abzulosen scheint, da ist es noch viel politischer als das Politische selbst, dann da ist es das sociale Element. Preface to *Das System der erworbenen Rechts* by Ferdinand Lassalle.

[27] And before Madison's century, Harrington had perceived its significance, H.A.L. Fisher, Republican Tradition in Europe, p. 51.

[28] Number 10.

[29] The theory of the economic interpretation of history as stated by Professor Seligman seems as nearly axiomatic as any proposition in social science can be: "The existence of man depends upon his ability to sustain himself; the economic life is therefore the fundamental condition of all life. Since human life, however, is the life of man in society, individual existence moves within the framework of the social structure and is modified by it. What the conditions of maintenance are to the individual, the similar relations of production and consumption are to the community. To economic causes, therefore, must be traced in the last instance those transformations in the structure of society which themselves condition the relations of social classes and the various manifestations of social life." *The Economic Interpretation of History*, p. 3.

The requirements for an economic interpretation of the formation and adoption of the Constitution may be stated in a hypothetical proposition which, although it cannot be verified absolutely from ascertainable data, will at once illustrate the problem and furnish a guide to research and generalisation.

It will be admitted without controversy that the Constitution was the creation of a certain number of men, and it was opposed by a certain number of men. Now, if it were possible to have an economic biography of all those connected with its framing and adoption, - perhaps about 160,000 men altogether, - the materials for scientific analysis and classification would be available. Such an economic biography would include a list of the real and personal property owned by all of these men and their families: lands and houses, with incumbrances, money at interest, slaves, capital invested in shipping and manufacturing, and in state and continental securities.

Suppose it could be shown from the classification of the men who supported and opposed the Constitution that there was no line of property division at all; that is, that men owning substantially the same amounts of the same kinds of property were equally divided on the matter of adoption or rejection - it would then become apparent that the Constitution had no ascertainable relation to economic groups or classes, but was the product of some abstract causes remote from the chief business of life - gaining a livelihood.

Suppose, on the other hand, that substantially all of the merchants, money lenders, security holders, manufacturers, shippers, capitalists, and financiers and their professional associates are to be found on one side in support of the Constitution and that substantially all or the major portion of the opposition came from the non-slave-holding farmers and the debtors - would it not be pretty conclusively demonstrated that our fundamental law was not the product of an abstraction known as the "whole people," but of a group of economic interests which must have expected beneficial results from its adoption? Obviously all the facts here desired cannot be discovered, but the data presented in the following chapters bear out the latter hypothesis, and thus a reasonable presumption in favour of the theory is created.

Of course it may be shown (and perhaps can be shown) that the farmers and debtors who opposed the Constitution were, in fact, benefited by the general improvement which resulted from its adoption. It may likewise be shown, to take an extreme case, that the English nation derived immense advantages from the Norman Conquest and the orderly administrative processes which were introduced, as it undoubtedly did; nevertheless, it does not follow that the vague thing known as "the advancement of general welfare" or some abstraction known as "justice" was the immediate, guiding purpose of the leaders in either of these great historic changes. The point is, that the direct, im- pelling motive in both cases was the economic advantages which the beneficiaries expected would accrue to themselves first, from their action. Further than this, economic interpretation cannot go. It may be that some larger world-process is working through each series of historical events; but ultimate causes lie beyond our horizon.

Chapter 2.

A Survey of Economic Interests in 1787.

The whole story of the economic interpretation of history rests upon the concept that social progress in general is the result of contending interests in society - some favourable, others opposed, to change. On this hypothesis, we are required to discover at the very outset of the present study what classes and social groups existed in the United States just previous to the adoption of the Constitution and which of them, from the nature of their property, might have expected to benefit immediately and definitely by the overthrow of the old system and the establishment of the new. On the other hand, it must be discovered which of them might have expected more beneficial immediate results, on the whole, from the maintenance of the existing legal arrangements.

The importance of a survey of the distribution of property in 1787 for economic as well as political history is so evident that it is strange that no attempt has been made to undertake it on a large scale. Not even a beginning has been made. It is, therefore, necessary for us to rely for the present upon the general statements of historians who have written more or less at length about the period under consideration; but in the meanwhile it can do no harm to suggest, by way of a preface, the outlines of such a survey and some of the chief sources of information.

I. In the first place, there were the broad interests of real property which constituted, in 1787, a far larger pro- portion of all wealth than it does at the present time. The size, value, and ownership of holdings and their geographical distribution ought to be ascertained. In the absence of a general census, the preparation of such an economic survey would entail an enormous labour, and it could never be more than approximately complete. Neither the census of 1790 nor the assessment for direct taxes under the law of 1798 covers this topic. The assessment rolls of the several States for taxation, wherever available, would yield the data desired, at least in part; but a multitude of local records would have to be consulted with great scrutiny and critical care.

II. In order to ascertain the precise force of personality in the formation and adoption of the Constitution, it would be necessary to discover not only the amount and geographical distribution[30] of money and public securities; but also the exact fields of operation in which personality looked for immediate and prospective gains. A complete analysis of the economic forces in the Constitution-making-process would require the following data:-

1. The geographic distribution of money on hand and loaned and the names of the holders. It is apparent that much of the material from which evidence on these points may be obtained has disappeared; but an intensive study of the tax returns of the States, the records of the local assessors, wills probated, mortgages recorded, and suits in courts over loans and mortgages, would no doubt produce an immense amount of illuminating information.

2. The geographic distribution and ownership of the public securities. Fortunately the unpublished and unworked records of the Treasury Department at Washington throw great light on this fundamental problem.

Shortly after the federal government was established the old debt was converted into a new consolidated, or funded, debt; and holders of public securities, State and continental, brought their papers to their local loan office (one for each state) or to the Treasury to have them recorded and transformed into the stocks of the new government.

---

[30] The question of geographic distribution will be considered below, Chap. X.

The records of this huge transaction (which was the first really great achievement of nascent capitalism in the United States), if they had been kept intact, would constitute, perhaps, the most wonderful single collection on economic history ever possessed by any country. Were they complete, they would form a veritable Domesday Book of the politics during the first years of the new government. But unfortunately they are not complete. The records of Hamilton's administration at the Treasury seem to have largely disappeared, and the records of the loan offices in the several States are generally fragmentary, although in one or two instances they are indeed monumental.

A complete set of these financial documents should show:

(1) the owners of certificates of the old government as issued, during the Revolution and afterward, to original holders;

(2) the transfers of certificates from original holders to other parties;

(3) the names of those who held certificates in 1787, when the Convention was called to frame the Constitution;

(4) the records of transactions in stocks between the announcement of the Convention's work and the adoption of Hamilton's funding system;

(5) the names of those who brought in securities for funding into the new debt;

(6) the names of those for whom the brokers, whose names appear in the loan office books, were, in fact, operating.

None of the records preserved at the Treasury Department presents all of the evidence required for the scientific study of a single State. Nearly one third of the operations were at the Treasury and of these only a meagre fragment seems to have escaped the ravages of time. In the documents of some of the commonwealths, however, it is possible to ascertain the names of hundreds of patriots who risked their money in original certificates or received certificates for services rendered The books of a few loan offices are so kept that it can be easily discovered who brought in securities to be funded into the new debt and also to whom these securities were originally issued.

In some States the ledgers were carefully preserved and it is possible to find out the names and addresses of the holders of securities funded at the local loan office and the amount held by each person. The ledgers of Connecticut, for example, offer a rich field for the study of the names and geographical distribution of public creditors, and the tracing of these interests through their myriad local ramifications would afford an interesting and profitable undertaking. But unfortunately multitudes of the most significant operations are forever lost; it is to be particularly deplored that the "powers of attorney" for the period are not forthcoming. Unless the Government at Washington follows the example of enlightened administrations in Europe and establishes a Hall of Records, the precious volumes which have come down to us will be worked only with great difficulty, if they do not disintegrate and disappear altogether.[31]

3. The geographic distribution of small mortgaged farms and their connection with various schemes for depreciation of the currency and impairment of the obligation of contract. No doubt work in local records would yield valuable results in this field.

4. Owners and operators in western lands. Speculation in western lands was one of the leading activities of capitalists in those days. As is well known, the soldiers were paid in part in land scrip and this scrip was

---

[31] A few years ago a Negro attendant at the Treasury sold a cart-load or more of these records to a junk dealer. He was imprisoned for the offence, but this is a small consolation for scholars. The present writer was able to use some of the records only after a vacuum cleaner had been brought in to excavate the ruins.

bought up at low prices by dealers, often with political connections. Furthermore, large areas had been bought outright for a few cents and acre and were being held for a rise in value. The chief obstacle in the way of rapid appreciation of these lands was the weakness of the national government which prevented the complete subjugation of the Indians, the destruction of old Indian claims, and the orderly settlement of the frontier. Every leading capitalist of the time thoroughly understood the relation of a new constitution to the rise in land values beyond the Aleghanies. This idea was expressed, for example, by Hugh Williamson, a member of the Convention from North Carolina and a land speculator in a letter to Madison.[32]

5. The geographic distribution of manufacturing establishments and the names of owners and investors. On this important topic a mass of printed and manuscript material exists, but no attempt has yet been made to catalogue the thousands of names of persons with a view to establishing political connections. To produce the materials for this study, searches must be made in the local records from New Hampshire to Georgia. Wills probated, trans- fers of property, law suits, private papers, advertisements in newspapers, shipping records, Hamilton's correspondence in the Manuscript Division of the Library of Congress, unclassified Treasury Records and correspondence, and innumerable other sources must be searched and lists of names and operations made.

Pending the enormous and laborious researches here enumerated, the following pages are offered merely as an indication of the way in which the superficial aspects of the subject may be treated.[33] In fact, they sketch the broad outlines of the study which must be filled in and corrected by detailed investigations.

The Disenfranchised

In an examination of the structure of American society in 1787, we first encounter four groups whose economic status had a definite legal expression: the slaves, the indented servants, the mass of men who could not qualify for voting under the property tests imposed by the state constitutions and laws, and women, disenfranchised and subjected to the discriminations of the common law. These groups were, therefore, not represented in the Convention which drafted the Constitution, except under the theory that representation has no relation to voting.

How extensive the disenfranchisement really was cannot be determined.[34] IN some states, for instance, Pennsylvania and Georgia, propertyless merchants in the towns could vote; but in other states the freehold qualifications certainly excluded a great number of the adult males.

In no state, apparently, had the working-class developed a consciousness of a separate interest or an organisation that commanded the attention of the politicians of the time. In turning over the hundreds of pages of writings left by eighteenth-century thinkers one cannot help being impressed with the fact that the existence and special problems of a working class, then already sufficiently numerous to form a considerable portion of society, were outside the realm of politics, except in so far as the future power of the proletariat was foreseen and feared.[35]

---

[32] See below, p. 50.

[33] See Curtis, *the Constitutional History of the United States*, Book I, Chaps II-VII; Fiske, *Critical Period of American History*; McMaster, *History of the People of the United States,* Vol I; Channing, *History of the united States*, Vol III.

[34] See below, Chaps. IV and IX.

[35] Working men in the cities were not altogether indifferent spectators. See Becker, *Political Parties in New York*. They would have doubtless voted with the major interests of the cities in favour of the Constitution as against the agrarians had they been enfranchised. In fact, this is what happened in New York. See below, Chap. IX.

When the question of the suffrage was before the Convention, Madison warned his colleagues against the coming industrial masses: "Viewing the subject in its merits alone, the freeholders of the Country would be safest depositories of Republican liberty. These will either combine under the influence of their common situation; in which case,[36] the rights of property and the public liberty will not be secure in their hands, or, which is more probable, they will become the tools of opulence and ambition; in which case there will be equal danger on another side."[37]

So far as social policy is concerned, however, the working class problem had not made any impression on the statesmen of the time. Hamilton in his report on manufactures,[38] dismisses the subject with scant notice. He ob- serves that one of the advantages of the extensive introduction of machinery will be "the employment of persons who would otherwise be idle, and in many cases, a burthen on the community, either from bias of temper, habit, infirmity of body, or some other cause, indisposing or disqualifying them for the toils of the country. It is worthy of remark, that, in general, women and children are rendered more useful, and the latter more early useful, by manufacturing establishments, than they would otherwise be. Of the number of persons employed in the cotton manufactories of Great Britain, it is computed that four-sevenths, nearly, are women and children; of whom the greatest proportion are children, many of them of a tender age." Apparently this advantage was, in Hamilton's view, to accrue principally to the fathers of families, for he remarks: "The husbandman himself experiences a new source of profit and support, from the increased industry of his wife and daughters, invited and stimulated by the demands of the neighbouring manufactories."

Passing beyond these groups which were politically non-existent, except in so far as those who possessed the ballot and economic power were compelled to safeguard their rights against assaults from such quarters, we come to the social groupings within the politically enfranchised mass. Here we find no legal class distinctions. Social distinctions were very sharp, it is true, as every student of manners and customs well knows; but there were no outward legal signs of special class privileges.

Groups of Real Property Holders

Nevertheless, the possessors of property were susceptible of classification into several rather marked groups, though of course they shade off into one another by imperceptible graduations. Broadly speaking, there were the interests of real and personal property. Here, however, qualifications must be made. There was no such identity of interest between the large planters and the small inland farmers of the south as existed in England between the knights and yeomen. The real property holders may be classified into three general groups: the small farmers, particularly back from the sea-coast, scattered from New Hampshire to Georgia, the manorial lords, such as we find along the banks of the Hudson,[39] and the slaveholding planters of the south.

1. The first of these groups, the small farmers, constituted a remarkable homogenous class. The inland section was founded and recruited by mechanics, the poorer whites, and European (particularly Scotch-Irish) immigrants. It had particular social and political views arising from the crude nature of its environment, but its active political doctrines were derived from an antagonism to the seaboard groups. One source of conflict was connected with the possession of the land itself. Mush of the western country had been taken up by speculators and the settlers were either squatters or purchasers from large holders. This is illustrated by the situation in Virginia, where, as Ambler points out, "liberality in granting her unoccupied lands did not prove

---

[36] "If the authority be in their hands by the rulle of suffrage," struck out in the Ms. See also the important note to this speech in Farrand, *Records*, Vol. II. P. 204, note 17.

[37] Farrand, *Records*, Vol II. P. 203.

[38] December 5, 1791. *State Papers: Finance*, Vol I, p. 126.

[39] Roosevelt, *Gouvernor Morris*, pp. 14 ff.

to be a good policy. True, large numbers of settlers were attracted to the state, where they made permanent homes, but much of the land fell into the hands of speculators. Companies were formed in Europe and America to deal in Virginia lands, which were bought up in large tracts at the trifling cost of two cents per acre. This wholesale engrossment soon consumed practically all the most desirable lands and force the home seeker to purchase from speculators or to settle as a squatter."[40] As the settler sought to escape from the speculator by moving westward, the frontier line of speculation advanced.

In addition to being frequently in debt for their lands, the small farmers were dependent upon the towns for most of the capital to develop their resources. They were, in other words, a large debtor class, to which must be added, of course, the urban dwellers who were in a like unfortunate condition.

That this debtor class had developed a strong consciousness of identical interests in the several states is clearly evident in local politics and legislation.[41] Shays' Rebellion in Massachusetts, the disturbances in Rhode Island, New Hampshire, and other northern states, the activities of the paper-money advocates in state legislatures, the innumerable schemes for the relief of debtors, such as the abolition of imprisonment, paper money, laws delaying the collection of debts, propositions requiring debtors to accept land in lieu of specie at a valuation fixed by a board of arbitration, these and many other schemes testify eloquently to the fact that the debtors were conscious of their status and actively engaged in establishing their interest in the form of legal provisions. Their philosophy was reflected in the writings of Luther martin, delegate to the Convention from Maryland, who disapproved of the Constitution, partly on the ground that it would put a stop to agrarian legislation.[42]

2. The second group of landed proprietors, the manorial lords of the Hudson valley region, constituted a peculiar aristocracy in itself and was the dominant class in the politics of New York during the period between the Revolu- ion and the adoption of the Constitution, as it had been before the War. It was unable or unwilling to block the emission of paper money, because the burden of that operation fell on the capitalists rather than itself. It also took advantage of its predominance to shift the burden of taxation from the land to imports,[43] and this fact contributed powerfully to its opposition to the Constitution, because it implied a transference of the weight of taxation for state purposes to the soil. Its spokesmen indulged in much high talk of state's rights, in which Federalist leaders refused to see more than a hollow sham made over to cover the rural gentry's economic supremacy.

3 The third group of landed proprietors were the slaveholders of the south. It seems curious at the first glance that the representatives of the southern states which sold raw materials and wanted competition in shipping were willing to join in a union that subjected them to commercial regulations devised immediately in behalf of northern interests. An examination of the records shows that they were aware of this apparent incongruity, but that there were overbalancing compensations to be secured in a strong federal government.[44]

---

[40] Ambler, *Sectionalism in Virginia*, p. 44.

[41] Libby has shown the degree of correspondence between the rural vote on paper money measures, designed for the relief of debtors, and the vote against the ratification of the Constitution. *Op cit.*, pp. 50 ff.

[42] See below, p. 205.

[43] The landholders were able to do this largely because New York City was the entry port for Connecticut and New Jersey. The opportunity to shift the taxes not only to the consumers, but to the consumers of neighbouring states, as too tempting to be resisted.

[44] For a paragraph on nascent capitalism in South Carolina, see W.A. Schaper, "Sectionalism in South Carolina," A*merican Historical Association Report (1900),* Vol. I. See the letter of Blount, Davie, and Williamson to the governor of North Carolina, below p. 169.

Money lending and the holding of public securities were not confined to the north by any means; although, perhaps, as Calhoun long afterward remarked,[45] the south was devoid of some of the artifices of commerce which characterised new England. Neither were attempts at relieving debtors by legislative enactment restricted to Massachusetts and Rhode island. The south had many men who were rich in personality, other than slaves, and it was this type, rather than the slaveholding planter as such, which was represented in the Convention that framed the Constitution. The majority of the southern delegates at Philadelphia in 1787 were from the towns or combined a wide range of personality operations with their planting. On this account there was mode identity of interest among Langdon of Portsmouth, Gerry of Boston, Hamilton of new York, Dayton of New Jersey, Robert Morris of Philadelphia, McHenry of Baltimore, Washington on the Potomac, Williamson of North Carolina, the Pinckeys of Charleston, and Pierce of Savannah than between these several men and their debt burdened neighbours at the back door. Thus nationalism was created by a welding of economic interests that cut through state boundaries.

The southern planter was also as much concerned in maintaining order against slave revolts as the creditor in Massachusetts was concerned in putting down Shays' "desperate debtors." And the possibilities of such servile insurrections were by no means remote. Every slave owner must have felt more secure in 1789 when he knew that the governor of his state could call in the strong arm of the federal administration in case a domestic disturbance got beyond the local police and militia. The north might make discriminatory commercial regulation, but they could be regarded as a sort of insurance against conflagrations that might bring ruin in their train. It was obviously better to ship products under adverse legislation than to have no products to ship.

Groups of Personal Property Interests.

A second group of interests was that of personal property as contrasted with real property. This embraced, particularly, money loaned, state and continental securities, stocks of goods, manufacturing plants, soldiers' scrip, and shipping. The relative proportion of personality to reality in 1787 has not been determined and it is questionable whether adequate data are available for settling such an important matter.[46]

Personality in Money. - Although personality in the form of money at interest or capital seeking investment did not constitute in 1787 anything like the same amount, relative to the value of real estate, which it does to-day, it must not be thought that it was by any means inconsiderable in any state. The tax returns of New Hampshire for 1793 report the value of all buildings and real estate as £893,327/16/10 and the amount of money on hand or at interest as £35,985/5/6. The Massachusetts tax returns of 1792 show £196,698/4/6 at interest and £95,474/4/5 on hand. The Connecticut returns for 1795 show £63,348/10/1 at interest.[47]

Money capital was suffering in two ways under the Articles of Confederation. It was handicapped in seeking profitable outlets by the absence of protection for manufacturers, the lack of security in investments in western lands, and discriminations against American shipping by foreign countries. It was also being positively attacked by the makers of paper money, stay laws, pine barren acts, and other devices for depreciating the currency or delaying the collection of debts. In addition there was a widespread de

---

[45] It is not without interest to not that about the time Calhoun made this criticism of New England capitalist devices he was attempting to borrow several thousand dollars from a Massachusetts mill owner to engage to railway enterprise in the south.

[46] See, however, *State Papers: Finance*, Vol. I, pp. 414 ff.

[47] *Ibid*, Vol I, pp. 442 ff.

rangement of the monetary system and the coinage due to the absence of uniformity and stability in the standards.[48]

Creditors, naturally enough, resisted all of these schemes in the state legislatures, and failing to find relief there at length turned to the idea of a national government so constructed as to prevent laws impairing the obligation of contract, emitting paper money, and other with benefiting debtors. It is idle to inquire whether the rapacity of the creditors or the total depravity of the debtors (a matter much discussed at the time) was responsible for this deep and bitter antagonism. It is sufficient for our purposes to discover its existence and to find its institutional reflex in the Constitution. It was to the interest of the creditors to see currency appreciate, to facilitate the process for securing possession of forfeited mortgaged property, and to hold the rigour of the law before the debtor who was untrue to his obligations. Whether the creditors were driven into class consciousness by the assaults of their debtors or attained it by the exercise of their wits is, for scientific purposes immaterial.

Personality in Public Securities. - Even more immediately concerned in the establishment of a stable national government were the holders of state and continental securities. The Government under the Articles of Confederation was not paying the interest on its debt and its paper had depreciated until it was selling at from one-sixth to one-twentieth of its par value.[49] Grave uncertainties as to the actions of legislature kept state paper at a low price, also, even where earnest attempts were being made to meet the obligations.

The advantage of a strong national government that could discharge this debt at its face value is obvious; and it was fully understood at the time. The importance of this element of personality in forcing on the revolution that overthrew the Articles of Confederation is all the more apparent when it is remembered that securities constituted a very large proportion of the intangible wealth. In Massachusetts, for example, it is set down in 1792 at a sum greater than all the money at interest and on hand in the state.[50]

The amount of the public securities of the United States and of the several states at the establishment of the new government was estimated by Hamilton, in his first report on credit, as Secretary of the Treasury.[51] the foreign debt, that is, money borrowed abroad, was fixed at $10,070,307 and arrears of interest up to December, 1789, were estimated at $1,640,071.62, making a total of $11,710,378.62. The domestic continental debt, including the registered debt, army certificates, etc., amounted to $27,383,917.74, to which was added arrears of interest to the amount of $13,030,168.2, making a total of $40,414,085.94. The amount of the state debts was unknown in 1790, but Hamilton placed it at about $25,000,000, which appears to have been rather high. The issue, later authorised to cover them was $21,5000,000 and the amount actually paid out was $18,271,786.47.[52]

The enormous total of the national debt after state and national securities were funded is shown by Hamilton's report of January 16, 1795:-

Foreign Debt	$13,754,379.35
Funded Domestic Debt	60,789,914.18

---

48 See the picturesque description of the monetary system of lack of system in Fiske, Critical Period of American History.

49 See below, p. 146.

50 *State Papers: Finance*, Vol. I, p. 451; see also below, pp. 261-2.

51 *State Papers: Finance*, Vol. I, p. 19.

52 W. De Knight, History of the Currency, p. 21.

Unsubscribed Debt	1,561,175.14
Total Unredeemed Debt	$76,096,468.67

In addition to this sum, there was an amount of $1,400,000 due to the Bank of the United States on account of the loan from that institution, but this was more than counterbalanced by the value of the stock.[53]

It is evident from this statement that a vast mass of state and continental securities was scattered throughout the country in 1787. The degree of its concentration or distribution cannot be determined until the Domesday Books of the Treasury Department have been carefully studied, and their incompleteness makes an absolute statement impossible. The value of this paper in the hands of the holders in the spring when the Convention met cannot be ascertained with mathematical precision, for prices varied from state to state. Furthermore, the prices obtained by the holders of public paper after Hamilton's funding system had gone into effect can only be roughly estimated, for it depends upon the market in which they were sold. For example, 6 per cents were bringing 17 shillings in the pound on March 7, 1791, and 22 shillings in the pound on October 3, 1792. On these dates, deferred sixes were 9/1 and 13/7, respectively, and 3 per cents were 9/1 and 13/1, respectively.[54]

If we leave out of account the foreign debt, it appears that some $60,000,000 worth of potential paper lay in the hands of American citizens in the spring of 1787. This paper was changing hands all of the time at varying prices. The common selling price in good markets before the movement for the Constitution got under way ranged from one-sixth to one-tenth it face value; and some of it sold as low as twenty to one. In fact, many holders regarded continental paper as worthless, as it might have been had the formation of the Constitution been indefinitely delayed.

It seems safe to hazard a guess, therefore, that at least $40,000,000 gain of the Constitution and the sound financial system which it made possible. This leaves out of account the large fortunes won by the manipulation of stocks after the government was established and particularly after the founding of the New York Stock Exchange in 1792.[55]

It should be pointed out, however, that this was not all gain for the original holders of public paper, that is, for those who had loaned the Revolutionary government money or had rendered it services during the War. Nevertheless, they would have lost all their continental securities under the prevailing methods of the Congress. As Pitkin points out, "The interest of the debt was unpaid, public credit was gone, the debt itself was considered of little value, and was sold at last by many of the original holders for about one-tenth of its

---

[53] *State Papers: Finance*, Vol. I, p. 325.

[54] *Ibid, Vol. I*, p. 231.

[55] Callender, not a very reliable authority on most matters concerning Hamilton, claims that twenty-five million dollars was made by the founding of the public debt, and that about ten million dollars more was made out of the state debt assumption process. He further declared that a public debt of eighty million dollars had been created of which only about thirty millions was all that was necessary. Gallatin held also that the unnecessary debt created by the assumption act amounted to about eleven million dollars. Callendar, *A History of the united States for 1796*, pp. 224 ff. The ethics of redeeming the debt at face value is not here considered although the present writer believes that the success of the national government could not have been secured under any other policy than that pursued by Hamilton. Callendar claims that those who held it were, in large measure, speculators and that they made huge fortunes out of the transaction. By a stroke of the pen the federal government created capital to the amount of millions in the hands of the holders.

nominal value."[56] From this point of view, the appreciation due to the adoption of the new government was so much clear gain, even to original holders; and in some states more than one-half of the paper had passed into the hands of speculators at low figures.

The significance of this huge national debt and of the enormous gain made in the appreciation of securities can be understood only in comparison with other forms of wealth at the time. Unfortunately, our statistics for the period of the formation of the Constitution are meagre, but under an act of Congress passed in 1798 a valuation of lands was made for the purposes of direct taxation. The surveys were made between the years 1798 and 1804. The following table[57] exhibits the value of lands (not including houses, which amounted to more than $140,00,000 in addition) in each of the estates at the close of the eighteenth century, and also the amount of money paid out by the loan offices of the respective states for the year 1795 in discharging the interest on the public debt and the payment of 2 per cent towards the reimbursement of the 6 per cent stocks held in the several commonwealths:-

	Value of Lands	Interest, Etc, Disbursed [58]
New Hampshire	$19,028,108.03	$20,000.00
Massachusetts	59,445,642.64	309,500.00
Rhode Island	8,082,355.21	31,700.00
Connecticut	40,163,955.34	79,600.00
Vermont	15,165,484.02	
New York	74,885,075.69	367,600.00
New Jersey	27,287,981.89	27,350.00
Pennsylvania	72,824,852.60	86,379.19
Delaware	4,053,248.42	2,980.00

---

[56] *A Statistical View of the Commerce of the united States, p. 31.*

[57] Tables from Pitkin, *A Statistical View of the Commerce of the United States, pp. 367-368,* and *An Account of the Receipts and Expenditures of the United States for the Year 1795, p. 65.*

[58] No table showing the capital amount on the loan office books of the states after the funding was complete was discovered, so that the interest payment is given here.

Maryland	21,634,004.57	74,000.00
Virginia	59,976,860.04	62,300.00
North Carolina	27,909,479.70	3,200.00
South Carolina	12,456,720.94	109,500.00
Georgia	10,263,506.95	6,800.00
Kentucky	20,268,325.07	
Tennessee	5,847,562.00	
Total	$479,293,263.13	$1,180,909.19

To the total amount of payments made through the loan offices must be added the payments made at the Treasury on the securities registered there, bringing the total annual interest and capital disbursements to $2,727,959.07.

It seems safe to assume from the table that $400,000,000 would cover the total taxable value of all the lands in the thirteen States in 1781.[59] Very probably the estimate could be much lower, but letting the figures stand at this amount, it would have represented one-tenth of the total taxable value of all the land in the thirteen United States at the time of the formation of the Constitution.

To put the matter in another way: The amount gained by public security holders through the adoption of the new system was roughly equivalent to the value of all the lands as listed for taxation in Connecticut. It was but little less than the value of the lands in New Hampshire, Vermont, and Rhode Island. It was about equivalent to one-half the value of the lands in New Hampshire, Vermont, and Rhode Island. It was about equivalent to one-half the value of the lands in New York and to two-thirds the value of the lands in Massachusetts. It amounted to at least ten dollars for every man, woman, and child in the whole United Stated from New Hampshire to Georgia.[60]

The significance of the figures showing the annual interest disbursement also the debt had been funded becomes evident only by comparison. Tench Coxe, as commissioner of the revenue, estimated the amount of goods, wares, and merchandise exported from the United States between October 1, 1791, and September 30, 1792, at $21,005,568. In other words, the annual interest on the domestic debt was more than one-tenth the total value of the goods exported annually. The average imports for each of the three years ending March 4,

---

[59] Undoubtedly a large appreciation had taken place between 1787 and 1800.

[60] "The public securities of the United States of America were a dead, inactive kind of property, previous to the establishment of the constitution of the new government; then they became the object of avarice. They before had an existence as to value, on the slender hope of having something done for them at some distant future period; and obtained a motion only from the sagacity of the few, who happened to be right in their conjectures respecting the then future events of American financeering. Upon the adoption of the new system of government they assumed all the properties of a rising credit, and became an immense active capital for commerce." James Sullivan, *An Inquiry into the Origin and Use of Money* (1792) Duane Pamphlets, Library of Congress.

1792, was $19,150,000, so that the interest on the domestic debt was more than one-tenth of the value of the goods imported into the United-States.[61]

One of the most potent effective forces of these public securities was the Society of the Cincinnati which was composed of the officers of the Revolutionary Army organised into local branches in the several States. Like other soldiers, the members of this order had been paid for their patriotic services partly in land warrants and depreciated paper; but unlike the privates, they were usually men of some means and were not compelled to sacrifice their holdings to speculators at outrageously low prices. The members of this Society appear in large numbers on the loan office records of the several States preserved in the Treasury Department; and many, if not all, of the State branches had funds derived from this source.

The political influence of the Society was recognised in the Convention. When the popular election of President was under consideration, Gerry objected to it. "The ignorance of the people," he said, "would put it in the power of some one set of men dispersed through the Union and acting in concert to delude them into any appointment. He observed that such a society of men existed in the Order of the Cincinnati. They were respectable, United, and in- fuential. They will in fact elect the chief Magistrate in every instance, if the election be referred to the people - His respect for the characters composing this Society could not blind him to the danger and impropriety of throwing such a power into their hands."[62] In this view Colonel Mason concurred.[63]

An observant French charge d'affaires, writing to his home secretary of state for foreign affairs in June, 1787, calls attention to the weight of the Order of the Cincinnati in the movement for a new government, but remarks that their power has been greatly exaggerated. "Les Cincinnati," he says, "c'est a dire les officiers de l'ancienne armee americaine, sont interesses a l'establissment d'un Gouvernement solide, puisqu'ils sont tous creanciers du public, mais, considerant la foiblesse du Conseil national et l'impossibilite d'etre payes par la presente administration, ils prosent de jeter tous les Etats dans une seule masse et de mettre a leur tete le gal. Washington avec toutes les prerogatives et les pouvoirs d'une tete couronne." He also says that they threaten a revolution by arms in case the Convention fails, but adds that this project is too extravagant to merit the least consideration.[64]

This society was, however, compactly organised. Correspondence among the members was frequent, extensive, and frank. Almost uniformly, they were in favour of a reconstruction of the national government on a stronger basis.[65] They were bitter in their denunciation of the popular movements in the States, particularly Shay's revolt in Massachusetts. War had given them a taste for strong measures, and the wretched provisions which had been made for paying them for their military services gave them an economic interest in the movement to secure a government with an adequate taxing power. Moreover, they were consolidated by the popular hostility to them on account of their "secret" and "aristocratic" character.

---

[61] Tench Coxe, *A View of the United States of America (1795)*, p. 360. Tucker, *Progress of the United States (1843)*, p. 205.

[62] Farrand, *Records*, Vol II, p. 114.

[63] *Ibid.*, Vol II, p. 119.

[64] *Ibid*, Vol. III, p. 43.

[65] A large majority of the officers of the army of the Revolution were in favour of the new Constitution. The Cincinnati were mostly among its warmest advocates; and as they were organised and were, many of them, of exalted private and public worth and could act in concert through all the States, their influence was foreseen and feared by its opponents." Blair, *The Virginia Convention of 1788*, Vol I. P. 36, note 41.

Personality in Manufacturing & Shipping.- The third group of personality interests which was not inconsiderable even at that time. A large amount of capital had been invested in the several branches of industry and a superficial study of the extensive natural resources at hand revealed the immense possibilities of capitalistic enterprise. The industrial revolution was then getting under way in England and the fame of Arkwright was being spread abroad in the land. In the survey of the economic interests of the members of the Federal Convention, given below, it is shown that a few leading men were directly connected with industrial concerns, although it is not apparent that the protection of industries was their chief consideration, in spite of the fact that they did undoubtedly contemplate such a system. But outside of the Convention vehement appeals were made by pamphleteers for protection, on the score that the discriminatory measures of Great Britain were disastrous to American economic independence.

As early as April, 1785, a memorial from prominent merchants and business men of Philadelphia was laid before the legislature of the State lamenting that Congress did not have "a full and entire power over the commerce of the United States," and praying that the legislature request Congress to lay a proposal conferring such a power before the States for their ratification. The memorialists assured the legislature that there was a "disposition in the mercantile interest of Pennsylvania favourable thereto."[66] Among the signers were T. Fitzsimmons and George Clymer, who were destined to sit in the constitutional Convention as representatives of the State of Pennsylvania an do the mercantile interest which they had so much at heart.

The supporters of the Constitution were so earnest and so persistent in their assertion that commerce was languishing and manufactures perishing for the lack of protection that there must have been some justification for their claims, although it is impossible to say how widespread the havoc really was. The exaggeration of danger threatened by a tariff reduction is not peculiar to our times; it was sharply marked in older days. The consumer suffered from the lack of the protection sought in 1787 by merchants and manufacturers is not apparent. Indeed the "mechanics and manufacturers of New York" in their humble petition to Congress for relief in 1789 complain that "their country-men have been deluded by an appearance of plenty; by the profusion of foreign articles which has deluged the country; and thus have mistaken excessive importation for a flourishing trade. To this deception they [the petitioners] impute the continuance of that immoderate prepossession in favour of foreign commodities which has been the principal cause of their distresses, and the subject of their complaint."[67]

That innumerable manufacturing, shipping, trading, and commercial interests did, however, look upon the adoption of the Constitution as the sure guarantee that protection could be procured against foreign competition, is fully evidenced in the memorials laid before the Congress in April, May, and June, 1789, asking for the immediate enactment of discriminatory tariff laws.[68]

The first of these petitions was from Baltimore in particular and Maryland generally, and was communicated to the House of Representatives on April 11, 1789, a few days after that body had settled down to business. The second was laid before the House a week later by a committee representing the mechanics and manufacturers of New York. On May 25, 1789, the shipwrights of Philadelphia laid their claims before Congress; and on June 5, the tradesmen and manufacturers of Boston put in their appearance. These petitions for protection from the four great trading and shipping centres of the country, Baltimore, Philadelphia, New York, and Boston, which had been most zealous in securing the establishment of the new government, are in themselves eloquent documents for the economic interpretation of the Constitution.

The first of these from Baltimore, bears the names of two members of the federal Convention from that State, Daniel Carrol and James McHenry, and the names of two or three hundred other citizens of that

---

[66] American Museum, Vol I, p. 3213. Other signers were C. Pettit, J. Ross, I. Hazelhurst, M. Lewis, T. Coxe, R. Wells, , J. M. Nesbit, J. Nixon, J. Wilcocks, S. Howell, and C. Biddle.

[67] *State Papers: Finance*, Vol I., p. 9.

[68] *American State Papers: Finance*, Vol I, pp. 5 ff.

community, the analysis of whose politico-economic connections would doubtless repay the detailed scrutiny which the painful labour would entail. The petition cites the sad state of decline in which manufacturing and trading interests have been since the close of the Revolution and the ineffectual attempts of the States acting alone to remedy the evils. "The happy period having now arrived," the memorialists exultingly exclaim, "when the United States are placed in a new situation; when the adoption of the General Government gives one sovereign Legislature the sole and exclusive power of laying duties upon imports; your petitioners rejoice at the prospect this affords them, that America, freed from the commercial shackles which have so long bound her, will see and pursue her true interest, becoming independent in fact as well as in name; and they confidently hope that the encouragement and protection of American manufactures will claim the earliest attention of the supreme Legislature of the nation.

The Maryland petitioners are conscious of no narrow motives in asking for relief at the hands of the government: "the number of her poor increasing for want of employment; foreign debts accumulating; houses and lands depreciating in value; trade and manufactures languishing and expiring" - these are the evidences of need for the expected legislation. They, therefore, ask for duties on all foreign articles that can be made in America, which will give" a just and decided preference to their labors." And lest Congress might not understand the precise character of the relief for which they ask, they append a long list of articles, which are, or can be, manufactured in Maryland, and on which protection is needed - including ships, hardware, clocks, boots, shoes, saddles, brushes, food-stuffs, and raw iron, to mention only a few.

The second petition, from the mechanics and manufacturers of New York, recites how the memorialists had expected great prosperity on the successful issue of the Revolution and had seen their hopes blasted "by a system of commercial usurpation, originating in prejudices, and fostered by a feeble government." They had struggled in vain against dire adversity and "wearied by their fruitless exertions, your petitioners have long looked forward with anxiety to the establishment of a government which would have the power to check the growing evil, and extend a protecting hand to the interests of commerce and the arts. Such a government is now established. On the promulgation of the Constitution just now commencing its operations, your petitioners discovered in its principles the remedy which they had so long and so earnestly desired. They embraced it with ardour, and have supported it with persevering attachment." Lest Congress might not have the information necessary for the formulation of a protective tariff on correct principles, the petitioners subjoined a list of articles manufactured in the state and susceptible of protection.

The petitioners from Philadelphia, humbly seeking protection for shipping, lament that the tonnage built at that harbour has fallen to about one-third the amount constructed before the Revolution, and call attention to the fact that the British navigation act totally prevents them from building for English customers. They add that they "have waited, with anxious expectation, for the sitting of the honourable Congress under the new Constitution of the United States, firmly relying that every exertion would be used to re-instate so necessary and useful a branch of business." Like the representatives from Baltimore and New York, they append for the information of Congress a list of suggestions as to the best method of protecting American shipping interests.

Finally come the manufacturers and ship-builders of Boston. Ship-building with them has also declined since the Revolution, and the revival of manufacturing in the north depends upon adequate protection from the federal government. Accordingly they request that "heavy duties may be laid on such articles as are manufactured by our own citizens, humbly conceiving that the impost is not solely considered by Congress as an object of *revenue,* but, in its operation, intended to *exclude* such importations, and, ultimately, establish these several branches of manufacture among ourselves." Rope-makers, hatters, pewterers, soap-boilers, and tallow-chandlers, wool card-makers, ship-carvers, sail-makers, cabinet-makers, coach-makers, tailors, cord-wainers, glue and starch makers, brass-founders, and coppersmiths are among the memorialists.

In the processions which celebrated the adoption of the Constitution in Boston, Philadelphia, Baltimore, Charleston, and New York, the several local manufacturing concerns were extensively represented by floats and bannermen, which shows that they were not unaware of the gain that had been made in their favour by the establishment of the new system. But it must not be supposed that the consolidation of interests in support of the Constitution was purely local in character. On the contrary it was nationwide.

Immediately after the Revolution the local groups were being welded into a national interest by correspondence committees. Before the formation of the Constitution, Boston merchants were sending out appeals to other merchants in the several states to join in a national movement for protection; and before the new government went into effect, they were active in stirring up united action among the merchants and manufacturers of the whole country. In 1788, a committee of the association of Boston merchants and manufacturers sent out a circular to "their brethren in the several seaports of the union," asking for cooperation in this grave juncture.[69] To this Boston appeal are appended the names of John Gray, Gibbins Sharp, Benjamin Austin, Jr., Larson Belcher, William Hawes, and Joshua Witherle - all of whom signed the petition addressed to Congress the following year asking for protection.[70]

During the struggle over the reconstruction, the advocates of a constitution made use of the argument that the consumption of foreign luxuries, manufactured stuffs, was one of the chief causes of the economic distress which was said to prevail; and declared that national legislation was the only source of relief from this heavy importation. A writer in the *American Museum* for February, 1787, complains that "the articles of rum and tea alone, which are drank in this country, would pay all its taxes. But when we add sugar, coffee, gauzes, silks, feathers, and the whole list of baubles and trinkets, what an enormous expense! No wonder you want paper currency. My countrymen are all grown very tasty. Feathers and jordans must all be imported. Certainly, gentlemen, the *devil* is among you. A Hampshireman, who drinks forty shillings worth of rum in a year and never thinks of the expense, will raise a mob to reduce the governor's salary."[71]

The Connecticut Courant, of November 12, 1787, in an argument for ratification declares: "In the harbour of New York there are now 60 ships of which 55 are British. The produce of South Carolina was shipped in 170 ships, of which 150 were British. Surely there is not any American who regards the interest of his country but must see the immediate necessity of an efficient federal government; without it the Northern states will soon be depopulated and dwindle into poverty, while the Southern ones will become silk worms to toil and labour for Europe."

It is worthy of remark, however, that the gloomy view of economic conditions persistently propagated by the advocates of a new national system was not entertained by all writers of eminence and authority. One of the members of the Convention, Franklin, early in 1787, before the calling of that assembly, declared that the country was, on the whole, so prosperous that there was every reason for profound thanksgiving.[72] He mentioned, it is true, that there were some who complained of hard times, slack trade, and scarcity of money,

---

[69] Carey, *American Museum*, Vol. IV, p. 348. See also Winsor, *Memorial History of Boston*, Vol. IV, p. 77.

[70] For illustrative evidence that the protection of manufactures and shipping was being widely agitated previous to the adoption of the Constitution, and that an extensive consciousness of identity of interest was being developed among the individuals concerned, see the articles in *The American Museum*, Vol. I, on American Manufactures; Winsor, *Memorial History Boston*, Vol. IV, Chap. III. See memorials in *The American Museum*, from Philadelphia mercantile interests (April 6,1785), Vol. I, p. 313; from Boston merchants, *ibid.*, Vol. I, p. 320. For the merchants' movement in New York, see the Magazine of American History, April, 1893, pp. 324 ff.

[71] Vol. I, p. 117.

[72] M. Carey, *The American Museum,* for January, 1787, Vol. 1. pp. 5 II.

but he was quick to add that there never was an age nor a country in which there were not some people so circumstanced as to find it hard to make a living and that "it is always in the power of a small number to make a great clamour." But taking the several classes in the community as a whole, prosperity, contended Franklin, was widespread and obvious. Never was the farmer paid better prices for his products, "as the published prices current abundantly testify. The lands he possesses are continually rising in value." In no part of Europe are the labouring poor so well paid, fed, or clothed. The fishing trade, he thinks, is in a rather bad way, and mercantile branches are overcrowded; but he is not distressed by the extensive importation of English goods, because this is nothing new, and America has prospered in spite of it.

It may very well be that Franklin's view of the general social conditions just previous to the formation of the Constitution is essentially correct and that the defects in the Articles of Confederation were not the serious menace to the social fabric which the loud complaints of advocate of change implied. It may be that II the critical period was not such a critical period after all; but a phantom of the imagination produced by some undoubted evils which could have been remedied without a political revolution. It does not seem to have occurred to those historians, who have repeated without examination Fiske's picturesque phrase that it is a serious matter to indict a whole system, an entire epoch, and a whole people. It does not appear that anyone has really inquired just what precise fact must be established to prove that "the bonds of the social order were dissolving." Certainly, the inflamed declarations of the Shaysites are not to be taken as representing accurately the state of the people, and just as certainly the alarmist letters and pamphlets of interested persons on the other side are not to be accepted without discount. When it is remembered that most of our history has been written by Federalists, it will become apparent that great care should be taken in accepting, without reserve, the gloomy picture of the social conditions prevailing under the Articles o Confederation. In fact, a very learned, though controversial, historian, Henry B. Dawson, in an article published more than forty years ago makes out quite a plausible cast (documented by minute research) for the statement that the "chaos" of which historians are wont to speak when dealing with the history of the years 1783-87, was a creation of their fancies.[73]

However this may be, and whether or not Franklin's view is correct,[74] it cannot be denied that the interests seeking protection were extensive and diversified. This is con- clusively shown by the petitions addressed to public bodies, by the number of influential men connected with the movement, and by the rapidity with which the new government under the Constitution responded to their demands.

Capital Invested In Western Lands. - Although companies had been formed to deal in western lands on a large scale before the Revolution, it was not until the close a, of the War that effective steps were taken toward settlement. At that time, says Professor Haskins, "the number of emigrants, the cheapness of the lands, and the lack of an established system of sale in small quantities offered many inducements for the formation of great land companies whose opportunities for speculation were increased by the depreciated currency and general ignorance concerning the West. ...'All I am now worth was gained by speculations in land,' wrote Timothy Pickering [a member of the Pennsylvania ratifying convention] in the same year [1796]; and many eminent men could have said the same, often with a later experience quite similar. Land speculation involved Washington, Franklin, Gallatin, Patrick Henry, Robert Morris, and James Wilson, as well as many less widely known."[75]

---

[73] The Historical Magazine (1871), Vol. IX, Second Series, pp. 157 ff.

[74] For an interesting and novel view of the state of commerce under the Articles of Confederation, see Channing, *History of the United States,* Vol. III, pp. 422 ff.

[75] Haskins, *The Yazoo Land Companies,* p. 62. American Historical Association Papers for 1891. See also the lists printed in A.M. Dyer, *First Ownership of Ohio Lands* (1911).

The situation was this: Congress under the Articles of Confederation adopted a policy of accepting certificates in part payment for lands; and it was hoped by some that the entire national debt might be extinguished in this way. However, the weakness of the Confederation, the lack of proper military forces, the uncertainty as to the frontiers kept the values of the large sections held for appreciation at an abnormally low price. Those who had invested their funds in these lands or taken stocks in the companies felt the adverse effects of the prevailing public policy, and foresaw the benefits which might be expected from a new and stable government. Their view was tersely put by Williamson, a member of the Convention from North Carolina, in a letter to Madison on June 2, 1788: " For myself, I conceive that my opinions are not biased by private Interests but having claims to a considerable Quantity of Land in the Western Country, I am fully persuaded that the Value of those Lands must be increased by an efficient federal Government."[76]

The weight of the several species of property in politics is not determined by the amount, but rather by the opportunities offered to each variety for gain and by the degree of necessity for defence against hostile legislation designed to depreciate values or close opportunities for increments. When viewed in this light the reason for the special pressure of personalty in politics in 1787 is apparent. It was receiving attacks on all hands from the depreciators and it found the way to profitable operations closed by governmental action or neglect. If we may judge from the politics of the Congress under the Articles of Confederation, two related groups were most active: those working for the establishment of a revenue sufficient to discharge the interest and principal of the public debt, and those working for commercial regulations advantageous to personalty operations in shipping and manufacturing and in western land speculations.[77]

It should be remembered also that personalty is usually more active than real property. It is centralized in the towns and can draw together for defence or aggression with greater facility. The expectation of profits from its manipulation was much larger in 1787 than from real property. It had a considerable portion of the professional classes in attached to it; its influence over the press was tremendous, not only through ownership, but also through advertising and other patronage.[78] It was, in short, the dynamic element in the movement for the new Constitution.

---

[76] *Documentary History of the Constitution,* Vol. IV, p. 678.

[77] But see Madison's view as to the chief reason for calling the Convention, below, p. 178.

[78] A study of the newspapers of the period shows a large number of prominent advocates of the Constitution among the merchants and brokers advertising in the, Federalist press.

Chapter 3.

The Movement for the Constitution.

Did the system of government prevailing in the United States in 1787 affect adversely any of the economic interests enumerated in the preceding chapter? Furthermore, were the leaders in the movement which led to the adoption of the Constitution representatives of the interests so affected?

Fortunately, it is not necessary to devote any considerable attention to the first of these questions. It is answered in part above, and all of the standard treatises show conclusively that the legal system prevailing at the opening of 1787 was unfavourable to the property rights of four powerful groups above enumerated.[79] That system was, in brief, as follows. There was a loose union of thirteen sovereign states under the Articles of Confederation. The national government consisted of a legislature of one house in which the states had an equal voting power. There was no executive department and no general judiciary. The central government had no power to regulate commerce or to tax directly; and in the absence of these powers all branches of the government were rendered helpless. Particularly, money could not be secured to pay the holders of public securities, either their interest or principal. Under this system, the state legislatures were substantially without restrictions or judicial control; private rights in property were continually attacked by stay laws, legal tender laws, and a whole range of measures framed in behalf of debtors; and in New England open rebellion had broken out.

That the economic groups in question looked to a new national government as the one source of relief and advantage, is shown in a hundred contemporary pamphlets and newspaper articles. It was in fact the topic of the times.

For example, a letter from Philadelphia, under date of August 29, 1787, sums up concisely the interests which were turning to the new Constitution: "The states neglect their roads and canals, till they see whether those necessary improvements will not become the objects of a national government. Trading and manufacturing companies suspend their voyages and manufactures till they see how far their commerce will be protected and promoted by a national system of commercial regulations. The lawful usurer locks up or buries his specie till he sees whether the new frame of government will deliver him from the curse or fear of paper money and the tender laws. ...The public creditor, who, from the deranged state of finances in every state and their total inability to support their partial funding systems, has reason to fear that his certificates will perish in his hands, now places all his hopes of justice in an enlightened and stable national government. The embarrassed farmer and the oppressed tenant, who wishes to become free by emigrating to a frontier country, wait to see whether they shall be protected by a national force from the Indians."[80]

A final answer to the second question propounded above would require an exhaustive analysis of the "movement for the Constitution," in the following form: -

1. A study of the economic forces in the Revolution and particularly in the Continental Congress that drafted the Articles of Confederation.
2. An inquiry into the first signs of discontent with the prevailing system, their geographic distribution, and their economic sources.
3. An examination of the several attempts in the Congress under the Articles of Confederation to secure the power to regulate commerce and establish a revenue for

---

[79] Bancroft, *op. cit.,* Book I, Chaps. II-VII; Fiske, *Critical Period;* Marshall, *Life of Washington* (1850 ed.), Vol. II, pp. 75 ff.

[80] The Connecticut Courant. September 10, 1787.

discharging the debt.
4. A description of the economic interests of all the members who were most active in these attempts.
5. A description of the economic forces in the communities whose representatives in Congress were zealous in securing a revision of the Articles.
6. A study of the nature and distribution of the several legislative attacks on private rights in property between 1783 and 1787.
7. A minute study of the personnel of the movement for revision and the economic interests of the leading spirits in Congress and the state legislatures and outside of legislative chambers.

Anyone superficially acquainted with the sources of American history will see at once the nature of the work which must be done to secure the raw materials for such a study. The enormous mass of unprinted papers of the Continental Congress in the Library at Washington would have to be thoroughly searched; proceedings in state legislatures during the years under consideration would have to be scrutinized; local archives and newspapers would have to be examined.

In the present state of our historical materials, therefore, all that can be attempted here is a superficial commentary on some of the outward aspects of the movement for the Constitution which are described in the conventional works on the subject. Many of the eminent men prominently identified with the events which led up to the Convention sir of 1787 were themselves members of that Assembly, and their economic interests are considered below in Chapter V. But it is not without significance to discover that some of to the leading men outside of the Convention who laboured for an overthrow of the old system were also directly interested in the results of their labours.

As early as January, 1781, General Philip Schuyler moved in the senate of New York " to request the eastern states to join in an early convention, which should form a perpetual league of incorporation, subservient, however, to the common interest of all the states; invite others to accede to it; erect Vermont into a state; devise a fund for the redemption of the common debts; substitute a permanent and uniform system for temporary expedients; and invest the confederacy with powers of coercion."[81] General Schuyler was a large holder of depreciated securities.[82]

In February, 1781, Congress recommended to the states that they vest in the national legislature a power to levy a duty to pay the principal and interest of the debt. In April, 1783, Congress again appealed to the states for authority to lay duties for the purpose of supplying a revenue with which to discharge the debt. Among the leaders in Congress who favoured this increase in power were Gorham, Higginson, Ellsworth, Dyer, Boudinot, Fitzsimons, Williamson, Izard, Johnson, and King, all of whom held securities which were daily depreciating under the failure of the government to meet its just obligations.[83]

In 1785, Governor Bowdoin, of Massachusetts, in his inaugural address urged the necessity of a stronger union with larger powers, and recommended a convention to de- liberate upon the whole matter.[84] Governor

---

[81] Bancroft, *op. cit.*. Vol. I, p. 29.

[82] See below, p. 109.

[83] Elliot's *Debates,* Vol. I, p. 95. See below, Chaps. V and VII.

[84] Bancroft, *op. cit.,* Vol. I, p. 190.

Bowdoin was a large holder of public securities.[85] The legislature of the commonwealth, thereupon, resolved that the Articles of Confederation were inadequate, and directed the representatives in Congress to take steps looking toward a strengthening of the union; but they failed to act.

Men less eminent than Bowdoin and Schuyler were being educated in Federalism by the march of events. In Boston merchants were petitioning Congress for relief from British discriminations[86]; in the Virginia legislature the representatives of the commercial interests were learning their lessons[87]; the demands for positive action were increasing daily in number. Every failure to find a remedy under the Articles of Confederation only served to augment the ranks of those who were ready for a complete reconstruction of the prevailing system.

A few illustrations will serve to show how the demand for reform was being fostered and also the connection between the leaders in the agitation and the personnel of the public bodies which later achieved the great work of framing and ratifying the Constitution. Even before the war was over and the Articles of Confederation tested in a time of peace, the inability of the government under it to afford defence to commerce on the high seas was deplored by merchants whose vessels were falling prey to the British. In April, 1782, a number of prominent merchants presented a petition to Congress in which they lamented the British depredations on American trade and the want of adequate naval protection at sea.[88] Among the signers of this petition were several men who were later known as warm as supporters of a strong federal government. One of them, Thomas Fitzsimons, was a member of the Convention of which drafted the Constitution; another, John Barclay, was a member of the Pennsylvania convention and voted in favour of the ratification of the new system of government.

Six years before the Convention met in Philadelphia, the disordered financial system under the Confederation was the subject of protest by interested parties. In 1781, "divers inhabitants of the state of Pennsylvania," were petitioning Congress to take some action designed to put the credit of the country on a sound basis.[89] Thus runs the petition. "Humbly sheweth that whereas you thought fit heretofore in the course of your wisdom to emit bills of credit for good and great purposes, but the same depreciating to such an amazing degree beyond the expectation of all living did therefore lay open wide door for the most monstrous and absurd injustices by fraudulent payments which we conclude is directly contrary to your good and great purposes in emitting the same, we therefore, not only firmly relying on the extraordinary clearness of the circumstances of our agrievances, but likewise on the uprightness of your understandings, Do therefore presume to pray your honours would be pleased to recommend to the several states to adopt such measures as they may think most likely to afford a safe and effectual redress to all such agrievances. ..."[90]

Among the signers to this petition are Thomas Bull, John Hannum, and Thomas Cheyney, who six years later as members of the Pennsylvania convention had the pleasure of voting for the ratification of an instrument of government that put an end to the evils against which they had so earnestly protested.

The failure of repeated attempts in Congress to secure an amendment authorizing the laying of impost duties, the refusal of the states to pay the requisitions made by Congress, and the obvious impossibility of

---

85   See below, p. 263.

86   See above, p. 46 *n.*

87   Ambler, *Sectionalism in Virginia,* p. 48.

88   Ms. Library of Congress: *Papers of the Continental Congress* (Memorials), No. 41. Vol. VI, p. 283. Simpson, *Eminent Philadelphians.*

89   *Ibid"* No. 42, Vol, VI, p, 254.

90   *Ibid"* No. 42, Vol, VI, p, 254.

gaining their ends through the ordinary channels of ratification by state legislatures, drove the advocates of these measures to desperation. Republican government, as it had been tried out, had failed to secure for personalty that protection and opportunity for advancement which it enjoyed under monarchy. The despair of the representatives of the property interests thus jeopardized and their readiness for some heroic measures were fully manifest in the correspondence of the time.

Washington, who was not given to undue alarms, wrote to John Jay from Mount Vernon, on August 1, 1786, to the effect that men of leadership were ready for drastic action: "What astonishing changes," he said, "a few years are capable of producing. I am told that even respectable characters speak of a monarchical form of Government without horror. From thinking proceeds speaking, thence to acting is often but a single step. But how irrevocable and tremendous! What a triumph for our enemies to verify their predictions - what a triumph for the advocates of despotism to find that we are incapable of governing ourselves, & that systems founded on the basis of equal liberty are merely ideal & fallacious! Would to God that wise measures may be taken in time to avert the consequences we have but too much reason to apprehend."[91]

Later in that year, General Knox, who was a holder of public securities, wrote to Washington in the following strain: "The people who are the insurgents [Shaysites] have never paid any, or but very little taxes - But they see the weakness of government; They feel at once their own poverty, compared with the opulent, and their own force, and they are determined to make use of the latter, in order to remedy the former. Their creed is 'That the property of the United States has been protected from the confiscations of Britain by the joint exertions of all, and therefore ought to be the common property of all. And he that attempts opposition to this creed is an enemy to equity and for justice, and ought to be swept from off the face of the earth.' In a word they are determined to annihilate all debts public and private and have agrarian Laws, which are easily effected by means of un-funded paper money which shall be a tender in all cases whatever –

"The numbers of these people may amount in Massachusetts to about one fifth part of several populous counties, and to them may be collected, people of similar sentiments, from the states of Rhode Island, Connecticut, and New Hampshire so as to constitute a body of 12 or 15000 desperate & unprincipled men - They are chiefly of the young and active part of the community, more easily collected than perhaps kept together afterwards - But they will probably commit overt acts of treason which will compel them to embody for their own safety - once embodied they will be constrained to submit to discipline for the same reason. Having proceeded to this length for which they are now ripe, we shall have a formidable rebellion against reason, the principle of all government, and the very name of liberty. This dreadful situation has alarmed every man of principle and property in New England. They start as from a dream, and ask what has been the cause of our - delusion? what is to afford us security against the violence of lawless men? Our government must be braced, changed, or altered to secure our lives and property. We imagined that the mildness of our government and *the virtue* of the people were so correspondent, that we were not as other nations requiring brutal force to support the laws - But we find that we are men, actual men, possessing all the turbulent passions be longing to that animal and that we must have a government proper and adequate for him. The people of Massachuse[tts] for instance, are far advanced in this doctrine and the men of reflection, & principle, are determined to endev[or] to establish a government which shall have the power to protect them in their lawful pursuits, and which will be efficient in all cases of internal commotions or foreign invasions -They mean that liberty shall be the basis, a liberty resulting from the equal and firm administration of the laws. They wish for a general government of unity as they see the local legislatures must naturally and necessarily tend to retard and frustrate all general government."[92]

---

[91] *Documentary History of the Constitution*, Vol. IV, p. 20.

[92] *Documentary History of the Constitution*, Vol. IV, p. 30.

A few months later, Madison, writing to Edmund Pendleton from New York, the seat of the government: corroborated the views expressed by Washington and Knox and set forth what he conceived to be the desperate state of republican government. His letter, dated February 24, 1787, three days after Congress had issued the call for a national Convention, ran as follows: "In general I find men of reflection much less sanguine as to a new than despondent as to the present System. Indeed the Present System neither has nor deserves advocates; and if some very strong props are not applied will quickly tumble to the ground. ...If the approaching Convention should not agree on some remedy, I am persuaded that some very different arrangement will ensue. The late turbulent scenes in Massachusetts & infamous ones in Rhode Island, have done inexpressible injury to the republican character in that part of the U. States; and a propensity towards Monarchy is said to have been produced by it in some leading minds. The bulk of the people will probably prefer the lesser evil of a partition of the Union into three more practicable and energetic Governments. The latter idea I find after long confinement to individual speculations & private circles, is beginning to show itself in the Newspapers."[93]

A few days after this letter was written by Madison, John Armstrong wrote to Washington from Carlisle that the suppression of the insurrection in Massachusetts had not allayed the fears of leading men in his state. "The alarming flame in Massachusetts," he says, "seems nearly extinguished, but if the subsequent measures of that State respecting the insurgents should be severe, amounting to *death,* Confiscation, or disfranchisement, the consequence may be bad, as tending to reinkindle the flame. Shall I tell you in *confidence,* I have now twice heard, nor from low authority (some principal men of that State) begin to talk of wishing one general *Head* to the Union, in the room of Congress!"[94]

By correspondence such as this just cited, by an increasing recognition of the desperate straights in which they were placed, a remarkable fusion of interested forces was effected. The wealth, the influence, and a major portion of the educated men of the country were drawn together in a compact group, "informed by a conscious solidarity of interests," as President Wilson has so tersely put it.[95] Having failed to obtain relief through the regular channels of amendment by Congress ratified by the state legislatures, the leaders struck out on a new path. Operating through the Virginia legislature, they secured a resolution inviting the sister commonwealths to send delegates to a convention at Annapolis to take into consideration the trade and commercial system of the United States.[96] The convention duly met, but the attendance was so slim that, as Professor Burgess has put it, "a coup d'etat attempted by so small a body could not but fail."[97]

Although the Annapolis convention was ostensibly concerned with commercial regulation primarily, there is no doubt that it was the creation of the men who had been working in Congress and out for a general revision of the whole system. There is no doubt also that it was not regarded as of much significance in itself, but rather as a preliminary to a national convention which would afford an opportunity for reconstructing the government. For this view we have a witness of high authority, James Madison, who in a letter of August 12,

---

[93] *ibid.,* Vol. IV, p. 83.

[94] *ibid.,* Vol. IV, p. 88.

[95] *Division and Reunion,* p. 12.

[96] James Monroe to James Madison. New York, September 3, 1786. "I consider the convention of Annapolis as a most important era in our affairs - the eastern men be assur'd mean it as leading further than the object originally comprehended. If they do not obtain that things shall be arranged to suit them in every respect, their intrigues will extend to the objects I have suggested above - Pennsylvania is their object - upon succeeding or failing with her they will gain or lose confidence - I doubt not the emissaries of foreign countries will be on the ground." *Documentary History of the Constitution,* Vol. IV, p. 25.

[97] *Political Science and Constitutional Law,* Vol. I, p. 103.

1786, to Jefferson, written a month before the Annapolis conference, said: "Many gentlemen, both within and without Congress, wish to make this meeting subservient to a plenipotentiary Convention for amending the Confederation. Tho' my wishes are in favour of such an event, yet I despair so much of its accomplishment at the present crisis that I do not extend my views beyond a commercial Reform."[98]

Under the influence of Hamilton, the conference at Annapolis contented itself with merely recommending that another convention be called "to devise such further pro- visions as shall appear to them necessary to render the constitution of the federal government adequate to the exigencies of the Union." Acting on this modest suggestion, Congress, in February, 1787, invited the states to send delegates to a Convention at Philadelphia for " the sole and express purpose of revising the Articles of Confederation."

Certain tentative conclusions emerge at this point.

Large an important groups of economic interests were adversely affected by the system of government under the Articles of Confederation, namely, those of public securities, shipping and manufacturing, money at interest; in short, capital as opposed to land.

The representatives of these important interests attempted through the regular legal channels to secure amendments to the Articles of Confederation which would safeguard their rights in the future, particularly those of the public creditors"

Having failed to realize their great purposes through the regular means, the leaders in the movement set to work to secure by a circuitous route the assemblying of a convention to "revise" the Articles of Confederation with the hope of obtaining, outside of the existing legal framework, the adoption of a revolutionary programme.

Ostensibly, however, the formal plan of approval by Congress and the state legislatures was to be preserved.

---

[98] *Writings of James Madison* (1865), Vol. I, p. 246.

Chapter 4.

Property Safeguard in the Election of Delegates.

Under the protection afforded by these outward signs of regularity, the leaders in the movement for the new Constitution set to work in their respective legislatures to secure the choice of delegates prepared to take the heroic measures which the circumstances demanded. The zealous and dynamic element, of course, was favoured by the inertness, ignorance, and indifference of the masses, and the confidence of the legislatures in their ability to exercise the ultimate control through the ratifying power. No special popular elections were called to complicate the problem of securing the right kind of a Convention and the leaders were confronted with the comparatively simple task of convincing the legislatures of the advisability of sending delegates. Naturally the most strenuous and interested advocates of change came forward as candidates.

The resolution of the Congress under the Articles of Confederation calling for the Convention provided that the delegates should be "appointed by the states." The actual selection was made in each case by the legislature, both houses participating, except in Georgia and Pennsylvania, which had unicameral assemblies. That is, the delegates to the federal Convention were selected in the same fashion as were United States Senators under the present Constitution, in all states, previous to the adoption of the principle of direct election. This fact in itself removed the choice of delegates one degree from the electorate.

A further safeguard against the injection of too much popular feeling into the choice of delegates to the convention was afforded by the property qualifications generally placed on voters and members of the legislatures by the state constitutions and laws in force in 1787.[99] In order to ascertain the precise character of the defence afforded to property by this barrier to universal manhood suffrage, it is necessary to inquire in detail into the qualifications then imposed.[100]

The New Hampshire constitution of 1784 was in force when the call for the election of delegates came. It provided that "no person shall be capable of being elected a senator who is not of the Protestant religion, and seized of a freehold estate in his own right of the value of two hundred pounds."[101] Members of the lower house were required to " possess an estate of the value of one hundred pounds, one, half of which to be a freehold." The suffrage was widely extended, for freeholders, tax payers, and even those who paid a poll tax could vote. Massachusetts conferred the suffrage upon all males possessing a freehold estate of the annual income of three pounds, or any estate of the value of sixty pounds. A senator was required to be " seized in his own right of a freehold within this commonwealth, of the value of three hundred pounds at least, or possessed of a personal estate of the value of six hundred pounds at least, or of both to the amount of the same sum." Every member of the house of representatives was required to be "seized in his own right of a free hold of the value of one hundred pounds, within the town he shall be chosen to represent, or any rateable estate to the value of two hundred pounds; and he shall cease to represent the said town immediately on his ceasing to be qualified as aforesaid."

Like the neighbouring state of Rhode Island, which sent no delegates to Philadelphia, Connecticut had continued after the Revolution under the old royal charter form of government without taking the trouble to

---

[99] On the suffrage and elections in general in the eighteenth century, see the state constitutions in the well-known collections of Poore and Thorpe; A.E. McKinley, *The Suffrage Franchise in the Thirteen English Colonies;* Paullin's "The First Elections under the Constitution," Iowa Journal of History and Politics, Vol. II; Jameson, ., Did the Fathers Vote," New England Magazine, January, 1890; Thorpe, *Constitutional History of the American People;* S.H. Miller, '.Legal Qualifications for Office;' *American Historical Association Report* (1899), Vol. I; F.A. Cleveland, *Growth of Democracy*; C. F. Bishop, *History of Elections in the American Colonies;* see below, Chap. IX.

[100] The data on the constitutions here given are taken from Thorpe's collection, *Charters, Constitutions,* etc.

[101] Senators were apportioned among the respective districts on the basis of public taxes paid by the said districts.

draft a constitution. Under this old system, the suffrage was restricted to holders of real or personal property of a certain value. According to McKinley, "The forty-shilling freehold, translated later into seven dollars income from land, was retained as one of the alternative qualifications of the suffrage until the amendment in 1845 of the constitution of 1818."[102] The alternative qualification here spoken of was the ownership of forty pounds' worth of personal property, which was established in 1702 and remained until after the Revolution. The Connecticut Register of the time thus quaintly describes the franchise: "The qualifications for freemen are that they be at least twenty-one years of age, possessed of freehold estate to the value of 40s. per ann. or £40 personal estate in the general list of estates in that year wherein they desire to be admitted Freemen; or are possessed of estate as aforesaid and by law excused from putting it into the list; and being of quiet and peaceable behaviour."[103]

New York gave a special position to the rights of property in the senate. Senators were required to be freeholders, and were chosen by freeholders "possessed of freeholds of the value of one hundred pounds." With regard to the of voter for members of the lower house, it was stipulated that "he shall have been a freeholder, possessing a freehold of the value of twenty pounds within said county, or have rented a tenement therein of the yearly value of forty to shillings, and been rated and actually paid taxes to this be state." An exception to this rule conferred the suffrage on all who were freemen in Albany, and in New York City, on or before October 14, 1775.

These qualifications worked an extensive disfranchisement in New York. "The census of 1790 shows that out of a population of thirty thousand [in New York City], there were but 1,209 freeholders of £100 valuation or over; 1,221 of £20, and 2,661 'forty-shilling' freeholders. Property interests - something like a landed aristocracy - controlled municipal elections."[104] Some notion of the extent to which the adult males would have voted if permitted, is afforded by the elections of 1788, at which members of the state ratifying convention were chosen under the universal manhood suffrage rule,[105] and members of the assembly were chosen under the regular property qualifications.

For example, Richard Harrison received 2677 votes as member of the convention, and 1500 votes as member of the state assembly.[106] In Albany County the vote for members of the assembly ran about 1600 under that for members of the convention.[107] It looks as if one could safely guess that about one-third more voters would have been active participants in elections if they had not been shut out b the prevailing property qualifications in New York.

New Jersey had a legislature of two houses, a council and a general assembly. Every member of the former had to be a freeholder and " worth at least one thousand pound proclamation money, or real and personal estate within the same county;" and every member of the latter body was required to possess at least half as much in real and personal property. As for the suffrage, the constitution provided " that all inhabitants of this colony, of full age, who are worth fifty pounds proclamation money clear estate in the same. ...shall be entitled to vote for Representatives in Council and Assembly."

---

[102] *The Suffrage Franchise in the English Colonies,* p. 414.

[103] *Greene's Register for the State of Connecticut,* for the Year 1786, p. 4.

[104] Magazine of American History, April, 1893, p. 311.

[105] See below, p. 241.

[106] New York Journal, June 5, 1788.

[107] *Ibid.*

The Delaware constitution of 1776 provided that members of both branches of the legislature should be chosen from among the freeholders of the county, and that " the right of suffrage in the election of members for both houses shall remain as exercised by law at present." The election law which then governed the suffrage in Delaware was the act of 1734 which enfranchised freeholders owning "fifty acres of land, with twelve acres cleared and improved, or otherwise worth £40 lawful money."[108]

The first constitution of Pennsylvania established in 1776 was the work of a radical party, and it provided for a single chambered legislature based on a widely extended suffrage. "Every freeman of the full age of twenty-one years," runs the instrument, "having resided in this state for the space of one whole year. ..and paid public taxes during that time, shall enjoy the right of an elector: *Provided* always that sons of freeholders of the age of twenty-one years shall be entitled to vote although they have not paid taxes."[109]

In Maryland a distinction was made between town and county in the choice of delegates to the lower house of the state legislature. Generally every freeman "having a freehold of fifty acres of land," or " having property in this state above the value of thirty pounds current money " could vote in the county in which he resided for members of the house of delegates. All persons qualified by the charter of Annapolis to vote for burgesses could vote for delegates from that city; and in Baltimore persons "having the same qualifications as electors in the county" could vote he for delegates. County delegates in the state legislature in were required to possess "real or personal property above the value of five hundred pounds current money." The senators were chosen indirectly by electors selected by the qualified voters for delegates. These senatorial electors of were to possess the qualifications of delegates, and senators themselves had to possess "real and personal property above the value of one thousand pounds current money."

The Virginia constitution of 1776 stipulated that members of both houses of the legislature must be " freeholders or duly qualified according to law;" and added that "the right of suffrage in the election of members of both houses shall remain as exercised at present." Under this provision, persons owning twenty-five acres of improved land or fifty acres of unimproved land were admitted to the suffrage, " together with certain artisans residing in Norfolk and Williamsburg."[110]

At the time of choosing delegates to the Convention, North Carolina was under the constitution of 1776, which prescribed property qualifications for members of the legislature and for voters as well. Each member of the senate was required to possess "not less than three hundred acres of land in fee," and each member of the lower house "not less than one hundred acres of land in fee or for the term of his own life." A freehold qualification of fifty acres of land was required of voters for senators, and the suffrage for voters for members of the lower house was extended to all freemen who paid "public taxes." In the towns entitled to representation the possession of a freehold or the payment of a public tax qualified for voting in the election of members of the lower house.

The legislature of South Carolina, that chose the representatives of that state to the Philadelphia Convention, was elected under the constitution of 1778 which prescribed high property qualifications.[111] "No person who resides in the parish for which he is elected shall take his seat in the senate, unless he possess a settled estate and freehold in his own right in the said parish or district of the value of two thousand pounds currency at least, clear of debt." Non-resident senators were required to be the holders of such an estate worth at least seven thousand pounds, clear of debt. The member of the lower house was required to possess an

---

[108] McKinley, *The Suffrage Franchise in the English Colonies*, p. 270.

[109] Tench Coxe fixes the number of "taxables" in Pennsylvania at 39,765 in 1770 and 91,177 in 1793. *A View of the United States*, p. 413.

[110] Ambler, *Sectionalism in Virginia*, p. 29, note 11; for details see McKinley, op. *cit.*, pp. 40 ff.

[111] Schaper, "Sectionalism in South Carolina," *American Historical Association Report* (1900), Vol. I, p. 368.

estate and slaves or realty worth one thousand pounds,[112] while each non-resident member of that house had to own a freehold estate worth at least three thousand five hundred pounds, clear of debt. The suffrage was restricted to persons owning fifty acres, or a town lot, or paying taxes equivalent to the taxes on fifty acres of land.

In 1787, the Georgia legislature consisted of one chamber, under the constitution of 1777, which stipulated that members of the house of representatives "Shall be of the Protestant religion, and of the age of twenty-one years, and shall be possessed in their own rights of two hundred and not fifty acres of land or some property to the amount of two hundred and fifty pounds." The suffrage was widely extended to every white male having in his own right property "of ten pounds value and liable to pay tax " or " being of any to mechanic trade."

From this review it is apparent that a majority of the states placed direct property qualifications on the voters, on and the other states eliminated practically all who were not taxpayers. Special safeguards for property were secured in the qualifications imposed on members of the legislatures as in New Hampshire, Massachusetts, New York, New Jersey, Maryland, North Carolina, South Carolina, and Georgia. Further safeguards were added by the qualifications imposed in the case of senators in New Hampshire, Massachusetts, New Jersey, New York, Maryland, North Carolina, and South Carolina.

While these qualifications operated to exclude a large portion of the adult males from participating in elections, the wide distribution of real property created an extensive electorate and in most rural regions gave the legislatures a broad popular basis.[113] Far from rendering to personal property that defence which was necessary to the full realization of its rights, these qualifications for electors admitted to the suffrage its most dangerous antagonists: the small farmers and many of the debtors who were the most active in all attempts to depreciate personalty by legislation. Madison with his usual acumen saw the inadequacy of such defence and pointed out in the Convention that the really serious assaults on property (having in mind of course, personalty) had come from the " freeholders."[114]

Nevertheless, in the election of delegates to the Conven- tion, the representatives of personalty in the legislature were able by the sheer weight of their combined intelligence and economic power to secure delegates from the urban centres or allied with their interests. Happily for them, all legislatures which they had to convince had not been elected on the issue of choosing delegates to a national Convention: and did not come from a populace stirred up on that question.[115] The call for the Convention went forth on February 2 1787, from Congress, and within a few months all the legislatures, except that of Rhode Island, had responded. Thus the heated popular discussion usually incident to such momentous political undertaking was largely avoided, an, an orderly and temperate procedure in the selection delegates was rendered possible.

---

[112] *Statutes at Large* (S.C.), Vol. IV, p. 93.

[113] See below, p. 242.

[114] *Ibid.*, p. 167.

[115] Some of the states selected delegates before Congress issued the call. Bancroft *op. cit.*,vol. I, pp. 269 ff.

Chapter 5.

The Economic Interests of the Members of the Convention.

Having shown that four groups of property rights were adversely affected by the government under the Articles of Confederation, and that economic motives were behind the movement for a reconstruction of the system, it is now necessary to inquire whether the members of the Convention which drafted the Constitution represented in their own property affiliations any or all of these groups. In other words, did the men who formulated the fundamental law of the land possess the kinds of property which were immediately and directly increased in value or made more secure by the results of their labours at Philadelphia? Did they have money at interest? Did they own public securities? Did they hold western lands for appreciation? Were they interested in shipping and manufactures?

The purpose of such an inquiry is not, of course, to show that the Constitution was made for the personal benefit of the members of the Convention. Far from it. Neither is it of any moment to discover how many hundred thousand dollars accrued to them as a result of the foundation of the new government. The only point here considered is: Did they represent distinct groups whose economic interests they understood and felt in concrete, definite form through their own personal experience with identical property rights, or were they working merely under the guidance of abstract principles of political science?

Unfortunately, the materials for such a study are very scanty, because the average biographer usually considers as negligible the processes by which his hero gained his livelihood. The pages which follow are, therefore, more an evidence of what ought to be done than a record of results actually accomplished. They would be meagre, indeed, were it not for the rich unpublished records of the Treasury Department which are here used for the first time in this connection; and they would doubtless have been fuller were it not for the fact that most of the books showing the central operations of the Treasury Department under Hamilton have disappeared. The names of the attending members of the Convention are given in alphabetical order.

Of **Abraham Baldwin's** private fortune there is little known. His father was evidently well-to-do, for he enjoyed the advantage of a classical education at Yale before he established himself in the practice of law at Savannah, Georgia. He soon rose to eminence in his profession, and was reckoned among the ablest and shrewdest lawyers of his adopted commonwealth. A short sketch of him states that by "his constant habits of economy and temperance," he accumulated enough to enable him to assist many young men in their education and establishment in business. When his father died, in 1787, he was able to pay the debts of the insolvent estate, and he educated his six half brothers and sisters "in a great measure at his own expense."[116]

Some portion of Baldwin's fortune was invested in public securities. He possessed a few thousand dollars worth of the stocks of the new government at its very inception, which doubtless represented old paper of the Confederation acquired by original subscription or by purchase. The ledgers and other principal records of Georgia are appar- ently unavailable - at all events a search at the Treasury Department failed to reveal them; but Baldwin held some paper which is entered on the books of his native state, Connecticut, in April, 1792: deferred 6 per cents, funded 6 per cents, and 3 per cents to the amount of about $2500.[117]

---

[116] Herring, *National Portrait Gallery,* Vol. IV.

[117] Ms. Treasury Department: *Connecticut Loan Office. Ledger B. Assumed Debt,* folio 135; *ibid., Ledger C,* folio 135; *ibid., Ledger A.* folio 136.

At later dates, 1797 and 1804, he appears on the Treasury Records for several thousand dollars worth of 6 per cents this and 3 per cents, but the sources of these sums are not apparent.[118] It is probable, however, that these stocks were the paper which Baldwin funded at the Treasury instead of a loan office. He was a member of Congress, and naturally would have transacted business with the agency nearest at hand. They may, of course, represent purchases for investment, made after the great appreciation had taken place.[119]

There is no exhaustive biography of **Richard Bassett**, of Delaware. A brief sketch of him relates that he "was born in 1745. He was the adopted son of Mr. Lawson, a lawyer, led who married Miss Inzer. The Inzer family was Herman's heir to Bohemia Manor. ...Mr. Bassett was educated and trained for the profession of law by Mr. Lawson, whose heir he became. By this inheritance he came into in possession of six thousand acres of Bohemia manor, which we are informed, embraced the fairest and best portion of he the Manor."[120] Through his inheritance and his accumulations in the practice of law, he became one of the wealthy men of his state. Another biographer notes that "His fortune was large and he entertained lavishly at his three homes in Wilmington, Dover, and at Bohemia Manor."[121] He was on intimate terms with the leading financial men the community; he was very active in securing a charter in Delaware for the Bank of North America when it was attacked by the Pennsylvania legislature, and was warmly thanked for his success by President Willing, in a letter dated February 6, 1786.[122]

Whether any considerable amount of Mr. Bassett's large fortune was invested in public securities at the inception the new government it is impossible to ascertain, on account of the meagre records of the state of Delaware preserved in the Treasury Department. In the later documents the central office of the Treasury there appears the remnant of "an old account" to the amount of a few hundred dollars worth of 3 per cents and 6 per cents under dates of 1796 a 1797.[123] A reasonable inference from the entry would be that Bassett, like other members of Congress, carried on transactions directly with the Treasury (whose early records are missing), and that these holdings were based on paper originally funded.

Gunning Bedford, of Delaware, was the son of a "substantial land owner"[124] and a Bedford of that name appears on the tax lists of Newcastle county for the year 1776 for the amount of sixteen pounds, a moderate

---

[118] *Ibid., Ledger E, Treasury,* Vol. 44, folio 46; *Ledger C. Treasury* 6 per cents, Vol. 42, folio 55; and Treasury Ledgers, *passim.* Consult Index.

[119] It is here assumed that when a member of the Convention appears upon the funding books of the new government he was a public creditor at the time of the Convention. Of course, it is possible that some of the members who are recorded as security holders possessed no paper when they went to Philadelphia, but purchased it afterward for speculation. But it is hardly to be supposed that many of them would sink to the level of mere speculators. There is plenty of evidence for the statement that many of the members did possess public paper *before* the meeting of the Convention, but the incompleteness of the old records prevents the fixing of the exact number. Those members who purchased after the Convention for speculation must have had idle capital seeking investment.

[120] *Papers of the Delaware Historical Society,* No. XXIX (1900).

[121] *National Encyclopaedia of Biography.* Vol. XI. p. 530.

[122] *History of the Bank of North America,* p. 68.

[123] Ms. Treasury Department: *Ledger E, Treasury,* Vol. 44, folio 26; and *ibid Ledger C, Treasury,* 6 per cents, Vol. 42, folio 33.

[124] *National Encyclopaedia of Biography.* Vol. XI, p. 530.

sum for those days.[125] He was a lawyer, but the extent of his practice is not known. He was of high standing in the community, and was elected governor of his state a few years after the Convention met. He took an interest in the financial affairs of the state, and under his administration as governor the Bank of Delaware was organized. How far Bedford had an interest in public securities cannot be determined on account of the fact that only a few scraps of the loan office papers for Delaware seem to be preserved in the Treasury Department. An old loan office volume shows a Gunning Bedford down for one $400 certificate of May, 1779[126] and large traces of the financial connections of the member of the Convention with the government are to be found in the Pennsylvania loan office records.[127]

John Blair, of Virginia, was born in that state about 1731. He received a collegiate education, prepared for the law, and "in a very few years rose to the head of his profession."[128] Pierce, in his notes on the men of the Convention, says: "Mr. Blair is one of the most respectable men in Virginia, both on account of his Family as well as fortune. He is one of the Judges of the Supreme Court of Virginia, and acknowledged to have a very extensive knowledge of the Laws. Mr. Blair is however no orator, but his good sense and most excellent principles compensate for other deficiencies."[129]

Blair took advantage of the excellent opportunity afforded by the formation of the new Constitution to profit by the rise of securities. He appears frequently in the fiscal transactions between the federal government and the Virginia loan office, of which a few illustrations need be given here. In March, 1791, he presented £577/16/7 in Virginia certificates toward the United States loan; and of these securities £249 had been invested by Blair himself in 1782. The remaining amount he had purchased on his own account.[130] In the same year an agent of Blair presented two small certificates which had evidently been purchased by the principal because they were issued to other parties in 1778.[131] In September of that year, Blair himself turned in nearly $10,000 worth of paper on the United States loan of which apart was purchased and a part original issues to the holder.[132]

William Blount, of North Carolina, was the son of Jacob Blount who died in 1789, "leaving a large estate."[133] Of the younger Blount's property interests in 1787 it is impossible to speak in detail. Very early after the establishment of the new government he was connected with land speculations on a large scale.[134] In 1790 he was appointed by Washington to the post of governor of the Territory South of the Ohio and it seems that

---

[125] Delaware Mss., *Tax Lists;* Library of Congress. This was probably the father of the member of the Convention.

[126] Ms. Treasury Department: *Loan Office, Delaware,* 1777-1784, see under date, May, 1779.

[127] *Journal C; Register of Certificates* (1777); and *Ledger C.*

[128] *Biographia Americana*, p. 48.

[129] Farrand, *Records vol.* III, p. 95.

[130] Ms. Treasury Department: *Loan Office (Va.) Register of Subscriptions,* 1791 see date March 8, 1791.

[131] *Ibid., Register of Certificates of Public Debt Presented.*

[132] *Ibid., Virginia Loan Office,* 1791, under date September 30, 1791.

[133] *National Encyclopaedia of Biography,* Vol. VII, p. 206.

[134] Haskins, *The Yazoo Companies,* p. 83.

he did not consider the employment of public office for personal gain as incompatible with the discharge of his administrative duties. In July, 1797 President Adams sent a message to Congress asserting that there was a conspiracy in the southwest to wrest New Orleans and the Floridas from the King of Spain and transfer then to the English crown, and adding that Blount, who was then a Senator from Tennessee, was implicated in the plot. The United States Senate immediately took action, and after inquiry expelled him by a vote of twenty-five to one on the charge of "high misdemeanour inconsistent with public trust and duty." When the sergeant-at-arms went to arrest him and take him to Philadelphia for trial he refused to go; and in his refusal he was warmly supported by his friends, of whom he had a legion, for, as his biographer remarks, "He was a man of commanding presence, courtly yet simple manners, and having a large salary and large private means, he entertained lavishly at his house."[135]

It does not appear that Blount combined dealings in loan, securities with speculations in land, for the loan office of North Carolina credits him with only a small holding, and the origin of that is not apparent.[136] It is true that the records Jacob of that state are incomplete, but Blount's appointment to the western post at the beginning of Washington's administration must have precluded extensive operations in securities.

David Brearley, of New Jersey, was the grandson of John Brearley, who "owned 1600 acres of land near Newton, N. J. ...a hundred acre plantation on the Delaware. .. besides several thousand acres of land near Lawrenceville."[137] A brief sketch of him states that he "received the honours of Princeton at the age of eighteen. On leaving that celebrated seminary, he commenced the study of law, and in a leans few years stood foremost at the bar of his native state."[138] In 1779 he was appointed chief justice of New Jersey, a post which he held until 1789 when he resigned to accept a position as judge of the United States district court of that state.[139]

Brearley died in the summer of 1790 and consequenty could not have established any fiscal relations with the new government. The incompleteness of the early loan office records for New Jersey, preserved in the Treasury Department, renders impossible a positive statement concerning Brearley's holdings of securities at the time of the Convention. Only one small entry appears in his name for a few hundred dollars in a certificate purchased in 1779;[140] his relatives however, appear frequently on the loan office books of his state; but their aggregate holdings were small. Joseph Brearley's name occurs several times, for example in July 1791, for $505.80 worth of 3 per cents;[141] David Brearley had son and a brother bearing that name.[142] Elizabeth Brearle

---

[135] *Encyclopaedia of Biography,* Vol. VII, p. 206.

[136] Ms. Treasury Department: *Loan Office, N.C.,* 1791-1797, folio 75.

[137] *The Brearley Family Genealogy* (Library of Congress).

[138] *Biographia Americana,* p. 49.

[139] L. Elmer, *Constitution and Government of New Jersey,* p. 274.

[140] Ms. Treasury Department: *Register-Loan Office, N.J.,* under date, Feb. 1779.

[141] *Ibid., Loan Office, N. J., Ledger* C/2, folio 38.

[142] *Brearley Family Genealogy* (L.C.).

is also among the small holders, and the Chief Justice first and second wife and a daughter bore that name.[143] The name of Zerujah Brearley - a sister of the member of the Convention[144] - also appears.

Jacob Broom, of Delaware, was born at Wilmington, in 1752. His father "originally a blacksmith was regarded as one of 'the gentry' of the day, and was 'a man of considerable substance, in real estate, silver, and gold,' although not one of the very wealthiest of his class. 'Class' distinctions, arising from birth, education, and worldly possessions were not wholly ignored at that time by those who came to this land to find a home, a sanctuary, and liberty. And so in the transactions of the period we find James Broom, Jacob's father, referred to as James Broom, Gentleman; and Jacob Broom as Surveyor. And both of these men had lands and houses to rent and sell and gold and silver to loan on good security. And both of them sold and rented and loaned."[145]

Broom was a man of diversified financial resources. He was interested in cotton mills and other enterprises. He was one of the original stockholders of the Insurance Company of North America organized at Philadelphia in 1792.[146] He was also one of the organizers and original stockholders of the Delaware Bank established under Bedford's administration.[147] As mentioned above, the fragmentary records of Delaware in the Treasury Department throw little light on the public security holders of that state at the time of the formation of the Constitution; but the ledgers of the central Treasury show that Broom was a holder of a small amount of 3 per cents in 1797 and that this was a remnant of an older account.[148] Broom was also willing to serve the new government in an official capacity, for he applied to Madison in April, 1789, for an appointment as collector at Wilmington.[149]

Pierce Butler, of South Carolina, was a descendant of the Duke of Ormond and was very vain of his noble birth.[150] William Pierce in his notes on the members of the Convention records that Butler "is a gentleman of fortune and takes rank among the first in South Carolina."[151] He was a large slave holder, having thirty-one in his possession at the time of the first census. He also possessed some public securities, for he was a stockholder and director of the first United States Bank, and must have purchased his shares on the same basis as other stockholders, that is, by the exchange of securities. He does not appear on the records of South Carolina, however, but his daughter, Sarah, had in 1792 a small amount of the assumed debt.[152]

---

143   See records in Treasury for N.J. Loan Office, *passim;* also *Family Genealogy.*

144   *Genealogy.*

145   W.W. Campbell, *Life and Character of Jacob Broom,* Papers of the Historical Society of Delaware, Vol. LI, pp. 10, 26.

146   *History of the Insurance Company of North America,* p. 138.

147   Campbell, *op. cit.,* p. 26.

148   Ms. Treasury Department: *Ledger E, Treasury,* 3%, Vol. 44, folio 57; also, *Ibid., Ledger C, Treasury,* 6%, Vol. 42, folio 67.

149   *Calendar Madison Correspondence,* under Broom.

150   *National Encyclopaedia of Biography,* Vol. II, p. 162.

151   Farrand, *Records,* Vol. III, p. 97.

152   Ms. Treasury Department: *Loan Office, S.C., 1791-1797,* folio 128. The entry in the ledger notes the residence of Sarah Butler as Charleston; there was another Sarah Butler in South Carolina at the time, but

Daniel Carroll, of Maryland, is recorded by his contemporary, Pierce, as "a man of large fortune and influence in his state."[153] His interests were wide and varied. He was a stockholder in the Potomac Company;[154] and he favoured the adoption of a protective tariff, for he was among the signers of the petition for such a measure laid before the first Congress under the new Constitution.[155] He was a holder of public securities, for his name occurs frequently in the Treasury records of the period.[156] His chief source of profit out of the new system was however in the location of the capitol at Washington, on land which he owned.[157] Incidentally, he was able to facilitate this last transaction, for he was a member of the Congress of 1789-1791 and was one of the commissioners appointed to layout the District of Columbia.

George Clymer, of Pennsylvania, was the son of "a well- to-do merchant and ship builder of Philadelphia" who had augmented his fortunes by marrying the daughter of a South fellow merchant of the same city.[158] On the early death of .1792 his parents he was placed under the guardianship of William Coleman, one of the first business men of his native city, whose counting house he entered to learn all the arts of mercantile pursuits and "the principal part of whose fortune he inherited."[159] Clymer's personal fortune was further enhanced by a happy marriage to Elizabeth Meredith, the daughter of Reese Meredith, "one of the principal merchants of Philadelphia."[160] He was thus a brother-in-law of Mr. Meredith the first treasurer of the Union, also a man of "large fortune."[161] For some time Clymer was associated profit in business with his father- and brother-in-law .[162]

Mr. Clymer's intimate associations were therefore mercantile and financial, and his large fortune and quick understanding of the needs of trade and commerce made him one of the first men of his city in the Revolution and gave him a wide influence during the critical period, the formation of the Constitution, and

---

according to the first Census she did not reside in that city. For the evidence that Sarah Butler was the daughter of Pierce Butler, see Salley, *South Carolina Marriages*, p. 108, for the record of her marriage.

[153]   Farrand, *Records*, Vol. III, p. 93.

[154]   Madison Ms: Letter to James Madison, October 28, 1787, Library of Congress.

[155]   *State Papers: Finance*, Vol. I, p. 6.

[156]   Ms. Treasury Department: *Loan Office, Maryland*, 1790-1797, folio 98; *Loan Office*, Penna., 1790-1791, folio 94; *Ledger C, 3% Stock (Pa.)*, folio 54. Alphabet to Dividend Book of Domestic Debt, Maryland, under "C " (book not found). Charles Carroll was also a holder of securities. Ms. Treasury Department; *Maryland Loan Office*, 1790-1797, folios 157 and 226 for over $5000 worth of sixes and threes.

[157]   Scharf, *History of Western Maryland*, Vol. I, p. 679; H. Crew, *History of Washington*, p. 108.

[158]   *Magazine of American History*, Vol. V, p. 196.

[159]   Sanderson, *Biography of the Signers* (1831 ed.), Vol. III, p. 147.

[160]   Sanderson, *ibid.*, p. 150.

[161]   Simpson, *Lives of Eminent Philadelphians* (1859 ed.), p. 693.

[162]   Sanderson, *ibid.*, p. 147.

the establishment of the new government, which he served as a member of Congress and later in several official capacities.

In all financial matters he took a deep interest. He helped to create the temporary Bank of Pennsylvania in 1780, and subscribed £5000 to its capital stock. When the Bank of North America was organized he became one of the directors and later was president of the Philadelphia Bank.[163]

Clymer turned his extensive financial experience to some account in handling the securities of the new government which he had been instrumental in framing, for he is recorded in the Pennsylvania books as holding, in August, 1791, over $3000 worth of 3 per cent securities.[164] If he held sixes deferred and funded, as may be assumed, although the incomplete records apparently do not permit of a verification or denial of this, he had in all over $10,000 worth of the government paper.

Wm. R. Davie, of North Carolina, was born in England in 1756 and was brought to America in 1763 by his father, who left him in care of his maternal uncle, William Richardson, a Presbyterian clergyman, who took charge of his education and on his death bequeathed to him his estate.[165] Davie chose the profession of law, and by a lucrative practice "he quickly accumulated a large estate."[166] He was of counsel in the famous case of Bayard *v.* Singleton, and he had the satisfaction of securing from the court an opinion declaring an act of the state legislature unconstitutional.[167] He held a fine plantation at Tivoli and at his death left a considerable estate which was the subject of litigation as late as 1892 in the Supreme Court of the United States. His personal property certainly was not small for he was able to pay $5000 for a thoroughbred colt.[168] His connections with the landed proprietors of his region were intimate and extensive and he is reported to have drawn all the wills made during his time in that part of the state.[169]

Jonathan Dayton, of New Jersey, was associated with, and agent for, John Cleves Symmes, in the purchase of an enormous tract of land in Ohio in July and October, 1787, the year of the Convention (formally consummated in 1788), and before the ensealing of the contract Symmes and his associates had paid into the Treasury $82,198 "one seventh in military rights and the residue in the public securities of the United States." The remainder was to be paid in gold or silver or the securities of the United States, and part, (one seventh) in military rights. In 1792 Symmes and Dayton complained that on account of the "advanced price of

---

[163] McMaster and Stone, *Pennsylvania and the Federal Constitution*, p. 705.

[164] Ms. Treasury Department: *Ledger C*, 3% Stock, *Pa.*, folio 231; see also *Ledger E, Treasury*, 3%, Vol. 44, folio 170; and *Ledger C, Treasury*, 6%, Vol. 42, folio 114. The existence of this latter small account in sixes in 1797 is the basis for the surmise above that Clymer held also his quota of sixes. With his business acumen he might very well have disposed of most of this stock after ..taking the rise" in 1787-1792, for he could have made more money in business than from the interest which the government paid.

[165] Peele, Lives *of Distinguished North Carolinians*, p. 59.

[166] *Ibid.*, p. 69.

[167] *Ibid.*, p. 69.

[168] *Ibid.*, p. 80.

[169] *Ibid.*, p. 78.

certificates," they must have easier terms. It is apparent from this record,[170] that they were engaged in buying up military certificates and government securities about the time of the meeting of the Convention.

Afterward, by collusion with Ludlow, the official surveyor, and the inadvertence of Hamilton, Secretary of the Treasury, Symmes, Dayton, and associates secured "the advantage of paying almost two-sevenths of their contract and above one-half of their actual payments in military warrants of one acre for an acre and a half of the supposed million, instead of one-seventh part of the actual payments" at a loss to the United States of more than $30,000.[171] In March and April, 1800, Dayton purchased about 15,000 acres of public lands with military certificates.[172]

If further evidence were needed that Dayton was speculating vigorously in government securities and military certificates, it is to be found in a suit brought by him and his partner, Lawrence, against Childs, a member of their concern in 1800, which was carried before Chancellor Livingston and later withdrawn. In this case Childs ex- hibited sixteen letters from Dayton, showing that while the latter was Speaker of the House of Representatives he had been engaged in speculations in public land warrants. Dayton was not unaware of the improper character of such transactions, for in a letter of April 17, 1796, he wrote to Childs: "The contents of this letter are of such a nature as to render it improper to be seen by any except yourself; burn it therefore, when you have perused it."[173]

The conclusive evidence of Dayton's extensive operatic in public securities during the period of the establishment of the new government and his term of service as Speaker is afforded by the records of the Treasury Department. Here he appears so frequently on the books of the loan offices of several states that some pages of this volume would be required to present the bare data of his transactions. However, a few examples of his dealings may be given by way of illustration. He appears on the loan office books of New York in February and March, 1791, for the following amounts: $17,060.82, $8530.40, $11,332.93, $7401.31, $3700.73, and $5100.61, totalling more than $50,000.[174] At another point he is recorded for more than $15,000;[175] and at another point for $6000.[176] Although Woods is not celebrated for the painstaking impartiality of his famous *History of Adam, Administration,* he is singularly accurate in one of his characterizations: "Jonathan Dayton, of New Jersey, the late speaker of Congress, is notorious from Boston to Georgia. The deeds of other members of Congress were scarcely known beyond the circle of their respective states, but the speculations of this man have rung throughout the western world."[177]

John Dickinson, of Delaware, was a member of one of the established landed families of the south. He was born in 1732, on a plantation in Talbot County, on the eastern shores of Maryland; and eight years after

---

[170] *State Papers: Public Lands,* Vol. I, pp. 104-106.

[171] *Ibid.,* p. 129.

[172] *Ibid.,* p. 118.

[173] John Wood, *Suppressed History of the Administration of John Adams,* pp. 149.

[174] Ms. Treasury Department: *N.Y. Loan Office,* 1791, folio 130.

[175] *Ibid., N.Y. Office, Deferred 6%,* 1790-1796, folio 208.

[176] *Ibid., Ledger B, New York Office, Deferred 6% Stock,* 1790, folio 55.

[177] J. Wood, *Suppressed History of the Administration of John Adams* (1846 ed.), p. 145.

his birth, his father, Samuel Dickinson moved from Maryland to Delaware "where he purchased a large estate in Kent County, near Dover."[178] Dickinson was a student of law in the Middle Temple and took up the practice of his profession in Philadelphia in 1757.[179] Within five years he had acquired an extensive practice and won a respectable standing at the bar.

If his personal fortunes, however, had not been sufficient to assure him a satisfactory position in the business and professional world at Philadelphia, his marriage into one of the first and wealthiest commercial families would have more than made up for his deficiencies.

In 1770 he married Mary Norris, and for a time lived at the family estate, Fairhill, one of the show places of the day: "This house," says Simpson,[180] "was in its day a very grand mansion and a place of great celebrity, with a large front of sixty feet. It was surrounded by forest and evergreen trees of majestic growth and well-arranged shrubbery. It commanded a beautiful prospect of the city, with a distant view of the Delaware. ...The mansion was two stories high and most substantially built, with a very wide hall running through its centre. The library was papered, but the parlors and hall were wainscotted with oak and red cedar unpainted, but polished with wax and kept in bright and handsome order by constant rubbing. The carriageway was finely graduated and wound through an extensive lawn, from its approach on the Germantown road which was bordered with shrubbery. The pleasure grounds, lawn, green house, and gardens, fish-ponds, and walk, embraced a large area of several acres in extent." It is true the vast estates bequeathed to Miss Norris by her father were transferred to collateral male heirs in order to preserve the family holding and name, but she retained the "considerable personal property" which her father left to her.[181] Dickinson was able to make a large gift to Dickinson College, named in his honour; and he and his wife were widely celebrated for their extensive benefactions.[182]

The meagreness of the Treasury records for Delaware make it impossible to determine whether Dickinson was engaged in fiscal operations along with his intimate friend, Robert Morris, Thomas Willing, George Clymer, and other prominent Philadelphia men of affairs. It is possible that he was not largely engaged in the public security transactions,[183] for he was an extremely cautious man in finances and had got into serious discredit with the patriot part; during the Revolution, because it was rumoured that he had advised his brother against accepting the payment of debt in paper which was sure to depreciate. He was also unhappily involved with Robert Morris to the amount of £7000 at the time of the latter's embarrassment, and may not have wished to incur further risks.[184]

Oliver Ellsworth, of Connecticut, was the son of a clever Connecticut farmer who inherited a hundred pounds and "had the industry and the shrewdness to accumulate a considerable estate and to win the

---

[178] Stille, *Life and Time& of John Dickinson*, p. 14.

[179] *Ibid*, p. 35.

[180] *Eminent Philadelphians*, p. 747.

[181] Stille, p. 331.

[182] *Ibid.*, p. 327.

[183] The Index in the Treasury Department gives the name of John Dickinson among the security holders, but the volume referred to was not found.

[184] Morris Ms. in the Library of Congress, *Private Letter Book,* Vol. III, p. 160.

reputation of an excellent farmer."[185] Oliver was educated at Yale and Princeton and became a lawyer in spite of his father's determination to force him into the ministry. Though he was almost brief-less during the early days of his practice, he had the good fortune to wed the daughter of William Wolcott, of East Windsor, "a gentleman of substance and distinction."[186] He is described by his biographer as a man of great purpose, left to persistency, and of little imagination, and he rose rapidly to wealth and power at the bar of his native state. "It is doubtful," says Brown, "if in the entire history of the Connecticut bar any other lawyer has ever in so short a time accumulated so great a practice. ...Measured either by the amount of his business or by his earnings, it was unrivalled in his own day and unexampled in the history of the colony. Naturally shrewd, and with nothing of the spendthrift in his nature, he quickly earned a competence, and by good management he increased it to a fortune which for the times and the country was quite uncommonly large. From a few documents still in existence it is clear that he had became something of a capitalist and investor. He bought debts lands and houses and loaned out money at interest. He was a stockholder in the Hartford Bank and one of the original subscribers to the stock of the old Hartford Broad-cloth Mill (1788)."

With that natural shrewdness and economy which his latest biographer ascribed to him, Ellsworth accumulated a by no means negligible amount in public securities from which he profited by the rise of credit that accompanied the establishment of the new government. He was among the first citizens of Connecticut to have his paper funded into the new government securities, for he appears in December, 1791, with $1330.50 in deferred sixes, $2660.98 in funded sixes, and $1995.75 in 3 per cents.[187] His wife, Abigail, and other members of her family, the Wolcott had also invested in securities.[188]

William Few, of Georgia, was almost unique among the members of the Convention in being a representative, in origin and education, of the small farming class. His father was a Maryland farmer who was led by a successive failure of crops to try his fortune in North Carolina, where young Few laboured with the axe and plough. Even here the elder Few did not prosper, and he became so deeply involved in debt that his son had to take over the management of his property. William, afterward, in 1776, settled in Georgia and soon became engaged in politics and the Revolutionary War.

At the close of the War, he relates, "I possessed not much property nor had I any expectation that I did not acquire by my own industry. I therefore determined to commence the practice of law, although I had never spent one hour in the office of an attorney to prepare for business, nor did know anything of the practice." He adds, however, that his practice grew in spite of his deficiencies and that his "pecuniary prospects were very flattering," by the time he was elected a member of the Convention. At all events he acquired a plantation in Columbia County, and after the expiration of his term as Senator in 1793, he retired there and engaged in agricultural pursuits. In 1799 he left Georgia for New York, where he managed his small fortune in real and personal property, according to his own estimate, about $100,000.[189]

Few's personal interest in the new government was probably rather small, but the absence of the full records of Georgia from the books of the Treasury Department renders impossible a categorical statement.

---

[185]   G. Brown, *The Life of Oliver Ellsworth*, p. 11.

[186]   Brown, *ibid.*, p. 23.

[187]   MB. Treasury Department: *Connecticut Loan Office, Ledgers A, B, and C,* folio 21 in each volume.

[188]   Consult same volumes through the Index.

[189]   Facts here are taken from his *Autobiography*, in the Magazine of America History. *Vol.* VII. pp. 343 ff.

He was connected with the Georgia Union Company, which was involved in the Yazoo land deals;[190] and he presented for funding a certificate of the issue of 1779 to the amount of $2170 nominal value, which he had secured from one Spears.[191] His name appears occasionally on other records for small amounts, and the index in the office of the Register of the Treasury cites him as being among the security holders recorded in a volume not found.[192]

Thomas Fitzsimons, of Pennsylvania, was intimately identified with the mercantile interests of his city. He is described as "an extensive merchant," and his family connections were with people engaged in his own line. He married the daughter of Robert Meade, and established business relations with his brother-in-law "who was one of the prominent merchants and ship-owners of Philadelphia."[193] It is recorded of him that "His influence in the country and, especially among merchants was second to none. ...Mr. Fitzsimons was one of those efficient and able men who laid the foundations of the commercial and financial systems of the United States."[194] It is not surprising to find that he was also a "conspicuous advocate of a protective tariff."[195]

Like his prominent associates in Philadelphia, Mr. Fitzsimmons combined mercantile and financial operations. He was "for a long time a director in the Bank of North America and President of the Insurance Company of North America, in which latter office he continued until his death."[196] Indeed he was so extensively involved in the speculations of Robert Morris that his resources were seriously crippled by the failure of that gentleman.[197]

His intimate knowledge of finance and his immediate business connections doubtless invited him to deal in public securities; and Maclay sets him down among the speculators as follows: "The Speaker gives me this day his opinion that Mr. Fitzsimons was concerned in this business [of speculating] as well as Mr. Morris, and that they stayed away (from Congress) for the double purpose of pursuing their speculation and remaining unsuspected."[198] It is probable that Maclay's version is correct, for in 1791 Fitzsimon's agent, Michael Conner, presented for him certificates of 1778 to the amount of nearly $12,000 nominal value which he had evidently

---

[190] Haskins, *The Yazoo Land Companies*, p, 81.

[191] Ms. Treasury Department; *Register of Certificates of Public Debt Presented to the Auditor of the Treasury*.

[192] Volume 31, folio 346.

[193] McMaster and Stone, *Pennsylvania and the Federal Constitution*, p. 706.

[194] Simpson, *Eminent Philadelphians*, p. 373.

[195] McMaster and Stone, *op. cit.*, p. 707.

[196] Simpson, *op cit.*, 373.

[197] Sumner, *The Financier and the Finances of the Revolution*, Vol. II, p. 294.

[198] Maclay, *Journal* (1890 ed.), p. 178.

bought up.[199] He appears also on the records of the 6 per cents and the threes for small amounts, and his operations extended beyond his native state.[200]

Fitzsimons was also involved extensively in land speculations with Robert Morris, for the latter in a letter of October 9, 1795, writes to James Marshall, their European agent, to the effect that Fitzsimons and he had put on sale in London "about 360,000 acres of land situated in Georgia."[201] But as pointed out above Fitzsimons' relations with Morris cost him dearly and snatched away from him all that he had made in public securities and more besides.

Benjamin Franklin, of Pennsylvania, in the midst of his varied activities as printer, diplomat, statesman, and philosopher, managed withal by thrift and investments to accumulate a considerable fortune for his day, about $150,000.[202] At his great age on the assembling of the Convention, it public would hardly have been practicable for him to have engaged in investments in public securities had he been so inclined; and he died in 1790, before the funding system went into effect. A short time before his death, however, he was interested in land speculations;[203] and in his will he bequeaths "lands near the Ohio" and three thousand acres granted by the State of Georgia to him.[204] He does not appear to have held any public paper.

Nicholas Gilman, of New Hampshire, was in public life which from his youth until his death. He entered the army at the age of twenty-one, and after the War he served in Congress and in other public positions. He does not seem to have been a man of much weight either in private life or the Convention. A French observer remarks of his election as a member of the Federal Convention: "Cette circonstance prouve qu'il n'y a pas un grand choix a faire dans cet Etat, ou que du moins les hommes des plus senses et les plus habiles ne sont pas asses riches pour accepter une place publique."[205]

In financial matters, there was no doubt of Gilman's ability. He managed to accumulate a considerable amount of public securities before the meeting of the Convention, and apparently added to his holdings later. In the Nicholas-Gilman papers preserved in the Library of Congress there is a list of certificates of the liquidated debt to the amount of $5400.67, declared to be the property of Nicholas Gilman, on December 9, 1786. This paper was bought up by Gilman, for the list of original holders is given. A receipt bearing the date of June 29, 1787, preserved in the above paper shows Nicholas Gilman to have received interest on $6654 of the public debt. He and the various members of the Gilman family of New Hampshire were extensively engaged in transactions in public securities.[206] One entry in the Treasury books of the new government shows

---

[199] Ms. Treasury Department: *Register of Certificates of Public Debt Presented to the Auditor of the Treasury*.

[200] Ibid., See *Ledger E, Treasury, 3%*, Vol. 44, folio 335. Also *Ledger C, Treasury, 6%*, Vol. 42, folio 300 for small entries.

[201] Morris Mss. in the Library of Congress: *Private Letter Book*, Vol. I, p. 529. Marshall (a brother of John Marshall) was the confidential and trusted agent of Morris in large transactions in land.

[202] Bigelow, *Life of Franklin*, Vol. III, p. 470.

[203] Haskins, *The Yazoo Land Companies*, p. 62.

[204] Bigelow, *Works*, Vol. X, pp. 206 ff.

[205] Farrand, *Records*, Vol. III, p. 232.

[206] Consult the Loan Office Records of New Hampshire in the Treasury Department, *passim*.

Nicholas Gilman to have $11,021.95 worth of 6 per cent Deferred Stock;[207] and he supplemented his purely fiscal operation by dealing in military certificates (that is, soldier's paper which could be bought from necessitous holders at a fraction of its value), and in public lands.[208]

While Oilman was quick to look after his own interests his devotion to his native state made him anxious for her towns to participate in the general prosperity enjoyed by holders of public securities after the formation of the Constitution. On September 3, 1787, he had already discovered the probable effect of the proposed Constitution not yet ready to lay before the people, upon the securities of the government. On that day he wrote to the President of New Hampshire advising the towns to buy up public securities at the prevailing low price in order to have paper to transfer to the federal government in lieu of taxes and other charges. He says: "I find many of the states are making provision to buy in their quota's of the final settlements, and I must ardently wish that the towns in New Hampshire may be so far awake to a sense of their interest as to part with their property freely in order to purchase their several quota's of the public securities now in circula- tion, while they are to be had at the present low rate which is in this place, at two shillings and six pence on the pound. If they suffer the present opportunity to pass and we should be so fortunate as to have an efficient Government, they will be obliged to buy them of brokers, hawkers, speculators, and jockeys at six or perhaps eight times their present value."[209]

Elbridge Gerry, of Massachusetts, was born in Marblehead in 1744. His father was a merchant of good standing and comfortable estate. His biographer states that after his graduation from Harvard, Elbridge "turned his attention to that line of life in which his father's prosperity seemed to hold out the greatest inducements to a young and enterprising mind; and he plunged at once into the most active pursuits of commerce. His fairness, correctness, and assiduity, and the extensive knowledge of commercial concerns which he acquired from his father's experience and his own exertions were crowned with good fortune, and while yet young in business and in years he acquired a considerable estate and a very high standing at Marblehead."[210]

As a merchant, Gerry was closely in touch with the needs of commerce, and was deeply impressed with the necessity for national resistance to the discriminations of Great Britain. In April, 1784, he presented a report to Congress in which he called attention to the fact that Great Britain had adopted regulations destructive to American commerce in the West India Islands, and that these measures of discrimination were growing into a system. "Unless the United States in Congress assembled," he urged, "shall be vested with powers competent to the protection of commerce, they can never command reciprocal advantages in trade; and without these, our foreign commerce must decline and eventually be annihilated." The West Indian trade affected New England particularly, and Gerry is thus reflecting a local interest in demanding a national system of commercial protection.[211]

In addition to his mercantile interests, Gerry was concerned in financial affairs. In the Convention he strongly urged inserting in the Constitution a clause conferring on the new government not only the power but also the obligation to provide fully for the holders of public securities. According to Madison's notes, "Mr.

---

[207] Ms. Treasury Department: *Ledger C, Treasury*, 6%. Vol. 42, folio 368.

[208] *State Papers: Public Lands,* Vol. I, p. 118.

[209] Hammond. *State Papers of New Hampshire*, Vol. XVIII. p. 790.

[210] Sanderson, *Lives of the Signers* (1831 ed.), V 01. I, p. 197; Austin, *Life of Gerry*.

[211] Sanderson, *Biography of the Signers,* Vol. I, p. 230.

Gerry considered giving the power only, without adopting the obligation, as destroying the security now enjoyed by the public creditors of the United States. He enlarged on the merit of this class of citizens, and the solemn faith which had been pledged under the existing Confederation."[212] Later in the Convention, when Colonel Mason objected to making the full discharge of the debt obligatory, Gerry again took exceptions. He said, " that for himself he had no interest in the question, being not possessed of more of the securities than would by the interest pay his taxes. He would observe, however, that as the public had received the value of the literal amount, they ought to pay that value to somebody. The frauds on the soldiers ought to have been foreseen. These poor and ignorant people could not but part with their securities. There are other creditors who will part with anything rather than be cheated out of the capital of their advances. ... If the public faith would admit, of which he was not clear, he would not object to a revision of the debt so far as to compel restitution to the ignorant and distressed who had been defrauded. As to the Stock-jobbers he saw no reason for the censures thrown on them. They kept up the value of the paper. Without them there would be no market."[213]

Gerry here explains to his colleagues that he is a holder of securities; but he modestly underestimates the amount, or his taxes were rather high, for the loan office records of Massachusetts show that the interest on his securities, issued pursuant to the act of Congress of April 28, 1784, was about $3500 a year, an amount which, even at the prevailing rate of depreciation, would have covered the taxes on a considerable estate.[214] The incompleteness of the records in the Treasury Department does not permit of an exact estimate of Gerry's holdings; but they must have been large, for the following items appear to his credit: $14,266.89 on the Liquidated Debt Book of the Massachusetts loan office,[215] $2648.50 worth of sixes and threes in 1790 on the Pennsylvania loan office books,[216] $409.50 in threes on the Pennsylvania ledger under the date of December 13, 1790,[217] and £3504/8/10 worth of old paper funded into federal securities in the Massachusetts loan office, August 24, 1791.[218] There may be of course some duplication of amounts but there can be no doubt that Gerry's interest income from confederate securities in one year shortly before the meeting of the Convention was about $3500, and also there can be no doubt that Gerry had bought largely with a view to speculation, for a very few of his certificates were issued to him originally. He had therefore more than an academic sympathy with the stockbrokers. Nevertheless, it should be noted that notwithstanding his large interests at stake, Gerry for several reasons strongly opposed the ratification of the Constitution.[219]

---

[212]   Farrand, *Records,* Vol. 11, p. 356.

[213]   *Ibid.,* 413.

[214]   Ms. Treasury Department: *Mass. Loan Office, Register of Certificates of Interest Issued* (Vellum bound), folios 15 ff.

[215]   *Ibid., Mass. Loan Office, Certificates for Liquidated Debt,* folios 3, 4, 5, 6, and 7. This paper had evidently been bought by Gerry for speculation.

[216]   *Ibid.. Loan Office, Pa.,* 1790-1791. folio 60.

[217]   *Ibid., Ledger C. 3% Stocks. Pa.,* folio 37.

[218]   *Ibid., Massachusetts Loan Office.* 1791, Item 582; this wall also paper bought up by Gerry for speculation.

[219]   Gerry was accused by Ellsworth *(q.v.)* of having turned against the new Constitution because the Convention refused to put the old continental paper money on the same basis as other securities. Toward the close of the Convention, "Gerry", says Ellsworth, " introduced a motion respecting the redemption of the old continental money - that it should be placed on a footing with other liquidated securities of the United States. As Mr. Gerry was supposed to be possessed of large quantities of this species of paper, his motion

However, Gerry during his entire public career seems to have intermixed his official relations with his private economic affairs. While he was a member of Congress, before the adoption of the Constitution, he became interested in the public lands. On March 1, 1785, Timothy Pickering,[220] one of the leading land operators of the period, wrote to Gerry: "As you have expressed your wishes to be concerned in the purchase of lands on the other side of the Alleghany mountains thro' our agency, we think it very material to your interest as well as our own that we be informed, if possible, what plan Congress will probably adopt in disposing of those lands which lie west of the Ohio. If they mean to permit adventurers to make a scramble. . it will behove us to engage seasonably with some enterprising, but confidential character, to explore the country and make locations. ...If there must be a scramble, we have an equal right with others, and, therefore, the information desired in the beginning of this letter may be of essential importance. Your answer to this letter will much oblige your sincere friends who wish to advance your interest with their own."[221]

Gerry was then a member of Congress, which had under consideration the disposal of the western lands. If this land company, of course, could secure inside information, it would be advantageous to Mr. Gerry who contemplated speculating in those lands, as well as to Mr. Pickering's agency.

Gerry undoubtedly took advantage of the opportunity to invest in western enterprises, for he was a shareholder in the Ohio Company, proprietors of lands on the Muskingum River[222] - a concern in which he apparently became interested while a member of the Congress under the Articles of Confederation, during the organization of the Company - and the procuring of the public grant.

Nathaniel Gorham, of Massachusetts, was a successful merchant at Charlestown, the place of his birth. He was prominent in the political life of his community, having served as a member of the legislature and the constitutional convention of his state.

In addition to his mercantile and political pursuits, Gorham engaged in land speculation on a large scale. In 1786, Massachusetts, by a compromise with New York, secured a large area of western country, and in April, 1788, "sold all land to Nathaniel Gorham, of Charlestown, and Oliver Phelps, of Granville, for a million dollars, to be paid in three annual instalments in the scrip of Massachusetts, known as consolidated securities, which were then much below par. . . . Behind Phelps and Gorham there was a syndicate of persons who desired to speculate in the lands, but who, in order not to compete with each other, had united and allowed these two to act for all."[223]

---

appeared to be founded in such bare-face selfishness and injustice, that it at once accounted for all his former plausibility and concession, while the rejection of it by the convention inspired its author wit the utmost rage and intemperate opposition to the whole system he had formerly praised." Ford, *Essays on the Constitution*, p. 174. Gerry indignantly denied that he ever made such a motion in the Convention, or that he held much continental money. *Ibid.*, p. 127. It does not appear in Farrand, *Records*, that any such motion was made in the Convention; and under the circumstances it seems not unjust to remark that Ellsworth's charges were made with very bad grace, particularly in vie of the fact that he and members of his family and intimate friends held considerable amounts of public securities. 'Bare-faced selfishness" was not monopolized by Gerry in the Convention.

[220] See above, p. 49.

[221] King, *Life* and *Correspondence*, Vol. I, p. 72.

[222] A.M. Dyer. *The Ownership of Ohio Lands*, p. 68.

[223] Sumner, *The Financier and the Finances of the Revolution*, Vol. II, pp. 253 ff. See Turner, *Pioneer History of the Holland Purchase of Western New York*, pp. 326 ff.

Robert Morris was one of Gorham's associates in this venture, and other prominent men were behind the project but the projectors were unable to realize fully on their scheme, because the rise of Massachusetts scrip, after the adoption of the Constitution, made it impossible for them to fulfil the original terms of their contract. Consequently, they received only a portion of the original purchase.

The unhappy outcome of this venture apparently left Gorham without a very large fortune at his death in 1796. He does not seem to have combined any considerable transactions in continental securities with those in state scrip; although he was doubtless a holder in some amount because his will shows him to have been possessed of twenty shares in United States Bank stock.[224] Inasmuch as holders of this paper secured it in exchange for old securities and some specie, it may be surmised that Gorham must have had some of the continental paper at the time of the establishment of the Bank, although it may be that he purchased the stock as an investment. The tangled state of his affairs at his death makes this latter conclusion improbable at least.

We have now come to the colossal genius of the new system, **Alexander Hamilton**. It is true, that he had little part in the formation of the Constitution, but it was his organizing ability that made it a real instrument bottomed on all the substantial interests of the time. It was he who saw most keenly the precise character of the social groups which would have to be rallied to the new government in order to draw support away from the states and give the federal system a firm foundation. He perceived that governments were not made out of thin air and abstract principles. He knew that the Constitution was designed to accomplish certain definite objects, affecting in its operation certain definite groups of property rights in society. He saw that these interests were at first inchoate, in process of organization, and he achieved the task of completing their consolidation and attaching them to the federal government.

He saw, in the first place, that the most easily consolidated and timorous group was composed of the creditors, the financiers, bankers, and money lenders. He perceived that they were concentrated in the towns and thus were easily drawn together. He saw that by identifying their interests with those of the new government, the latter would be secure; they would not desert the ship in which they were all afloat. It has been charged that he leaned always on the side of the financial interest against the public as represented in the government; but it must be remembered that at the time the new system went into effect, the public had no credit, and financiers were not willing to forego their gains and profits for an abstraction. It is charged against him that he did not buy up government paper in behalf the public at the most favourable terms; but to have done so would have diminished the profits of the very financiers whose good will was necessary to the continuance of the government.

The second group of interests which Hamilton saw ready for organization were the merchants and manufacturers who wished protective tariffs. He would have been blind, indeed, if he had not discovered and interpreted the widespread movement for protection which was swiftly gathering headway during the years preceding the formation of the Constitution. He was not blind. His first report on manufactures show how keenly alive he was to the extent and diversity of the groups whose financial advantage lay in a system of protection. Whether this was for the good of the whole people need not be argued here. Hamilton's relations were with the immediate beneficiaries. They were the men who were to throw their weight on the side of the new government. How persistently Hamilton sought to inform himself of the precise nature of the interests needing protection in the separate localities, from New Hampshire to Georgia, is evidenced by his unpublished correspondence with businessmen in all the commercial centres.[225]

The third interest which Hamilton consolidated was composed of the land speculators and promoters and embraced all the leading men of the time - Washington, Franklin, Robert Morris, James Wilson, William Blount, and other men of eminence.[226] This dealing in land was intimately connected with public securities,

---

[224] T. Wyman, *Genealogies and Estates of Charlestown*, Vol. 1, p. 424.

[225] To be found in the Hamilton Mss, Library of Congress.

[226] Haskins, *The Yazoo Land Companies*.

for a large portion of the lands were bought with land warrants purchased from the soldiers, and with other stocks bought on the open market at low prices. Hamilton saw clearly the connection of this interest with the new government, and his public land policies were directed especially to obtaining the support of this type of operators.[227]

Without the conciliation and positive support of these powerful elements in American society, the new government could not have been founded or continued. With keen insight, Hamilton saw this. He made no attempt to conceal it; for whatever may have been his faults he did not add the crime of demogogy. It is true that in private he often expressed a contempt for popular rule which is absent from his public papers; but his public papers contain a plain statement of his policies, and show why he considered them necessary to the strength and stability of the government.

Thousands of small farmers and debtors and labouring mechanics were opposed to his policies, but they did not have the organization or consciousness of identity of interests which was necessary to give them weight in the councils of the new government. They were partly disfranchised under the existing laws, and they had no leaders worthy of mention. The road to power and glory did not yet lie in championing their cause. It required the astute leadership of Jefferson, and the creation of a federal machine under his direction, to consolidate the heterogeneous petty interests against the Federalist group.

But during Hamilton's administration, representatives of these smaller interests began to attack his policies as inimical to public interest, *i.e.*, their own interests; and out of this attack grew the charge that Hamilton himself was privately engaged in augmenting his personal fortune by the methods which he had created for the advantage of public creditors and financiers generally. Although this charge, even if true, should not be allowed to obscure the real greatness of Hamilton's masterly mind, and has little bearing upon a scientific application of the economic interpretation to the period, it deserves examination at length.

Rumors that Hamilton was personally interested in securities were persistent from the beginning of his career as Secretary of the Treasury, and in his famous Reynolds pamphlet, published in 1797, he precisely states the charge against himself: "Merely because I retained an opinion once common to me and the most influential of those who opposed me, that the public debt ought to be provided for on the basis of the contract upon which it was created, I have been wickedly accused with wantonly increasing the public burthen many millions in order to promote a stock-jobbing interest of myself and friends."[228] That this heavy burden was necessary to secure the support of the financial interests concerned, and that their support was absolutely indispensable to the establishment of the new national system on substantial basis, was admitted by many of Hamilton' worst enemies; but this did not prevent their attacking the Secretary on mere rumours of private peculations.

It now remains to examine the evidence against Hamilton, and state the case fairly so far as our existing records will allow. In 1793, Hamilton was accused of a criminal violation of the laws, and laid under the suspicion of being a defaulter. The House of Representatives was so impressed with the charges that it appointed a committee to investigate the conduct of the Treasury Department, particularly with regard to the charge that Hamilton had made the public moneys "subservient to loans, discounts, and accommodations" to himself and friends.

The result of this investigation was a vindication of the Secretary by the committee on the basis of affidavits from the officers and employees of the various banks involved, public and private. Hamilton cites the report of this committee of the House as containing the "materials of a complete exculpation."[229] But this

---

[227] *State Papers: Finance,* Vol. I, p. 8.

[228] Hamilton, *Works* (Lodge ed.), Vol. VI, p. 453.

[229] *Ibid.,* Vol. VI, p. 454; *Annals of Congress,* Vol. III, pp. 900 ff.

investigation does not cover the dealings which Hamilton might have had with stock brokers and other persons handling public securities.

Evidences of such relations would not have been contained in the public and private papers available to the committee. Indeed, on account of his intimate business relations with all the leaders who were buying and selling public securities, and, on account of the fact that he could have seen them personally at New York and Philadelphia, it would not have been necessary for him to make any written record of such transactions. But of the larger charges brought against him in Congress we may regard this report as a complete vindication.

The direct charge, however, that Hamilton had violated the solemn obligations of his own office by buying up public securities, as distinct from the charge that he had employed his high authority in the interests of his friends and his class, first took on a serious form in 1797, when the notorious pamphleteer J.T. Callender, in his *History of the United States for the Year* 1796 published a series of papers purporting to show that in 1791 and 1792 Hamilton had been engaged in speculative ventures with one James Reynolds and Mr. Duer.[230] It appears that in 1792 a Mr. Clingman, then in jail for a crooked transaction with the government, got into communication with Speaker Muhlenburg and hinted that a fellow-prisoner, Reynolds, had been associated with Hamilton in security operations, and had in his possession papers that would establish the facts in the case. Muhlenburg communicated with Monroe and Venable, and the three heard from Reynolds and his wife grave charges against the Secretary.

On learning of these serious charges, Muhlenburg, Venable, and Monroe confronted Hamilton with them and the Secretary explained that the whole charge of speculation was false and that his relations with the Reynolds grew out of an unhappy amour with Mrs. Reynolds. The three investigators accepted this explanation, although Monroe prosecuted further inquiries which resulted in his accumulating additional charges. The papers in the case, it was agreed by Hamilton and his three investigators,[231] were to be kept secret and out of the reach of publication. It turned out, however, that Monroe, angered by the abuse heaped upon him later by the Federalists, gave the documents out for publication, much to the scandal of the country. Hamilton promptly replied in a pamphlet in which he denied any improper financial relations with Reynolds, and explained in painful detail his affair with Reynolds' wife.[232]

When all the external and internal evidence is taken in this case, and the documents connected with it are carefully analyzed, it will be apparent that a decision will rest upon the answer to this question: "Shall Hamilton's testimony as to speculations outweigh that of an undoubted rascal and his wife?" Mr. F.T. Fox, in a recent study of the matter, attempts to convict Hamilton on the internal evidence of his vindication; and apparently does so. But on an examination of Mr. Fox's brief against the Secretary, it soon comes out that he has made a mistake in the crucial dates on which turns his whole case.[233] Consequently, this particular matter rests just where it did more than a hundred years ago. Fair-minded men will be inclined to exonerate Hamilton of the charge brought in the Reynolds indictment.

---

[230] See below. p. 112.

[231] Mr. Lodge calls the three investigators "inquisitors," but this seems like a strong word to apply to members of Congress engaged in running down rumours relative to the official conduct of a government officer. *Works* (Lodge ed.), Vol. VI, p. 450 note. The impropriety of Monroe's action in allowing the story to escape is another matter.

[232] The pamphlet by Hamilton in his defence in printed in the Lodge edition, Vol. VI, pp. 449 ff.

[233] Compare the date of the receipts on page 20 of Mr. Fox's *A Study in Hamilton* with the date in the pamphlet (Lodge ed.), Vol. VI, p. 494.

That Hamilton himself made any money in stocks which he held personally has never been proved by reference to any authentic evidence. He did hold a small amount of public securities, for in a letter of June 26, 1792, to William Seton, he says, "All my property in the funds is about $800, 3 per cents. These at a certain period I should have sold, had I not been unwilling to give occasion to cavil."[234] The origin of this holding is not explained. Even if it was derived from the funding under the acts of August, 1790, and the 6 per cents, funded and deferred were added, it would not have made more than a trifling amount.

That Hamilton ever held any considerable sum in securities seems highly improbable, for he was at no time a rich man, and at his death left a small estate. Though he lived well, and had a large income apart from his paltry salary as Secretary, his earnings as an eminent lawyer may very well account for such sources of revenue as he may have enjoyed. Certainly, had he seen fit to employ his remarkable talents in private enterprise, he might have died one of the rich men of his day. However this may be, the question may be legitimately asked whether Hamilton had any personal connections with any of the security operations which were carried on during his administration of the Treasury? Hamilton's defenders, in response to such an inquiry, will cite his famous reply to Henry Lee in 1789, when the latter asked him for his opinion about the probable rise of public securities: "I am sure you are sincere when you say that you would not subject me to an impropriety, nor do I know that there would be any in answering your queries; but you remember the saying with regard to Caesar's wife. I think the spirit of it applicable to every man concerned in the administration of the finances of the country. With respect to the conduct of such men, suspicion is ever eagle-eyed, and the most innocent things may be misinterpreted."[235]

On the other hand, Maclay, who, as United States Senator during the funding operations, had opportunities for first-hand information, answers the above question in the affirmative. He says, in his record of the Senate on February 1, 1790: "If I needed proof of the baseness of Hamilton, I have it in the fullest manner. His price was communicated in manuscript as far as Philadelphia. Thomas Willing, in a letter to the speaker of the Representatives, after passing many eulogiums on Hamilton's plan, concludes, 'For I have seen in manuscript his whole price,' and it has been used as the basis of the most abandoned system of speculation ever broached in our country."[236] What Maclay doubtless means here is that Hamilton had communicated to one of the leading financiers of Philadelphia, a partner of Robert Morris and dealer in securities,[237] his proposed plans for redemption of the public debt in full, previous to their publication in the first report to the House on public credit, January 9, 1790. On the question as to how much credence should be given to the assertions of the querulous Maclay, students of history will differ, and impartial scholars will seek further evidence.

Far from admitting any truth in Maclay's allegations, Hamilton's friends would indignantly deny that he had any private connections with security operations in any form. Hamilton's son, in his *Reminiscences*, states that "Hamilton requested his father-in-law, General Schuyler, not to permit his son to speculate in the public securities lest it should be inferred that their speculations were made upon information furnished by Hamilton; or were made in part on Hamilton's account. Schuyler inhibited any speculations; as Van

---

[234] *Works of Hamilton* (Lodge ed.), Vol. VIII, p. 268. Perhaps the remnant of an old account of Hamilton on the Treasury Books in 1797 refers to this petty holding. Ms. Treasury Department: *Ledger E, Treasury,* 3%, Vol. 44, folio 434.

[235] J. A. Hamilton, *Reminiscences*, p. 18.

[236] W. Maclay, *Journal* (1890 ed.), p. 188.

[237] *State Papers: Finance,* Vol. I, p. 188.

Rensellaer Schuyler, my uncle, told me, complaining at the same time that, but for this inhibition, he would have made a large sum of money."[238]

The General, however, evidently did not regard this inhibition as binding upon himself, for he appears upon the records as one of the large dealers in public paper in New York. Examples of his extensive financial transactions can be readily found by reference to the old loan books in the Treasury Department; there appear in March, October, and November, 1791, the following amounts to his credit : $23,189.21; $15,594.61, $8036.50, $20,689.21.[239]

Neither did Hamilton deem it necessary to inhibit his brother-in-law, J.B. Church, from dealing in securities. During Hamilton's administration of the Treasury, Church was a large holder of public securities.[240] One entry credits him with $28,187.91 worth. Moreover, while Secretary of the Treasury, through his agents, Thomas Willing in Philadelphia, and Wm. Seton in New York, Hamilton bought and sold for his brother-in-law. In the Hamilton Mss. in the Library of Congress is preserved a letter from Thomas Willing bearing the date of February 24, 1790, and addressed to Hamilton, which shows that the former was then selling stocks under the latter's orders for Church.[241]

At a later date, Hamilton was engaged in an extended correspondence with William Seton of the New York Bank which shows that the latter was buying United States Bank stocks for Church, under Hamilton's orders. On November 21, 1793, Seton writes that he has not been able to make an investment for Mr. Church

---

[238] *Reminiscences of J. A. Hamilton,* p. 18.

[239] Ms. Treasury Department: *N. Y. Loan Office,* 1791, folio 24. See also the volume of *N. Y. Loan Office Receipts* in the Mss. Division of the Library of Congress for General Schuyler's receipts for interest on securities. The intimate correspondence between Hamilton and General Schuyler during the period of the formation of the Constitution was destroyed by a son of one of the latter's executors. American Historical Review, Vol. X, p. 181. See Tuckerman, *Life of General Schuyler.*

[240] Ms. Treasury Department: *N. Y. Office, Deferred 6%,* 1790-1796, folio 325.

[241] PHILADELPHIA, Feby. 24th, 1790.

[ALEXANDER HAMILTON, Esq., Secretary of the Treasury at New York.]

SIR: I have had this day the honor of yours inclosing your power of substitution on behalf of Mr. Church. At present the sale of stock, and indeed every other money transaction is nearly at a stand. The produce of the State and the sale of Bills of Exchange will alone command it, until we receive a supply from sea.

Mr. Constable has informed me of the purchase he had made of 20 shares and when they appear the transfer will be compleated.

I observe what you say respecting the sale of what remains of Mr. Church's shares and shall do whatever may be in my power to dispose of them, whenever I receive the certificates and your orders to make the sale. I am, Sir, with great respect,

Yr Obedt Servt

Hamilton Mss., Vol. XXIII, p. 1.   THOS. WILLING.

on account of the high price of bank stock.[242] Five days later Seton writes to Hamilton that he thinks it will be possible in a day or two to purchase stock for Mr. Church "under your limits;" and adds, after further remarks, "I therefore feel loth to enter into the market without further orders from you."[243] Here follow, voluminous correspondence showing Seton's successful purchases.

Hamilton's operations for his brother-in-law, Church also extended to speculations in public lands; for in the Hamilton Manuscripts there is a letter bearing the date of August 24, 1792, from William Henderson to him relative to the purchase of large quantities of land (45,000 acres),[244] It appears that Hamilton, Church, and General Schuyler were involved in this negotiation, and that Church was the principal.

Hamilton was also personally interested in western land schemes, for he held five shares of the Ohio Company, pro- prietors of land on the Muskingum River.[245] Although this concern was organized before the formation of the Constitution, Hamilton as Secretary of the Treasury was called upon to pass upon the validity of claims involving thousands of acres. He felt the delicacy of this situation, for on May 9, 1792, he wrote to Washington that he regretted that he was required by law to decide a case in which he was an interested, party, and stated that he had left the matter to be adjusted by the accounting officers of the Treasury acting under an opinion of the Attorney General.[246]

Although Hamilton showed great hesitancy in passing upon his own land claims while Secretary, he did not deem it incompatible with his official duties to communicate occasionally with friends as to the probable prices of public securities and bank stock.

For the communication to Willing, mentioned above,[247] we have, of course, only Maclay's testimony; and if his statement is true Hamilton transmitted official secrets of the most significant character to a financier who, however great his integrity, was in a position to take advantage of them, and was engaged in dealing in securities on his own account and for Hamilton's brother-in-law, Church, under Hamilton's orders. When we remember that Maclay's journal was private in its nature, not intended for publication, and not given to the world until long after all the men mentioned in it were dead, we are constrained to give some credence to his straightforward statements like the one in question, even though he was a bitter enemy of the Federalist leaders. But we are not constrained to attribute to Hamilton any improper motives. Those who assume that the Secretary of the Treasury could have carried out his enormous reorganization of the finances without conferring with the leading financiers of the time have only an elementary knowledge of Treasury administration.

As Secretary, he often found it necessary to set rumours at rest. An instance is afforded in a letter written by Hamilton, on August 17, 1791, to Rufus King, in which he mentioned having given out his opinion on prices to counteract an undue rise in script on the stock market, and concluded by giving King his standard of prices on that day, saying "I give you my standard that you may be able if necessary to contradict insinuations of an estimation on my part short of that standard for the purpose of depressing the funds."[248]

---

[242] Library of Congress: *Hamilton Mss.*, Vol. XX, p. 180.

[243] *Ibid.*, Vol. XX, pp. 182 ff. Lodge omits references to this correspondence on Seton's part, although he gives selected letters from Hamilton to Seton. *Works, of Alexander Hamilton*, Vol. VIII, pp. 231 ff.

[244] Library of Congress: *Hamilton Mss.*, Vol. XXIII, p. 180.

[245] A.M. Dyer. *The Ownership of Ohio Lands.* p. 69.

[246] Mss. Library of Congress: *Treasury Department. 1790-1792* (Washington papers), folio 291.

[247] P. 108.

[248] *Life and Correspondence of Rufus King*, Vol. I, p. 402.

This letter from Hamilton was evidently drawn by one from King bearing the date of August 15, 1791, in which the latter cautions the former against giving out any statements which might affect prices, and informs him that his opinions had been quoted in efforts to depress stocks.[249] King also adds that Duer had been injured in attempts to raise prices, but is of the opinion that "his conduct has been as correct as any buyer's and seller's could be." King had little liking for popular vagaries in finance, for he tells Hamilton that "the fall of Bank certificates may have some good effects; it will operate to deter our industrious citizens from meddling in future with the funds, and teach them contentment in their proper avocations." On the same day that Hamilton replied to King's letter which had informed him of Duer's danger, he wrote to Duer cautioning him against pushing prices too high and repeating earlier warnings. He says: "I will honestly own I had serious fears for you - for your purse and for your reputa- tion; and with an anxiety for both, I wrote you in earnest terms. You are sanguine, my friend. You ought to be aware of it yourself and to be on your guard against the propensity. ...I do not widely differ from you about the real value of bank script. I should rather call it about 190, to be within bounds, with hopes of better things, and I sincerely wish you may be able to support it at what you mention."[250] There is of course, little beyond friendly advice in this, although Hamilton's enemies may see impropriety in his communicating his own price to a man deeply engaged in speculation.

There is some evidence, however, which may reasonably be interpreted to imply that Hamilton might have used his official power in behalf of Duer. In reply to a letter from Duer (after his disastrous failure) making some request which is not explained by Mr. Lodge, the Secretary says: "Your letter of the 11th got to hand this day. I am affected beyond measure at its contents, especially as it is too late to have any influence upon the event you were apprehensive of, Mr. Wolcott's instructions having gone off yesterday."[251] Wolcott was Hamilton's subordinate in the Treasury Department, and evidently he had issued some instructions which affected Duer's fortunes. Wolcott was the auditor of the Treasury whose duty it was under the act of September 2, 1789, "to receive all public accounts and after examination to certify the balance, and transmit the accounts with the vouchers and certificates to the Comptroller for his decision thereon." This connection with Duer is the sole piece of evidence of what might be termed the possible use of the Secretary's office in a private matter. The nature of this is not clear, and the plan was not carried out.

The conclusion to be reached from this evidence is that Hamilton did not have in 1787 any more than a petty amount of public securities which might appreciate under a new system; that he did have some western land; but that an extensive augmentation of his personal fortune was no consideration with him. The fact that he died a poor man is conclusive evidence of this fact. That he was sway throughout the period of the formation of the Constitution by large policies of government - not by any of the personal interests so often ascribed to him - must therefore be admitted. Nevertheless, it is apparent from the additional evidence given here that it was no mere abstract political science which dominated his principles of government. He knew at first hand the stuff of which government is made.

William C. Houston, of New Jersey, was of no consequence in the Convention, and little is known of his economic interests. He was a Princeton graduate, and was for a time professor of mathematics and natural philosophy. He entered the practice of law at Trenton, and from 1784 until his death in 1788 he was clerk of the Supreme Court of his state. On account of ill health he was unable to remain through the sessions of the Convention. A search among the New Jersey loan office records in the Treasury Department failed to reveal Houston as a holder of securities but the records for that state are incomplete and Houston's death in 1788

---

[249] Library of Congress, *Hamilton Mss.*, Vol. XVI, p. 126. The editor of King's letters says this letter is lost.

[250] Hamilton's *Works* (Lodge ed.), Vol. VIII, p. 234.

[251] *Ibid.*, Vol. VIII, p. 240, date March 14, 1792.

would have prevented his appearing on the Treasury Records of the new government. A William Houston is recorded in the New York books for small amount of deferred sixes,[252] but, although William Churchill Houston had a son by that name, the identity of the son and the public creditor cannot be established.

Houston was, however, interested in the possibilities of western land speculations, for his biographer relates that he, "joined with others in procuring for John Fitch, the steam-boat inventor, the office of Deputy Surveyor. After the treaty of peace with England, the question of how the lands northwest of the Ohio should be disposed of was mooted in Congress. It was thought that they would be sold to pay the debts of the confederacy. Fitch was a land jobber and supposed that a good operation might be made by a pre-survey of the country, so that when the Land Offices were opened, warrants might be taken out immediately for choice tracts. He found no difficulty in forming a company to forward such an enterprise. It was composed of Dr. John Ewing, Rev. Nathaniel Irwin, Wm. C. Houston. ...These gentlemen put £20 each in a fund to pay expenses."[253] How far this venture was carried and whether Houston acquired lands through it is not related. As a member of the Congress under the Articles of Confederation, he doubtless learned of the advantages to be gained in the West.

William Houstoun, of Georgia, took some part in the proceedings of the Convention, but he was of little weight. He was the son of a royal officer in the government of Georgia; and he received his education in England and studied law at the Inner Temple. His colleague Pierce records that "Mr. Houstoun is an Attorney at Law, and has been a member of Congress for the state of Georgia. He is a gentleman of family, and was educated in England. As to his legal or political knowledge, he has little to boast of."[254] The meagre biographical details available do not permit a statement of his economic interests; and the paucity of the records of the Georgia loan office in the Treasury Department make it impossible to say whether he was among the beneficiaries through the appreciation of public securities. An index to a volume of Treasury Records not found (Vol. XXV folio 44) contains the name of William Houstown, but whether this holder of public debt and the member of the Convention were identical cannot be determined.

Jared Ingersoll, of Pennsylvania, was the son of Jared Ingersoll of Connecticut, sometime agent of that colony commissioner in England and later admiralty judge, Pennsylvania. He graduated at Yale and studied in the Middle Temple. At the bar in Philadelphia he "soon rose to first rank. His practice was larger than any others. His opinions were taken on all important controversies, his services engaged in every great litigation."[255] Ingersoll was a man of considerable wealth, but he does not seem to be involved in the large transactions in public securities which engaged the attention of his intimate friends in the Convention.[256] He does not appear on the Pennsylvania books as a holder of securities. If he held any, his transactions must have been with the Treasury direct, and this would have been very convenient as it was located in Philadelphia

---

[252] *Ms.* Treasury Department: *Ledger B. N.Y. Office. 1790. Deferred 6% Stock;* folio 260; also *N.Y. Office. Deferred 6%. 1790-1796.* folio 144.

[253] T.A. Glenn, *William Churchill Houston*, pp. 71-72 (Privately printed), copy in Library of Congress.

[254] Farrand, *Records,* Vol. III, p. 97.

[255] Simpson. *Eminent Philadelphians.* p. 596.

[256] His private fortune was much impaired by the failure of Robert Morris, for whom he had pledged his faith in several transactions. Morris Mss. Library of Congress: *Private Letter Book.* Vol. II. pp. 193, 261, 327, 351, 414.

during the funding process. Ingersoll was a son-in-law of Charles Pettit, one of the security operators in Philadelphia.[257]

Daniel of St. Thomas Jenifer, of Maryland, is reported by Pierce to have been "a gentleman of fortune" in his state.[258] He was a planter and a slave-holder; the census of 1790 records his holding twenty slaves on one plantation under an overseer, but the number on his own plantation is illegible.[259] It is probable also that he held a small amount of public securities at the establishment of the new government. He died in the latter part of the year 1790, but his son,[260] Daniel Jenifer, Jr., appears on the loan office records as the holder of nearly six thousand dollars' worth of paper in December, 1790,[261] which he disposed of the following year.[262]

William Samuel Johnson, of Connecticut, was a son of Samuel Johnson, a clergyman of Stratford, Connecticut, and a gentleman of some means. He was a graduate of Yale, and entered the practice of law. He refused to aid in the Revolutionary cause, because he could not "conscientiously" take up arms against England, and he lived in retirement until the War was over. After the establishment of independence he resumed the prominent position in public life which he had enjoyed before the struggle; and according to his biographer he took "the highest rank in his profession and became the renowned and high-minded advocate who was always crowded with cases and had his clients in New York as well as in every part of Connecticut."[263] He added to his own patrimony by marrying the daughter of a " wealthy gentleman " of Stratford.

Johnson was a member of the first Senate under the new Constitution, and he was included by Jefferson in the list of men "operating in securities."[264] It is highly probable that he did not aid the Revolutionary cause by investing his money in the original paper; and he does not appear on the Treas- ury Books for large amounts of stock,[265] but there is every reason for believing that he carried on extensive operations through his son Robert Charles Johnson. The latter was speculating extensively in New York and Connecticut immediately after the establishment of the new government, and two entries show a credit to the father through the Son.[266] The loan office books under the date of December 13, 1791, credit Robert Charles Johnson, of Stratford, Gentleman, with nearly fifty thousand dollars' worth of sixes and threes.[267] Connecticut loan office receipts

---

[257] H. Binney, *Leaders of the Old Philadelphia Bar.* p. 83; *State Papers: Finance,* Vol. I. p. 81.

[258] Farrand, *Records.* Vol. III. p. 93.

[259] *Census of 1790: Heads of Families.* p. 51; consult Index.

[260] J Appleton. *Encyclopaedia of American Biography.* Vol. III. p. 426.

[261] Ms. Treasury Department: *Maryland Loan Office,* 1790-1797, folio 14.

[262] *Ibid.,* folio 134.

[263] Beardsley. *Life and Times of William Samuel Johnson,* pp. 8-9.

[264] *Writings of Jefferson* (Ford ed.), Vol. I, p. 223.

[265] Ms. Treasury Department: *Ledger B, New York Office, Deferred 6%,* 1790, folios 10, 152, 457.

[266] Folios 152 and 457 of above *Ledger B.*

[267] MB. Treasury Department; *Connecticut Loan Office, Ledger A,* folio 15; *Ledger B,* folio 15; *Ledger C,* folio 15. *Connecticut Loan Office Receipts,* Library of Congress, MBB. Division.

confirm this evidence of his extensive holdings. The New York loan office also Shows large transactions in the name of Robert Charles Johnson.[268]

Rufus King, of Massachusetts, was born in Scarborough, Maine, then in the province of Massachusetts, March 24, 1755. His father, in 1740, was "in prosperous business as a trader and factor for Ebenezer Thornton, one of the principal merchants in Boston for whom he purchased and prepared large quantities of timber." On settling at Scarborough, his father became "both a farmer and a merchant, and in each capacity was so successful as to become the owner of three thousand acres of land divided into several valuable farms and to be the largest exporter of lumber from Maine."

Rufus was educated at Harvard. When his father died in 1775 he left a good estate which was divided among several children. Rufus King was also fortunate in his marriage; his wife was Mary Alsop. Her father at first sympathized with the movement against Great Britain, but, "taking umbrage at the manner in which the New York convention had conveyed their adhesion to the Declaration of Independence to the Congress, and besides unwilling to close the door of reconciliation with Great Britain, "-he retired to Middletown, Connecticut, and stayed until after the War was over, when he returned to New York, resumed business, and became president of the Chamber of Commerce. According to King himself, his wife "was the only child of Mr. John Alsop, a very respectable and eminent merchant in this city [New York]. Mr. Alsop declined business in 1775 with a very handsome fortune."[269] King thus had extensive mercantile and other business interests which were largely managed for him by others, so that he was able to devote most of his time to politics.

Nevertheless, he did not neglect matters of private economy. Robert and Gouverneur Morris were engaged in 1788 in a plan to associate a number of Americans in a project to purchase up the debt (or portions thereof) of the United States due to France. Wadsworth, General Knox, Osgood, and Colonel Duer were involved in it. It was first proposed to send Gouverneur Morris as minister to Holland to further the scheme. The originators of the plan finally hit upon the appointment of Rufus King. King replied to the overture: "I told Col. Duer that I was not indisposed to a foreign appointment - that the honour and duties of such an office wd. be my sovereign rule of Cond. and that if in perfect consistence with the duties and dignity of the office, I cd. promote the interest of my friends, it wd. be a great satisfaction to me. But that I desired not to be considered as giving an answer any way at present, that the opinions of Mr. Jay and Col. Hamilton were of consequence in my mind. That previous to any decision on my part I must be ascertained of their opinions."[270]

Whether King engaged in this ambitious project or not, there is evidence to show that he was a considerable holder of government paper shortly after its establishment. It may be that apart of his fortune had been invested originally in public securities, although this is not apparent from the early loan office books in the Treasury Department. Jefferson puts King down among the holders of bank stock and public

---

[268] *Ibid., New York Loan Office, 6% Ledger,* 1791-1797, folio 161; *ibid., New York Office, Deferred 6%,* 1790-1796, folio 107- two entries of about 525,000 each. *Ledger B, New York Office, Deferred 6% Stock,* 1790, folios, 152,457. *Ledger E, Treasury, 3%,* Vol. 44, folio 529. There can be no question of the identity of the Robert Charles Johnson who appears on the public security records and the Robert Charles Johnson who was the son of William Samuel, The cross entries between father and son in the records constitute one piece of evidence. The residence of Robert Charles in Stratford presents another, for that was the family place. Furthermore, the signature to the Loan Office Receipts is the signature of Robert Charles, son of William Samuel Johnson.

[269] Rufus King, *Life and Correspondence.* Vol. I, 132.

[270] *Life and Correspondence of King,* Vol. I, p. 624.

securities;[271] and he is correct in his statement. King was director in the first United States bank.[272] He was also a large holder of government securities - one entry records more than $10,000 worth to his credit.[273] King thought that speculations should be reserved to the experienced, and rejoiced in the hope that one of the crashes would teach the ordinary industrious citizens " contentment in their proper avocations."[274]

John Langdon, of New Hampshire, was born on the family farm near Portsmouth in 1740, and "after a mercantile education in the counting room of Daniel Rindge, he entered upon a sea-faring life, but was driven from it by the revolutionary troubles." He must have prospered, however, before the War blighted his trade, for when the news of the fall of Ticonderoga reached Exeter, he rose in the legislature of which he was the speaker and said: "I have a thousand dollars in hard money; I will pledge my plate for three thousand more. I have seventy hogsheads of Tobago rum which will be sold for the most they will bring. They are at the service of the state. If we succeed. ..I will be remunerated; if we do not then the property will be of no value to me."[275]

After the war, Langdon's various mercantile and commercial enterprises took on new life, and there is every evidence that in his worldly affairs he was uniformly prosperous. A French report to the Ministry of Foreign Affairs on the Congress of 1788 speaks of John Langdon as a man of great wealth and pressing commercial interests: "M.L. a fait une grande fortune dans le commerce, c' est le Rob. Morris de son Etat, faisant une grande depense et s'attachant beau coup de citoyens par ses liberalites."[276]

John Langdon-Elwyn, grandson of John Langdon, in whose family were preserved the valuable private papers of the elder Langdon, wrote, sometime in the early part of the nineteenth century, a pamphlet on his celebrated grandfather. The author of this useful brochure "was nineteen years of age at the time of his grandfather's death. A critical observer of men and affairs, his opportunities as a member of the family of Governor Langdon give the production of his pamphlet a special significance."[277] This writer characterizes John Langdon as "a man that loved money, at an age when it gets the upper hand, that was prone to banking and funding, to whom such atmospheres were familiar and congenial, that knew how to make it and keep it, and felt no envy of others that did so too."[278]

That Langdon was deeply concerned in the financial operations connected with the new government is evidenced in many sources. According to his grandson, quoted above "He voted for this bank [the first United

---

[271] *Writings* (Ford ed.), Vol. I, p. 223. Maclay makes some quite uncomplimentary remarks about King, *Journal*, p. 315.

[272] Dunlap's Daily Advertiser, October 23, 1791.

[273] Ms. Treasury Department: *N.Y. Office, 6%, Ledger,* 1791-1799, folio 14. *Ibid., Ledger B, N.Y. Office, Deferred* 6%, 1790, folio 60; *ibid., Deferred* 6%, 1790-1796, folio 14. The Treasury Index gives a number of references to volumes not found.

[274] See above, p. 112.

[275] C.W. Brewster, *Rambles about Old Portsmouth* (1859), pp. 360-361.

[276] Farrand, *Records,* Vol. III, p. 233.

[277] Batchelor, *New Hampshire State Papers,* Vol. XXI, p. 804 note.

[278] *Ibid.,* Vol. XX, p. 868.

States Bank] and was we suppose an original subscriber of some account ...We believe he had been concerned in the Bank of North America: the first real National Bank: He was an intimate friend of Robert Morris."[279]

Maclay also adds his testimony to that of Langdon's grandson. When he was a Senator, Langdon lodged in New York with a Mr. Hazard who followed the business of buying up government certificates of public debt which had been "issued in place of the paper money of the old Congress and bore interest for their face value," and had depreciated to even as low as seven cents on the dollar. Maclay writes: "Mr. Hazard told me he had made a business of it; it is easy to guess for whom. I told him, 'You are then among the happy few who have been let into the secret.' He seemed abashed and I checked by my forwardness much more information which he seemed disposed to give."[280]

The loan office books of New Hampshire show that Langdon was a large creditor of the new government, and indeed he was one of the heavy original contributors who risked their fortunes on the outcome of the War.[281] One entry in the New Hampshire ledger credits him with more than $25,000 worth of sixes and threes;[282] and there are other entries as well. His brother, Woodbury Langdon, was also among the holders of public paper.

With that patriotism to his state and thrift in her interest that characterized his colleague, Gilman, Langdon sought to give the commonwealth some advantage in the various speculations in securities. On January 7, 1791, he wrote to the President of New Hampshire advising him of the approaching passage of the National Bank bill and advising that the state use its continental securities and some cash to buy stock in the new Bank. He says that the stock "would undoubtedly sell for specie at par at any time. ..; and in all probability it would soon sell above par, the state would therefore run no risque of looseing."[283]

John Lansing, of New York, was a lawyer at Albany and the mayor of that city. William Pierce, in his notes on the Convention, speaks of him in the following language: " His legal knowledge, I am told, is not extensive nor his education a good one. He is however a man of good sense, plain in his manners, and sincere in his friendships."[284] Lansing was one of the stout opponents of the Constitution and left the Convention early. He was there long enough however to learn (what was not a very deep secret) the certain effect of an efficient government on continental securities; for in January, 1791, immediately after the establishment of the new financial system, he appeared at the New York loan office with paper to fund to the amount of over seven thousand dollars.[285] All the members of the Lansing family in Albany seem to have taken advantage of the opportunity to augment their fortunes.[286]

---

[279] Batchellor, *New Hampshire State Papers,* Vol. XX, p. 872.

[280] *Journal of William Maclay* (1890 ed.), p. 178.

[281] Ms. Treasury Department: See *Loan Office Certificate Book,* New Hampshire (Loan of 1777 *passim*).

[282] *Ibid., New Hampshire Loan Office, Journal A,* folio 4, date March, 1791, and *passim.*

[283] Hammond, *State Papers of New Hampshire,* Vol. XVIII, p. 824.

[284] Farrand, *Records,* Vol. III, p. 90.

[285] Ms. Treasury Department: *New York Loan Office,* 1791, folio 97.

[286] Johannis, Garrit, Abraham, John J., Henry R., and other Lansings appear on *Ledger C, Funded 6%,* 1790, Ms. Treasury Department. Consult Index.

William Livingston, of New Jersey, was a member of the distinguished Livingston family which was among the largest proprietors in New York. He graduated at Yale, and in 1745 married Miss French "whose father had been large proprietor of land in New Jersey." He entered the practice of law in 1748 "and soon became a prominent member of the bar and employed in most of the important legal controversies of that day in New York and New Jersey." He apparently accumulated a comfortable fortune, but had lost a portion of it in 1773 by the failure of his debtors, and the necessity of accepting depreciated continental currency.[287]

Whether Livingston held any of the securities of the confederacy, it is impossible apparently to determine, for his death in the summer of 1790, before the funding system went into effect, would have precluded his appearing on the Ledger records. It is probable, however, that he did not entertain views in regard to the relation of public and private affairs different from those of his eminent colleagues. This theory will seem justified when it is understood that his son and heir, Brockholst Livingston, a new York lawyer, was among the heaviest security holders in that city; and in view of the wide reaching ramifications of his operations and his connections with Le Roy and Bayard was reckoned among the princely speculators of his day. One entry in 1791 credits him with about $70,000 worth; another in the same year, in conjunction with Le Roy and Bayard, with nearly $30,000.[288] At a slightly later date, 1792 and 1793, his 6 per cents alone amount to more than $100,000,[289] and he appears frequently in the records of other states. How much of this was his own paper and how much was for friends who did not wish to appear among the records cannot be determined.

James Madison, of Virginia, was a descendant of one of the old landed families of Virginia whose wealth consisted principally of plantations and slaves, and whose personal property was relatively small in amount. Madison's father "was a large landed proprietor occupied mainly ,with the care and management of his extensive rural concerns." Madison graduated at Princeton and studied law, but the practice of his profession did not appeal to him. His inclinations were all toward politics, for which he was prepared by long and profound researches in history, law, and political economy. He was constantly in public life, and seems to have relied upon the emoluments of office and 'his father's generosity as a source of income. The postponement of his marriage until 1794 enabled him to devote himself to political pursuits rather than commercial or economic interests of any kind. He does not appear to have been a holder of public securities; for the small amounts 'credited to James Madison on the books of the Treasury Department[290] seem to have belonged to his father, also named James Madison.[291]

Having none of the public securities, Madison was able later to take a more disinterested view of the funding system "proposed by Hamilton; and the scramble of politicians and speculators which accompanied the establishment of the new government did more than anything else to disgust him with the administration party and drive him into opposition. Writing to Jefferson in July, 1791, he said: "The subscriptions [to the Bank] are consequently a mere scramble for so much public plunder, which will be engrossed by those already loaded with the spoils of individuals. ...It pretty clearly appears, also, in what proportions the public debt lies in the Country, what sort of hands hold it, and by whom the people of the United States are to be governed.

---

[287] L. Elmer, *The Constitution and Government of New Jersey* (1872), pp. 57-59.

[288] MB. Treasury Department: *Ledger B, N.Y. Office, Deferred 6% Stock, 1790"*, folios, 72, 306, etc.

[289] *Ibid., N.Y., 6%, Ledger*, 1791-1797, folio 123.

[290] *Ibid., Virginia Loan Office*, 1791, under date of September 30, 1791; *Ledger A, ..Funded 6% Stock*, 1790, folio 123.

[291] In a letter of February 13, 1791, Madison advises his father to fund his Virginia ,certificates at Richmond: 'I do not see what better you can do with your certificates than to subscribe them to the public fund at Richmond.' *Writings of James Madison* (1865 ed.), Vol. I. p. 529.

Of all the shameful circumstances of this business, it is among the greatest to see the members of the legislature who were most active in pushing this job openly grasping its emoluments. Schuyler is to be put at the head of the Directors, if the weight of the New York subscribers can effect it. Nothing new is talked of here. In fact, stock-jobbing' drowns every other subject. The Coffee-House is in an eternal buzz with the gamblers."[292]

Alexander Martin, of North Carolina, was a graduate of Princeton, and practised law. He was for a time governor of his state. Later he served in the United States Senate, and supported Adams and the alien and sedition laws; but was defeated for election in 1799.[293] Martin was among the well-to-do planters and slave-owners of his state;[294] but his tastes do not seem to have turned to dealings in public securities, for the Index to the holders of the public debt preserved in the Treasury Department does not contain his name, and a search among the papers of North Carolina fails to reveal any record of his transactions.

Luther Martin, of Maryland, was a descendant of English ancestors who had obtained "large grants of land in New Jersey [and] removed their domestic establishment there when a greater part of the colonial domain was a dense wilderness." He was a graduate of Princeton and took up the practice of law. Being the third of nine children, and having little or no assistance from his parents, who were in pinched circumstances, he was thrown upon his own resources. He commenced his career in Virginia " where he soon acquired a full and lucrative practice, amounting, as he informs us, to about one thousand pounds per annum; which, however, was after a period diminished by the disturbance growing out of the American Revolution."[295]

Luther Martin's fortune was never very large, although he had among his clients men of great wealth and influence, like Robert Morris.[296] The census of 1790 records his owning only six slaves,[297] and his holdings of public securities were apparently meagre - a few thousand dollars at most. One entry of sixes and threes on June 15, 1791, credits him with $1992.67, and he occasionally appears in other records.[298] He was always more or less in sympathy with poor debtors, and was unwilling to preclude altogether the issue of paper money or moderate impairments of contract. He was accordingly a bitter opponent of the adoption of the Constitution in his state.[299]

George Mason, of Virginia, was born in 1725. He was the son of a rich slave owning and planting family of Dogue's Neck, and on account of the early death of his father he came into his vast estate on attaining his majority.[300] His family fortunes were augmented by speculations in western lands. He married the daughter

---

[292] *Writings* (1865 ed.), Vol. I. p. 538.

[293] *National Encyclopaedia of Biography,* Vol. IV, p. 420.

[294] *The Census of 1790 - Heads of Families.* p. 168, places the number of Martin's slaves at 47.

[295] Herring, *National Portrait Gallery,* Vol. IV.

[296] See Index to *Private Letter Books* of Robert Morris, Library of Congress: Mss. Division.

[297] *Census of 1790 - Heads of Families.* Maryland, p. 18.

[298] Ms. Treasury Department: *Maryland Loan Office,* 1790-1797, folios, 80.81; 194.

[299] See below, p. 205.

[300] Rowland, *The Life of George Mason.* Vol. I. pp. 48 ff. 55 ff.

of a Maryland merchant, from whom a large estate came into his family.[301] He was a member of the Ohio Company which was organized in 1749, and obtained a grant of " six hundred thousand acres of and, lying mostly west of the mountains and south of the Ohio."[302] In 1754 he also secured a patent for about fifteen hundred acres of land in Northern Neck.[303] He was constantly increasing his holdings,[304] and in 1769 " he seems to have come into possession of two thousand acres of land in the district of Kentucky."[305] As a member of the Virginia; legislature he drew a bill "to encourage the making of hemp, woollen, linen, and other manufactures."[306]

His property at the time of the establishment of the Constitution was unquestionably large, for at his death in 1792 "he devised to his sons alone, some fifteen thousand acres, the greater part of his own acquisition, of the very best land in the Potomac region. Most of these estates were well improved, with large and comfortable mansions and all necessary outbuildings. But he left to be divided among his children what was solely acquired by himself: sixty thousand of among the finest acres in Kentucky, some three hundred slaves, more than fifty thousand dollars' worth of other personal property, and at least thirty thousand dollars of debts due on his books, while his own indebtedness was absolutely nothing."[307] Very little of this personal property seems to have been in public securities, for a search in the records of the Treasury Department shows one small entry of a few hundred dollars' worth of threes and sixes to his credit.[308]

Mason frankly admitted his personal interest in certain landed property to be among his many objections to the Constitution - which he refused to approve and the adoption of which he bitterly opposed. Speaking on the dangers from the supremacy of the federal courts, in the Virginia ratifying convention, he said: "I am personally endangered as an inhabitant of Northern Neck. The people of that part will be obliged, by the operation of this power, to pay the quit rent of their lands. ...Lord Fairfax's title was clear and undisputed. After the revolution we taxed his lands as private property. After his death, an act of Assembly was made, in 1782, to sequester the quit rents due, at his death, in the hands of his debtors. Next year an act was made restoring them to the executor of the proprietor. Subsequent to this, the treaty of peace was made, by which it was agreed that there should be no further confiscations. But after this an act of Assembly was passed, confiscating his whole property. As Lord Fairfax's title was indisputably good, and as treaties are to be the supreme law of the land, will not his representatives be able to recover all in the federal court? How will gentlemen like to pay an additional tax on lands in the Northern Neck?"[309]

Mason proposed to limit the judicial power in such a manner that it should "extend to no case where the cause of action shall have originated before the ratification of this Constitution, except in suits for debts due

---

[301] *Ibid.,* I. p. 56.

[302] Rowland, *The Life of George Mason,* Vol. 1. p. 58.

[303] *Ibid.,* 1. p. 60.

[304] *Ibid.,* 1. pp. 117, 154.

[305] *Ibid.,* 1. p. 119.

[306] *Ibid.,* 1. p. 270.

[307] *Ibid.,* Vol. II, p. 368.

[308] Ms. Treasury Department: *Ledger A, Funded 6% Stock,* 1790, folio 130; See *Loan Office Virginia,* 1790-1798, folio 132. The Index gives references to other volumes not found, Vols. 41, 43, 45, folios 93, 15, and 18 respectively.

[309] Elliot, *Debates* (1836 ed.), Vol. III. pp. 528-529.

the United States, disputes between states about their territory, and disputes between persons claiming lands under grants of different states." He expressed a fear that under the Constitution as it stood the titles to all the country between the Blue Ridge and Alleghany Mountains would be upset in the federal courts and that the vast Indiana purchase would be rendered a subject of dispute.[310]

James McClurg, of Virginia, was an accomplished man of letters and distinguished physician of his native state. He was born there in 1747, studied at the college of William and Mary, and finished his training in medicine at Edinburgh and Paris. He established himself in the practice first a Williamsburg, and about 1783 he settled in Richmond, where he took first rank as a physician, scholar, and man of the world.[311]

McClurg's knowledge of government was not academic. He knew the subject practically, as well as theoretically for as early as November 23, 1790, he was engaged in operations in federal securities.[312] And on February 17, 1791, he presented to the local loan office Virginia certificates to the amount of $26,819, all of which, except a few hundred pounds originally subscribed by himself, he had evidently bought for speculation.[313] McClurg was also an investor in stock in the first United States Bank and one of the, directors.[314]

James McHenry, of Maryland, received a classical education in Ireland, the country of his birth, and came to Baltimore in 1771. He studied medicine with Dr. Benjamin Rush at Philadelphia and became an army surgeon during the War. He was for a time secretary to Washington and later to Lafayette, and from 1783 to 1786 he was a member of Congress from Maryland.[315]

McHenry was the son of Daniel McHenry, a Baltimore merchant, who achieved "considerable financial success"[316] and was in business with his son, John, a brother of James until his death in 1782. John and James began buying town property, and when the former died in 1790, the latter inherited the entire estate, as John had never married. The death of James' father, says Steiner, left him financially independent.

McHenry's personal property must have been considerable. A casual letter of August 4, 1792, shows that one Dickinson owed him an amount secured by a bond for £5000.[317] He was one of the original stockholders of the Insurance Company of North America organized in 1792.[318]

---

[310] *Ibid..* p. 529.

[311] Duyckinck, *Cyclopaedia of American Literature* (1855 ed.), Vol. I, p. 283.

[312] Ms. Treasury Department: *Ledger A, Funded 6% Stock,* 1790, folio 18.

[313] *Ibid., Loan Office: Register of Subscriptions, Virginia* (1791), see date, no folio given.

[314] Dunlap's Daily Advertiser, October 23, 1791.

[315] Magazine of American History, Vol. VII, p. 104.

[316] Steiner, *The Life and Correspondence of James McHenry*, p. 2.

[317] *Hamilton Mss.*, Library of Congress, Vol. XXIII, p. 156.

[318] T. Montgomery, *History of the Insurance Company of North America*, p. 142.

It is not apparent that he was among the original holders of federal securities, but an entry in 1797 records an old account to the amount of $6970.90, brought forward.[319]

McHenry's early mercantile interests left a deep impression on him, and he sympathized with the efforts made in his state to secure an adequate protective tariff. Indeed, he was among the signers of the memorial from Baltimore laid before Congress on April 11, 1789, praying for the protection and encouragement of American manufactures.[320]

John Francis Mercer, of Maryland, was born in Virginia and graduated at William and Mary College in 1775. He served in the army and after the war studied law with Jefferson. He moved to Maryland in 1786. He seems to have been a man of some fortune, for he held six slaves,[321] and a moderate amount of public securities.[322] His sympathies, however, were with the popular party in Maryland. He joined with Luther Martin in violent opposition to the adoption of the Constitution. In 1801 he was elected governor of the state, and as governor he attacked the property quali- fications on voters under the constitution of the commonwealth, at length securing the repeal of the provisions.

Thomas Mifflin, of Pennsylvania, was born in Philadelphia in 1744 and graduated at the College of Philadelphia where he distinguished himself as a student of the classics. His father introduced him to a mercantile life by placing him in the counting house of William Coleman, one of the most eminent merchants of his native city. "When was twenty-one years of age he visited Europe to improve his knowledge of commercial affairs, and after his return home he entered into business with his brother, the Connection continuing until after the Revolution."[323]

Mifflin was deeply interested in the protection of American manufactures. He was prominently identified with the Philadelphia Society for the Encouragement of Manufactures and Useful Arts, organized in the summer of 1787. In fact he presided at the meeting at which it was established in August of that year, during the sessions of the Convention.[324]

General Mifflin was a holder of public securities, but does not appear that his paper aggregated more than petty sum. He and Jonathan Mifflin are down for a few hundred dollars' worth of continental paper in 1788;[325] and he held in his own name another small account in 1791.[326] It is, therefore, apparent that General Mifflin appreciated the position of the powerful class of security holders who looked to the Convention for relief, and had a more than abstract interest in the establishment of public credit.

---

[319]   Ms. Treasury Department: *Ledger E, Treasury, 3%.* Vol. 45, folio 22.

[320]   *State Papers: Finance,* Vol. I. p. 8.

[321]   *Census of 1790- Heads of Families, Maryland,* p. 41.

[322]   Ms. Treasury Department: *Loan Office Maryland, 1790-1797, S%,* folios 72, 135, and other loan office records of that state, *passim.*

[323]   McMaster and Stone, *Pennsylvania and the Federal Constitution,* p. 701.

[324]   *The American Museum,* Vol. II, p. 248.

[325]   Ms. Treasury Department: *Pa. Loan Office Certificates,* 1788, folio 45.

[326]   *Ibid.: Ledger C, 3% Stock, Pa.,* folio 48. John F. Mifflin was a holder paper to the amount of several thousand dollars funded in 1790. *Ibid., Loan office Pa., 1790-1791,* folio 6; *Ledger C, 3% Stock, Pa.,* folio 6.

Gouverneur Morris, of Pennsylvania, was born in 1752 the family manor house at Morrisania. He "belonged by birth to that powerful landed aristocracy whose rule was known by New York alone among all the northern colonies." He graduated at King's College, entered the practice of law, and very soon began to take a hand in colonial politics, attacking with great vehemence the propositions of the paper money party. "He criticised unsparingly the attitude of a majority of his fellow citizens in wishing such a measure of relief, not only for their short-sighted folly, but also for their criminal and selfish dishonesty in trying to procure a temporary benefit for themselves at the lasting expense of the community."[327]

He was a member of the Continental Congress and was regarded as a considerable expert in financial affairs. He assisted Robert Morris in the establishment of the Bank of North America, and seems to have been able, in the midst of his public engagements, to augment his private fortunes and to engage in divers economic enterprises. At the time of the formation of the Constitution, he had accumulated enough to purchase the family estate from his elder brother, and "he had for some time been engaged in various successful commercial ventures with his friend Robert Morris, including an East India voyage on a large scale, shipments of tobacco to France, and a share in iron works on the Delaware river, and had become quite a rich man."[328] He declared in the Convention that he did not hold any public securities, and the records seem to bear out his assertion, although his name does appear on an index to a volume of Treasury Records not found.

Of all the members of the Convention, *Robert Morris* of Pennsylvania, had the most widely diversified economic interests. He was born of humble parents in Liverpool in 1734, and came to America at an early age. The death of his father, about 1750, left him a small estate of a few thousand dollars, which stood him in good stead in his relations with the Willings, whose counting house he had entered to learn mercantile arts, in which he showed an early proficiency.[329]

In the course of his long career he owned and directed ships trading with the East and West Indies, engaged in iron and several other branches of manufacturing, bought and sold thousands of acres of land in all parts of the country, particularly in the west and south, and speculated in lots in Washington as soon as he learned of the establishment of the capital there. He was instrumental in organizing the Bank of North America in Philadelphia, with Thomas Willing, his partner, as first President, and Thomas Fitzsimons, an associate in his land and speculative enterprises, as one of the directors,[330] and was in short a merchant prince, a captain of industry, a land speculator, a financier: and a broker combined.[331] Had he been less ambitious he would have died worth millions instead of in poverty and debt, after having served a term in a' debtor's cell.

It is impossible to gauge correctly the extent of his land speculations, for they ran into the millions of acres. Before and after the adoption of the Constitution, he was busy interesting his colleagues in every kind of enterprise that promised to be profitable. James Marshall, a brother of John Marshall, was his chief agent, and carried on operations for him in the United States and Europe. Marshal was given the power of attorney by Morris and his wife to sell enormous quantities of lands and other properties, and received from his

---

[327] Roosevelt, G. *Morris*, pp. 1, 24.

[328] *Ibid.*, p. 167.

[329] Oberholtzer, *Robert Morris*, p. 4.

[330] *Ibid.*, p. 108.

[331] For his multifarious operations see Oberholtzer, *Robert Morris* ; Sumner, *The Financier and the Finances of the American Revolution*, 2 vols.

principal letters of introduction to European capitalists and persons of prominence, including Mr. Pinckney, the representative of the United States in France.[332]

The exact extent of Morris' speculations in the securities of the new government is a matter beyond the scope of the present inquiry, but it is sufficient for our purposes to know that he held practically every kind of continental security, that his deals in stocks mounted upward into the tens of thousands of dollars,[333] and that in the Convention and in the first Senate under the Constitution, of which he was a member, he was uniformly strenuous in his support of public credit. No man of his time had such wide-reaching interests or involved in his personal affairs so many eminent men, like Hamilton, John Marshall, Thomas Fitzsimons, Thomas Willing, Gouverneur Morris, John Langdon, and Robert Clymer, all closely identified with the new system of government.

It may be truly said therefore that Morris was an effective representative of the speculative land operators, the holders of securities, the dealers in public paper, and the mercantile groups seeking protection for manufactures - in short every movable property interest in the country. It was fortunate for the new government to have in its support a man whose economic power and personal acquaintanceship extended from New Hampshire to Georgia. It seems fair to say that no man contributed more to the establishment of our Constitution and the stability of our national institutions than Robert Morris, " the Patriot Financier."

Washington, therefore, showed his acumen when, first President of the United States, he selected Morris for the office of Secretary of the Treasury; but the latter, on a count of the pressing nature of his private business, was unable to accept the post thus tendered. Indeed, he wisely concluded that he could be more serviceable to the new government in his capacity as senator from Pennsylvania and in this position he lent his powerful support to the funding system, the new Bank, and the establishment of protective tariff. "Morris and Hamilton together worked out a tariff bill," says Oberholtzer.[334] "But for the influence of the Senator from Pennsylvania the measure, important because it would provide the national government with ample revenues, and because it had protective features of utility in the development of the country industries, could not have passed Congress in the form which would have commended it to the Secretary of the Treasury.....All witnesses agree that Robert Morris was a stupendous political force in Washington's administration, and his influence did not decrease when, in December, 1790, the capital was removed to Philadelphia, where he resumed his princely entertainment of public men, surrendering his home on Market Street to Washington, and becoming the President most intimate friend and closest companion."

William Paterson was born in the north of Ireland, came this country in 1747, graduated at Princeton in 1763, and received his license to practise law in 1769. His father was merchant, and he was himself for a time engaged in the mercantile business.[335] A by no means extensive search has failed to bring out any of Paterson's later economic interests.

---

[332] Library of Congress: *Morris Mss.* Consult the Index to the three volumes of - Morris' *Letter Books of Private Correspondence* for references, under "James Marshall." Only by turning over this enormous mass of correspondence can one gain a correct notion of the ramifications of Morris' interests and the number of prominent men involved in his schemes.

[333] *Hamilton Mss.*, Library of Congress, Vol. XXII, p. 179; two minor illustrations of his operations may be given: January 1, 1791, $7588.78, July 1,1792, $26,408.66. See also the enormous transactions in the name of Willing and Morris scattered through the books of nearly every state. Ms. Treasury Department: *Ledger C, 8%, Pa.*, folio 334; *Register of Certificates of Public Debt Presented: Auditor of Treasury*; folios not given. Consult Index to holders of old securities in the Treasury Department.

[334] *Op. cit.*, pp. 237 ff.

[335] L. Elmer, *The Constitution and Government of New Jersey*, p. 77.

William Pierce, of Georgia, does not seem to have made any considerable impression on his age, for the biographical material relating to him is meagre indeed. His economic interests do not appear to have been looked into, although it is known that he was "in business in Savannah as the head of the house of William Pierce and Company."[336] His private fortune was probably not large, for he applied to Madison in 1788 for a position as collector in his district.[337]

Charles Cotesworth Pinckney was the son of "Chief Justice Pinckney, a man of great integrity and of considerable eminence under the Provincial Government." He received a fine classical and legal education in England. He began the practice of law in the provincial courts in 1770, and very soon "began to acquire business and reputation." After the Revolutionary war " his business was large and its profits commensurate - reaching in one year the amount of four thousand guineas, a considerable sum for that day." He became "a considerable landholder in the city of Charleston. He had numerous tenants living on his property. ...His benevolence was of the most enlarged character, and was experienced not only by the poor and such as were dependent on him, but in his liberal support of churches, seminaries of learning, and every object of public utility."[338] He also held a country estate at Pinckney Island, and is recorded in the first census as the owner of forty-five slaves.[339]

Pinckney had a large practice for the merchants of Charleston, and his knowledge of maritime law must have been extensive.[340] Through this direct experience, he must have learned the importance of a national commercial system not only to merchants and manufacturers, but also to those having occasion to appear in the courts. In the midst of the local conflict between the creditors and debtors, he took a firm stand against any weakening of public and private credit.

The significance and importance of the public credit he understood from first-hand knowledge, for his holding public securities were large when compared with the average holdings in the South. Shortly after the establishment of Hamilton's funding system, Pinckney is credited with over ten thousand dollars' worth of sixes and threes on the loan office books of his state.[341]

---

[336] American Historical Review, Vol. III, p. 312.

[337] *Calendar of Madison Correspondence*, Library of Congress. Mss.

[338] Herring, *National Portrait Gallery*, Vol. IV.

[339] *Census of 1790 -Head, of Families, 8.C .*, p. 33.

[340] Speaking of the nature of the practice in Charleston just after the Revolution, Charles Fraser says, in *Reminiscences of Charleston,* p. 71: "It was stated by the Duc de Liancourt, who was well acquainted with most or all of the gentlemen named, that General Pinckney, Mr. Rutledge, Mr. Pringle, and Mr. Holmes, made from eighteen to twenty-three thousand dollars a year. ...The extensive commercial business of Charleston at that time opened a wide field of litigation. Our courts were constantly employed in heavy insurance cases - in questions of charter party, foreign and inland bills of exchange, and in adjusting foreign claims. There was also a good deal of business in admiralty, and, occasionally, a rich prize case."

[341] Ms. Treasury Department: *Loan Office, S.C., 1791-1797*, folio 38. For other entries, *Loan Office, S.C .*, folio 70; a later entry of $8721.53 in trust for Mary Pinckney, *ibid.,* folio 152.

Charles Pinckney, like his distinguished cousin, was also an eminent lawyer in Charleston and enjoyed a large practice with the merchants. He was likewise a land-owner on a considerable scale, for the census of 1790 records number of his slaves as fifty-two.[342]

Charles Pinckney was also identified with the conservative forces of the state in their fight against the debtor or paper money party, and he thoroughly understood the meaning of the sacredness of private and public obligations. He was a holder of government securities on a large scale, his transac- ions early in the history of the new system amounting to more than fourteen thousand dollars.[343] In common with the men of his party he naturally feared the effect of popular lawmaking upon the value of personalty.[344]

Edmund Randolph was a grandson of Sir John Randolph, English gentleman of ancient and honourable lineage. Through an uncle he inherited "three farms. ..Negroes, and other property;" but this estate was burdened with debt.[345] As a lawyer, however, he enjoyed a magnificent practice which furnished him a considerable revenue. When charged with having defrauded the Treasury of the United States during his official service as Secretary of State, he advanced as a counter claim the fact that the condition of, his fortune was evidence that he could not have engrossed any large government funds. He reported on that occasion (1801) that in money claims he had £14,200 Virginia currency which he traced "to the best of all resources, the independent labours of my own hands."[346] About that time, his other property which had come to him by way of inheritance amounted to "some seven thousand acres of land, several houses, and near two hundred Negroes. The slaves had long been an incumbrance on account of his refusal to sell their increase and his inability while at Philadelphia to hire them properly."[347]

Indeed, Randolph was apparently never very prosperous. He held ten or fifteen thousand dollars' worth of public securities about the time of the establishment of the new government;[348] but he seems to have been in debt to Hamilton for a considerable sum that gave him some embarrassment On April 23, 1793, he wrote to Hamilton asking an extension of time on the paper, saying: "I am extremely thankful to you for your readiness to accommodate me the subject of the bills. ...The sum which I want to sell is much less than £2600 stg. It is only £1300; as prefer waiting for a rise. ..."[349]

George Read, of Delaware, was the grandson of a "wealthy citizen of Dublin." His father had migrated to America and established himself as "a respectable planter" in Delaware. George studied law under John Moland, a distinguished attorney in Philadelphia, and began business for himself in Newcastle in 1754 where

---

[342] *Census of 1790 - Heads of Families, S.C.,* p. 34.

[343] Ms. Treasury Department: *Loan office, 8.C.,* 1791-1797, folio 221.

[344] *Madison Mss.,* Library of Congress, under date of March 28, 1789.

[345] M. Conway. *Edmund Randolph.* p. 48.

[346] *Ibid..* p. 372.

[347] *Ibid.,* p. 384.

[348] Ms. Treasury Department: *Current Accounts, Va.,* 1791-1796, folios 6, 13, 21; *Ledger B, Assumed Debt, Va.,* folio 87.

[349] *Hamilton Mss.,* Library of Congress. Vol. XX, p. 57.

he soon acquired a lucrative practice.350 Although he surrendered all claim his father's estate on the ground that he had received his portion in his education,351 Read managed to accumulate a modest competence.

Of his economic position, so far as it was reflected in his style of living, a descendant writes: "The mansion of Mr. Read commanded an extensive view of the river Delaware ...It was an old-fashioned brick structure, looking very comfortable but with no pretensions to elegance. ...Here Mr. Read resided for many years in the style of the colonial gentry who, when having no more than the moderate income of Mr. Read, maintained a state and etiquette which have long disappeared. ...How could this be, Mr. Read not being affluent? His income would buy more then that now, and he had a small farm. ..and besides he generally owned his servants." In addition to his income from official positions and his practice, Read possessed some capital for investment, because he appears among the sub- scribers to the stock of the Bank of North America issued in 1784.352

A small part of his worldly goods he had invested in the securities of the Continental Congress in 1779, during the dark days of the Revolution when the chances of ever recovering it were slight indeed. He was among those who risked their lives and fortunes in the Revolutionary cause, and has the honour of being one of the signers of the Declaration of Independence. The loan office of Delaware records that in March and April, 1779, Read subscribed for $2000 worth of certificates, and that Mary Read subscribed for $11,500 worth of the same paper.353 The incompleteness of the records of Delaware in the Treasury department prevents the tracing of these securities, but an entry of 1797 shows Read as holding a small account (old) of threes.354 At all events, Read had felt personally the inconveniences of depreciated paper, and knew the value of a stable government to every owner of personal property.

John Rutledge, of South Carolina, was the son of Dr. John Rutledge, a native of Ireland who settled in Carolina about 1735. He was educated under a classical tutor and pursued the study of law in the Temple. He opened his practice in Charleston in 1761, and a biographer relates that "instead of rising by degrees to the head of his profession, he burst forth at once the able lawyer and accomplished scholar. Business flowed in upon him. He was employed in the most difficult causes and retained with the largest fees that were usually given."355

Rutledge was elected president of South Carolina the first constitution, and when a new frame of government was made by the legislature, in some respects more democratic, he vetoed it, preferring "a compound or mixed government to a simple democracy, or one verging towards it.356 "However

---

350   Sanderson, *Biography of the Signers* (1831 ed.), Vol. III, p. 351.

351   W.T. Read, *Life of George Read*, p. 575.

352   *History of the Bank of North America*, p. 147.

353   Ms. Treasury Department: *Loan Office, Delaware, 1777-1781*" *passim*. His mother and daughter bore the name of "Mary." J. W. Reed, *The Reed Family*, pp. 433 and 436.

354   *Ibid., ledger E, Treasury*. 3%. Vol. 45, folio 202. The Index gives references to several other volumes which were not found.

355   Herring, *National Portrait Gallery*. Vol. IV.

356   Flanders. *Lives of the Chief Justices*. Vol. I. p. 551.

unexceptionable democratic power may appear at first view," said Rutledge, "its defects have been arbitrary, severe, and destructive."

He resigned because he was unable to prevent the adoption of the new constitution; but he was soon elected governor under it; and inasmuch as it provided that no person could be governor unless he held in his own right, on his election, "a settled plantation or freehold. .. value of at least ten thousand pounds currency, clear of debt," it must be assumed that Rutledge was the owner of a considerable plantation and a number of slaves. Indeed, the census of 1790 records the number at twenty-six, which, though small, was considerable for a man whose interests were not primarily in planting.[357] Unlike his other colleagues from South Carolina, John Rutledge does not seem to have invested in securities, though several members of the ledge family appear on the records.

Roger Sherman, the shoemaker of New Milford,[358] Connecticut, was one of the very few men of the Convention who had risen from poverty to affluence largely through his own efforts, and had none of the advantages of education and support which a family patrimony can give. But as his biographer remarks of him: "In regard to worldly circumstances, Sherman was very happily situated. Beginning life with- out the aid of patrimonial wealth or powerful connections, with nothing but his good sense and good principles, he, by his industry and skilful management, always lived in a comfortable manner, and his property was gradually increasing."[359]

In common with other far-seeing business men of his day, Sherman seems to have invested a portion of his accumulations in public securities, for shortly after Hamilton's fiscal system went into effect he funded nearly eight thousand dollars' worth of paper at the loan office of his native state.[360]

Richard Dobbs Spaight, of North Carolina, was of respectable origin. His father had been secretary of the colony under the crown, and his mother was a sister of Dobbs, a royal governor of the colony. He came into his father's estate early; he studied in Ireland, and finished his education at the University of Glasgow. At the time of the Convention, he was, according to Pierce, a "worthy man, of some abilities, and fortune."[361] He was among the large planters of his state, and is recorded to have held seventy-one slaves.[362] He seems to have taken no share in the public security transactions. At least a search in the incomplete records does not reveal him as an original holder- but an old account of 3 per cents for the sum of a few dollars, shows that he was not unaware of the relations of public credit to stable institutions.[363] It was largely through his influence that Washington went to North Carolina to aid in the fight for the adoption of the Constitution by that state.

---

[357]   *Census of 1790 - Heads of Families. S.C.,* p. 42.

[358]   When Roger Sherman resided in Park Lane and ran a store in New Milford, Connecticut, he lost money through the depreciation of bills of credit, and he thereupon declared a war on paper money which he continued to the end of his days. *Proceedings of the American Antiquarian Society.* 1906-1907, pp. 214 ff.

[359]   Sanderson, *Lives of the Signers,* Vol. II, p. 66.

[360]   Ms. Treasury Department: *Loan Office: Connecticut, Ledgers A, B, and C, Threes and Sixes,* folio 28 in each; January, 1792.

[361]   Farrand. *Records,* Vol. III, p. 95.

[362]   *Census of 1790 - Heads of Families, N.C.,* p. 130.

[363]   Ms. Treasury Department: *Ledger E. Treasury,* 3%. Vol. 45, folio 308.

Caleb Strong, of Massachusetts, was the descendant of an old and honourable family of Northampton, the place of his birth. He was educated at Harvard and entered the practice of law.³⁶⁴ He early began a public career for which he showed remarkable aptitudes, and was rewarded by election to the convention which drafted the constitution of his state, to the federal Convention, to the first United States Senate, and later to the office of governor of the commonwealth. Whether he inherited a fortune or accumulated considerable wealth in the practice of law is not recorded by his biographer, Senator Lodge,³⁶⁵ but he took advantage of his superior knowledge of public affairs, and bought up £3271/0/6 worth of certificates of issues up to May, 1787, which he funded into federal securities in September, 1791.³⁶⁶

Washington, of Virginia, was probably the richest man in the United States in his time, and his financial ability was not surpassed among his countrymen anywhere. He possessed, in addition to his great estate on the Potomac, a large amount of fluid capital which he judiciously invested in western lands, from which he could reasonably expect a large appreciation with the establishment of stable government and the advance of the frontier.

Perhaps the best way to illustrate his economic interests is to give the data from the schedule of his property attached to his will, drawn up in 1799. He possessed in Virginia, counting the enormous holdings on the Ohio, and the Great Kenhawa, more than 35,000 acres, valued at $200,000; in Maryland, 1119 acres, at $9828; in Pennsylvania, 234 acres, at $1404; in New York, about 1000 acres, at $6000; in the Northwest Territory, 3051 acres, at $15,255; in Kentucky, 5000 acres, at $10,000; property in Washington, at $19,132; in Alexandria, at $4000; in Winchester, at $400; at Bath, $800. He held $6246 worth of United States securities; and of this holding he said: "These are the sums which are actually funded; and though no more in the aggregate than 7566 dollars, stand me in at least ten thousand pounds, Virginia money; being the amount of bonded and other debts due me and discharged during the war when money had depreciated in that rate - and was so settled by the public authority." He held $10,666 worth of shares in the Potomac Company presented to him by the state of Virginia (which he left to establish a national university); $500 worth of James River Company shares; $6800 worth of stock in the Bank of Columbia, and $1000 worth of stock in the Bank of Alexandria. His own slaves were to be emancipated on the death of his wife. His livestock he estimated at $15,653 - making a grand total at a conservative estimate of $530,000.³⁶⁷

Washington was also a considerable money lender and suffered from the paper money operations of the Virginia legislature. He "had bonds and mortgages to 'nigh £10,000' paid off in depreciated paper currency worth at times as little as 2/6 in the pound, and when he attended the federal Convention he was in arrears for two years' taxes through having been unable to sell the products of his farms."³⁶⁸

If anyone in the country had a just reason for being disgusted with the imbecilities of the Confederation it was Washington. He had given the best years of life to the Revolutionary cause, and had refused all remuneration for his great services. He was paid his personal expenses to the amount of $64,355.30 in paper that steadily depreciated. M. Otto writing to Vergennes on February 10, 1787, says of Washington's losses: " I

---

364   *Encyclopaedia of National Biography.* Vol. I. p. 110.

365   *Massachusetts Historical Society Proceedings. 1791-1835.* Vol. I, pp. 290 ff.

366   Ms. Treasury Department: *Mass. Loan Office.* 1791, Vol. III. item No. 1284.

367   Sparks, *Life of Washington,* Appendix, No. IX.

368   W.C. Ford, *The Federalist,* p. xi, note 3.

have before me a letter of this honoured man in which he complains of being obliged to sell at a rate of twenty for one the certificates which Congress sent to him in payment for the arrearages due him."[369]

Hugh Williamson, of North Carolina, was the son of "an industrious tradesman" of Dublin, who settled in America about 1730 - five years before Hugh was born. The latter received a fine education and graduated at the College of Philadelphia in 1757. About this time his father died, leaving him sole executor of the estate, the settlement of which required the greater part of two years.[370] He studied divinity, but later turned to medicine and went to Edinburgh to pursue his studies in that subject. He practised for a time in Philadelphia, but afterward went South to reside.

During the Revolutionary War he engaged in mercantile speculations in Charleston and later at Edenton, "from which he afterward traded to the neutral islands in the West Indies." While continuing his mercantile connections with his brother, "then also engaged in the West India trade, he determined to resume the practice of medicine; this he did with the same success as he had done formerly at Philadelphia." He was an opponent of the emission of paper money in North Carolina and published an essay against fiat currency.

He happily combined a theoretical and practical knowledge of finance, for he seems to have accumulated a large amount of public securities. He appears frequently on the records of the Treasury Department; for example in December, 1791, for $2444.84 worth of sixes and threes.[371] Furthermore, his correspondence with Hamilton and others shows that he had "the smallest of two large trunks" full of 6 per cents, threes, and deferred stock which he had delivered to Hamilton for transfer to the New York loan office, in 1793.[372]

Williamson also engaged in western land speculations, and was not unaware of the advantage to that class of property which the new Constitution afforded. On June 2, 1788, he wrote to Madison from New York, "For myself, I conceive that my opinions are not biased by private interests, but having claims to a considerable quantity of land in the Western Country, I am fully persuaded that the value of those lands must be increased by an efficient federal government."[373] After his long and assiduous public services, Williamson settled in New York, where he engaged in historical writing and the management of the considerable fortune which he had accumulated in the midst of his pressing public duties.[374]

James Wilson, of Pennsylvania, was born in Scotland in 1742 and received a fine classical education there. He came to America in 1766, began the study of law with John Dickinson, and was admitted to the bar in 1767. He developed a lucrative practice at Carlisle, where he first settled; but in 1778 he removed to Philadelphia where he established a close connection with the leading merchants and men of affairs including Robert Morris, George Clymer, and General Mifflin.[375] He was one of the directors of the Bank of North

---

[369] Bancroft, *History of the Constitution* (1882 ed.), Vol. II, p. 411.

[370] D. Hosack, *Biographical Memoir of Hugh Williamson*, p. 18.

[371] MB. Treasury Department: *Loan Office, N.C.*, 1791, folio 3.

[372] *Hamilton Mss.*, Library of Congress, Vol. XXIV, pp. 70 ff.

[373] *Documentary History of the Constitution*, Vol. IV, p. 678.

[374] Hosack, *op. cit.*, p. 85.

[375] Simpson, *Eminent Philadelphians*, p. 966.

America on its incorporation in 1781;[376] and he also appears among the original stockholders of the Insurance Company of North America, organized in 1792.[377]

Wilson's largest interest seems to have been in public lands, for he was among the members of the Georgia Land Company, a highly speculative concern tainted with fraud, to put it mildly, for ten shares, £25,000 cash and 750,000 acres.[378] Haskins says, "James Wilson, of the Supreme Court of the United States, held shares to the amount of at least one million acres and it is asserted was influential in securing the grants."[379]

Wilson does not appear to have been a large holder of public securities; for a search in the records of the Pennsylvania loan office preserved in the Department of the Treasury reveals only a trivial amount of 3 per cents to his credit, on June 2, 1791.[380] It may be that the extent of his other operations prevented his taking advantage of the opportunities offered in this line.

George Wythe, of Virginia, was born in 1726 on the shores of the Chesapeake in the colony of Virginia. "He was descended from a respectable family and inherited from his father, who was a farmer, an estate amply sufficient for all the purposes of ease and independence, although it was seriously impaired by the Revolution." He studied law, and "by reason of his extensive learning, correctness of elocution, and his logical style of argument, he quickly arrived at the head of the bar."[381] His second wife "was a lady of a wealthy and respectable family of Taliafero, residing near Williamsburg." He was a slave-owner, but he emancipated his slaves and made provisions to keep them from want. His public security holding was not large. On March 12, 1791, he presented Virginia certificates to the amount of £513/2/8 which he had acquired from their original owners.[382]

Robert Yates, of New York, was born in Schenectady, and received a classical education at New York City. He read law and began the practice at Albany where he soon built up an extensive business. He was made a judge of the Supreme Court under the state constitution of 1777, but his salary was small. "Indeed before the scale of depreciation of continental money had been settled, he received one year's salary in that money at its *nominal* value, the whole of which was just sufficient (as he humorously observed), to purchase a pound of green tea for his wife.'" He refused to enrich himself by speculating in confiscated estates, a favourite occupation of some of his friends, and "he died poor."[383] He opposed the adoption of the

---

[376]   Oberholtzer, *Robert Morris*, p. 108.

[377]   *History of the Insurance Company of North America*, p. 146.

[378]   *State Papers: Public Lands,* Vol. I, p. 141.

[379]   *Yazoo Land Companies*, p. 83.

[380]   Ms. Treasury Department: *Ledger C, 3% Stock, Pa.,* folio 195.

[381]   Sanderson, *Biography of the Signers* (1831 ed.), Vol. IV, pp. 172 ff.

[382]   Ms. Treasury Department: *Loan Office: Register of Subscriptions, V /I., 1791,* **lee** date. Also *Ledger A, Assumed Debt, Va.,* folio 32.

[383]   *Appendix to the Secret Proceedings and Debates of the Federal Convention* (1821, Albany).

Constitution, and apparently took no part in the transactions in public securities; but several members of the Yates family, Richard, Adolphus, and Christopher were large operators.[384]

A survey of the economic interests of the members of the Convention presents certain conclusions:

- A majority of the members were lawyers by profession.
- Most of the members came from towns, on or near the coast, that is, from the regions in which personalty was largely concentrated.
- Not one member represented in his immediate personal economic interests the small farming or mechanic classes.
- The overwhelming majority of members, at least five-sixths, were immediately, directly, and personally interested in the outcome of their labours at Philadelphia, and were to a greater or less extent economic beneficiaries from the adoption of the Constitution.

    1. Public security interests were extensively represented in the Convention.[385]

        Of the fifty-five members who attended no less than forty appear on the Records of the Treasury Department for sums varying from a few dollars up to more than one hundred thousand dollars.

        Among the minor holders were Bassett, Blount, Brearley, Broom, Butler, Carroll, Few, Hamilton, L. Martin, Mason, Mercer, Mifflin, Read, Spaight, Wilson, and Wythe. Among the larger holders (taking the sum of about $5000 as the criterion) were Baldwin, Blair, Clymer, Dayton, Ellsworth, Fitzsimmons, Gilman, Gerry, Gorham, Jenifer, Johnson, King, Langdon, Lansing, Livingston,[386] McClurg, R. Morris, C.C. Pinckney, C. Pinckney, Randolph, Sherman, Strong, Washington, and Williamson.

        It is interesting to note that, with the exception of New York, and possibly Delaware, each state had one or more prominent representatives in the Convention who held more than a negligible amount of securities, and who could therefore speak with feeling and authority on the question of providing in the new Constitution for the full discharge of the public debt:

        Langdon and Gilman, of New Hampshire.
        Gerry, Strong, and King, of Massachusetts.
        Ellsworth, Sherman, and Johnson, of Connecticut.
        Hamilton, of New York. Although he held no large amount personally, he was the special pleader for the holders of public securities and the maintenance of public faith.
        Dayton, of New Jersey.
        Robert Morris, Clymer, and Fitzsimons, of Pennsylvania. Mercer and Carroll, of Maryland.
        Blair, McClurg, and Randolph, of Virginia. Williamson, of North Carolina.
        The two Pinckneys, of South Carolina. Few and Baldwin, of Georgia.

    2. Personalty invested in lands for speculation was represented by at least fourteen members: Blount, Dayton, Few, Fitzsimons, Franklin, Oilman, Gerry, Gorham, Hamilton, Mason, R. Morris, Washington, Williamson, and Wilson.

---

[384] Records of the New York Loan Office in the Treasury Department.

[385] See above, p. 75. *n.* 3.

[386] See above, p. 124. Livingston's holdings are problematical.

3. Personalty in the form of money loaned at interest was represented by at least twenty-four members: Bassett, Broom, Butler, Carroll, Clymer, Davie, Dickinson, Ellsworth, Few, Fitzsimons, Franklin, Oilman, Ingersoll, Johnson, King, Langdon, Mason, McHenry, C.C. Pinckney, C. Pinckney, Randolph, Read, Washington, and Williamson.
4. Personalty in mercantile, manufacturing, and shipping lines was represented by at least eleven members: Broom, Clymer, Ellsworth, Fitzsimons, Gerry, King, Langdon, McHenry, Miffiin, G. Morris, and R. Morris.
5. Personalty in slaves was represented by at least fifteen members: Butler, Davie, Jenifer, A. Martin, L. Martin, Mason, Mercer, C.C. Pinckney, C. Pinckney, Randolph, Read, Rutledge, Spaight, Washington, and Wythe.

It cannot be said, therefore, that the members of the Convention were "disinterested." On the contrary, we are forced to accept the profoundly significant conclusion that they knew through their personal experiences in economic affairs the precise results which the new government that they were setting up was designed to attain. As a group of doctrinaires, like the Frankfort assembly of 1848, they would have failed miserably; but as practical men they were able to build the new government upon the only foundations which could be stable: fundamental economic interests.[387]

---

[387] The fact that a few members of the Convention, who had considerable economic interests at stake. refused to support the Constitution does not invalidate the general conclusions here presented. In the cases of Yates, Lansing, Luther Martin, and Mason, definite economic reasons for their action are forthcoming; but this is a minor detail.

Chapter 6

The Constitution as an Economic Document.

It is difficult for the superficial student of the Constitution, who has read only the commentaries of the legists, to conceive of that instrument as an economic document. It places no property qualifications on voters or officers; it gives no outward recognition of any economic groups in society; it mentions no special privileges to be conferred upon any class. It betrays no feeling, such as vibrates through the French constitution of 1791; its language is cold, formal, and severe.

The true inwardness of the Constitution is not revealed by an examination of its provisions as simple propositions of law; but by along and careful study of the voluminous correspondence of the period,[388] contemporary newspapers and pamphlets, the records of the debates in the Convention at Philadelphia and in the several state conventions, and particularly, *The Federalist,* which was widely circulated during the struggle over ratification. The correspondence shows the exact character of the evils which the Constitution was intended to remedy; the records of the proceedings in the Philadelphia Convention reveal the succes- sive steps in the building of the framework of the government under the pressure of economic interests; the pamphlets and newspapers disclose the ideas of the contestants over the ratification; and *The Federalist* presents the political science of the new system as conceived by three of the profoundest thinkers of the period, Hamilton, Madison, and Jay.

Doubtless, the most illuminating of these sources on the economic character of the Constitution are the records of the debates in the Convention, which have come down to us in fragmentary form; and a thorough treatment of material forces reflected in the several clauses of the instrument of government created by the grave assembly at Philadelphia would require a rewriting of the history of the proceedings in the light of the great interests represented there.[389] But an entire volume would scarcely suffice to present the results of such a survey, and an undertaking of this character is accordingly impossible here.

The Federalist, on the other hand, presents in a relatively brief and systematic form an economic interpretation of the Constitution by the men best fitted, through an intimate knowledge of the ideals of the framers, to expound the political science of the new government. This wonderful piece of argumentation by Hamilton, Madison, and Jay is in fact the finest study in the economic interpretation of politics which exists in any language; and whoever would understand the Constitution as an economic document need hardly go beyond it. It is true that the tone of the writers is somewhat modified on account of the fact that they are appealing to the voters to ratify the Constitution, but at the same time they are, by the force of circumstances, compelled to convince large economic groups that safety and strength lie in the adoption of the new system.

Indeed, every fundamental appeal in it is to some material and substantial interest. Sometimes it is to the people at large in the name of protection against invading armies and European coalitions. Sometimes it is to the commercial classes whose business is represented as prostrate before the follies of the Confederation.

---

[388] A great deal of this valuable material has been printed in the *Documentary History of the Constitution,* Vols. IV and V; a considerable amount has been published in the letters and papers of the eminent men of the period; but an enormous mass still remains in manuscript form. Fortunately, such important papers as those of Washington, Hamilton, Madison, and others are in the Library of Congress; but they are not complete, of course.

[389] From this point of view, the old conception of the battle at Philadelphia as a contest between small and large states - as political entities - will have to be severely modified. See Professor Farrand's illuminating paper on the so-called compromises of the Constitution in the *Report of the American Historical Association,* 1903, Vol. I, pp. 73 ff. J.C. Welling, 'States' Rights Conflict over the Public Lands," *ibid.* (1888), pp. 184 ff.

Now it is to creditors seeking relief against paper money and the assaults of the agrarians in general; now it is to the holders of federal securities which are depreciating toward the vanishing point. But above all, it is to the owners of personalty anxious to find a foil against the attacks of levelling democracy, that the authors of *The Federalist* address their most cogent arguments in favour of ratification. It is true there is much discussion of the details of the new frame-work of government, to which even some friends of reform took exceptions; but Madison and Hamilton both knew that these were incidental matters when compared with the sound basis upon which the superstructure rested.

In reading the pages of this remarkable work as a study in political economy, it is important to bear in mind that the system, which the authors are describing, consisted of two fundamental parts - one positive, the other negative:

   I.   A government endowed with certain positive powers, but so constructed as to break the force of majority rule and prevent invasions of the property rights of minorities.
   II. Restrictions on the state legislatures which had been so vigorous in their attacks on capital.

Under some circumstances, action is the immediate interest of the dominant party; and whenever it desires to make an economic gain through governmental functioning, it must have, of course, a system endowed with the requisite powers.

Examples of this are to be found in protective tariffs, in ship subsidies, in railway land grants, in river and harbour improvements, and so on through the catalogue of so-called "paternalistic" legislation. Of course it may be shown that the " general good " is the ostensible object of any particular act; but the general good is a passive force, and unless we know who are the several individuals that benefit in its name, it has no meaning. When it is so analysed, immediate and remote beneficiaries are discovered; and the former are usually found to have been the dynamic element in securing the legislation. Take for example, the economic interests of the advocates who appear in tariff hearings at Washington.

On the obverse side, dominant interests quite as often benefit from the prevention of governmental action as from positive assistance. They are able to take care of themselves if let alone within the circle of protection created by the law. Indeed, most owners of property have as much to fear from positive governmental action as from their inability to secure advantageous legislation. Particularly is this true where the field of private property is already extended to cover practically every form of tangible and intangible wealth. This was clearly set forth by Hamilton:

"It may perhaps be said that the power of preventing bad laws includes that of preventing good ones. ...But this objection will have little weight with those who can properly estimate the mischiefs of that inconstancy and mutability in the laws which form the greatest blemish in the character and genius of our governments. They will consider every institution calculated to restrain the excess of law-making, and to keep things in the same state in which they happen to be at any given period, as more likely to do good than harm. ...The injury which may possibly be done by defeating a few good laws will be amply compensated by the advantage of preventing a number of bad ones."[390]

The Underlying Political Science Of The Constitution.[391]

Before taking up the economic implications of the structure of the federal government, it is important to ascertain what, in the opinion of *The Federalist*, is the basis of all government. The most philosophical

---

[390] *The Federalist,* No.73.

[391] See J.A. Smith, *The Spirit of American Government.*

examination of the foundations of political science is made by Madison in the tenth number. Here he lays down, in no uncertain language, the principle that the first and elemental concern of every government is economic.

1. "The first object of government," he declares, is the protection of " the diversity in the faculties of men, from which the rights of property originate." The chief business of government, from which, perforce, its essential nature must be derived, consists in the control and adjustment of conflicting economic interests. After enumerating the various forms of propertied interests which spring up inevitably in modern society, he adds: " The regulation of these various and interfering interests forms the principal task of modern legislation, and involves the spirit of party and faction in the ordinary operations of the government."[392]

2. What are the chief causes of these conflicting political forces with which the government must concern itself? Madison answers. Of course fanciful and frivolous distinctions have sometimes been the cause of violent conflicts; "but the most common and durable source of factions has been the various and unequal distribution of property. Those who hold and those who are without property have ever formed distinct interests in society. Those who are creditors, and those who are debtors, fall under a like discrimination. A landed interest, a manufacturing interest, a mercantile interest, a moneyed interest, with many lesser interests grow up of necessity in civilized nations, and divide them into different classes actuated by different sentiments and views."

3. The theories of government which men entertain are emotional reactions to their property interests. "From the protection of different and unequal faculties of acquiring property, the possession of different degrees and kinds of property immediately results; *and from the influence of these on the sentiments and views of the respective proprietors, ensues a division of society into different interests and parties."* Legislatures reflect these interests. "What," he asks, "are the different classes of legislators but advocates and parties to the causes which they determine." There is no help for it. "The causes of faction cannot be removed," and "we well know that neither moral nor religious motives can be relied on as an adequate control."

4. Unequal distribution of property is inevitable, and from it contending factions will rise in the state. The government will reflect them, for they will have their separate principles and "sentiments"; but the supreme danger will arise from the fusion of certain interests into an overbearing majority, which Madison, in another place, prophesied would be the landless proletariat,[393] - an overbearing majority which will make its "rights" paramount, and sacrifice the "rights" of the minority. "To secure the public good," he declares, "and private rights against the danger of such a faction and at the same time preserve the spirit and the form of popular government is then the great object to which our inquiries are directed."

5. How is this to be done? Since the contending classes cannot be eliminated and their interests are bound to be reflected in politics, the only way out lies in making it difficult for enough contending interests to fuse into a majority, and in balancing one over against another. The machinery for doing *this is* created by the new Constitution and by the Union.

    (a) Public views are to be refined and enlarged "by passing them through the medium of a chosen body of citizens."
    (b) The very size of the Union will enable the inclusion of more interests so that the danger

---

[392] See Noah Webster's consideration of the subject of government and property; Ford, *Pamphlets on the Constitution*, pp. 57 ff.

[393] Farrand, *Records*, Vol. II, p. 203.

of an overbearing majority is not so great. "The smaller the society, the fewer probably will be the distinct parties and interests composing it; the fewer the distinct parties and interests, the more frequently will a majority be found of the same party. ...Extend the sphere, and you take in a greater variety of parties and interests; you make it less probable that a majority of the whole will have a common motive to invade the rights of other citizens; or if such a common motive exists, it will be more difficult for all who feel it to discover their strength and to act in unison with each other." Q.E.D., " in the extent and proper structure of the Union, therefore, we behold a republican remedy for the diseases most incident to republican government."[394]

I. The Structure Of Government Or The Balance Of Powers

The fundamental theory of political economy thus stated by Madison was the basis of the original American conception of the balance of powers which is formulated at length in four numbers of *The Federalist* and consists of the following elements:

1. No mere parchment separation of departments of government will be effective. "The legislative department is everywhere extending the sphere of its activity, and drawing all power into its impetuous vortex. The founders of our republic...seem never for a moment to have turned their eyes from the danger to liberty from the overgrown and all-grasping prerogative of an hereditary magistrate, supported and fortified by an hereditary branch of the legislative authority. They seem never to have recollected the danger from legislative usurpations, which, by assembling all power in the same hands, must lead to the same tyranny as is threatened by executive usurpations."[395]

2. Some sure mode of checking usurpations in the government must be provided, other than frequent appeals to the people. "There appear to be insuperable objections against the proposed recurrence to the people as a provision in all cases for keeping the several departments of power within their constitutional limits."[396] In a contest between the legislature and the other branches of the government, the former would doubtless be victorious on account of the ability of the legislators to plead their cause with the people.

3. What then can be depended upon to keep the govern- ment in close rein? "The only answer that can be given is, that as all these exterior provisions are found to be inadequate, the defect must be supplied by so contriving the interior structure of the government as that its several constituent parts may, by their mutual relations, be the means of keeping each other in their proper places. ...It is of great importance

---

[394] This view was set forth by Madison in a letter to Jefferson in 1788. ..Wherever the real power in a Government lies, there is the danger of oppression. In our Governments the real power lies in the majority of the Community, and the invasion of private rights is *chiefly* to be apprehended, not from acts of Government contrary to the sense of its constituents, but from acts in which the Government is the mere instrument of the major number of the constituents. This is a truth of great importance, but not yet sufficiently attended to, and is probably more strongly impressed upon my mind by facts, and reflections suggested by them, than on yours which has contemplated abuses of power issuing from a very different Quarter. Wherever there is an interest and power to do wrong, wrong will generally be done, and not less readily by a powerful and interested party than by a powerful and interested prince." *Documentary History of the Constitution,* Vol. V. p.88.

[395] *The Federalist,* No. 48.

[396] *Ibid.,* No. 49.

in a republic not only to guard the society against the oppression of its rulers, but to guard one part of the society against the injustice of the other part. Different interests necessarily exist in different classes of citizens. If a majority be united by a common interest, the rights of, the minority will be insecure."[397] There are two ways of obviating this danger: one is by establishing a monarch independent of popular will, and the other is by reflecting these contending interests (so far as their representatives may be enfranchised) in the very structure of the government itself so that a majority cannot dominate the minority - which minority is of course composed of those who possess property that may be attacked. "Society itself will be broken into so many parts, interests, and classes of citizens, that the rights of individuals, or of the minority, will be in little danger from interested combinations of the majority."[398]

4. The structure of the government as devised at Philadelphia reflects these several interests and makes improbable any danger to the minority from the majority. "The House of Representatives being to be elected immediately by the people, the Senate by the State legislatures, the President by electors chosen for that purpose by the people, there would be little probability of a common interest to cement these different branches in a predilection for any particular class of electors."[399]

5. All of these diverse interests appear in the amend- ing process but they are further reinforced against majorities. An amendment must receive a two-thirds vote in each of the two houses so constituted and the approval of three-fourths of the states.

6. The economic corollary of this system is as follows: Property interests may, through their superior weight in power and intelligence, secure advantageous legislation whenever necessary and they may at the same time obtain immunity from control by parliamentary majorities.

If we examine carefully the delicate instrument by which the framers sought to check certain kinds of positive action that might be advocated to the detriment of established and acquired rights, we cannot help marvelling at their skill. Their leading idea was to break up the attacking forces at the starting point: the source of political authority for the several branches of the government. This disintegration of positive action at the source was further facilitated by the differentiation in the terms given to the respective departments of the government. And the crowning counterweight to "an interested and over-bearing majority," as Madison phrased it, was secured in the peculiar position assigned to the judiciary, and the use of the sanctity and mystery of the law as a foil to democratic attacks.

It will be seen on examination that no two of the leading branches of the government are derived from the same source. The House of Representatives springs from the mass of the people whom the states may see fit to enfranchise. The Senate is elected by the legislatures of the states, which were, in 1787, almost uniformly based on property qualifications, sometimes with a differentiation between the sources of the upper and lower houses. The President is to be chosen by electors selected as the legis- latures of the states may determine - at all events by an authority one degree removed from the voters at large. The judiciary is to be chosen by the President and the Senate, both removed from direct popular control and holding for longer terms than the House.

A sharp differentiation is made in the terms of the several authorities, so that a complete renewal of the government at one stroke is impossible. The House of Representatives is chosen for two years; the Senators

---

[397] *The Federalist*, No. 51.

[398] *Ibid.*, No. 51.

[399] *Ibid.*, No. 60.

for six, but not at one election, for one-third go out every two years. The President is chosen for four years. The judges of the Supreme Court hold for life. Thus "popular distempers," as eighteenth century publicists called them, are not only restrained from working their havoc through direct elections, but they are further checked by the requirement that they must last six years in order to make their effects felt in the political department of the government, providing they can break through the barriers imposed by the indirect election of the Senate and the President. Finally, there is the check of judicial control that can be overcome only through the manipulation of the appointing power which requires time, or through the operation of a cumbersome amending system.

The keystone of the whole structure is, in fact, the system provided for judicial control - the most unique contribution to the science of government which has been made by American political genius. It is claimed by some recent writers that it was not the intention of the framers of the Constitution to confer upon the Supreme Court the power of passing upon the constitutionality of statutes enacted by Congress; but in view of the evidence on the other side, it is incumbent upon those who make this assertion to bring forward positive evidence to the effect that judicial control was not a part of the Philadelphia programme.[400] Certainly, the authors of *The Federalist* entertained no doubts on the, point, and they conceived it to be such an excellent principle that they were careful to explain it to the electors to whom they addressed their arguments.

After elaborating fully the principle of judicial control over legislation under the Constitution, Hamilton enumerates the advantages to be derived from it. Speaking on the point of tenure during good behaviour, he says: "In a monarchy it is an excellent barrier to the despotism of the prince; in a republic it is no less an excellent barrier to the encroachments and oppressions of the representative body. ...If, then, the courts of justice are to be considered as the bulwarks of a limited Constitution against legislative encroachments, this consideration will afford a strong argument for the permanent tenure of judicial offices, since nothing will contribute so much as this to that independent spirit in the judges which must be essential to the faithful performance of so arduous a duty. ...But it is not with a view to infractions of the Constitution only that the independence of the judges may be an essential safeguard against the effects of occasional ill humours in the society. These sometimes extend no farther than to the injury of private rights of particular classes of citizens, by unjust and partial laws. Here also the firmness of the judicial magistracy is of vast importance in mitigating the severity and confining the operation of such laws. It not only serves to moderate the immediate mischiefs of those which may have been passed, but it operates as a check upon the legislative body in passing them; who, perceiving that obstacles to the success of iniquitous intention are to be ex- pected from the scruples of the courts, are in a manner compelled, by the very motives of injustice they meditate, to qualify their attempts. This is a circumstance calculated to have more influence upon the character of our governments than but few may be aware of."[401]

Nevertheless, it may be asked why, if the protection of property rights lay at the basis of the new system, there is in the Constitution no provision for property qualifications for voters or for elected officials and representatives. This is, indeed, peculiar when it is recalled that the constitutional history of England is in a large part a record of conflict over the weight in the government to be enjoyed by definite economic groups, and over the removal of the property qualifications early imposed on members of the House of Commons and on the voters at large. But the explanation of the absence of property qualifications from the Constitution is not difficult.

The members of the Convention were, in general, not opposed to property qualifications as such, either for officers or voters. "Several propositions," says Mr. S.H. Miller, " were made in the federal Convention in regard to property qualifications. A motion was carried instructing the committee to fix upon such

---

[400] Beard, *The Supreme Court and the Constitution*. See also the criticisms of this work by Professor W.F. Dodd, in the American Historical Review for January, 1913.

[401] Number 78.

qualifications for members of Congress. The committee could not agree upon the amount and reported in favour of leaving the matter to the legislature. Charles Pinckney objected to this plan as giving too much power to the first legislature. ...Ellsworth objected to a property qualification on account of the difficulty of fixing the amount. If it was made high enough for the South, it would not be applicable to the Eastern States. Franklin was the only speaker who opposed the proposition to require property on principle, saying that' some of the reflected in the Convention could, in truth, see no safeguard at all in a freehold qualification against the assaults on vested personalty rights which had been made by the agrarians in every state. And it was obviously impossible to establish a personalty test, had they so desired, for there would have been no chance of securing a ratification of the Constitution at the hands of legislatures chosen by free-holders, or at the hands of conventions selected by them.

A very neat example of this antagonism between realty and personalty in the Convention came out on July 26, when Mason made, and Charles Pinckney supported, a motion imposing landed qualifications on members of Congress and excluding from that body "persons having unsettled accounts with or being indebted to the United States." In bringing up this motion Mason "observed that persons of the latter descriptions had frequently got into the state legislatures in order to promote laws that might shelter their delinquencies; and that this evil had crept into Congress if report was to be regarded."[402]

Gouverneur Morris was on his feet in an instant. If qualifications were to be imposed, they should be laid on electors, not elected persons. The disqualification would fall upon creditors of the United States, for there were but few who owed the government anything. He knew that under this rule very few members of the Convention could get into the new government which they were establishing. "As to persons having unsettled accounts, he believed them to be pretty many. He thought, however, that such a discrimination would be both odious and useless and in many instances unjust and cruel. The delay of settlement had been more the fault of the public than of individuals. What will be done with those patriotic Citizens who have lent money or services or property to their country, without having been yet able to obtain a liquidation of their claims? Are they to be excluded?" On thinking it over, Morris added to his remarks on the subject, saying, "It was a precept of great antiquity as well as of high authority that we should not be righteous overmuch. He thought we ought to be equally on our guard against being wise overmuch. ... The parliamentary qualifications quoted by Colonel Mason had been disregarded in practice; and was but a scheme of the landed against the moneyed interest."[403]

Gerry thought that the inconvenience of excluding some worthy creditors and debtors was of less importance than the advantages offered by the resolution, but, after some reflection, he added that "if property be one object of government, provisions for securing it cannot be improper."

King sagely remarked that there might be a great danger in imposing a landed qualification, because II it would exclude the moneyed interest, whose aids may be essential in particular emergencies to the public safety."

Madison had no confidence in the effectiveness of the landed qualification and moved to strike it out, adding, "Landed possessions were no certain evidence of real wealth. Many enjoyed them to a great extent who were more in debt than they were worth. The unjust laws of the states had proceeded more from this class of men than any others. It had often happened that men who had acquired landed property on credit got into the Legislatures with a view of promoting an unjust protection against their Creditors. In the next place, if a small quantity of land should be made the standard, it would be no security; if a large one, it would exclude the proper representatives of those classes of Citizens who were not landholders." For these and other reasons

---

[402] Farrand, *Records,* Vol. II, p. 121.

[403] *Ibid.* pp. 121-122.

he opposed the landed qualifications and suggested that property qualifications on the voters would be better.[404]

The motion to strike out the "landed" qualification for legislators was carried by a vote of ten to one; the proposition to strike out the disqualification of persons having unsettled accounts with the United States was carried by a vote of nine to two. Finally the proposition to exclude persons who were indebted to the United States was likewise defeated by a vote of nine to two, after Pinckney had called attention to the fact that "it would exclude persons who had purchased confiscated property or should purchase Western territory of the public and might be some obstacle to the sale of the latter."

Indeed, there was little risk to personalty in thus allowing the Constitution to go to the states for approval without any property qualifications on voters other than those which the state might see fit to impose. Only one branch of new government, the House of Representatives, was required to be elected by popular vote; and, in case popular choice of presidential electors might be established, a safeguard was secured by the indirect process. Two controlling bodies, the Senate and Supreme Court, were removed altogether from the possibility of popular election except by constitutional amendment. Finally, the conservative members of the Convention were doubly fortified in the fact that nearly all of the state constitutions then in force provided real or personal property qualifications for voters anyway, and radical democratic changes did not seem perilously near.[405]

II. THE POWERS CONFERRED UPON THE FEDERAL GOVERNMENT

1. The powers for positive action conferred upon the new government were few, but they were adequate to the purposes of the framers. They included, first, the power to lay and collect taxes; but here the rural interests were conciliated by the provision that direct taxes must be apportioned among the states according to population, counting three-fifths of the slaves. This, in the opinion of contemporaries eminently qualified to speak, was designed to prevent the populations of the manufacturing states from shifting the burdens of taxation to the sparsely settled agricultural regions.[406]

   In a letter to the governor of their state, three delegates from North Carolina, Blount, Spaight, and Williamson, explained the advantage of this safeguard on taxation to the southern planters and farmers: "We had many things to hope from a National Government and the chief thing we had to fear from such a Government was the risque of unequal or heavy Taxation, but we hope you will believe as we do that the Southern states in general and North Carolina in particular are well secured on that head by the proposed system. It is provided in the 9th section of article the first that no Capitation or direct Tax shall be laid except in proportion to the number of inhabitants, in which number five blacks are only counted as three. If a land tax is laid, we are to pay the same rate; for example, fifty citizens of North Carolina can be taxed no more for all their Lands than fifty Citizens in one of the Eastern States. This must be greatly in our favour, for as most of their farms are small and many of them live in Towns we certainly have, one with another, land of twice the value that they possess. When it is also considered that five Negroes are only to be charged the same Poll Tax as three whites, the advantage must be considerably increased under the proposed Form of Government. The Southern states have also a better

---

404 Debate in Farrand, *Records,* Vol. II, pp. 123-124.

405 See above, pp. 65 ff. The members of the Convention could not foresee the French Revolution which was to break out just as the new federal government was being put into operation in 1789.

406 It was a curious turn of fortune that this provision prevented the agrarians and populists in 1894 from shifting a part of the burden of taxes to the great cities of the East. Thus the *Zweck im Recht* is sometimes reversed.

security for the return of slaves who might endeavour to escape than they had under the original Confederation."[407]

The taxing power was the basis of all other positive powers, and it afforded the revenues that were to discharge the public debt in full. Provision was made for this discharge in Article VI to the effect that "All debts contracted and engagements entered into before the adoption of this Constitution shall be valid against the United States under this Constitution as under the Confederation."

But the cautious student of public economy, remembering the difficulties which Congress encountered under the Articles of Confederation in its attempts to raise the money to meet the interest on the debt, may ask how the framers of the Constitution could expect to overcome the hostile economic forces which had hitherto blocked the payment of the requisitions. The answer is short. Under the Articles, Congress had no power to lay and collect taxes immediately it could only make requisitions on the state legislatures. Inasmuch as most of the states relied largely on direct taxes for their revenues, the demands of Congress were keenly felt and stoutly resisted. Under the new system, however, Congress is authorized to lay taxes on its own account, but it is evident that the framers contemplated placing practically all of the national burden on the consumer. The provision requiring the apportionment of direct taxes on a basis of population obviously implied that such taxes were to be viewed as a last resort when indirect taxes failed to provide the required revenue.

With his usual acumen, Hamilton conciliates the freeholders and property owners in general by pointing out that they will not be called upon to support the national government by payments proportioned to their wealth.[408] Experience has demonstrated that it is impracticable to raise any considerable sums by direct taxation. Even where the government is strong, as in Great Britain, resort must be had chiefly to indirect taxation. The pockets of the farmers "will reluctantly yield but scanty supplies, in the unwelcome shape of impositions on their houses and lands; and personal property is too precarious and invisible a fund to be laid hold of in any other way than by the imperceptible agency of taxes on consumption." Real and personal property are thus assured a generous immunity from such burdens as Congress had attempted to impose under the Articles; taxes under the new system will, therefore, be less troublesome than under the old.

2. Congress was given, in the second place, plenary power to raise and support military and naval forces, for the defence of the country against foreign and domestic foes. These forces were to be at the disposal of the President in the execution of national laws; and to guard the states against renewed attempts of "desperate debtors" like Shays, the United States guaranteed to every commonwealth a republican form of government and promised to aid in quelling internal disorder on call of the proper authorities.

The army and navy are considered by the authors of *The Federalist* as genuine economic instrumentalities. As will be pointed out below, they regarded trade and commerce as the fundamental cause of wars between nations; and the source of domestic insurrection they traced to class conflicts within society. "Nations in general," says Jay, "will make war whenever they have a prospect of getting anything by it";[409] and it is obvious that the United States dissevered and discordant will be the easy prey to the commercial ambitions of their neighbors and rivals.

The material gains to be made by other nations at the expense of the United States are so apparent that the former cannot restrain themselves from aggression. France and Great Britain feel the pressure of our rivalry in the fisheries; they and other European nations are our competitors in navigation and the carrying trade; our independent voyages to China interfere with the monopolies enjoyed by other countries there; Spain would like to shut the Mississippi against us on one side and Great Britain fain would close the St. Lawrence

---

[407] Clark, *The Records of North Carolina*, V 01. XX, p. 778.

[408] *The Federalist*, Number 12.

[409] *The Federalist*, No.4.

on the other. The cheapness and excellence of our productions will excite their jealousy, and the enterprise and address of our merchants will not be consistent with the wishes or policy of the sovereigns of Europe. But, adds the commentator, by way of clinching the argument, "if they see that our national government is efficient and well administered, our trade prudently regulated, our militia properly organized and disciplined, our resources and finances discreetly managed, our credit re-established, our people free, contented, and united, they will be much more disposed to cultivate our friendship than provoke our resentment."[410]

All the powers of Europe could not prevail against us. "Under a vigorous national government the natural strength and resources of the country, directed to a common interest, would baffle all the combinations of European jealousy to restrain our growth. ...An active commerce, an ex- tensive navigation, and a flourishing marine would then be the offspring of moral and physical necessity. We might defy the little arts of the little politicians to control or vary the irresistible and unchangeable course of nature."[411] In the present state of disunion the profits of trade are snatched from us; our commerce languishes; and poverty threatens to overspread a country which might outrival the world in riches. The army and navy are to be not only instruments of defence in protecting the United States against the commercial and territorial ambitions of other countries; but they may be used also in forcing open foreign markets.

What discriminatory tariffs and navigation laws may not accomplish the sword may achieve. The authors of *The Federalist* do not contemplate that policy of mild and innocuous isolation which was later made famous by Washington's farewell address.[412] On the contrary - they do not expect the United States to change human nature and make our commercial classes less ambitious than those of other countries to extend their spheres of trade. A strong navy will command the respect of European states. "There can be no doubt that the continuance of the Union under an efficient government would put it within our power, at a period not very distant, to create a navy which, if it could not vie with those of the great maritime powers, would at least be of respectable weight if thrown into the scale of either of two contending parties. ...A few ships of the line sent opportunely to the reinforcement of either side, would often be sufficient to decide the fate of a campaign, on the event of which interests of the greatest magnitude were suspended. Our position is, in this respect, a most commanding one. And if to this consideration we add that of the usefulness of supplies from this country in the prosecution of military operations in the West Indies, it will be readily perceived that a situation so favourable would enable us to bargain with great advantage for commercial privileges. A price would be set not only upon our friendship, but upon our neutrality. By a steady adherence to the Union, we may hope, ere long, to become the arbiter of Europe in America, and to be able to incline the balance of European competitions in this part of the world as our interest may dictate."[413]

As to dangers from class wars within particular states, the authors of *The Federalist* did not deem it necessary to make extended remarks: the recent events in New England were only too vividly impressed upon the public mind. "The tempestuous situation from which Massachusetts has scarcely emerged," says Hamilton, "evinces that dangers of this kind are not merely speculative. Who can

---

[410] *Ibid.*

[411] *The Federalist*, No. 11.

[412] Washington's farewell address which was partially written by Hamilton is one of the most ingenious partisan documents ever written. It, too, has its economic interpretation.

[413] *The Federalist*, No. 11.

determine what might have been the issue of her late convulsions, if the malcontents had been headed by a Caesar or by a Cromwell."[414] The strong arm of the Union must be available in such crises.

In considering the importance of defence against domestic insurrection, the authors of *The Federalist* do not overlook an appeal to the slave-holders' instinctive fear of a servile revolt. Naturally, it is Madison whose interest catches this point and drives it home, by appearing to discount it. In dealing with the dangers of insurrection, he says: "I take no notice of an unhappy species of population abounding in some of the states who, during the calm of regular government are sunk below the level of men; but who, in the tempestuous scenes of civil violence, may emerge into human character and give a superiority of strength to any party with which they may associate themselves."[415]

3. In addition to the power to lay and collect taxes and raise and maintain armed forces on land and sea, the Constitution vests in Congress plenary control over foreign and interstate commerce, and thus authorizes it to institute protective and discriminatory laws in favour of American interests,[416] and to create a wide sweep for free trade throughout the whole American empire. A single clause thus reflects the strong impulse of economic forces in the towns and young manufacturing centres. In a few simple words the mercantile and manufacturing interests wrote their *Zweck im Recht;* and they paid for their victory by large concessions to the slave-owning planters of the south.[417]

While dealing with commerce in *The Federalist*[418] Hamilton does not neglect the subject of interstate traffic and intercourse. He shows how free trade over a wide range will be to reciprocal advantage, will give great diversity to commercial enterprise, and will render stagnation less liable by offering more distant markets when local demands fall off. "The speculative trader," he concludes, "will at once perceive the force of these observations and will acknowledge that the aggregate balance of the commerce of the United States would bid fair to be much more favourable than that of the thirteen states without union or with partial unions."

4. Another great economic antagonism found its expression in the clause conferring upon Congress the power to dispose of the territories and make rules and regulations for their government and admission to the Union. In this contest, the interests of the states which held territories came prominently to the front; and the ambiguity of the language used in the Constitution on this point may be attributed to the inability of the contestants to reach precise conclusions.[419] The leaders were willing to risk the proper management of the land problem after the new government was safely launched; and they were correct in their estimate of their future political prowess.

These are the great powers conferred on the new government: taxation, war, commercial control, and disposition of western lands. Through them public creditors may be paid in full, domestic peace maintained, advantages obtained in dealing with foreign nations, manufactures protected, and the development of the territories go forward with full swing. The remaining powers are minor and need not be examined here. What

---

[414] *Ibid.*, No. 21.

[415] *The Federalist,* No. 43.

[416] *Ibid.*, No. 35.

[417] See the entire letter of Blount, Spaight, and Williamson, cited above, p. 169.

[418] No.11.

[419] J.C. Welling, "States' Rights Conflict over the Public Lands," *Report of the American Historical Association* (1888), pp. 174 ff.

implied powers lay in the minds of the framers likewise need not be inquired into; they have long been the subject of juridical speculation.

None of the powers conferred by the Constitution on Congress permits a direct attack on property. The federal government is given no general authority to define property. It may tax, but indirect taxes must be uniform, and these are to fall upon consumers. Direct taxes may be laid, but resort to this form of taxation is rendered practically impossible, save on extraordinary occasions, by the provision that they must be apportioned according to population – so that numbers cannot transfer the burden to accumulated wealth. The slave trade may be destroyed, it is true, after the lapse of a few years; but slavery as a domestic institution is better safeguarded than before.

Even the destruction of the slave trade had an economic basis, although much was said at the time about the ethics of the clause. In the North where slavery, though widespread, was of little economic consequence, sympathy with the unfortunate Negroes could readily prevail. Maryland and Virginia, already overstocked with slaves beyond the limits of land and capital, had prohibited the foreign trade in Negroes, because the slave-holders, who predominated in the legislatures, were not willing to see the value of their chattels reduced to a vanishing point by excessive importations. South Carolina and Georgia, where the death rate in the rice swamps and the opening of adjoining territories made a strong demand for the increase of slave property, on the other hand, demanded an open door for slave-dealers.

South Carolina was particularly determined,[420] and gave northern representatives to understand that if they wished to secure their commercial privileges, they must make concessions to the slave trade. And they were met half way. Ellsworth said: "As slaves multiply so fast in Virginia and Maryland that it is cheaper to raise than import them, whilst in the sickly rice swamps foreign supplies are necessary, if we go no farther than is urged, we shall be unjust towards South Carolina and Georgia. Let us not inter-meddle. As population increases; poor labourers will be so plenty as to render slaves useless."[421]

General Pinckney taunted the Virginia representatives in the Convention, some of whom were against slavery as well as importation, with disingenuous interestedness. "South Carolina and Georgia cannot do without slaves. As to Virginia she will gain by stopping the importations. Her slaves will rise in value and she has more than she wants. It would be unequal to require South Carolina and Georgia to confederate on such unequal terms."

III. Restrictions Laid Upon State Legislatures

Equally important to personalty as the positive powers conferred upon Congress to tax, support armies, and regulate commerce were the restrictions imposed on the states.[422] Indeed, we have the high authority of Madison for the statement that of the forces which created the Constitution, those property interests seeking protection against omnipotent legislatures were the most active.

In a letter to Jefferson, written in October, 1787, Madison elaborates the principle of federal judicial control over state legislation, and explains the importance of this new institution in connection with the restrictions laid down in the Constitution on laws affecting private rights. "The mutability of the laws of the States," he says, "is found to be a serious evil. The injustice of them has been so frequent and so flagrant as to

---

[420] Farrand, *Records*, Vol. II, p. 371.

[421] *Ibid.*, p. 371.

[422] There are, of course, some restrictions on Congress laid down in the Constitution; but the powers of the national legislature are limited and the restrictions are not of the same significance. Radical action on the part of the national legislature was anticipated in the structure of the government itself, but specific provision had to be made against the assaults of popular majorities in state legislatures on property rights.

alarm the most steadfast friends of Republicanism. I am persuaded I do not err in saying that the evils issuing from these sources contributed more to that uneasiness which produced the Convention, and prepared the public mind for a general reform, than those which accrued to our national character and interest from the inadequacy of the Confederation to its immediate objects. A reform, therefore, which does not make provision for private rights must be materially defective."[423]

Two small clauses embody the chief demands of personalty against agrarianism: the emission of paper money is pro- hibited and the states are forbidden to impair the obligation of contract. The first of these means a return to a specie basis - when coupled with the requirement that the gold and silver coin of the United States shall be the legal tender. The Shays and their paper money legions, who assaulted the vested rights of personalty by the process of legislative depreciation, are now subdued forever, and money lenders and security holders may be sure of their operations. Contracts are to be safe, and whoever engages in a financial operation, public or private, may know that state legislatures cannot destroy overnight the rules by which the game is played.

A principle of deep significance is written in these two brief sentences. The economic history of the states between the Revolution and the adoption of the Constitution is compressed in them. They appealed to every money lender, to every holder of public paper, to every man who had any personalty at stake. The intensity of the economic interests reflected in these two prohibitions can only be felt by one who has spent months in the study of American agrarianism after the Revolution. In them personalty won a significant battle in the conflict of 1787-1788.

The authors of *The Federalist* advance in support of these two clauses very substantial arguments which bear out the view here expressed. "The loss which America has sustained since the peace, from the pestilential effects of paper money on the necessary confidence between man and man, on the necessary confidence in the public councils, on the industry and morals of the people, and on the character of republican government, constitutes an enormous debt against the States chargeable with this unadvised measure, which must long remain unsatisfied; or rather an accumulation of guilt which can be expiated no otherwise than by a voluntary sacrifice on the altar of justice of the power which has been the instrument of it." Speaking on the contract clause - that "additional bulwark in favour of personal security and private rights" - Madison is sure that the "sober people of America are weary of the fluctuating policy which has directed the public councils," and will welcome a reform that will "inspire a general prudence and industry and give a regular course to the business of society."[424]

Hamilton on several occasions laid great stress on the contract clause as one of the features of the Constitution which had warmly commended it to its supporters. In a communication to Washington, dated May 29, 1790, he wrote: "This, to the more enlightened part of the community, was not one of the least recommendations of that Constitution. The too frequent inter-meddlings of the state legislatures in relation to private contracts were extensively felt and seriously lamented; and a Constitution which promised a preventative was, by those who felt and thought in that manner, eagerly embraced."[425]

There was not a little discussion of the obligation of contract clause in the contemporary press during the period of ratification, and there can be no doubt that it was favourably viewed by the supporters of the Constitution as an added safeguard against paper money and stay laws. A writer in the New Hampshire Spy, on November 3, 1787, in commending the new frame of government to his fellow citizens, calls particular attention to this provision: "It also expressly prohibits those destructive laws in the several states which alter

---

[423] *Writings of James Madison* (1865), Vol. I, p. 350. This entire letter deserves careful study by anyone who would understand the Constitution as an economic document.

[424] *The Federalist*, No. 44.

[425] Ms. Library of Congress: *Treasury Department Ledgers*, 1789-1790 (Washington Papers), folio 297.

or impair the obligation of contracts; so that in future anyone may be certain of an exact fulfilment of any contract that may be entered into or the penalty that may be stipulated for in case of failure."

Another writer of the period approves the same principle with more vigour. "My countrymen, the devil is among you. Make paper as much as you please. Make it a tender in all *future* contracts, or let it rest on its own credit - but remember that *past* contracts are sacred things - and that legislatures have no right to interfere with them - they have no right to say, a debt shall be paid at a discount, or in any manner which the parties never intended. ...To pay *bona fide* contracts for cash, in paper of little value, or in old horses, would be a dishonest attempt in an individual: but for legislatures to frame laws to support and encourage such detestable villainy, is like a judge who should inscribe the arms of a rogue over the seat of justice."[426]

The full import of the obligation of contract clause was doubtless better understood by Chief Justice Marshall than by any man of that generation. He had taken an active part in the adoption of the Constitution in his state, and he had studied long and arduously the history of the period for his classic defence of Federalism, *The Life of Washington*. In more than one decision he applied the clause with great effect, and voiced the views of his Federalist contemporaries on this point, explaining the deep-seated social antagonism which is reflected in it.[427] And when at length, in his declining years, he saw it attacked in the legislatures by Jacksonian democracy, and beheld the Supreme Court itself surrendering the position which he had earlier taken, he spread on record in a dissenting opinion a warning and a protest which for cogency and vigour equals any of his great dissertations delivered in the name of the Court.

In the case of Ogden *v.* Saunders, decided in the January term of 1827, the Supreme Court was compelled to pass upon the issue: "Does a bankrupt law which applies to contracts made *after* its passage impair the obligation of those contracts?" The newer school on the bench, Washington, Johnson, Trimble, and Thompson were of opinion that such a law did not impair the obligation of contract and was valid. Marshall, Duvall, and Story dissented. The Chief Justice took the high ground that the obligation of a contract inhered In the contract Itself, and could not be changed by any external legislation whatever. Therefore, obviously, legislation affecting adversely the obligation of "future contracts was just as unconstitutional as legislation attacking contracts already made. In other words, Marshall, who ought to have known what the framers of the Constitution intended better than any man on the supreme bench, believed that it was designed to bring under the ban substantially all legislation which affected personalty adversely - in other words that it was similar in character to the due process clause of the Fourteenth Amendment. Speaking on the contract clause he said with great solemnity: "We cannot look back to the history of the times when the august spectacle was exhibited of the assemblage of the whole people by their representatives in convention, in order to unite thirteen independent sovereignties under one government, so far as might be necessary for the purposes of union, without being sensible of the great importance attached to the tenth section of the first article. The power of changing the relative situation of debtor and creditor, of interfering with contracts, a power which comes home to every man, touches the interest of all, and controls the conduct of every individual in those things which he supposes to be proper for his own exclusive management, had been used to such an excess by the state legislatures as to break in upon the ordinary intercourse of society, and destroy all confidence between man and man. The mischief had become so great, so alarming as not only to impair commercial intercourse, and threaten the existence of credit, but to sap the morals of the people, and destroy the sanctity of private faith. To guard against the continuance of the evil was an object of deep interest with all the truly wise, as well as virtuous, of this great community, and was one of the important benefits expected from a reform of the government."[428]

---

[426] *The American Museum,* Vol. I, p. 118.

[427] See below, p. 295.

[428] Ogden vs. Saunders, 12 Wheaton, pp. 213 ff.

The Economics Of International Politics

The authors of *The Federalist* carry over into the field of international politics the concept of economic antagonisms which lie at the basis of their system of domestic politics. Modern wars spring primarily out of commercial rivalry, although the ambitions of princes have often been a source of international conflict. "Has commerce hitherto done anything more than change the objects of war?" asks Hamilton. "Is not the love of wealth as domineering and enterprising a passion as that of power or glory? Have there not been as many wars founded upon commercial motives, since that has become the prevailing system of nations, as were before occasioned by the cupidity of territory or dominion? Has not the spirit of commerce, in many instances, administered new incentives to the appetite, both for the one and for the other?"[429] Let history answer. Carthage, a commercial republic, was an aggressor in a war that ended in her destruction. The furious contests of Holland and England were over the dominion of the sea. Commerce has been for ages the predominant pursuit of England, and she has been constantly engaged in wars.

Even the Hapsburg-Bourbon wars have in a large measure grown out of commercial considerations.

In this world-wide and age-long conflict of nations for commercial advantages, the United States cannot expect to become a non-resistant, an idle spectator. Even were pacific ideals to dominate American policy, she could not overcome the scruples of her ambitious rivals. In union, therefore, is strength against aggression and in support of offensive operations. Moreover, the Union will be better able to settle disputes amicably because of the greater show of power which it can make. "Acknowledgements, explanations, and compensations are often accepted as satisfactory from a strong united nation, which would be rejected as unsatisfactory if offered by a state or a confederacy of little consideration or power."[430]

Turning from the material causes of foreign wars the authors of *The Federalist* examine the possible sources of danger from domestic discord among the states, regarded as independent sovereignties. And how may such domestic discord arise? The North will probably grow strong and formidable and be tempted to despoil the South: nor "does it appear to be a rash conjecture," says Jay, "that its young swarms might often be tempted to gather honey in the more blooming fields and milder air of their luxurious and more delicate neighbours."[431]

Then the apple of discord may be thrown among the states by foreign countries if several confederacies take the place of union. And what is this apple of discord? Each of the proposed confederacies, says Jay, "would have its commerce with foreigners to regulate by distinct treaties; and as their productions and commodities are different and proper for different markets, so would those treaties be essentially different." Treaties are subject to the law of greatest economic pressure. "Different commercial concerns," he continues, "must create different interests, and of course different degrees of political attachment to and connection with different foreign nations."[432] The degrees of political attachment also follow the law of greatest economic pressure; and if foreign nations come to blows among themselves, their allies in America are likely to be drawn into the conflict. Thus domestic discord may arise among the states indirectly through their material connections with other countries.

---

[429] *The Federalist*, No. 6.

[430] *The Federalist*, No. 3.

[431] *Ibid.*, No. 5.

[432] *Ibid.*

But internecine warfare will more probably arise from causes operating within the states; and what may be the real sources of such conflict? asks Hamilton.[433] They are numerous: lust for power and dominion, the desire for equality and safety, the ambitions of leaders. Has it not invariably been found, he adds, "that momentary passions, and immediate interests have a more active and imperious control over human conduct than general and remote considerations of policy, utility, or justice? ...Has commerce hitherto done anything more than change the objects of war? Is not the love of wealth as domineering and enterprising a passion as that of power or glory? Have there not been as many wars founded upon commercial motives since that has become the prevailing system of nations, as were before occasioned by the cupidity of territory or dominion?"

Of course such acute observers as the authors of *The Federalist* do not omit to remark that the personal ambitions of monarchs have been a cause of wars, and the passions of men for leadership have been a source of domestic insurrections. But they are quick to add that the ag- grandizement and support of their particular families are among the motives that have led monarchs to undertake wars of conquest;[434] and as to personal element in domestic insurrections, Hamilton expresses a doubt whether Massachusetts would recently have been plunged into civil war "if Shays had not been a *desperate debtor.*"[435]

Turning from the question as to the extent of the economic motive in the personal element, Hamilton makes an inquiry into the more probable sources of wars among the states in case a firmer union, endowed with adequate powers, is not established. These he enumerates:[436]

1. "Territorial disputes have at all times been found one of the most fertile sources of hostility among nations." The several states have an interest in the Western Territories, and " to reason from the past to the future, we shall have good ground to apprehend that the sword would sometimes be appealed to as the arbiter of their differences."

2. "The competitions of commerce would be another fruitful source of contention." Each state will pursue a policy conducive to its own advantage, and "the spirit of enterprize, which characterizes the commercial part of America, has left no occasion of displaying itself unimproved. It is not at all probable that this unbridled spirit would pay much respect to those regulations of trade by which particular states might endeavour to secure exclusive benefits to their own citizens." The economic motive will thus probably override all considerations of interstate comity and all considerations of international law. But that is not all; says Hamilton, in italics, "*We should be ready to denominate injuries those things which were in reality the justifiable acts of independent sovereignties consulting a distinct interest.*" Commerce will have little respect for the right of other peoples to protect their interests, and it will stigmatise as an "injury" anything which blocks its enterprise.

3. "The public debt of the Union would be a further cause of collision between the separate states or confederacies." Some states would oppose paying the debt. Why? Because they are "less impressed with the importance of national credit, or because their citizens have little, if any, immediate interest in the question." But other states, "a numerous body of whose citizens are creditors to the public beyond the proportion of the state in the total amount of the national debt, would be strenuous for some equitable and effective provision." In other words, citizens who had nothing at stake would be indifferent, and

---

433   *Ibid.* No. 6.

434   *The Federalist,* No. 4.

435   *Ibid.,* No. 6.

436   *Ibid.,* No. 7.

those who had something to lose would clamour. Foreign powers also might intervene, and the "double contingency of external invasion and internal contention " would be hazarded.

4. "Laws in violation of private contracts, as they amount to aggressions on the rights of those states whose citizens are injured by them, may be considered as another probable source of hostility." Had there not been plenty of evidence to show that state legislatures, if unrestrained, by some higher authority, would attack private rights in property? And had there not been a spirit of retaliation also? "We reasonably infer that in similar cases, under other circumstances, a war, not of *parchment,* but of the sword, would chastise such atrocious breaches of moral obligation and social justice."

These, then, are the four leading sources of probable conflict among the states if not united into a firm union: territory, commerce, the national debt, and violations of contractual rights in property - all as severely economic as could well be imagined.

To carry the theory of the economic interpretation of the Constitution out into its ultimate details would require a monumental commentary, such as lies completely beyond the scope of this volume. But enough has been said to show that the concept of the Constitution as a piece of abstract legislation reflecting no group interests and recognizing no economic antagonisms is entirely false. It was an economic document drawn with superb skill by men whose property interests were immediately at stake; and as such it appealed directly and unerringly to identical interests in the country at large.

Chapter 7.

The Political Doctrines of the Members of the Convention.

Having examined the economic implications of the constitution in the light of the greatest of all commentaries, *The Federalist,* it is now interesting to inquire whether the members of the Convention at large entertained substantially identical views as to the political science of the system. There are several difficulties in the way of such an investigation. Not all of the delegates, indeed not all of the most influential, were speech makers or writers or philosophers. As intensely practical men they were concerned with tangible results, not with the manner in which political scientists might view the details of their operations. There is, accordingly, a considerable danger of attempting too much in making generalizations, and to obviate this as far as possible, the method of taking the members in alphabetical order is adopted, and the evidence of the views entertained by each is fully documented.[437]

The leaders in politics and political philosophy in the eighteenth century were not far removed from that frank recognition of class rights which characterized English society, and they were not under the necessity of obscuring - at least to the same extent as modern partisan writers - the essential economic antagonisms featuring in law and constitution making. Their clarity of thought was greatly facilitated by the disfranchisement of the property-less, which made it unnecessary for political writers to address themselves to the proletariat and to explain dominant group interests in such a manner as to make them appear in the garb of "public policy."

There does not appear, of course, in the writings of American political scientists in the eighteenth century, that sharp recognition of class rights which characterizes the feudal legists, because within the propertied interests politically represented in the government, there were divisions which had to be glossed over; and there were also mutterings of unrest on the part of the disfranchised which later broke out in the storm that swept away the property qualifications on voters and introduced political equalitarianism. Under these circumstances the supporters of the Constitution had to be somewhat circumspect in the expression of their views; but, happily for science, the proceedings at Philadelphia during the drafting of the Constitution were secret, and they were able to discuss with utmost frankness the actual politico-economic results which they desired to reach. Fortunately, also, fragmentary reports of these proceedings have come down to us, and have been put in a definitive form by Professor Farrand.

Abraham Baldwin, of Georgia, did not indulge in any lengthy disquisitions on government in the Convention, and his literary remains are apparently very meagre. However, his view that the Senate of the United States ought to, represent property came out in the debate on June 29, over a motion by Ellsworth to the effect that the "rule of suffrage in the second branch be the same as that established by the Articles of Confederation." Baldwin immediately opposed the proposition, saying, "He thought the second branch ought to be the representation of property, and that in forming it therefore some reference ought to be had to the relative wealth of their constituents, and to the principles on which the senate of Massachusetts was constituted."[438] At the time the senate of that commonwealth rested upon special freehold and personalty qualifications,[439] and the members were apportioned among the several districts on the basis of the amount

---

[437] A few whose views were not ascertained are omitted.

[438] Farrand, *Records,* Vol. I, p. 469.

[439] Above, p. 65.

of taxes paid by each. It is thus apparent that Baldwin wished the Senate of the new government to be based frankly upon property.

Gunning Bedford, of Delaware, did not participate extensively in the debates of the Convention, but it seems from the character of the few remarks that he made that he favoured a more democratic form than was finally adopted, although he signed the Constitution. This inference is drawn from a brief notice of his objection to the establishment of a council of revision composed of the executive and a certain number of the judiciary to exercise a sort of censorship over the acts of Congress. Madison records as follows: "Mr. Bedford was opposed to every check on the Legislative, even the Council of Revision first proposed. He thought it would be sufficient to mark out in the Constitution the boundaries to the Legislative Authority, which would give all the requisite security to the rights of the other departments. The Representatives of the People were the best judges of what was for their interest, and ought to be under no external control whatever. The two branches would produce a sufficient control within the Legislature itself."[440]

Jacob Broom was among those who wished to "lessen the dependence of the general government on the people," to use Jefferson's phrase, by lengthening the terms of public officers. He seconded Read's motion to increase the term of Senators to nine years;[441] he opposed the election of the executive by popular vote, and supported Luther Martin's resolution in favour of election by electors appointed by the legislatures of the several states;[442] he wished to give life tenure to the executive, that is, during good behavior,[443] and he favoured the suggestion that Congress should be given a negative over state legislatures.[444] Broom seldom spoke in the Convention, but there is no doubt that he believed in a restricted and well "balanced" democracy.

Pierce Butler, of South Carolina, on more than one occasion urged the desirability of making property at least one of the elements in the distribution of representation. On June 6, when Charles Pinckney moved that the lower house of the national legislature should be chosen by the state legislatures and not by the people, Butler said: "I am against determining the mode of election until the ratio of representation is fixed - if that proceeds on a principle favourable to wealth as well as numbers of free inhabitants, I am content to unite with Delaware (Mr. Read) in abolishing the state legislatures and becoming one nation instead of a confederation of republics."[445] In connection with a discussion of the Senate, "he urged that the second branch ought to represent the states according to their property."[446] Later in the sessions of the Convention he again "warmly urged the justice and necessity of regarding wealth in the apportionment of representation."[447] He was also

---

[440] Farrand, *Records,* Vol. I, p. 100.

[441] Farrand, *Records,* Vol. I. p. 421.

[442] *Ibid.,* Vol. II, p. 32.

[443] *Ibid.,* Vol. II, p. 33.

[444] *Ibid.,* Vol. II, p. 390.

[445] *Ibid.,* Vol. I, p. 144.

[446] *Ibid.,* p. 529.

[447] *Ibid.,* p. 562.

particularly solicitous about slave property, and he declared that "the security which the southern states want is that their Negroes may not be taken from them."[448]

Daniel Carroll favoured the popular election of the execu- tive, but he advocated a three-fourths vote in Congress to overcome the executive veto. Speaking on this point, " He remarked that as a majority was now to be the quorum, seventeen in the larger and eight in the smaller house he might carry points. The advantage that might be taken of this seemed to call for greater impediments to improper laws."[449] Carroll did not indulge in any philosophic reflections in the Convention so that his "political science," if he had worked out any definite system, is not apparent in the records.

George Clymer entertained the notions of government which were common to the Federalists of his time. He held that "a representative of the people is appointed to think *for* and not *with* his constituents";[450] and invariably, during the course of his career, he "showed a total disregard to the opinions of his constituents when opposed to the matured decisions of his own mind." It was on these principles that he "warmly opposed the proposition introducing a clause in the Constitution which conferred upon the people the unalienable right of instructing their representatives."[451]

W.R. Davie, although he is reputed to have been an accomplished orator and profound student, does not figure extensively in Madison's meagre records. At no point does he expound any philosophy of government. His views were always practical. On the proposition to count slaves in apportioning representation, he threw down the gauntlet to the Convention, and declared that if the rate was not at least three-fifths, North Carolina would not federate.[452]

As to the basis of government Davie "seemed to think that wealth or property ought to be represented in the second branch; and numbers in the first branch."[453]

Davie fully understood the significance of the obligation of contract clause which was designed as a check on the propensities of popular legislatures to assault private rights in property, particularly personalty. Speaking in the convention of North Carolina on this clause, he said: "That section is the best in the Constitution. It is founded on the strongest principles of justice. It is a section, in short, which I thought would have endeared the Constitution to this country."[454] Davie undoubtedly understood and approved the doctrines of balanced classes in the government, as expounded in Adams' *Defence of American Constitutions*.[455]

---

[448] *Ibid.*, p. 605.

[449] *Ibid.*, Vol. II. p. 300.

[450] Sanderson, *op. cit.*, p. 168.

[451] *Ibid.*, p. 169.

[452] Farrand, *Records,* Vol. I, p. 693.

[453] *Ibid.*, Vol. I, p. 642.

[454] Farrand, *Records.* Vol. III. p. 350.

[455] McRee, *Life and Correspondence of James Iredell.* Vol. II. pp. 161. 168. 78.

At no time does Davie appear to have courted popular favour in his native state, for a writer speaking of his candidacy for the legislature in 1798 says: "The true Whigs,' as they styled themselves, dined together under the oaks and toasted Mr. Jefferson. The other party, who were called 'aristocrats,' ate and drank in the house on entirely different principles. General Davie dined in the house with the 'aristocrats.' The 'true Whigs' took offence at this and resolved to oppose his selection, and it was only with much address that they were kept quiet. ...If any person had had the impudence to dispute the election, General Davie would certainly not have been returned. The rabble, which in all places is the majority, would have voted against him."[456]

John Dickinson, of Delaware, frankly joined that minority which was outspoken in its belief in a monarchy - an action that comported with his refusal to sign the Declaration of Independence and his reluctance to embark upon the stormy sea of Revolution. At the very opening of the Convention, on June 2, he expressed his preference for a regal government, although he admitted that the existing state of affairs would not permit its establishment in America. Madison -records him as saying: "A limited Monarchy he considered as one of the best Governments in the world. It was not certain that the same blessings were derivable from any, other form. It was certain that equal blessings had never yet been derived from any of the republican form. A limited monarchy, however, was out of the question."[457]

Dickinson was also among the members of the Convention who wished to establish a property qualification for voters because he thought no other foundation for government would be secure. In the debate on this subject on August 7, according to Madison's notes: "Mr. Dickinson had a very different idea of the tendency of vesting the right of suffrage in the freeholders of the Country. He considered them as the best guardians of liberty; And the restriction of the right to them as a necessary defence agst. the dangerous influence of those multitudes without property & without principle, with which our Country like all others, will in time abound. As to the unpopularity of the innovation it was in his opinion chemirical. The great mass of our Citizens is composed at this time of freeholders, and will be pleased with it."[458]

According to King's notes: "Dickinson - It is said yr. restraining by ye Constitution the rights of Election to Freeholders, is a step towards aristocracy - is this true, No. - we are safe by trusting the owners of the soil - the Owners of the Country - it will not be unpopular - because the Freeholders are the most numerous at this Time -The Danger to Free Governments has not been from Freeholders, but those who are not Freeholders - there is no Danger - because our Laws favour the Division of property -The Freehold will be parcelled among all the worthy men in the State - The Merchants & Mechanicks are safe - They may become Freeholders besides they are represented in ye State Legislatures, which elect the Senate of the U.S.[459] No member of the Convention distrusted anything savouring of "levelling democracy" more than,

Oliver Ellsworth Later as Chief Justice he denounced from the bench Jefferson and the French party as "the apostles of anarchy bloodshed, and atheism."[460] In the Convention, he opposed the popular election

---

[456] Peele. *Lives of Distinguished North Carolinians,* p. 75. Davie's great collection of papers was destroyed in Sherman's raid. *Ibid.,* p.

[457] Farrand, *Records,* Vol. I, p. 86.

[458] *Ibid.,* Vol. II, p. 202.

[459] Farrand, *Ibid.,* Vol. II, p. 207.

[460] H.J. Ford, *Rise and Growth of American Politics,* p. 113.

of the President[461] and favoured associating the judges with the executive in the exercise of a veto power over acts of Congress.[462] He believed in the restriction of the suffrage to those who paid taxes,[463] He was a warm advocate of judicial control, in general, and thoroughly understood the political significance of the system.[464]

Thomas Fitzsimons, the wealthy merchant and stockbroker from Pennsylvania, was, after his kind, not a loquacious man, but rather a man of action - a practical man; and the records of the Convention contain no lengthy speech by him. When Gouverneur Morris, on August 7, proposed to restrain the right to vote to freeholders, Fitzsimons seconded the motion, apparently without saying anything on the point.[465] While he thus sympathized with the movement to set the Constitution frankly on a property basis, Fitzsimons was naturally more interested in such matters as protection to manufactures and harbour improvements.[466]

Benjamin Franklin, who at the time of the Convention was so advanced in years as to be of little real weight in the formation of the Constitution, seems to have entertained a more hopeful view of democracy than any other member of that famous group. He favoured a single-chambered legislature,[467] opposed an absolute veto in the executive,[468] and resisted the attempt to place property qualifications on the suffrage.[469] He signed the Constitution when it was finished, but he was accounted by his contemporaries among the doubters, and was put forward by the opponents of ratification in Pennsylvania as a candidate for the state convention, but was defeated.[470]

Elbridge Gerry, of Massachusetts, participated extensively in the debates of the Convention, but his general view of government was doubtless stated in his speech on May 31, when he expressed himself as not liking the election of members of the lower house by popular vote. He said on this point: "The evils we experience flow from the excess of democracy. The people do not want virtue; but are the dupes of pretended patriots. In Massts. it has been fully confirmed by experience that they are daily misled into the most baneful measures and opinions by the false reports circulated by designing men, and which no one on the spot can refute. One principal evil arises from the want of due provision for those employed in the administration of Government. It would seem to be a maxim of democracy to starve the public servants. He mentioned the popular clamour in Massts. for the reduction of salaries and the attack made on that of the Govr. though secured by the spirit of the Constitution itself. He had, he said, been too republican heretofore: he was still, however, republican, but had been taught by experience the danger of the levelling spirit."[471]

---

[461] Farrand, *Records,* Vol, II, pp. 67,68, 63, 101, 108, 111.

[462] *Ibid.,* Vol. II, p. 73.

[463] *Ibid.,* Vol. II, p. 207.

[464] Beard, *The Supreme Court and the Constitution,* pp. 71-72.

[465] Farrand, *Records,* Vol. II, p. 201.

[466] *Ibid.,* pp. 362, 629, 689.

[467] *Ibid.,* Vol. I, p. 48; Vol. III, p. 297.

[468] *Ibid.,* Vol. I, pp. 94, 99.

[469] *Ibid.,* Vol. II, p. 204.

[470] Scharf and Wescott, *History of Philadelphia,* Vol. I, p. 447.

[471] Farrand, *Records, Vol.* I, p. 48.

When the proposition that Senators should be elected by the state legislatures was up for consideration, "Mr. Gerry insisted that the commercial and monied interest wd. be more secure in hands of the State Legislatures, than of the people at large. The former have more sense of character and will be restrained by that from injustice. The people are for paper money when the Legislatures are agst. it. In Massts. the County Conventions had declared a wish for a depreciating paper that wd. sink itself. Besides, in some States there are two Branches in the Legislature, one of which is somewhat aristocratic. There wd. therefore be so far a better chance of refinement in the choice."[472]

Nicholas Gilman was by temper and interest a man of affairs, more concerned with the stability of public securities and the development of western land schemes than with political theorizing. From Madison's record he does not appear to have said anything in the Convention.

Nathaniel Gorham was opposed to property qualifications on the suffrage in the federal Constitution and the association of the judiciary with the executive in the exercise of the veto power.[473] Speaking on the latter point, however, he said, "All agree that a check on the legislature is necessary. But there are two objections against admitting the judges to share in it which no observations on the other side seem to obviate. The 1st is that the judges ought to carry into the exposition of the laws no prepossessions with regard to them; 2d that as the judges will outnumber the executive, the revisionary check would be thrown entirely out of the executive hands, and instead of enabling him to defend himself would enable the judges to sacrifice him."

Alexander Hamilton had a profound admiration for the British constitution. "The House of Lords," he said in the Convention, "is a noble institution. Having nothing to hope for by a change and a sufficient interest by means of their property, in being faithful to the national interest, they form a permanent barrier against every pernicious innovation whether attempted on the part of the Crown or of the Commons."[474] Doubtless his maturely considered system of government was summed up in the following words: "All communities divide themselves into the few and the many. The first are the rich and well born, the other the mass of the people. The voice of the people has been said to be the voice of God; and however generally this maxim has been quoted and believed, it is not true in fact. The people are turbulent and changing; they seldom judge or determine right. Give therefore to the first class a distinct, permanent share in the government. They will check the unsteadiness of the second, and as they cannot receive any advantage by a change, they therefore will ever maintain good government. Can a democratic assembly who annually revolve in the mass of the people, be supposed steadily to pursue the public good? Nothing but a permanent body can check the imprudence of democracy. ... It is admitted that you cannot have a good executive upon a democratic plan."[475] In consonance with these principles Hamilton outlined his scheme of government which included an assembly to consist of persons elected for three years by popular vote, a senate chosen for life or during good behaviour by electors chosen by the voters, and a president also elected for life or during good behaviour by electors chosen by the voters. The Convention failed to adopt his programme, and he entertained a rather uncertain view of the Constitution as it was finally drafted, doubting its stability and permanency.

William Houstoun, of Georgia, seems to have spoken only once or twice; but he gave an indication of his political science in a remark which he made to the effect that the Georgia constitution "was a very bad one,

---

[472] *Ibid., Vol.* I, p. 154.

[473] *Ibid., Vol.* II, p. 122 and pp. 73-79.

[474] *Ibid.,* Vol. I. pp. 288 .

[475] *Ibid.,* Vol I, pp. 299 ff.

and he hoped it would be revised and amended."[476] The constitution to which he alludes was the radical instrument made in 1777, which provided for a legislature with a single chamber and an unusually wide extension of the suffrage.[477]

Jared Ingersoll, in spite of his great abilities as a student and lawyer, seems to have taken no part at all in the debates of the Convention. Such at least is the view to which Madison's records lead. Something is known, however, of the political principles which he entertained. Though he became intimately associated with President Reed on his migration to Philadelphia in 1778, he never accepted the extreme democratic principles embodied in the constitution of that state in 1776.[478] His biographer, after making an exception of Ingersoll's services in the Convention, says: "I am not aware that he held or sought a position in any popular or representative body whatever. He was what is called conservative in politics; that is to say, he was not by constitutional temper a rebuilder or reconstructor of anything that had been once reasonably well built; nor was his favourite order of political architecture, the democratic. After the great subversion in 1801 he was found as rarely as anybody in Pennsylvania on the side of the majority. He was known to be inclined to the contrary, so far that with or without his consent he was selected in that state, in the year 1812, as the opposition or anti-Madisonian candidate for the office of Vice-President of the United States."[479]

Rufus King correctly understood the idea of a balanced government independent of " popular whims "and endowed with plenty of strength. He favoured a long term for the President, and speaking on the executive department in the Convention he "expressed his apprehensions that an extreme caution in favour of liberty might enervate the government we were forming. He wished the house to recur to the primitive axiom that the three great departments of governments should be separate and independent: that the executive and the judiciary should be so, as well as the legislative: that the executive should be equally so with the judiciary ... He [the executive] ought not to be impeachable unless he hold his office during good behaviour, a tenure which would be most agreeable to him; provided an independent and effectual forum could be devised; But under no circumstances ought he to be impeachable by the legislature. This would be destructive of his independence and of the principles of the constitution. He relied on the vigour of the executive as a great security for the public liberties."[480] King also believed in the principle of judicial control - that most effective check on the popular attacks on property through legislatures.[481]

It was largely on King's initiative that the prohibition against interference with contracts was placed in the Constitution.[482]

---

[476] Farrand, *op. cit.*, Vol. II, p. 48.

[477] See above, p. 70.

[478] H. Binney, *Leaders of the Old Bar of Philadelphia*, p. 86.

[479] *Ibid.*, p. 87.

[480] Farrand. *Records*. Vol. II. p. 66.

[481] Beard, *The Supreme Court and the Constitution*, p. 29.

[482] Farrand, *Records,* Vol. II. p. 439.

William Livingston took a middle ground between the "high-toned" system of John Adams and the simple democracy of such writers as "Centinel" of Pennsylvania.[483] *The Defence of the Constitutions* he impatiently characterized as "rubbage"; and a "Humiliating and mortify- ing acknowledgement that man is incapable of governing himself." But for the opposite party that would set up a simple democratic government through legislative majorities, Livingston had just as little patience. "The security of the liberties of a people or state depends wholly on a proper delegation of power. The several component powers of government should be so distributed that no one man, or body of men, should possess a larger share thereof than what is absolutely necessary for the administration of government. ...The people ever have been and ever will be unfit to retain the exercise of power in their own hands; they must of necessity delegate it somewhere. ... But it has been found from experience that a government by representation, consisting of a single house of representatives, is in some degree liable to the same inconvenience which attend a pure democracy; a few leading men influence the majority to pass laws calculated not for the public good, but to promote some sinister views of their own. To prevent this, another representative branch is added these two separate houses form mutual checks upon each other; but this expedient has not been found to be altogether effectual. If the legislative power, even tho' vested in two distinct houses is left without any control, they will inevitably encroach upon the executive and judicial; ... But further, as prejudices always prevail, more or less, in all popular governments, it is necessary that a check be placed somewhere in the hands of a power not immediately dependent upon the breath of the people, in order to stem the torrent, and prevent the mischiefs which blind passions and rancorous prejudices might otherwise occasion. The executive and judicial powers should of course then be vested with this check or control on the legislature; and that they may be enabled fully to effect this beneficial pur- pose, they should be rendered as independent as possible. ... Tho' it is so short a time since our governments have been put in motion, yet examples have not been wanting of the prevalence of this dangerous thirst after more power in some of our legislatures; a negative therefore lodged in the hands of the executive and judicial powers, is absolutely necessary in order that they may be able to defend themselves from the encroachments of the legislature."[484] Livingston thought that there were some grave defects in the Constitution as drafted at Philadelphia and proposed some emendations. He believed that the President should enjoy the appointing power without any control by the Senate; he thought the Chief Justice should hold office during good behaviour and be empowered to appoint his colleagues; and he further held that the President, the Chief Justice, and a Superintendent of Finance should be organized into a council of revision to pass upon the acts of Congress.

James McClurg, of Virginia, left the Convention during the early part of August, and was silent on most of the questions before that body. On July 17th, he proposed that the term of the executive should be changed from seven years to "good behaviour";[485] and he was particularly anxious to have the executive independent of the legislature. He said that he II was not so much afraid of the shadow of monarchy as to be unwilling to approach it; nor so wedded to republican government as not to be sensible of the tyrannies that had been and may be exercised under that form. It was an essential object with him to make the executive independent of

---

[483] See below, p. 312.

[484] *Observations on Government, Including Some Animadversions on Mr. Adams's Defence of the Constitutions of Government of the United States of America.* etc., published in 1787, by Livingston. under the pen-name of "A Farmer of New Jersey." The pamphlet is sometimes ascribed to J. Stevens, but there is good authority for believing that Livingston is the author. It is not inconsistent with his notions on judicial control; see American Historical Review. Vol. IV, pp. 460 ff.

[485] Farrand. *Records,* Vol. II. p. 33.

the legislature; and the only mode left for effecting it, after the vote destroying his ineligibility the second time, was to appoint him during good behaviour."[486]

That McClurg had small respect for legislatures in general is shown by a letter which he wrote to Madison from Virginia on August 7, 1787, in which he said: "The necessity of some independent power to control the Assembly by negative, seems now to be admitted by the most zealous Republicans - they only differ about the mode of constituting such a power. B. Randolph seems to think that a magistrate annually elected by the people might exercise such a control as independently as the King of G.B. I hope that our representative, Marshall, will be a powerful aid to Mason in the next Assembly. He has observ'd the continual depravation of Mens manners, under the corrupting influence of our Legislature; & is convinc'd that nothing but the adoption of some efficient plan from the Convention can prevent Anarchy first, & civil convulsions afterwards."[487]

James McHenry belonged to the conservative party of his state and opposed "radical alterations" in the constitution of that commonwealth as it stood in November, 1791.[488]

Writing in February, 1787, on the property qualifications placed on voters and representatives in Maryland, McHenry explained that "These disabilities, exclusions, and qualifications have for their object an upright legislature, endowed with faculties to judge of the things most proper to promote the public good." He was warmly opposed to the doctrine that the people had a right to instruct their representatives.[489] Democracy was, in his opinion, synonymous with "confusion and licentiousness."[490]

James Madison was the systematic philosopher of the Convention and set forth his views with such cogency and consistency on so many different topics that no short quotations will suffice to state his doctrines. His general scheme of political science was, however, embodied in the tenth number of *The Federalist*, which has been discussed above and need not be reconsidered here.[491]

Alexander Martin was among the silent members of the Convention, for Madison records only an occasional and incidental participation by him in the proceedings.

Luther Martin was the champion of the extreme states' that rights' view, and entertained rather democratic notions for his time, although, in arguing against the clause prohibiting Congress to issue paper money, he held that, "considering the administration of the government would be principally the in the hands of the wealthy," there could be little danger from an abuse of this power. Martin was in fact a champion of paper money in his state, and he opposed that part of the Constitution which prohibited the emission of bills of credit. As a representative of the more radical section of his community, he was against the clauses restricting the states to the use of the gold and silver coin of the United States, and was opposed to the clause forbidding the impairment of the obligation of contract. Speaking on the latter point he said: "There might be times of such great public calamities and distress, and of such extreme scarcity of specie, as should render it

---

[486] Farrand, *Records,* Vol. II, p. 36.

[487] *Documentary History of the Constitution,* Vol. IV, p. 245.

[488] Letter to Hamilton, Library of Congress, *Hamilton Mss.,* Vol. XXIII, p. 93.

[489] *American Museum,* Vol. IV, p. 333.

[490] Steiner, *Life* and *Correspondence.* p. 527.

[491] Above. p. 156. Mr. E. W. Crecraft, of Columbia University, has in preparation a dissertation on Madison's political philosophy.

the duty of a government for the preservation of even the most valuable part of its citizens in some measure to interfere in their favour, by passing laws totally or partially stopping the courts of justice, or authorizing the debtor to pay by instalments, or by delivering up his property to his creditors at a reasonable and honest valuation. The times have been such as to render regulations of this kind necessary in most or all of the states, to prevent the wealthy creditor and the moneyed man from totally destroying the poor, though even industrious debtor. Such times may again arrive. ...I apprehend, Sir, the principal cause of complaint among the people at large, is the public and private debt with which they are oppressed, and which in the present scarcity of cash threatens them with destruction, unless they can obtain so much indulgence in point of time that by industry and frugality they may extricate themselves."[492]

As might have been expected, a man entertaining such radical notions about the power and duty of a government to interfere with the rights of personalty in behalf of the debtor could not have accepted the instrument framed at Philadelphia. In fact, Martin refused to sign the Constitution; he wrote a vehement protest against it to the legislature of his state; he worked assiduously against its ratification; and as a member of the state convention, he voted against its approval by his commonwealth - but in vain.

George Mason thoroughly understood the doctrine of a balanced government. Speaking in the Convention on the function of the upper house, he said: "One important object in constituting the senate was to secure the rights of property. To give them weight and firmness for this purpose a considerable duration in office was thought necessary. But a longer term than six years would be of no avail in this respect, if needy persons should be appointed. He suggested therefore the propriety of annexing to the office a qualification of property. He thought this would be very practicable; as the rules of taxation would supply a scale for measuring the degree of wealth possessed by every man."[493] On another occasion, he presented a motion requiring "certain qualifications of landed property, in members of the legislature."[494] Although Mason refused to sign the Constitution, his reasons were based on personal economic interests, not on any objections to its checks on democratic legislatures.[495]

J.F. Mercer, of Maryland, who opposed the Constitution in its final form and became the belligerent anti-federalist leader in that state, does not appear to have been so warmly -devoted to the " people's cause," behind the closed doors of the Convention, for he took exceptions to the proposition that the determination of the qualifications of voters should be left to the several states. But his particular objection was "to the mode of election by the people. The people cannot know and judge of the characters of candidates. The worst possible choice will be made."[496]

Thomas Mifflin took no part worthy of mention in the proceedings of the Convention, and expounded no views of government during the debates.

Gouverneur Morris, of Pennsylvania, was the leader of those who wanted to base the new system upon a freehold suffrage qualification; and, on August 7, he made a motion to this effect. In the course of the discussion which followed, Morris said: "He had long learned not to be the dupe of words. The sound of Aristocracy, therefore, had no effect on him. It was the thing, not the name, to which he was opposed, and one of his principal objections to the Constitution as it is now before us, is that it threatens this Country with an

---

[492] Farrand, *Records,* Vol. III, pp. 214 ff.

[493] Farrand, *Records,* Vol. I, p. 428.

[494] *Ibid.,* Vol. II. p. 121.

[495] See above, p. 128.

[496] Farrand, *Records,* Vol. II, p. 205.

Aristocracy. The Aristocracy will grow out of the House of Representatives. Give the votes to people who have no property, and they will sell them to the rich who will be able to buy them. We should not confine our attention to the present moment. The time is not distant when this Country will abound with mechanics & manufacturers who will receive their bread from their employers. Will such men be the secure & faithful Guardians of liberty. Will they be the impregnable barrier agst. aristocracy? - He was as little duped by the association of the words, 'taxation & Representation' -The man who does not give his vote freely is not represented. It is the man who dictates the vote. Children do not vote. Why? because they want prudence, because they have no will of their own. The ignorant & the dependent can be as little trusted with the public interest. He did not conceive the difficulty of defining 'freeholders' to be insuperable. Still less that the restriction could be unpopular. 9/10 of the people are at present freeholders and these will certainly be pleased with it. As to Merchts. &c. if they have wealth & value the right they can acquire it. If not they don't deserve it."[497]

In all the proceedings of the Convention, Morris took deep interest and expressed his views freely, always showing his thorough distrust of democratic institutions. As his biographer, Mr. Roosevelt puts it, "He throughout appears as the *advocatus diaboli;* he puts the lowest interpretation upon every act, and frankly avows his disbelief in all generous and unselfish motives. His continual allusions to the overpowering influence of the baser passions, and to their mastery of the human race at all times, drew from Madison, although the two men generally acted together, a protest against his 'forever inculcating the utter political depravity of men, and the necessity of opposing one vice and interest as the only possible check to another vice and interest.'"[498]

This protest from Madison, however, betrays inconsistency, for on more than one occasion in the Convention he expounded principles substantially identical with those which he reprobated in Morris.[499] Indeed, what appeared to be cynical eccentricity on the part of the latter was nothing more than unusual bluntness in setting forth Federalist doctrines.

Robert Morris, the merchant prince and speculator of Pennsylvania, seems to have broken his rule of absolute silence only two or three times in the Convention, and he apparently made no speech at all. He nominated Washington as president of the assembly, and seconded Read's motion that Senators should hold office during good behavior.[500] There is no doubt that Morris appreciated the relative weight of speeches and private negotiations.[501]

In the proceedings of the Convention, **William Paterson** was chiefly concerned with protecting the rights of small states; but he signed the Constitution, and after its adoption became an ardent Federalist, serving as an associate justice of the Supreme Court. On the bench he was one of the most scholarly and eminent supporters of the doctrine of judicial control over legislation.[502]

---

[497] Farrand, *Records,* Vol. II. pp. 202 if.

[498] Roosevelt, *Gouverneur Morris,* p. 140.

[499] See *The Federalist,* No.51.

[500] Farrand, *Records,* Vol. I, p. 409. 4

[501] For an example see *ibid.,* p. 11, note. He also entertained Washington during the sessions of the Convention. *American Historical Association Report* (1902), Vol. I, p.92.

[502] Beard, *The Supreme Court and the Constitution,* p. 37.

William Pierce took little part in the proceedings of the -Convention. On the question of states' rights he held a broad view, saying, " state distinctions must be sacrificed so far as the general government shall render it necessary - without, however, destroying them altogether. Al- though I am here as a representative from a small state, consider myself as a citizen of the United States, whose general interest I will always support."[503] On no occasion apparently, did Pierce indulge in any general reflections on the basis of all government. He did not sign the Constitution, but he explained this fact by saying, "I was absent in New York on a piece of business so necessary that it became unavoidable. I approve of its principles and would have signed it with all my heart had I been present. To say, however, that I consider it as perfect would be to make an acknowledgement immediately opposed to my judgement."[504]

Charles Pinckney was among the members of the Convention who thought that it was desirable to fix the property: qualifications of members of the national legislature firmly in the Constitution. Speaking on the subject of property and government he said: "The Committee as he had conceived were instructed to report the proper qualification of property for the members of the Natl. Legislature; in stead of which they have referred the task to the Natl Legislature itself. Should it be left on this footing, the first Legislature will meet without any particular qualifications of property; and if it should happen to consist of rich men they might fix such qualifications as may be too favourable to the rich; if of poor men, an opposite extreme might be run into. He was opposed to the establishment of an undue aristocratic influence in the Constitution, but he thought it essential that the members of the Legislature, the Executive, and the Judges - should be possessed of competent property to make them independent & respectable. It was prudent when such great powers were to be trusted to connect the tie of property with that of reputation in securing a faithful administration. The Legislature would have the fate of the Nation put into their hands. The President would also have a very great influence on it. The Judges would have not only important causes between Citizen & Citizen but also where foreigners were concerned. They will even be the Umpires between the U. States and individual States as well as between one State & another. Were he to fix the quantum of property which should be required, he should not think of less than one hundred thousand dollars for the President, half of that sum for each of the Judges, and in like proportion for the members of the Natl. Legislature. He would however leave the sum blank. His motion was that the President of the U.S., the Judges, and members of the Legislature should be required to swear that they were respectively possessed of a clear unincumbered Estate to the amount of -------- in the case of the President, &c &c -"[505]

Pinckney, in fact, had no confidence in popular government, for on March 28, 1788, he wrote to Madison: "Are you not abundantly impressed that the theoretical nonsense of an election of Congress by the people in the first instance is clearly and practically wrong, that it will in the end be the means of bringing our councils into contempt." [506]

General Charles Cotesworth Pinckney entertained views with regard to the special position that should be enjoyed by property, which were substantially identical with those held by his cousin. He proposed that no salary should be paid to members of the Senate. As this branch, he said, "was meant to represent the wealth of the country, it ought to be composed of persons of wealth; and if no allowance was to be made the

---

[503] Farrand, *Records, Vol.* I, p. 474.

[504] *Ibid., Vol.* III, p. 100.

[505] *Ibid.,* Vol. II, p. 248.

[506] *Madison* Mss., Library of Congress; date of March 28, 1788.

wealthy alone would undertake the service."[507] General Pinckney also wished to extend property qualifications not only to members of the legislature but also to the executive and judicial departments.[508]

Edmund Randolph was not only fully aware of the d tress to which property had been put under the Articles Confederation, but he also understood the elements of "balanced" government. Speaking on the subject of the structure of the Senate, he said: "If he was to give an opinion as to the number of the second branch, he should say that it ought to be much smaller than that of the first, so small as to be exempt from the passionate proceedings to which numerous assemblies are liable. He observed that the general object was to provide a cure for the evils under which the U.S. Laboured; that in tracing these evils their origin every man had found it in the turbulence and follies of democracy: that some check therefore was to be sought for agst. this tendency of our governments: and that a good Senate seemed most likely to answer the purpose, ...Mr. Randolph was for the term of 7 years. The Democratic licentiousness of the State Legislatures proved the necessity of a firm Senate. The object of this 2d. branch is to control the democratic branch of the Natl. Legislature If it be not a firm body, the other branch being more numerous, and coming immediately from the people, will over whelm it. The Senate of Maryland constituted on like principles had been scarcely able to stem the popular torrent. No mischief can be apprehended, as the concurrence of the other branch, and in some measure, of the Executive, will in all cases be necessary. A firmness & independence may be the more necessary also in this branch, as it ought to guard the Constitution agst. encroachments of the Ex- ecutive who will be apt to form combinations with the demagogues of the popular branch."[509]

George Read was most outspoken in his desire to see the Articles of Confederation completely discarded. He said that "he was against patching up the old federal system: he hoped the idea would be dismissed. It would be like putting new cloth on an old garment. The Confederation was founded on temporary principles. It cannot last; it cannot be amended."[510] He favoured vesting an absolute veto power in the executive;[511] and he proposed that Senators should hold office during good behaviour.[512]

John Rutledge held that the apportionment of representatives should be on a basis of wealth and population.[513] He favoured a property qualification for the legislative, executive, and judicial departments;[514] and he thought that Senators should not be paid.[515] In fact, he was one of the most ardent champions of the rights of property in government in the Convention. He was strictly opposed to the introduction of sentimental considerations in politics, for, speaking on an aspect of slavery and the Constitution, he said: "Religion & humanity had nothing to do with this question - Interest alone is the governing principle with Nations - The

---

[507] Farrand, *Records,* Vol. I, p. 426.

[508] *Ibid.,* Vol. 11, p. 122.

[509] *Ibid.,* Vol. I, p. 51 and p. 218.

[510] *Ibid.,* Vol. I, p. 136.

[511] *Ibid.,* Vol. II, p. 200.

[512] *Ibid.,* Vol. I, p. 409.

[513] *Ibid.,* Vol. I, p. 582.

[514] *Ibid.,* Vol. II, p. 249.

[515] *Ibid.,* Vol. I, p. 211.

true question at present is whether the Southn. States shall or shall not be parties to the Union. If the Northern States consult their interests they will not oppose the increase of Slaves which will increase the commodities of which they will become the carriers."[516]

Roger Sherman believed in reducing the popular influence in the new government to the minimum. When it was proposed that the members of the first branch of the national legislature should be elected, Sherman said that he was "opposed to the election by the people, insisting that it ought to be by the state legislatures. The people, he said, immediately should have as little to do as may be about the government. They want information and are constantly liable to be misled."[517]

Richard Dobbs Spaight does not seem to have made any very lengthy speeches in the Convention, but his occasional motions show that he was not among those who believed in "frequent recurrence to the people." On September 6, he moved that the length of the President's term be increased to seven years, and finding this lost he attempted to substitute six years for four.[518] Spaight was the one member of the Convention, however, who came out clearly and denounced judicial control;[519] but he nevertheless proved a stout champion of the Constitution in North Carolina - defending it warmly against charges to the effect that it was aristocratic in character.[520]

Caleb Strong carried into the Convention the old Massachusetts tradition in favour of frequent elections. He favoured a one year term for representatives,[521] voted against a seven year term for President,[522] and also opposed a seven year term for Senators.[523] He supported the Constitution, however, in his native state, and was a member of the convention that ratified it.

George Washington's part in the proceedings of the Convention was almost negligible, and it does not appear that in public document or private letter he ever set forth any coherent theory of government. When he had occasion to dwell upon the nature of the new system he indulged in the general language of the bench rather than that of the penetrating observer. For example, in his Farewell Address, which was written largely by Hamilton, he spoke of the government's being "the offspring of our own choice, uninfluenced and unawed, adopted upon full investigation, and mature deliberation, completely free in its principles, in the distribution of its powers, uniting security with energy."[524] He feared, however, the type of politics represented by the Democratic Societies which sprang up during his administration, and looked upon criticism of the government

---

[516] *Ibid.,* Vol. II, p. 364.

[517] Farrand, *Records,* Vol. I, p. 48; also, p. 154.

[518] *Ibid.,* Vol. II, p. 525.

[519] Beard, *The Supreme Court and the Constitution,* p. 53.

[520] Elliot, *Debates,* Vol. IV, p. 207.

[521] Farrand, *Records,* Vol. I, 361.

[522] *Ibid.,* p. 72.

[523] *Ibid.,* p. 219.

[524] *Writings* (Sparks ed., 1848). Vol. XII, p. 222; see below, p. 299.

as akin to sedition.[525] Like Jefferson, he also viewed with apprehension the growth of an urban population, for in a letter to La Fayette at the time of the French Revolution, he said, "The tumultuous populace of large cities are ever to be dreaded. Their indiscriminate violence prostrates for the time all public authority."[526]

Hugh Williamson was against placing property qualifications on voters for members of Congress;[527] and he was opposed to the association of the judges with the executive in the exercise of the veto power.[528] He preferred to insert a provision requiring a two-thirds vote for every "effective act of the legislature."[529] He was, however, an opponent of the paper money party in North Carolina[530] and in the Convention he supported a proposition forbidding the states to pass ex post facto laws, on the ground that " the judges can take hold of it."[531]

James Wilson was among the philosophers of the period who had seriously pondered on politics in its historical and practical aspects. In the Convention he took a democratic view on several matters. He favoured the annual election of representatives by the people,[532] he advocated the popular election of United States Senators,[533] and he believed also the popular election of the President.[534] He furthermore opposed the proposition to place property qualifications voters.[535] His check on popular legislation was to be found judicial control, at first in the association of the judges with the executive in its exercise, and later in its simple direct form.[536] In fact, Wilson shared the apprehensions his colleagues as to the dangers of democratic legislature though he did not frankly advocate direct property checks.[537] He doubtless believed that judicial control would be sufficient.

George Wythe was a representative of the old school of lawyers in Virginia, and he was a profound student of historical jurisprudence, although he apparently made no attempt to apply his learning to any of

---

[525] *Ibid..* Vol. X, p. 429.

[526] *Ibid..* Vol. X, p. 179.

[527] Farrand, *Records.* Vol. II. pp. 201, 250.

[528] *Ibid.,* Vol. I, p. 140.

[529] *Ibid..* Vol. I, p. 140.

[530] Above, p. 146.

[531] Farrand, Vol. II, 376.

[532] Farrand, *Record."* V 01. I, p. 49 and *passim.*

[533] *Ibid.,* p. 52 and *passim.*

[534] *Ibid.,* p. 68 and *passim.*

[535] *Ibid.,* Vol. I, p. 375; Vol. II, p. 125 and *passim.*

[536] *Ibid.,* Vol. I, p. 98; Beard, *The Supreme Court and the Constitution,* p. 42.

[537] *Lectures on Law* (1804 ed.) Vol. I, pp. 398 ff.

the general political questions before the Convention. He was a warm advocate of the doctrine of judicial control and gave practical effect to principles while on the bench in Virginia.[538]

The conclusion seems warranted that the authors of *The Federalist* generalized the political doctrines of the members of the Convention with a high degree of precision, in spite of the great diversity of opinion which prevailed on many matters.

---

[538] Beard, *The Supreme Court and the Constitution*, p. 48.

Chapter 8.

The Process of Ratification.

On the 17th day of September, 1787, the Convention at Philadelphia finished its work and transmitted the new Constitution to Congress, with the suggestion that "it should afterwards be submitted to a convention of delegates chosen in each state by the people thereof, under the recommendation of Its legislature for their assent and ratification and that each convention assenting to and ratifying the same should give notice thereof to the United States in Congress assembled." The Philadelphia Convention further proposed that when nine states had ratified the new instrument, it should go into effect as between the states ratifying the same. Eleven days later, on September 28, the Congress, then sitting in New York, resolved to accept the advice of the Convention, and sent the Constitution to the state legislatures to be transmitted by them to conventions chosen by the voters of the respective commonwealths.

This whole process was a departure from the provisions of the then fundamental law of the land - the Articles of Confederation - which provided that all alterations and amendments should be made by Congress and receive the approval of the legislature of every state. If today the Congress of the United States should call a national convention to "revise" the Constitution, and such a convention should throwaway the existing instrument of government entirely and submit a new frame of government to a popular referendum, disregarding altogether the process of amendment now provided, we should have something analogous to the great political transformation of 1787-89. The revolutionary nature of the work of the Philadelphia Convention is correctly characterized by Professor John W. Burgess when he states that had such acts been performed Julius or Napoleon, they would have been pronounced *coups d' etat*.[539]

This revolutionary plan of procedure was foreshadow in the Virginia proposals at the opening of the Convention and was, therefore, contemplated by some of the leaders from the beginning. When it was under consideration on June 5, Sherman, of Connecticut, opposed it on the ground that it was unnecessary and that regular provisions we already made in the Articles for amendments. Madison wanted to establish the Constitution on some foundation other than mere legislative approval. Gerry "observed that in the Eastern states the Confederation had been sanctioned by the people themselves. He seemed afraid, of referring the new system to them. The people in that quarter have, at this time, the wildest ideas of government in the world. They were for abolishing the senate in Massachusetts." King thought that "a convention being a single house, the adoption may be more easily carried through it than through the legislatures where there are several branches. The legislatures also being to lose power will be most likely to raise objections."[540]

On July 23 the resolution regarding ratification came before the Convention again for discussion,[541] when it was moved that the Constitution be referred to the state legislatures. One of the principal objections urged against this plan was the possibility of a later legislature's repealing the ratification by a preceding body of the same authority; but the chief problem was whether there was more likelihood of securing a confirmation by legislatures or by conventions. "Whose opposition will be most likely to be excited against the system?" asked

---

[539] What they [the Convention] actually did, stripped of all fiction and verbiage, was to assume constituent powers, ordain a constitution of government and of liberty, and demand a *plebiscite* thereon over the heads of all existing legally organized powers. Had Julius or Napoleon committed these acts they would have been pronounced coupa *d'etat." Political Science and Comparative Constitutional Law,* Vol. I, p. 105.

[540] Farrand, *Records,* Vol. I, p. 123.

[541] *Ibid.,* Vol. II, p. 89.

Randolph. "That of the local demagogues who will be degraded by it from the importance they now hold. These will spare no efforts to impede that progress in the popular mind which will be necessary to the adoption of the plan. ...It is of great importance, therefore, that the consideration of this subject should be transferred from the legislatures where this class of men have their full influence to a field in which their efforts can be less mischievous: It is, moreover, worthy of consideration that some of the states are averse to any change in their constitution, and will not take the requisite steps unless expressly called upon to refer the question to the people."

Mr. Gorham, of Massachusetts, was of the same opinion. He "was against referring the plan to the legislatures.

1. Men chosen by the people for the particular purpose will discuss the subject more candidly than members of the legislature who are to lose the power which is to be given up to the general government.
2. Some of the legislatures are composed of several branches. It will consequently be more difficult in these cases to get the plan through the legislatures than through a convention.
3. In the states many of the ablest men are excluded from the legislatures, but may be elected into a convention. Among these be ranked many of the clergy who are generally friends to good government.
4. The legislatures will interrupted with a variety of little business; by artfully pressing which, designing men will find means to delay from year to year, if not to frustrate altogether, the national system.
5. If the last article of the Confederation is to be pursued the unanimous concurrence of the states will be necessary."

In the Convention, Ellsworth preferred to trust the legislatures rather than popularly elected conventions. "I thought more was to be expected from the legislature than from the people. The prevailing wish of the people in the eastern states is to get rid of the public debt; and the idea of strengthening the national government carries with it that of strengthening the public debt." After the plan of ratification by conventions was carried in spite of Ellsworth's objections, he defended it in his appeal to the populace by saying: "It proves the honesty and patriotism of the gentlemen who composed the general Convention that they chose to submit their system to the people rather than to the legislatures, whose decisions are often influenced by men in the higher departments of government, who have provided well for themselves and dread any change least they should be injured by its operation. I would not wish to exclude from a state convention those gentlemen who compose the higher branches of the assemblies in the several states, but choose to see them stand on an even floor with their brethren, where the artifice of a small number cannot negative a vast majority of the people. This danger was foreseen by the federal convention and they have wisely avoided it by appealing directly to the people."[542]

A study of the opinions of the members of the Convention shows that four leading reasons led to the agreement on ratification by state conventions. It permitted the disregard of the principle of unanimous approval by the states. A firmer foundation would be laid for the Constitution if it had the sanction of special conventions rather than temporary legislatures. One of the first objects of the Constitution was to restrict the authority of state legislatures, and it could hardly be expected that they would voluntarily commit suicide. Another leading purpose of the Convention was to pay the public debt at par, and the members had learned from the repeated appeals to the state legislatures for funds to meet this national obligation that no relief was to be expected from this source. There was a better chance of getting the right kind of citizens elected to a convention than to a legislature. By separating the election of delegates to state conventions from the election of members to the state legislatures, the supporters of the Constitution were better able to concentrate their campaign of education. As for the provision of the Articles of Confederation requiring the approval of every state for any amendment in the Articles, the urgent necessities of the advocates of the new system could not permit such a mere technicality to stand in their way.

---

[542] Farrand. *Records*. Vol. III, p. 137.

The question of their legal right to cast aside their instructions and draft a totally new instrument was more or less troublesome for those who entertained a strict regard for the observance of the outward signs of propriety. No doubt the instructions of the delegations from the several states limited them to the "revision" of the Articles of Confederation, and it is highly improbable that in the state of public temper then prevailing a Convention would have assembled at all if its revolutionary purposes had been understood. During the debates behind closed doors Mr. Paterson declared that the delegates were bound by their instructions, but Randolph replied that "he was not scrupulous on the point of power"; and Hamilton agreed with this view saying, " We owed it to our country to do on this emergency whatever we should deem essential to its happiness. The states sent us here to provide for the exigencies of the union. To rely on and propose any plan not adequate to these exigencies merely because it was not clearly within our powers would be to sacrifice the means to the end."[543]

Outside the halls of the Convention it also became necessary to defend this revolutionary departure from their instructions. Madison took up the cause in *The Federalist*[544] and made out an unanswerable case for his side, frankly pleading the justification of revolution if the legal arguments which he advanced were deemed insufficient.

At the outset he is unwilling to admit that the Convention had broken with its instructions and performed a revolutionary act. He, accordingly, puts forward a legal and moral justification first, based upon an analysis of the instructions of the delegates. They were bound, he shows, to make such revisions in the Articles as would render them adequate to the exigencies of the union; but an adequate government, he pleads, could not be made by revising the Articles, and the Convention was either compelled to sacrifice the greater for the less by strictly obeying its instructions or to do its whole duty by sacrificing the letter of the law. Then he clinches the argument: "Let them declare whether it was of most importance to the happiness of the people of America that the Articles of Confederation should be disregarded and an adequate government be provided and the Union preserved; or that an adequate government should be omitted and the Articles of Confederation preserved."

But Madison, after having paid his respects to Legality, hastens to add that in all great changes in government "forms ought to give way to substance." A rigid adherence to mere technicalities "would render nominal and nugatory the transcendent and precious right of the people' to abolish or alter their governments as to them shall seem most likely to effect their safety and happiness.'" That is, the right of revolution is, at bottom, the justification for all great political changes. If it is argued that this right of revolution should not be exercised by a small group of men, such as the Convention of fifty-odd delegates at Philadelphia, Madison replies that it is impossible for the whole people to move forward in concert, and "it is therefore essential that such changes be instituted by some informal and unauthorized propositions made by some patriotic and respectable citizen or number of citizens." This was the manner in which the recent revolt against England was carried out; and in the present case the people had the right to pass upon the work of the Philadelphia assembly.

The opponents of the Constitution were able to see the significance of that clause of the Constitution which cast aside the legal system under which they were living and provided that the new instrument should go into effect when ratified by nine states - as between those states. "Cornelius," in Massachusetts, exhibited great anxiety on this point, and in his letters of December 11 and 18, 1787, he asked concerning this departure: "Will not the adoption of this constitution in the manner here prescribed be justly considered as a perfidious violation of that fundamental and solemn compact by which the United States hold an existence and claim to be a people? If a nation may easily discharge itself from obligations to abide by its most solemn and fundamental compacts, may it not with still greater ease do the same in matters of less importance? And if

---

[543]   Farrand. *Records,* Vol. I, pp. 255 II. ; p.283.

[544]   No. 40.

nations may set the example, may not particular states, citizens, and subjects follow? What then will become of public and private faith? Where is the ground of allegiance that is due to government? Are not the bonds of civil society dissolved? Or is allegiance founded only in power? Has moral obligation no place in civil government? In mutual compacts can one party be bound while the other is free? Or, can one party disannul such compact, without the consent of the other? If so, Constitutions and national compacts are, I conceive, of no avail; and oaths of allegiance must be preposterous things."[545]

On all hands the "unconstitutional" procedure of the Convention was attacked by the Anti-Federalists. "A system of consolidation," says another writer, "has been formed with the most profound secrecy and without the least authority: And has been suddenly and without any previous notice transmitted by the federal convention for ratification - Congress not disposed to give any opinion on the plan, have transmitted it to the legislatures - The legislatures have followed the example and sent it to the people. The people of this state, unassisted by Congress or their legislature, have not had time to investigate the subject, have referred to the newspapers for information, have been divided by contending writers, and under such circumstances have elected members for the state convention -and these members are to consider whether they will accept the plan of the federal convention, with all its imperfections, and bind the people by a system of government, of the nature and principles of which they have not at present a clearer idea than they have of the Copernican system."[546]

Whatever was thought of the merits of the controversy over the proposed plan of ratification, it was accepted by the state legislatures which were invited by Congress to transmit the Constitution to special conventions. It remains to inquire, therefore, what methods were employed in calling these conventions and setting the seal of approval on the new and revolutionary proposals of the Philadelphia assembly.

The resolution calling the convention in New Hampshire to pass upon the federal Constitution was adopted by the legislature on December 14, 1787. The time for holding the elections was left to the selectmen of the several towns, who were instructed to warn the duly qualified voters of the event. The date for the meeting of the convention was fixed on the second Wednesday of February, 1788.[547] Four hundred copies of the Constitution were ordered to be printed for distribution.

The elections seem to have been held about mid-January, for the New Hampshire Spy, for January 25, 1788, contains a long list of delegates already chosen, and adds that "several of the towns not mentioned in the above list were to have had their meetings this week."

A majority of the members of the state convention so chosen, writes a student, who has inquired into the personnel of that body, "were undoubtedly opposed to the Constitution. ...The talent of the convention was decidedly on the side of the Federalists and a majority of the ablest members were in favour of ratification. ...For a time the friends of the Constitution had hopes of securing its ratification without a recess of the convention. Although the greater number of the members from the upper part of the state came down rather opposed to its adoption, yet on the final question it was hoped that a majority would be found to favour it. But these hopes proved delusive. While some of the members who came to the convention instructed to vote against the Constitution had been led by the discussions to a change of opinion and now favoured it, they still felt bound by their instructions, and frankly said that if a final vote was to be taken before they had an

---

[545] Herding, *The Federal Constitution in Massachusetts.* pp. 118-119.

[546] The Massachusetts Centinel, January 2, 1788.

[547] Batchellor, *State Papers of New Hampshire,* Vol. XXI, pp. 151-165; *Documentary History of the Constitution,* 11, p. 141.

opportunity to consult their constituents their vote would be adverse to ratification."[548] Under these circumstances the Federalists adjourned the convention and set to work to convert the enemy. When the convention reassembled a few months later, they were able to carry the day by the uncomfortably small margin of 57 to 47.[549]

In Massachusetts the Federalists lost no time in moving for a convention. As early as October 20, 1787, they carried a favourable resolution in the senate of the state, and secured the concurrence of the house four days later. This resolve provided that the delegates should be chosen by those inhabitants "qualified by law to vote in the election of representatives," and the elections should take place "as soon as may be" in the several towns and districts. The date for the meeting of the delegates was fixed as the second Wednesday in January next. On January 9, 1788, the Convention met at Boston; and a real battle of wits ensued.

As in New Hampshire, the delegates, when they came together fresh from their constituents, appeared to be opposed to adopting the new instrument of government. A careful scholar, who has studied the period intensively, takes this view: "Had a vote been taken on the adoption of the Constitution as soon as the convention assembled, there can be no question but that it would have been overwhelmingly against the proposed plan."[550]

Even after powerful influences had been brought to bear, the margin for the Federalists was uncomfortably close - 187 to 168. Harding remarks: "The majority in favour of ratification, it will be seen was only nineteen. The nine delegates whose names were returned to the convention, but who were not present when the vote was taken, might almost have turned the scale in the other direction. Bearing in mind that it was mainly the Anti-federalist towns that were unrepresented, it may be safely asserted that out of the forty-six delinquent corporations there were enough which were Anti-federalist to have procured the rejection of the constitution. This calculation, however, is based on the assumption that a corresponding increase did not take place in the Federalist representation. Had all the towns entitled to send representatives done so, and had all the delegates been present to cast their votes, it is probable that the final result would not have been changed, though the Federalist majority would have been cut down to scarcely more than a bare half-dozen."[551]

After turning over the debates in the Massachusetts convention, one can scarcely escape the conclusion that the victory in eloquence, logic, and pure argumentation lay on the side of the Federalists; and it would not be worth while to consider at all the charges that improper influence was brought to bear on the delegates, were it not for the fact that they were made at the time and have lasted in the literature on the ratification in Massachusetts. We have "the sober assertion of a reputable historical writer within the last thirty years "to the effect" that enough members of the Massachusetts convention were bought with money from New York to secure the ratification of the new system by Massachusetts."[552] Harding, after making an examination of the charges, dismissed them as "baseless"; and quite properly, for whoever would convict men of such high standing in the community as King, Gorham, and Strong of being associated with such a reprehensible transaction should produce more than mere unsubstantiated evidence.

---

[548]   J.B. Walker, *A History of the New Hampshire Convention*, pp. 22 ff.

[549]   Four members are not recorded, and ..there is a pretty well authenticated tradition that a certain prominent federalist of Concord gave a dinner party on the last day of the session at which several members reckoned as opposed to ratification were present and discussing the dinner when the final vote was taken." *Ibid.*, p. 43, note.

[550]   Harding, *The Federal Constitution in Massachusetts*, p. 67.

[551]   Harding, *op. cit.*, p. 99.

[552]   Harding, *op. cit.*, p. 101.

The legislature of Connecticut, determined not to be behindhand in setting the approval of the state on the new instrument, called a convention on October 11, 1787.[553] A month was given to the electors to deliberate over the choice of delegates who were to decide the momentous issue. The election was held on November 12; the convention assembled on January 3, 1788; and after a few days' discussion gave its assent on January 9, 1788, by a vote of 128 to 40.[554]

In New York the voters were given more time than in Connecticut to consider the new Constitution before they were called upon to settle the question of ratification at the polls by choosing delegates to the state convention. It was not until February 1, 1788, that the legislature of that commonwealth issued the call for the special election to be held on the last Tuesday of the following April.[555]

The contest in New York was hot from the start. Governor " Clinton, in his message to the legislature in January, 1788, did not mention the Constitution - an omission which gave the Federalists some hope as they had feared an executive attack. The resolution calling the state convention passed the lower house by a narrow margin; and in the senate a motion to postpone the matter was almost carried, receiving nine out of nineteen votes.[556]

When, at length, the convention assembled, at least two- thirds of the sixty-four members were found to be against ratification. Such is the view of, Bancroft, and the contemporary press bears out his conclusion.[557] Nevertheless, by much eloquence and no little manoeuvring, the Federalist champions were able to obtain a majority of 30 to 27. The assent of the requisite number of opponents was secured only after an agreement that a circular should be issued recommending the call of another national convention at once to revise the Constitution as adopted.

In pursuance of this agreement, the legislature at its next session, on February 5, 1789, called upon Congress to summon another convention to revise the new instrument of government at once. The address of the legislature stated that the Constitution had been ratified "in the fullest confidence of obtaining a revision of the said Constitution by a general convention, and in confidence that certain powers in and by the said Constitution granted would not be exercised until a convention should have been called and convened for proposing amendments to the said Constitution." The legislature went on to say that it complied with the unanimous sense of the state convention, " who all united in opinion that such a revision was necessary to recommend the said Constitution to the approbation and support of a numerous body of their constituents, and a majority of the members of which conceived several articles of the Constitution so exceptionable, that nothing but such confidence and an invincible reluctance to separate from our sister states could have prevailed upon a sufficient number to assent to it without stipulating for previous amendments."[558]

---

[553] *Documentary History of the Constitution*, Vol. II, pp. 86-87; Connecticut Courant, October 22, 1787.

[554] Bancroft, *op. cit.*, Vol. II, p. 257.

[555] *Debates and Proceedings of the New York State Convention* (1905 ed.), p. 3.

[556] Bancroft, *op. cit.*, Vol. 11, p. 340.

[557] Ibid., p. 340; and see below, p. 244.

[558] *State Papers: Miscellaneous*, Vol. 1, p. 7. For valuable side-lights on the opposition to the Constitution, see E. P. Smith's essay, 'The Movement towards a Second Constitutional Convention," in Jameson, *Essays in the Constitutional History of the United States*, pp. 46 ff.

The commonwealth of New Jersey made haste to ratify the new Constitution as soon as possible after its transmission by Congress. On November 1, 1787, the legislature issued the call for the convention, ordering the inhabitants who were "entitled to vote for representatives in General Assembly," to elect delegates on the fourth Tuesday in the following November, *i.e.*, November 27. The date for the meeting of the convention was fixed as the second Tuesday in December, the 11th, and on the 18th day of that month, the members, "Having maturely deliberated on and considered the aforesaid proposed Constitution," unanimously agreed to its adoption.[559]

The legislature of Delaware, influenced by "the sense and desire of great numbers of the people of the state, signified in petitions to their general assembly," adopted a resolution on November 10, 1787, calling for the election of delegates within a few days - that is on November 26 - for the state convention to pass upon the Constitution. The convention met at Dover on December 3; and after four days' deliberation on the matter adopted the Constitution by unanimous vote on December 6, 1787.[560]

"In Pennsylvania the proceedings connected with the ratification were precipitous and narrowly escaped being irregular. Before it was known that Congress would even transmit the Constitution to the states for their consideration, George Clymer,[561] who had been a member of the national Convention and was then serving in the Pennsylvania legislature, " rose in his place and moved that a state convention of deputies be called, that they meet at Philadelphia, and that they be chosen in the same manner and on the same day as the members of the next general assembly."[562] In vain did the opponents urge that this was irregular, that it was not known whether Congress would act favourably, and that deliberation rather than haste should characterize such a weighty procedure. The legislature, nevertheless, resolved to call the convention, and adjourned until the afternoon, leaving the date of the convention and manner of selecting delegates to be settled later. The opposition thereupon decided to secure delay by staying, away and preventing the transaction of business for want of a quorum.

Meanwhile the news reached Philadelphia that Congress had sent the Constitution to the states for their consideration. The Federalists in the legislature, now having secured the sanction of regularity, determined not to brook further delay, so they sent officers after some of the recalcitrants, who thought "filibustering" justifiable in view of the importance of securing more deliberation before acting. These officers, ably assisted by a Federalist mob "broke into their lodgings, seized them, dragged them through the streets to the State house, and thrust them into the assembly room, with clothes torn and faces white with rage. The quorum was now complete."[563] The legislature (September 29) fixed the election of delegates to the state convention at a date five weeks distant, November 6, 1787. Thus the people of the state were given a little over a month to deliberate on this momentous issue before selecting their agents to voice their will. Some Federalists, like Tench Coxe, expressed regret at the necessity of adopting these high-handed methods; but the stress was so great that it did not admit of delay.

---

[559] *Documentary History of the Constitution,* Vol. II, pp. 46 ff.

[560] Bancroft, *History of the Constitution of the United States,* Vol. II, p. 250; *Documentary History of the Constitution,* Vol. II, p. 25; *Delaware State Council Minutes, 1776-1792,* pp. 1081-82 *(Delaware Historical Society Papers);* Connecticut Courant, Dec. 24, 1787.

[561] See above, p. 82.

[562] McMaster and Stone, *Pennsylvania and the Federal Constitution,* p. 3.

[563] McMaster and Stone, *op. cit.,* p. 4.

After the convention assembled, the Federalists continued their irregular practices, although from the vote on the Constitution in the convention this latter manipulation seems to have been a work of supererogation. Everything was done that could be done to keep the public out of the affair. "Thomas Lloyd applied to the convention for the place of assistant clerk. Lloyd was a shorthand writer of considerable note, and when the convention refused his request, determined to report the debates and print them on his own account. His advertisement promised that the debates should be accurately taken in shorthand and published in one volume octavo at the rate of one dollar the hundred pages. These fine promises, however, were never fulfilled. Only one thin volume ever came out, and that contains merely the speeches of Wilson and a few of those of Thomas M'Kean. The reason is not far to seek. He was bought up by the Federalists, and in order to satisfy the public was suffered to publish one volume containing nothing but speeches made by the two federal leaders."[564] The Federalists appear to have suppressed other attempts at issuing the debates, and they " withdrew their subscriptions from every publica- tion that warmly supported the Anti-federal cause."[565] The Constitution was ratified by a vote of 46 to 23.

Against these precipitous actions on the part of the Federalists in carrying the ratification of the Constitution, a minority of the state convention, twenty-one members, protested in an address to the people after the day had been lost. The protestants told how the federal Convention had been called by Congress, and then recited the facts as they viewed them: "So hastily and eagerly did the states comply [with the call of Congress for the Convention] that their legislatures, without the slightest authority, without ever stopping to consult the people, appointed delegates, and the conclave met at Philadelphia. To it came a few men of character, some more noted for cunning than patriotism, and some who had always been enemies to the independence of America. The doors were shut, secrecy was enjoined, and what then took place no man could tell. But it was well known that the sittings were far from harmonious. Some left the dark conclave before the instrument was framed. Some had the firmness to withhold their hands when it was framed. But it came forth in spite of them, and was not many hours old when the meaner tools of despotism were carrying petitions about for the people to sign praying the legislature to call a convention to consider it. The convention was called by a legislature made up in part of members who had been dragged to their seats and kept there against their wills, and so early a day was set for the election of delegates that many a voter did not know of it until it was passed. Others kept away from the polls because they were ignorant of the new plan; some because they disliked it, and some because they did not think the convention legally called. Of the seventy thousand freemen entitled to vote but thirteen thousand voted."[566] For a long time the war of the dissenters against the Constitution went on in Pennsylvania, breaking out in occasional riots, and finally in the Whiskey Rebellion in Washington's administration; but they were at length beaten, out-generalled, and outclassed in all the arts of political management.

In November, 1787, the Maryland legislature, after hearing Luther Martin's masterly indictment of the Constitution and McHenry's effective reply, "unanimously ordered a convention of the people of the state; it copied the example set by Virginia of leaving the door open for amendments; and by a majority of one the day

---

[564]   *Ibid.*, p. 14.

[565]   *Ibid.*, p. 15.

[566]   McMaster and Stone, *op. cit.*, p. 20. The following year [1788] when the ratification of the Constitution was celebrated in Philadelphia, James Wilson, in an oration on the great achievement said: ..A people free and enlightened, establishing and ratifying a system of government which they have previously Considered, examined, and approved! This is the spectacle which we are assembled to celebrate; and it is the most dignified one that has yet appeared on our globe. ... What is the object exhibited to our contemplation? A whole people exercising its first and greatest power - performing an act of sovereignty, original and unlimited! ...Happy Country! May thy happiness be perpetual!" *Works* (1804 ed.), Vol. III, pp. 299 ff.

for the choice and the day for the meeting of its convention were postponed till the next April."[567] Several months were thus given for deliberation, in marked contrast to the speedy despatch of the business in Delaware, New Jersey, Connecticut, Pennsylvania, and Massachusetts. The elections were duly held on the first Monday in April, 1788; and the convention assembled on April 21. The opponents of the Constitution, Chase, Mercer, and Martin, hurled themselves against it with all their might; but, it is related, "the friends to the federal government 'remained inflexibly silent.'"[568] After a week's sessions, "the malcontents having tired themselves out," the convention ratified the Constitution by a vote of "sixty-three against eleven on the afternoon of Saturday, April 26. The instrument was formally sealed on the 28th.

The legislature of Virginia, by a resolution passed on October 25, 1787, and a law enacted on December 12th, called a convention to be elected in March, 1788, and to assemble on June 2, 1788.[569] In no state were the forces for and against the Constitution more ably marshalled and led. In no state was there higher order of debate in the convention than took place in Virginia, the birthplace of the constitution. It was a magnificent battle of talents that was waged during those June days, from the 2nd until the 25th. Then "the roll was called; and from the cities of Richmond and Williamsburg, from the counties near the ocean, from the northern neck, and from the counties between the Blue Ridge and the Alleghanies, eighty-nine delegates voted for the Constitution. From the other central and southern border counties of Kentucky, seventy-nine cried No." The margin of victory was small, but it was safe.

North Carolina was recalcitrant. The call for the convention was issued by the legislature on December 6, 1787;[570] the election was held on the last Friday and Saturday of March, 1788; and the convention assembled on July 21, 1788. In this body II the Anti-federalists obtained a large majority. They permitted the whole subject to be de- bated until the 2d of August; still it had been manifested from the first that they would not allow of an unconditional ratification." On that day the convention deferred the ratification of the Constitution by a vote of 184 to 84[571]; and adjourned *sine die*. The new federal government was inaugurated without North Carolina; but the economic pressure which it brought to bear on that state, combined with the influence of eminent Federalists (including Washington), and the introduction of constitutional amendments in Congress, brought her into the union on November 21, 1789.[572]

South Carolina was one of the most deliberative of all the states, for it was not until January 18, 1788, that the legislature by unanimous resolution called a convention which was elected in April, and organized in Charleston, on May 13 of that year. The discussion there was evidently of a high order. Those who participated

---

[567] Bancroft, *op. cit.*, V 01. II, p. 278; *Votes and Proceedings of the Senate of Maryland, November Session*, 1781, pp. 511.

[568] *Ibid.*, p. 283.

[569] Bancroft, *op. cit.*, Voi. II. p. 316. The resolution provided that the "election shall be held in the month of March next on the first day of the court to be held for each county, city, or corporation respectively." The qualifications of voters were 'the same as those now established by law." Blair, *The Virginia Convention of 1788.* Vol. I, p. 56-57. Only freeholders were eligible to seats in the Convention. *Ibid..* p. 56. Hening, *Statutes at Large,* Vol. XII, p. 462.

[570] *Laws of North Carolina* (1821), Vol. I, p. 597; *North Carolina Assembly Journals,* 1785-98, p. 22.

[571] Bancroft, *op. cit.*, Vol. II, p. 349.

[572] Hugh Williamson, writing to Madison on May 21, 1789, said: ..Our people near the sea-coast are in great pain on the idea of being shut out from the Union. They say that unless they can continue in the coasting trade without the alien duty, they must starve with their families or remove from the state. Can no exception be made in favour of such apparent aliens for so long a period as the first of January next?" *Madison Mss.*, Library of Congress.

in it took first rank in the commonwealth, and the defenders of the new system put forth efforts worthy of the distinguished forensic leaders of the Charleston bar. The opponents exhausted the armoury of their arguments, and seeing the tide running against them, they sought an adjournment of five months for further deliberation; but a motion to this effect was lost by a vote of 89 to 135. Finally at five o'clock on the tenth day of the sessions, May 23, the Constitution was carried by a large majority - 149 to 73.[573]

The legislature of Georgia, on October 26, 1787, called for a state convention to be chosen "in the same manner as representatives are elected," at the next General Election, held on the first Tuesday in December, *i.e.*, December 4, 1787.

The convention was duly chosen, and met at Augusta on December 25 ; and after "having taken into serious consideration the said constitution" for four or five days, solemnly ratified the instrument on January 2, 1788.[574]

Rhode Island was the last of the thirteen states to accept the Constitution. She had refused to send delegates to the federal Convention; and the triumphant paper money party there would have none of the efficiency promised by the new system. It was not until May 29, 1790, that Rhode Island ratified the Constitution, and this action was brought about by the immediate prospect of coercion on the part of the government of the United States,[575] combined with the threat of the city of Providence to join with the other towns which were Federalist in opinion, in a movement to secede from the state and seek the protection of the federal government.[576] Without these material considerations pressing upon them, the agrarians of that commonwealth would have delayed ratification indefinitely; but they could not contend against a great nation and a domestic insurrection.

A survey of the facts here presented yields several important generalizations:

Two states, Rhode Island and North Carolina refused to ratify the Constitution until after the establishment of the new government which set in train powerful economic forces against them in their isolation.

In three states, New Hampshire, New York, and Massachusetts, the popular vote as measured by the election of delegates to the conventions was adverse to the Constitution; and ratification was secured by the conversion of opponents and often the repudiation of their tacit (and in some cases express) instructions.

In Virginia the popular vote was doubtful.

In the four states which ratified the constitution with facility, Connecticut, New Jersey, Georgia, and Delaware, only four or five weeks were allowed to elapse before the legislatures acted, and four or five weeks more before the elections to the conventions were called; and about an equal period between the elections and the meeting of the conventions. This facility of action may have been due to the general sentiment in favour of the Constitution; or the rapidity of action may account for the slight development of the opposition.

---

[573] Bancroft, *op. cit.*, Vol. II, p. 293.

[574] *Documentary History of the Constitution.* Vol. II. pp. 82 ff.

[575] F.G. Bates, *Rhode Island and the Union.* pp. 192 ff.

[576] *Ibid.*, p. 197.

In two commonwealths, Maryland and South Carolina, deliberation and delays in the election and the assembling of the conventions resulted in an undoubted majority in favour, of the new instrument; but for the latter state the popular vote has never been figured out.[577]

In one of the states, Pennsylvania, the proceedings connected with the ratification of the Constitution were conducted with unseemly haste.

---

[577] See below, p. 248.

Chapter 9.

The popular Vote of the Constitution.

In the adoption of the Constitution, says James Wilson, we have the gratifying spectacle of "a whole people exercising its first and greatest power - performing an act of sovereignty original and unlimited."[578] Without questioning the statement that for juristic purposes the Constitution may be viewed as an expression of the will of the whole people, a historical view of the matter requires an analysis of "the people" into its constituent elements. In other words, how many of "the people" favoured the adoption of the Constitution, and how many opposed it?

At the very outset, it is necessary to recall that the question whether a constitutional Convention should be held was not submitted to popular vote, and that it was not specially passed upon by the electors in choosing the members of the legislatures which selected the delegates.[579]

In the second place, the Constitution was not submitted to popular ratification. The referendum was not unknown at that time, but it was not a fixed principle of American politics.[580] At all events, such a procedure does not seem to have crossed the minds of the members of the Convention, and long afterward, Marshall stated that ratification by state conventions was the only mode conceivable.[581] In

view of the fact that there was no direct popular vote taken on the Constitution, it is therefore impossible to ascertain the exact number of "the people" who favoured its adoption.

The voters, who took part in the selection of delegates to the ratifying conventions in the states, may be considered as having been divided into four elements: those who were consciously in favour of the Constitution, those who were just as consciously against it, those who were willing to leave the matter to the discretion of their elected representatives, and those who voted blindly.

The proportions which these four groups bear to one another cannot be determined, but certain facts may be brought out which will throw light on the great question: How many of the people favoured the adoption of the Constitution?

The first fact to be noted in this examination is that a considerable proportion of the adult white male population was debarred from participating in the elections of delegates to the ratifying state conventions by the prevailing property qualifications on the suffrage. The determination of these suffrage qualifications was left to the state legislatures; and in general they adopted the property restrictions already imposed on voters for members of the lower branch of the state legislatures.

In New Hampshire the duly qualified voters for members of the lower house were authorized to vote for members of the convention, and those Tories and sympathizers with Great Britain who were excluded by law

---

[578] See above, p. 234.

[579] *Ibid.*, p. 72.

[580] Dodd, *The Revision and Amendment of Constitutions;* and Garner, in The American Political Science Review, February, 1907.

[581] McCulloch *v.* Maryland, 4 Wheaton, 316. 239

were also admitted for this special election.[582] In Massachusetts the voters were those "qualified by law to vote in the election of representatives."[583] In Connecticut, those " qualified by law to vote in town meetings" were enfranchised.[584] In New Jersey, those who were "entitled to vote for representatives in general assembly;"[585] and in Delaware, those "qualified by law to vote for Representatives to the General Assembly"[586] were empowered to vote for delegates to their respective conventions. In Pennsylvania, voters for members of the assembly selected the delegates to the convention.[587] In Maryland, voters for members of the lower house;[588] in Virginia, those possessing the "qualifications now established by law;"[589] in North Carolina, those entitled to vote for members of the House of Commons;[590] in South Carolina, those voting for members of the lower house; and in Georgia, those voting for members of the legislature (one branch) were admitted to participation in the election of delegates to their respective state conventions.[591]

In New York alone was the straight principle of manhood suffrage adopted in the election of delegates to the ratifying convention. Libby seems inclined to hold that this exception was made by the landed aristocracy in the state legislature because it was opposed to the Constitution and wished to use its semi-servile tenants in the elections; but this problem has not yet been worked out, and any final conclusion as to the " politics " of this move is at present mere guess-work.[592]

It is impossible to say just what proportion of the adult males twenty-one years of age was disfranchised by these qualifications. When it is remembered that only about 3 per cent of the population dwelt in towns of over 8000 inhabitants in 1790, and that freeholds were widely distributed, especially in New England, it will become apparent that nothing like the same proportion was disfranchised as would be today under similar qualifications. Dr. Jameson estimates that probably one-fifth of the adult males were shut out in Massachusetts,[593] and it would probably be safe to say that nowhere were more than one-third of the adult males disfranchised by the property qualifications.

---

[582] Batchellar, *State Papers of New Hampshire,* Val. XXI, p. 165.

[583] *Debates and Proceedings in the Convention of the Commonwealth of Massachusetts in* 1788 (1856), p. 23.

[584] Connecticut Courant, October 22,1787.

[585] *Documentary History of the Constitution,* Vol. II, p. 61.

[586] Delaware State Council Minutes, 1776-1792, pp. 1080-1082.

[587] McMaster and Stone, Pennsylvania and the Federal Constitution, p. 72.

[588] Votes and Proceedings of the Senate of Maryland, November Session, 1787, pp. 5 ff.

[589] Above, p. 69. Blair, The Virginia Convention of 1788, Vol. I, pp. 56-57. Only freeholders could sit in the Convention.

[590] North Carolina Assembly Journals, 1785-1789, p. 22.

[591] Documentary History of the Constitution, Vol. II, p. 83.

[592] Libby, Geographical Distribution of the Vote on the Federal Constitution, p.26, and note.

[593] Article cited below, p. 243.

Far more were disfranchised through apathy and lack of understanding of the significance of politics. It is a note- worthy fact that only a small proportion of the population entitled to vote took the trouble to go to the polls until the hot political contests of the Jeffersonian era. Where voting was *viva voce* at the town hall or the county seat, the journey to the polls and the delays at elections were very troublesome. At an election in Connecticut in 1775, only 3477 voters took part, out of a population of nearly 200,000, of whom 40,797 were males over twenty years of age. How many were disfranchised by the property qualifications and how many stayed away through indifference cannot be shown.[594]

Dr. Jameson, by most ingenious calculations, reaches the conclusion that in Massachusetts about 55,000 men in round numbers or about 16 or 17 per cent of the population were entitled to vote under the law. Assuming that 16 per cent were entitled to vote, he inquires into the number who actually exercised the franchise in the years from 1780 to 1790 in elections for governor; and his inquiry yields some remarkable results. To give his conclusions in his own words: "Something like three per cent [of the population, or about one-fifth or one-sixth of those entitled to vote] took part in the first election in the autumn of 1780. During the next six years the figures remain at about two per cent only. In 1784, only 7631 votes were cast in the whole state; in the spring of 1786 only a little over eight thousand. Then came Shays' Rebellion and the political excitement of that winter brings up the votes in the spring election of '87 to a figure nearly three times as high as in '86, and amounting to something between five and six per cent of the population. The political discussions of the next two winters respecting the new federal government keep the figure up to five per cent. Then it drops to something between three and four and there it remains until 1794."[595]

For the purposes of a fine analysis of the economic forces in the ratifying process, it would be of the highest value to have the vote on delegates to the state conventions in each town and county throughout the whole country; but unfortunately no such figures are compiled and much of the original materials upon which the statistical tables could be based have doubtless disappeared.[596] Even such tables would be unsatisfactory because in several instances there were no contests and the issue of adoption or rejection of the Constitution was not squarely put before the voters.

In a few instances, however, the number of voters participating in the election of delegates to the state conventions has come down to us. In Boston, for example, where the fight was rather warm, and some 2700 men were entitled to vote, only 760 electors turned out to pass upon the momentous issue of the national Constitution - about half as many as voted in the next gubernatorial election.[597]

The treatises on the Constitution do not give any figures on the popular vote for delegates to the state convention in New York, but the following partial list taken from contemporary papers shows that in some of the counties the vote ran to almost 10 per cent of the population, while in others the percentage of the electorate participating (even under the universal manhood suffrage provision) was about that in Massachusetts, namely, 5 per cent. It will be noted also that the distribution of representation in the convention was grossly unequal and decidedly unfavourable to the Anti-Federalists. The classification into Federalist and Anti-Federalist is based upon the election returns as reported in the contemporary press, not on the vote in the state-ratifying convention.

---

[594] McKinley, *Suffrage Franchise in the English Colonies*, p. 420.

[595] Dr. J. F. Jameson, "Did the Fathers Vote," New England Magazine, January, 1890.

[596] A detailed statement of the vote in many Connecticut towns on the members of the state convention could doubtless be compiled after great labour from the local records described in the report on the public archives of Connecticut. *Report of the American Historical Association for 1906*, Vol. II.

[597] Harding, *The Federal Constitution in Massachusetts*, p. 55, note 3. The Connecticut Courant gives the number as 763, December 17, 1787.

Federalist

	Population 1790	Highest Federalist Vote	Highest Antifederalist Vote	Delegates in Convention[598]	Ratio of Delegates to Population
New York County	33,131	2735[599]	134	9	3,681
Westchester	23,941	694[600]	399	6	3,990
Queens[601]	16,014			4	4,003
Kings	4,495			2	2,247
Richmond	3,385			2	1,917
				23	

Antifederalist

	Population 1790	Highest Federalist Vote	Highest Antifederalist Vote	Delegates in Convention	Ratio of Delegates to Population
Albany	75,921	2627[602]	4681	7	10,845
Ulster	79,397	68[603]	1372	6	4,899
Dutchess	45,266	892[604]	1765	7	6,466

---

[598] Elliot, *Debates*, Vol. II, p. 206.

[599] Daily Advertiser, May 30, 1788.

[600] *Ibid.*, June 3.

[601] Queens vote was divided in the Convention.

[602] Daily Advertiser, June 4.

[603] *Ibid.*, June 4.

[604] *Ibid.*, June 6.

Orange	18,478		340[605]	4	4,619
Columbia	27,732	1498[606]	1863	3	9,244
Montgomery	28,839	811[607]	1209	6	4,806
Suffolk	16,440			5	3,288
Washington[608]	15,647			4	3,911
				41	

Several conclusions are obvious from this table. Measured by the popular vote, New York was overwhelmingly against the ratification of the Constitution. With the apportionment of representation against them, the Anti-Federalists elected nearly twice as many delegates as the Federalists. The popular vote in favour of ratification was largely confined to the urban centres of New York City and Albany City, thus correcting assumptions based on the convention vote alone.

But with this decided popular vote against them the Federalists were able to carry through their program by a narrow margin of thirty to twenty-seven. Why did so many Anti-Federalists whose popular mandate was clear and unmistakable, for there was a definite fight at the polls on the issue, go over to their enemies? Three Anti-Federalist members, who did go over and carry the day for the Federalists, John DeWitt, John Smith, and Melancton Smith, later appeared as holders of public securities;[609] but this does not explain the event.[610]

In Pennsylvania, the vote on the election of delegates to ratify the Constitution was apparently very slight. The dissenting minority in their famous manifesto declared: "The election for members of the convention was held at so early a period and the want of information was so great that some of us did not know of it until after it was over. ... We apprehend that no change can take place that will affect the internal government or constitution of this commonwealth unless a majority of the people should evidence a wish for such a change; but on examining the number of votes given for members of the present State convention, we find that of upwards of seventy thousand freemen who are entitled to vote in Pennsylvania, the whole convention has been elected by about thirteen thousand voters, and though two-thirds of the members of the convention have thought proper to ratify the proposed Constitution, yet those two-thirds were elected by the votes of only six

---

[605] *Ibid.*, June 14.

[606] New York Journal, June 5, 1788.

[607] *Ibid.*, June 5.

[608] The Journal for June 5 reports the Anti-Federalist ticket carried in Washington County by a vote of two to one.

[609] See below. p. 270.

[610] See a forthcoming dissertation on this subject by Wm. Feigenbaum. There was a threat of secession on the part of some New York City interests in case the Constitution was defeated. Weight was given to this threat by the news of the ratification from New Hampshire and Virginia. The possibility of retaining New York as the seat of the new Government was used by Jay, Hamilton, and Duane as an argument in favour of ratification. James Madison, *Writings*, Vol. I, p. 405.

thousand and eight hundred freemen."⁶¹¹ Though the partisan source of these figures might lead one to question their accuracy, nevertheless it is hardly probable that they would have greatly exaggerated figures that were open to all.

Philadelphia was the scene of perhaps the hottest contest over the election of delegates that occurred anywhere. The city had at that time a population of about 28,000 inhabitants. At the election, the candidate who stood the highest at the polls, George Latimer, received 1215 votes while his leading opponent received only 235 votes.⁶¹² Thus a total of 1450 votes was cast in the election - about 5 per cent of the population.

The total population of the state in 1790 was 434,373, and allowing for the difficulty of journeying to the polls in the rural districts, it seems that the estimate of the dissenters was probably not far from correct.

It appears that in Baltimore 1347 voters participated in the election of representatives from that city. McHenry at the head of the poll received 962 votes and it was known that he favoured unconditional ratification of the Constitution. His leading opponent received 385 votes.⁶¹³ This vote was taken after a considerable demonstration, for a newspaper report says that "On the same day, the ship builders, the tradesmen concerned in navigation, the merchants, the manufacturers and several thousand inhabitants walked in procession through the different streets of the town." Baltimore had at that time a population of 13,000 so that a very large proportion of the adult males took part in the election.

Further light is thrown on the vote in Maryland by an opponent of ratification in along paper printed in the Maryland Journal of May 16, 1788, signed "Republican." The author, says Steiner, "asserts that the 'common class' of people knew little of the Constitution. The two thousand copies of that document printed by order of the Assembly were too few to go far. The Annapolis paper is of small circulation, and the two Baltimore ones are never seen on the Eastern Shore, while the severe weather during the past winter prevented any newspapers from being sent over thither. Of the 25,000 voters in the state, only 6000 voted at the election and 4,000 of these votes were cast in Baltimore town and seven of the counties. The rich and wealthy worked for the Constitution to prevent the loss of their debts, and in some counties the opposition had named no candidates."⁶¹⁴

In South Carolina, the distribution of representation in the convention was such as to give a decided preponderance to the personalty districts along the sea-board. The convention of 1788 was composed of approximately twice the number of the house of representatives in 1794 and the apportionment was similar in character. In the latter year, R.G. Harper, under the pen-name of "Appius" pointed out the great disparity in the weight of the upper and lower districts in the legislature: "The lower country, including the three districts of Charleston, Beaufort, and Georgetown [which were strongly in favour of ratification of the Constitution], contains 28,694 white inhabitants, and it elects seventy representatives and twenty senators. Divide 149,596, the whole number in the state, by 28,694, those of the lower country, and the result will be more than five, from whence it appears, that a large majority of both branches of the legislature is elected by less than one-fifth of the people."⁶¹⁵ The upper district [largely Anti-Federal], on the other hand, contained 120,902 white inhabitants, and sent only fifty-four members to the house of representatives. On this basis, the seventy-three votes cast in the convention against ratification may in fact have represented a majority of the white

---

611   McMaster and Stone, *op. cit.*, p. 460.

612   Scharf and Wescott, *History of Philadelphia*, Vol. I, p. 447.

613   Hartford Courant, April 28, 1788.

614   American Historical Review, Vol. V, p. 221.

615   Appius," To the Citizens of South Carolina (1794). Library of Congress, Duane Pamphlets, V 01. 83.

inhabitants and voters in the state.[616] While one hesitates to generalize about the vote cast in favour of the Constitution on the basis of the fragmentary evidence available, it seems worth while, nevertheless, to put together several related facts bearing on the matter. In addition to the conclusion, brought out by Dr. Jameson, that about 5 per cent of the population voted in Massachusetts in the period under consideration, we have other valuable data. Dr. Paullin has shown that the electoral vote in the presidential election of 1788 in New Hampshire was 2.8 per cent of the free population; that the vote in Madison's electoral district in Virginia in the same election was 2.7 per cent of the white population; that the vote in the first congressional election in Maryland was 3.6 per cent of the white population and that the vote in the same congressional election in Massachusetts was 3 per cent.[617] Speaking of the exercise of the franchise as a whole in the period, Dr. Paullin says, " The voting was done chiefly by a small minority of interested property holders, a disproportionate share of whom in the northern states resided in the towns, and the wealthier and more talented of whom like a closed corporation controlled politics."

In view of these figures, in view of the data given above on the election of delegates (to the ratifying conventions) in the cities of Boston, Philadelphia, and Baltimore, in view of the fact that the percentage participating in the country was smaller than in the towns, and in view of the fact that only 3 per cent of the population resided in cities of over 8000, it seems a safe guess to say that not more than 5 per cent of the population in general, or in round numbers, 160,000 voters, expressed an opinion one way or another on the Constitution. In other words, it is highly probable that not more than one-fourth or one-fifth of the adult white males took part in the election of delegates to the state conventions. If anything, this estimate is high.

Now in four of the states, New Hampshire, Massachusetts, New York, and Virginia, the conventions at the time of their election were either opposed to the ratification of the Constitution or so closely divided that it was hard to tell which way the final vote would go. These four states, with Rhode Island and North Carolina,[618] which were at first against ratification, possessed about three-fifths of the population - in round numbers 1,900,000 out of 3,200,000 free persons. Of the 1,900,000 population in these states we may, with justice it seems, set off at least 900,000, that is, 45,000 voters as representing the opposition. Add to these the voters in Pennsylvania who opposed the ratification of the Constitution, approximately 6000, and we have 51,000 dissenting voters, against ratification. Adding the dissenters in Maryland, South Carolina,[619] and Connecticut, and taking the other states as unanimous, we may reasonably conjecture that of the estimated 160,000 who voted in the election of delegates, not more than 100,000 men favoured the adoption of the Constitution at the time it was put into effect - about one in six of the adult males.

Admitting that these figures are rough guesses, it appears, nevertheless, that the Constitution was not "an expression of the clear and deliberate will of the whole people," nor of a majority of the adult males, nor at the outside of one - fifth of them.

Indeed, it may very well be that a majority of those who voted were against the adoption of the Constitution as it then stood. Such a conjecture can be based on the frank statement of no less an authority

---

[616] By a careful study of local geography and the distribution of representation this could be accurately figured out.

[617] "The First Elections under the Constitution," *Iowa Journal of History and Politics*, Val. II, pp. 3 ff.

[618] It will be recalled that the Constitution was put into effect without either North Carolina or Rhode Island.

[619] See above, p. 248.

than the great Chief Justice Marshall who took a prominent part in the movement which led to the formation and ratification of the new instrument of government.[620]

At all events, the disfranchisement of the masses through property qualifications and ignorance and apathy contributed largely to the facility with which the personalty - interest representatives carried the day. The latter were alert everywhere, for they knew, not as a matter of theory, but as a practical matter of dollars and cents, the value of the new Constitution. They were well informed. They were "conscious of the identity of their interests. They were well organized. They knew for weeks in advance, even before the Constitution was sent to the states for ratification, what the real nature of the contest was. They resided for the most part in the towns, or the more thickly populated areas, and they could marshall their forces quickly and effectively. They had also the advantage of appealing to all discontented persons who exist in large numbers in every society and are ever anxious for betterment through some change in political machinery.

Talent, wealth, and professional abilities were, generally speaking, on the side of the Constitutionalists. The money to be spent in the campaign of education was on their side also; and it was spent in considerable sums for pamphleteering, organizing parades and demonstrations, and engaging the interest of the press. A small percentage of the enor- mous gain to come through the appreciation of securities alone would have financed no mean campaign for those days.

The opposition on the other hand suffered from the difficulties connected with getting a backwoods vote out to the town and county elections. This involved sometimes long journeys in bad weather, for it will be remembered that the elections were held in the late fall and winter. There were no such immediate personal gains to be made through the defeat of the Constitution, as were to be made by the security holders on the other side. It was true the debtors knew that they would probably have to settle their accounts in full and the small farmers were aware that taxes would have to be paid to discharge the national debt if the Constitution was adopted; and the debtors everywhere waged war against the Constitution - of this there is plenty of evidence.[621] But they had no money to carry on their campaign ; they were poor and uninfluential - the strongest battalions were not on their side. The wonder is that they came so near defeating the Constitution at the polls.

---

[620] See below. p. 299.

[621] Libby, *op. cit.,* pp. 50 ff.

Chapter 10.

The Economics of the Vote on the Constitution.

As in natural science no organism is pretended to be understood as long as its merely superficial aspects are described, so in history no movement by a mass of people can be correctly comprehended until that mass is resolved into its component parts. To apply this concept to the problem before us: no mathematically exact conclusion can be reached concerning the material interests reflected in the Constitution until "the people" who favoured its adoption and "the people" who opposed it are individualized and studied as economic beings dependent upon definite modes and processes of gaining a livelihood. A really fine analytical treatment of this problem would, therefore, require a study of the natural history of the (approximately) 160,000 men involved in the formation and adoption of the Constitution; but for the present we must rely on rougher generalizations, drawn from incomplete sources.

It would be fortunate if we had a description of each of the state conventions similar to that made of the Philadelphia Convention;[622] but such a description would require a study of the private economy of several hundred men, with considerable scrutiny. And the results of such a search would be on the whole less fruitful than those secured by the study of the Philadelphia Convention, because so many members of the state-ratifying bodies were obscure persons of whom biography records nothing and whose property holdings do not appear in any of the documents that have come down to us. In a few instances, as in the case of Pennsylvania, a portion of this work has been done in a fragmentary way - as regards economic matters; and it may be hoped that a penetrating analysis of the public security holdings and other property interests of the members of all state conventions may sometime be made - as far as the sources will allow. Nevertheless, for the purposes of this study, certain general truths concerning the conflict over the ratification of the Constitution in the several states have already been established by scholars like Libby, Harding, Ambler.

The first of these authors, Dr. Libby, has made a painstaking study of the *Geographical Distribution of the Vote on the Constitution,* in which he sets forth the economic characteristics of the areas for and against the adoption of the Constitution. These conclusions are all utilized in this chapter; but they are supplemented by reference to the later researches of Harding[623] and Ambler,[624] and by a large amount of new illustrative materials here presented for the first time. The method followed is to exhibit, in general, the conflict of economic interests in each of the several states over the adoption of the Constitution.

New Hampshire. -There were three rather sharply marked economic districts in New Hampshire which found political expression in the convention that ratified the Constitution. Two of the three were the sea-coast area and the interior or middle region. "The former," says Libby, " the coast area, represented the commercial and urban interests; here were to be found most of the professional men, leaders of thought, men of wealth and influence. The second section, the interior, was composed of those representing the small farmers; a population cut off from the outside world by lack of good roads, and which raised little for market except to exchange for the few things that could not be produced at home. The former class, progressive and liberal and familiar with the practical details of government, as a rule voted for the Constitution. The latter, conservative

---

[622] Above, Chapter v. 253

[623] *Massachusetts* and *the Federal Constitution* (Harvard Studies).

[624] *Sectionalism in Virginia.*

by environment and having little knowledge of what went on outside the narrow bounds of the home village or township, quite as generally voted against the Constitution."[625]

The third region in New Hampshire (whose representatives favoured ratification) was "the Connecticut valley or border district " whose interests were akin to those of the sea towns because it had commercial connection with the outside world through the Connecticut River. It was to this region particularly that Oliver Ellsworth must have appealed in his open letter to the citizens of New Hampshire in which he said: " New York, the trading towns on the Connecticut River, and Boston are the sources from which a great part of your foreign supplies will be obtained, and where your produce will be exposed for market. In all these places an import is collected, of which, as consumers, you pay a share without deriving any public benefit. You cannot expect any alteration in the private systems of these states unless effected by the proposed government."[626]

Several economic facts of prime significance in the ratification of the Constitution in New Hampshire are afforded by the tax returns of 1793. These show that of the £61,711/ 9/5 " total value of stock in trade " in the state in that year (Vermont being then cut off) no less than £42,512/0/5 or over two-thirds was in Rockingham county, the seat of the commercial town of Portsmouth, whose citizens were the lead- ing agitators for the new system, and whose delegates in the state convention were overwhelmingly in favour of ratification. Moreover, of the total amount of the "money on hand or at interest" in the state, £35,985/5/6, about two-thirds, £22,770/9/4 was in Rockingham county. It is of further significance that of the £893,327/16/10 worth of real estate and buildings in the state, less than one-half, £317,970/7/2, was in that county.[627] Thus the stronghold of Federalism possessed about two-thirds of all the personalty and only about one-half of the realty values in the commonwealth.

All personalty was not equally interested in ratifying the Constitution, as pointed out above; holders of public paper multiplied their values from six to twenty times in securing the establishment of the new system. Further interesting data would be revealed, therefore, if we could discover the proportion of public securities to other personalty and their geographic distribution.[628] The weight of the securities in New Hampshire is shown by the fact that the tax list for 1793 gives only £35,985 as the total amount of money on hand or at interest (including public securities)[629] in the state, while the accounts of the Treasury department show that $20,000 in interest on the public debt went to the loan office of that state to discharge that annual federal obligation.[630] It is highly probable that the tax list is very low, but even at that the public securities constituted a considerable mass of the capital of the commonwealth. The leading supporters of the Con- stitution in New Hampshire were large holders of public paper,[631] and there is no doubt that as personalty was the dynamic element in the movement for the Constitution, so securities were the dynamic element in the personalty.

---

[625] Libby, *op. cit.*, pp. 7-8.

[626] *Ibid.*, p. 11.

[627] Data given here are from *State Papers: Finance,* Vol. I, p. 442. It should be remembered that the figures would have been relatively different in 1787 on account of the union of Vermont with New Hampshire, but they are doubtless roughly correct.

[628] Some painstaking research in the Treasury Department would produce valuable data toward the solution of this problem.

[629] *State Papers: Finance,* Vol. I, p. 442 (public funds included. see p. 419).

[630] See above for the table, p. 36.

[631] Ms. Treasury Department: New Hampshire Loan Office Books.

Massachusetts. -The vote in Massachusetts on the Constitution was clearly along class or group lines: those sections in which were to be found the commerce, money, securities - in a word, personalty - were in favour of the ratification of the new instrument of government; and those sections which were predominantly rural and possessed little personalty were against it. Libby classifies ...the sections on the basis of the vote as follows: -

Eastern section.	Yeas, 73 per cent	Nays, 27 per cent
Middle section.	Yeas, 14 per cent	Nays, 86 per cent
Western section.	Yeas, 42 per cent	Nays, 58 per cent

Speaking of this table he says: "Such striking differences as these indicate clearly that there is something fundamental , lying back of the vote. Each of these sections is an economic and social unit, the first representing the coast region, the second the interior, and the third the Connecticut valley and border districts of the state. In the eastern section the interests were commercial; there was the wealth, the influence, the urban population of the state. ...The middle section of Massachusetts represented the interior agricultural interests of the state - the small farmers. From this section came a large part of the Shays faction in 1786. The Connecticut valley or western district may be subdivided into the northern, most interior, and predominantly Anti-federal section, and the southern section, nearest the coast and predominantly Federal, with the trading towns of the Connecticut River in its southeastern part."[632]

Harding, after an independent study of the opposition to the Constitution in Massachusetts, comes to substantially the same conclusion. Among the weighty elements in the struggle he places "the conflict of interest, partly real and partly fancied, between the agricultural and the commercial sections of the state." Underlying the whole opposition, he continues, "was the pronounced antagonism between the aristocratic and the democratic elements of society in Massachusetts. ...Massachusetts was not alone in this experience; in most, if not all, of the states a similar contest had arisen since the war. The men who at Philadelphia had put their names to the new Constitution were, it seems quite safe to affirm, at that time identified with the aristocratic interest. ...There can be no question that this feeling [of antagonism between democracy and aristocracy] underlay most of the opposition in the Massachusetts convention."[633]

Of course this second element of opposition - aristocracy *versus* democracy - introduced by Harding is really nothing but the first under another guise; for the aristocratic party was the party of wealth with its professional dependents; and the democratic party was the agrarian element which, by the nature of economic circumstances, could have no large body of professional adherents. This economic foundation of the class division was fully understood by Adams and set forth with unmistakable clearness in his *Defence of the American Constitutions*. Hamilton, Madison, and all thinkers among the Federalists understood it also. To speak of a democratic interest apart from its economic sources is therefore a work of supererogation; and it does not add, in fact, to an exposition of the real forces at work. Harding himself recognizes this and explains it in a luminous fashion in his introductory chapter.

And what were the economic and social antecedents of the opponents of the Constitution in the Massachusetts convention? Harding, with his customary directness, meets the inquiry: "A half-dozen obscure men, it must be answered, whose names are utterly unknown, even to most students of this period." He

---

[632] Libby, *op. cit.*, p. 12.

[633] *The Federal Constitution in Massachusetts*, p. 75.

continues: "William Widgery (or Wedgery) of New Gloucester, Maine, was one of these.[634] A poor, friendless, uneducated boy, he had emigrated from England before the Revolution, had served as a lieutenant on board a privateer in that contest, had then settled in Maine, had acquired some property, and by 1788 had served one term in the Massachusetts legislature. ... Samuel Thompson, of Topsham, Maine, was another of the anti-federalist leaders. A self-made man, he had the obstinacy of opinion which such men often show. ...He "was wealthy for the times, but inclined to be niggardly. ... Another determined opponent of the proposed Constitution was Samuel Nasson (or Nason) of Sanford, Maine. Born in New Hampshire and a saddler by trade, he became a store keeper in Maine, served awhile in the War ...and finally settled down as a trader at Sanford. ...In 1787 he served a term in the General Court, but declined a re-election because he felt 'the want of a proper education.' ... From Massachusetts proper, Dr. John Taylor, of Douglas, Worcester County, was the most prominent opponent of the new Constitution. ...But the slightest information, it seems, can now be gathered as to his history and personality. He had been one of the popular majority in the legislature of 1787 where he had taken an active part in procuring the extension of the Tender Law. ...Another delegate from this part of the state who was prominent in the opposition was Captain Phanuel Bishop, of Rehoboth, Bristol County. In him the Rhode Island virus may be seen at work. ...He was a native of Massachusetts and had received a public school education. When or why he had been dubbed Captain is not now apparent. Belknap styles him 'a noted insurgent'; and he had evidently ridden into office on the crest of the Shaysite wave. His first legislative experience had been in the Senate of 1787 where he had championed the debtor's cause."[635]

This completes the list of leaders who fought bitterly against the Constitution to the end in Massachusetts, according to a careful student of the ratification in that state: three self-made men from the Maine regions and two representatives of the debtor's cause. Nothing could be more eloquent than this description of the alignment.

Neither Harding nor Libby has, however, made analysis of the facts disclosed by the tax lists of Massachusetts or the records in the Treasury Department at Washington, which show unquestionably that the live and persistent economic force which organized and carried through the ratification was the personalty interests and particularly the public security interests. As has been pointed out, these had the most to gain immediately from the Constitution. Continental paper bought at two and three shillings in the pound was bound to rise rapidly with the establishment of the federal government. No one knew this better than the members of the federal Convention from Massachusetts and their immediate friends and adherents in Boston.

- Of the total amount of funded 6 per cents in the state, £113,821, more than one-half, £65,730, was concentrated in the two counties, Essex and Suffolk, of which Boston was the urban centre – the two counties whose delegates in the state convention were almost unanimous in supporting the Constitution.
- Of the total amount of 3 per cents, £73,100, more than one-half, £43,857, was in these two counties.
- Of the deferred stock, amounting to £59,872, more than one-half, £32,973, was in these two counties.
- Of the total amount of all other securities of the state or the United States in the commonwealth, £94,893, less than one-third or £30,329, was in these counties.
- Of the total amount of money at interest in the state, £196,698, only about one-third, £63,056, was in these two counties, which supports the above conjecture that public securities were the active element.[636]

---

[634] As to the opposition in Maine, see General Knox's view, below, p. 301.

[635] *The Federal Constitution in Massachusetts*, pp. 63-66.

[636] *State Papers: Finance*, Vol. I, pp. 451. Of course some changes in distribution may have occurred between 1789 and 1792, but this may be taken approximately correct.

Further confirmation for this conjecture seems to be afforded by the following tables, showing the distribution of the vote and of public securities.[637] The first group shows the votes of the delegates from Essex and Suffolk counties - the Federalist strongholds - on the ratification, and also the amount of public securities in each as revealed by the tax lists of 1792:

Essex

For the Constitution — 38 votes — Against 6 votes

Suffolk

For the Constitution — 34 votes — Against 5 votes

Table of public securities listed for taxation in each of these counties.

	Suffolk £	Essex £
Funded Sixes	29,228	36,502
Funded Threes	17,096	26,761
Funded, not on interest	14,854	18,119
Other Securities	14,056	16,273
Money at Interest	29,941	33,115

Now let us take the vote in the convention and the property in two counties which were heavily against the Constitution.[638] The vote is as follows:

Worcester

For the Constitution — 7 votes — Against 43 votes

Berkshire

For the Constitution — 7 votes — Against 15 votes

The table of public securities and money in these counties follow:

	Worcester £	Berkshire £
Funded Sixes	12,924	981

---

[637] *State Papers: Finance,* Vol. I, p. 443; Libby, *op. cit.,* p. 107 for the vote.

[638] Libby, *op. cit.,* for vote, p. 107; *State Papers: Finance,* Vol. I. pp. 450 and 449 for taxes lists.

Funded Threes	8,184	665
Funded, not on interest	5,736	384
Other Securities	10,903	602
Money at Interest	25,594	6,298

Now if we take the securities in these two counties which went heavily against the Constitution several economic facts are worthy of notice. Of the total amount of 6 per cents in the state, only £13,905, or about one-eighth is to be found in them. Of the 3 per cents, we find £8,849, or about one-eighth of the total amount in the commonwealth. But if we take money at interest, we find £31,892, or about one-sixth of the total amount in the state. This is not surprising, for Worcester was the centre of the Shays rebellion in behalf of debtors, and a large portion of their creditors were presumably in the neighbourhood.[639]

"The courts were burdened with suits for ordinary debts by means of which creditors sought to put in more lasting form the obligations which their debtors could not at that time meet. In Worcester county alone, with a population of less than 50,000, more than 2000 actions were entered in 1784, and during the next year 1700 more were put on the list."[640]

These figures, like all other statistics, should be used with care, and it would require a far closer analysis than can be made here to work out all of their political implications. We should have a thorough examination of such details as the distribution of the public securities among towns and individual holders; and such a work is altogether worthy of a Quetelet.

Meanwhile, it may be said with safety that the communities in which personalty was relatively more powerful favoured the ratification of the Constitution, and that in these communities large quantities of public securities were held. Moreover, there was undoubtedly a vital connection between the movement in support of the Constitution and public security holding, or to speak concretely, among the leading men in Massachusetts who laboured to bring about the ratification was a large number of public creditors.

For example, Boston had twelve representatives in the state-ratifying convention, all of whom voted in favour of the Constitution. Of these twelve men the following were holders of public securities:[641]

Samuel Adams   John Coffin Jones
James Bowdoin, Sr.   William Phillips
Thomas Dawes, Jr.   Thomas Russell
Christopher Gore   John Winthrop

In other words, at least eight out of the twelve men representing the chief financial centre of the state were personally interested in the fate of the new Constitution. How deeply, it is impossible to say, for the

---

[639] The full significance of the Worcester vote and property lists would involve an analysis of the distribution of each among the towns.

[640] *American Antiquarian Society Proceedings* (1911), p. 65.

[641] Ms. Treasury Department: *Index to the Three Per Cents (Mass.)*. Gore, Dawes, and Phillips appear on the New Hampshire Journals and other Massachusetts Records.

Ledgers seem to have disappeared from the Treasury Department and only the Index to the funded debt remains. Supplementary records, however, show some of them to have been extensively engaged in dealing in paper. The four men who, apparently, were not security holders were John Hancock, Caleb Davis, Charles Jarvis, and Rev. Samuel Stillman.[642]

The towns surrounding Boston in Suffolk county also returned a number of men who were holders of securities:[643]

Fisher Ames, Dedham	Benj. Lincoln, Hingham
John Baxter, Medfield	Rev. Daniel Shute, Hingham
James Bowdoin, Jr., Dorchester	Increase Sumner, Roxbury
Richard Cranch, Braintree	Cotton Tufts, Weymouth
J. Fisher, Franklin	Ebenezer Wales, Dorchester
William Heath, Roxbury	Ebenezer Warren, Foxboro
Thomas Jones, Hull	Rev. Anthony Wibird, Braintree

In other words, twenty-two of the thirty-four men from Boston and Suffolk county who voted in favour of the ratification of the Constitution in the Massachusetts convention were holders of public securities, and all of the twenty-two except two (Wales and Warren) probably benefited from the appreciation of the funds which resulted from the ratification.[644]

To recapitulate. There were thirty-nine members of the Massachusetts convention from Suffolk county, which includes Boston. Of these, thirty-four voted for the ratification of the Constitution, and of the thirty-four who so voted, two-thirds, or twenty-two to be exact, were holders of public paper.

That other supporters of the Constitution from other Massachusetts counties held paper so extensively is not to be expected, and a casual glance through the records shows that this surmise is probably true. Boston was the centre of the Federalist agitation, and it supplied the sinews of war for the campaign which finally secured the adoption of the new system of government.

Connecticut. -The vote on the Constitution in Connecticut was so largely in favour of ratification that no very clear lines of cleavage are apparent on the surface.[645] The opposition, as measured by the vote of the

---

[642] The *Index* shows several holders by the name of Davis: Jonathan, James, Aaron, Susanna, John, Nathl., Joseph. Moses, Thomas, Saml., Wendell, and John G. Whether they were relatives of Caleb is not apparent. Leonard and Nathl. Jarvis also appear on the Book. Also Mary and Belcher Hancock.

[643] All of these men except Wales and Warren appear on the *Index to the Three Per Cents (Mass.)*. Wales and Warren appear on the books as holders of old certificates *(Loan Office Certificates. 1779-1788. Mas..)*; and it does not appear when or how they disposed of their holdings.

[644] See above, p. 75, note 3.

[645] On September 3, 1787, the Connecticut Courant in a letter from Philadelphia (Aug. 24) says: "One of the first objects with the national government to be elected under the new constitution, it is said, will be to provide funds for the payment of the national debt, and thereby restore the credit of the United States, which has been so much impaired by the individual states. Every holder of a public security of any kind is,

delegates in the Convention, was "scattered and unimportant. Its two chief centres were in New Haven county on the coast, and in five or six towns on the Connecticut river at the northern boundary, connecting with a group of opposition towns in Massachusetts."[646] It is worthy of note that the considerable towns for the time, Windsor, Norwalk, Stamford, Litchfield, Hartford, and New Haven were for the Constitution, while much of the opposition came from small inland towns like Cornwall, Norfolk, and Sharon.[647]

The map facing this page shows that the Federalist towns were the financial centres of the time in Connecticut. The representatives of the "shaded" towns in the state convention voted against the Constitution; those from the partially "shaded" towns were divided; and those from the plain white towns voted for the Constitution.[648] Each black dot represents a holder of one 6 per cent assumed debt bond.[649] It is apparent at a glance that there must have been some relation between security-holding and the "sentiments," to Madison's term,[650] of the respective proprietors. Hartford alone had almost as many security holders as all of the Anti-Federalist towns combined. It would be interesting to have a map showing the distribution of all other forms of, wealth as well as the assumed debt.

What a more searching study would produce were we able to carry the contest back into the town meetings that chose the delegates cannot be conjectured. But the local evidence - even that which was recorded - has largely the disappeared or would require years of search to unearth. Moreover, the tax system in Connecticut at the time was not such as to yield the data most needed for such an inquiry, for "loans to the state and the United States were exempt from assessment."[651] Whether this grew out of a public policy or the fact that the chief politicians of the day were large holders of securities - evidenced by the records the in the Treasury Department at Washington - is also a matter for conjecture. No documents, no history.

Nevertheless, as in Massachusetts, the public securities formed a dynamic element in the movement for ratification. One hundred and twenty-eight members of the Connecticut convention voted in favour of the new system. Of these men at least sixty-five held public paper in some amount (ranging from a few dollars to tens of thousands) previous to or about the time of the adoption of the Constitution. They are given here in alphabetical order with the names of the towns which they represented.

> In the original work, this table was in the format of Christian name/s, Surname, Town. The Table has been formatted with Surname, Christian Name/s, town. Anybody using this text in Microsoft Word,

---

therefore, deeply interested in the cordial reception and speedy establishment of a vigorous continental government."

[646] Libby, *op. cit.*, p. 14.

[647] *Ibid.*, p, 113.

[648] Towns not represented or not voting in the convention are counted *against the* Constitution.

[649] The assumed debt is taken because the Ledgers of that debt are in excellent shape and apparently complete. They do not contain, however, half of the security holders in that state. Several of the towns that had no assumed debt-holders were represented in the convention by holders of other paper. See table, p. 267.

[650] See above, p. 15.

[651] *State Papers: Finance,* Vol. I, p. 423.

or other compatible word processor will be able to sort the list by either surname or town if they wish. Editor.

Beardsley, Nehemiah	New Fairfield
Bradley, Philip, B.	Ridgefield
Brainerd, Hezekiah	Haddam
Brinsmade, Daniel	Washington
Buckingham, Gideon	Milford
Burr, Thaddeus	Fairfield
Burrall, Charles	Canaan
Canfield, Samuel	New Milford
Carver, Samuel	Bolton
Chapman, Jabez	East Haddam
Cleaveland, Moses	Canterbury
Coit, Wheeler	Preston
Crocker, Seth	Wilington
Davenport, James	Stamford
Davenport, John	Stamford
Dow, Benjamin	Voluntown
Dunlop, Joshua	Plainfield
Dyer, Eliphalet	Windham
Edwards, Pierpont	New Haven
Ellsworth, Oliver	Winsor
Fitch, Jabez	Greenwich
Foor, Daniel	Colchester
Foot, Isaac	Stafford
Griswold, Mathew, (President of the Convention)	Lyme
Hale, Nathan	Canaan
Hall, Asaph	Goshen
Halsey, Jeremiah,	Preston
Hart, William	Saybrook
Higgins, Cornelius	Haddam
Hinman, Benjamin	Southbury
Holt, Caleb	Willington
Huntington, Jedediah	Norwich
Huntington, Samuel	Norwich
Hyde, Eli	Franklin
Johnson, Wm. Samuel	Stratford

Law, Richard	New London
Lee, Andrew	Lisbon
Mills, Elisha	Stratford
Mitchel, Stephen	Wethersfield
Mosely, Josiah	Glastonbury
Newberry, Roger	Winsor
Noyes, Wm.	Lyme
Parsons, Samuel H.	Middletown
Phelps, Charles	Stonnington
Phelps, John	Stafford
Porter, Joshua	Salisbury
Ripley, Jeremiah	Coventry
Root, Ephraim	Coventry
Root, Jesse	Hartford
Sanford, Lemuel	Reading
Sheldon, Epaphras	Torrington
Sherman, Roger	New Haven
Smith, Simeon	Ashford
Sturges, Jonathan	Fairfield
Throop, Dyar	East Haddam
Treadwell, John	Farmington
Wadsworth, Jeremiah	Hartford
Warner, Ichabod	Bolton
Watson, John	East Winsor
West, Jeremiah	Tolland
White, Ebenezer	Chatham
Williams, William	Lebanon
Woolbridge, Joseph	Groton
Wolcott, Erastus	East Wonsor
Wolcott, Oliver	Lichfield[652]

It must not be thought that the ramifications of economic interest ends with these names.[653] A large number of men, who do not appear on the records as holding securities personally, belonged to families having

---

[652] The sources for the information as to these securities are in the Treasury Department: *Connecticut Loan Office, 1781-178"* (Register of Certificates) ; *Connecticut Loan Office, Ledger B, Assumed Debt; Ledger C, 1790-1796; Ledger A, ac 1790-1797; Loan Office Certificates 011779*, etc.

[653] No doubt a study of local economic interests in Connecticut would yield highly important data. See, for example, the early capitalist enterprises connected with, the navigation of the Connecticut River. *Proceedings of the American Antiquarian Society, 1903-1904*, p. 404. Such local histories as E.D. Larned, *A*

such holdings. For example, John Chester, of Wethersfield, is apparently not on the books, but he was a colonel in the war and doubtless received the soldiers' certificates or other paper at some period. Thomas Chester and Sarah Chester of Wethersfield appear on the records. Whether there were family connections might be ascertained by a study of local history. It is evident what infinite pains would be required to trace out all of these genealogical data.

New York. - There can be no question about the predominance of personalty in the contest over the ratification in New York. That state, says Libby, "presents the problem in its simplest form. The entire mass of interior counties...were solidly Anti-federal, comprising the agricultural portion of the state, the last settled and the most thinly populated. There were however in this region two Federal cities (not represented in the convention [as such]), Albany in Albany county and Hudson in Columbia county.

...The Federal area centred about New York city and county: to the southwest lay Richmond county (Staten Island); to the southeast Kings county, and to the north-east Westchester county; while still further extending this area, at the northeast lay the divided county of Dutchess, with a vote in the convention of 4 to 2 in favour of the Constitution, and at the southeast were the divided counties of Queens and Suffolk. ...These radiating strips of territory with New York city as a centre form a unit, in general favourable to the new Constitution; and it is significant of this unity that Dutchess, Queens, and Suffolk counties broke away from the anti-Federal phalanx and joined the Federalists, securing thereby the adoption of the Constitution."[654]

Unfortunately the exact distribution of personalty in New York and particularly in the wavering districts which went over to the Federalist party cannot be ascertained, for the system of taxation in vogue in New York at the period of the adoption of the Constitution did not require a state record of property.[655] The data which proved so fruitful in Massachusetts are not forthcoming, therefore, in the case of New York; but it seems hardly necessary to demonstrate the fact that New York City was the centre of personalty for the state and stood next to Philadelphia as the great centre of operations in public stock.

This somewhat obvious conclusion is reinforced by the evidence relative to the vote on the legal tender bill which the paper money party pushed through in 1786. Libby's analysis of this vote shows that "No vote was cast against the bill by members of counties north of the county of New York. In the city and county of New York and in Long Island and Staten Island, the combined vote was 9 to 5 against the measure. Comparing this vote with the in vote on the ratification in 1788, it will be seen that of the Federal counties 3 voted against paper money and 1 for it; of the divided counties 1 (Suffolk) voted against paper money and 2 (Queens and Dutchess) voted for it. Of the anti-Federal counties none had members voting against paper money. The merchants as a body were opposed to the issue of paper money and the Chamber of Commerce adopted a memorial against the issue."[656]

Public security interests were identified with the sound money party. There were thirty members of the New York constitutional convention who voted in favour of the ratification of the Constitution and of these no less than sixteen were holders of public securities:[657]

History of Windham County, contain veritable mines of information on the economic interests of men prominent in local politics.

[654] Libby, *op. cit.,* p. 18. Libby here takes the vote in the New York convention, but that did not precisely represent the popular vote. Above, p. 244.

[655] *State Papers: Finance,* Vol. I, p. 425.

[656] Libby, *op. cit.,* p. 59.

[657] Those marked "C6," Ms; Treasury Department: *New York, 6% Funds,* 1790; "N.Y. 3" *ibid.,* 3% *Funds;* "R," *New York Loan Office Receipts,* Ms. Division, Library of Congress. Melancton Smith appears on

James Duane, New York (C6)
John DeWitt, Dutchess (N.Y. 3)
Alexander Hamilton,[658] New York
Richard Harrison, New York (C6)
Jonathan Havens, Suffolk (C6 as Trustee for a religious society).
John Jay, New York (C6)
Samuel Jones, Queens (C6)
Philip Livingston, Westchester (C6)
Robert R. Livingston, New York (N.Y. 3)
Nicholas Low, New York (C6)
Richard Morris,[659] New York (C6)
Isaac Roosevelt, New York (R)
Gozen Ryerss, Richmond (N.Y. 3)
John Smith, Suffolk (C6)
Melancton Smith, Dutchess (Conn.)
Philip Van Cortland, Westchester (C6)
Jesse Woodhull, Orange (C6)

New Jersey. - New Jersey was among the states which pushed through the ratification of the Constitution without giving the agrarian party time to organize its forces; and, from the records, the vote in the state convention was unanimous. This unanimity is rather startling in view of the fact that the year before a paper money party had been able to force through an emission bill by a narrow margin. Either there was a violent reaction against inflation, or the Federalist campaign had been highly organized. What little opposition appears to have been raised in that state seems to have been by the debtor and paper money class.[660]

It must be admitted, however, that no detailed study of the ratification in New Jersey has ever been made. Libby passes it over briefly; and the older writers like Bancroft and Curtis dismiss it with their usual lightness of touch. Unfortunately for such a study, the records of the convention in that state are no more than bare minutes; and the materials in the Treasury Department from the New Jersey loan office are extremely fragmentary. Until extended search in local and state history is made on the points here raised, New Jersey must be dismissed cursorily.

There were thirteen counties in the state represented in the Convention, and each of nine counties had one or more representatives who had learned the elementary lessons in public finance through holding at least some small amounts of public securities - often certificates of only trivial value.

The meagre character of the records of that state do not permit of a satisfactory statement. There were three delegates from Bergen county; of these John Fell appears on the Register of Land Office Certificates; there is no record of Peter Zabriskie either as a subscriber to original funds or as owner of securities; but a Jacob Zabriskie appears on a later Ledger. From Essex county, John Chetwood and David Crane appear among the holders; from Middlesex, John Beatty, John Neilson, and Benjamin Manning - the entire delegation; from Somerset, Fred. Frelinghuysen; from Gloucester, Andw. Hunter; from Salem, Edmund

---

the Ledgers of the Connecticut Loan Office; and *N.Y. Loan Office,* 1791, folio 138, for $10,000 worth of sixes and threes.

[658] See above, p. 107.

[659] Not present on final vote, but see Elliot, *Debates,* Vol. II, p. 411.

[660] Libby, *op. cit.,* pp. 60-61. Writing on October 14, 1787, Madison said, 'I do not learn that any opposition is likely to be made [to the ratification] in New Jersey," *Writings of James Madison,* Vol. I, p. 342.

Wetherby; from Hunterdon, David Brearley and Joshua Corshon; from Morris, John Jacob Faesch; and from Sussex, Robert Ogden and Thomas Anderson, and even the Secretary, Saml. W. Stockton, was a considerable holder. Thus every county except Cumberland, Cape-of-May, Burlington, and Monmouth had its spokesmen for public creditors.[661]

Delaware. - Although there had been a strong paper money party in Delaware it does not seem to have manifested any considerable influence in the ratification of the Constitution, for that commonwealth was the first to set its seal on the new instrument, and it did so with apparent unanimity. No detailed scrutiny of the local contests over the election of delegates has ever been made; and the records of the loan office of that state preserved in the Treasury Department are defective. The records for taxation are also of little help. The absence of any contest of course contributes to obscuring the economic forces which may have been at work.[662]

Pennsylvania. - In strong contrast to the uniformity in Delaware is the sharp division which existed in Pennsylvania. There, says Libby, "the opposition to the Constitution came from those counties belonging to the great interior highland of the state, extending from the head waters of the Schuylkill to the Alleghany and Monongahela rivers, with only Huntingdon county (one vote - Federal) interrupting the continuity from east to west. ... The Federal area contained...York, Lancaster, Chester, Montgomery, Philadelphia, Bucks, Luzerne, and Northampton, and the largest population, most of the men of wealth and influence and the commercial classes of the state. Pittsburgh with 400 inhabitants was Federal in an Anti-Federal county."[663]

Each of the eastern counties of Pennsylvania was represented in the state convention by one or more members who held public securities.[664] From Philadelphia city and county, five of the ten members, all of whom favoured ratifica- tion, were interested in stocks, George Latimer, James Wilson, Thomas M'Kean, Samuel Ashmead, and Enoch Edwards. From Bucks came John Barclay, a large dealer, to whose credit $17,056.56 is set down in one entry. Two of the six members from Chester, John Hannum and Thomas Bull, were security holders. James Morris, of Montgomery county, John Black and David Grier, from York, Timothy Pickering, from Luzerne, Stephen Balliet, David Deshler, and Joseph Horsfield of Northampton (three of the four from that county) were interested. From Lancaster came Jasper Yeates, a large holder (one entry

---

[661] These records are drawn principally from incomplete lists of early certificates issued, or from some later funding books in the Treasury Department. The real weight of securities in the New Jersey convention must remain problematical, at least, for the present. The amounts set down to the names above recorded are for the most part insignificant - a few hundred or thousand dollars at the most, and often smaller. The point, it may be repeated, is not the amount but the practical information derived from holding even one certificate of the nominal value of $10.

[662] Dr. Jameson says of the records of the Delaware convention; "Neither Journal nor debates, has, I believe, ever been published," *American Historical Association Report* (1902), Vol. I, p. 165.

[663] Libby, *op. cit.*, pp. 26 ff.

[664] The Massachusetts Gazette, on October 19, 1787, prints a letter from Philadelphia (dated October 5) in which the activities of speculators in public securities are fully set forth; ..Since the grand federal convention has opened the budget and published their scheme of government, all goes well here. Continental loan office certificates and all such securities have risen twenty-five per cent. Even the old emission which has long lain dormant begins to show its head. Last week many thousand pounds' worth of it were bought up. Moneyed men have their agents employed to buy up all the continental securities they can -foreseeing the rapid rise of our funds. Such men as have the cash to spare will certainly make large fortunes. ...We send our factors to the distant towns who know nothing of the rise and buy them cheap; for there is no buying them on reasonable terms in Philadelphia, as the wealthy men are purchasing them to lay up. Thus we go on - pray how is it with you?"

$11,986.65), Robert Coleman, Sebastian Graft', and John Hubley (four of the six delegates), who had a first-hand knowledge of the relation of a new and stable government to public paper.

In other words at least nineteen out of the forty-six men who voted for the Constitution in the Pennsylvania convention were interested in public paper at or about the time of the adoption of the Constitution. Their names follow with the references to each,[665] but it is not to be supposed that this list is complete, for the records of Pennsylvania are not full, and a great many of the transactions in that state were not with the local loan office, but directly with the Treasury, a part of whose early records were probably burned in one of the fires at the Treasury Building:

>Samuel Ashmead (I)   Robert Coleman (R)
>Stephen Balliet (LT)   David Deshler (M)
>John Barclay (JA)   Enoch Edwards (JA)
>John Black (M)   Sebastian Graff (I)
>Thomas Bull (I)   David Grier (I)
>John Hannum (3 C)   Thomas M'Kean (M)
>Joseph Horsfield (M)   James Morris (I)
>John Hubley (77) Timothy Pickering (I)
>George Latimer (JB)   James Wilson (I)
>Jasper Yeates (JA)

Fortunately, also other data are easily available for the study of the economic interests of the members of the Pennsylvania convention. McMaster and Stone[666] have appended to their work on the ratification of the Constitution in that state brief biographical sketches of the members of the convention, in which many clues are given to their respective economic interests. The following table is prepared from these biographies, and every effort is made to state in the language of the authors the exact occupation and interests of the delegates. These details are given so that the student may draw his conclusions independently.

Members Who Voted In Favour Of Ratification

John Allison "received a thorough English and classical education;" laid out the town of Greencastle in 1781; in the War, rank of Colonel.

John Arndt. Father a mill owner on the Bush kill; for a time a commissary of supplies during the War; "advanced large sums of money to the government, most of which was refunded to him;" devoted the latter years of his life to "'mercantile pursuits."

Samuel Ashmead. "Little is known of his early history, save that he received a good education and was brought up to mercantile pursuits." [Securities.]

---

[665] Ms. Treasury Department: 'I," *Index to Funded* 6 C; "JA," *Journal A,* 1790-1791 (sixes and threes); "JB," *Journal B;* "R," *Register Loan Office Certificates, 1788;* "77," *Register Certificates of 1777;* "3C," *Ledger C, 3% Stock;* "LT," *Treasury Ledger;* ..M," *Miscellaneous.*

[666] *Pennsylvania and the Federal Constitution.* It will be noted that there were at least seven members of the Order of Cincinnati in the convention, all of whom were in favour of the Constitution.

Hilary Baker	"received a good classical education, entered mercantile life, became an iron merchant, which business he carried on for some years."
Stephen Balliet	"acquired a very limited education and was brought up to mercantile life under his father;" an agent for forfeited estates in Northampton county. Held many offices. Colonel in War .[Securities.]
John Barclay	"was a son of Alexander Barclay, an officer of In the Crown under the proprietary government, and received a classical education." Captain in the War and member of the Cincinnati. Sometime president of the Bank of the Northern Liberties. [Securities.]
John Black	was a graduate of Nassau Hall. Was an eminent Presbyterian clergyman in his time. [Securities.]
John Boyd.	Little known of early life and education. In the War. Member of the Cincinnati. After the War "entered into merchandising at the town of Northumberland" and was interested in a mill.
Thomas Bull.	"Meagre education" and "learned the trade of a stone-mason. Prior to the Revolution he was the manager of Warwick Furnace." Resumed this place after service in the War. [Securities.]
Thomas Campbell	"was a farmer by occupation." Captain in the War and member of the Cincinnati.
Stephen Chambers.	A lawyer. Captain in the War and member of the Cincinnati.
Thomas Cheyney,	"An intelligent and progressive farmer." Grandfather bequeathed to his father half of a large tract of land in Thombury.
Robert Coleman.	"By his energy and indomitable perseverance became the most enterprising and successful iron-master in Pennsylvania." [Securities.]!
David Deshler	was a shop-keeper and afterwards operated grist and saw mills. He "advanced money out of his private means at a time when not only the United States treasury but also that of Pennsylvania was empty." [Securities.]
Richard Downing	operated " a fulling, grist, and saw mill."
Enoch Edwards	"received a classical education, studied medicine, and was in practice when he went into the War serving as & ha surgeon. [Securities.]
Benjamin Elliott	"settled in the town of Huntingdon prior to the Revolution." Held many local offices. Regular occupation, if any, not given.
William Gibbons	resided for a time in Philadelphia, and later moved to "a fine farm left him by his parents." Later held local offices. Lieutenant Colonel.
Sebastian Graff.	Son of a Lancaster "shopkeeper," and was in "active business when the War broke out." [Securities.]

George Gray. "The fifth of that name in the line of descent from George Gray, a wealthy member of the Society of Friends." Office-holder; in the War; apparently a gentleman of means.

David Grier. Classical education. Lawyer. Served in the War, rank of Colonel. [Securities.]

John Hannum. Settled on a large farm. Local office-holder. In the War, rank of Colonel. [Securities.]

Thomas Hartley. Classical education. Lawyer. In the War, rank of Colonel; member of the Cincinnati. Purchased a tract of one thousand acres of land during the Revolution.

Joseph Horsfield. Man of good education. Local postmaster under Washington. [Securities.]

John Hubley was a lawyer by profession. [Securities.]

John Hunn was a captain in the merchant marine service at the outbreak of the War. Engaged in privateering during the war and saw service in the field also.

George Latimer was a merchant, bank director, and wealthy capitalist. [Securities.]

Thomas M'Kean received a classical education. Was a lawyer. Extensive office-holder. In the War, and a member of the Cincinnati. Capitalist of some quality. [Securities.]

William MacPherson was the Bon of a noted " privateersman in the French and Spanish wars." Educated at the College of New Jersey. Officer in the British Army; but joined the American cause. Major and member of the Cincinnati. Man of some means.

James Morris possessed "a house and gristmill and ninety-four acres of land "which his father had given him. [Securities.]

F.A. Muhlenberg. Studied at the University of Halle. Clergyman, but entered into the politics of the Revolutionary War. Extensive office-holder.

John Neville. Soldier and large landholder. Office-holder and member of the Cincinnati.

Benjamin Pedan. Farmer and office-holder.

Timothy Pickering. Harvard graduate. In the War, rank of Adjutant-general; member of the Cincinnati. Lawyer and office-holder and land speculator. [Securities.]

John Richards owned a fine estate. He was "a progressive farmer, a store-keeper, and iron-master."

Jonathan Roberts was brought up as a farmer. Office-holder.

Benjamin Rush. graduate of the College of New Jersey and distinguished physician in Philadelphia.

Thomas Scott	settled in Western Pennsylvania as a farmer. Became local office-holder and later (1791) entered the practice of law.
Henry Slagle	was a provincial magistrate. Joined the Revolutionary cause and held a number of political offices and was connected with the loan office.
Abraham Stout	seems to have been "an influential farmer."
Anthony Wayne	was the son of a farmer and surveyor. Soldier, and a member of the Cincinnati.
James Wilson.	Lawyer. Member of the constitutional Convention of 1787. Wealthy land speculator. [Securities.]
William Wilson.	Officer in the War. Office-holder. In mercantile business and millowner.
Henry Wynkoop.	Collegiate education. Major in the War and office-holder.
Thomas Yardley,	farmer owning a large tract of land.
Jasper Yeates,	educated at the College of Philadelphia, lawyer, judge, and man of large means for his time. [Securities.]

Opponents Of Ratification

John Baird	"took up land" and "appears to have been a man of mark west of the Alleghanies." Held local offices.
Richard Bard	was a farmer and proprietor of a mill. "
John Bishop	"was brought up as a farmer, an occupation he was engaged in all his life. ...He had extensive business connections, and became an iron-master. He was a large landholder." Advanced large sums of money to the Revolutionary cause.
Nathaniel Breading	received a classical education, taught school, was in the War, and held local offices. "In deference to" his constituents he did not sign the ratification."
William Brown	descendant of a farmer; was a frontiersman; in the War.
James Edgar	was born on a farm and died on a farm.
William Findley	received a fair English education and "towards the close of the war he removed with his family to Western Pennsylvania and took up a tract of land. ..on which he resided until his death."
John Andre Hanna	received a good classical education; admitted to the bar and was a successful lawyer at Harrisburg.
John Harris	was a farmer and laid out Mifflintown.
Joseph Hiester	acquired the rudiments of a good education, and " until near age he worked upon his father's farm when he went to Reading and learned merchandising." Was in the War.
Jonathan Hoge.	Nothing known.
Abraham Lincoln	was brought up on a farm and died on a farm. Local office-holder.
John Ludwig	was a substantial farmer. Was in the War. Local office-holder.
Nicholas Lotz	was a millwright by occupation and established a mill near Reading. Was in the War.
James Marshel	"moved to the western country some three years prior to the Revolution, and settled in what is now Cross Creek Township." Frontiersman and local officer.
James Martin	was born in the Cumberland valley and resided in what was then (1772) Colerain township. Was in the War.

	For the Constitution	Against
Adam Orth		was "brought up amid the dangers and struggles of Pennsylvania pioneer life. He received the limited education of the' back settlements.' ...He was one of the pioneers in the manufacture of iron in Lebanon county."

Adam Orth — was "brought up amid the dangers and struggles of Pennsylvania pioneer life. He received the limited education of the' back settlements.' ...He was one of the pioneers in the manufacture of iron in Lebanon county."

John Reynolds. Joseph Powell.

John Smilie. His father settled in Lancaster county and evidently was a farmer. In 1781 John Smilie "removed with his family to then Westmoreland county," which meant that he went to the frontier. Office-holder.

William Todd went to Western Pennsylvania about 1765 and later "removed to Westmoreland county where he settled upon land subsequently warranted to him."

John Whitehill, "son of an Irish immigrant who settled on Pequea Creek in 1723. "Received a good education. Local office holder. At his death he left "a large landed estate."

Robert Whitehill, brother of the above Whitehill. "In the el spring of 1771 he removed to Cumberland county, locating on a farm two miles west of Harrisburg." Extensive public career. "Died at his residence in Cumberland county two miles west of the Susquehanna." Evidently dependent largely upon agriculture, but farmer of some means.

Obviously such a table is more or less superficial so far as economic aspects are concerned, for the forms of wealth possessed by each member and the numerical proportions of the several forms at the time of, the Pennsylvania state convention are not apparent. More than the ordinary margin must therefore be allowed for error on both sides. Evidently also it is difficult to classify these men from the meagre data given; but the following table may be taken to be roughly correct as to the men about whom we have some economic facts.

	For the Constitution	Against
Merchants	4	1
Lawyers	8	1
Doctors	2	
Clergymen	2	
Farmers	10	13
Capitalists	12	3
Total Classifiable	38	18

Of the thirty-eight in favour of the Constitution, who may be reasonably classified, ten, or one-fourth, represented agricultural interests primarily. Of the eighteen, opposed to the Constitution, who may be satisfactorily classified, thirteen or more than two-thirds were primarily identified with agricultural interests. Of the forty-six favourable, twenty were capitalists and lawyers; of the twenty-three opposed, four were in these categories. When all allowance for error is made, the result is highly significant and bears out the general conclusion that the Constitution was a reflex of personalty rather than realty interests.

Maryland. - In Maryland the mercantile interests of the towns were all on the side of the Constitution; and as the urban centres were the seats of operations in public securities these too must be thrown into the balance. The opposition came from the rural districts and particularly from the paper money constituencies.

Libby discovered there, "a correspondence between the friends of paper money and debt laws and the Anti-Federal party of 1788, both as to leaders and to the rank and file of the respective parties."[667]

But it should be noted that we are now leaving the regions of small farms and of estates tilled by free labour and are coming into the districts where slavery and the plantation system dominate rural economy. Indeed, the slave-holding plantations were so extensive and the small farming class so restricted that the paper money party would have been seriously weakened had it not been for the fact that their ranks were recruited from other sources. A contemporary, speaking of the election of delegates to the convention, says: "Baltimore and Hartford counties alone are clearly anti-Federal, in which are many powerful and popular men who have speculated deeply in British confiscated property and for that reason are alarmed at shutting the door against state paper money. The same men, their relations and particular friends are more violently anti-Federal because they paid considerable sums into the treasury in depreciated continental currency and are scared at the sweeping clause...which may bring about a due execution of the treaty between Great Britain and America to their loss.[668]

Virginia. - Fortunately, for Virginia we have a somewhat detailed study of the economic forces in the politics of that commonwealth by Dr. Charles H. Ambler. By way of preparation he examines the geographical distribution of economic characteristics, and takes up first the Tidewater region. Of this portion of the state, he says, "The industrial, social and political life of the Tidewater centred in the large estate. ...The society which developed in the Tidewater resembled that of the mother country. It consisted of several strata separated by no clearly marked lines. Along the large rivers there were the great landowners who lived in a style of luxury and extravagance beyond the means of other inhabitants. Immediately below them were the half-breeds, persons descended from the younger sons and daughters of the landed proprietors. They had all the pride and social tastes of the upper class but not its wealth. Then came the 'pretenders,' men of industry and enterprise but not of established families, ...Below these classes were the 'yeomen,' most of whom were very poor. The system of entail and primogeniture operated to preserve these strata intact."[669] The Tidewater region was almost solid in favour of ratifying the constitution.

The second geographical division of Virginia, according to Dr. Ambler, was the Piedmont region, which resembled in many respects the Tidewater but had some decided characteristics of its own. "Although one and two-thirds times as large as the Tidewater, the Piedmont, in 1790 contained a much smaller Negro slave population. Immigrants from the northern colonies, who, as will be shown, had pushed into the Valley, came into the Piedmont from the rear. For the most part they were conscientiously opposed to slave-holding and consequently did not become tobacco-growers. On the other hand the poorer whites of the Tidewater had been pushed by the gradual advance of the plantation into the less desirable lands of the Piedmont. Lack of ability and the presence of conscientious scruples prevented them from becoming large planters. These elements constituted a large and influential democratic and non-slaveholding population in the Piedmont."[670] This region was largely against ratifying the Constitution.

Beyond the Piedmont lay the Valley which was largely settled by Scotch-Irish and Germans, and the economic basis was the small farm with all that it implies. Here the political theories, says Ambler " differed

---

[667] Libby, *op. cit.*, p. 66.

[668] Letter, quoted in Libby, *op cit.* p. 65.

[669] *Sectionalism* in Virginia, pp. 6-9; p. 58,

[670] Ambler, *op. cit.*, pp. 8, 59.

widely from those entertained in the east. The Germans and the Scotch-Irish brought to the Valley the sacred traditions of the years of religious wars which taught hatred to an established church, antipathy to a government by the privileged, and; a love for civic and personal liberty. To the Scotch-Irish, the political leaders, civil liberty meant freedom of person, the right of fee-simple possession, and an open door to civic honors."[671] The markets for this region were at Baltimore and Philadelphia. This fact, coupled with several peculiar social characteristics may partially account for the heavy vote for the Constitution; but the sentiment in favour of the new government in this region has not yet been traced to economic reasons.

To the far West lay the Kentucky region whose frontier economic characteristics need no description. There the sentiment was almost solid against the ratification of the Constitution.

At the time of the movement for the adoption of a new national Constitution, the self-sufficient western regions of Virginia were practically indifferent; and the eastern section was the part of the state in which there was a conscious determination to bring about a change. At this time, says Ambler, "The towns of the Tidewater chafed under the British restrictions upon trade and desired better commercial relations between the states. Of the numerous petitions to the assembly on these subjects, that from Norfolk was, perhaps, the most significant. It claimed that the restrictions on the West India trade and the foreign commercial monopolies were producing injury to Virginia, and asked for restriction on British trade and better commercial relations between the states. ...Petitions of a similar tone came from Fredericksburg, Falmouth, Alexandria, and Port Royal."[672]

Against the indifference and opposition of the western districts, the east prevailed in the contest over the proposition to send delegates to the federal Convention and Washington, Madison, Mason, Henry, Randolph, Wythe, and Blair were named - "all residents of the Tidewater, except Henry and Madison."[673] This result was partly due to the fact that the Tidewater region was over-represented in the state legislature according to population, and partly to the superior cohesion of the interests affected.[674]

The same economic antagonism that was manifested in the selection of delegates to the federal Convention was again manifested in the state convention called to ratify the Constitution. "The democratic leaders of the interior, says Ambler, "declared that it [the Constitution] sacrificed the state's sovereignty. Accordingly they made a desperate fight to secure the election of delegates pledged to vote against ratification. When the canvass was ended it was not known which side would be successful, so evenly were the friends and enemies of the new plan of federal government matched. From the Tidewater came a strong delegation favourable to ratification. It numbered among its members the most prominent characters of the Virginia bar, former sympathizers with Great Britain, and representatives of interests essentially commercial. The other delegates favourable to ratification came from the Valley and the north-western part of the state. Most of them had seen service in the Revolutionary armies and were largely under the influence of Washington. The Kentucky country and the Piedmont sent delegates opposed to ratification. ... The vote on the ratification was: ayes 89, nays 79 ... practically all the lower Tidewater [being] in favour of ratification. Only two delegates from

---

[671] *Ibid.*, pp. 15-16.

[672] Ambler, *op. cit.*, pp. 48-52.

[673] Henry not only refused to attend but opposed the adoption of the Constitution with all his might.

[674] *Ibid.*, p. 36.

Shenandoah Valley and that part of the Trans-Alleghany north of the Great Kanawha voted nay. The democratic Piedmont and the Kentucky country was almost unanimous in opposition to the Constitution."[675]

These conclusions reached by Ambler closely support Libby's survey. In speaking of the distribution of the vote on the Constitution in Virginia, he says: "Four well-marked sections are to be noted. ...The first, the eastern, comprised all the counties in tidewater Virginia. Its vote on the Constitution stood 80 per cent for and 20 per cent against ratification. This was the region of the large towns, and where commercial interests were predominant. The middle district, lying farther west to the Blue Ridge mountains, represented the interior farming interests of the state; the class of small farmers made up the principal part of its population. Its vote on the Constitution stood 26 per cent for and 74 per cent against adoption. The third, the West Virginia district is really double, composed of the Shenandoah Valley, in which lay the bulk of the population and the sparsely settled Trans-Alleghany region. This, also, was an agricultural section with a population chiefly Scotch-Irish and Germans from Pennsylvania. Its vote stood 97 per cent for and 3 per cent against the Constitution.[676] ...The fourth, or Kentucky district comprised all that territory west of the great Kanawha to the Cumberland River. Its vote stood 10 per cent for and 90 per cent against. ...The question of the opening of the Mississippi river was the decisive one in determining the vote of this section."[677]

That public securities also carried some weight in the Virginia counties which were strongly favourable to the Constitution is shown by the following table of the delegates (all, except Thomas Read, favourable to the Constitution) to the state convention from the towns and the seaboard or tidewater regions. Those italicised were holders of paper to some amount and appear on the *Index to Virginia Funds* C in the Mss. of the Treasury Department. Those not italicised were not discovered on the books.

Fairfax County	-	*David Stuart* and *Charles Simms*.
King George	-	Burdet Ashton and William Thornton.
Westmoreland	-	*Henry Lee* and *Bushrod Washington*.
Northumberland	-	Walter Jones and Thomas Gaskins.
Richmond County	-	*Walker Tomlin* (as Executor) and *William Peachy* (as Executor).
Lancaster	-	James Gordon and Henry Towles.
Gloucester	-	*Warner Lewis* and Thomas Smith.
York	-	*John Blair* and *George Wyeth*.
Princess Anne	-	Anthony Walke and Thomas Walke.
Norfolk	-	James Webb and James Taylor. (Portsmouth.)
Henrico- (Richmond City) -		*Edmund Randolph* and *John Marshall*.
James City	-	*Nathl. Burwell* and *Robert Andrews*.
Elizabeth City	-	Miles King and Worlich Westwood.
Charlotte	-	*Paul Carrington* and Thomas Read.[678]

North Carolina. - North Carolina was at first overwhelmingly Anti-Federal. It had peculiar economic characteristics. Though in the south, it had a large body of small farmers; and the great slave-tilled plantation

---

[675] Ambler, *op. cit.*, pp. 53 ff.

[676] For an explanation of the Federalist complexion of this region see Ambler's explanation, *Sectionalism in Virginia*, p. 16.

[677] Libby, *op. cit.*, pp. 34-35.

[678] Voted against ratification.

was not such a marked feature of its economy as it was of South Carolina. It had small mercantile interests as compared with Massachusetts, New York, Maryland, Pennsylvania, and South Carolina, with their considerable seaport towns. And perhaps most significant of all was the fact that a very large proportion of the public securities in that state were bought up by speculators from northern cities[679] and therefore not held by native inhabitants in the centres of influence. This must have had a very deadening effect on the spirit of the movement for ratification.

Owing to these peculiarities, it is impossible to layout North Carolina into such sharply differentiated economic regions as some of the other commonwealths. Nevertheless, certain lines are marked out by Libby in his survey of the vote in 1789 when the Constitution was finally ratified. "The counties around Albemarle and Pamlico Sounds constituted the bulk of the federal area. ...This region was the earliest settled, the most densely populated, and represented most of the mercantile and commercial interests of the state." With this region went some additional inland districts when the swing to the Federalists carried the state for ratification. The second region was in the centre of the state where the "interests were wholly agricultural;" this region was strongly Anti-Federal. To it was added the Tennessee region, also Anti-Federal, for the same reasons that carried western Virginia against the Constitution.[680]

South Carolina. - South Carolina presents the economic elements in the ratification with the utmost simplicity. There we find two rather sharply marked districts in antagonism over the Constitution. "The rival sections," says Libby, "were the coast or lower district and the upper, or more properly, the middle and upper country. The coast region was the first settled and contained a larger portion of the wealth of the state; its mercantile and commercial interests were important; its church was the Episcopal, supported by the state." This region, it is scarcely necessary to remark, was overwhelmingly in favour of the Constitution. The upper area, against the Constitution, "was a frontier section, the last to receive settlement; its lands were fertile and its mixed population were largely small farmers. ...There was no established church, each community supported its own church and there was a great variety in the district."[681]

A contemporary writer, R.G. Harper, calls attention to the fact that the lower country, Charleston, Beaufort, and Georgetown, which had 28,694 white inhabitants, and about seven-twelfths of the representation in the state convention, paid £28,081/5/10 taxes in 1794, while the upper country, with 120,902 inhabitants, and five-twelfths of the representation in the convention, paid only £8,390/13/3 taxes.[682]

The lower districts in favour of the Constitution therefore possessed the wealth of the state and a disproportionate share in the convention - on the basis of the popular distribution of representation.[683]

These divisions of economic interest are indicated by the abstracts of the tax returns for the state in 1794 which show that of £127,337 worth of stock in trade, faculties, etc. listed for taxation in the state, £109,800

---

[679] This is evident from the records in the Treasury Department.

[680] Libby, *op. cit.*, pp. 38 ff.

[681] *Ibid.*, p. 42--43.

[682] Appius," *To the Citizens of South Carolina* (1794), Library of Congress, Duane Pamphlets, V 01. 83.

[683] See above, p. 248.

worth was in Charleston, city and county - the stronghold of Federalism. Of the valuation of lots in towns and villages to the amount of £656,272 in the state, £549,909 was located in that city and county.[684]

The records of the South Carolina loan office preserved in the Treasury Department at Washington show that the public securities of that state were more largely in the hands of inhabitants than was the case in North Carolina. They also show a heavy concentration in the Charleston district.

At least fourteen of the thirty-one members of the state-ratifying convention from the parishes of St. Philip and Saint Michael, Charleston (all of whom favoured ratification) held over $75,000 worth of public securities, which amount was distributed unevenly among the following men:

John Blake	Isaac Motte
Danl. Cannon	C. C. Pinckney
Edw. Darrell	John Pringle
John F. Grimke	David Ramsay
Wm. Johnson	Nathaniel Russel
Thomas Jones	Josiah Smith
Lewis Morris	Danl. de Soussure[685]

Georgia. - Georgia was one of the states that gave a speedy and unanimous consent to the adoption of the Constitution. If there was any considerable contest there, no record of it appears on the surface; and no thorough research has ever been made into the local unprinted records.[686] Libby dismisses the state with the suggestion that the pressing dangers from the Indians on the frontiers, which were formidable and threatening in the summer and autumn of 1787, were largely responsible for the swift and favourable action of the state in ratifying the new instrument of government that promised protection under national arms,[687]

Three conclusions seem warranted by the data presented in this chapter:

Inasmuch as the movement for the ratification of the Constitution centred particularly in the regions in which mercantile, manufacturing, security, and personalty interests generally had their greatest strength, it is

---

[684] *State Papers: Finance,* Vol. I, p. 462. In 1783 an attempt to establish a bank .I with 5100,000 capital was made in Charleston, S.C., but it failed. "Soon after ! the adoption of the funding system, three banks were established in Charleston whose capitals in the whole amounted to twenty times the sum proposed in 1783." D. Ramsay, *History of South Carolina* (1858 ed.), Vol. II, p. 106.

[685] Ms. Treasury Department: *South Carolina Loan Office Ledger,* consult Index. No general search was made for other names.

[686] On the subject of ratification in Georgia, Dr. Jameson says: "Nothing of either journal or debates is known to have been printed, unless in some contemporary newspaper outside the state; the Georgia newspapers seem to have nothing of the sort." *American Historical Association Report* (1902), Vol. I, p. 167.

[687] This danger may have had some influence in the concessions made by the Georgia delegates in the Convention for they were kept informed of the Indian troubles in the summer of 1787. Force Transcripts, *Georqia Records,* 1781-1789: Library of Congress.

impossible to escape the conclusion that holders of personalty saw in the new government a strength and defence to their advantage.

Inasmuch as so many leaders in the movement for ratification were large security holders, and inasmuch as securities constituted such a large proportion of personalty, this economic interest must have formed a very considerable dynamic element, if not the preponderating element, in bringing about the adoption of the new system.

The state conventions do not seem to have been more "disinterested" than the Philadelphia convention; but in fact the leading champions of the new government appear to have been, for the most part, men of the same practical type, with actual economic advantages at stake.

The opposition to the Constitution almost uniformly came from the agricultural regions, and from the areas in which debtors had been formulating paper money and other depreciatory schemes.[688]

---

[688] Some holders of public securities are found among the opponents of the Constitution, but they are not numerous.

Chapter 11.

The Economic Conflict Over Ratification As Viewed By Contemporaries.

Having discovered the nature of the social conflict connected with the formation and adoption of the Constitution, and having shown the probable proportion of the people who participated in the conflict and the several group-interests into which they fell, it is interesting, though not fundamentally important, to inquire whether the leading thinkers of the time observed the nature of the antagonisms present in the process. A full statement of the results of such an inquiry would require far more space than is at command in this volume; and consequently only a few illustrative and representative opinions can be given.

No one can pore for weeks over the letters, newspapers, and pamphlets of the years 1787-1789 without coming to the conclusion that there was a deep-seated conflict between a popular party based on paper money and agrarian interests, and a conservative party centred in the towns and resting on financial, mercantile, and personal property interests generally. It is true that much of the fulmination in pamphlets was concerned with controversies over various features of the Constitution; but those writers who went to the bottom of matters, such as the authors of *The Federalist,* and the more serious Anti-Federalists, gave careful attention to the basic elements in the struggle as well as to the " incidental controversial details.

The superficiality of many of the ostensible reasons put forth by the opponents of the Constitution was penetrated by Madison. Writing to Jefferson, in October, 1788, he says: "The little pamphlet herewith inclosed will give you a collective view of the alterations which have been proposed by the State Conventions for the new Constitution. Various and numerous as they appear, they certainly omit many of the true grounds of opposition. The articles relating to Treaties, to paper money, and to contracts, created more enemies than all the errors in the system, positive and negative, put together."[689]

Naturally the more circumspect of the pamphleteers who lent their support to the new system were careful about a too precise alignment of forces, for their strength often lay in the conciliation of opponents rather than in exciting a more deep-seated antagonism. But even in such conciliatory publications the material advantages to be expected from the adoption of the Constitution are constantly put forward.

Take, for example, this extract from a mollifying "Address to the Freemen of America" issued while the Convention was in the midst of its deliberations: "Let the public creditor, who lent his money to his country , and the soldier and citizen who yielded their services, come forward next and contribute their aid to establish an effective federal government. It is from the united power and resources of America only that they can expect permanent and substantial justice. ...Let the citizens of America who inhabit the western counties of our states fly to a federal power for protection [against the Indians]. ...Let the farmer who groans beneath the weight of direct taxation seek relief from a government whose extensive jurisdiction will enable it to extract the resources of our country by means of imposts and customs. Let the merchant, who complains of the restrictions and exclusions imposed upon his vessels by foreign nations, unite his influence in establishing a power that shall retaliate those injuries and insure him success in his honest pursuits by a general system of commercial regulations. Let the manufacturer and mechanic, who are everywhere languishing for want of employment, direct their eyes to an assembly of the states. It will be in their power only to encourage such arts and manufactures as are essential to the prosperity of our country.[690]

---

[689] *Writings.* Vol. I, p. 423.

[690] Address to the Freemen of America," *The American Museum for* June, 1787, Vol. I, p. 494.

It is in the literature of the contest in the states where the battle over ratification was hottest that we find the most frank recognition of the fact that one class of property interests was in conflict with another. This recognition appears not so much in attacks on opponents as in appeals to the groups which have the most at stake in the outcome of the struggle, although virulent abuse of debtors and paper money advocates is quite common. Merchants, money lenders, public creditors are constantly urged to support the Constitution on the ground that their economic security depends upon the establishment of the new national government.

Perhaps the spirit of the battle over ratification is best reflected in the creed ironically attributed to each of the contending parties by its opponents. The recipe for an Anti-Federalist essay which indicates in a very concise way the class-bias that actuated the opponents of the Constitution, ran in this manner: "Wellborn, nine times - Aristocracy, eighteen times -Liberty of the Press, thirteen times repeated - Liberty of Conscience, once - Negro slavery, once mentioned - Trial by jury, seven times - Great Men, six times repeated - Mr .Wilson, forty times - put them altogether and dish them up at pleasure."[691]

To this sarcastic statement of their doctrines, the Anti-Federalists replied by formulating the "Political Creed of Every Federalist" as follows: "I believe in the infallibility, all-sufficient wisdom, and infinite goodness of the late convention; or in other words, I believe that some men are of so perfect a nature that it is absolutely impossible for them to commit errors or design villainy. I believe that the great body of the people are incapable of judging in their nearest concerns, and that, therefore, they ought to be guided by the opinions of their superiors. ...I believe that aristocracy is the best form of government. ... I believe that trial by jury and the freedom of the press ought to be exploded from every wise government. ...I believe that the new constitution will prove the bulwark of liberty - the balm of misery - the essence of justice - and the astonishment of all mankind. In short, I believe that it is the best form of government which has ever been offered to the world. I believe that to speak, write, read, think, or hear any thing against the proposed government is damnable heresy, execrable rebellion, and high treason, against the sovereign majesty of the convention - And lastly I believe that every person who differs from me in belief is an infernal villain. AMEN."[692]

Marshall's Analysis Of The Conflict

It must not be thought that this antagonism of economic interests which, in the language of controversy, frequently took on the form of a war between "aristocracy" and "democracy" was observed only by partisans whose views were distorted by the heat of battle. On the contrary, it was understood by the keenest thinkers- in fact, one may say that the more profound the wisdom of the observer, the clearer was his comprehension of the issues at stake. Next to Madison, whose concept of the Constitution-making process has already been fully discussed,[693] John Marshall probably understood best the nature of the new instrument, the social forces which produced it, and the great objects it was designed to accomplish. In speaking from the bench, as Chief Justice, he used, of course, the language of jurisprudence and spoke of the Constitution as a creation of the

---

[691] New Hampshire Spy, November 30, 1787.

[692] *American Museum,* July, 1788, Vol. IV, p. 85.

[693] Above, p. 156.

whole people.[694] But as a historian of great acumen, in which capacity he was not hampered by the traditional language of the bench and bar, Marshall sketched with unerring hand the economic conflict which led to the adoption of the Constitution, and impressed itself upon the nature of that instrument. In his masterly *Life of Washington,* he sets forth this conflict in unmistakable terms:

1. In the first place, the mercantile interest was sorely tried under the Articles of Confederation. There "was a general discontent with the course of trade. It had commenced with the native merchants of the north who found themselves incapable of contending in their own ports with foreigners; and was soon communicated to others. The gazettes of Boston contained some very animated and angry addresses which produced resolutions for the government of the citizens of that town, applications to their state legislature, a petition to congress, and a circular letter to the merchants of the several sea ports throughout the United States. ...The merchants of the city of Philadelphia presented a memorial to the legislature of that state, in which, after lamenting it as a fundamental defect in the constitution that full and entire power over the commerce of the United States had not been originally vested in Congress ...they prayed that the legislature would endeavour to procure from Congress a recommendation to the several states to vest in that body the necessary powers over the commerce of the United States."[695]

2. The public creditors had lost faith in the old government. "That the debt of the United States should have greatly depreciated will excite no surprise when it is recollected that the government of the Union possessed no funds, and without the assent of jealous and independent sovereigns could acquire none to pay the accruing interest; but the depreciation of the debt due from those states, which made an annual and adequate provision for the interest, can be ascribed only to a want of confidence in the governments which were controlled by no fixed principles; and it is therefore not entirely unworthy of attention. In many of those states which had repelled every attempt to introduce into circulation a depreciated medium of commerce or to defeat the annual provision of funds for the payment of the interest, the debt sunk in value to ten, five, and even less than four shillings in the pound. However unexceptionable might be the conduct of the existing legislature, the hazard from those which were to follow was too great to be encountered without an immense premium."

3. A profound division ensued throughout the United States based on different views of the rights of property. "At length," continues Marshall, "two great parties were formed in every state which were distinctly marked and which pursued distinct objects with systematic arrange- ment. The one struggled with unabated zeal for the exact observance of public and private engagements. By those belonging to it, the faith of a nation or of a private man was deemed a sacred pledge, the violation of which was equally forbidden by the principles of moral justice and of sound policy. The distresses of individuals were, they thought, to be alleviated only by industry and frugality, not by a relaxation of the laws or by a sacrifice of the rights of others. They were consequently the uniform friends of a regular administration of justice, and of a vigorous course of taxation which would enable the state to comply with its engagements. By a natural association of ideas, they were also, with very few exceptions, in favour of enlarging the powers of the federal government. ...

   "The other party marked out for themselves a more indulgent course. Viewing with extreme tenderness the case of the debtor, their efforts were unceasingly directed to his relief. To exact a faithful compliance with contracts was, in their opinion, a harsh measure which the people would not bear. They were uniformly in favour of relaxing the administration of justice, of affording facilities for the payment

---

[694] McCulloch *v.* Maryland, 4 Wheaton, 316; below, p. 299.

[695] Vol. II (1850 ed.), p. 99 ff.

of debts, or of suspending their collection, and of remitting taxes. The same course of opinion led them to resist every attempt to transfer from their own hands into those of congress powers which by others were deemed essential to the preservation of the union. In many of these states, the party last mentioned constituted a decided majority of the people, and in all of them it was very powerful. The emission of paper money, the delay of legal proceedings, and the suspension of the collection of taxes were the fruits of their rule wherever they were completely predominant. ...Throughout the union, a contest between these parties was periodically revived; and the public mind was perpetually agitated with hopes and fears on subjects which essentially affected the fortunes of a considerable proportion of society."

4. Finally, so sharp was this division into two parties on the lines of divergent views of property rights, that the Constitution, far from proceeding from "the whole people," barely escaped defeat altogether.' So positive is this statement by the great Chief Justice and so decidedly does it contradict his juristic theory of the nature of the supreme law that the two should be studied together. For this reason, the two views enunciated by Marshall are printed in parallel columns:

"So balanced were the parties in some of them [the states] that even after the subject had been discussed for a considerable time, the fate of the constitution could scarcely be conjectured; and so small in many instances, was the majority in its favour, as to afford strong ground for the opinion that, had the influence of character been removed, the intrinsic merits of the instrument would not have secured its adoption. Indeed it is scarcely to be doubted that in some of the adopting states a majority of the people were in the opposition. In all of them, the numerous amendments which were proposed demonstrate the reluctance with which the new government was accepted; and that a dread of dismemberment, not an approbation of the particular system under consideration, had induced an acquiescence in it. . . . North Carolina and Rhode Island did not at first accept the constitution, and New York was apparently dragged into it by a repugnance to being excluded from the confederacy." Marshall, in his *Life of Washington,* written in 1804-07.	"The government [of the United States] proceeds directly from the people; it is' ordained and established' in the name of the people; and it is declared to be ordained 'in order to form a more perfect union, establish justice, insure domestic tranquillity, and secure the blessings of liberty' to themselves and to their posterity. ... The government of the Union then (whatever may be the influence of this fact on the case) is, emphatically and truly, a government of the people. In form and substance it emanates from them. Its powers are granted by them and are to be exercised directly on them and for their benefit. ...It is the government of all; its powers are delegated by all; it represents all, and acts for all." Marshall, in McCulloch *V8.* Maryland (4 Wbeaton, 316), in 1819.

The Conflict In The States

Turning aside from these more general observations on the nature of the conflict over the ratification of the Constitution, let us now take up the struggle in the several states and examine the views entertained by some of the representative participants in it.

New Hampshire. -That New Hampshire was rather sharply divided into an "aristocratic" and a "country" party at the period of the adoption of the Constitution was remarked by an observing Frenchman;[696] and the New Hampshire Spy, published at Portsmouth, in the issue of October 27, 1787, aligns the mercantile and mechanical interest on the side of the new Constitution, adding that the "honest farmer" can have no objections, either. "The *honest man,*" runs the plea, "can have no objection to a federal government, for while it obliges him to pay a sacred regard to past contracts, it will eventually secure him in his person and his property. The *mercantile interest* have suffered enough *to induce* them to wish for, and espouse a federal reform. ... The *mechanical interest* can have no aversion to it, when they are informed that an efficient government will protect and encourage commerce, which is the very soul of mechanism. ...Nor can the *honest farmer* have any objection; the increase of commerce will naturally increase the demand for such articles as he may have for sale; he will be enabled to pay his taxes and, if economy shakes hands with industry, increase his farm and live independent of troublesome creditors. Since then no one respectable order of citizens can have any just reason to reject the new Constitution, we may venture to conclude that none but *fools, blockheads,* and *mad men* will dare oppose it."

Massachusetts. -The contest over the Constitution in Massachusetts was a sharp conflict between the personalty interests on the one hand and the small farmers and debtors on the other, and this fact seems to have been recognized by every thoughtful leader on both sides. This view of the social struggle was set forth on so many occasions and by so many eminent observers that it is difficult to select from the mass of material the most typical statement of the situation. Perhaps that by General Knox is not excelled for its clarity and conciseness. Writing to Washington, January 14, 1788, a few days after the state convention had begun its labours, he describes the alignment over ratification as follows:

"There are three parties existing in that state [Massachusetts] at present, differing in their numbers and greatly differing in their wealth and talents.

"The 1st. is the commercial part of the state to which are added all the men of considerable property, the clergy, the lawyers - including all the judges of all the courts, and all the officers of the late army, and also the neighbourhood of all the great towns - its numbers may include 3/7ths of the state. This party are for vigorous government, perhaps many of them would have been still more pleased with the new Constitution had it been more analogous to the British Constitution.

"The 2d party are the eastern part of the state lying beyond New Hampshire formerly the province of Main - This party are chiefly looking towards the erection of a new state and the majority of them will adopt or reject the new Constitution as it may facilitate or retard their designs - this party 2/7ths.

"The 3d party are the Insurgents or their favourers, the great majority of whom are for an annihilation of debts, public and private, and therefore they will not approve the new Constitution - this party 2/7ths."[697]

---

[696] Farrand. *Records.* Vol. III. p. 232. Speaking of New Hampshire, Madison says. ..The opposition [to the Constitution]. I understand. is composed precisely of the same description of characters with that of Massachusetts and stands contrasted to all the wealth, abilities, and respectability of the State." *Writings.* Vol. I, p. 383.

[697] *Documentary History of the Constitution.* Vol. IV. p. 442.

Several months before Knox had formulated this view of the conflict, indeed, early in the struggle over ratification, the Federalist agitators were busy with appeals to practical economic interests. The Massachusetts Gazette of October 26, 1787, for example, contains a letter signed by "Marcus" in which the groups likely to be affected advantageously by the new Constitution are enumerated and an argument directed to each of them: "It is the interest of the merchants to encourage the new constitution, because commerce may then be a national object, and nations will form treaties with us. It is the interest of the mechanicks to join the mercantile interest, because it is not their interest to quarrel with their bread and butter. It is the interest of the farmer because the prosperity of commerce gives vent to his produce, raises the value of his lands, and commercial duties will alleviate the burden of his taxes. It is the interest of the landholder, because thousands in Europe, with moderate fortunes will migrate to this country if an efficient government gives them a prospect of tranquillity. It is the interest of all gentlemen and men of property, because they will see many low demagogues reduced to their tools, whose upstart dominion insults their feelings, and whose passions for popularity will dictate laws, which ruin the minority of creditors and please the majority of debtors. It is the interest of the American soldier as the military profession will then be respectable and Florida may be conquered in a campaign. The spoils of the West-Indies and South America may enrich the next generation of Cincinnati.

It is the interest of the lawyers who have ability and genius, because the dignities in the Supreme Court will interest professional ambition and create emulation which is not now felt. ...It is the interest of the clergy, as civil tumults excite every passion -the soul is neglected and the clergy starve. It is the interest of all men whose education has been liberal and extensive because there will be a theatre for the display of talents."

In fact-, from the very beginning of the movement, the most eminent advocates of a new system were aware of the real nature of the struggle which lay before them. They knew that there was a deep-seated antagonism between the "natural aristocracy" and the "turbulent democracy" which was giving the government of Massachusetts trouble. Such an analysis of the difficulty is set forth by Stephen Higginson, a leading Federalist of Boston, in March, 1787: "The people of the interior parts of these states [New England] have by far too much political knowledge and too strong a relish for unrestrained freedom, to be governed by our feeble system, and too little acquaintance with real sound policy or rational freedom and too little virtue to govern themselves. They have become too well acquainted with their own weight in the political scale under such governments as ours and have too high a taste for luxury and dissipation to sit down contented in their proper line, when they see others possessed of much more property than themselves. With these feelings and sentiments they will not be quiet while such distinctions exist as to rank and property; and sensible of their own force, they will not rest easy till they possess the reins of Government and have divided property with their betters, or they shall be compelled by force to submit to their proper stations and mode of living."[698]

Discerning opponents of the Constitution, as well as its advocates, were aware of the alignment of forces in the battle. Rufus King explained to Madison in January, 1788, that the opposition was grounded on antagonism to property rather than to the outward aspects of the new system. "Apprehension that the liberties of the people are in danger," he said, "and a distrust of men of property or education have a more powerful effect upon the minds of our opponents than any specific objections against the Constitution. ...The opposition

---

[698] *Report of the Manuscripts Commission of the American Historical Association,* December 20, 1896, p. 754. A writer in the Chronicle of Freedom (reprinted in the Massachusetts Centinel, October, 27, 1787) complains of the dangers to the freedom of the press from the new Constitution and continues: "One thing, however, is calculated to alarm our fears on this head; - I mean the fashionable language which now prevails so much and is so frequent in the mouths of some who formerly held very different opinions; -That common people have no business to trouble themselves about government." The Massachusetts Centinel (November 24, 1787) declares it to be "a notorious fact that three of the principle enemies of the proposed constitution were heart and hand with the insurgents last winter."

complains that the lawyers, judges, clergymen, merchants, and men of education are all in favour of the Constitution - and for that reason they appear to be able to make the worse appear the better cause."[699]

The correctness of King's observation is sustained by a vigorous writer in the Boston Gazette and Country Journal of November 26, 1787, who charges the supporters of the Constitution with attempting to obscure the real nature of the instrument, and enumerates the interests advocating its adoption. "At length," says the writer, "the luminary of intelligence begins to beam its effulgent rays upon this important production; the deceptive mists cast before the eyes of the people by the delusive machinations of its INTERESTED advocates begins to dissipate, as darkness flies before the burning taper. ...Those furious zealots who are for cramming it down the throats of the people without allowing them either time or opportunity to scan or weigh it in the balance of their intelligences, bear the same marks in their features as those who have been long wishing to erect an aristocracy in THIS COMMONWEALTH - their menacing cry is for a RIGID government, it matters little to them of what kind, provided it answers THAT description. ...They incessantly declare that none can discover any defect in the system but bankrupts who wish no government and officers of the present government who fear to lose a part of their power. ...It may not be improper to scan the characters of its most strenuous advocates: it will first be allowed that many undesigning citizens may wish its adoption from the best motives, but these are modest and silent, when compared to the greater number, who endeavor to suppress all attempts for investigations; these violent partizans are for, having the people gulp down the gilded pill blindfolded, whole, and without any qualification whatever, these consist generally, of the NOBLE order of C-s, holders of public securities, men of great wealth and expectations of public office, B-k-s and L--y-s: these with their train of dependents from [form] the aristocratick combination."

Probably the most reasoned statement of the antagonism of realty and personalty in its relation to the adoption of the Constitution in Massachusetts was made in the letters of "Cornelius" on December 11 and 18, 1787: "I wish," he said, " there never might be any competition between the landed and the mercantile interests, nor between any different classes of men whatever. Such competition will, however, exist, so long as occasion and opportunity for it is given, and while human nature remains the same that it has ever been. The citizens in the seaport towns are numerous; they live compact; their interests are one; there is a constant connection and intercourse between them; they can, on any occasion, centre their votes where they please. This is not the case with those who are in the landed interest; they are scattered far and wide; they have but little intercourse and connection with each other. ...I conceive a foundation is laid for throwing the whole power of the federal government into the hands of those who are in the mercantile interest; and for the landed, which is the great interest at of this country, to lie unrepresented, forlorn, and without hope. It grieves me to suggest an idea of this kind: But I believe it to be important and not the mere phantom of imagination, or the result of an uneasy and restless disposition."[700]

Connecticut. -There was no such spirited battle of wits over ratification in Connecticut as occurred in Massachusetts. Nevertheless, Ellsworth, in that state, produced a remarkable series of essays in support of the new Constitution which were widely circulated and read. In these papers there is revealed a positive antagonism between agrarianism and personalty, but an attempt is made at conciliation by subtly blending the two interests. Ellsworth opens: "The writer of the following passed the first part of his life in mercantile employments, and by Industry and economy acquired a sufficient sum on retiring from trade to purchase and stock a decent plantation, on which he now lives in the state of a farmer. By his present employment he is interested in the prosperity of agriculture and those who derive a support from cultivating the earth. An acquaintance with business has freed him from many prejudices and jealousies which he sees in his neighbours who have not intermingled with mankind nor learned by experience the method of managing an extensive

---

[699] *Life and Letters,* Vol. I, pp. 314 ff.

[700] Harding, *The Federal Constitution in Massachusetts,* pp. 123-124.

circulating property. Conscious of an honest intention he wishes to address his brethren on some political subjects which now engage the public attention and will in the sequel greatly influence the value of landed property."[701]

The fact that the essential implications of this statement about his primary economic interests being those of a farmer are untrue does not affect the point here raised: Ellsworth recognised that the opposition was agrarian in character, and he simulated the guise of a farmer to conciliate it. Later on Ellsworth classifies the opposition. In the first rank he puts the Tories as leading in resisting the adoption of the Constitution because it would embarrass Great Britain. In the second class, Ellsworth puts those who owe money. "Debtors in desperate circumstances," he says, "who have not resolution to be either honest or industrious will be the next men to take alarm. They have long been upheld by the property of their creditors and the mercy of the public, and daily destroy a thousand honest men who are unsuspicious. Paper money and tender acts is the only atmosphere in which they can breathe and live. This is now so generally known that by being a friend to such measures, a man effectually advertises himself as a bankrupt. ...There is another kind of people who will be found in the opposition: Men of much self-importance and supposed skill in politics who are not of sufficient consequence to obtain public employment, but can spread jealousies in the little districts of country where they are placed. These are always jealous of men in place and of public measures, and aim at making themselves consequential by distrusting everyone in the higher offices of society. ...But in the present case men who have lucrative and influential state offices, if they act from principles of self interest will be tempted to oppose an alteration which would doubtless be beneficial to the people. To sink from a controulment of finance or any other great departments of the state, thro' want of ability or opportunity to act a part in the federal system must be a terrifying consideration."[702]

Leaving aside the Tories and office-holders, it is apparent that the element which Ellsworth considers the most weighty in the opposition is the agrarian party. The correctness of his analysis is supported by collateral pieces of evidence. Sharon, one of the leading paper money towns which opposed the ratification of the Constitution in Connecticut had voted to assist Shays and had repeatedly attempted to secure paper emission legislation.[703] In a few letters and speeches against the Constitution the plaintive note of the agrarian is discernible. The opponents of the Constitution in Connecticut found no skilled champions such as led the fight in Pennsylvania and Massachusetts; and no such spirited discussion took place. The debates in the state ratifying convention were not recorded (save for a few fragments); but the contest in the legislature over the proposition to send delegates to the Philadelphia Convention showed that the resistance came from the smaller agrarian interests similar to those in Rhode Island and Massachusetts which had stood against the whole movement.

Mr. Granger from Suffield was opposed to the proposition to send delegates to Philadelphia because "he conceived it would be disagreeable to his constituents; he thought the liberties of the people would be endangered by it; ...and concluded by saying that he imagined these things would have a tendency to produce a regal government in this country." Mr. Humphrey from the inland town of Norfolk sided with Mr. Granger and "concluded by saying that he approved the wisdom and policy of Rhode Island in refusing to send delegates to the convention and that the conduct of that state in this particular, was worthy of imitation." Mr. Perkins

---

[701] Ford, *Essays on the Constitution.* p. 139.

[702] Ford, *Essays on the Constitution,* pp. 144 ff.

[703] Libby, *op. cit.,* p. 58.

of Enfield "was opposed to the measure and said that the state would send men that had been delicately bred and who were in affluent circumstances, that could not feel for the people in this day of distress."[704]

New York. -When it is remembered that the greatest piece of argumentation produced by the contest over ratification, *The Federalist,* was directed particularly to the electorate in New York, although widely circulated elsewhere, it will appear a work of supererogation to inquire whether the leaders in that commonwealth understood the precise nature of the social conflict which was being waged.[705] Nevertheless, it may be worth while to present Hamilton's analysis of it. On the side of the Constitution, he placed the "very great weight of influence of the persons who framed it, particularly in the universal popularity of General Washington - the good will of the commercial interest throughout the states which will give all its efforts to the establishment of a government capable of regulating, protecting, and extending the commerce of the Union - the good will of most men of property in the several states who wish a government of the Union able to protect them against domestic violence and the depredations which the democratic spirit is apt to make on property. - a strong belief in the people at large of the insufficiency of the present confederation to preserve the existence of the Union."

Over against these forces in favour of the Constitution, Hamilton places the antagonism of some inconsiderable men in office under state governments, the influence of some considerable men playing the part of the demagogue for their own aggrandizement; - "and add to these causes the democratical jealousy of the people which may be alarmed at the appearance of institutions that may seem calculated to place the power of the community in a few hands and raise a few individuals to stations of great pre-eminence."[706]

New Jersey and Delaware. - *The* speedy ratification of the Constitution in these states gave no time for the development of a sharp antagonism, even had there been an economic basis for it. In the absence of this actual conflict over the Constitution we can hardly expect to find any consideration of the subject by contemporary writers of note.[707]

Pennsylvania. -The opposition between town and country, between personalty and realty in other words, was so marked in this commonwealth during the struggle over the ratification of the Constitution that it was patent to all observers and was the subject of frequent and extensive comment by leaders on both sides. On September 28, 1787, Tench Coxe wrote to Madison describing the disturbance over the resolution in the state legislature calling the ratifying convention, and after reciting the events of the day he added, "It appears from these facts that the Western people [i.e. the agrarians] have a good deal of jealousy about the new Constitution and it is very clear that the men who have been used to lead the Constitutional [or radical

---

[704] Connecticut Courant, May 21, 1787.

[705] See above, p. 156.

[706] *Documentary History of the Constitution,* Vol. IV, p. 288. On the antagonism in New York see some clues afforded in an article in The Magazine of American History, April, 1893, pp. 326 ff.

[707] Dickinson's Fabius letters were printed after the ratification by Delaware and were directed to the "general public" rather than fellow-citizens in that commonwealth. Among the opponents to the Constitution, he put "men without principles or fortunes who think they may have a chance to mend their circumstances with impunity under a weak government." Ford, *Pamphlets on the Constitution,* p.166.

party][708] are against it decidedly."[709] A month later Coxe again writes to Madison: "The opposition here has become more open. It is by those leaders of the constitutional [local radical] interest who have acted in concert with the Western interest. The people of the party in the city are chiefly federal, tho' not so I fear in the Counties."[710]

Writing about the same time from Philadelphia to Washington, Gouverneur Morris, said: "With respect to this state, I am far from being decided in my opinion that they will consent. It is true that the City and its Neighbourhood was enthusiastic in the cause; but I dread the cold and sower temper of the back counties and still more the wicked industry of those who have long habituated themselves to live on the public, and cannot bear the idea of being removed from power and profit of state government which has been and still is the means of supporting themselves, their families, and their dependents."[711] Such comments on the nature of the alignment of forces might be multiplied from the writings of other Federalist leaders in Pennsylvania, but it appears to be unnecessary to say more.

The leaders on the other side were constantly discanting upon the opposition between town and country. The recalcitrant members of the legislature in their protest to the people against the hasty calling of the state convention declared, "We lamented at the time [of the selection of delegates to the national Convention] that a majority of our legislature appointed men to represent this state who were all citizens of Philadelphia, none of them calculated to represent the landed interests of Pennsylvania, and almost all of them of one political party, men who have been uniformly opposed to that [state] constitution for which you have on every occasion manifested your attachment."[712] The author of the famous "Centinel" letters saw in the movement favourable to the new Constitution a design of "the wealthy and ambitious who in every community think they have a right to lord it over their fellow creatures."[713] In fact the most philosophic argument against the adoption of the new system on account of its intrinsic nature was made by the author of these letters. At the opening of his series, Centinel inveighs against the precipitancy which characterized the movements of the Federalists, and then attacks the Constitution as the work of an active minority. "The late revolution," he says, "having effaced in a great measure all former habits and the present institutions are so recent that there exists not that great reluctance to innovation, so remarkable in old communities and which accords with reason, for the most comprehensive mind cannot foresee the full operation of material changes on civil polity. ...The wealthy and ambitious, who in every community think they have a right to lord it over their fellow creatures have availed

---

[708] See Harding, "Party struggles over the First Pennsylvania Constitution," *American Historical Association Report* (1894).

[709] *Documentary History of the Constitution,* Vol. IV, p. 305.

[710] *Ibid.,* Vol. IV, p. 339.

[711] *Ibid.,* Vol. IV, p. 358.

[712] McMaster and Stone, *op. cit.,* p. 73.

[713] *Ibid.,* p. 567.

themselves very successfully of this favourable disposition; for the people thus unsettled in their sentiments have been prepared to accede to any extreme of government. All the distresses and difficulties they experience, proceeding from various causes, have been ascribed to the impotency of the present confederation, and thence they have been led to expect full relief from the adoption of the proposed system of government ; and in the other event immediately ruin and annihilation as a nation."[714]

After warning his countrymen against being lulled into false security by the use of the great names of Washington and Franklin in support of the Constitution, Centinel takes up the fundamental element in the new system: the balance of powers as expounded in Adams' *Defence of the Constitutions*; and shows the inherent antagonism between "democracy" and the Federalist concept of government in a manner that would do honour to the warmest advocate of the initiative and referendum in our time. Mr. Adams' *sine qua non* of good government is three balancing powers; whose repelling qualities are to produce an equilibrium of interests and thereby promote the happiness of the whole community. He asserts that the administrators of every government will ever be actuated by views of private interest and ambition to the prejudice of the public good; that therefore the only effectual method to secure the rights of the people and promote their welfare is to create an opposition of interests between the members of two distinct bodies in the exercise of the powers of government, and balanced by those of a third. This hypothesis supposes human wisdom competent to the task of instituting three co-equal orders in government and a corresponding weight in the community to enable them respectively to exercise their several parts and whose views and interests should be so distinct as to prevent a coalition of any two of them for the destruction of the third. Mr. Adams, although he has traced the constitution of every form of government that ever existed, as far as history affords materials, has not been able to adduce a single instance of such a government; he indeed says the British constitution is such in theory but this is rather a confirmation that his principles are chimerical and not to be reduced to practice. If such an organization of power were practicable how long would it continue? Not a day-for there is so great a disparity in the talents, wisdom, and industry of mankind, that the scale would presently preponderate to one or the other body, and with every accession of power the means of further increase would be greatly extended. The state of society in England is much more favourable to such a scheme of government than that of America. There they have a powerful hereditary nobility, and real distinctions of rank and interests; but even there, for want of that perfect equality of power and distinction of interests in the three orders of government, they exist but in name; the only operative and efficient check upon the conduct of administration is the sense of the people at large. ...If the administrators of every government are actuated by views of private interest and ambition, how is the welfare and happiness of the community to be the result or such jarring adverse interests?"[715]

In opposition to the Adams-Madison theory of balanced economic interests and innocuous legislatures, which was the essence of the Federalist doctrine, Centinel expounded his reasons for believing that distinct property groups should not be set against one another in the government, and that trust in the political capacity of the broad undifferentiated mass of the community should be the basis of the Constitution; but it should be noted that his undifferentiated mass was composed largely of property holders. "I believe," he says "that it will be found that the form of government which holds those entrusted with power in the greatest responsibility to their constituents, the best calculated for freemen. A republican or free government can only exist where the body of the people are virtuous and *where property is pretty equally divided*. In such a government the people are sovereign and their sense or opinion is the criterion of every public measure; for when this ceases to be the case, the nature of the government is changed and an aristocracy, monarchy, or

---

[714] *Ibid.*, p. 367.

[715] McMaster and Stone, *op. cit.*, pp. 568-569.

despotism will rise on its ruins. The highest responsibility is to be attained in a simple structure of government, for the great body of the people never steadily attend to the operations of government, and for the want of due information are liable to be imposed upon. If you complicate the plan by various orders, the people will be perplexed and divided in their sentiment about the sources of abuses or misconduct; some will impute it to the senate, others to the house of representatives, and so on, that the interposition of the people may be rendered imperfect or perhaps wholly abortive. But if imitating the constitution of Pennsylvania, you vest all the legislative power in one body of men (separating the executive and the judicial), elected for a short period, and necessarily excluded by rotation from permanency and guarded from precipitancy and surprise by delays imposed on its proceedings, you will create the most perfect responsibility; for then, whenever the people feel a grievance, they cannot mistake the authors and will apply the remedy with certainty and effect, discarding them at the next election."[716]

It is evident that a considerable number of the voters in Pennsylvania clearly understood the significance of the division of powers created by the Constitution. In a petition circulated and extensively signed by Philadelphia citizens immediately after the completion of the labours of the Convention and directed to the state ratifying convention, the memorialists expressed their approval of the Constitution, and added: "The division of the power of the United States into three branches gives the sincerest satisfaction to a great majority of our citizens, who have long suffered many inconveniences from being governed by a single legislature. All single governments are tyrannies - whether they be lodged in one man - a few men - or a large body of the people."[717]

Maryland. -The contest in Maryland over the ratification was keen and spirited and every side of the question was threshed out in newspaper articles and pamphlets.[718] Through all the controversy ran the recognition of the fact that it was a struggle between debtors and creditors, between people of substance and the agrarians. Alexander Hanson in his considerable tract in favour of the ratification, dedicated to Washington, treats the charge that the Constitution was an instrument of property as worthy of a dignified answer. "You have been told," he says, "that the proposed plan was calculated peculiarly for the rich. In all governments, not merely despotic, the wealthy must, in most things, find an advantage from the possession of that which is too much the end and aim of mankind. In the proposed plan there is nothing like a discrimination in their favour. ...Is it a just cause of reproach that the Constitution effectually secures property? Or would the objectors introduce a general scramble?"[719]

Recognizing the importance of the interests at stake, another Federalist writer, "Civis," in the Maryland Journal of February 1, 1788, appeals to the voters for delegates to the coming state convention to be circumspect in order to procure the ratification of the Constitution. He laments that "men of property, character, and abilities have too much retired from public employment since the conclusion of the war," but expresses the hope "that, in this all-im- portant crisis, they will again step forth, with a true patriotic ardour, and snatch their dear country from the dreadful and devouring jaws of anarchy and ruin." He cautions the citizens against voting for undesirable persons: "The characters whom I would especially point out as your particular aversion, in the present critical conjuncture, are all those in desperate or embarrassed

---

[716] *Ibid.*, pp. 569-570.

[717] Connecticut Courant, Oct. 1, 1787.

[718] See the valuable articles on "Maryland's Adoption of the Constitution," by Dr. Steiner in the American Historical Review, Vol. V.

[719] Ford, *Pamphlets on the Constitution,* p. 254.

circumstances, who may have been advocates for paper money, the truck-bill, or insolvent act; and who may expect to escape in the general ruin of the country."

On the other hand many opponents of the Constitution in Maryland definitely declared the contest to be one between property and the people of little substance. Such was practically the view of Luther Martin[720] in basing his resistance on the ground that the new system prevented the states from interfering with property rights. The spirit of this opposition was also well reflected in a reply to the letter of "Civis," mentioned above, which took the form of an ironical appeal to the voters to support only men of property and standing for the coming state convention. "Choose no man in debt," it runs, "because being in debt proves that he wanted understanding to take care of his own affairs. ...A man in debt can scarcely be honest. ...Vote for no man who was in favour of paper money, for no *honest* man was for that measure. None but *debtors* and desperate wretches advocated the diabolical scheme. ...Elect no man who supported the law allowing insolvent debtors to discharge their persons from perpetual imprisonment, by *honestly* delivering up *all* their property to the use of their creditors. The legislature *have* no right to interfere with *private* contracts, and debtors might safely trust to the humanity and clemency of their creditors who will not keep them in gaol all their lives, unless they deserve it. ...Men of great property are deeply interested in the welfare of the state; and they are the most competent judges of the form of government, best calculated to preserve their property, and such liberties as it is proper for the common and inferior class *of* people to enjoy. Men of wealth possess natural and acquired understanding, as they manifest by amassing riches, or by keeping and increasing those they derive from their ancestors, and they are best acquainted with the wants, the wishes, and desires of the people, and they are always ready to relieve them in their private and public stations."[721]

Virginia. -Madison remarked that he found in his state "men of intelligence, patriotism, property, and independent circumstances"[722] divided over the ratification of the Constitution although in some other commonwealths, men of this stamp were " zealously attached " to the new government. This general reflection is not borne out however by some of his contemporaries. Marshall, as we have noted above,[723] regarded the conflict as being between two rather sharply divided parties, those who favoured maintaining public and private rights in their full integrity and those who proposed to attack them through legislation.[724] In fact, Madison himself at a later date declared that "the superiority of abilities" was on the side of the Constitution.[725] Charles Lee claimed that " except a few characters, the members [of the Virginia convention] with the most knowl- edge and abilities and personal influence are also in favour of the Constitution."[726] In the opposition Patrick Henry put the whole mass of small farmers. "I believe it to be a fact," he declared in the Virginia convention, "that the great body of yeomanry are in decided opposition to it. I may say with confidence that, for nineteen counties adjacent to each other, nine-tenths of the people are conscientiously opposed to it. I

---

[720] See above, p. 205.

[721] Maryland Journal, March 21, 1788.

[722] *Documentary History of the Constitution*, Vol. IV, p. 398. For the economics of this, see above, p. 30.

[723] P. 295.

[724] "It is currently reported, "says the New Hampshire Spy, on December 7. 1787, "that there are only two men in Virginia who are not in debt, to be found among the enemies to the federal constitution. Debtors, speculators in papers, and states demagogues act consistently in opposing it."

[725] *Documentary History of the Constitution*, V 01. IV. p. 584.

[726] *Ibid.*, p. 577.

may be mistaken but I give you it as my opinion; and my opinion is founded on personal knowledge in some measure, and other good authority. ...You have not solid reality - the hearts and hands of the men who are to be governed."[727]

North Carolina. - It would have been strange if the leaders for and against the Constitution in this commonwealth had not taken cognizance of the nature of the conflict they were waging. The popular paper money and debtor party had been powerful and active and had aroused the solicitude of all men of substance; and the representatives of the latter, as practical men, knew what they were doing in supporting an overthrow of the old system. "It is essential to the interests of agriculture and commerce," exclaimed Davie, in the state ratifying convention, "that the hands of the states should be bound from making paper money, instalment laws, and pine-barren acts. By such iniquitous laws the merchant or farmer may be defrauded of a considerable part of his just claims. But in the federal court, real money will be recovered with that speed which is necessary to accommodate the circumstances of individuals."[728] Speaking on the same theme, paper money, Gover- nor Johnston said: "Every man of property - every man of considerable transactions, whether a merchant, planter, mechanic, or of any other condition - must have felt the baneful influence of that currency."[729]

The recognition of the nature of the clash of interests is manifest in scattered correspondence, as well as in speeches. For example, in a letter to Iredell, January 15, 1788, Maclaine says: "In New Hanover county the people if left to themselves are in favour of the change. Some demagogues, a few persons who are in debt, and every public officer, except the clerk of the county court, are decidedly against any change; at least against any that will answer the purpose. Our friend Huske is the loudest man in Wilmington against the new constitution. Whether ambition, or avarice, or a compound of both actuates him I leave you to judge. ... I expect in a few weeks *The Federalist* in a volume. He is certainly a judicious and ingenious writer, though not well calculated for the common people. ...Your old friend Huske and Col. Read have joined all the low scoundrels in the County [i.e. the country party] and by every underhand means are prejudicing the common people against the new constitution. The former is a candidate for the county."[730]

This conflict between the town and country is explained by Iredell's biographer: "Soon after the [Revolutionary] War commenced a feud between the town of Wilmington and the county of New Hanover. The leading men' upon 'Change' were either Tories or those whose lukewarmness had provoked suspicion: the agrestic population could but illy brook their prosperity. From that day to the present [1857] the politics of the burgess have been antagonistical to those of the former. The merchants have ever been the predominant class in the borough: daily intercourse has enabled them with facility to form combinations that have given them the control of the moneyed institutions while their patronage has added a potent influence with the press."[731]

---

[727] Elliot, *Debates,* Vol. III. p. 592. See W.C. Ford, 'The Federal Constitution in Virginia," in the *Proceedings of the Massachusetts Historical Society* for October, " 1903.

[728] Elliot. *Debates*. Vol. IV. p. 159.

[729] Elliot. *Debates,* Vol. IV, p. 90.

[730] McRee, *Life and Correspondence of James Iredell,* Vol. II, pp. 216, 219.

[731] McRee, *op. cit.,* Vol. II, p. 164 note.

South Carolina. -The materials bearing on the ratification of the Constitution in South Carolina which are available to the northern student are relatively scanty.[732] Nevertheless, in view of the marked conflict between the agrarian back-country and the commercial seaboard, it may easily be imagined that it was not unobserved by the leaders in the contest over ratification who championed the respective regions. This antagonism came out in a pamphlet war over the amendment of the state constitution which was being waged about the time of the adoption of the new federal system. In this war, "Appius," the spokesman for the reform party is reported to have declared that "wealth ought not to be represented; that a rich citizen ought to have fewer votes than his poor neighbour; that wealth should be stripped of as many advantages as possible and it will then have more than enough; and finally, that in giving property the power of protecting itself, government becomes an aristocracy."[733]

"Appius," after this general statement of his theory, then explains wherein the distribution of economic interests engendered antagonism in politics in that state. "The upper and lower countries, have opposite habits and views in almost every particular. One is accustomed to expense, the other to frugality. One will be inclined to numerous offices, large salaries, and an expensive government; the other, from the moderate fortunes of the inhabitants, and their simple way of life will prefer low taxes, small salaries, and a very frugal civil establishment. One imports almost every article of consumption and pays for it in produce; the other is far removed from navigation, has very little to export, and must therefore supply its own wants. Consequently one will favour commerce, the other manufactures; one wishes slaves, the other will be better without them."[734] In view of this opposition of interests, "Appius" holds that there should be a redistribution of representatives which will give the back-country its proper proportion and enable the majority to rule.

To this argument Ford replies in the language of Federalism. The rights of property are anterior to constitutions; the state constitution recognizes and guarantees these rights; the substantial interests of the minority must be forever immune from attacks by majorities. Otherwise the weaker party in society," he declares, "would literally have no right whatever: neither life, liberty, or property would be guaranteed to them by the social compact, seeing the majority are not bound by it, but might destroy the whole and by the same rule any part of it at pleasure. ... Virtue and vice would lose their distinction; the most vicious views would be sanctified if pursued by the greater number, and the most virtuous resistance punishable in the less. If the principles of justice are derived from a higher source than human institutions (and who will deny it?) I contend that the majority have no right to infringe them."[735] Hence, any change in the system which deprives the seaboard minority of their preponderance in the state government cannot be too severely reprobated.

It can hardly be supposed that an economic antagonism in the state that was so clearly recognized by publicists in 1794, and that manifested itself in the vote on the ratification of the Federal Constitution six years before, was overlooked in the earlier contest.

Indeed, evidence that it was not appears in a pamphlet written in defence of the Constitution by Dr. David Ram- say, who was afterward a member of the ratifying convention in South Carolina. He particularly warns his fellow-citizens against the debtor element. "Be on your guard," he says, "against the misrepresentations of men who are involved in debt; such may wish to see the Constitution rejected because of the following clause,

---

[732] See W. A. Schaper, "Sectionalism in South Carolina," *American Historical Association Report* (1900), Vol. I.

[733] Summary by T. Ford, *The Constitutionalist* (1794), p. 21.

[734] Ford, *op. cit.*, pp. 21-22.

[735] *Op. cit.*, p. 13.

no state shall emit bills of credit, make anything but gold and silver coin a tender in payment of debts, pass any ex post facto law, or law impairing the obligation of contracts.' This will doubtless bear hard on debtors who wish to defraud their creditors, but it will be real service to the honest part of the community. Examine well the characters and circumstances of men who are averse to the new constitution. Perhaps you will find that the above clause is the real ground of the opposition of some of them, though they may artfully cover it with a splendid profession of zeal for state privileges and general liberty."[736]

Georgia. -The speedy and unanimous ratification of the Constitution in Georgia seems to have prevented any very vigorous pamphleteering on the question. Indeed, the energies of the state were being strained to the limit in pre- paring for defence against the Indians, and there was little time for theorizing. Foreign invasion generally silences domestic discord.

Conclusions.

At the close of this long and arid survey - partaking of the nature of catalogue - it seems worth while to bring together the important conclusions for political science which the data presented appear to warrant.

The movement for the Constitution of the United States was originated and carried through principally by four groups of personalty interests which had been adversely affected under the Articles of Confederation: money, public securities, manufactures, and trade and shipping.

The first firm steps toward the formation of the Constitution were taken by a small and active group of men immediately interested through their personal possessions in the outcome of their labours.

No popular vote was taken directly or indirectly on the proposition to call the Convention which drafted the Constitution.

A large propertyless mass was, under the prevailing suffrage qualifications, excluded at the outset from participation (through representatives) in the work of framing the Constitution.

The members of the Philadelphia Convention which drafted the Constitution were, with a few exceptions, immediately, directly, and personally interested in, and derived economic advantages from, the establishment of the new system.

The Constitution was essentially an economic document based upon the concept that the fundamental private rights of property are anterior to government and morally beyond the reach of popular majorities.

The major portion of the members of the Convention are on record as recognizing the claim of property to a special and defensive position in the Constitution.

---

[736] Ford, *Pamphlets on the Constitution,* p. 379. On May 24, 1788, after the Constitution had been approved in South Carolina, General Pinckney wrote to Rufus King, saying, "The Anti-Federalists had been most mischievously industrious in prejudicing the minds of our citizens against the Constitution. Pamphlets, speeches, & Protests from the disaffected in Pennsylvania were circulated throughout the state, particularly in the back country." King, *Life and Correspondence,"* Vol. I, p. 329.

In the ratification, of the Constitution, about three-fourths of the adult males failed to vote on the question, having abstained from the elections at which delegates to the state conventions were chosen, either on account of their indifference or their disfranchisement by property qualifications.

The Constitution was ratified by a vote of probably not more than one-sixth of the adult males. It is questionable whether a majority of the voters participating in the elections for the state conventions in New York, Massachusetts, New Hampshire, Virginia, and South Carolina, actually approved the ratification of the Constitution.

The leaders who supported the Constitution in the ratifying conventions represented the same economic groups as the members of the Philadelphia Convention; and in a large number of instances they were also directly and personally interested in the outcome of their efforts.

In the ratification, it became manifest that the line of cleavage for and against the Constitution was between substantial personalty interests on the one hand and the small farming and debtor interests on the other.

The Constitution was not created by "the whole people" as the jurists have said; neither was it created by "the states" as Southern nullifiers long contended; but it was the work of a consolidated group whose interests knew no state boundaries and were truly national in their scope.

THE END

BOOK TWO
HISTORY
OF THE
UNITED STATES

PREFACE

As things now stand, the course of instruction in American history in our public schools embraces three distinct treatments of the subject. Three separate books are used. First, there is the primary book, which is usually a very condensed narrative with emphasis on biographies and anecdotes. Second, there is the advanced text for the seventh or eighth grade, generally speaking, an expansion of the elementary book by the addition of forty or fifty thousand words. Finally, there is the high school manual. This, too, ordinarily follows the beaten path, giving fuller accounts of the same events and characters. To put it bluntly, we do not assume that our children obtain permanent possessions from their study of history in the lower grades. If mathematicians followed the same method, high school texts on algebra and geometry would include the multiplication table and fractions.

There is, of course, a ready answer to the criticism advanced above. It is that teachers have learned from bitter experience how little history their pupils retain as they pass along the regular route. No teacher of history will deny this. Still it is a standing challenge to existing methods of historical instruction. If the study of history cannot be made truly progressive like the study of mathematics, science, and languages, then the historians assume a grave responsibility in adding their subject to the already overloaded curriculum. If the successive historical texts are only enlarged editions of the first text—more facts, more dates, more words—then history deserves most of the sharp criticism which it is receiving from teachers of science, civics, and economics.

In this condition of affairs we find our justification for offering a new high school text in American history. Our first contribution is one of omission. The time-honored stories of exploration and the biographies of heroes are left out. We frankly hold that, if pupils know little or nothing about Columbus, Cortes, Magellan, or Captain John Smith by the time they reach the high school, it is useless to tell the same stories for perhaps the fourth time. It is worse than useless. It is an offense against the teachers of those subjects that are demonstrated to be progressive in character.

In the next place we have omitted all descriptions of battles. Our reasons for this are simple. The strategy of a campaign or of a single battle is a highly technical, and usually a highly controversial, matter about which experts differ widely. In the field of military and naval operations most writers and teachers of history are mere novices. To dispose of Gettysburg or the Wilderness in ten lines or ten pages is equally absurd to the serious student of military affairs. Any one who compares the ordinary textbook account of a single Civil War campaign with the account given by Ropes, for instance, will ask for no further comment. No youth called upon to serve our country in arms would think of turning to a high school manual for information about the art of warfare. The dramatic scene or episode, so useful in arousing the interest of the immature pupil, seems out of place in a book that deliberately appeals to boys and girls on the very threshold of life's serious responsibilities.

It is not upon negative features, however, that we rest our case. It is rather upon constructive features.

First. We have written a topical, not a narrative, history. We have tried to set forth the important aspects, problems, and movements of each period, bringing in the narrative rather by way of illustration.

Second. We have emphasized those historical topics which help to explain how our nation has come to be what it is to-day.

Third. We have dwelt fully upon the social and economic aspects of our history, especially in relation to the politics of each period.

Fourth. We have treated the causes and results of wars, the problems of financing and sustaining armed forces, rather than military strategy. These are the subjects which belong to a history for civilians. These are matters which civilians can understand—matters which they must understand, if they are to play well their part in war and peace.

Fifth. By omitting the period of exploration, we have been able to enlarge the treatment of our own time. We have given special attention to the history of those current questions which must form the subject matter of sound instruction in citizenship.

Sixth. We have borne in mind that America, with all her unique characteristics, is a part of a general civilization. Accordingly we have given diplomacy, foreign affairs, world relations, and the reciprocal influences of nations their appropriate place.

Seventh. We have deliberately aimed at standards of maturity. The study of a mere narrative calls mainly for the use of the memory. We have aimed to stimulate habits of analysis, comparison, association, reflection, and generalization—habits calculated to enlarge as well as inform the mind. We have been at great pains to make our text clear, simple, and direct; but we have earnestly sought to stretch the intellects of our readers—to put them upon their mettle. Most of them will receive the last of their formal instruction in the high school. The world will soon expect maturity from them. Their achievements will depend upon the possession of other powers than memory alone. The effectiveness of their citizenship in our republic will be measured by the excellence of their judgment as well as the fullness of their information.

C.A.B.
M.R.B.

NEW YORK CITY,
February 8, 1921.

PART I. THE COLONIAL PERIOD

CHAPTER I

THE GREAT MIGRATION TO AMERICA

The tide of migration that set in toward the shores of North America during the early years of the seventeenth century was but one phase in the restless and eternal movement of mankind upon the surface of the earth. The ancient Greeks flung out their colonies in every direction, westward as far as Gaul, across the Mediterranean, and eastward into Asia Minor, perhaps to the very confines of India. The Romans, supported by their armies and their government, spread their dominion beyond the narrow lands of Italy until it stretched from the heather of Scotland to the sands of Arabia. The Teutonic tribes, from their home beyond the Danube and the Rhine, poured into the empire of the Cæsars and made the beginnings of modern Europe. Of this great sweep of races and empires the settlement of America was merely a part. And it was, moreover, only one aspect of the expansion which finally carried the peoples, the institutions, and the trade of Europe to the very ends of the earth.

In one vital point, it must be noted, American colonization differed from that of the ancients. The Greeks usually carried with them affection for the government they left behind and sacred fire from the altar of the parent city; but thousands of the immigrants who came to America disliked the state and disowned the church of the mother country. They established compacts of government for themselves and set up altars of their own. They sought not only new soil to till but also political and religious liberty for themselves and their children.

THE AGENCIES OF AMERICAN COLONIZATION

It was no light matter for the English to cross three thousand miles of water and found homes in the American wilderness at the opening of the seventeenth century. Ships, tools, and supplies called for huge outlays of money. Stores had to be furnished in quantities sufficient to sustain the life of the settlers until they could gather harvests of their own. Artisans and laborers of skill and industry had to be induced to risk the hazards of the new world. Soldiers were required for defense and mariners for the exploration of inland waters. Leaders of good judgment, adept in managing men, had to be discovered. Altogether such an enterprise demanded capital larger than the ordinary merchant or gentleman could amass and involved risks more imminent than he dared to assume. Though in later days, after initial tests had been made, wealthy proprietors were able to establish colonies on their own account, it was the corporation that furnished the capital and leadership in the beginning.

The Trading Company.—English pioneers in exploration found an instrument for colonization in companies of merchant adventurers, which had long been employed in carrying on commerce with foreign countries. Such a corporation was composed of many persons of different ranks of society—noblemen, merchants, and gentlemen—who banded together for a particular undertaking, each contributing a sum of money and sharing in the profits of the venture. It was organized under royal authority; it received its charter, its grant of land, and its trading privileges from the king and carried on its operations under his supervision and control. The charter named all the persons originally included in the corporation and gave them certain powers in the management of its affairs, including the right to admit new members. The company was in fact a little government set up by the king. When the members of the corporation remained in England, as in the case of the Virginia Company, they operated through agents sent to the colony. When they came over the seas themselves and settled in America, as in the case of Massachusetts, they became the direct government of the country they possessed. The stockholders in that instance became the voters and the governor, the chief magistrate.

Four of the thirteen colonies in America owed their origins to the trading corporation. It was the London Company, created by King James I, in 1606, that laid during the following year the foundations of Virginia at Jamestown. It was under the auspices of their West India Company, chartered in 1621, that the Dutch planted the settlements of the New Netherland in the valley of the Hudson. The founders of Massachusetts were Puritan leaders and men of affairs whom King Charles I incorporated in 1629 under the title: "The governor and company of the Massachusetts Bay in New England." In this case the law did but incorporate a group drawn together by religious ties. "We must be knit together as one man," wrote John Winthrop, the first Puritan governor in America. Far to the south, on the banks of the Delaware River, a Swedish commercial company in 1638 made the beginnings of a settlement, christened New Sweden; it was destined to pass under the rule of the Dutch, and finally under the rule of William Penn as the proprietary colony of Delaware.

In a certain sense, Georgia may be included among the "company colonies." It was, however, originally conceived by the moving spirit, James Oglethorpe, as an asylum for poor men, especially those imprisoned for debt. To realize this humane purpose, he secured from King George II, in 1732, a royal charter uniting several gentlemen, including himself, into "one body politic and corporate," known as the "Trustees for establishing the colony of Georgia in America." In the structure of their organization and their methods of government, the trustees did not differ materially from the regular companies created for trade and colonization. Though their purposes were benevolent, their transactions had to be under the forms of law and according to the rules of business.

The Religious Congregation.—A second agency which figured largely in the settlement of America was the religious brotherhood, or congregation, of men and women brought together in the bonds of a common religious faith. By one of the strange fortunes of history, this institution, founded in the early days of Christianity, proved to be a potent force in the origin and growth of self-government in a land far away from Galilee. "And the multitude of them that believed were of one heart and of one soul," we are told in the Acts describing the Church at Jerusalem. "We are knit together as a body in a most sacred covenant of the Lord ... by virtue of which we hold ourselves strictly tied to all care of each other's good and of the whole," wrote John Robinson, a leader among the Pilgrims who founded their tiny colony of Plymouth in 1620. The Mayflower Compact, so famous in American history, was but a written and signed agreement, incorporating the spirit of obedience to the common good, which served as a guide to self-government until Plymouth was annexed to Massachusetts in 1691.

Three other colonies, all of which retained their identity until the eve of the American Revolution, likewise sprang directly from the congregations of the faithful: Rhode Island, Connecticut, and New Hampshire, mainly offshoots from Massachusetts. They were founded by small bodies of men and women, "united in solemn covenants with the Lord," who planted their settlements in the wilderness. Not until many a year after Roger Williams and Anne Hutchinson conducted their followers to the Narragansett country was Rhode Island granted a charter of incorporation (1663) by the crown. Not until long after the congregation of Thomas Hooker from Newtown blazed the way into the Connecticut River Valley did the king of England give Connecticut a charter of its own (1662) and a place among the colonies. Half a century elapsed before the towns laid out beyond the Merrimac River by emigrants from Massachusetts were formed into the royal province of New Hampshire in 1679.

Even when Connecticut was chartered, the parchment and sealing wax of the royal lawyers did but confirm rights and habits of self-government and obedience to law previously established by the congregations. The towns of Hartford, Windsor, and Wethersfield had long lived happily under their "Fundamental Orders" drawn up by themselves in 1639; so had the settlers dwelt peacefully at New Haven under their "Fundamental Articles" drafted in the same year. The pioneers on the Connecticut shore had no difficulty in agreeing that "the Scriptures do hold forth a perfect rule for the direction and government of all men."

The Proprietor.—A third and very important colonial agency was the proprietor, or proprietary. As the name, associated with the word "property," implies, the proprietor was a person to whom the king granted property in lands in North America to have, hold, use, and enjoy for his own benefit and profit, with the right to hand the estate down to his heirs in perpetual succession. The proprietor was a rich and powerful person, prepared to furnish or secure the capital, collect the ships, supply the stores, and assemble the settlers necessary to found and sustain a plantation beyond the seas. Sometimes the proprietor worked alone. Sometimes two or more were associated like partners in the common undertaking.

Five colonies, Maryland, Pennsylvania, New Jersey, and the Carolinas, owe their formal origins, though not always their first settlements, nor in most cases their prosperity, to the proprietary system. Maryland, established in 1634 under a Catholic nobleman, Lord Baltimore, and blessed with religious toleration by the act of 1649, flourished under the mild rule of proprietors until it became a state in the American union. New Jersey, beginning its career under two proprietors, Berkeley and Carteret, in 1664, passed under the direct government of the crown in 1702. Pennsylvania was, in a very large measure, the product of the generous spirit and tireless labors of its first proprietor, the leader of the Friends, William Penn, to whom it was granted in 1681 and in whose family it remained until 1776. The two Carolinas were first organized as one colony in 1663 under the government and patronage of eight proprietors, including Lord Clarendon; but after more than half a century both became royal provinces governed by the king.

THE COLONIAL PEOPLES

The English.—In leadership and origin the thirteen colonies, except New York and Delaware, were English. During the early days of all, save these two, the main, if not the sole, current of immigration was from England. The colonists came from every walk of life. They were men, women, and children of "all sorts and conditions." The major portion were yeomen, or small land owners, farm laborers, and artisans. With them were merchants and gentlemen who brought their stocks of goods or their fortunes to the New World. Scholars came from Oxford and Cambridge to preach the gospel or to teach. Now and then the son of an English nobleman left his baronial hall behind and cast his lot with America. The people represented every religious faith—members of the Established Church of England; Puritans who had labored to reform that church; Separatists, Baptists, and Friends, who had left it altogether; and Catholics, who clung to the religion of their fathers.

New England was almost purely English. During the years between 1629 and 1640, the period of arbitrary Stuart government, about twenty thousand Puritans emigrated to America, settling in the colonies of the far North. Although minor additions were made from time to time, the greater portion of the New England people sprang from this original stock. Virginia, too, for a long time drew nearly all her immigrants from England alone. Not until the eve of the Revolution did other nationalities, mainly the Scotch-Irish and Germans, rival the English in numbers.

The populations of later English colonies—the Carolinas, New York, Pennsylvania, and Georgia—while receiving a steady stream of immigration from England, were constantly augmented by wanderers from the older settlements. New York was invaded by Puritans from New England in such numbers as to cause the Anglican clergymen there to lament that "free thinking spreads almost as fast as the Church." North Carolina was first settled toward the northern border by immigrants from Virginia. Some of the North Carolinians, particularly the Quakers, came all the way from New England, tarrying in Virginia only long enough to learn how little they were wanted in that Anglican colony.

The Scotch-Irish.—Next to the English in numbers and influence were the Scotch-Irish, Presbyterians in belief, English in tongue. Both religious and economic reasons sent them across the sea. Their Scotch ancestors, in the days of Cromwell, had settled in the north of Ireland whence the native Irish had been driven by the conqueror's sword. There the Scotch nourished for many years enjoying in peace their own form of religion and growing prosperous in the manufacture of fine linen and woolen cloth. Then the blow fell. Toward the end of the seventeenth century their religious worship was put under the ban and the export of their cloth was forbidden by the English Parliament. Within two decades twenty thousand Scotch-Irish left Ulster alone, for America; and all during the eighteenth century the migration continued to be heavy. Although no exact record was kept, it is reckoned that the Scotch-Irish and the

Scotch who came directly from Scotland, composed one-sixth of the entire American population on the eve of the Revolution.

These newcomers in America made their homes chiefly in New Jersey, Pennsylvania, Maryland, Virginia, and the Carolinas. Coming late upon the scene, they found much of the land immediately upon the seaboard already taken up. For this reason most of them became frontier people settling the interior and upland regions. There they cleared the land, laid out their small farms, and worked as "sturdy yeomen on the soil," hardy, industrious, and independent in spirit, sharing neither the luxuries of the rich planters nor the easy life of the leisurely merchants. To their agriculture they added woolen and linen manufactures, which, flourishing in the supple fingers of their tireless women, made heavy inroads upon the trade of the English merchants in the colonies. Of their labors a poet has sung:

"O, willing hands to toil;Strong natures tuned to the harvest-song and bound to the kindly soil;Bold pioneers for the wilderness, defenders in the field."

The Germans.—Third among the colonists in order of numerical importance were the Germans. From the very beginning, they appeared in colonial records. A number of the artisans and carpenters in the first Jamestown colony were of German descent. Peter Minuit, the famous governor of New Motherland, was a German from Wesel on the Rhine, and Jacob Leisler, leader of a popular uprising against the provincial administration of New York, was a German from Frankfort-on-Main. The wholesale migration of Germans began with the founding of Pennsylvania. Penn was diligent in searching for thrifty farmers to cultivate his lands and he made a special effort to attract peasants from the Rhine country. A great association, known as the Frankfort Company, bought more than twenty thousand acres from him and in 1684 established a center at Germantown for the distribution of German immigrants. In old New York, Rhinebeck-on-the-Hudson became a similar center for distribution. All the way from Maine to Georgia inducements were offered to the German farmers and in nearly every colony were to be found, in time, German settlements. In fact the migration became so large that German princes were frightened at the loss of so many subjects and England was alarmed by the influx of foreigners into her overseas dominions. Yet nothing could stop the movement. By the end of the colonial period, the number of Germans had risen to more than two hundred thousand.

The majority of them were Protestants from the Rhine region, and South Germany. Wars, religious controversies, oppression, and poverty drove them forth to America. Though most of them were farmers, there were also among them skilled artisans who contributed to the rapid growth of industries in Pennsylvania. Their iron, glass, paper, and woolen mills, dotted here and there among the thickly settled regions, added to the wealth and independence of the province.

Unlike the Scotch-Irish, the Germans did not speak the language of the original colonists or mingle freely with them. They kept to themselves, built their own schools, founded their own newspapers, and published their own books. Their clannish habits often irritated their neighbors and led to occasional agitations against "foreigners." However, no serious collisions seem to have occurred; and in the days of the Revolution, German soldiers from Pennsylvania fought in the patriot armies side by side with soldiers from the English and Scotch-Irish sections.

Other Nationalities.—Though the English, the Scotch-Irish, and the Germans made up the bulk of the colonial population, there were other racial strains as well, varying in numerical importance but contributing their share to colonial life.

From France came the Huguenots fleeing from the decree of the king which inflicted terrible penalties upon Protestants.

From "Old Ireland" came thousands of native Irish, Celtic in race and Catholic in religion. Like their Scotch-Irish neighbors to the north, they revered neither the government nor the church of England imposed upon them by the sword. How many came we do not know, but shipping records of the colonial period show that boatload after boatload left the southern and eastern shores of Ireland for the New

World. Undoubtedly thousands of their passengers were Irish of the native stock. This surmise is well sustained by the constant appearance of Celtic names in the records of various colonies.

The Jews, then as ever engaged in their age-long battle for religious and economic toleration, found in the American colonies, not complete liberty, but certainly more freedom than they enjoyed in England, France, Spain, or Portugal. The English law did not actually recognize their right to live in any of the dominions, but owing to the easy-going habits of the Americans they were allowed to filter into the seaboard towns. The treatment they received there varied. On one occasion the mayor and council of New York forbade them to sell by retail and on another prohibited the exercise of their religious worship. Newport, Philadelphia, and Charleston were more hospitable, and there large Jewish colonies, consisting principally of merchants and their families, flourished in spite of nominal prohibitions of the law.

Though the small Swedish colony in Delaware was quickly submerged beneath the tide of English migration, the Dutch in New York continued to hold their own for more than a hundred years after the English conquest in 1664. At the end of the colonial period over one-half of the 170,000 inhabitants of the province were descendants of the original Dutch—still distinct enough to give a decided cast to the life and manners of New York. Many of them clung as tenaciously to their mother tongue as they did to their capacious farmhouses or their Dutch ovens; but they were slowly losing their identity as the English pressed in beside them to farm and trade.

The melting pot had begun its historic mission.

THE PROCESS OF COLONIZATION

Considered from one side, colonization, whatever the motives of the emigrants, was an economic matter. It involved the use of capital to pay for their passage, to sustain them on the voyage, and to start them on the way of production. Under this stern economic necessity, Puritans, Scotch-Irish, Germans, and all were alike laid.

Immigrants Who Paid Their Own Way.—Many of the immigrants to America in colonial days were capitalists themselves, in a small or a large way, and paid their own passage. What proportion of the colonists were able to finance their voyage across the sea is a matter of pure conjecture. Undoubtedly a very considerable number could do so, for we can trace the family fortunes of many early settlers. Henry Cabot Lodge is authority for the statement that "the settlers of New England were drawn from the country gentlemen, small farmers, and yeomanry of the mother country.... Many of the emigrants were men of wealth, as the old lists show, and all of them, with few exceptions, were men of property and good standing. They did not belong to the classes from which emigration is usually supplied, for they all had a stake in the country they left behind." Though it would be interesting to know how accurate this statement is or how applicable to the other colonies, no study has as yet been made to gratify that interest. For the present it is an unsolved problem just how many of the colonists were able to bear the cost of their own transfer to the New World.

Indentured Servants.—That at least tens of thousands of immigrants were unable to pay for their passage is established beyond the shadow of a doubt by the shipping records that have come down to us. The great barrier in the way of the poor who wanted to go to America was the cost of the sea voyage. To overcome this difficulty a plan was worked out whereby shipowners and other persons of means furnished the passage money to immigrants in return for their promise, or bond, to work for a term of years to repay the sum advanced. This system was called indentured servitude.

It is probable that the number of bond servants exceeded the original twenty thousand Puritans, the yeomen, the Virginia gentlemen, and the Huguenots combined. All the way down the coast from Massachusetts to Georgia were to be found in the fields, kitchens, and workshops, men, women, and children serving out terms of bondage generally ranging from five to seven years. In the proprietary colonies the proportion of bond servants was very high. The Baltimores, Penns, Carterets, and other promoters anxiously sought for workers of every nationality to till their fields, for land without labor was worth no more than land in the moon. Hence the gates of the proprietary colonies were flung wide open. Every inducement was offered to immigrants in the form of cheap land, and special efforts were made to increase the population by importing servants. In Pennsylvania, it was not uncommon to find a master with fifty bond servants on his estate. It has been estimated that two-thirds of all the immigrants into Pennsylvania between the opening of the eighteenth century and the outbreak of the Revolution were in bondage. In the other Middle colonies the number was doubtless not so large; but it formed a considerable part of the population.

The story of this traffic in white servants is one of the most striking things in the history of labor. Bondmen differed from the serfs of the feudal age in that they were not bound to the soil but to the master. They likewise differed from the negro slaves in that their servitude had a time limit. Still they were subject to many special disabilities. It was, for instance, a common practice to impose on them penalties far heavier than were imposed upon freemen for the same offense. A free citizen of Pennsylvania who indulged in horse racing and gambling was let off with a fine; a white servant guilty of the same unlawful conduct was whipped at the post and fined as well.

The ordinary life of the white servant was also severely restricted. A bondman could not marry without his master's consent; nor engage in trade; nor refuse work assigned to him. For an attempt to escape or indeed for any infraction of the law, the term of service was extended. The condition of white bondmen in Virginia, according to Lodge, "was little better than that of slaves. Loose indentures and harsh laws put them at the mercy of their masters." It would not be unfair to add that such was their lot in all other colonies. Their fate depended upon the temper of their masters.

Cruel as was the system in many ways, it gave thousands of people in the Old World a chance to reach the New—an opportunity to wrestle with fate for freedom and a home of their own. When their weary years of servitude were over, if they survived, they might obtain land of their own or settle as free mechanics in the towns. For many a bondman the gamble proved to be a losing venture because he found himself unable to rise out of the state of poverty and dependence into which his servitude carried him. For thousands, on the contrary, bondage proved to be a real avenue to freedom and prosperity. Some of the best citizens of America have the blood of indentured servants in their veins.

The Transported—Involuntary Servitude.—In their anxiety to secure settlers, the companies and proprietors having colonies in America either resorted to or connived at the practice of kidnapping men, women, and children from the streets of English cities. In 1680 it was officially estimated that "ten thousand persons were spirited away" to America. Many of the victims of the practice were young children, for the traffic in them was highly profitable. Orphans and dependents were sometimes disposed of in America by relatives unwilling to support them. In a single year, 1627, about fifteen hundred children were shipped to Virginia.

In this gruesome business there lurked many tragedies, and very few romances. Parents were separated from their children and husbands from their wives. Hundreds of skilled artisans—carpenters, smiths, and weavers—utterly disappeared as if swallowed up by death. A few thus dragged off to the New World to be sold into servitude for a term of five or seven years later became prosperous and returned home with fortunes. In one case a young man who was forcibly carried over the sea lived to make his way back to England and establish his claim to a peerage.

Akin to the kidnapped, at least in economic position, were convicts deported to the colonies for life in lieu of fines and imprisonment. The Americans protested vigorously but ineffectually against this practice. Indeed, they exaggerated its evils, for many of the "criminals" were only mild offenders against unduly harsh and cruel laws. A peasant caught shooting a rabbit on a lord's estate or a luckless servant girl who purloined a pocket handkerchief was branded as a criminal along with sturdy thieves and incorrigible rascals. Other transported offenders were "political criminals"; that is, persons who criticized or opposed the government. This class included now Irish who revolted against British rule in Ireland; now Cavaliers who championed the king against the Puritan revolutionists; Puritans, in turn, dispatched after the monarchy was restored; and Scotch and English subjects in general who joined in political uprisings against the king.

The African Slaves.—Rivaling in numbers, in the course of time, the indentured servants and whites carried to America against their will were the African negroes brought to America and sold into slavery. When this form of bondage was first introduced into Virginia in 1619, it was looked upon as a temporary necessity to be discarded with the increase of the white population. Moreover it does not appear that those planters who first bought negroes at the auction block intended to establish a system of permanent bondage. Only by a slow process did chattel slavery take firm root and become recognized as the leading source of the labor supply. In 1650, thirty years after the introduction of slavery, there were only three hundred Africans in Virginia.

The great increase in later years was due in no small measure to the inordinate zeal for profits that seized slave traders both in Old and in New England. Finding it relatively easy to secure negroes in Africa, they crowded the Southern ports with their vessels. The English Royal African Company sent to America annually between 1713 and 1743 from five to ten thousand slaves. The ship owners of New England were not far behind their English brethren in pushing this extraordinary traffic.

As the proportion of the negroes to the free white population steadily rose, and as whole sections were overrun with slaves and slave traders, the Southern colonies grew alarmed. In 1710, Virginia sought to curtail the importation by placing a duty of £5 on each slave. This effort was futile, for the royal governor promptly vetoed it. From time to time similar bills were passed, only to meet with royal disapproval. South Carolina, in 1760, absolutely prohibited importation; but the measure was killed by the British crown. As late as 1772, Virginia, not daunted by a century of rebuffs, sent to George III a petition in this vein: "The importation of slaves into the colonies from the coast of Africa hath long been considered as a trade of great inhumanity and under its present encouragement, we have too much reason to fear, will endanger the very existence of Your Majesty's American dominions.... Deeply impressed with these sentiments, we most humbly beseech Your Majesty to remove all those restraints on Your Majesty's governors of this colony which inhibit their assenting to such laws as might check so very pernicious a commerce."

All such protests were without avail. The negro population grew by leaps and bounds, until on the eve of the Revolution it amounted to more than half a million. In five states—Maryland, Virginia, the two Carolinas, and Georgia—the slaves nearly equalled or actually exceeded the whites in number. In South Carolina they formed almost two-thirds of the population. Even in the Middle colonies of Delaware and Pennsylvania about one-fifth of the inhabitants were from Africa. To the North, the proportion of slaves steadily diminished although chattel servitude was on the same legal footing as in the South. In New York approximately one in six and in New England one in fifty were negroes, including a few freedmen.

The climate, the soil, the commerce, and the industry of the North were all unfavorable to the growth of a servile population. Still, slavery, though sectional, was a part of the national system of economy. Northern ships carried slaves to the Southern colonies and the produce of the plantations to Europe. "If the Northern states will consult their interest, they will not oppose the increase in slaves which will increase the commodities of which they will become the carriers," said John Rutledge, of South Carolina, in the convention which framed the Constitution of the United States. "What enriches a part enriches the whole and the states are the best judges of their particular interest," responded Oliver Ellsworth, the distinguished spokesman of Connecticut.

References

E. Charming, *History of the United States*, Vols. I and II.
J.A. Doyle, *The English Colonies in America* (5 vols.).
J. Fiske, *Old Virginia and Her Neighbors* (2 vols.).
A.B. Faust, *The German Element in the United States* (2 vols.).
H.J. Ford, *The Scotch-Irish in America*.

L. Tyler, *England in America* (American Nation Series).
R. Usher, *The Pilgrims and Their History*.

Questions

1. America has been called a nation of immigrants. Explain why.

2. Why were individuals unable to go alone to America in the beginning? What agencies made colonization possible? Discuss each of them.

3. Make a table of the colonies, showing the methods employed in their settlement.

4. Why were capital and leadership so very important in early colonization?

5. What is meant by the "melting pot"? What nationalities were represented among the early colonists?

6. Compare the way immigrants come to-day with the way they came in colonial times.

7. Contrast indentured servitude with slavery and serfdom.

8. Account for the anxiety of companies and proprietors to secure colonists.

9. What forces favored the heavy importation of slaves?

10. In what way did the North derive advantages from slavery?

Research Topics

The Chartered Company.—Compare the first and third charters of Virginia in Macdonald, *Documentary Source Book of American History*, 1606-1898, pp. 1-14. Analyze the first and second Massachusetts charters in Macdonald, pp. 22-84. Special reference: W.A.S. Hewins, *English Trading Companies*.

Congregations and Compacts for Self-government.—A study of the Mayflower Compact, the Fundamental Orders of Connecticut and the Fundamental Articles of New Haven in Macdonald, pp. 19, 36, 39. Reference: Charles Borgeaud, *Rise of Modern Democracy*, and C.S. Lobingier, *The People's Law*, Chaps. I-VII.

The Proprietary System.—Analysis of Penn's charter of 1681, in Macdonald, p. 80. Reference: Lodge, *Short History of the English Colonies in America*, p. 211.

Studies of Individual Colonies.—Review of outstanding events in history of each colony, using Elson, *History of the United States*, pp. 55-159, as the basis.

Biographical Studies.—John Smith, John Winthrop, William Penn, Lord Baltimore, William Bradford, Roger Williams, Anne Hutchinson, Thomas Hooker, and Peter Stuyvesant, using any good encyclopedia.

Indentured Servitude.—In Virginia, Lodge, *Short History*, pp. 69-72; in Pennsylvania, pp. 242-244. Contemporary account in Callender, *Economic History of the United States*, pp. 44-51. Special reference: Karl Geiser, *Redemptioners and Indentured Servants* (Yale Review, X, No. 2 Supplement).

Slavery.—In Virginia, Lodge, *Short History*, pp. 67-69; in the Northern colonies, pp. 241, 275, 322, 408, 442.

The People of the Colonies.—Virginia, Lodge, *Short History*, pp. 67-73; New England, pp. 406-409, 441-450; Pennsylvania, pp. 227-229, 240-250; New York, pp. 312-313, 322-335.

CHAPTER II

COLONIAL AGRICULTURE, INDUSTRY, AND COMMERCE

THE LAND AND THE WESTWARD MOVEMENT

The Significance of Land Tenure.—The way in which land may be acquired, held, divided among heirs, and bought and sold exercises a deep influence on the life and culture of a people. The feudal and aristocratic societies of Europe were founded on a system of landlordism which was characterized by two distinct features. In the first place, the land was nearly all held in great estates, each owned by a single proprietor. In the second place, every estate was kept intact under the law of primogeniture, which at the death of a lord transferred all his landed property to his eldest son. This prevented the subdivision of estates and the growth of a large body of small farmers or freeholders owning their own land. It made a form of tenantry or servitude inevitable for the mass of those who labored on the land. It also enabled the landlords to maintain themselves in power as a governing class and kept the tenants and laborers subject to their economic and political control. If land tenure was so significant in Europe, it was equally important in the development of America, where practically all the first immigrants were forced by circumstances to derive their livelihood from the soil.

Experiments in Common Tillage.—In the New World, with its broad extent of land awaiting the white man's plow, it was impossible to introduce in its entirety and over the whole area the system of lords and tenants that existed across the sea. So it happened that almost every kind of experiment in land tenure, from communism to feudalism, was tried. In the early days of the Jamestown colony, the land, though owned by the London Company, was tilled in common by the settlers. No man had a separate plot of his own. The motto of the community was: "Labor and share alike." All were supposed to work in the fields and receive an equal share of the produce. At Plymouth, the Pilgrims attempted a similar experiment, laying out the fields in common and distributing the joint produce of their labor with rough equality among the workers.

In both colonies the communistic experiments were failures. Angry at the lazy men in Jamestown who idled their time away and yet expected regular meals, Captain John Smith issued a manifesto: "Everyone that gathereth not every day as much as I do, the next day shall be set beyond the river and forever banished from the fort and live there or starve." Even this terrible threat did not bring a change in production. Not until each man was given a plot of his own to till, not until each gathered the fruits of his own labor, did the colony prosper. In Plymouth, where the communal experiment lasted for five years, the results were similar to those in Virginia, and the system was given up for one of separate fields in which every person could "set corn for his own particular." Some other New England towns, refusing to profit by the experience of their Plymouth neighbor, also made excursions into common ownership and labor, only to abandon the idea and go in for individual ownership of the land. "By degrees it was seen that even the Lord's people could not carry the complicated communist legislation into perfect and wholesome practice."

Feudal Elements in the Colonies—Quit Rents, Manors, and Plantations.—At the other end of the scale were the feudal elements of land tenure found in the proprietary colonies, in the seaboard regions of the South, and to some extent in New York. The proprietor was in fact a powerful feudal lord, owning land granted to him by royal charter. He could retain any part of it for his personal use or dispose of it all in large or small lots. While he generally kept for himself an estate of baronial proportions, it was impossible for him to manage directly any considerable part of the land in his dominion. Consequently he either sold it in parcels for lump sums or granted it to individuals on condition that they make to him an annual payment in money, known as "quit rent." In Maryland, the proprietor sometimes collected as high as £9000 (equal to about $500,000 to-day) in a single year from this source. In Pennsylvania, the quit rents brought a handsome annual tribute into the exchequer of the Penn family. In the royal provinces, the king of England claimed all revenues collected in this form from the land, a sum amounting to £19,000 at the time of the Revolution. The quit rent,—"really a feudal payment from freeholders,"—was thus a material source of income for the crown as well as for the proprietors. Wherever it was laid, however, it proved to be a burden, a source of constant irritation; and it became a formidable item in the long list of grievances which led to the American Revolution.

Something still more like the feudal system of the Old World appeared in the numerous manors or the huge landed estates granted by the crown, the companies, or the proprietors. In the colony of Maryland alone there were sixty manors of three thousand acres each, owned by wealthy men and tilled by tenants holding small plots under certain restrictions of tenure. In New York also there were many manors of wide extent, most of which originated in the days of the Dutch West India Company, when extensive concessions were made to patroons to induce them to bring over settlers. The Van Rensselaer, the Van Cortlandt, and the Livingston manors were so large and populous that each was entitled to send a representative to the provincial legislature. The tenants on the New York manors were in somewhat the same position as serfs on old European estates. They were bound to pay the owner a rent in money and kind; they ground their grain at his mill; and they were subject to his judicial power because he held court and meted out justice, in some instances extending to capital punishment.

The manors of New York or Maryland were, however, of slight consequence as compared with the vast plantations of the Southern seaboard—huge estates, far wider in expanse than many a European barony and tilled by slaves more servile than any feudal tenants. It must not be forgotten that this system of land tenure became the dominant feature of a large section and gave a decided bent to the economic and political life of America.

The Small Freehold.—In the upland regions of the South, however, and throughout most of the North, the drift was against all forms of servitude and tenantry and in the direction of the freehold; that is, the small farm owned outright and tilled by the possessor and his family. This was favored by natural circumstances and the spirit of the immigrants. For one thing, the abundance of land and the scarcity of labor made it impossible for the companies, the proprietors, or the crown to develop over the whole continent a network of vast estates. In many sections, particularly in New England, the climate, the stony soil, the hills, and the narrow valleys conspired to keep the farms within a moderate compass. For another thing, the English, Scotch-Irish, and German peasants, even if they had been tenants in the Old World, did not propose to accept permanent dependency of any kind in the New. If they could not get freeholds, they would not settle at all; thus they forced proprietors and companies to bid for their enterprise by selling land in small lots. So it happened that the freehold of modest proportions became the cherished unit of American farmers. The people who tilled the farms were drawn from every quarter of western Europe; but the freehold system gave a uniform cast to their economic and social life in America.

Social Effects of Land Tenure.—Land tenure and the process of western settlement thus developed two distinct types of people engaged in the same pursuit—agriculture. They had a common tie in that they both cultivated the soil and possessed the local interest and independence which arise from that occupation. Their methods and their culture, however, differed widely.

The Southern planter, on his broad acres tilled by slaves, resembled the English landlord on his estates more than he did the colonial farmer who labored with his own hands in the fields and forests. He sold his rice and tobacco in large amounts directly to English factors, who took his entire crop in exchange for goods and cash. His fine clothes, silverware, china, and cutlery he bought in English markets. Loving the ripe old culture of the mother country, he often sent his sons to Oxford or Cambridge for their education. In short, he depended very largely for his prosperity and his enjoyment of life upon close relations with the Old World. He did not even need market towns in which to buy native goods, for they were made on his own plantation by his own artisans who were usually gifted slaves.

The economic condition of the small farmer was totally different. His crops were not big enough to warrant direct connection with English factors or the personal maintenance of a corps of artisans. He needed local markets, and they sprang up to meet the need. Smiths, hatters, weavers, wagon-makers, and potters at neighboring towns supplied him with the rough products of their native skill. The finer goods, bought by the rich planter in England, the small farmer ordinarily could not buy. His wants were restricted to staples like tea and sugar, and between him and the European market stood the merchant. His community was therefore more self-sufficient than the seaboard line of great plantations. It was more isolated, more provincial, more independent, more American. The planter faced the Old East. The farmer faced the New West.

The Westward Movement.—Yeoman and planter nevertheless were alike in one respect. Their land hunger was never appeased. Each had the eye of an expert for new and fertile soil; and so, north and south, as soon as a foothold was secured on the Atlantic coast, the current of migration set in westward, creeping through forests, across rivers, and over mountains. Many of the later immigrants, in their search for cheap lands, were compelled to go to the border; but in a large part the path breakers to the West were native Americans of the second and third generations. Explorers, fired by curiosity and the lure of the mysterious unknown, and hunters, fur traders, and squatters, following their own sweet wills, blazed the trail, opening paths and sending back stories of the new regions they traversed. Then came the regular settlers with lawful titles to the lands they had purchased, sometimes singly and sometimes in companies.

In Massachusetts, the westward movement is recorded in the founding of Springfield in 1636 and Great Barrington in 1725. By the opening of the eighteenth century the pioneers of Connecticut had pushed north and west until their outpost towns adjoined the Hudson Valley settlements. In New York, the inland movement was directed by the Hudson River to Albany, and from that old Dutch center it radiated in every direction, particularly westward through the Mohawk Valley. New Jersey was early filled to its borders, the beginnings of the present city of New Brunswick being made in 1681 and those of Trenton in 1685. In Pennsylvania, as in New York, the waterways determined the main lines of advance. Pioneers, pushing up through the valley of the Schuylkill, spread over the fertile lands of Berks and Lancaster counties, laying out Reading in 1748. Another current of migration was directed by the Susquehanna, and, in 1726, the first farmhouse was built on the bank where Harrisburg was later founded. Along the southern tier of counties a thin line of settlements stretched westward to Pittsburgh, reaching the upper waters of the Ohio while the colony was still under the Penn family.

In the South the westward march was equally swift. The seaboard was quickly occupied by large planters and their slaves engaged in the cultivation of tobacco and rice. The Piedmont Plateau, lying back from the coast all the way from Maryland to Georgia, was fed by two streams of migration, one westward from the sea and the other southward from the other colonies—Germans from Pennsylvania and Scotch-Irish furnishing the main supply. "By 1770, tide-water Virginia was full to overflowing and the 'back country' of the Blue Ridge and the Shenandoah was fully occupied. Even the mountain valleys ... were claimed by sturdy pioneers. Before the Declaration of Independence, the oncoming tide of home-seekers had reached the crest of the Alleghanies."

Beyond the mountains pioneers had already ventured, harbingers of an invasion that was about to break in upon Kentucky and Tennessee. As early as 1769 that mighty Nimrod, Daniel Boone, curious to hunt buffaloes, of which he had heard weird reports, passed through the Cumberland Gap and brought back news of a wonderful country awaiting the plow. A hint was sufficient. Singly, in pairs, and in groups, settlers followed the trail he had blazed. A great land corporation, the Transylvania Company, emulating the merchant adventurers of earlier times, secured a huge grant of territory and sought profits in quit rents from lands sold to farmers. By the outbreak of the Revolution there were several hundred people in the Kentucky region. Like the older colonists, they did not relish quit rents, and their opposition wrecked the Transylvania Company. They even carried their protests into the Continental Congress in 1776, for by that time they were our "embryo fourteenth colony."

INDUSTRIAL AND COMMERCIAL DEVELOPMENT

Though the labor of the colonists was mainly spent in farming, there was a steady growth in industrial and commercial pursuits. Most of the staple industries of to-day, not omitting iron and textiles, have their beginnings in colonial times. Manufacturing and trade soon gave rise to towns which enjoyed an importance all out of proportion to their numbers. The great centers of commerce and finance on the seaboard originated in the days when the king of England was "lord of these dominions."

Textile Manufacture as a Domestic Industry.—Colonial women, in addition to sharing every hardship of pioneering, often the heavy labor of the open field, developed in the course of time a national industry which was almost exclusively their own. Wool and flax were raised in abundance in the North and South. "Every farm house," says Coman, the economic historian, "was a workshop where the women spun and wove the serges, kerseys, and linsey-woolseys which served for the common wear." By the close of the seventeenth century, New England manufactured cloth in sufficient quantities to export it to the Southern colonies and to the West Indies. As the industry developed, mills were erected for the more difficult process of dyeing, weaving, and fulling, but carding and spinning continued to be done in the home. The Dutch of New Netherland, the Swedes of Delaware, and the Scotch-Irish of the interior "were not one whit behind their Yankee neighbors."

The importance of this enterprise to British economic life can hardly be overestimated. For many a century the English had employed their fine woolen cloth as the chief staple in a lucrative foreign trade, and the government had come to look upon it as an object of special interest and protection. When the colonies were established, both merchants and statesmen naturally expected to maintain a monopoly of increasing value; but before long the Americans, instead of buying cloth, especially of the coarser varieties, were making it to sell. In the place of customers, here were rivals. In the place of helpless reliance upon English markets, here was the germ of economic independence.

If British merchants had not discovered it in the ordinary course of trade, observant officers in the provinces would have conveyed the news to them. Even in the early years of the eighteenth century the royal governor of New York wrote of the industrious Americans to his home government: "The consequence will be that if they can clothe themselves once, not only comfortably, but handsomely too, without the help of England, they who already are not very fond of submitting to government will soon think of putting in execution designs they have long harboured in their breasts. This will not seem strange when you consider what sort of people this country is inhabited by."

The Iron Industry.—Almost equally widespread was the art of iron working—one of the earliest and most picturesque of colonial industries. Lynn, Massachusetts, had a forge and skilled artisans within fifteen years after the founding of Boston. The smelting of iron began at New London and New Haven about 1658; in Litchfield county, Connecticut, a few years later; at Great Barrington, Massachusetts, in 1731; and near by at Lenox some thirty years after that. New Jersey had iron works at Shrewsbury within ten years after the founding of the colony in 1665. Iron forges appeared in the valleys of the Delaware and the Susquehanna early in the following century, and iron masters then laid the foundations of fortunes in a region destined to become one of the great iron centers of the world. Virginia began iron working in the year that saw the introduction of slavery. Although the industry soon lapsed, it was renewed and flourished in the eighteenth century. Governor Spotswood was called the "Tubal Cain" of the Old Dominion because he placed the industry on a firm foundation. Indeed it seems that every colony, except Georgia, had its iron foundry. Nails, wire, metallic ware, chains, anchors, bar and pig iron were made in large quantities; and Great Britain, by an act in 1750, encouraged the colonists to export rough iron to the British Islands.

Shipbuilding.—Of all the specialized industries in the colonies, shipbuilding was the most important. The abundance of fir for masts, oak for timbers and boards, pitch for tar and turpentine, and hemp for rope made the way of the shipbuilder easy. Early in the seventeenth century a ship was built at New Amsterdam, and by the middle of that century shipyards were scattered along the New England coast at Newburyport, Salem, New Bedford, Newport, Providence, New London, and New Haven. Yards at Albany and Poughkeepsie in New York built ships for the trade of that colony with England and the Indies. Wilmington and Philadelphia soon entered the race and outdistanced New York, though unable to equal the pace set by New England. While Maryland, Virginia, and South Carolina also built ships, Southern interest was mainly confined to the lucrative business of producing ship materials: fir, cedar, hemp, and tar.

Fishing.—The greatest single economic resource of New England outside of agriculture was the fisheries. This industry, started by hardy sailors from Europe, long before the landing of the Pilgrims, flourished under the indomitable seamanship of the Puritans, who labored with the net and the harpoon in almost every quarter of the Atlantic. "Look," exclaimed Edmund Burke, in the House of Commons, "at the manner in which the people of New England have of late carried on the whale fishery. Whilst we follow them among the tumbling mountains of ice and behold them penetrating into the deepest frozen recesses of Hudson's Bay and Davis's Straits, while we are looking for them beneath the arctic circle, we hear that they have pierced into the opposite region of polar cold, that they are at the antipodes and engaged under the frozen serpent of the south.... Nor is the equinoctial heat more discouraging to them than the accumulated winter of both poles. We know that, whilst some of them draw the line and strike the harpoon on the coast of Africa, others run the longitude and pursue their gigantic game along the coast of Brazil. No sea but what is vexed by their fisheries. No climate that is not witness to their toils. Neither the perseverance of Holland nor the activity of France nor the dexterous and firm sagacity of English enterprise ever carried this most perilous mode of hard industry to the extent to which it has been pushed by this recent people."

The influence of the business was widespread. A large and lucrative European trade was built upon it. The better quality of the fish caught for food was sold in the markets of Spain, Portugal, and Italy, or exchanged for salt, lemons, and raisins for the American market. The lower grades of fish were carried to the West Indies for slave consumption, and in part traded for sugar and molasses, which furnished the raw materials for the thriving rum industry of New England. These activities, in turn, stimulated shipbuilding, steadily enlarging the demand for fishing and merchant craft of every kind and thus keeping the shipwrights, calkers, rope makers, and other artisans of the seaport towns rushed with work. They also increased trade with the mother country for, out of the cash collected in the fish markets of Europe and the West Indies, the colonists paid for English manufactures. So an ever-widening circle of American enterprise centered around this single industry, the nursery of seamanship and the maritime spirit.

Oceanic Commerce and American Merchants.—All through the eighteenth century, the commerce of the American colonies spread in every direction until it rivaled in the number of people employed, the capital engaged, and the profits gleaned, the commerce of European nations. A modern historian has said: "The enterprising merchants of New England developed a network of trade routes that covered well-nigh half the world." This commerce, destined to be of such significance in the conflict with the mother country, presented, broadly speaking, two aspects.

On the one side, it involved the export of raw materials and agricultural produce. The Southern colonies produced for shipping, tobacco, rice, tar, pitch, and pine; the Middle colonies, grain, flour, furs, lumber, and salt pork; New England, fish, flour, rum, furs, shoes, and small articles of manufacture. The variety of products was in fact astounding. A sarcastic writer, while sneering at the idea of an American union, once remarked of colonial trade: "What sort of dish will you make? New England will throw in fish and onions. The middle states, flax-seed and flour. Maryland and Virginia will add tobacco. North Carolina, pitch, tar, and turpentine. South Carolina, rice and indigo, and Georgia will sprinkle the whole composition with sawdust. Such an absurd jumble will you make if you attempt to form a union among such discordant materials as the thirteen British provinces."

On the other side, American commerce involved the import trade, consisting principally of English and continental manufactures, tea, and "India goods." Sugar and molasses, brought from the West Indies, supplied the flourishing distilleries of Massachusetts, Rhode Island, and Connecticut. The carriage of slaves from Africa to the Southern colonies engaged hundreds of New England's sailors and thousands of pounds of her capital.

The disposition of imported goods in the colonies, though in part controlled by English factors located in America, employed also a large and important body of American merchants like the Willings and Morrises of Philadelphia; the Amorys, Hancocks, and Faneuils of Boston; and the Livingstons and Lows of New York. In their zeal and enterprise, they were worthy rivals of their English competitors, so celebrated for world-wide commercial operations. Though fully aware of the advantages they enjoyed in

British markets and under the protection of the British navy, the American merchants were high-spirited and mettlesome, ready to contend with royal officers in order to shield American interests against outside interference.

Measured against the immense business of modern times, colonial commerce seems perhaps trivial. That, however, is not the test of its significance. It must be considered in relation to the growth of English colonial trade in its entirety—a relation which can be shown by a few startling figures. The whole export trade of England, including that to the colonies, was, in 1704, £6,509,000. On the eve of the American Revolution, namely, in 1772, English exports to the American colonies alone amounted to £6,024,000; in other words, almost as much as the whole foreign business of England two generations before. At the first date, colonial trade was but one-twelfth of the English export business; at the second date, it was considerably more than one-third. In 1704, Pennsylvania bought in English markets goods to the value of £11,459; in 1772 the purchases of the same colony amounted to £507,909. In short, Pennsylvania imports increased fifty times within sixty-eight years, amounting in 1772 to almost the entire export trade of England to the colonies at the opening of the century. The American colonies were indeed a great source of wealth to English merchants.

Intercolonial Commerce.—Although the bad roads of colonial times made overland transportation difficult and costly, the many rivers and harbors along the coast favored a lively waterborne trade among the colonies. The Connecticut, Hudson, Delaware, and Susquehanna rivers in the North and the many smaller rivers in the South made it possible for goods to be brought from, and carried to, the interior regions in little sailing vessels with comparative ease. Sloops laden with manufactures, domestic and foreign, collected at some city like Providence, New York, or Philadelphia, skirted the coasts, visited small ports, and sailed up the navigable rivers to trade with local merchants who had for exchange the raw materials which they had gathered in from neighboring farms. Larger ships carried the grain, live stock, cloth, and hardware of New England to the Southern colonies, where they were traded for tobacco, leather, tar, and ship timber. From the harbors along the Connecticut shores there were frequent sailings down through Long Island Sound to Maryland, Virginia, and the distant Carolinas.

Growth of Towns.—In connection with this thriving trade and industry there grew up along the coast a number of prosperous commercial centers which were soon reckoned among the first commercial towns of the whole British empire, comparing favorably in numbers and wealth with such ports as Liverpool and Bristol. The statistical records of that time are mainly guesses; but we know that Philadelphia stood first in size among these towns. Serving as the port of entry for Pennsylvania, Delaware, and western Jersey, it had drawn within its borders, just before the Revolution, about 25,000 inhabitants. Boston was second in rank, with somewhat more than 20,000 people. New York, the "commercial capital of Connecticut and old East Jersey," was slightly smaller than Boston, but growing at a steady rate. The fourth town in size was Charleston, South Carolina, with about 10,000 inhabitants. Newport in Rhode Island, a center of rum manufacture and shipping, stood fifth, with a population of about 7000. Baltimore and Norfolk were counted as "considerable towns." In the interior, Hartford in Connecticut, Lancaster and York in Pennsylvania, and Albany in New York, with growing populations and increasing trade, gave prophecy of an urban America away from the seaboard. The other towns were straggling villages. Williamsburg, Virginia, for example, had about two hundred houses, in which dwelt a dozen families of the gentry and a few score of tradesmen. Inland county seats often consisted of nothing more than a log courthouse, a prison, and one wretched inn to house judges, lawyers, and litigants during the sessions of the court.

The leading towns exercised an influence on colonial opinion all out of proportion to their population. They were the centers of wealth, for one thing; of the press and political activity, for another. Merchants and artisans could readily take concerted action on public questions arising from their commercial operations. The towns were also centers for news, gossip, religious controversy, and political discussion. In the market places the farmers from the countryside learned of British policies and laws, and so, mingling with the townsmen, were drawn into the main currents of opinion which set in toward colonial nationalism and independence.

References

J. Bishop, *History of American Manufactures* (2 vols.).

E.L. Bogart, *Economic History of the United States*.

P.A. Bruce, *Economic History of Virginia* (2 vols.).

E. Semple, *American History and Its Geographical Conditions*.

W. Weeden, *Economic and Social History of New England*. (2 vols.).

Questions

1. Is land in your community parceled out into small farms? Contrast the system in your community with the feudal system of land tenure.

2. Are any things owned and used in common in your community? Why did common tillage fail in colonial times?

3. Describe the elements akin to feudalism which were introduced in the colonies.

4. Explain the success of freehold tillage.

5. Compare the life of the planter with that of the farmer.

6. How far had the western frontier advanced by 1776?

7. What colonial industry was mainly developed by women? Why was it very important both to the Americans and to the English?

8. What were the centers for iron working? Ship building?

9. Explain how the fisheries affected many branches of trade and industry.

10. Show how American trade formed a vital part of English business.

11. How was interstate commerce mainly carried on?

12. What were the leading towns? Did they compare in importance with British towns of the same period?

Research Topics

Land Tenure.—Coman, *Industrial History* (rev. ed.), pp. 32-38. Special reference: Bruce, *Economic History of Virginia*, Vol. I, Chap. VIII.

Tobacco Planting in Virginia.—Callender, *Economic History of the United States*, pp. 22-28.

Colonial Agriculture.—Coman, pp. 48-63. Callender, pp. 69-74. Reference: J.R.H. Moore, *Industrial History of the American People*, pp. 131-162.

Colonial Manufactures.—Coman, pp. 63-73. Callender, pp. 29-44. Special reference: Weeden, *Economic and Social History of New England*.

Colonial Commerce.—Coman, pp. 73-85. Callender, pp. 51-63, 78-84. Moore, pp. 163-208. Lodge, *Short History of the English Colonies*, pp. 409-412, 229-231, 312-314.

Chapter III

SOCIAL AND POLITICAL PROGRESS

Colonial life, crowded as it was with hard and unremitting toil, left scant leisure for the cultivation of the arts and sciences. There was little money in private purses or public treasuries to be dedicated to schools, libraries, and museums. Few there were with time to read long and widely, and fewer still who could devote their lives to things that delight the eye and the mind. And yet, poor and meager as the intellectual life of the colonists may seem by way of comparison, heroic efforts were made in every community to lift the people above the plane of mere existence. After the first clearings were opened in the forests those efforts were redoubled, and with lengthening years told upon the thought and spirit of the land. The appearance, during the struggle with England, of an extraordinary group of leaders familiar with history, political philosophy, and the arts of war, government, and diplomacy itself bore eloquent testimony to the high quality of the American intellect. No one, not even the most critical, can run through the writings of distinguished Americans scattered from Massachusetts to Georgia—the Adamses, Ellsworth, the Morrises, the Livingstons, Hamilton, Franklin, Washington, Madison, Marshall, Henry, the Randolphs, and the Pinckneys—without coming to the conclusion that there was something in American colonial life which fostered minds of depth and power. Women surmounted even greater difficulties than the men in the process of self-education, and their keen interest in public issues is evident in many a record like the *Letters* of Mrs. John Adams to her husband during the Revolution; the writings of Mrs. Mercy Otis Warren, the sister of James Otis, who measured her pen with the British propagandists; and the patriot newspapers founded and managed by women.

THE LEADERSHIP OF THE CHURCHES

In the intellectual life of America, the churches assumed a rôle of high importance. There were abundant reasons for this. In many of the colonies—Maryland, Pennsylvania, and New England—the religious impulse had been one of the impelling motives in stimulating immigration. In all the colonies, the clergy, at least in the beginning, formed the only class with any leisure to devote to matters of the spirit. They preached on Sundays and taught school on week days. They led in the discussion of local problems and in the formation of political opinion, so much of which was concerned with the relation between church and state. They wrote books and pamphlets. They filled most of the chairs in the colleges; under clerical guidance, intellectual and spiritual, the Americans received their formal education. In several of the provinces the Anglican Church was established by law. In New England the Puritans were supreme, notwithstanding the efforts of the crown to overbear their authority. In the Middle colonies, particularly, the multiplication of sects made the dominance of any single denomination impossible; and in all of them there was a growing diversity of faith, which promised in time a separation of church and state and freedom of opinion.

The Church of England.—Virginia was the stronghold of the English system of church and state. The Anglican faith and worship were prescribed by law, sustained by taxes imposed on all, and favored by the governor, the provincial councilors, and the richest planters. "The Established Church," says Lodge, "was one of the appendages of the Virginia aristocracy. They controlled the vestries and the ministers, and the parish church stood not infrequently on the estate of the planter who built and managed it." As in England, Catholics and Protestant Dissenters were at first laid under heavy disabilities. Only slowly and on sufferance were they admitted to the province; but when once they were even covertly tolerated, they pressed steadily in, until, by the Revolution, they outnumbered the adherents of the established order.

The Church was also sanctioned by law and supported by taxes in the Carolinas after 1704, and in Georgia after that colony passed directly under the crown in 1754—this in spite of the fact that the majority of the inhabitants were Dissenters. Against the protests of the Catholics it was likewise established in Maryland. In New York, too, notwithstanding the resistance of the Dutch, the Established Church was fostered by the provincial officials, and the Anglicans, embracing about one-fifteenth of the population, exerted an influence all out of proportion to their numbers.

Many factors helped to enhance the power of the English Church in the colonies. It was supported by the British government and the official class sent out to the provinces. Its bishops and archbishops in England were appointed by the king, and its faith and service were set forth by acts of Parliament. Having its seat of power in the English monarchy, it could hold its clergy and missionaries loyal to the crown and so counteract to some extent the independent spirit that was growing up in America. The Church, always a strong bulwark of the state, therefore had a political rôle to play here as in England. Able bishops and far-seeing leaders firmly grasped this fact about the middle of the eighteenth century and redoubled their efforts to augment the influence of the Church in provincial affairs. Unhappily for their plans they failed to calculate in advance the effect of their methods upon dissenting Protestants, who still cherished memories of bitter religious conflicts in the mother country.

Puritanism in New England.—If the established faith made for imperial unity, the same could not be said of Puritanism. The Plymouth Pilgrims had cast off all allegiance to the Anglican Church and established a separate and independent congregation before they came to America. The Puritans, essaying at first the task of reformers within the Church, soon after their arrival in Massachusetts, likewise flung off their yoke of union with the Anglicans. In each town a separate congregation was organized, the male members choosing the pastor, the teachers, and the other officers. They also composed the voters in the town meeting, where secular matters were determined. The union of church and government was thus complete, and uniformity of faith and life prescribed by law and enforced by civil authorities; but this worked for local autonomy instead of imperial unity.

The clergy became a powerful class, dominant through their learning and their fearful denunciations of the faithless. They wrote the books for the people to read—the famous Cotton Mather having three hundred and eighty-three books and pamphlets to his credit. In coöperation with the civil officers they enforced a strict observance of the Puritan Sabbath—a day of rest that began at six o'clock on Saturday evening and lasted until sunset on Sunday. All work, all trading, all amusement, and all worldly conversation were absolutely prohibited during those hours. A thoughtless maid servant who for some earthly reason smiled in church was in danger of being banished as a vagabond. Robert Pike, a devout Puritan, thinking the sun had gone to rest, ventured forth on horseback one Sunday evening and was luckless enough to have a ray of light strike him through a rift in the clouds. The next day he was brought into court and fined for "his ungodly conduct." With persons accused of witchcraft the Puritans were still more ruthless. When a mania of persecution swept over Massachusetts in 1692, eighteen people were hanged, one was pressed to death, many suffered imprisonment, and two died in jail.

Just about this time, however, there came a break in the uniformity of Puritan rule. The crown and church in England had long looked upon it with disfavor, and in 1684 King Charles II annulled the old charter of the Massachusetts Bay Company. A new document issued seven years later wrested from the Puritans of the colony the right to elect their own governor and reserved the power of appointment to the king. It also abolished the rule limiting the suffrage to church members, substituting for it a simple property qualification. Thus a royal governor and an official family, certain to be Episcopalian in faith and monarchist in sympathies, were forced upon Massachusetts; and members of all religious denominations, if they had the required amount of property, were permitted to take part in elections. By this act in the name of the crown, the Puritan monopoly was broken down in Massachusetts, and that province was brought into line with Connecticut, Rhode Island, and New Hampshire, where property, not religious faith, was the test for the suffrage.

Growth of Religious Toleration.—Though neither the Anglicans of Virginia nor the Puritans of Massachusetts believed in toleration for other denominations, that principle was strictly applied in Rhode Island. There, under the leadership of Roger Williams, liberty in matters of conscience was established in the beginning. Maryland, by granting in 1649 freedom to those who professed to believe in Jesus Christ, opened its gates to all Christians; and Pennsylvania, true to the tenets of the Friends, gave freedom of conscience to those "who confess and acknowledge the one Almighty and Eternal God to be the creator, upholder, and ruler of the World." By one circumstance or another, the Middle colonies were thus early characterized by diversity rather than uniformity of opinion. Dutch Protestants, Huguenots, Quakers, Baptists, Presbyterians, New Lights, Moravians, Lutherans, Catholics, and other denominations became too strongly intrenched and too widely scattered to permit any one of them to rule, if it had desired to do so. There were communities and indeed whole sections where one or another church prevailed, but in no colony was a legislature steadily controlled by a single group. Toleration encouraged diversity, and diversity, in turn, worked for greater toleration.

The government and faith of the dissenting denominations conspired with economic and political tendencies to draw America away from the English state. Presbyterians, Quakers, Baptists, and Puritans had no hierarchy of bishops and archbishops to bind them to the seat of power in London. Neither did they look to that metropolis for guidance in interpreting articles of faith. Local self-government in matters ecclesiastical helped to train them for local self-government in matters political. The spirit of independence which led Dissenters to revolt in the Old World, nourished as it was amid favorable circumstances in the New World, made them all the more zealous in the defense of every right against authority imposed from without.

SCHOOLS AND COLLEGES

Religion and Local Schools.—One of the first cares of each Protestant denomination was the education of the children in the faith. In this work the Bible became the center of interest. The English version was indeed the one book of the people. Farmers, shopkeepers, and artisans, whose life had once been bounded by the daily routine of labor, found in the Scriptures not only an inspiration to religious conduct, but also a book of romance, travel, and history. "Legend and annal," says John Richard Green, "war-song and psalm, state-roll and biography, the mighty voices of prophets, the parables of Evangelists, stories of mission journeys, of perils by sea and among the heathen, philosophic arguments, apocalyptic visions, all were flung broadcast over minds unoccupied for the most part by any rival learning.... As a mere literary monument, the English version of the Bible remains the noblest example of the English tongue." It was the King James version just from the press that the Pilgrims brought across the sea with them.

For the authority of the Established Church was substituted the authority of the Scriptures. The Puritans devised a catechism based upon their interpretation of the Bible, and, very soon after their arrival in America, they ordered all parents and masters of servants to be diligent in seeing that their children and wards were taught to read religious works and give answers to the religious questions. Massachusetts was scarcely twenty years old before education of this character was declared to be compulsory, and provision was made for public schools where those not taught at home could receive instruction in reading and writing.

Outside of New England the idea of compulsory education was not regarded with the same favor; but the whole land was nevertheless dotted with little schools kept by "dames, itinerant teachers, or local parsons." Whether we turn to the life of Franklin in the North or Washington in the South, we read of tiny schoolhouses, where boys, and sometimes girls, were taught to read and write. Where there were no schools, fathers and mothers of the better kind gave their children the rudiments of learning. Though illiteracy was widespread, there is evidence to show that the diffusion of knowledge among the masses was making steady progress all through the eighteenth century.

Religion and Higher Learning.—Religious motives entered into the establishment of colleges as well as local schools. Harvard, founded in 1636, and Yale, opened in 1718, were intended primarily to train "learned and godly ministers" for the Puritan churches of New England. To the far North, Dartmouth, chartered in 1769, was designed first as a mission to the Indians and then as a college for the sons of New England farmers preparing to preach, teach, or practice law. The College of New

Jersey, organized in 1746 and removed to Princeton eleven years later, was sustained by the Presbyterians. Two colleges looked to the Established Church as their source of inspiration and support: William and Mary, founded in Virginia in 1693, and King's College, now Columbia University, chartered by King George II in 1754, on an appeal from the New York Anglicans, alarmed at the growth of religious dissent and the "republican tendencies" of the age. Two colleges revealed a drift away from sectarianism. Brown, established in Rhode Island in 1764, and the Philadelphia Academy, forerunner of the University of Pennsylvania, organized by Benjamin Franklin, reflected the spirit of toleration by giving representation on the board of trustees to several religious sects. It was Franklin's idea that his college should prepare young men to serve in public office as leaders of the people and ornaments to their country.

Self-education in America.—Important as were these institutions of learning, higher education was by no means confined within their walls. Many well-to-do families sent their sons to Oxford or Cambridge in England. Private tutoring in the home was common. In still more families there were intelligent children who grew up in the great colonial school of adversity and who trained themselves until, in every contest of mind and wit, they could vie with the sons of Harvard or William and Mary or any other college. Such, for example, was Benjamin Franklin, whose charming autobiography, in addition to being an American classic, is a fine record of self-education. His formal training in the classroom was limited to a few years at a local school in Boston; but his self-education continued throughout his life. He early manifested a zeal for reading, and devoured, he tells us, his father's dry library on theology, Bunyan's works, Defoe's writings, Plutarch's *Lives*, Locke's *On the Human Understanding*, and innumerable volumes dealing with secular subjects. His literary style, perhaps the best of his time, Franklin acquired by the diligent and repeated analysis of the *Spectator*. In a life crowded with labors, he found time to read widely in natural science and to win single-handed recognition at the hands of European savants for his discoveries in electricity. By his own efforts he "attained an acquaintance" with Latin, Italian, French, and Spanish, thus unconsciously preparing himself for the day when he was to speak for all America at the court of the king of France.

Lesser lights than Franklin, educated by the same process, were found all over colonial America. From this fruitful source of native ability, self-educated, the American cause drew great strength in the trials of the Revolution.

THE COLONIAL PRESS

The Rise of the Newspaper.—The evolution of American democracy into a government by public opinion, enlightened by the open discussion of political questions, was in no small measure aided by a free press. That too, like education, was a matter of slow growth. A printing press was brought to Massachusetts in 1639, but it was put in charge of an official censor and limited to the publication of religious works. Forty years elapsed before the first newspaper appeared, bearing the curious title, *Public Occurrences Both Foreign and Domestic*, and it had not been running very long before the government of Massachusetts suppressed it for discussing a political question.

Publishing, indeed, seemed to be a precarious business; but in 1704 there came a second venture in journalism, *The Boston News-Letter*, which proved to be a more lasting enterprise because it refrained from criticizing the authorities. Still the public interest languished. When Franklin's brother, James, began to issue his *New England Courant* about 1720, his friends sought to dissuade him, saying that one newspaper was enough for America. Nevertheless he continued it; and his confidence in the future was rewarded. In nearly every colony a gazette or chronicle appeared within the next thirty years or more. Benjamin Franklin was able to record in 1771 that America had twenty-five newspapers. Boston led with five. Philadelphia had three: two in English and one in German.

Censorship and Restraints on the Press.—The idea of printing, unlicensed by the government and uncontrolled by the church, was, however, slow in taking form. The founders of the American colonies had never known what it was to have the free and open publication of books, pamphlets, broadsides, and newspapers. When the art of printing was first discovered, the control of publishing was vested in clerical authorities. After the establishment of the State Church in England in the reign of Elizabeth, censorship of the press became a part of royal prerogative. Printing was restricted to Oxford, Cambridge, and London; and no one could publish anything without previous approval of the official censor. When the Puritans were in power, the popular party, with a zeal which rivaled that of the crown, sought, in turn, to silence royalist and clerical writers by a vigorous censorship. After the restoration of the monarchy, control of the press was once more placed in royal hands, where it remained until 1695, when Parliament, by failing to renew the licensing act, did away entirely with the official censorship. By that time political parties were so powerful and so active and printing presses were so numerous that official review of all published matter became a sheer impossibility.

In America, likewise, some troublesome questions arose in connection with freedom of the press. The Puritans of Massachusetts were no less anxious than King Charles or the Archbishop of London to shut out from the prying eyes of the people all literature "not mete for them to read"; and so they established a system of official licensing for presses, which lasted until 1755. In the other colonies where there was more diversity of opinion and publishers could set up in business with impunity, they were nevertheless constantly liable to arrest for printing anything displeasing to the colonial governments. In 1721 the editor of the *Mercury* in Philadelphia was called before the proprietary council and ordered to apologize for a political article, and for a later offense of a similar character he was thrown into jail. A still more famous case was that of Peter Zenger, a New York publisher, who was arrested in 1735 for criticising the administration. Lawyers who ventured to defend the unlucky editor were deprived of their licenses to practice, and it became necessary to bring an attorney all the way from Philadelphia. By this time the tension of feeling was high, and the approbation of the public was forthcoming when the lawyer for the defense exclaimed to the jury that the very cause of liberty itself, not that of the poor printer, was on trial! The verdict for Zenger, when it finally came, was the signal for an outburst of popular rejoicing. Already the people of King George's province knew how precious a thing is the freedom of the press.

Thanks to the schools, few and scattered as they were, and to the vigilance of parents, a very large portion, perhaps nearly one-half, of the colonists could read. Through the newspapers, pamphlets, and almanacs that streamed from the types, the people could follow the course of public events and grasp the significance of political arguments. An American opinion was in the process of making—an independent opinion nourished by the press and enriched by discussions around the fireside and at the taverns. When the day of resistance to British rule came, government by opinion was at hand. For every person who could hear the voice of Patrick Henry and Samuel Adams, there were a thousand who could see their appeals on the printed page. Men who had spelled out their letters while poring over Franklin's *Poor Richard's Almanac* lived to read Thomas Paine's thrilling call to arms.

THE EVOLUTION IN POLITICAL INSTITUTIONS

Two very distinct lines of development appeared in colonial politics. The one, exalting royal rights and aristocratic privileges, was the drift toward provincial government through royal officers appointed in England. The other, leading toward democracy and self-government, was the growth in the power of the popular legislative assembly. Each movement gave impetus to the other, with increasing force during the passing years, until at last the final collision between the two ideals of government came in the war of independence.

The Royal Provinces.—Of the thirteen English colonies eight were royal provinces in 1776, with governors appointed by the king. Virginia passed under the direct rule of the crown in 1624, when the charter of the London Company was annulled. The Massachusetts Bay corporation lost its charter in 1684, and the new instrument granted seven years later stripped the colonists of the right to choose their chief executive. In the early decades of the eighteenth century both the Carolinas were given the provincial instead of the proprietary form. New Hampshire, severed from Massachusetts in 1679, and Georgia, surrendered by the trustees in 1752, went into the hands of the crown. New York, transferred to the Duke of York on its capture from the Dutch in 1664, became a province when he took the title of James II in 1685. New Jersey, after remaining for nearly forty years under proprietors, was brought directly under the king in 1702. Maryland, Pennsylvania, and Delaware, although they retained their proprietary character until the Revolution, were in some respects like the royal colonies, for their governors were as independent of popular choice as were the appointees of King George. Only two colonies, Rhode Island and Connecticut, retained full self-government on the eve of the Revolution. They alone had governors and legislatures entirely of their own choosing.

The chief officer of the royal province was the governor, who enjoyed high and important powers which he naturally sought to augment at every turn. He enforced the laws and, usually with the consent of a council, appointed the civil and military officers. He granted pardons and reprieves; he was head of the highest court; he was commander-in-chief of the militia; he levied troops for defense and enforced martial law in time of invasion, war, and rebellion. In all the provinces, except Massachusetts, he named the councilors who composed the upper house of the legislature and was likely to choose those who favored his claims. He summoned, adjourned, and dissolved the popular assembly, or the lower house; he laid before it the projects of law desired by the crown; and he vetoed measures which he thought objectionable. Here were in America all the elements of royal prerogative against which Hampden had protested and Cromwell had battled in England.

The colonial governors were generally surrounded by a body of office-seekers and hunters for land grants. Some of them were noblemen of broken estates who had come to America to improve their fortunes. The pretensions of this circle grated on colonial nerves, and privileges granted to them, often at the expense of colonists, did much to deepen popular antipathy to the British government. Favors extended to adherents of the Established Church displeased Dissenters. The reappearance of this formidable union of church and state, from which they had fled, stirred anew the ancient wrath against that combination.

The Colonial Assembly.—Coincident with the drift toward administration through royal governors was the second and opposite tendency, namely, a steady growth in the practice of self-government. The voters of England had long been accustomed to share in taxation and law-making through representatives in Parliament, and the idea was early introduced in America. Virginia was only twelve years old (1619) when its first representative assembly appeared. As the towns of Massachusetts multiplied and it became impossible for all the members of the corporation to meet at one place, the representative idea was adopted, in 1633. The river towns of Connecticut formed a representative system under their "Fundamental Orders" of 1639, and the entire colony was given a royal charter in 1662. Generosity, as well as practical considerations, induced such proprietors as Lord Baltimore and William Penn to invite their colonists to share in the government as soon as any considerable settlements were made. Thus by one process or another every one of the colonies secured a popular assembly.

It is true that in the provision for popular elections, the suffrage was finally restricted to property owners or taxpayers, with a leaning toward the freehold qualification. In Virginia, the rural voter had to be a freeholder owning at least fifty acres of land, if there was no house on it, or twenty-five acres with a house twenty-five feet square. In Massachusetts, the voter for member of the assembly under the charter of 1691 had to be a freeholder of an estate worth forty shillings a year at least or of other property to the value of forty pounds sterling. In Pennsylvania, the suffrage was granted to freeholders owning fifty acres or more of land well seated, twelve acres cleared, and to other persons worth at least fifty pounds in lawful money.

Restrictions like these undoubtedly excluded from the suffrage a very considerable number of men, particularly the mechanics and artisans of the towns, who were by no means content with their position. Nevertheless, it was relatively easy for any man to acquire a small freehold, so cheap and abundant was land; and in fact a large proportion of the colonists were land owners. Thus the assemblies, in spite of the limited suffrage, acquired a democratic tone.

The popular character of the assemblies increased as they became engaged in battles with the royal and proprietary governors. When called upon by the executive to make provision for the support of the administration, the legislature took advantage of the opportunity to make terms in the interest of the taxpayers. It made annual, not permanent, grants of money to pay official salaries and then insisted upon electing a treasurer to dole it out. Thus the colonists learned some of the mysteries of public finance, as well as the management of rapacious officials. The legislature also used its power over money grants to force the governor to sign bills which he would otherwise have vetoed.

Contests between Legislatures and Governors.—As may be imagined, many and bitter were the contests between the royal and proprietary governors and the colonial assemblies. Franklin relates an amusing story of how the Pennsylvania assembly held in one hand a bill for the executive to sign and, in the other hand, the money to pay his salary. Then, with sly humor, Franklin adds: "Do not, my courteous reader, take pet at our proprietary constitution for these our bargain and sale proceedings in legislation. It is a happy country where justice and what was your own before can be had for ready money. It is another addition to the value of money and of course another spur to industry. Every land is not so blessed."

It must not be thought, however, that every governor got off as easily as Franklin's tale implies. On the contrary, the legislatures, like Cæsar, fed upon meat that made them great and steadily encroached upon executive prerogatives as they tried out and found their strength. If we may believe contemporary laments, the power of the crown in America was diminishing when it was struck down altogether. In New York, the friends of the governor complained in 1747 that "the inhabitants of plantations are generally educated in republican principles; upon republican principles all is conducted. Little more than a shadow of royal authority remains in the Northern colonies." "Here," echoed the governor of South Carolina, the following year, "levelling principles prevail; the frame of the civil government is unhinged; a governor, if he would be idolized, must betray his trust; the people have got their whole administration in their hands; the election of the members of the assembly is by ballot; not civil posts only, but all ecclesiastical preferments, are in the disposal or election of the people."

Though baffled by the "levelling principles" of the colonial assemblies, the governors did not give up the case as hopeless. Instead they evolved a system of policy and action which they thought could bring the obstinate provincials to terms. That system, traceable in their letters to the government in London, consisted of three parts: (1) the royal officers in the colonies were to be made independent of the legislatures by taxes imposed by acts of Parliament; (2) a British standing army was to be maintained in America; (3) the remaining colonial charters were to be revoked and government by direct royal authority was to be enlarged.

Such a system seemed plausible enough to King George III and to many ministers of the crown in London. With governors, courts, and an army independent of the colonists, they imagined it would be easy to carry out both royal orders and acts of Parliament. This reasoning seemed both practical and logical. Nor was it founded on theory, for it came fresh from the governors themselves. It was wanting in one respect only. It failed to take account of the fact that the American people were growing strong in the practice of self-government and could dispense with the tutelage of the British ministry, no matter how excellent it might be or how benevolent its intentions.

References

A.M. Earle, *Home Life in Colonial Days*.

A.L. Cross, *The Anglican Episcopate and the American Colonies* (Harvard Studies).

E.G. Dexter, *History of Education in the United States*.

C.A. Duniway, *Freedom of the Press in Massachusetts*.

Benjamin Franklin, *Autobiography*.

E.B. Greene, *The Provincial Governor* (Harvard Studies).

A.E. McKinley, *The Suffrage Franchise in the Thirteen English Colonies* (Pennsylvania University Studies).

M.C. Tyler, *History of American Literature during the Colonial Times* (2 vols.).

Questions

1. Why is leisure necessary for the production of art and literature? How may leisure be secured?

2. Explain the position of the church in colonial life.

3. Contrast the political rôles of Puritanism and the Established Church.

4. How did diversity of opinion work for toleration?

5. Show the connection between religion and learning in colonial times.

6. Why is a "free press" such an important thing to American democracy?

7. Relate some of the troubles of early American publishers.

8. Give the undemocratic features of provincial government.

9. How did the colonial assemblies help to create an independent American spirit, in spite of a restricted suffrage?

10. Explain the nature of the contests between the governors and the legislatures.

Research Topics

Religious and Intellectual Life.—Lodge, *Short History of the English Colonies*: (1) in New England, pp. 418-438, 465-475; (2) in Virginia, pp. 54-61, 87-89; (3) in Pennsylvania, pp. 232-237, 253-257; (4) in New York, pp. 316-321. Interesting source materials in Hart, *American History Told by Contemporaries*, Vol. II, pp. 255-275, 276-290.

The Government of a Royal Province, Virginia.—Lodge, pp. 43-50. Special Reference: E.B. Greene, *The Provincial Governor* (Harvard Studies).

The Government of a Proprietary Colony, Pennsylvania.—Lodge, pp. 230-232.

Government in New England.—Lodge, pp. 412-417.

The Colonial Press.—Special Reference: G.H. Payne, *History of Journalism in the United States* (1920).

Colonial Life in General.—John Fiske, *Old Virginia and Her Neighbors*, Vol. II, pp. 174-269; Elson, *History of the United States*, pp. 197-210.

Colonial Government in General.—Elson, pp. 210-216.

CHAPTER IV

THE DEVELOPMENT OF COLONIAL NATIONALISM

It is one of the well-known facts of history that a people loosely united by domestic ties of a political and economic nature, even a people torn by domestic strife, may be welded into a solid and compact body by an attack from a foreign power. The imperative call to common defense, the habit of sharing common burdens, the fusing force of common service—these things, induced by the necessity of resisting outside interference, act as an amalgam drawing together all elements, except, perhaps, the most discordant. The presence of the enemy allays the most virulent of quarrels, temporarily at least. "Politics," runs an old saying, "stops at the water's edge."

This ancient political principle, so well understood in diplomatic circles, applied nearly as well to the original thirteen American colonies as to the countries of Europe. The necessity for common defense, if not equally great, was certainly always pressing. Though it has long been the practice to speak of the early settlements as founded in "a wilderness," this was not actually the case. From the earliest days of Jamestown on through the years, the American people were confronted by dangers from without. All about their tiny settlements were Indians, growing more and more hostile as the frontier advanced and as sharp conflicts over land aroused angry passions. To the south and west was the power of Spain, humiliated, it is true, by the disaster to the Armada, but still presenting an imposing front to the British empire. To the north and west were the French, ambitious, energetic, imperial in temper, and prepared to contest on land and water the advance of British dominion in America.

RELATIONS WITH THE INDIANS AND THE FRENCH

Indian Affairs.—It is difficult to make general statements about the relations of the colonists to the Indians. The problem was presented in different shape in different sections of America. It was not handled according to any coherent or uniform plan by the British government, which alone could speak for all the provinces at the same time. Neither did the proprietors and the governors who succeeded one another, in an irregular train, have the consistent policy or the matured experience necessary for dealing wisely with Indian matters. As the difficulties arose mainly on the frontiers, where the restless and pushing pioneers were making their way with gun and ax, nearly everything that happened was the result of chance rather than of calculation. A personal quarrel between traders and an Indian, a jug of whisky, a keg of gunpowder, the exchange of guns for furs, personal treachery, or a flash of bad temper often set in motion destructive forces of the most terrible character.

On one side of the ledger may be set innumerable generous records—of Squanto and Samoset teaching the Pilgrims the ways of the wilds; of Roger Williams buying his lands from the friendly natives; or of William Penn treating with them on his arrival in America. On the other side of the ledger must be recorded many a cruel and bloody conflict as the frontier rolled westward with deadly precision. The Pequots on the Connecticut border, sensing their doom, fell upon the tiny settlements with awful fury in 1637 only to meet with equally terrible punishment. A generation later, King Philip, son of Massasoit, the friend of the Pilgrims, called his tribesmen to a war of extermination which brought the strength of all New England to the field and ended in his own destruction. In New York, the relations with the Indians, especially with the Algonquins and the Mohawks, were marked by periodic and desperate wars. Virginia and her Southern neighbors suffered as did New England. In 1622 Opecacano, a brother of Powhatan, the friend of the Jamestown settlers, launched a general massacre; and in 1644 he attempted a war of extermination. In 1675 the whole frontier was ablaze. Nathaniel Bacon vainly attempted to stir the colonial governor to put up an adequate defense and, failing in that plea, himself headed a revolt and a successful expedition against the Indians. As the Virginia outposts advanced into the Kentucky country, the strife with the natives was transferred to that "dark and bloody ground"; while to the southeast, a desperate struggle with the Tuscaroras called forth the combined forces of the two Carolinas and Virginia.

From such horrors New Jersey and Delaware were saved on account of their geographical location. Pennsylvania, consistently following a policy of conciliation, was likewise spared until her western vanguard came into full conflict with the allied French and Indians. Georgia, by clever negotiations and treaties of alliance, managed to keep on fair terms with her belligerent Cherokees and Creeks. But neither diplomacy nor generosity could stay the inevitable conflict as the frontier advanced, especially after the French soldiers enlisted the Indians in their imperial enterprises. It was then that desultory fighting became general warfare.

Early Relations with the French.—During the first decades of French exploration and settlement in the St. Lawrence country, the English colonies, engrossed with their own problems, gave little or no thought to their distant neighbors. Quebec, founded in 1608, and Montreal, in 1642, were too far away, too small in population, and too slight in strength to be much of a menace to Boston, Hartford, or New York. It was the statesmen in France and England, rather than the colonists in America, who first grasped the significance of the slowly converging empires in North America. It was the ambition of Louis XIV of France, rather than the labors of Jesuit missionaries and French rangers, that sounded the first note of colonial alarm.

Evidence of this lies in the fact that three conflicts between the English and the French occurred before their advancing frontiers met on the Pennsylvania border. King William's War (1689-1697), Queen Anne's War (1701-1713), and King George's War (1744-1748) owed their origins and their endings mainly to the intrigues and rivalries of European powers, although they all involved the American colonies in struggles with the French and their savage allies.

The Clash in the Ohio Valley.—The second of these wars had hardly closed, however, before the English colonists themselves began to be seriously alarmed about the rapidly expanding French dominion in the West. Marquette and Joliet, who opened the Lake region, and La Salle, who in 1682 had gone down the Mississippi to the Gulf, had been followed by the builders of forts. In 1718, the French founded New Orleans, thus taking possession of the gateway to the Mississippi as well as the St. Lawrence. A few years later they built Fort Niagara; in 1731 they occupied Crown Point; in 1749 they formally announced their dominion over all the territory drained by the Ohio River. Having asserted this lofty claim, they set out to make it good by constructing in the years 1752-1754 Fort Le Bœuf near Lake Erie, Fort Venango on the upper waters of the Allegheny, and Fort Duquesne at the junction of the streams forming the Ohio. Though they were warned by George Washington, in the name of the governor of Virginia, to keep out of territory "so notoriously known to be property of the crown of Great Britain," the French showed no signs of relinquishing their pretensions.

The Final Phase—the French and Indian War.—Thus it happened that the shot which opened the Seven Years' War, known in America as the French and Indian War, was fired in the wilds of Pennsylvania. There began the conflict that spread to Europe and even Asia and finally involved England and Prussia, on the one side, and France, Austria, Spain, and minor powers on the other. On American soil, the defeat of Braddock in 1755 and Wolfe's exploit in capturing Quebec four years later were the dramatic features. On the continent of Europe, England subsidized Prussian arms to hold France at bay. In India, on the banks of the Ganges, as on the banks of the St. Lawrence, British arms were triumphant. Well could the historian write: "Conquests equaling in rapidity and far surpassing in magnitude those of Cortes and Pizarro had been achieved in the East." Well could the merchants of London declare that under the administration of William Pitt, the imperial genius of this world-wide conflict, commerce had been "united with and made to flourish by war."

From the point of view of the British empire, the results of the war were momentous. By the peace of 1763, Canada and the territory east of the Mississippi, except New Orleans, passed under the British flag. The remainder of the Louisiana territory was transferred to Spain and French imperial ambitions on the American continent were laid to rest. In exchange for Havana, which the British had seized during the war, Spain ceded to King George the colony of Florida. Not without warrant did Macaulay write in after years that Pitt "was the first Englishman of his time; and he had made England the first country in the world."

THE EFFECTS OF WARFARE ON THE COLONIES

The various wars with the French and the Indians, trivial in detail as they seem to-day, had a profound influence on colonial life and on the destiny of America. Circumstances beyond the control of popular assemblies, jealous of their individual powers, compelled coöperation among them, grudging and stingy no doubt, but stillcoöperation. The American people, more eager to be busy in their fields or at their trades, were simply forced to raise and support armies, to learn the arts of warfare, and to practice, if in a small theater, the science of statecraft. These forces, all cumulative, drove the colonists, so tenaciously provincial in their habits, in the direction of nationalism.

The New England Confederation.—It was in their efforts to deal with the problems presented by the Indian and French menace that the Americans took the first steps toward union. Though there were many common ties among the settlers of New England, it required a deadly fear of the Indians to produce in 1643 the New England Confederation, composed of Massachusetts, Plymouth, Connecticut, and New Haven. The colonies so united were bound together in "a firm and perpetual league of friendship and amity for offense and defense, mutual service and succor, upon all just occasions." They made provision for distributing the burdens of wars among the members and provided for a congress of commissioners from each colony to determine upon common policies. For some twenty years the Confederation was active and it continued to hold meetings until after the extinction of the Indian peril on the immediate border.

Virginia, no less than Massachusetts, was aware of the importance of intercolonial coöperation. In the middle of the seventeenth century, the Old Dominion began treaties of commerce and amity with New York and the colonies of New England. In 1684 delegates from Virginia met at Albany with the agents of New York and Massachusetts to discuss problems of mutual defense. A few years later the Old Dominion coöperated loyally with the Carolinas in defending their borders against Indian forays.

The Albany Plan of Union.—An attempt at a general colonial union was made in 1754. On the suggestion of the Lords of Trade in England, a conference was held at Albany to consider Indian relations, to devise measures of defense against the French, and to enter into "articles of union and confederation for the general defense of his Majesty's subjects and interests in North America as well in time of peace as of war." New Hampshire, Massachusetts, Connecticut, Rhode Island, New York, Pennsylvania, and Maryland were represented. After a long discussion, a plan of union, drafted mainly, it seems, by Benjamin Franklin, was adopted and sent to the colonies and the crown for approval. The colonies, jealous of their individual rights, refused to accept the scheme and the king disapproved it for the reason, Franklin said, that it had "too much weight in the democratic part of the constitution." Though the Albany union failed, the document is still worthy of study because it forecast many of the perplexing problems that were not solved until thirty-three years afterward, when another convention of which also Franklin was a member drafted the Constitution of the United States.

The Military Education of the Colonists.—The same wars that showed the provincials the meaning of union likewise instructed them in the art of defending their institutions. Particularly was this true of the last French and Indian conflict, which stretched all the way from Maine to the Carolinas and made heavy calls upon them all for troops. The answer, it is admitted, was far from satisfactory to the British government and the conduct of the militiamen was far from professional; but thousands of Americans got a taste, a strong taste, of actual fighting in the field. Men like George Washington and Daniel Morgan learned lessons that were not forgotten in after years. They saw what American militiamen could do under favorable circumstances and they watched British regulars operating on American soil. "This whole transaction," shrewdly remarked Franklin of Braddock's campaign, "gave us Americans the first suspicion that our exalted ideas of the prowess of British regular troops had not been well founded." It was no mere accident that the Virginia colonel who drew his sword under the elm at Cambridge and took command of the army of the Revolution was the brave officer who had "spurned the whistle of bullets" at the memorable battle in western Pennsylvania.

Financial Burdens and Commercial Disorder.—While the provincials were learning lessons in warfare they were also paying the bills. All the conflicts were costly in treasure as in blood. King Philip's war left New England weak and almost bankrupt. The French and Indian struggle was especially expensive. The twenty-five thousand men put in the field by the colonies were sustained only by huge outlays of money. Paper currency streamed from the press and debts were accumulated. Commerce was driven from its usual channels and prices were enhanced. When the end came, both England and America were staggering under heavy liabilities, and to make matters worse there was a fall of prices accompanied by a commercial depression which extended over a period of ten years. It was in the midst of this crisis that measures of taxation had to be devised to pay the cost of the war, precipitating the quarrel which led to American independence.

The Expulsion of French Power from North America.—The effects of the defeat administered to France, as time proved, were difficult to estimate. Some British statesmen regarded it as a happy circumstance that the colonists, already restive under their administration, had no foreign power at hand to aid them in case they struck for independence. American leaders, on the other hand, now that the soldiers of King Louis were driven from the continent, thought that they had no other country to fear if they cast off British sovereignty. At all events, France, though defeated, was not out of the sphere of American influence; for, as events proved, it was the fortunate French alliance negotiated by Franklin that assured the triumph of American arms in the War of the Revolution.

COLONIAL RELATIONS WITH THE BRITISH GOVERNMENT

It was neither the Indian wars nor the French wars that finally brought forth American nationality. That was the product of the long strife with the mother country which culminated in union for the war of independence. The forces that created this nation did not operate in the colonies alone. The character of the English sovereigns, the course of events in English domestic politics, and English measures of control over the colonies—executive, legislative, and judicial—must all be taken into account.

The Last of the Stuarts.—The struggles between Charles I (1625-49) and the parliamentary party and the turmoil of the Puritan régime (1649-60) so engrossed the attention of Englishmen at home that they had little time to think of colonial policies or to interfere with colonial affairs. The restoration of the monarchy in 1660, accompanied by internal peace and the increasing power of the mercantile classes in the House of Commons, changed all that. In the reign of Charles II (1660-85), himself an easy-going person, the policy of regulating trade by act of Parliament was developed into a closely knit system and powerful agencies to supervise the colonies were created. At the same time a system of stricter control over the dominions was ushered in by the annulment of the old charter of Massachusetts which conferred so much self-government on the Puritans.

Charles' successor, James II, a man of sterner stuff and jealous of his authority in the colonies as well as at home, continued the policy thus inaugurated and enlarged upon it. If he could have kept his throne, he would have bent the Americans under a harsh rule or brought on in his dominions a revolution like that which he precipitated at home in 1688. He determined to unite the Northern colonies and introduce a more efficient administration based on the pattern of the royal provinces. He made a martinet, Sir

Edmund Andros, governor of all New England, New York, and New Jersey. The charter of Massachusetts, annulled in the last days of his brother's reign, he continued to ignore, and that of Connecticut would have been seized if it had not been spirited away and hidden, according to tradition, in a hollow oak.

For several months, Andros gave the Northern colonies a taste of ill-tempered despotism. He wrung quit rents from land owners not accustomed to feudal dues; he abrogated titles to land where, in his opinion, they were unlawful; he forced the Episcopal service upon the Old South Church in Boston; and he denied the writ of *habeas corpus* to a preacher who denounced taxation without representation. In the middle of his arbitrary course, however, his hand was stayed. The news came that King James had been dethroned by his angry subjects, and the people of Boston, kindling a fire on Beacon Hill, summoned the countryside to dispose of Andros. The response was prompt and hearty. The hated governor was arrested, imprisoned, and sent back across the sea under guard.

The overthrow of James, followed by the accession of William and Mary and by assured parliamentary supremacy, had an immediate effect in the colonies. The new order was greeted with thanksgiving. Massachusetts was given another charter which, though not so liberal as the first, restored the spirit if not the entire letter of self-government. In the other colonies where Andros had been operating, the old course of affairs was resumed.

The Indifference of the First Two Georges.—On the death in 1714 of Queen Anne, the successor of King William, the throne passed to a Hanoverian prince who, though grateful for English honors and revenues, was more interested in Hanover than in England. George I and George II, whose combined reigns extended from 1714 to 1760, never even learned to speak the English language, at least without an accent. The necessity of taking thought about colonial affairs bored both of them so that the stoutest defender of popular privileges in Boston or Charleston had no ground to complain of the exercise of personal prerogatives by the king. Moreover, during a large part of this period, the direction of affairs was in the hands of an astute leader, Sir Robert Walpole, who betrayed his somewhat cynical view of politics by adopting as his motto: "Let sleeping dogs lie." He revealed his appreciation of popular sentiment by exclaiming: "I will not be the minister to enforce taxes at the expense of blood." Such kings and such ministers were not likely to arouse the slumbering resistance of the thirteen colonies across the sea.

Control of the Crown over the Colonies.—While no English ruler from James II to George III ventured to interfere with colonial matters personally, constant control over the colonies was exercised by royal officers acting under the authority of the crown. Systematic supervision began in 1660, when there was created by royal order a committee of the king's council to meet on Mondays and Thursdays of each week to consider petitions, memorials, and addresses respecting the plantations. In 1696 a regular board was established, known as the "Lords of Trade and Plantations," which continued, until the American Revolution, to scrutinize closely colonial business. The chief duties of the board were to examine acts of colonial legislatures, to recommend measures to those assemblies for adoption, and to hear memorials and petitions from the colonies relative to their affairs.

The methods employed by this board were varied. All laws passed by American legislatures came before it for review as a matter of routine. If it found an act unsatisfactory, it recommended to the king the exercise of his veto power, known as the royal disallowance. Any person who believed his personal or property rights injured by a colonial law could be heard by the board in person or by attorney; in such cases it was the practice to hear at the same time the agent of the colony so involved. The royal veto power over colonial legislation was not, therefore, a formal affair, but was constantly employed on the suggestion of a highly efficient agency of the crown. All this was in addition to the powers exercised by the governors in the royal provinces.

Judicial Control.—Supplementing this administrative control over the colonies was a constant supervision by the English courts of law. The king, by virtue of his inherent authority, claimed and exercised high appellate powers over all judicial tribunals in the empire. The right of appeal from local courts, expressly set forth in some charters, was, on the eve of the Revolution, maintained in every colony. Any subject in England or America, who, in the regular legal course, was aggrieved by any act of a colonial legislature or any decision of a colonial court, had the right, subject to certain regulations, to carry his case to the king in council, forcing his opponent to follow him across the sea. In the exercise of appellate power, the king in council acting as a court could, and frequently did, declare acts of colonial legislatures duly enacted and approved, null and void, on the ground that they were contrary to English law.

Imperial Control in Operation.—Day after day, week after week, year after year, the machinery for political and judicial control over colonial affairs was in operation. At one time the British governors in the colonies were ordered not to approve any colonial law imposing a duty on European goods imported in English vessels. Again, when North Carolina laid a tax on peddlers, the council objected to it as "restrictive upon the trade and dispersion of English manufactures throughout the continent." At other times, Indian trade was regulated in the interests of the whole empire or grants of lands by a colonial legislature were set aside. Virginia was forbidden to close her ports to North Carolina lest there should be retaliation.

In short, foreign and intercolonial trade were subjected to a control higher than that of the colony, foreshadowing a day when the Constitution of the United States was to commit to Congress the power to regulate interstate and foreign commerce and commerce with the Indians. A superior judicial power, towering above that of the colonies, as the Supreme Court at Washington now towers above the states, kept the colonial legislatures within the metes and bounds of established law. In the thousands of appeals, memorials, petitions, and complaints, and the rulings and decisions upon them, were written the real history of British imperial control over the American colonies.

So great was the business before the Lords of Trade that the colonies had to keep skilled agents in London to protect their interests. As common grievances against the operation of this machinery of control arose, there appeared in each colony a considerable body of men, with the merchants in the lead, who chafed at the restraints imposed on their enterprise. Only a powerful blow was needed to weld these bodies into a common mass nourishing the spirit of colonial nationalism. When to the repeated minor irritations were added general and sweeping measures of Parliament applying to every colony, the rebound came in the Revolution.

Parliamentary Control over Colonial Affairs.—As soon as Parliament gained in power at the expense of the king, it reached out to bring the American colonies under its sway as well. Between the execution of Charles I and the accession of George III, there was enacted an immense body of legislation regulating the shipping, trade, and manufactures of America. All of it, based on the "mercantile" theory then prevalent in all countries of Europe, was designed to control the overseas plantations in such a way as to foster the commercial and business interests of the mother country, where merchants and men of finance had got the upper hand. According to this theory, the colonies of the British empire should be confined to agriculture and the production of raw materials, and forced to buy their manufactured goods of England.

The Navigation Acts.—In the first rank among these measures of British colonial policy must be placed the navigation laws framed for the purpose of building up the British merchant marine and navy—arms so essential in defending the colonies against the Spanish, Dutch, and French. The beginning of this type of legislation was made in 1651 and it was worked out into a system early in the reign of Charles II (1660-85).

The Navigation Acts, in effect, gave a monopoly of colonial commerce to British ships. No trade could be carried on between Great Britain and her dominions save in vessels built and manned by British subjects. No European goods could be brought to America save in the ships of the country that produced them or in English ships. These laws, which were almost fatal to Dutch shipping in America, fell with severity upon the colonists, compelling them to pay higher freight rates. The adverse effect, however, was short-lived, for the measures stimulated shipbuilding in the colonies, where the abundance of raw materials gave the master builders of America an advantage over those of the mother country. Thus the colonists in the end profited from the restrictive policy written into the Navigation Acts.

The Acts against Manufactures.—The second group of laws was deliberately aimed to prevent colonial industries from competing too sharply with those of England. Among the earliest of these measures may be counted the Woolen Act of 1699, forbidding the exportation of woolen goods from the colonies and even the woolen trade between towns and colonies. When Parliament learned, as the result of an inquiry, that New England and New York were making thousands of hats a year and sending large numbers annually to the Southern colonies and to Ireland, Spain, and Portugal, it enacted in 1732 a law declaring that "no hats or felts, dyed or undyed, finished or unfinished" should be "put upon any vessel or laden upon any horse or cart with intent to export to any place whatever." The effect of this measure upon the hat industry was almost ruinous. A few years later a similar blow was given to the iron industry. By an act of 1750, pig and bar iron from the colonies were given free entry to England to encourage the production of the raw material; but at the same time the law provided that "no mill or other engine for slitting or rolling of iron, no plating forge to work with a tilt hammer, and no furnace for making steel" should be built in the colonies. As for those already built, they were declared public nuisances and ordered closed. Thus three important economic interests of the colonists, the woolen, hat, and iron industries, were laid under the ban.

The Trade Laws.—The third group of restrictive measures passed by the British Parliament related to the sale of colonial produce. An act of 1663 required the colonies to export certain articles to Great Britain or to her dominions alone; while sugar, tobacco, and ginger consigned to the continent of Europe had to pass through a British port paying custom duties and through a British merchant's hands paying the usual commission. At first tobacco was the only one of the "enumerated articles" which seriously concerned the American colonies, the rest coming mainly from the British West Indies. In the course of time, however, other commodities were added to the list of enumerated articles, until by 1764 it embraced rice, naval stores, copper, furs, hides, iron, lumber, and pearl ashes. This was not all. The colonies were compelled to bring their European purchases back through English ports, paying duties to the government and commissions to merchants again.

The Molasses Act.—Not content with laws enacted in the interest of English merchants and manufacturers, Parliament sought to protect the British West Indies against competition from their French and Dutch neighbors. New England merchants had long carried on a lucrative trade with the French islands in the West Indies and Dutch Guiana, where sugar and molasses could be obtained in large quantities at low prices. Acting on the protests of English planters in the Barbadoes and Jamaica, Parliament, in 1733, passed the famous Molasses Act imposing duties on sugar and molasses imported into the colonies from foreign countries—rates which would have destroyed the American trade with the French and Dutch if the law had been enforced. The duties, however, were not collected. The molasses and sugar trade with the foreigners went on merrily, smuggling taking the place of lawful traffic.

Effect of the Laws in America.—As compared with the strict monopoly of her colonial trade which Spain consistently sought to maintain, the policy of England was both moderate and liberal. Furthermore, the restrictive laws were supplemented by many measures intended to be favorable to colonial prosperity. The Navigation Acts, for example, redounded to the advantage of American shipbuilders and the producers of hemp, tar, lumber, and ship stores in general. Favors in British ports were granted to colonial producers as against foreign competitors and in some instances bounties were paid by England to encourage colonial enterprise. Taken all in all, there is much justification in the argument advanced by some modern scholars to the effect that the colonists gained more than they lost by British trade and industrial legislation. Certainly after the establishment of independence, when free from these old restrictions, the Americans found themselves handicapped by being treated as foreigners rather than favored traders and the recipients of bounties in English markets.

Be that as it may, it appears that the colonists felt little irritation against the mother country on account of the trade and navigation laws enacted previous to the close of the French and Indian war. Relatively few were engaged in the hat and iron industries as compared with those in farming and planting, so that England's policy of restricting America to agriculture did not conflict with the interests of the majority of the inhabitants. The woolen industry was largely in the hands of women and carried on in connection with their domestic duties, so that it was not the sole support of any considerable number of people.

As a matter of fact, moreover, the restrictive laws, especially those relating to trade, were not rigidly enforced. Cargoes of tobacco were boldly sent to continental ports without even so much as a bow to the English government, to which duties should have been paid. Sugar and molasses from the French and Dutch colonies were shipped into New England in spite of the law. Royal officers sometimes protested against smuggling and sometimes connived at it; but at no time did they succeed in stopping it. Taken all in all, very little was heard of "the galling restraints of trade" until after the French war, when the British government suddenly entered upon a new course.

SUMMARY OF THE COLONIAL PERIOD

In the period between the landing of the English at Jamestown, Virginia, in 1607, and the close of the French and Indian war in 1763—a period of a century and a half—a new nation was being prepared on this continent to take its place among the powers of the earth. It was an epoch of migration. Western Europe contributed emigrants of many races and nationalities. The English led the way. Next to them in numerical importance were the Scotch-Irish and the Germans. Into the melting pot were also cast Dutch, Swedes, French, Jews, Welsh, and Irish. Thousands of negroes were brought from Africa to till Southern fields or labor as domestic servants in the North.

Why did they come? The reasons are various. Some of them, the Pilgrims and Puritans of New England, the French Huguenots, Scotch-Irish and Irish, and the Catholics of Maryland, fled from intolerant governments that denied them the right to worship God according to the dictates of their consciences. Thousands came to escape the bondage of poverty in the Old World and to find free homes in America. Thousands, like the negroes from Africa, were dragged here against their will. The lure of adventure appealed to the restless and the lure of profits to the enterprising merchants.

How did they come? In some cases religious brotherhoods banded together and borrowed or furnished the funds necessary to pay the way. In other cases great trading companies were organized to found colonies. Again it was the wealthy proprietor, like Lord Baltimore or William Penn, who undertook to plant settlements. Many immigrants were able to pay their own way across the sea. Others bound themselves out for a term of years in exchange for the cost of the passage. Negroes were brought on account of the profits derived from their sale as slaves.

Whatever the motive for their coming, however, they managed to get across the sea. The immigrants set to work with a will. They cut down forests, built houses, and laid out fields. They founded churches, schools, and colleges. They set up forges and workshops. They spun and wove. They fashioned ships and sailed the seas. They bartered and traded. Here and there on favorable harbors they established centers of commerce—Boston, Providence, New York, Philadelphia, Baltimore, and Charleston. As soon as a firm foothold was secured on the shore line they pressed westward until, by the close of the colonial period, they were already on the crest of the Alleghanies.

Though they were widely scattered along a thousand miles of seacoast, the colonists were united in spirit by many common ties. The major portion of them were Protestants. The language, the law, and the literature of England furnished the basis of national unity. Most of the colonists were engaged in the same hard task; that of conquering a wilderness. To ties of kinship and language were added ties created by necessity. They had to unite in defense; first, against the Indians and later against the French. They were all subjects of the same sovereign—the king of England. The English Parliament made laws for them and the English government supervised their local affairs, their trade, and their manufactures. Common forces assailed them. Common grievances vexed them. Common hopes inspired them.

Many of the things which tended to unite them likewise tended to throw them into opposition to the British Crown and Parliament. Most of them were freeholders; that is, farmers who owned their own land and tilled it with their own hands. A free soil nourished the spirit of freedom. The majority of them were Dissenters, critics, not friends, of the Church of England, that stanch defender of the British monarchy. Each colony in time developed its own legislature elected by the voters; it grew accustomed to making laws and laying taxes for itself. Here was a people learning self-reliance and self-government. The attempts to strengthen the Church of England in America and the transformation of colonies into royal provinces only fanned the spirit of independence which they were designed to quench.

Nevertheless, the Americans owed much of their prosperity to the assistance of the government that irritated them. It was the protection of the British navy that prevented Holland, Spain, and France from wiping out their settlements. Though their manufacture and trade were controlled in the interests of the mother country, they also enjoyed great advantages in her markets. Free trade existed nowhere upon the earth; but the broad empire of Britain was open to American ships and merchandise. It could be said, with good reason, that the disadvantages which the colonists suffered through British regulation of their industry and trade were more than offset by the privileges they enjoyed. Still that is somewhat beside the point, for mere economic advantage is not necessarily the determining factor in the fate of peoples. A thousand circumstances had helped to develop on this continent a nation, to inspire it with a passion for independence, and to prepare it for a destiny greater than that of a prosperous dominion of the British empire. The economists, who tried to prove by logic unassailable that America would be richer under the British flag, could not change the spirit of Patrick Henry, Samuel Adams, Benjamin Franklin, or George Washington.

References

G.L. Beer, *Origin of the British Colonial System* and *The Old Colonial System*.

A. Bradley, *The Fight for Canada in North America*.

C.M. Andrews, *Colonial Self-Government* (American Nation Series).

H. Egerton, *Short History of British Colonial Policy*.

F. Parkman, *France and England in North America* (12 vols.).

R. Thwaites, *France in America* (American Nation Series).

J. Winsor, *The Mississippi Valley* and *Cartier to Frontenac*.

Questions

1. How would you define "nationalism"?

2. Can you give any illustrations of the way that war promotes nationalism?

3. Why was it impossible to establish and maintain a uniform policy in dealing with the Indians?

4. What was the outcome of the final clash with the French?

5. Enumerate the five chief results of the wars with the French and the Indians. Discuss each in detail.

6. Explain why it was that the character of the English king mattered to the colonists.

7. Contrast England under the Stuarts with England under the Hanoverians.

8. Explain how the English Crown, Courts, and Parliament controlled the colonies.

9. Name the three important classes of English legislation affecting the colonies. Explain each.

10. Do you think the English legislation was beneficial or injurious to the colonies? Why?

Research Topics

Rise of French Power in North America.—Special reference: Francis Parkman, *Struggle for a Continent*.

The French and Indian Wars.—Special reference: W.M. Sloane, *French War and the Revolution*, Chaps. VI-IX. Parkman, *Montcalm and Wolfe*, Vol. II, pp. 195-299. Elson, *History of the United States*, pp. 171-196.

English Navigation Acts.—Macdonald, *Documentary Source Book*, pp. 55, 72, 78, 90, 103. Coman, *Industrial History*, pp. 79-85.

British Colonial Policy.—Callender, *Economic History of the United States*, pp. 102-108.

The New England Confederation.—Analyze the document in Macdonald, *Source Book*, p. 45. Special reference: Fiske, *Beginnings of New England*, pp. 140-198.

The Administration of Andros.—Fiske, *Beginnings*, pp. 242-278.

Biographical Studies.—William Pitt and Sir Robert Walpole. Consult Green, *Short History of England*, on their policies, using the index.

PART II. CONFLICT AND INDEPENDENCE

CHAPTER V

THE NEW COURSE IN BRITISH IMPERIAL POLICY

On October 25, 1760, King George II died and the British crown passed to his young grandson. The first George, the son of the Elector of Hanover and Sophia the granddaughter of James I, was a thorough German who never even learned to speak the language of the land over which he reigned. The second George never saw England until he was a man. He spoke English with an accent and until his death preferred his German home. During their reign, the principle had become well established that the king did not govern but acted only through ministers representing the majority in Parliament.

GEORGE III AND HIS SYSTEM

The Character of the New King.—The third George rudely broke the German tradition of his family. He resented the imputation that he was a foreigner and on all occasions made a display of his British sympathies. To the draft of his first speech to Parliament, he added the popular phrase: "Born and educated in this country, I glory in the name of Briton." Macaulay, the English historian, certainly of no liking for high royal prerogative, said of George: "The young king was a born Englishman. All his tastes and habits, good and bad, were English. No portion of his subjects had anything to reproach him with.... His age, his appearance, and all that was known of his character conciliated public favor. He was in the bloom of youth; his person and address were pleasing; scandal imputed to him no vice; and flattery might without glaring absurdity ascribe to him many princely virtues."

Nevertheless George III had been spoiled by his mother, his tutors, and his courtiers. Under their influence he developed high and mighty notions about the sacredness of royal authority and his duty to check the pretensions of Parliament and the ministers dependent upon it. His mother had dinned into his ears the slogan: "George, be king!" Lord Bute, his teacher and adviser, had told him that his honor required him to take an active part in the shaping of public policy and the making of laws. Thus educated, he surrounded himself with courtiers who encouraged him in the determination to rule as well as reign, to subdue all parties, and to place himself at the head of the nation and empire.

Political Parties and George III.—The state of the political parties favored the plans of the king to restore some of the ancient luster of the crown. The Whigs, who were composed mainly of the smaller freeholders, merchants, inhabitants of towns, and Protestant non-conformists, had grown haughty and overbearing through long continuance in power and had as a consequence raised up many enemies in their own ranks. Their opponents, the Tories, had by this time given up all hope of restoring to the throne the direct Stuart line; but they still cherished their old notions about divine right. With the accession of

George III the coveted opportunity came to them to rally around the throne again. George received his Tory friends with open arms, gave them offices, and bought them seats in the House of Commons.

The British Parliamentary System.—The peculiarities of the British Parliament at the time made smooth the way for the king and his allies with their designs for controlling the entire government. In the first place, the House of Lords was composed mainly of hereditary nobles whose number the king could increase by the appointment of his favorites, as of old. Though the members of the House of Commons were elected by popular vote, they did not speak for the mass of English people. Great towns like Leeds, Manchester, and Birmingham, for example, had no representatives at all. While there were about eight million inhabitants in Great Britain, there were in 1768 only about 160,000 voters; that is to say, only about one in every ten adult males had a voice in the government. Many boroughs returned one or more members to the Commons although they had merely a handful of voters or in some instances no voters at all. Furthermore, these tiny boroughs were often controlled by lords who openly sold the right of representation to the highest bidder. The "rotten-boroughs," as they were called by reformers, were a public scandal, but George III readily made use of them to get his friends into the House of Commons.

GEORGE III'S MINISTERS AND THEIR COLONIAL POLICIES

Grenville and the War Debt.—Within a year after the accession of George III, William Pitt was turned out of office, the king treating him with "gross incivility" and the crowds shouting "Pitt forever!" The direction of affairs was entrusted to men enjoying the king's confidence. Leadership in the House of Commons fell to George Grenville, a grave and laborious man who for years had groaned over the increasing cost of government.

The first task after the conclusion of peace in 1763 was the adjustment of the disordered finances of the kingdom. The debt stood at the highest point in the history of the country. More revenue was absolutely necessary and Grenville began to search for it, turning his attention finally to the American colonies. In this quest he had the aid of a zealous colleague, Charles Townshend, who had long been in public service and was familiar with the difficulties encountered by royal governors in America. These two men, with the support of the entire ministry, inaugurated in February, 1763, "a new system of colonial government. It was announced by authority that there were to be no more requisitions from the king to the colonial assemblies for supplies, but that the colonies were to be taxed instead by act of Parliament. Colonial governors and judges were to be paid by the Crown; they were to be supported by a standing army of twenty regiments; and all the expenses of this force were to be met by parliamentary taxation."

Restriction of Paper Money (1763).—Among the many complaints filed before the board of trade were vigorous protests against the issuance of paper money by the colonial legislatures. The new ministry provided a remedy in the act of 1763, which declared void all colonial laws authorizing paper money or extending the life of outstanding bills. This law was aimed at the "cheap money" which the Americans were fond of making when specie was scarce—money which they tried to force on their English creditors in return for goods and in payment of the interest and principal of debts. Thus the first chapter was written in the long battle over sound money on this continent.

Limitation on Western Land Sales.—Later in the same year (1763) George III issued a royal proclamation providing, among other things, for the government of the territory recently acquired by the treaty of Paris from the French. One of the provisions in this royal decree touched frontiersmen to the quick. The contests between the king's officers and the colonists over the disposition of western lands had been long and sharp. The Americans chafed at restrictions on settlement. The more adventurous were continually moving west and "squatting" on land purchased from the Indians or simply seized without authority. To put an end to this, the king forbade all further purchases from the Indians, reserving to the crown the right to acquire such lands and dispose of them for settlement. A second provision in the same proclamation vested the power of licensing trade with the Indians, including the lucrative fur business, in the hands of royal officers in the colonies. These two limitations on American freedom and enterprise were declared to be in the interest of the crown and for the preservation of the rights of the Indians against fraud and abuses.

The Sugar Act of 1764.—King George's ministers next turned their attention to measures of taxation and trade. Since the heavy debt under which England was laboring had been largely incurred in the defense of America, nothing seemed more reasonable to them than the proposition that the colonies should help to bear the burden which fell so heavily upon the English taxpayer. The Sugar Act of 1764 was the result of this reasoning. There was no doubt about the purpose of this law, for it was set forth clearly in the title: "An act for granting certain duties in the British colonies and plantations in America ... for applying the produce of such duties ... towards defraying the expenses of defending, protecting and securing the said colonies and plantations ... and for more effectually preventing the clandestine conveyance of goods to and from the said colonies and plantations and improving and securing the trade between the same and Great Britain." The old Molasses Act had been prohibitive; the Sugar Act of 1764 was clearly intended as a revenue measure. Specified duties were laid upon sugar, indigo, calico, silks, and many other commodities imported into the colonies. The enforcement of the Molasses Act had been utterly neglected; but this Sugar Act had "teeth in it." Special precautions as to bonds, security, and registration of ship masters, accompanied by heavy penalties, promised a vigorous execution of the new revenue law.

The strict terms of the Sugar Act were strengthened by administrative measures. Under a law of the previous year the commanders of armed vessels stationed along the American coast were authorized to stop, search, and, on suspicion, seize merchant ships approaching colonial ports. By supplementary orders, the entire British official force in America was instructed to be diligent in the execution of all trade and navigation laws. Revenue collectors, officers of the army and navy, and royal governors were curtly ordered to the front to do their full duty in the matter of law enforcement. The ordinary motives for the discharge of official obligations were sharpened by an appeal to avarice, for naval officers who seized offenders against the law were rewarded by large prizes out of the forfeitures and penalties.

The Stamp Act (1765).—The Grenville-Townshend combination moved steadily towards its goal. While the Sugar Act was under consideration in Parliament, Grenville announced a plan for a stamp bill. The next year it went through both Houses with a speed that must have astounded its authors. The vote in the Commons stood 205 in favor to 49 against; while in the Lords it was not even necessary to go through the formality of a count. As George III was temporarily insane, the measure received royal assent by a commission acting as a board of regency. Protests of colonial agents in London were futile. "We might as well have hindered the sun's progress!" exclaimed Franklin. Protests of a few opponents in the Commons were equally vain. The ministry was firm in its course and from all appearances the Stamp Act hardly roused as much as a languid interest in the city of London. In fact, it is recorded that the fateful measure attracted less notice than a bill providing for a commission to act for the king when he was incapacitated.

The Stamp Act, like the Sugar Act, declared the purpose of the British government to raise revenue in America "towards defraying the expenses of defending, protecting, and securing the British colonies and plantations in America." It was a long measure of more than fifty sections, carefully planned and skillfully drawn. By its provisions duties were imposed on practically all papers used in legal transactions,—deeds, mortgages, inventories, writs, bail bonds,—on licenses to practice law and sell liquor, on college diplomas, playing cards, dice, pamphlets, newspapers, almanacs, calendars, and advertisements. The drag net was closely knit, for scarcely anything escaped.

The Quartering Act (1765).—The ministers were aware that the Stamp Act would rouse opposition in America—how great they could not conjecture. While the measure was being debated, a friend of General Wolfe, Colonel Barré, who knew America well, gave them an ominous warning in the Commons. "Believe me—remember I this day told you so—" he exclaimed, "the same spirit of freedom which actuated that people at first will accompany them still ... a people jealous of their liberties and who will vindicate them, if ever they should be violated." The answer of the ministry to a prophecy of force was a threat of force. Preparations were accordingly made to dispatch a larger number of soldiers than usual to the colonies, and the ink was hardly dry on the Stamp Act when Parliament passed the Quartering Act ordering the colonists to provide accommodations for the soldiers who were to enforce the new laws. "We have the power to tax them," said one of the ministry, "and we will tax them."

COLONIAL RESISTANCE FORCES REPEAL

Popular Opposition.—The Stamp Act was greeted in America by an outburst of denunciation. The merchants of the seaboard cities took the lead in making a dignified but unmistakable protest, agreeing not to import British goods while the hated law stood upon the books. Lawyers, some of them incensed at the heavy taxes on their operations and others intimidated by patriots who refused to permit them to use stamped papers, joined with the merchants. Aristocratic colonial Whigs, who had long grumbled at the administration of royal governors, protested against taxation without their consent, as the Whigs had done in old England. There were Tories, however, in the colonies as in England—many of them of the official class—who denounced the merchants, lawyers, and Whig aristocrats as "seditious, factious and republican." Yet the opposition to the Stamp Act and its accompanying measure, the Quartering Act, grew steadily all through the summer of 1765.

In a little while it was taken up in the streets and along the countryside. All through the North and in some of the Southern colonies, there sprang up, as if by magic, committees and societies pledged to resist the Stamp Act to the bitter end. These popular societies were known as Sons of Liberty and Daughters of Liberty: the former including artisans, mechanics, and laborers; and the latter, patriotic women. Both groups were alike in that they had as yet taken little part in public affairs. Many artisans, as well as all the women, were excluded from the right to vote for colonial assemblymen.

While the merchants and Whig gentlemen confined their efforts chiefly to drafting well-phrased protests against British measures, the Sons of Liberty operated in the streets and chose rougher measures. They stirred up riots in Boston, New York, Philadelphia, and Charleston when attempts were made to sell the stamps. They sacked and burned the residences of high royal officers. They organized committees of inquisition who by threats and intimidation curtailed the sale of British goods and the use of stamped papers. In fact, the Sons of Liberty carried their operations to such excesses that many mild opponents of the stamp tax were frightened and drew back in astonishment at the forces they had unloosed. The Daughters of Liberty in a quieter way were making a very effective resistance to the sale of the hated goods by spurring on domestic industries, their own particular province being the manufacture of clothing, and devising substitutes for taxed foods. They helped to feed and clothe their families without buying British goods.

Legislative Action against the Stamp Act.—Leaders in the colonial assemblies, accustomed to battle against British policies, supported the popular protest. The Stamp Act was signed on March 22, 1765. On May 30, the Virginia House of Burgesses passed a set of resolutions declaring that the General Assembly of the colony alone had the right to lay taxes upon the inhabitants and that attempts to impose them otherwise were "illegal, unconstitutional, and unjust." It was in support of these resolutions that Patrick Henry uttered the immortal challenge: "Cæsar had his Brutus, Charles I his Cromwell, and George III...." Cries of "Treason" were calmly met by the orator who finished: "George III may profit by their example. If that be treason, make the most of it."

The Stamp Act Congress.—The Massachusetts Assembly answered the call of Virginia by inviting the colonies to elect delegates to a Congress to be held in New York to discuss the situation. Nine colonies responded and sent representatives. The delegates, while professing the warmest affection for the king's person and government, firmly spread on record a series of resolutions that admitted of no double meaning. They declared that taxes could not be imposed without their consent, given through their respective colonial assemblies; that the Stamp Act showed a tendency to subvert their rights and liberties; that the recent trade acts were burdensome and grievous; and that the right to petition the king and Parliament was their heritage. They thereupon made "humble supplication" for the repeal of the Stamp Act.

The Stamp Act Congress was more than an assembly of protest. It marked the rise of a new agency of government to express the will of America. It was the germ of a government which in time was to supersede the government of George III in the colonies. It foreshadowed the Congress of the United States under the Constitution. It was a successful attempt at union. "There ought to be no New England men," declared Christopher Gadsden, in the Stamp Act Congress, "no New Yorkers known on the Continent, but all of us Americans."

The Repeal of the Stamp Act and the Sugar Act.—The effect of American resistance on opinion in England was telling. Commerce with the colonies had been effectively boycotted by the Americans; ships lay idly swinging at the wharves; bankruptcy threatened hundreds of merchants in London, Bristol, and Liverpool. Workingmen in the manufacturing towns of England were thrown out of employment. The government had sown folly and was reaping, in place of the coveted revenue, rebellion.

Perplexed by the storm they had raised, the ministers summoned to the bar of the House of Commons, Benjamin Franklin, the agent for Pennsylvania, who was in London. "Do you think it right," asked Grenville, "that America should be protected by this country and pay no part of the expenses?" The answer was brief: "That is not the case; the colonies raised, clothed, and paid during the last war twenty-five thousand men and spent many millions." Then came an inquiry whether the colonists would accept a modified stamp act. "No, never," replied Franklin, "never! They will never submit to it!" It was next suggested that military force might compel obedience to law. Franklin had a ready answer. "They cannot force a man to take stamps.... They may not find a rebellion; they may, indeed, make one."

The repeal of the Stamp Act was moved in the House of Commons a few days later. The sponsor for the repeal spoke of commerce interrupted, debts due British merchants placed in jeopardy, Manchester industries closed, workingmen unemployed, oppression instituted, and the loss of the colonies threatened. Pitt and Edmund Burke, the former near the close of his career, the latter just beginning his, argued cogently in favor of retracing the steps taken the year before. Grenville refused. "America must learn," he wailed, "that prayers are not to be brought to Cæsar through riot and sedition." His protests were idle. The Commons agreed to the repeal on February 22, 1766, amid the cheers of the victorious majority. It was carried through the Lords in the face of strong opposition and, on March 18, reluctantly signed by the king, now restored to his right mind.

In rescinding the Stamp Act, Parliament did not admit the contention of the Americans that it was without power to tax them. On the contrary, it accompanied the repeal with a Declaratory Act. It announced that the colonies were subordinate to the crown and Parliament of Great Britain; that the king and Parliament therefore had undoubted authority to make laws binding the colonies in all cases whatsoever; and that the resolutions and proceedings of the colonists denying such authority were null and void.

The repeal was greeted by the colonists with great popular demonstrations. Bells were rung; toasts to the king were drunk; and trade resumed its normal course. The Declaratory Act, as a mere paper resolution, did not disturb the good humor of those who again cheered the name of King George. Their confidence was soon strengthened by the news that even the Sugar Act had been repealed, thus practically restoring the condition of affairs before Grenville and Townshend inaugurated their policy of "thoroughness."

RESUMPTION OF BRITISH REVENUE AND COMMERCIAL POLICIES

The Townshend Acts (1767).—The triumph of the colonists was brief. Though Pitt, the friend of America, was once more prime minister, and seated in the House of Lords as the Earl of Chatham, his severe illness gave to Townshend and the Tory party practical control over Parliament. Unconvinced by the experience with the Stamp Act, Townshend brought forward and pushed through both Houses of Parliament three measures, which to this day are associated with his name. First among his restrictive laws was that of June 29, 1767, which placed the enforcement of the collection of duties and customs on colonial imports and exports in the hands of British commissioners appointed by the king, resident in the colonies, paid from the British treasury, and independent of all control by the colonists. The second measure of the same date imposed a tax on lead, glass, paint, tea, and a few other articles imported into the colonies, the revenue derived from the duties to be applied toward the payment of the salaries and other expenses of royal colonial officials. A third measure was the Tea Act of July 2, 1767, aimed at the tea trade which the Americans carried on illegally with foreigners. This law abolished the duty which the East India Company had to pay in England on tea exported to America, for it was thought that English tea merchants might thus find it possible to undersell American tea smugglers.

Writs of Assistance Legalized by Parliament.—Had Parliament been content with laying duties, just as a manifestation of power and right, and neglected their collection, perhaps little would have been heard of the Townshend Acts. It provided, however, for the strict, even the harsh, enforcement of the law. It ordered customs officers to remain at their posts and put an end to smuggling. In the revenue act of June 29, 1767, it expressly authorized the superior courts of the colonies to issue "writs of assistance," empowering customs officers to enter "any house, warehouse, shop, cellar, or other place in the British colonies or plantations in America to search for and seize" prohibited or smuggled goods.

The writ of assistance, which was a general search warrant issued to revenue officers, was an ancient device hateful to a people who cherished the spirit of personal independence and who had made actual gains in the practice of civil liberty. To allow a "minion of the law" to enter a man's house and search his papers and premises, was too much for the emotions of people who had fled to America in a quest for self-government and free homes, who had braved such hardships to establish them, and who wanted to trade without official interference.

The writ of assistance had been used in Massachusetts in 1755 to prevent illicit trade with Canada and had aroused a violent hostility at that time. In 1761 it was again the subject of a bitter controversy which arose in connection with the application of a customs officer to a Massachusetts court for writs of assistance "as usual." This application was vainly opposed by James Otis in a speech of five hours' duration—a speech of such fire and eloquence that it sent every man who heard it away "ready to take up arms against writs of assistance." Otis denounced the practice as an exercise of arbitrary power which had cost one king his head and another his throne, a tyrant's device which placed the liberty of every man in jeopardy, enabling any petty officer to work possible malice on any innocent citizen on the merest suspicion, and to spread terror and desolation through the land. "What a scene," he exclaimed, "does this open! Every man, prompted by revenge, ill-humor, or wantonness to inspect the inside of his neighbor's house, may get a writ of assistance. Others will ask it from self-defense; one arbitrary exertion will provoke another until society is involved in tumult and blood." He did more than attack the writ itself. He said that Parliament could not establish it because it was against the British constitution. This was an assertion resting on slender foundation, but it was quickly echoed by the people. Then and there James Otis sounded the call to America to resist the exercise of arbitrary power by royal officers. "Then and there," wrote John Adams, "the child Independence was born." Such was the hated writ that Townshend proposed to put into the hands of customs officers in his grim determination to enforce the law.

The New York Assembly Suspended.—In the very month that Townshend's Acts were signed by the king, Parliament took a still more drastic step. The assembly of New York, protesting against the "ruinous and insupportable" expense involved, had failed to make provision for the care of British troops in accordance with the terms of the Quartering Act. Parliament therefore suspended the assembly until it promised to obey the law. It was not until a third election was held that compliance with the Quartering Act was wrung from the reluctant province. In the meantime, all the colonies had learned on how frail a foundation their representative bodies rested.

Renewed Resistance in America

The Massachusetts Circular (1768).—Massachusetts, under the leadership of Samuel Adams, resolved to resist the policy of renewed intervention in America. At his suggestion the assembly adopted a Circular Letter addressed to the assemblies of the other colonies informing them of the state of affairs in Massachusetts and roundly condemning the whole British program. The Circular Letter declared that

Parliament had no right to lay taxes on Americans without their consent and that the colonists could not, from the nature of the case, be represented in Parliament. It went on shrewdly to submit to consideration the question as to whether any people could be called free who were subjected to governors and judges appointed by the crown and paid out of funds raised independently. It invited the other colonies, in the most temperate tones, to take thought about the common predicament in which they were all placed.

The Dissolution of Assemblies.—The governor of Massachusetts, hearing of the Circular Letter, ordered the assembly to rescind its appeal. On meeting refusal, he promptly dissolved it. The Maryland, Georgia, and South Carolina assemblies indorsed the Circular Letter and were also dissolved at once. The Virginia House of Burgesses, thoroughly aroused, passed resolutions on May 16, 1769, declaring that the sole right of imposing taxes in Virginia was vested in its legislature, asserting anew the right of petition to the crown, condemning the transportation of persons accused of crimes or trial beyond the seas, and beseeching the king for a redress of the general grievances. The immediate dissolution of the Virginia assembly, in its turn, was the answer of the royal governor.

The Boston Massacre.—American opposition to the British authorities kept steadily rising as assemblies were dissolved, the houses of citizens searched, and troops distributed in increasing numbers among the centers of discontent. Merchants again agreed not to import British goods, the Sons of Liberty renewed their agitation, and women set about the patronage of home products still more loyally.

On the night of March 5, 1770, a crowd on the streets of Boston began to jostle and tease some British regulars stationed in the town. Things went from bad to worse until some "boys and young fellows" began to throw snowballs and stones. Then the exasperated soldiers fired into the crowd, killing five and wounding half a dozen more. The day after the "massacre," a mass meeting was held in the town and Samuel Adams was sent to demand the withdrawal of the soldiers. The governor hesitated and tried to compromise. Finding Adams relentless, the governor yielded and ordered the regulars away.

The Boston Massacre stirred the country from New Hampshire to Georgia. Popular passions ran high. The guilty soldiers were charged with murder. Their defense was undertaken, in spite of the wrath of the populace, by John Adams and Josiah Quincy, who as lawyers thought even the worst offenders entitled to their full rights in law. In his speech to the jury, however, Adams warned the British government against its course, saying, that "from the nature of things soldiers quartered in a populous town will always occasion two mobs where they will prevent one." Two of the soldiers were convicted and lightly punished.

Resistance in the South.—The year following the Boston Massacre some citizens of North Carolina, goaded by the conduct of the royal governor, openly resisted his authority. Many were killed as a result and seven who were taken prisoners were hanged as traitors. A little later royal troops and local militia met in a pitched battle near Alamance River, called the "Lexington of the South."

The *Gaspee* Affair and the Virginia Resolutions of 1773.—On sea as well as on land, friction between the royal officers and the colonists broke out into overt acts. While patrolling Narragansett Bay looking for smugglers one day in 1772, the armed ship, *Gaspee*, ran ashore and was caught fast. During the night several men from Providence boarded the vessel and, after seizing the crew, set it on fire. A royal commission, sent to Rhode Island to discover the offenders and bring them to account, failed because it could not find a single informer. The very appointment of such a commission aroused the patriots of Virginia to action; and in March, 1773, the House of Burgesses passed a resolution creating a standing committee of correspondence to develop coöperation among the colonies in resistance to British measures.

The Boston Tea Party.—Although the British government, finding the Townshend revenue act a failure, repealed in 1770 all the duties except that on tea, it in no way relaxed its resolve to enforce the other commercial regulations it had imposed on the colonies. Moreover, Parliament decided to relieve the British East India Company of the financial difficulties into which it had fallen partly by reason of the Tea Act and the colonial boycott that followed. In 1773 it agreed to return to the Company the regular import duties, levied in England, on all tea transshipped to America. A small impost of three pence, to be collected in America, was left as a reminder of the principle laid down in the Declaratory Act that Parliament had the right to tax the colonists.

This arrangement with the East India Company was obnoxious to the colonists for several reasons. It was an act of favoritism for one thing, in the interest of a great monopoly. For another thing, it promised to dump on the American market, suddenly, an immense amount of cheap tea and so cause heavy losses to American merchants who had large stocks on hand. It threatened with ruin the business of all those who were engaged in clandestine trade with the Dutch. It carried with it an irritating tax of three pence on imports. In Charleston, Annapolis, New York, and Boston, captains of ships who brought tea under this act were roughly handled. One night in December, 1773, a band of Boston citizens, disguised as Indians, boarded the hated tea ships and dumped the cargo into the harbor. This was serious business, for it was open, flagrant, determined violation of the law. As such the British government viewed it.

RETALIATION BY THE BRITISH GOVERNMENT

Reception of the News of the Tea Riot.—The news of the tea riot in Boston confirmed King George in his conviction that there should be no soft policy in dealing with his American subjects. "The die is cast," he stated with evident satisfaction. "The colonies must either triumph or submit.... If we take the resolute part, they will undoubtedly be very meek." Lord George Germain characterized the tea party as "the proceedings of a tumultuous and riotous rabble who ought, if they had the least prudence, to follow their mercantile employments and not trouble themselves with politics and government, which they do not understand." This expressed, in concise form, exactly the sentiments of Lord North, who had then for three years been the king's chief minister. Even Pitt, Lord Chatham, was prepared to support the government in upholding its authority.

The Five Intolerable Acts.—Parliament, beginning on March 31, 1774, passed five stringent measures, known in American history as the five "intolerable acts." They were aimed at curing the unrest in America. The *first* of them was a bill absolutely shutting the port of Boston to commerce with the outside world. The *second*, following closely, revoked the Massachusetts charter of 1691 and provided furthermore that the councilors should be appointed by the king, that all judges should be named by the royal governor, and that town meetings (except to elect certain officers) could not be held without the governor's consent. A *third* measure, after denouncing the "utter subversion of all lawful government" in the provinces, authorized royal agents to transfer to Great Britain or to other colonies the trials of officers or other persons accused of murder in connection with the enforcement of the law. The *fourth* act legalized the quartering of troops in Massachusetts towns. The *fifth* of the measures was the Quebec Act, which granted religious toleration to the Catholics in Canada, extended the boundaries of Quebec southward to the Ohio River, and established, in this western region, government by a viceroy.

The intolerable acts went through Parliament with extraordinary celerity. There was an opposition, alert and informed; but it was ineffective. Burke spoke eloquently against the Boston port bill, condemning it roundly for punishing the innocent with the guilty, and showing how likely it was to bring grave consequences in its train. He was heard with respect and his pleas were rejected. The bill passed both houses without a division, the entry "unanimous" being made upon their journals although it did not accurately represent the state of opinion. The law destroying the charter of Massachusetts passed the Commons by a vote of three to one; and the third intolerable act by a vote of four to one. The triumph of the ministry was complete. "What passed in Boston," exclaimed the great jurist, Lord Mansfield, "is the overt act of High Treason proceeding from our over lenity and want of foresight." The crown and Parliament were united in resorting to punitive measures.

In the colonies the laws were received with consternation. To the American Protestants, the Quebec Act was the most offensive. That project they viewed not as an act of grace or of mercy but as a direct attempt to enlist French Canadians on the side of Great Britain. The British government did not grant religious toleration to Catholics either at home or in Ireland and the Americans could see no good motive in granting it in North America. The act was also offensive because Massachusetts, Connecticut, and Virginia had, under their charters, large claims in the territory thus annexed to Quebec.

To enforce these intolerable acts the military arm of the British government was brought into play. The commander-in-chief of the armed forces in America, General Gage, was appointed governor of Massachusetts. Reinforcements were brought to the colonies, for now King George was to give "the rebels," as he called them, a taste of strong medicine. The majesty of his law was to be vindicated by force.

From Reform to Revolution in America

The Doctrine of Natural Rights.—The dissolution of assemblies, the destruction of charters, and the use of troops produced in the colonies a new phase in the struggle. In the early days of the contest with the British ministry, the Americans spoke of their "rights as Englishmen" and condemned the acts of Parliament as unlawful, as violating the principles of the English constitution under which they all lived. When they saw that such arguments had no effect on Parliament, they turned for support to their "natural rights." The latter doctrine, in the form in which it was employed by the colonists, was as English as the constitutional argument. John Locke had used it with good effect in defense of the English revolution in the seventeenth century. American leaders, familiar with the writings of Locke, also took up his thesis in the hour of their distress. They openly declared that their rights did not rest after all upon the English constitution or a charter from the crown. "Old Magna Carta was not the beginning of all things," retorted Otis when the constitutional argument failed. "A time may come when Parliament shall declare every American charter void, but the natural, inherent, and inseparable rights of the colonists as men and as citizens would remain and whatever became of charters can never be abolished until the general conflagration." Of the same opinion was the young and impetuous Alexander Hamilton. "The sacred rights of mankind," he exclaimed, "are not to be rummaged for among old parchments or musty records. They are written as with a sunbeam in the whole volume of human destiny by the hand of divinity itself, and can never be erased or obscured by mortal power."

Firm as the American leaders were in the statement and defense of their rights, there is every reason for believing that in the beginning they hoped to confine the conflict to the realm of opinion. They constantly avowed that they were loyal to the king when protesting in the strongest language against his policies. Even Otis, regarded by the loyalists as a firebrand, was in fact attempting to avert revolution by winning concessions from England. "I argue this cause with the greater pleasure," he solemnly urged in his speech against the writs of assistance, "as it is in favor of British liberty ... and as it is in opposition to a kind of power, the exercise of which in former periods cost one king of England his head and another his throne."

Burke Offers the Doctrine of Conciliation.—The flooding tide of American sentiment was correctly measured by one Englishman at least, Edmund Burke, who quickly saw that attempts to restrain the rise of American democracy were efforts to reverse the processes of nature. He saw how fixed and rooted in the nature of things was the American spirit—how inevitable, how irresistible. He warned his countrymen that there were three ways of handling the delicate situation—and only three. One was to remove the cause of friction by changing the spirit of the colonists—an utter impossibility because that spirit was grounded in the essential circumstances of American life. The second was to prosecute American leaders as criminals; of this he begged his countrymen to beware lest the colonists declare that "a government against which a claim of liberty is tantamount to high treason is a government to which submission is equivalent to slavery." The third and right way to meet the problem, Burke concluded, was to accept the American spirit, repeal the obnoxious measures, and receive the colonies into equal partnership.

Events Produce the Great Decision.—The right way, indicated by Burke, was equally impossible to George III and the majority in Parliament. To their narrow minds, American opinion was contemptible and American resistance unlawful, riotous, and treasonable. The correct way, in their view, was to dispatch more troops to crush the "rebels"; and that very act took the contest from the realm of opinion. As John Adams said: "Facts are stubborn things." Opinions were unseen, but marching soldiers were visible to the veriest street urchin. "Now," said Gouverneur Morris, "the sheep, simple as they are, cannot be gulled as heretofore." It was too late to talk about the excellence of the British constitution. If any one is bewildered by the controversies of modern historians as to why the crisis came at last, he can clarify his understanding by reading again Edmund Burke's stately oration, *On Conciliation with America*.

References

G.L. Beer, *British Colonial Policy* (1754-63).

E. Channing, *History of the United States*, Vol. III.

R. Frothingham, *Rise of the Republic*.

G.E. Howard, *Preliminaries of the Revolution* (American Nation Series).

J.K. Hosmer, *Samuel Adams*.

J.T. Morse, *Benjamin Franklin*.

M.C. Tyler, *Patrick Henry*.

J.A. Woodburn (editor), *The American Revolution* (Selections from the English work by Lecky).

Questions

1. Show how the character of George III made for trouble with the colonies.

2. Explain why the party and parliamentary systems of England favored the plans of George III.

3. How did the state of English finances affect English policy?

4. Enumerate five important measures of the English government affecting the colonies between 1763 and 1765. Explain each in detail.

5. Describe American resistance to the Stamp Act. What was the outcome?

6. Show how England renewed her policy of regulation in 1767.

7. Summarize the events connected with American resistance.

8. With what measures did Great Britain retaliate?

9. Contrast "constitutional" with "natural" rights.

10. What solution did Burke offer? Why was it rejected?

Research Topics

Powers Conferred on Revenue Officers by Writs of Assistance.—See a writ in Macdonald, *Source Book*, p. 109.

The Acts of Parliament Respecting America.—Macdonald, pp. 117-146. Assign one to each student for report and comment.

Source Studies on the Stamp Act.—Hart, *American History Told by Contemporaries*, Vol. II, pp. 394-412.

Source Studies of the Townshend Acts.—Hart, Vol. II, pp. 413-433.

American Principles.—Prepare a table of them from the Resolutions of the Stamp Act Congress and the Massachusetts Circular. Macdonald, pp. 136-146.

An English Historian's View of the Period.—Green, *Short History of England*, Chap. X.

English Policy Not Injurious to America.—Callender, *Economic History*, pp. 85-121.

A Review of English Policy.—Woodrow Wilson, *History of the American People*, Vol. II, pp. 129-170.

The Opening of the Revolution.—Elson, *History of the United States*, pp. 220-235.

CHAPTER VI

THE AMERICAN REVOLUTION

Resistance and Retaliation

The Continental Congress.—When the news of the "intolerable acts" reached America, every one knew what strong medicine Parliament was prepared to administer to all those who resisted its authority. The cause of Massachusetts became the cause of all the colonies. Opposition to British policy, hitherto local and spasmodic, now took on a national character. To local committees and provincial conventions was added a Continental Congress, appropriately called by Massachusetts on June 17, 1774, at the instigation of Samuel Adams. The response to the summons was electric. By hurried and irregular methods delegates were elected during the summer, and on September 5 the Congress duly assembled in Carpenter's Hall in Philadelphia. Many of the greatest men in America were there—George Washington and Patrick Henry from Virginia and John and Samuel Adams from Massachusetts. Every shade of opinion was represented. Some were impatient with mild devices; the majority favored moderation.

The Congress drew up a declaration of American rights and stated in clear and dignified language the grievances of the colonists. It approved the resistance to British measures offered by Massachusetts and promised the united support of all sections. It prepared an address to King George and another to the people of England, disavowing the idea of independence but firmly attacking the policies pursued by the British government.

The Non-Importation Agreement.—The Congress was not content, however, with professions of faith and with petitions. It took one revolutionary step. It agreed to stop the importation of British goods into America, and the enforcement of this agreement it placed in the hands of local "committees of safety and inspection," to be elected by the qualified voters. The significance of this action is obvious. Congress threw itself athwart British law. It made a rule to bind American citizens and to be carried into effect by American officers. It set up a state within the British state and laid down a test of allegiance to the new order. The colonists, who up to this moment had been wavering, had to choose one authority or the other. They were for the enforcement of the non-importation agreement or they were against it. They either bought English goods or they did not. In the spirit of the toast—"May Britain be wise and America be free"—the first Continental Congress adjourned in October, having appointed the tenth of May following for the meeting of a second Congress, should necessity require.

Lord North's "Olive Branch."—When the news of the action of the American Congress reached England, Pitt and Burke warmly urged a repeal of the obnoxious laws, but in vain. All they could wring from the prime minister, Lord North, was a set of "conciliatory resolutions" proposing to relieve from taxation any colony that would assume its share of imperial defense and make provision for supporting the local officers of the crown. This "olive branch" was accompanied by a resolution assuring the king of support at all hazards in suppressing the rebellion and by the restraining act of March 30, 1775, which in effect destroyed the commerce of New England.

Bloodshed at Lexington and Concord (April 19, 1775).—Meanwhile the British authorities in Massachusetts relaxed none of their efforts in upholding British sovereignty. General Gage, hearing that military stores had been collected at Concord, dispatched a small force to seize them. By this act he precipitated the conflict he had sought to avoid. At Lexington, on the road to Concord, occurred "the little thing" that produced "the great event." An unexpected collision beyond the thought or purpose of any man had transferred the contest from the forum to the battle field.

The Second Continental Congress.—Though blood had been shed and war was actually at hand, the second Continental Congress, which met at Philadelphia in May, 1775, was not yet convinced that conciliation was beyond human power. It petitioned the king to interpose on behalf of the colonists in order that the empire might avoid the calamities of civil war. On the last day of July, it made a temperate but firm answer to Lord North's offer of conciliation, stating that the proposal was unsatisfactory because it did not renounce the right to tax or repeal the offensive acts of Parliament.

Force, the British Answer.—Just as the representatives of America were about to present the last petition of Congress to the king on August 23, 1775, George III issued a proclamation of rebellion. This announcement declared that the colonists, "misled by dangerous and ill-designing men," were in a state of insurrection; it called on the civil and military powers to bring "the traitors to justice"; and it threatened with "condign punishment the authors, perpetrators, and abettors of such traitorous designs." It closed with the usual prayer: "God, save the king." Later in the year, Parliament passed a sweeping act destroying all trade and intercourse with America. Congress was silent at last. Force was also America's answer.

AMERICAN INDEPENDENCE

Drifting into War.—Although the Congress had not given up all hope of reconciliation in the spring and summer of 1775, it had firmly resolved to defend American rights by arms if necessary. It transformed the militiamen who had assembled near Boston, after the battle of Lexington, into a Continental army and selected Washington as commander-in-chief. It assumed the powers of a government and prepared to raise money, wage war, and carry on diplomatic relations with foreign countries.

Events followed thick and fast. On June 17, the American militia, by the stubborn defense of Bunker Hill, showed that it could make British regulars pay dearly for all they got. On July 3, Washington took command of the army at Cambridge. In January, 1776, after bitter disappointments in drumming up recruits for its army in England, Scotland, and Ireland, the British government concluded a treaty with the Landgrave of Hesse-Cassel in Germany contracting, at a handsome figure, for thousands of soldiers and many pieces of cannon. This was the crowning insult to America. Such was the view of all friends of the colonies on both sides of the water. Such was, long afterward, the judgment of the conservative historian Lecky: "The conduct of England in hiring German mercenaries to subdue the essentially English population beyond the Atlantic made reconciliation hopeless and independence inevitable." The news of this wretched transaction in German soldiers had hardly reached America before there ran all down the coast the thrilling story that Washington had taken Boston, on March 17, 1776, compelling Lord Howe to sail with his entire army for Halifax.

The Growth of Public Sentiment in Favor of Independence.—Events were bearing the Americans away from their old position under the British constitution toward a final separation. Slowly and against their desires, prudent and honorable men, who cherished the ties that united them to the old order and dreaded with genuine horror all thought of revolution, were drawn into the path that led to the great decision. In all parts of the country and among all classes, the question of the hour was being debated. "American independence," as the historian Bancroft says, "was not an act of sudden passion nor the work of one man or one assembly. It had been discussed in every part of the country by farmers and merchants, by mechanics and planters, by the fishermen along the coast and the backwoodsmen of the West; in town meetings and from the pulpit; at social gatherings and around the camp fires; in county conventions and conferences or committees; in colonial congresses and assemblies."

Paine's "Commonsense."—In the midst of this ferment of American opinion, a bold and eloquent pamphleteer broke in upon the hesitating public with a program for absolute independence, without fears and without apologies. In the early days of 1776, Thomas Paine issued the first of his famous tracts, "Commonsense," a passionate attack upon the British monarchy and an equally passionate plea for

American liberty. Casting aside the language of petition with which Americans had hitherto addressed George III, Paine went to the other extreme and assailed him with many a violent epithet. He condemned monarchy itself as a system which had laid the world "in blood and ashes." Instead of praising the British constitution under which colonists had been claiming their rights, he brushed it aside as ridiculous, protesting that it was "owing to the constitution of the people, not to the constitution of the government, that the Crown is not as oppressive in England as in Turkey."

Having thus summarily swept away the grounds of allegiance to the old order, Paine proceeded relentlessly to an argument for immediate separation from Great Britain. There was nothing in the sphere of practical interest, he insisted, which should bind the colonies to the mother country. Allegiance to her had been responsible for the many wars in which they had been involved. Reasons of trade were not less weighty in behalf of independence. "Our corn will fetch its price in any market in Europe and our imported goods must be paid for, buy them where we will." As to matters of government, "it is not in the power of Britain to do this continent justice; the business of it will soon be too weighty and intricate to be managed with any tolerable degree of convenience by a power so distant from us and so very ignorant of us."

There is accordingly no alternative to independence for America. "Everything that is right or natural pleads for separation. The blood of the slain, the weeping voice of nature cries 'tis time to part.' ... Arms, the last resort, must decide the contest; the appeal was the choice of the king and the continent hath accepted the challenge.... The sun never shone on a cause of greater worth. 'Tis not the affair of a city, a county, a province or a kingdom, but of a continent.... 'Tis not the concern of a day, a year or an age; posterity is involved in the contest and will be more or less affected to the end of time by the proceedings now. Now is the seed-time of Continental union, faith, and honor.... O! ye that love mankind! Ye that dare oppose not only the tyranny, but the tyrant, stand forth.... Let names of Whig and Tory be extinct. Let none other be heard among us than those of a good citizen, an open and resolute friend, and a virtuous supporter of the rights of mankind and of the free and independent states of America." As more than 100,000 copies were scattered broadcast over the country, patriots exclaimed with Washington: "Sound doctrine and unanswerable reason!"

The Drift of Events toward Independence.—Official support for the idea of independence began to come from many quarters. On the tenth of February, 1776, Gadsden, in the provincial convention of South Carolina, advocated a new constitution for the colony and absolute independence for all America. The convention balked at the latter but went half way by abolishing the system of royal administration and establishing a complete plan of self-government. A month later, on April 12, the neighboring state of North Carolina uttered the daring phrase from which others shrank. It empowered its representatives in the Congress to concur with the delegates of the other colonies in declaring independence. Rhode Island, Massachusetts, and Virginia quickly responded to the challenge. The convention of the Old Dominion, on May 15, instructed its delegates at Philadelphia to propose the independence of the United Colonies and to give the assent of Virginia to the act of separation. When the resolution was carried the British flag on the state house was lowered for all time.

Meanwhile the Continental Congress was alive to the course of events outside. The subject of independence was constantly being raised. "Are we rebels?" exclaimed Wyeth of Virginia during a debate in February. "No: we must declare ourselves a free people." Others hesitated and spoke of waiting for the arrival of commissioners of conciliation. "Is not America already independent?" asked Samuel Adams a few weeks later. "Why not then declare it?" Still there was uncertainty and delegates avoided the direct word. A few more weeks elapsed. At last, on May 10, Congress declared that the authority of the British crown in America must be suppressed and advised the colonies to set up governments of their own.

Independence Declared.—The way was fully prepared, therefore, when, on June 7, the Virginia delegation in the Congress moved that "these united colonies are and of right ought to be free and independent states." A committee was immediately appointed to draft a formal document setting forth the reasons for the act, and on July 2 all the states save New York went on record in favor of severing their political connection with Great Britain. Two days later, July 4, Jefferson's draft of the Declaration of Independence, changed in some slight particulars, was adopted. The old bell in Independence Hall, as it is now known, rang out the glad tidings; couriers swiftly carried the news to the uttermost hamlet and farm. A new nation announced its will to have a place among the powers of the world.

To some documents is given immortality. The Declaration of Independence is one of them. American patriotism is forever associated with it; but patriotism alone does not make it immortal. Neither does the vigor of its language or the severity of its indictment give it a secure place in the records of time. The secret of its greatness lies in the simple fact that it is one of the memorable landmarks in the history of a political ideal which for three centuries has been taking form and spreading throughout the earth, challenging kings and potentates, shaking down thrones and aristocracies, breaking the armies of irresponsible power on battle fields as far apart as Marston Moor and Château-Thierry. That ideal, now so familiar, then so novel, is summed up in the simple sentence: "Governments derive their just powers from the consent of the governed."

Written in a "decent respect for the opinions of mankind," to set forth the causes which impelled the American colonists to separate from Britain, the Declaration contained a long list of "abuses and usurpations" which had induced them to throw off the government of King George. That section of the Declaration has passed into "ancient" history and is seldom read. It is the part laying down a new basis for government and giving a new dignity to the common man that has become a household phrase in the Old World as in the New.

In the more enduring passages there are four fundamental ideas which, from the standpoint of the old system of government, were the essence of revolution: (1) all men are created equal and are endowed by their Creator with certain unalienable rights including life, liberty, and the pursuit of happiness; (2) the purpose of government is to secure these rights; (3) governments derive their just powers from the consent of the governed; (4) whenever any form of government becomes destructive of these ends it is the right of the people to alter or abolish it and institute new government, laying its foundations on such principles and organizing its powers in such form as to them shall seem most likely to effect their safety and happiness. Here was the prelude to the historic drama of democracy—a challenge to every form of government and every privilege not founded on popular assent.

The Establishment of Government and the New Allegiance

The Committees of Correspondence.—As soon as debate had passed into armed resistance, the patriots found it necessary to consolidate their forces by organizing civil government. This was readily effected, for the means were at hand in town meetings, provincial legislatures, and committees of correspondence. The working tools of the Revolution were in fact the committees of correspondence—small, local, unofficial groups of patriots formed to exchange views and create public sentiment. As early as November, 1772, such a committee had been created in Boston under the leadership of Samuel Adams. It held regular meetings, sent emissaries to neighboring towns, and carried on a campaign of education in the doctrines of liberty.

Upon local organizations similar in character to the Boston committee were built county committees and then the larger colonial committees, congresses, and conventions, all unofficial and representing the revolutionary elements. Ordinarily the provincial convention was merely the old legislative assembly freed from all royalist sympathizers and controlled by patriots. Finally, upon these colonial assemblies was built the Continental Congress, the precursor of union under the Articles of Confederation and ultimately under the Constitution of the United States. This was the revolutionary government set up within the British empire in America.

State Constitutions Framed.—With the rise of these new assemblies of the people, the old colonial governments broke down. From the royal provinces the governor, the judges, and the high officers fled in haste, and it became necessary to substitute patriot authorities. The appeal to the colonies advising them to adopt a new form of government for themselves, issued by the Congress in May, 1776, was quickly acted upon. Before the expiration of a year, Virginia, New Jersey, Pennsylvania, Delaware, Maryland, Georgia, and New York had drafted new constitutions as states, not as colonies uncertain of their destinies. Connecticut and Rhode Island, holding that their ancient charters were equal to their needs, merely renounced their allegiance to the king and went on as before so far as the form of government was concerned. South Carolina, which had drafted a temporary plan early in 1776, drew up a new and more complete constitution in 1778. Two years later Massachusetts with much deliberation put into force its fundamental law, which in most of its essential features remains unchanged to-day.

The new state constitutions in their broad outlines followed colonial models. For the royal governor was substituted a governor or president chosen usually by the legislature; but in two instances, New York and Massachusetts, by popular vote. For the provincial council there was substituted, except in Georgia, a senate; while the lower house, or assembly, was continued virtually without change. The old property restriction on the suffrage, though lowered slightly in some states, was continued in full force to the great discontent of the mechanics thus deprived of the ballot. The special qualifications, laid down in several constitutions, for governors, senators, and representatives, indicated that the revolutionary leaders were not prepared for any radical experiments in democracy. The protests of a few women, like Mrs. John Adams of Massachusetts and Mrs. Henry Corbin of Virginia, against a government which excluded them from political rights were treated as mild curiosities of no significance, although in New Jersey women were allowed to vote for many years on the same terms as men.

By the new state constitutions the signs and symbols of royal power, of authority derived from any source save "the people," were swept aside and republican governments on an imposing scale presented for the first time to the modern world. Copies of these remarkable documents prepared by plain citizens were translated into French and widely circulated in Europe. There they were destined to serve as a guide and inspiration to a generation of constitution-makers whose mission it was to begin the democratic revolution in the Old World.

The Articles of Confederation.—The formation of state constitutions was an easy task for the revolutionary leaders. They had only to build on foundations already laid. The establishment of a national system of government was another matter. There had always been, it must be remembered, a system of central control over the colonies, but Americans had had little experience in its operation. When the supervision of the crown of Great Britain was suddenly broken, the patriot leaders, accustomed merely to provincial statesmanship, were poorly trained for action on a national stage.

Many forces worked against those who, like Franklin, had a vision of national destiny. There were differences in economic interest—commerce and industry in the North and the planting system of the South. There were contests over the apportionment of taxes and the quotas of troops for common defense. To these practical difficulties were added local pride, the vested rights of state and village politicians in their provincial dignity, and the scarcity of men with a large outlook upon the common enterprise.

Nevertheless, necessity compelled them to consider some sort of federation. The second Continental Congress had hardly opened its work before the most sagacious leaders began to urge the desirability of a permanent connection. As early as July, 1775, Congress resolved to go into a committee of the whole on the state of the union, and Franklin, undaunted by the fate of his Albany plan of twenty years before, again presented a draft of a constitution. Long and desultory debates followed and it was not until late in 1777 that Congress presented to the states the Articles of Confederation. Provincial jealousies delayed ratification, and it was the spring of 1781, a few months before the surrender of Cornwallis at Yorktown, when Maryland, the last of the states, approved the Articles. This plan of union, though it was all that could be wrung from the reluctant states, provided for neither a chief executive nor a system of federal courts. It created simply a Congress of delegates in which each state had an equal voice and gave it the right to call upon the state legislatures for the sinews of government—money and soldiers.

The Application of Tests of Allegiance.—As the successive steps were taken in the direction of independent government, the patriots devised and applied tests designed to discover who were for and who were against the new nation in the process of making. When the first Continental Congress agreed not to allow the importation of British goods, it provided for the creation of local committees to enforce the rules. Such agencies were duly formed by the choice of men favoring the scheme, all opponents being excluded from the elections. Before these bodies those who persisted in buying British goods were summoned and warned or punished according to circumstances. As soon as the new state constitutions were put into effect, local committees set to work in the same way to ferret out all who were not outspoken in their support of the new order of things.

These patriot agencies, bearing different names in different sections, were sometimes ruthless in their methods. They called upon all men to sign the test of loyalty, frequently known as the "association test." Those who refused were promptly branded as outlaws, while some of the more dangerous were thrown into jail. The prison camp in Connecticut at one time held the former governor of New Jersey and the mayor of New York. Thousands were black-listed and subjected to espionage. The black-list of Pennsylvania contained the names of nearly five hundred persons of prominence who were under suspicion. Loyalists or Tories who were bold enough to speak and write against the Revolution were suppressed and their pamphlets burned. In many places, particularly in the North, the property of the loyalists was confiscated and the proceeds applied to the cause of the Revolution.

The work of the official agencies for suppression of opposition was sometimes supplemented by mob violence. A few Tories were hanged without trial, and others were tarred and feathered. One was placed upon a cake of ice and held there "until his loyalty to King George might cool." Whole families were driven out of their homes to find their way as best they could within the British lines or into Canada, where the British government gave them lands. Such excesses were deplored by Washington, but they were defended on the ground that in effect a civil war, as well as a war for independence, was being waged.

The Patriots and Tories.—Thus, by one process or another, those who were to be citizens of the new republic were separated from those who preferred to be subjects of King George. Just what proportion of the Americans favored independence and what share remained loyal to the British monarchy there is no way of knowing. The question of revolution was not submitted to popular vote, and on the point of numbers we have conflicting evidence. On the patriot side, there is the testimony of a careful and informed observer, John Adams, who asserted that two-thirds of the people were for the American cause and not more than one-third opposed the Revolution at all stages.

On behalf of the loyalists, or Tories as they were popularly known, extravagant claims were made. Joseph Galloway, who had been a member of the first Continental Congress and had fled to England when he saw its temper, testified before a committee of Parliament in 1779 that not one-fifth of the American people supported the insurrection and that "many more than four-fifths of the people prefer a union with Great Britain upon constitutional principles to independence." At the same time General Robertson, who had lived in America twenty-four years, declared that "more than two-thirds of the people would prefer the king's government to the Congress' tyranny." In an address to the king in that year a committee of American loyalists asserted that "the number of Americans in his Majesty's army exceeded the number of troops enlisted by Congress to oppose them."

The Character of the Loyalists.—When General Howe evacuated Boston, more than a thousand people fled with him. This great company, according to a careful historian, "formed the aristocracy of the province by virtue of their official rank; of their dignified callings and professions; of their hereditary wealth and of their culture." The act of banishment passed by Massachusetts in 1778, listing over 300 Tories, "reads like the social register of the oldest and noblest families of New England," more than one out of five being graduates of Harvard College. The same was true of New York and Philadelphia; namely, that the leading loyalists were prominent officials of the old order, clergymen and wealthy merchants.

With passion the loyalists fought against the inevitable or with anguish of heart they left as refugees for a life of uncertainty in Canada or the mother country.

Tories Assail the Patriots.—The Tories who remained in America joined the British army by the thousands or in other ways aided the royal cause. Those who were skillful with the pen assailed the patriots in editorials, rhymes, satires, and political catechisms. They declared that the members of Congress were "obscure, pettifogging attorneys, bankrupt shopkeepers, outlawed smugglers, etc." The people and their leaders they characterized as "wretched banditti ... the refuse and dregs of mankind." The generals in the army they sneered at as "men of rank and honor nearly on a par with those of the Congress."

Patriot Writers Arouse the National Spirit.—Stung by Tory taunts, patriot writers devoted themselves to creating and sustaining a public opinion favorable to the American cause. Moreover, they had to combat the depression that grew out of the misfortunes in the early days of the war. A terrible disaster befell Generals Arnold and Montgomery in the winter of 1775 as they attempted to bring Canada into the revolution—a disaster that cost 5000 men; repeated calamities harassed Washington in 1776 as he was defeated on Long Island, driven out of New York City, and beaten at Harlem Heights and White Plains. These reverses were almost too great for the stoutest patriots.

Pamphleteers, preachers, and publicists rose, however, to meet the needs of the hour. John Witherspoon, provost of the College of New Jersey, forsook the classroom for the field of political controversy. The poet, Philip Freneau, flung taunts of cowardice at the Tories and celebrated the spirit of liberty in many a stirring poem. Songs, ballads, plays, and satires flowed from the press in an unending stream. Fast days, battle anniversaries, celebrations of important steps taken by Congress afforded to patriotic clergymen abundant opportunities for sermons. "Does Mr. Wiberd preach against oppression?" anxiously inquired John Adams in a letter to his wife. The answer was decisive. "The clergy of every denomination, not excepting the Episcopalian, thunder and lighten every Sabbath. They pray for Boston and Massachusetts. They thank God most explicitly and fervently for our remarkable successes. They pray for the American army."

Thomas Paine never let his pen rest. He had been with the forces of Washington when they retreated from Fort Lee and were harried from New Jersey into Pennsylvania. He knew the effect of such reverses on the army as well as on the public. In December, 1776, he made a second great appeal to his countrymen in his pamphlet, "The Crisis," the first part of which he had written while defeat and gloom were all about him. This tract was a cry for continued support of the Revolution. "These are the times that try men's souls," he opened. "The summer soldier and the sunshine patriot will, in this crisis, shrink from the service of his country; but he that stands it now deserves the love and thanks of men and women." Paine laid his lash fiercely on the Tories, branding every one as a coward grounded in "servile, slavish, self-interested fear." He deplored the inadequacy of the militia and called for a real army. He refuted the charge that the retreat through New Jersey was a disaster and he promised victory soon. "By perseverance and fortitude," he concluded, "we have the prospect of a glorious issue; by cowardice and submission the sad choice of a variety of evils—a ravaged country, a depopulated city, habitations without safety and slavery without hope.... Look on this picture and weep over it." His ringing call to arms was followed by another and another until the long contest was over.

MILITARY AFFAIRS

The Two Phases of the War.—The war which opened with the battle of Lexington, on April 19, 1775, and closed with the surrender of Cornwallis at Yorktown on October 19, 1781, passed through two distinct phases—the first lasting until the treaty of alliance with France, in 1778, and the second until the end of the struggle. During the first phase, the war was confined mainly to the North. The outstanding features of the contest were the evacuation of Boston by the British, the expulsion of American forces from New York and their retreat through New Jersey, the battle of Trenton, the seizure of Philadelphia by the British (September, 1777), the invasion of New York by Burgoyne and his capture at Saratoga in October, 1777, and the encampment of American forces at Valley Forge for the terrible winter of 1777-78.

The final phase of the war, opening with the treaty of alliance with France on February 6, 1778, was confined mainly to the Middle states, the West, and the South. In the first sphere of action the chief events were the withdrawal of the British from Philadelphia, the battle of Monmouth, and the inclosure of the British in New York by deploying American forces from Morristown, New Jersey, up to West Point. In the West, George Rogers Clark, by his famous march into the Illinois country, secured Kaskaskia and Vincennes and laid a firm grip on the country between the Ohio and the Great Lakes. In the South, the second period opened with successes for the British. They captured Savannah, conquered Georgia, and restored the royal governor. In 1780 they seized Charleston, administered a crushing defeat to the American forces under Gates at Camden, and overran South Carolina, though meeting reverses at Cowpens and King's Mountain. Then came the closing scenes. Cornwallis began the last of his operations. He pursued General Greene far into North Carolina, clashed with him at Guilford Court House, retired to the coast, took charge of British forces engaged in plundering Virginia, and fortified Yorktown, where he was penned up by the French fleet from the sea and the combined French and American forces on land.

The Geographical Aspects of the War.—For the British the theater of the war offered many problems. From first to last it extended from Massachusetts to Georgia, a distance of almost a thousand miles. It was nearly three thousand miles from the main base of supplies and, though the British navy kept the channel open, transports were constantly falling prey to daring privateers and fleet American war vessels. The sea, on the other hand, offered an easy means of transportation between points along the coast and gave ready access to the American centers of wealth and population. Of this the British made good use. Though early forced to give up Boston, they seized New York and kept it until the end of the war; they took Philadelphia and retained it until threatened by the approach of the French fleet; and they captured and held both Savannah and Charleston. Wars, however, are seldom won by the conquest of cities.

Particularly was this true in the case of the Revolution. Only a small portion of the American people lived in towns. Countrymen back from the coast were in no way dependent upon them for a livelihood. They lived on the produce of the soil, not upon the profits of trade. This very fact gave strength to them in the contest. Whenever the British ventured far from the ports of entry, they encountered reverses. Burgoyne was forced to surrender at Saratoga because he was surrounded and cut off from his base of supplies. As soon as the British got away from Charleston, they were harassed and worried by the guerrilla warriors of Marion, Sumter, and Pickens. Cornwallis could technically defeat Greene at Guilford far in the interior; but he could not hold the inland region he had invaded. Sustained by their own labor, possessing the interior to which their armies could readily retreat, supplied mainly from native resources, the Americans could not be hemmed in, penned up, and destroyed at one fell blow.

The Sea Power.—The British made good use of their fleet in cutting off American trade, but control of the sea did not seriously affect the United States. As an agricultural country, the ruin of its commerce was not such a vital matter. All the materials for a comfortable though somewhat rude life were right at hand. It made little difference to a nation fighting for existence, if silks, fine linens, and chinaware were cut off. This was an evil to which submission was necessary.

Nor did the brilliant exploits of John Paul Jones and Captain John Barry materially change the situation. They demonstrated the skill of American seamen and their courage as fighting men. They raised the rates of British marine insurance, but they did not dethrone the mistress of the seas. Less spectacular, and more distinctive, were the deeds of the hundreds of privateers and minor captains who overhauled British supply ships and kept British merchantmen in constant anxiety. Not until the French fleet was thrown into the scale, were the British compelled to reckon seriously with the enemy on the sea and make plans based upon the possibilities of a maritime disaster.

Commanding Officers.—On the score of military leadership it is difficult to compare the contending forces in the revolutionary contest. There is no doubt that all the British commanders were men of experience in the art of warfare. Sir William Howe had served in America during the French War and was accounted an excellent officer, a strict disciplinarian, and a gallant gentleman. Nevertheless he loved ease, society, and good living, and his expulsion from Boston, his failure to overwhelm Washington by sallies from his comfortable bases at New York and Philadelphia, destroyed every shred of his military reputation. John Burgoyne, to whom was given the task of penetrating New York from Canada, had likewise seen service in the French War both in America and Europe. He had, however, a touch of the theatrical in his nature and after the collapse of his plans and the surrender of his army in 1777, he devoted his time mainly to light literature. Sir Henry Clinton, who directed the movement which ended in the capture of Charleston in 1780, had "learned his trade on the continent," and was regarded as a man of discretion and understanding in military matters. Lord Cornwallis, whose achievements at Camden and Guilford were blotted out by his surrender at Yorktown, had seen service in the Seven Years' War and had undoubted talents which he afterward displayed with great credit to himself in India. Though none of them, perhaps, were men of first-rate ability, they all had training and experience to guide them.

The Americans had a host in Washington himself. He had long been interested in military strategy and had tested his coolness under fire during the first clashes with the French nearly twenty years before. He had no doubts about the justice of his cause, such as plagued some of the British generals. He was a stern but reasonable disciplinarian. He was reserved and patient, little given to exaltation at success or depression at reverses. In the dark hour of the Revolution, "what held the patriot forces together?" asks Beveridge in his *Life of John Marshall*. Then he answers: "George Washington and he alone. Had he died or been seriously disabled, the Revolution would have ended.... Washington was the soul of the American cause. Washington was the government. Washington was the Revolution." The weakness of Congress in furnishing men and supplies, the indolence of civilians, who lived at ease while the army starved, the intrigues of army officers against him such as the "Conway cabal," the cowardice of Lee at Monmouth, even the treason of Benedict Arnold, while they stirred deep emotions in his breast and aroused him to make passionate pleas to his countrymen, did not shake his iron will or his firm determination to see the war through to the bitter end. The weight of Washington's moral force was immeasurable.

Of the generals who served under him, none can really be said to have been experienced military men when the war opened. Benedict Arnold, the unhappy traitor but brave and daring soldier, was a druggist, book seller, and ship owner at New Haven when the news of Lexington called him to battle. Horatio Gates was looked upon as a "seasoned soldier" because he had entered the British army as a youth, had been wounded at Braddock's memorable defeat, and had served with credit during the Seven Years' War; but he was the most conspicuous failure of the Revolution. The triumph over Burgoyne was the work of other men; and his crushing defeat at Camden put an end to his military pretensions. Nathanael Greene was a Rhode Island farmer and smith without military experience who, when convinced that war was coming, read Cæsar's *Commentaries* and took up the sword. Francis Marion was a shy and modest planter of South Carolina whose sole passage at arms had been a brief but desperate brush with the Indians ten or twelve years earlier. Daniel Morgan, one of the heroes of Cowpens, had been a teamster with Braddock's army and had seen some fighting during the French and Indian War, but his military knowledge, from the point of view of a trained British officer, was negligible. John Sullivan was a successful lawyer at Durham, New Hampshire, and a major in the local militia when duty summoned him to lay down his briefs and take up the sword. Anthony Wayne was a Pennsylvania farmer and land surveyor who, on hearing the clash of arms, read a few books on war, raised a regiment, and offered himself for service. Such is the story of the chief American military leaders, and it is typical of them all. Some had seen fighting with the French and Indians, but none of them had seen warfare on a large scale with regular troops commanded according to the strategy evolved in European experience. Courage, native ability, quickness of mind, and knowledge of the country they had in abundance, and in battles such as were fought during the Revolution all those qualities counted heavily in the balance.

Foreign Officers in American Service.—To native genius was added military talent from beyond the seas. Baron Steuben, well schooled in the iron régime of Frederick the Great, came over from Prussia, joined Washington at Valley Forge, and day after day drilled and manœuvered the men, laughing and cursing as he turned raw countrymen into regular soldiers. From France came young Lafayette and the stern De Kalb, from Poland came Pulaski and Kosciusko;—all acquainted with the arts of war as waged in Europe and fitted for leadership as well as teaching. Lafayette came early, in 1776, in a ship of his own, accompanied by several officers of wide experience, and remained loyally throughout the war sharing the hardships of American army life. Pulaski fell at the siege of Savannah and De Kalb at Camden. Kosciusko survived the American war to defend in vain the independence of his native land. To these distinguished foreigners, who freely threw in their lot with American revolutionary fortunes, was due much of that spirit and discipline which fitted raw recruits and temperamental militiamen to cope with a military power of the first rank.

The Soldiers.—As far as the British soldiers were concerned their annals are short and simple. The regulars from the standing army who were sent over at the opening of the contest, the recruits drummed up by special efforts at home, and the thousands of Hessians bought outright by King George presented few problems of management to the British officers. These common soldiers were far away from home and enlisted for the war. Nearly all of them were well disciplined and many of them experienced in actual campaigns. The armies of King George fought bravely, as the records of Bunker Hill, Brandywine, and Monmouth demonstrate. Many a man and subordinate officer and, for that matter, some of the high officers expressed a reluctance at fighting against their own kin; but they obeyed orders.

The Americans, on the other hand, while they fought with grim determination, as men fighting for their homes, were lacking in discipline and in the experience of regular troops. When the war broke in upon them, there were no common preparations for it. There was no continental army; there were only local bands of militiamen, many of them experienced in fighting but few of them "regulars" in the military sense. Moreover they were volunteers serving for a short time, unaccustomed to severe discipline, and impatient at the restraints imposed on them by long and arduous campaigns. They were continually leaving the service just at the most critical moments. "The militia," lamented Washington, "come in, you cannot tell how; go, you cannot tell where; consume your provisions; exhaust your stores; and leave you at last at a critical moment."

Again and again Washington begged Congress to provide for an army of regulars enlisted for the war, thoroughly trained and paid according to some definite plan. At last he was able to overcome, in part at least, the chronic fear of civilians in Congress and to wring from that reluctant body an agreement to grant half pay to all officers and a bonus to all privates who served until the end of the war. Even this scheme, which Washington regarded as far short of justice to the soldiers, did not produce quick results. It was near the close of the conflict before he had an army of well-disciplined veterans capable of meeting British regulars on equal terms.

Though there were times when militiamen and frontiersmen did valiant and effective work, it is due to historical accuracy to deny the time-honored tradition that a few minutemen overwhelmed more numerous forces of regulars in a seven years' war for independence. They did nothing of the sort. For the victories of Bennington, Trenton, Saratoga, and Yorktown there were the defeats of Bunker Hill, Long Island, White Plains, Germantown, and Camden. Not once did an army of militiamen overcome an equal number of British regulars in an open trial by battle. "To bring men to be well acquainted with the duties of a soldier," wrote Washington, "requires time.... To expect the same service from raw and undisciplined recruits as from veteran soldiers is to expect what never did and perhaps never will happen."

How the War Was Won.—Then how did the American army win the war? For one thing there were delays and blunders on the part of the British generals who, in 1775 and 1776, dallied in Boston and New York with large bodies of regular troops when they might have been dealing paralyzing blows at the scattered bands that constituted the American army. "Nothing but the supineness or folly of the enemy could have saved us," solemnly averred Washington in 1780. Still it is fair to say that this apparent supineness was not all due to the British generals. The ministers behind them believed that a large part of the colonists were loyal and that compromise would be promoted by inaction rather than by a war vigorously prosecuted. Victory by masterly inactivity was obviously better than conquest, and the slighter the wounds the quicker the healing. Later in the conflict when the seasoned forces of France were thrown into the scale, the Americans themselves had learned many things about the practical conduct of campaigns. All along, the British were embarrassed by the problem of supplies. Their troops could not forage with the skill of militiamen, as they were in unfamiliar territory. The long oversea voyages were uncertain at best and doubly so when the warships of France joined the American privateers in preying on supply boats.

The British were in fact battered and worn down by a guerrilla war and outdone on two important occasions by superior forces—at Saratoga and Yorktown. Stern facts convinced them finally that an immense army, which could be raised only by a supreme effort, would be necessary to subdue the colonies if that hazardous enterprise could be accomplished at all. They learned also that America would then be alienated, fretful, and the scene of endless uprisings calling for an army of occupation. That was a price which staggered even Lord North and George III. Moreover, there were forces of opposition at home with which they had to reckon.

Women and the War.—At no time were the women of America indifferent to the struggle for independence. When it was confined to the realm of opinion they did their part in creating public sentiment. Mrs. Elizabeth Timothee, for example, founded in Charleston, in 1773, a newspaper to espouse the cause of the province. Far to the north the sister of James Otis, Mrs. Mercy Warren, early begged her countrymen to rest their case upon their natural rights, and in influential circles she urged the leaders to stand fast by their principles. While John Adams was tossing about with uncertainty at the Continental Congress, his wife was writing letters to him declaring her faith in "independency."

When the war came down upon the country, women helped in every field. In sustaining public sentiment they were active. Mrs. Warren with a tireless pen combatted loyalist propaganda in many a drama and satire. Almost every revolutionary leader had a wife or daughter who rendered service in the "second line of defense." Mrs. Washington managed the plantation while the General was at the front and went north to face the rigors of the awful winter at Valley Forge—an inspiration to her husband and his men. The daughter of Benjamin Franklin, Mrs. Sarah Bache, while her father was pleading the American cause in France, set the women of Pennsylvania to work sewing and collecting supplies. Even near the firing line women were to be found, aiding the wounded, hauling powder to the front, and carrying dispatches at the peril of their lives.

In the economic sphere, the work of women was invaluable. They harvested crops without enjoying the picturesque title of "farmerettes" and they canned and preserved for the wounded and the prisoners of war. Of their labor in spinning and weaving it is recorded: "Immediately on being cut off from the use of English manufactures, the women engaged within their own families in manufacturing various kinds of cloth for domestic use. They thus kept their households decently clad and the surplus of their labors they sold to such as chose to buy rather than make for themselves. In this way the female part of families by their industry and strict economy frequently supported the whole domestic circle, evincing the strength of their attachment and the value of their service."

For their war work, women were commended by high authorities on more than one occasion. They were given medals and public testimonials even as in our own day. Washington thanked them for their labors and paid tribute to them for the inspiration and material aid which they had given to the cause of independence.

THE FINANCES OF THE REVOLUTION

When the Revolution opened, there were thirteen little treasuries in America but no common treasury, and from first to last the Congress was in the position of a beggar rather than a sovereign. Having no authority to lay and collect taxes directly and knowing the hatred of the provincials for taxation, it resorted mainly to loans and paper money to finance the war. "Do you think," boldly inquired one of the delegates, "that I will consent to load my constituents with taxes when we can send to the printer and get a wagon load of money, one quire of which will pay for the whole?"

Paper Money and Loans.—Acting on this curious but appealing political economy, Congress issued in June, 1776, two million dollars in bills of credit to be redeemed by the states on the basis of their respective populations. Other issues followed in quick succession. In all about $241,000,000 of continental paper was printed, to which the several states added nearly $210,000,000 of their own notes. Then came interest-bearing bonds in ever increasing quantities. Several millions were also borrowed from France and small sums from Holland and Spain. In desperation a national lottery was held, producing meager results. The property of Tories was confiscated and sold, bringing in about $16,000,000. Begging letters were sent to the states asking them to raise revenues for the continental treasury, but the states, burdened with their own affairs, gave little heed.

Inflation and Depreciation.—As paper money flowed from the press, it rapidly declined in purchasing power until in 1779 a dollar was worth only two or three cents in gold or silver. Attempts were made by Congress and the states to compel people to accept the notes at face value; but these were like attempts to make water flow uphill. Speculators collected at once to fatten on the calamities of the republic. Fortunes were made and lost gambling on the prices of public securities while the patriot army, half clothed, was freezing at Valley Forge. "Speculation, peculation, engrossing, forestalling," exclaimed Washington, "afford too many melancholy proofs of the decay of public virtue. Nothing, I am convinced, but the depreciation of our currency ... aided by stock jobbing and party dissensions has fed the hopes of the enemy."

The Patriot Financiers.—To the efforts of Congress in financing the war were added the labors of private citizens. Hayn Solomon, a merchant of Philadelphia, supplied members of Congress, including Madison, Jefferson, and Monroe, and army officers, like Lee and Steuben, with money for their daily needs. All together he contributed the huge sum of half a million dollars to the American cause and died broken in purse, if not in spirit, a British prisoner of war. Another Philadelphia merchant, Robert Morris, won for himself the name of the "patriot financier" because he labored night and day to find the money to meet the bills which poured in upon the bankrupt government. When his own funds were exhausted, he borrowed from his friends. Experienced in the handling of merchandise, he created agencies at important points to distribute supplies to the troops, thus displaying administrative as well as financial talents.

Women organized "drives" for money, contributed their plate and their jewels, and collected from door to door. Farmers took worthless paper in return for their produce, and soldiers saw many a pay day pass without yielding them a penny. Thus by the labors and sacrifices of citizens, the issuance of paper money, lotteries, the floating of loans, borrowings in Europe, and the impressment of supplies, the Congress staggered through the Revolution like a pauper who knows not how his next meal is to be secured but is continuously relieved at a crisis by a kindly fate.

THE DIPLOMACY OF THE REVOLUTION

When the full measure of honor is given to the soldiers and sailors and their commanding officers, the civilians who managed finances and supplies, the writers who sustained the American spirit, and the women who did well their part, there yet remains the duty of recognizing the achievements of diplomacy. The importance of this field of activity was keenly appreciated by the leaders in the Continental Congress. They were fairly well versed in European history. They knew of the balance of power and the sympathies, interests, and prejudices of nations and their rulers. All this information they turned to good account, in opening relations with continental countries and seeking money, supplies, and even military assistance. For the transaction of this delicate business, they created a secret committee on foreign correspondence as early as 1775 and prepared to send agents abroad.

American Agents Sent Abroad.—Having heard that France was inclining a friendly ear to the American cause, the Congress, in March, 1776, sent a commissioner to Paris, Silas Deane of Connecticut, often styled the "first American diplomat." Later in the year a form of treaty to be presented to foreign powers was drawn up, and Franklin, Arthur Lee, and Deane were selected as American representatives at the court of "His Most Christian Majesty the King of France." John Jay of New York was chosen minister to Spain in 1779; John Adams was sent to Holland the same year; and other agents were dispatched to Florence, Vienna, and Berlin. The representative selected for St. Petersburg spent two fruitless years there, "ignored by the court, living in obscurity and experiencing nothing but humiliation and failure." Frederick the Great, king of Prussia, expressed a desire to find in America a market for Silesian linens and woolens, but, fearing England's command of the sea, he refused to give direct aid to the Revolutionary cause.

Early French Interest.—The great diplomatic triumph of the Revolution was won at Paris, and Benjamin Franklin was the hero of the occasion, although many circumstances prepared the way for his success. Louis XVI's foreign minister, Count de Vergennes, before the arrival of any American representative, had brought to the attention of the king the opportunity offered by the outbreak of the war between England and her colonies. He showed him how France could redress her grievances and "reduce the power and greatness of England"—the empire that in 1763 had forced upon her a humiliating peace "at the price of our possessions, of our commerce, and our credit in the Indies, at the price of Canada, Louisiana, Isle Royale, Acadia, and Senegal." Equally successful in gaining the king's interest was a curious French adventurer, Beaumarchais, a man of wealth, a lover of music, and the author of two popular plays, "Figaro" and "The Barber of Seville." These two men had already urged upon the king secret aid for America before Deane appeared on the scene. Shortly after his arrival they made confidential arrangements to furnish money, clothing, powder, and other supplies to the struggling colonies, although official requests for them were officially refused by the French government.

Franklin at Paris.—When Franklin reached Paris, he was received only in private by the king's minister, Vergennes. The French people, however, made manifest their affection for the "plain republican" in "his full dress suit of spotted Manchester velvet." He was known among men of letters as an author, a scientist, and a philosopher of extraordinary ability. His "Poor Richard" had thrice been translated into French and was scattered in numerous editions throughout the kingdom. People of all ranks—ministers, ladies at court, philosophers, peasants, and stable boys—knew of Franklin and wished him success in his mission. The queen, Marie Antoinette, fated to lose her head in a revolution soon to follow, played with fire by encouraging "our dear republican."

For the king of France, however, this was more serious business. England resented the presence of this "traitor" in Paris, and Louis had to be cautious about plunging into another war that might also end disastrously. Moreover, the early period of Franklin's sojourn in Paris was a dark hour for the American Revolution. Washington's brilliant exploit at Trenton on Christmas night, 1776, and the battle with Cornwallis at Princeton had been followed by the disaster at Brandywine, the loss of Philadelphia, the defeat at Germantown, and the retirement to Valley Forge for the winter of 1777-78. New York City and Philadelphia—two strategic ports—were in British hands; the Hudson and Delaware rivers were blocked; and General Burgoyne with his British troops was on his way down through the heart of northern New York, cutting New England off from the rest of the colonies. No wonder the king was cautious. Then the unexpected happened. Burgoyne, hemmed in from all sides by the American forces, his flanks harried, his foraging parties beaten back, his supplies cut off, surrendered on October 17, 1777, to General Gates, who had superseded General Schuyler in time to receive the honor.

Treaties of Alliance and Commerce (1778).—News of this victory, placed by historians among the fifteen decisive battles of the world, reached Franklin one night early in December while he and some friends sat gloomily at dinner. Beaumarchais, who was with him, grasped at once the meaning of the situation and set off to the court at Versailles with such haste that he upset his coach and dislocated his arm. The king and his ministers were at last convinced that the hour had come to aid the Revolution. Treaties of commerce and alliance were drawn up and signed in February, 1778. The independence of the United States was recognized by France and an alliance was formed to guarantee that independence. Combined military action was agreed upon and Louis then formally declared war on England. Men who had, a few short years before, fought one another in the wilderness of Pennsylvania or on the Plains of

Abraham, were now ranged side by side in a war on the Empire that Pitt had erected and that George III was pulling down.

Spain and Holland Involved.—Within a few months, Spain, remembering the steady decline of her sea power since the days of the Armada and hoping to drive the British out of Gibraltar, once more joined the concert of nations against England. Holland, a member of a league of armed neutrals formed in protest against British searches on the high seas, sent her fleet to unite with the forces of Spain, France, and America to prey upon British commerce. To all this trouble for England was added the danger of a possible revolt in Ireland, where the spirit of independence was flaming up.

The British Offer Terms to America.—Seeing the colonists about to be joined by France in a common war on the English empire, Lord North proposed, in February, 1778, a renewal of negotiations. By solemn enactment, Parliament declared its intention not to exercise the right of imposing taxes within the colonies; at the same time it authorized the opening of negotiations through commissioners to be sent to America. A truce was to be established, pardons granted, objectionable laws suspended, and the old imperial constitution, as it stood before the opening of hostilities, restored to full vigor. It was too late. Events had taken the affairs of America out of the hands of British commissioners and diplomats.

Effects of French Aid.—The French alliance brought ships of war, large sums of gold and silver, loads of supplies, and a considerable body of trained soldiers to the aid of the Americans. Timely as was this help, it meant no sudden change in the fortunes of war. The British evacuated Philadelphia in the summer following the alliance, and Washington's troops were encouraged to come out of Valley Forge. They inflicted a heavy blow on the British at Monmouth, but the treasonable conduct of General Charles Lee prevented a triumph. The recovery of Philadelphia was offset by the treason of Benedict Arnold, the loss of Savannah and Charleston (1780), and the defeat of Gates at Camden.

The full effect of the French alliance was not felt until 1781, when Cornwallis went into Virginia and settled at Yorktown. Accompanied by French troops Washington swept rapidly southward and penned the British to the shore while a powerful French fleet shut off their escape by sea. It was this movement, which certainly could not have been executed without French aid, that put an end to all chance of restoring British dominion in America. It was the surrender of Cornwallis at Yorktown that caused Lord North to pace the floor and cry out: "It is all over! It is all over!" What might have been done without the French alliance lies hidden from mankind. What was accomplished with the help of French soldiers, sailors, officers, money, and supplies, is known to all the earth. "All the world agree," exultantly wrote Franklin from Paris to General Washington, "that no expedition was ever better planned or better executed. It brightens the glory that must accompany your name to the latest posterity." Diplomacy as well as martial valor had its reward.

PEACE AT LAST

British Opposition to the War.—In measuring the forces that led to the final discomfiture of King George and Lord North, it is necessary to remember that from the beginning to the end the British ministry at home faced a powerful, informed, and relentless opposition. There were vigorous protests, first against the obnoxious acts which precipitated the unhappy quarrel, then against the way in which the war was waged, and finally against the futile struggle to retain a hold upon the American dominions. Among the members of Parliament who thundered against the government were the first statesmen and orators of the land. William Pitt, Earl of Chatham, though he deplored the idea of American independence, denounced the government as the aggressor and rejoiced in American resistance. Edmund Burke leveled his heavy batteries against every measure of coercion and at last strove for a peace which, while giving independence to America, would work for reconciliation rather than estrangement. Charles James Fox gave the colonies his generous sympathy and warmly championed their rights. Outside of the circle of statesmen there were stout friends of the American cause like David Hume, the philosopher and historian, and Catherine Macaulay, an author of wide fame and a republican bold enough to encourage Washington in seeing it through.

Against this powerful opposition, the government enlisted a whole army of scribes and journalists to pour out criticism on the Americans and their friends. Dr. Samuel Johnson, whom it employed in this business, was so savage that even the ministers had to tone down his pamphlets before printing them. Far more weighty was Edward Gibbon, who was in time to win fame as the historian of the *Decline and Fall of the Roman Empire*. He had at first opposed the government; but, on being given a lucrative post, he used his sharp pen in its support, causing his friends to ridicule him in these lines:

"King George, in a frightLest Gibbon should writeThe story of England's disgrace,Thought no way so sureHis pen to secureAs to give the historian a place."

Lord North Yields.—As time wore on, events bore heavily on the side of the opponents of the government's measures. They had predicted that conquest was impossible, and they had urged the advantages of a peace which would in some measure restore the affections of the Americans. Every day's news confirmed their predictions and lent support to their arguments. Moreover, the war, which sprang out of an effort to relieve English burdens, made those burdens heavier than ever. Military expenses were daily increasing. Trade with the colonies, the greatest single outlet for British goods and capital, was paralyzed. The heavy debts due British merchants in America were not only unpaid but postponed into an indefinite future. Ireland was on the verge of revolution. The French had a dangerous fleet on the high seas. In vain did the king assert in December, 1781, that no difficulties would ever make him consent to a peace that meant American independence. Parliament knew better, and on February 27, 1782, in the House of Commons was carried an address to the throne against continuing the war. Burke, Fox, the younger Pitt, Barré, and other friends of the colonies voted in the affirmative. Lord North gave notice then that his ministry was at an end. The king moaned: "Necessity made me yield."

In April, 1782, Franklin received word from the English government that it was prepared to enter into negotiations leading to a settlement. This was embarrassing. In the treaty of alliance with France, the United States had promised that peace should be a joint affair agreed to by both nations in open conference. Finding France, however, opposed to some of their claims respecting boundaries and fisheries, the American commissioners conferred with the British agents at Paris without consulting the French minister. They actually signed a preliminary peace draft before they informed him of their operations. When Vergennes reproached him, Franklin replied that they "had been guilty of neglecting *bienséance* [good manners] but hoped that the great work would not be ruined by a single indiscretion."

The Terms of Peace (1783).—The general settlement at Paris in 1783 was a triumph for America. England recognized the independence of the United States, naming each state specifically, and agreed to boundaries extending from the Atlantic to the Mississippi and from the Great Lakes to the Floridas. England held Canada, Newfoundland, and the West Indies intact, made gains in India, and maintained her supremacy on the seas. Spain won Florida and Minorca but not the coveted Gibraltar. France gained nothing important save the satisfaction of seeing England humbled and the colonies independent.

The generous terms secured by the American commission at Paris called forth surprise and gratitude in the United States and smoothed the way for a renewal of commercial relations with the mother country. At the same time they gave genuine anxiety to European diplomats. "This federal republic is born a pigmy," wrote the Spanish ambassador to his royal master. "A day will come when it will be a giant; even a colossus formidable to these countries. Liberty of conscience and the facility for establishing a new population on immense lands, as well as the advantages of the new government, will draw thither farmers and artisans from all the nations. In a few years we shall watch with grief the tyrannical existence of the same colossus."

Summary of the Revolutionary Period

The independence of the American colonies was foreseen by many European statesmen as they watched the growth of their population, wealth, and power; but no one could fix the hour of the great event. Until 1763 the American colonists lived fairly happily under British dominion. There were collisions from time to time, of course. Royal governors clashed with stiff-necked colonial legislatures. There were protests against the exercise of the king's veto power in specific cases. Nevertheless, on the whole, the relations between America and the mother country were more amicable in 1763 than at any period under the Stuart régime which closed in 1688.

The crash, when it came, was not deliberately willed by any one. It was the product of a number of forces that happened to converge about 1763. Three years before, there had come to the throne George III, a young, proud, inexperienced, and stubborn king. For nearly fifty years his predecessors, Germans as they were in language and interest, had allowed things to drift in England and America. George III decided that he would be king in fact as well as in name. About the same time England brought to a close the long and costly French and Indian War and was staggering under a heavy burden of debt and taxes. The war had been fought partly in defense of the American colonies and nothing seemed more reasonable to English statesmen than the idea that the colonies should bear part of the cost of their own defense. At this juncture there came into prominence, in royal councils, two men bent on taxing America and controlling her trade, Grenville and Townshend. The king was willing, the English taxpayers were thankful for any promise of relief, and statesmen were found to undertake the experiment. England therefore set out upon a new course. She imposed taxes upon the colonists, regulated their trade and set royal officers upon them to enforce the law. This action evoked protests from the colonists. They held a Stamp Act Congress to declare their rights and petition for a redress of grievances. Some of the more restless spirits rioted in the streets, sacked the houses of the king's officers, and tore up the stamped paper.

Frightened by uprising, the English government drew back and repealed the Stamp Act. Then it veered again and renewed its policy of interference. Interference again called forth American protests. Protests aroused sharper retaliation. More British regulars were sent over to keep order. More irritating laws were passed by Parliament. Rioting again appeared: tea was dumped in the harbor of Boston and seized in the harbor of Charleston. The British answer was more force. The response of the colonists was a Continental Congress for defense. An unexpected and unintended clash of arms at Lexington and Concord in the spring of 1775 brought forth from the king of England a proclamation: "The Americans are rebels!"

The die was cast. The American Revolution had begun. Washington was made commander-in-chief. Armies were raised, money was borrowed, a huge volume of paper currency was issued, and foreign aid was summoned. Franklin plied his diplomatic arts at Paris until in 1778 he induced France to throw her sword into the balance. Three years later, Cornwallis surrendered at Yorktown. In 1783, by the formal treaty of peace, George III acknowledged the independence of the United States. The new nation, endowed with an imperial domain stretching from the Atlantic Ocean to the Mississippi River, began its career among the sovereign powers of the earth.

In the sphere of civil government, the results of the Revolution were equally remarkable. Royal officers and royal authorities were driven from the former dominions. All power was declared to be in the people. All the colonies became states, each with its own constitution or plan of government. The thirteen states were united in common bonds under the Articles of Confederation. A republic on a large scale was instituted. Thus there was begun an adventure in popular government such as the world had never seen. Could it succeed or was it destined to break down and be supplanted by a monarchy? The fate of whole continents hung upon the answer.

References

J. Fiske, *The American Revolution* (2 vols.).

H. Lodge, *Life of Washington* (2 vols.).

W. Sumner, *The Financier and the Finances of the American Revolution*.

O. Trevelyan, *The American Revolution* (4 vols.). A sympathetic account by an English historian.

M.C. Tyler, *Literary History of the American Revolution* (2 vols.).

C.H. Van Tyne, *The American Revolution* (American Nation Series) and *The Loyalists in the American Revolution*.

Questions

1. What was the non-importation agreement? By what body was it adopted? Why was it revolutionary in character?

2. Contrast the work of the first and second Continental Congresses.

3. Why did efforts at conciliation fail?

4. Trace the growth of American independence from opinion to the sphere of action.

5. Why is the Declaration of Independence an "immortal" document?

6. What was the effect of the Revolution on colonial governments? On national union?

7. Describe the contest between "Patriots" and "Tories."

8. What topics are considered under "military affairs"? Discuss each in detail.

9. Contrast the American forces with the British forces and show how the war was won.

10. Compare the work of women in the Revolutionary War with their labors in the World War (1917-18).

11. How was the Revolution financed?

12. Why is diplomacy important in war? Describe the diplomatic triumph of the Revolution.

13. What was the nature of the opposition in England to the war?

14. Give the events connected with the peace settlement; the terms of peace.

Research Topics

The Spirit of America.—Woodrow Wilson, *History of the American People*, Vol. II, pp. 98-126.

American Rights.—Draw up a table showing all the principles laid down by American leaders in (1) the Resolves of the First Continental Congress, Macdonald, *Documentary Source Book*, pp. 162-166; (2) the Declaration of the Causes and the Necessity of Taking Up Arms, Macdonald, pp. 176-183; and (3) the Declaration of Independence.

The Declaration of Independence.—Fiske, *The American Revolution*, Vol. I, pp. 147-197. Elson, *History of the United States*, pp. 250-254.

Diplomacy and the French Alliance.—Hart, *American History Told by Contemporaries*, Vol. II, pp. 574-590. Fiske, Vol. II, pp. 1-24. Callender, *Economic History of the United States*, pp. 159-168; Elson, pp. 275-280.

Biographical Studies.—Washington, Franklin, Samuel Adams, Patrick Henry, Thomas Jefferson—emphasizing the peculiar services of each.

The Tories.—Hart, *Contemporaries*, Vol. II, pp. 470-480.

Valley Forge.—Fiske, Vol. II, pp. 25-49.

The Battles of the Revolution.—Elson, pp. 235-317.

An English View of the Revolution.—Green, *Short History of England*, Chap. X, Sect. 2.

English Opinion and the Revolution.—Trevelyan, *The American Revolution*, Vol. III (or Part 2, Vol. II), Chaps. XXIV-XXVII.

PART III. THE UNION AND NATIONAL POLITICS

CHAPTER VII

THE FORMATION OF THE CONSTITUTION

The Promise and the Difficulties of America

The rise of a young republic composed of thirteen states, each governed by officials popularly elected under constitutions drafted by "the plain people," was the most significant feature of the eighteenth century. The majority of the patriots whose labors and sacrifices had made this possible naturally looked upon their work and pronounced it good. Those Americans, however, who peered beneath the surface of things, saw that the Declaration of Independence, even if splendidly phrased, and paper constitutions, drawn by finest enthusiasm "uninstructed by experience," could not alone make the republic great and prosperous or even free. All around them they saw chaos in finance and in industry and perils for the immediate future.

The Weakness of the Articles of Confederation.—The government under the Articles of Confederation had neither the strength nor the resources necessary to cope with the problems of reconstruction left by the war. The sole organ of government was a Congress composed of from two to seven members from each state chosen as the legislature might direct and paid by the state. In determining all questions, each state had one vote—Delaware thus enjoying the same weight as Virginia. There was no president to enforce the laws. Congress was given power to select a committee of thirteen—one from each state—to act as an executive body when it was not in session; but this device, on being tried out, proved a failure. There was no system of national courts to which citizens and states could appeal for the protection of their rights or through which they could compel obedience to law. The two great powers of government, military and financial, were withheld. Congress, it is true, could authorize expenditures but had to rely upon the states for the payment of contributions to meet its bills. It could also order the establishment of an army, but it could only request the states to supply their respective quotas of soldiers. It could not lay taxes nor bring any pressure to bear upon a single citizen in the whole country. It could act only through the medium of the state governments.

Financial and Commercial Disorders.—In the field of public finance, the disorders were pronounced. The huge debt incurred during the war was still outstanding. Congress was unable to pay either the interest or the principal. Public creditors were in despair, as the market value of their bonds sank to twenty-five or even ten cents on the dollar. The current bills of Congress were unpaid. As some one complained, there was not enough money in the treasury to buy pen and ink with which to record the transactions of the shadow legislature. The currency was in utter chaos. Millions of dollars in notes issued by Congress had become mere trash worth a cent or two on the dollar. There was no other expression of contempt so forceful as the popular saying: "not worth a Continental." To make matters worse, several of the states were pouring new streams of paper money from the press. Almost the only good money in circulation consisted of English, French, and Spanish coins, and the public was even defrauded by them because money changers were busy clipping and filing away the metal. Foreign commerce was unsettled. The entire British system of trade discrimination was turned against the Americans, and Congress, having no power to regulate foreign commerce, was unable to retaliate or to negotiate treaties which it could enforce. Domestic commerce was impeded by the jealousies of the states, which erected tariff barriers against their neighbors. The condition of the currency made the exchange of money and goods extremely difficult, and, as if to increase the confusion, backward states enacted laws hindering the prompt collection of debts within their borders—an evil which nothing but a national system of courts could cure.

Congress in Disrepute.—With treaties set at naught by the states, the laws unenforced, the treasury empty, and the public credit gone, the Congress of the United States fell into utter disrepute. It called upon the states to pay their quotas of money into the treasury, only to be treated with contempt. Even its own members looked upon it as a solemn futility. Some of the ablest men refused to accept election to it, and many who did take the doubtful honor failed to attend the sessions. Again and again it was impossible to secure a quorum for the transaction of business.

Troubles of the State Governments.—The state governments, free to pursue their own course with no interference from without, had almost as many difficulties as the Congress. They too were loaded with revolutionary debts calling for heavy taxes upon an already restive population. Oppressed by their financial burdens and discouraged by the fall in prices which followed the return of peace, the farmers of several states joined in a concerted effort and compelled their legislatures to issue large sums of paper money. The currency fell in value, but nevertheless it was forced on unwilling creditors to square old accounts.

In every part of the country legislative action fluctuated violently. Laws were made one year only to be repealed the next and reënacted the third year. Lands were sold by one legislature and the sales were canceled by its successor. Uncertainty and distrust were the natural consequences. Men of substance longed for some power that would forbid states to issue bills of credit, to make paper money legal tender in payment of debts, or to impair the obligation of contracts. Men heavily in debt, on the other hand, urged even more drastic action against creditors.

So great did the discontent of the farmers in New Hampshire become in 1786 that a mob surrounded the legislature, demanding a repeal of the taxes and the issuance of paper money. It was with difficulty that an armed rebellion was avoided. In Massachusetts the malcontents, under the leadership of Daniel Shays, a captain in the Revolutionary army, organized that same year open resistance to the government of the state. Shays and his followers protested against the conduct of creditors in foreclosing mortgages upon the debt-burdened farmers, against the lawyers for increasing the costs of legal proceedings, against the senate of the state the members of which were apportioned among the towns on the basis of the amount of taxes paid, against heavy taxes, and against the refusal of the legislature to issue paper money. They seized the towns of Worcester and Springfield and broke up the courts of justice. All through the western part of the state the revolt spread, sending a shock of alarm to every center and section of the young republic. Only by the most vigorous action was Governor Bowdoin able to quell the uprising; and when that task was accomplished, the state government did not dare to execute any of the prisoners because they had so many sympathizers. Moreover, Bowdoin and several members of the legislature who had been most zealous in their attacks on the insurgents were defeated at the ensuing election. The need of national assistance for state governments in times of domestic violence was everywhere emphasized by men who were opposed to revolutionary acts.

Alarm over Dangers to the Republic.—Leading American citizens, watching the drift of affairs, were slowly driven to the conclusion that the new ship of state so proudly launched a few years before was careening into anarchy. "The facts of our peace and independence," wrote a friend of Washington, "do not at present wear so promising an appearance as I had fondly painted in my mind. The prejudices, jealousies, and turbulence of the people at times almost stagger my confidence in our political establishments; and almost occasion me to think that they will show themselves unworthy of the noble prize for which we have contended."

Washington himself was profoundly discouraged. On hearing of Shays's rebellion, he exclaimed: "What, gracious God, is man that there should be such inconsistency and perfidiousness in his conduct!

It is but the other day that we were shedding our blood to obtain the constitutions under which we now live—constitutions of our own choice and making—and now we are unsheathing our sword to overturn them." The same year he burst out in a lament over rumors of restoring royal government. "I am told that even respectable characters speak of a monarchical government without horror. From thinking proceeds speaking. Hence to acting is often but a single step. But how irresistible and tremendous! What a triumph for our enemies to verify their predictions! What a triumph for the advocates of despotism to find that we are incapable of governing ourselves!"

Congress Attempts Some Reforms.—The Congress was not indifferent to the events that disturbed Washington. On the contrary it put forth many efforts to check tendencies so dangerous to finance, commerce, industries, and the Confederation itself. In 1781, even before the treaty of peace was signed, the Congress, having found out how futile were its taxing powers, carried a resolution of amendment to the Articles of Confederation, authorizing the levy of a moderate duty on imports. Yet this mild measure was rejected by the states. Two years later the Congress prepared another amendment sanctioning the levy of duties on imports, to be collected this time by state officers and applied to the payment of the public debt. This more limited proposal, designed to save public credit, likewise failed. In 1786, the Congress made a third appeal to the states for help, declaring that they had been so irregular and so negligent in paying their quotas that further reliance upon that mode of raising revenues was dishonorable and dangerous.

THE CALLING OF A CONSTITUTIONAL CONVENTION

Hamilton and Washington Urge Reform.—The attempts at reform by the Congress were accompanied by demand for, both within and without that body, a convention to frame a new plan of government. In 1780, the youthful Alexander Hamilton, realizing the weakness of the Articles, so widely discussed, proposed a general convention for the purpose of drafting a new constitution on entirely different principles. With tireless energy he strove to bring his countrymen to his view. Washington, agreeing with him on every point, declared, in a circular letter to the governors, that the duration of the union would be short unless there was lodged somewhere a supreme power "to regulate and govern the general concerns of the confederated republic." The governor of Massachusetts, disturbed by the growth of discontent all about him, suggested to the state legislature in 1785 the advisability of a national convention to enlarge the powers of the Congress. The legislature approved the plan, but did not press it to a conclusion.

The Annapolis Convention.—Action finally came from the South. The Virginia legislature, taking things into its own hands, called a conference of delegates at Annapolis to consider matters of taxation and commerce. When the convention assembled in 1786, it was found that only five states had taken the trouble to send representatives. The leaders were deeply discouraged, but the resourceful Hamilton, a delegate from New York, turned the affair to good account. He secured the adoption of a resolution, calling upon the Congress itself to summon another convention, to meet at Philadelphia.

A National Convention Called (1787).—The Congress, as tardy as ever, at last decided in February, 1787, to issue the call. Fearing drastic changes, however, it restricted the convention to "the sole and express purpose of revising the Articles of Confederation." Jealous of its own powers, it added that any alterations proposed should be referred to the Congress and the states for their approval.

Every state in the union, except Rhode Island, responded to this call. Indeed some of the states, having the Annapolis resolution before them, had already anticipated the Congress by selecting delegates before the formal summons came. Thus, by the persistence of governors, legislatures, and private citizens, there was brought about the long-desired national convention. In May, 1787, it assembled in Philadelphia.

The Eminent Men of the Convention.—On the roll of that memorable convention were fifty-five men, at least half of whom were acknowledged to be among the foremost statesmen and thinkers in America. Every field of statecraft was represented by them: war and practical management in Washington, who was chosen president of the convention; diplomacy in Franklin, now old and full of honor in his own land as well as abroad; finance in Alexander Hamilton and Robert Morris; law in James Wilson of Pennsylvania; the philosophy of government in James Madison, called the "father of the Constitution." They were not theorists but practical men, rich in political experience and endowed with deep insight into the springs of human action. Three of them had served in the Stamp Act Congress: Dickinson of Delaware, William Samuel Johnson of Connecticut, and John Rutledge of South Carolina. Eight had been signers of the Declaration of Independence: Read of Delaware, Sherman of Connecticut, Wythe of Virginia, Gerry of Massachusetts, Franklin, Robert Morris, George Clymer, and James Wilson of Pennsylvania. All but twelve had at some time served in the Continental Congress and eighteen were members of that body in the spring of 1787. Washington, Hamilton, Mifflin, and Charles Pinckney had been officers in the Revolutionary army. Seven of the delegates had gained political experience as governors of states. "The convention as a whole," according to the historian Hildreth, "represented in a marked manner the talent, intelligence, and especially the conservative sentiment of the country."

THE FRAMING OF THE CONSTITUTION

Problems Involved.—The great problems before the convention were nine in number: (1) Shall the Articles of Confederation be revised or a new system of government constructed? (2) Shall the government be founded on states equal in power as under the Articles or on the broader and deeper foundation of population? (3) What direct share shall the people have in the election of national officers? (4) What shall be the qualifications for the suffrage? (5) How shall the conflicting interests of the commercial and the planting states be balanced so as to safeguard the essential rights of each? (6) What shall be the form of the new government? (7) What powers shall be conferred on it? (8) How shall the state legislatures be restrained from their attacks on property rights such as the issuance of paper money? (9) Shall the approval of all the states be necessary, as under the Articles, for the adoption and amendment of the Constitution?

Revision of the Articles or a New Government?—The moment the first problem was raised, representatives of the small states, led by William Paterson of New Jersey, were on their feet. They feared that, if the Articles were overthrown, the equality and rights of the states would be put in jeopardy. Their protest was therefore vigorous. They cited the call issued by the Congress in summoning the convention which specifically stated that they were assembled for "the sole and express purpose of revising the Articles of Confederation." They cited also their instructions from their state legislatures, which authorized them to "revise and amend" the existing scheme of government, not to make a revolution in it. To depart from the authorization laid down by the Congress and the legislatures would be to exceed their powers, they argued, and to betray the trust reposed in them by their countrymen.

To their contentions, Randolph of Virginia replied: "When the salvation of the republic is at stake, it would be treason to our trust not to propose what we find necessary." Hamilton, reminding the delegates that their work was still subject to the approval of the states, frankly said that on the point of their powers he had no scruples. With the issue clear, the convention cast aside the Articles as if they did not exist and proceeded to the work of drawing up a new constitution, "laying its foundations on such principles and organizing its powers in such form" as to the delegates seemed "most likely to affect their safety and happiness."

A Government Founded on States or on People?—The Compromise.—Defeated in their attempt to limit the convention to a mere revision of the Articles, the spokesmen of the smaller states redoubled their efforts to preserve the equality of the states. The signal for a radical departure from the Articles on this point was given early in the sessions when Randolph presented "the Virginia plan." He proposed that the new national legislature consist of two houses, the members of which were to be apportioned among the states according to their wealth or free white population, as the convention might decide. This plan was vehemently challenged. Paterson of New Jersey flatly avowed that neither he nor his state would ever bow to such tyranny. As an alternative, he presented "the New Jersey plan" calling for a national legislature of one house representing states as such, not wealth or people—a legislature in which all states, large or small, would have equal voice. Wilson of Pennsylvania, on behalf of the more populous states, took up the gauntlet which Paterson had thrown down. It was absurd, he urged, for 180,000 men in one state to have the same weight in national counsels as 750,000 men in another state. "The gentleman from New Jersey," he said, "is candid. He declares his opinion boldly.... I will be equally candid.... I will never confederate on his principles." So the bitter controversy ran on through many exciting sessions.

Greek had met Greek. The convention was hopelessly deadlocked and on the verge of dissolution, "scarce held together by the strength of a hair," as one of the delegates remarked. A crash was averted only by a compromise. Instead of a Congress of one house as provided by the Articles, the convention agreed upon a legislature of two houses. In the Senate, the aspirations of the small states were to be satisfied, for each state was given two members in that body. In the formation of the House of Representatives, the larger states were placated, for it was agreed that the members of that chamber were to be apportioned among the states on the basis of population, counting three-fifths of the slaves.

The Question of Popular Election.—The method of selecting federal officers and members of Congress also produced an acrimonious debate which revealed how deep-seated was the distrust of the capacity of the people to govern themselves. Few there were who believed that no branch of the government should be elected directly by the voters; still fewer were there, however, who desired to see all branches so chosen. One or two even expressed a desire for a monarchy. The dangers of democracy were stressed by Gerry of Massachusetts: "All the evils we experience flow from an excess of democracy. The people do not want virtue but are the dupes of pretended patriots.... I have been too republican heretofore but have been taught by experience the danger of a leveling spirit." To the "democratic licentiousness of the state legislatures," Randolph sought to oppose a "firm senate." To check the excesses of popular government Charles Pinckney of South Carolina declared that no one should be elected President who was not worth $100,000 and that high property qualifications should be placed on members of Congress and judges. Other members of the convention were stoutly opposed to such "high-toned notions of government." Franklin and Wilson, both from Pennsylvania, vigorously championed popular election; while men like Madison insisted that at least one part of the government should rest on the broad foundation of the people.

Out of this clash of opinion also came compromise. One branch, the House of Representatives, it was agreed, was to be elected directly by the voters, while the Senators were to be elected indirectly by the state legislatures. The President was to be chosen by electors selected as the legislatures of the states might determine, and the judges of the federal courts, supreme and inferior, by the President and the Senate.

The Question of the Suffrage.—The battle over the suffrage was sharp but brief. Gouverneur Morris proposed that only land owners should be permitted to vote. Madison replied that the state legislatures, which had made so much trouble with radical laws, were elected by freeholders. After the debate, the delegates, unable to agree on any property limitations on the suffrage, decided that the House of Representatives should be elected by voters having the "qualifications requisite for electors of the most numerous branch of the state legislature." Thus they accepted the suffrage provisions of the states.

The Balance between the Planting and the Commercial States.—After the debates had gone on for a few weeks, Madison came to the conclusion that the real division in the convention was not between the large and the small states but between the planting section founded on slave labor and the commercial North. Thus he anticipated by nearly three-quarters of a century "the irrepressible conflict." The planting states had neither the free white population nor the wealth of the North. There were, counting Delaware, six of them as against seven commercial states. Dependent for their prosperity mainly upon the sale of tobacco, rice, and other staples abroad, they feared that Congress might impose restraints upon their enterprise. Being weaker in numbers, they were afraid that the majority might lay an unfair burden of taxes upon them.

Representation and Taxation.—The Southern members of the convention were therefore very anxious to secure for their section the largest possible representation in Congress, and at the same time to restrain the taxing power of that body. Two devices were thought adapted to these ends. One was to count the slaves as people when apportioning representatives among the states according to their respective populations; the other was to provide that direct taxes should be apportioned among the states, in proportion not to their wealth but to the number of their free white inhabitants. For obvious reasons the Northern delegates objected to these proposals. Once more a compromise proved to be the solution. It was agreed that not all the slaves but three-fifths of them should be counted for both purposes—representation and direct taxation.

Commerce and the Slave Trade.—Southern interests were also involved in the project to confer upon Congress the power to regulate interstate and foreign commerce. To the manufacturing and trading states this was essential. It would prevent interstate tariffs and trade jealousies; it would enable Congress to protect American manufactures and to break down, by appropriate retaliations, foreign discriminations against American commerce. To the South the proposal was menacing because tariffs might interfere with the free exchange of the produce of plantations in European markets, and navigation acts might confine the carrying trade to American, that is Northern, ships. The importation of slaves, moreover, it was feared might be heavily taxed or immediately prohibited altogether.

The result of this and related controversies was a debate on the merits of slavery. Gouverneur Morris delivered his mind and heart on that subject, denouncing slavery as a nefarious institution and the curse of heaven on the states in which it prevailed. Mason of Virginia, a slaveholder himself, was hardly less outspoken, saying: "Slavery discourages arts and manufactures. The poor despise labor when performed by slaves. They prevent the migration of whites who really strengthen and enrich a country."

The system, however, had its defenders. Representatives from South Carolina argued that their entire economic life rested on slave labor and that the high death rate in the rice swamps made continuous importation necessary. Ellsworth of Connecticut took the ground that the convention should not meddle with slavery. "The morality or wisdom of slavery," he said, "are considerations belonging to the states. What enriches a part enriches the whole." To the future he turned an untroubled face: "As population increases, poor laborers will be so plenty as to render slaves useless. Slavery in time will not be a speck in our country." Virginia and North Carolina, already overstocked with slaves, favored prohibiting the traffic in them; but South Carolina was adamant. She must have fresh supplies of slaves or she would not federate.

So it was agreed that, while Congress might regulate foreign trade by majority vote, the importation of slaves should not be forbidden before the lapse of twenty years, and that any import tax should not exceed $10 a head. At the same time, in connection with the regulation of foreign trade, it was stipulated that a two-thirds vote in the Senate should be necessary in the ratification of treaties. A further concession to the South was made in the provision for the return of runaway slaves—a provision also useful in the North, where indentured servants were about as troublesome as slaves in escaping from their masters.

The Form of the Government.—As to the details of the frame of government and the grand principles involved, the opinion of the convention ebbed and flowed, decisions being taken in the heat of debate, only to be revoked and taken again.

The Executive.—There was general agreement that there should be an executive branch; for reliance upon Congress to enforce its own laws and treaties had been a broken reed. On the character and functions of the executive, however, there were many views. The New Jersey plan called for a council selected by the Congress; the Virginia plan provided that the executive branch should be chosen by the Congress but did not state whether it should be composed of one or several persons. On this matter the convention voted first one way and then another; finally it agreed on a single executive chosen indirectly by electors selected as the state legislatures might decide, serving for four years, subject to impeachment, and endowed with regal powers in the command of the army and the navy and in the enforcement of the laws.

The Legislative Branch—Congress.—After the convention had made the great compromise between the large and small commonwealths by giving representation to states in the Senate and to population in the House, the question of methods of election had to be decided. As to the House of Representatives it was readily agreed that the members should be elected by direct popular vote. There was also easy agreement on the proposition that a strong Senate was needed to check the "turbulence" of the lower house. Four devices were finally selected to accomplish this purpose. In the first place, the Senators were not to be chosen directly by the voters but by the legislatures of the states, thus removing their election one degree from the populace. In the second place, their term was fixed at six years instead of two, as in the case of the House. In the third place, provision was made for continuity by having only one-third of the members go out at a time while two-thirds remained in service. Finally, it was provided that Senators must be at least thirty years old while Representatives need be only twenty-five.

The Judiciary.—The need for federal courts to carry out the law was hardly open to debate. The feebleness of the Articles of Confederation was, in a large measure, attributed to the want of a judiciary to hold states and individuals in obedience to the laws and treaties of the union. Nevertheless on this point the advocates of states' rights were extremely sensitive. They looked with distrust upon judges appointed at the national capital and emancipated from local interests and traditions; they remembered with what insistence they had claimed against Britain the right of local trial by jury and with what consternation they had viewed the proposal to make colonial judges independent of the assemblies in the matter of their salaries. Reluctantly they yielded to the demand for federal courts, consenting at first only to a supreme court to review cases heard in lower state courts and finally to such additional inferior courts as Congress might deem necessary.

The System of Checks and Balances.—It is thus apparent that the framers of the Constitution, in shaping the form of government, arranged for a distribution of power among three branches, executive, legislative, and judicial. Strictly speaking we might say four branches, for the legislature, or Congress, was composed of two houses, elected in different ways, and one of them, the Senate, was made a check on the President through its power of ratifying treaties and appointments. "The accumulation of all powers, legislative, executive, and judicial, in the same hands," wrote Madison, "whether of one, a few, or many, and whether hereditary, self-appointed, or elective, may justly be pronounced the very definition of tyranny." The devices which the convention adopted to prevent such a centralization of authority were exceedingly ingenious and well calculated to accomplish the purposes of the authors.

The legislature consisted of two houses, the members of which were to be apportioned on a different basis, elected in different ways, and to serve for different terms. A veto on all its acts was vested in a President elected in a manner not employed in the choice of either branch of the legislature, serving for four years, and subject to removal only by the difficult process of impeachment. After a law had run the gantlet of both houses and the executive, it was subject to interpretation and annulment by the judiciary, appointed by the President with the consent of the Senate and serving for life. Thus it was made almost impossible for any political party to get possession of all branches of the government at a single popular election. As Hamilton remarked, the friends of good government considered "every institution calculated to restrain the excess of law making and to keep things in the same state in which they happen to be at any given period as more likely to do good than harm."

The Powers of the Federal Government.—On the question of the powers to be conferred upon the new government there was less occasion for a serious dispute. Even the delegates from the small states agreed with those from Massachusetts, Pennsylvania, and Virginia that new powers should be added to those intrusted to Congress by the Articles of Confederation. The New Jersey plan as well as the Virginia plan recognized this fact. Some of the delegates, like Hamilton and Madison, even proposed to give Congress a general legislative authority covering all national matters; but others, frightened by the specter of nationalism, insisted on specifying each power to be conferred and finally carried the day.

Taxation and Commerce.—There were none bold enough to dissent from the proposition that revenue must be provided to pay current expenses and discharge the public debt. When once the dispute over the apportionment of direct taxes among the slave states was settled, it was an easy matter to decide that Congress should have power to lay and collect taxes, duties, imposts, and excises. In this way the national government was freed from dependence upon stubborn and tardy legislatures and enabled to collect funds directly from citizens. There were likewise none bold enough to contend that the anarchy of state tariffs and trade discriminations should be longer endured. When the fears of the planting states were allayed and the "bargain" over the importation of slaves was reached, the convention vested in Congress the power to regulate foreign and interstate commerce.

National Defense.—The necessity for national defense was realized, though the fear of huge military establishments was equally present. The old practice of relying on quotas furnished by the state legislatures was completely discredited. As in the case of taxes a direct authority over citizens was demanded. Congress was therefore given full power to raise and support armies and a navy. It could employ the state militia when desirable; but it could at the same time maintain a regular army and call directly upon all able-bodied males if the nature of a crisis was thought to require it.

The "Necessary and Proper" Clause.—To the specified power vested in Congress by the Constitution, the advocates of a strong national government added a general clause authorizing it to make all laws "necessary and proper" for carrying into effect any and all of the enumerated powers. This clause, interpreted by that master mind, Chief Justice Marshall, was later construed to confer powers as wide as the requirements of a vast country spanning a continent and taking its place among the mighty nations of the earth.

Restraints on the States.—Framing a government and endowing it with large powers were by no means the sole concern of the convention. Its very existence had been due quite as much to the conduct of the state legislatures as to the futilities of a paralyzed Continental Congress. In every state, explains Marshall in his *Life of Washington*, there was a party of men who had "marked out for themselves a more indulgent course. Viewing with extreme tenderness the case of the debtor, their efforts were unceasingly directed to his relief. To exact a faithful compliance with contracts was, in their opinion, a harsh measure which the people could not bear. They were uniformly in favor of relaxing the administration of justice, of affording facilities for the payment of debts, or of suspending their collection, and remitting taxes."

The legislatures under the dominance of these men had enacted paper money laws enabling debtors to discharge their obligations more easily. The convention put an end to such practices by providing that no state should emit bills of credit or make anything but gold or silver legal tender in the payment of debts. The state legislatures had enacted laws allowing men to pay their debts by turning over to creditors land or personal property; they had repealed the charter of an endowed college and taken the management from the hands of the lawful trustees; and they had otherwise interfered with the enforcement of private agreements. The convention, taking notice of such matters, inserted a clause forbidding states "to impair the obligation of contracts." The more venturous of the radicals had in Massachusetts raised the standard of revolt against the authorities of the state. The convention answered by a brief sentence to the effect that the President of the United States, to be equipped with a regular army, would send troops to suppress domestic insurrections whenever called upon by the legislature or, if it was not in session, by the governor of the state. To make sure that the restrictions on the states would not be dead letters, the federal Constitution, laws, and treaties were made the supreme law of the land, to be enforced whenever necessary by a national judiciary and executive against violations on the part of any state authorities.

Provisions for Ratification and Amendment.—When the frame of government had been determined, the powers to be vested in it had been enumerated, and the restrictions upon the states had been written into the bond, there remained three final questions. How shall the Constitution be ratified? What number of states shall be necessary to put it into effect? How shall it be amended in the future?

On the first point, the mandate under which the convention was sitting seemed positive. The Articles of Confederation were still in effect. They provided that amendments could be made only by unanimous adoption in Congress and the approval of all the states. As if to give force to this provision of law, the call for the convention had expressly stated that all alterations and revisions should be reported to Congress for adoption or rejection, Congress itself to transmit the document thereafter to the states for their review.

To have observed the strict letter of the law would have defeated the purposes of the delegates, because Congress and the state legislatures were openly hostile to such drastic changes as had been made. Unanimous ratification, as events proved, would have been impossible. Therefore the delegates decided that the Constitution should be sent to Congress with the recommendation that it, in turn, transmit the document, not to the state legislatures, but to conventions held in the states for the special object of deciding upon ratification. This process was followed. It was their belief that special conventions would be more friendly than the state legislatures.

The convention was equally positive in dealing with the problem of the number of states necessary to establish the new Constitution. Attempts to change the Articles had failed because amendment required the approval of every state and there was always at least one recalcitrant member of the union. The opposition to a new Constitution was undoubtedly formidable. Rhode Island had even refused to take part in framing it, and her hostility was deep and open. So the convention cast aside the provision of the Articles of Confederation which required unanimous approval for any change in the plan of government; it decreed that the new Constitution should go into effect when ratified by nine states.

In providing for future changes in the Constitution itself the convention also thrust aside the old rule of unanimous approval, and decided that an amendment could be made on a two-thirds vote in both houses of Congress and ratification by three-fourths of the states. This change was of profound significance. Every state agreed to be bound in the future by amendments duly adopted even in case it did not approve them itself. America in this way set out upon the high road that led from a league of states to a nation.

THE STRUGGLE OVER RATIFICATION

On September 17, 1787, the Constitution, having been finally drafted in clear and simple language, a model to all makers of fundamental law, was adopted. The convention, after nearly four months of debate in secret session, flung open the doors and presented to the Americans the finished plan for the new government. Then the great debate passed to the people.

The Opposition.—Storms of criticism at once descended upon the Constitution. "Fraudulent usurpation!" exclaimed Gerry, who had refused to sign it. "A monster" out of the "thick veil of secrecy," declaimed a Pennsylvania newspaper. "An iron-handed despotism will be the result," protested a third. "We, 'the low-born,'" sarcastically wrote a fourth, "will now admit the 'six hundred well-born' immediately to establish this most noble, most excellent, and truly divine constitution." The President will become a king; Congress will be as tyrannical as Parliament in the old days; the states will be swallowed up; the rights of the people will be trampled upon; the poor man's justice will be lost in the endless delays of the federal courts—such was the strain of the protests against ratification.

Defense of the Constitution.—Moved by the tempest of opposition, Hamilton, Madison, and Jay took up their pens in defense of the Constitution. In a series of newspaper articles they discussed and expounded with eloquence, learning, and dignity every important clause and provision of the proposed plan. These papers, afterwards collected and published in a volume known as *The Federalist*, form the finest textbook on the Constitution that has ever been printed. It takes its place, moreover, among the wisest and weightiest treatises on government ever written in any language in any time. Other men, not so gifted, were no less earnest in their support of ratification. In private correspondence, editorials, pamphlets, and letters to the newspapers, they urged their countrymen to forget their partisanship and accept a Constitution which, in spite of any defects great or small, was the only guarantee against dissolution and warfare at home and dishonor and weakness abroad.

The Action of the State Conventions.—Before the end of the year, 1787, three states had ratified the Constitution: Delaware and New Jersey unanimously and Pennsylvania after a short, though savage, contest. Connecticut and Georgia followed early the next year. Then came the battle royal in Massachusetts, ending in ratification in February by the narrow margin of 187 votes to 168. In the spring came the news that Maryland and South Carolina were "under the new roof." On June 21, New

Hampshire, where the sentiment was at first strong enough to defeat the Constitution, joined the new republic, influenced by the favorable decision in Massachusetts. Swift couriers were sent to carry the news to New York and Virginia, where the question of ratification was still undecided. Nine states had accepted it and were united, whether more saw fit to join or not.

Meanwhile, however, Virginia, after a long and searching debate, had given her approval by a narrow margin, leaving New York as the next seat of anxiety. In that state the popular vote for the delegates to the convention had been clearly and heavily against ratification. Events finally demonstrated the futility of resistance, and Hamilton by good judgment and masterly arguments was at last able to marshal a majority of thirty to twenty-seven votes in favor of ratification.

The great contest was over. All the states, except North Carolina and Rhode Island, had ratified. "The sloop Anarchy," wrote an ebullient journalist, "when last heard from was ashore on Union rocks."

The First Election.—In the autumn of 1788, elections were held to fill the places in the new government. Public opinion was overwhelmingly in favor of Washington as the first President. Yielding to the importunities of friends, he accepted the post in the spirit of public service. On April 30, 1789, he took the oath of office at Federal Hall in New York City. "Long live George Washington, President of the United States!" cried Chancellor Livingston as soon as the General had kissed the Bible. The cry was caught by the assembled multitude and given back. A new experiment in popular government was launched.

References

M. Farrand, *The Framing of the Constitution of the United States*.

P.L. Ford, *Essays on the Constitution of the United States*.

The Federalist (in many editions).

G. Hunt, *Life of James Madison*.

A.C. McLaughlin, *The Confederation and the Constitution* (American Nation Series).

Questions

1. Account for the failure of the Articles of Confederation.

2. Explain the domestic difficulties of the individual states.

3. Why did efforts at reform by the Congress come to naught?

4. Narrate the events leading up to the constitutional convention.

5. Who were some of the leading men in the convention? What had been their previous training?

6. State the great problems before the convention.

7. In what respects were the planting and commercial states opposed? What compromises were reached?

8. Show how the "check and balance" system is embodied in our form of government.

9. How did the powers conferred upon the federal government help cure the defects of the Articles of Confederation?

10. In what way did the provisions for ratifying and amending the Constitution depart from the old system?

11. What was the nature of the conflict over ratification?

Research Topics

English Treatment of American Commerce.—Callender, *Economic History of the United States*, pp. 210-220.

Financial Condition of the United States.—Fiske, *Critical Period of American History*, pp. 163-186.

Disordered Commerce.—Fiske, pp. 134-162.

Selfish Conduct of the States.—Callender, pp. 185-191.

The Failure of the Confederation.—Elson, *History of the United States*, pp. 318-326.

Formation of the Constitution.—(1) The plans before the convention, Fiske, pp. 236-249; (2) the great compromise, Fiske, pp. 250-255; (3) slavery and the convention, Fiske, pp. 256-266; and (4) the frame of government, Fiske, pp. 275-301; Elson, pp. 328-334.

Biographical Studies.—Look up the history and services of the leaders in the convention in any good encyclopedia.

Ratification of the Constitution.—Hart, *History Told by Contemporaries*, Vol. III, pp. 233-254; Elson, pp. 334-340.

Source Study.—Compare the Constitution and Articles of Confederation under the following heads: (1) frame of government; (2) powers of Congress; (3) limits on states; and (4) methods of amendment. Every line of the Constitution should be read and re-read in the light of the historical circumstances set forth in this chapter.

CHAPTER VIII

THE CLASH OF POLITICAL PARTIES

THE MEN AND MEASURES OF THE NEW GOVERNMENT

Friends of the Constitution in Power.—In the first Congress that assembled after the adoption of the Constitution, there were eleven Senators, led by Robert Morris, the financier, who had been delegates to the national convention. Several members of the House of Representatives, headed by James Madison, had also been at Philadelphia in 1787. In making his appointments, Washington strengthened the new system of government still further by a judicious selection of officials. He chose as Secretary of the Treasury, Alexander Hamilton, who had been the most zealous for its success; General Knox, head of the War Department, and Edmund Randolph, the Attorney-General, were likewise conspicuous friends of the experiment. Every member of the federal judiciary whom Washington appointed, from the Chief Justice, John Jay, down to the justices of the district courts, had favored the ratification of the Constitution; and a majority of them had served as members of the national convention that framed the document or of the state ratifying conventions. Only one man of influence in the new government, Thomas Jefferson, the Secretary of State, was reckoned as a doubter in the house of the faithful. He had expressed opinions both for and against the Constitution; but he had been out of the country acting as the minister at Paris when the Constitution was drafted and ratified.

An Opposition to Conciliate.—The inauguration of Washington amid the plaudits of his countrymen did not set at rest all the political turmoil which had been aroused by the angry contest over ratification. "The interesting nature of the question," wrote John Marshall, "the equality of the parties, the animation produced inevitably by ardent debate had a necessary tendency to embitter the dispositions of the vanquished and to fix more deeply in many bosoms their prejudices against a plan of government in opposition to which all their passions were enlisted." The leaders gathered around Washington were well aware of the excited state of the country. They saw Rhode Island and North Carolina still outside of the union.[1] They knew by what small margins the Constitution had been approved in the great states of Massachusetts, Virginia, and New York. They were equally aware that a majority of the state conventions, in yielding reluctant approval to the Constitution, had drawn a number of amendments for immediate submission to the states.

The First Amendments—a Bill of Rights.—To meet the opposition, Madison proposed, and the first Congress adopted, a series of amendments to the Constitution. Ten of them were soon ratified and became in 1791 a part of the law of the land. These amendments provided, among other things, that Congress could make no law respecting the establishment of religion, abridging the freedom of speech or of the press or the right of the people peaceably to assemble and petition the government for a redress of grievances. They also guaranteed indictment by grand jury and trial by jury for all persons charged by federal officers with serious crimes. To reassure those who still feared that local rights might be invaded by the federal government, the tenth amendment expressly provided that the powers not delegated to the United States by the Constitution, nor prohibited by it to the states, are reserved to the states respectively or to the people. Seven years later, the eleventh amendment was written in the same spirit as the first ten, after a heated debate over the action of the Supreme Court in permitting a citizen to bring a suit against "the sovereign state" of Georgia. The new amendment was designed to protect states against the federal judiciary by forbidding it to hear any case in which a state was sued by a citizen.

Funding the National Debt.—Paper declarations of rights, however, paid no bills. To this task Hamilton turned all his splendid genius. At the very outset he addressed himself to the problem of the huge public debt, daily mounting as the unpaid interest accumulated. In a *Report on Public Credit* under date of January 9, 1790, one of the first and greatest of American state papers, he laid before Congress the outlines of his plan. He proposed that the federal government should call in all the old bonds, certificates of indebtedness, and other promises to pay which had been issued by the Congress since the beginning of the Revolution. These national obligations, he urged, should be put into one consolidated debt resting on the credit of the United States; to the holders of the old paper should be issued new bonds drawing interest at fixed rates. This process was called "funding the debt." Such a provision for the support of public credit, Hamilton insisted, would satisfy creditors, restore landed property to its former value, and furnish new resources to agriculture and commerce in the form of credit and capital.

Assumption and Funding of State Debts.—Hamilton then turned to the obligations incurred by the several states in support of the Revolution. These debts he proposed to add to the national debt. They were to be "assumed" by the United States government and placed on the same secure foundation as the continental debt. This measure he defended not merely on grounds of national honor. It would, as he foresaw, give strength to the new national government by making all public creditors, men of substance in their several communities, look to the federal, rather than the state government, for the satisfaction of their claims.

Funding at Face Value.—On the question of the terms of consolidation, assumption, and funding, Hamilton had a firm conviction. That millions of dollars' worth of the continental and state bonds had passed out of the hands of those who had originally subscribed their funds to the support of the government or had sold supplies for the Revolutionary army was well known. It was also a matter of common knowledge that a very large part of these bonds had been bought by speculators at ruinous figures—ten, twenty, and thirty cents on the dollar. Accordingly, it had been suggested, even in very respectable quarters, that a discrimination should be made between original holders and speculative purchasers. Some who held this opinion urged that the speculators who had paid nominal sums for their bonds should be reimbursed for their outlays and the original holders paid the difference; others said that the government should "scale the debt" by redeeming, not at full value but at a figure reasonably above the market price. Against the proposition Hamilton set his face like flint. He maintained that the government was honestly bound to redeem every bond at its face value, although the difficulty of securing revenue made necessary a lower rate of interest on a part of the bonds and the deferring of interest on another part.

Funding and Assumption Carried.—There was little difficulty in securing the approval of both houses of Congress for the funding of the national debt at full value. The bill for the assumption of state debts, however, brought the sharpest division of opinions. To the Southern members of Congress assumption was a gross violation of states' rights, without any warrant in the Constitution and devised in the interest of Northern speculators who, anticipating assumption and funding, had bought up at low prices the Southern bonds and other promises to pay. New England, on the other hand, was strongly in favor of assumption; several representatives from that section were rash enough to threaten a dissolution of the union if the bill was defeated. To this dispute was added an equally bitter quarrel over the location of the national capital, then temporarily at New York City.

A deadlock, accompanied by the most surly feelings on both sides, threatened the very existence of the young government. Washington and Hamilton were thoroughly alarmed. Hearing of the extremity to which the contest had been carried and acting on the appeal from the Secretary of the Treasury, Jefferson intervened at this point. By skillful management at a good dinner he brought the opposing leaders together; and thus once more, as on many other occasions, peace was purchased and the union saved by compromise. The bargain this time consisted of an exchange of votes for assumption in return for votes for the capital. Enough Southern members voted for assumption to pass the bill, and a majority was mustered in favor of building the capital on the banks of the Potomac, after locating it for a ten-year period at Philadelphia to satisfy Pennsylvania members.

The United States Bank.—Encouraged by the success of his funding and assumption measures, Hamilton laid before Congress a project for a great United States Bank. He proposed that a private corporation be chartered by Congress, authorized to raise a capital stock of $10,000,000 (three-fourths in new six per cent federal bonds and one-fourth in specie) and empowered to issue paper currency under proper safeguards. Many advantages, Hamilton contended, would accrue to the government from this institution. The price of the government bonds would be increased, thus enhancing public credit. A national currency would be created of uniform value from one end of the land to the other. The branches of the bank in various cities would make easy the exchange of funds so vital to commercial transactions on a national scale. Finally, through the issue of bank notes, the money capital available for agriculture and industry would be increased, thus stimulating business enterprise. Jefferson hotly attacked the bank on the ground that Congress had no power whatever under the Constitution to charter such a private corporation. Hamilton defended it with great cogency. Washington, after weighing all opinions, decided in favor of the proposal. In 1791 the bill establishing the first United States Bank for a period of twenty years became a law.

The Protective Tariff.—A third part of Hamilton's program was the protection of American industries. The first revenue act of 1789, though designed primarily to bring money into the empty treasury, declared in favor of the principle. The following year Washington referred to the subject in his address to Congress. Thereupon Hamilton was instructed to prepare recommendations for legislative action. The result, after a delay of more than a year, was his *Report on Manufactures*, another state paper worthy, in closeness of reasoning and keenness of understanding, of a place beside his report on public credit. Hamilton based his argument on the broadest national grounds: the protective tariff would, by encouraging the building of factories, create a home market for the produce of farms and plantations; by making the United States independent of other countries in times of peace, it would double its security in time of war; by making use of the labor of women and children, it would turn to the production of goods persons otherwise idle or only partly employed; by increasing the trade between the North and South it would strengthen the links of union and add to political ties those of commerce and intercourse. The revenue measure of 1792 bore the impress of these arguments.

THE RISE OF POLITICAL PARTIES

Dissensions over Hamilton's Measures.—Hamilton's plans, touching deeply as they did the resources of individuals and the interests of the states, awakened alarm and opposition. Funding at face value, said his critics, was a government favor to speculators; the assumption of state debts was a deep design to undermine the state governments; Congress had no constitutional power to create a bank; the law creating the bank merely allowed a private corporation to make paper money and lend it at a high rate of interest; and the tariff was a tax on land and labor for the benefit of manufacturers.

Hamilton's reply to this bill of indictment was simple and straightforward. Some rascally speculators had profited from the funding of the debt at face value, but that was only an incident in the restoration of public credit. In view of the jealousies of the states it was a good thing to reduce their powers and pretensions. The Constitution was not to be interpreted narrowly but in the full light of national needs. The bank would enlarge the amount of capital so sorely needed to start up American industries, giving markets to farmers and planters. The tariff by creating a home market and increasing opportunities for employment would benefit both land and labor. Out of such wise policies firmly pursued by the government, he concluded, were bound to come strength and prosperity for the new government at home, credit and power abroad. This view Washington fully indorsed, adding the weight of his great name to the inherent merits of the measures adopted under his administration.

The Sharpness of the Partisan Conflict.—As a result of the clash of opinion, the people of the country gradually divided into two parties: Federalists and Anti-Federalists, the former led by Hamilton, the latter by Jefferson. The strength of the Federalists lay in the cities—Boston, Providence, Hartford, New York, Philadelphia, Charleston—among the manufacturing, financial, and commercial groups of the population who were eager to extend their business operations. The strength of the Anti-Federalists lay mainly among the debt-burdened farmers who feared the growth of what they called "a money power" and planters in all sections who feared the dominance of commercial and manufacturing interests. The farming and planting South, outside of the few towns, finally presented an almost solid front against assumption, the bank, and the tariff. The conflict between the parties grew steadily in bitterness, despite the conciliatory and engaging manner in which Hamilton presented his cause in his state papers and despite the constant efforts of Washington to soften the asperity of the contestants.

The Leadership and Doctrines of Jefferson.—The party dispute had not gone far before the opponents of the administration began to look to Jefferson as their leader. Some of Hamilton's measures he had approved, declaring afterward that he did not at the time understand their significance. Others, particularly the bank, he fiercely assailed. More than once, he and Hamilton, shaking violently with anger, attacked each other at cabinet meetings, and nothing short of the grave and dignified pleas of Washington prevented an early and open break between them. In 1794 it finally came. Jefferson resigned as Secretary of State and retired to his home in Virginia to assume, through correspondence and negotiation, the leadership of the steadily growing party of opposition.

Shy and modest in manner, halting in speech, disliking the turmoil of public debate, and deeply interested in science and philosophy, Jefferson was not very well fitted for the strenuous life of political contest. Nevertheless, he was an ambitious and shrewd negotiator. He was also by honest opinion and matured conviction the exact opposite of Hamilton. The latter believed in a strong, active, "high-toned" government, vigorously compelling in all its branches. Jefferson looked upon such government as dangerous to the liberties of citizens and openly avowed his faith in the desirability of occasional popular uprisings. Hamilton distrusted the people. "Your people is a great beast," he is reported to have said. Jefferson professed his faith in the people with an abandon that was considered reckless in his time.

On economic matters, the opinions of the two leaders were also hopelessly at variance. Hamilton, while cherishing agriculture, desired to see America a great commercial and industrial nation. Jefferson was equally set against this course for his country. He feared the accumulation of riches and the growth of a large urban working class. The mobs of great cities, he said, are sores on the body politic; artisans are usually the dangerous element that make revolutions; workshops should be kept in Europe and with them the artisans with their insidious morals and manners. The only substantial foundation for a republic, Jefferson believed to be agriculture. The spirit of independence could be kept alive only by free farmers, owning the land they tilled and looking to the sun in heaven and the labor of their hands for their sustenance. Trusting as he did in the innate goodness of human nature when nourished on a free soil, Jefferson advocated those measures calculated to favor agriculture and to enlarge the rights of persons rather than the powers of government. Thus he became the champion of the individual against the interference of the government, and an ardent advocate of freedom of the press, freedom of speech, and freedom of scientific inquiry. It was, accordingly, no mere factious spirit that drove him into opposition to Hamilton.

The Whisky Rebellion.—The political agitation of the Anti-Federalists was accompanied by an armed revolt against the government in 1794. The occasion for this uprising was another of Hamilton's measures, a law laying an excise tax on distilled spirits, for the purpose of increasing the revenue needed to pay the interest on the funded debt. It so happened that a very considerable part of the whisky manufactured in the country was made by the farmers, especially on the frontier, in their own stills. The new revenue law meant that federal officers would now come into the homes of the people, measure their liquor, and take the tax out of their pockets. All the bitterness which farmers felt against the fiscal measures of the government was redoubled. In the western districts of Pennsylvania, Virginia, and North Carolina, they refused to pay the tax. In Pennsylvania, some of them sacked and burned the houses of the tax collectors, as the Revolutionists thirty years before had mobbed the agents of King George sent over to sell stamps. They were in a fair way to nullify the law in whole districts when Washington called out the troops to suppress "the Whisky Rebellion." Then the movement collapsed; but it left behind a deep-seated resentment which flared up in the election of several obdurate Anti-Federalist Congressmen from the disaffected regions.

FOREIGN INFLUENCES AND DOMESTIC POLITICS

The French Revolution.—In this exciting period, when all America was distracted by partisan disputes, a storm broke in Europe—the epoch-making French Revolution—which not only shook the thrones of the Old World but stirred to its depths the young republic of the New World. The first scene in this dramatic affair occurred in the spring of 1789, a few days after Washington was inaugurated. The king of France, Louis XVI, driven into bankruptcy by extravagance and costly wars, was forced to resort to his people for financial help. Accordingly he called, for the first time in more than one hundred fifty years, a meeting of the national parliament,the "Estates General," composed of representatives of the "three estates"—the clergy, nobility, and commoners. Acting under powerful leaders, the commoners, or "third estate," swept aside the clergy and nobility and resolved themselves into a national assembly. This stirred the country to its depths.

Great events followed in swift succession. On July 14, 1789, the Bastille, an old royal prison, symbol of the king's absolutism, was stormed by a Paris crowd and destroyed. On the night of August 4, the feudal privileges of the nobility were abolished by the national assembly amid great excitement. A few days later came the famous Declaration of the Rights of Man, proclaiming the sovereignty of the people and the privileges of citizens. In the autumn of 1791, Louis XVI was forced to accept a new constitution for France vesting the legislative power in a popular assembly. Little disorder accompanied these startling changes. To all appearances a peaceful revolution had stripped the French king of his royal prerogatives and based the government of his country on the consent of the governed.

American Influence in France.—In undertaking their great political revolt the French had been encouraged by the outcome of the American Revolution. Officers and soldiers, who had served in the American war, reported to their French countrymen marvelous tales. At the frugal table of General Washington, in council with the unpretentious Franklin, or at conferences over the strategy of war, French noblemen of ancient lineage learned to respect both the talents and the simple character of the leaders in the great republican commonwealth beyond the seas. Travelers, who had gone to see the experiment in republicanism with their own eyes, carried home to the king and ruling class stories of an astounding system of popular government.

On the other hand the dalliance with American democracy was regarded by French conservatives as playing with fire. "When we think of the false ideas of government and philanthropy," wrote one of Lafayette's aides, "which these youths acquired in America and propagated in France with so much enthusiasm and such deplorable success—for this mania of imitation powerfully aided the Revolution, though it was not the sole cause of it—we are bound to confess that it would have been better, both for themselves and for us, if these young philosophers in red-heeled shoes had stayed at home in attendance on the court."

Early American Opinion of the French Revolution.—So close were the ties between the two nations that it is not surprising to find every step in the first stages of the French Revolution greeted with applause in the United States. "Liberty will have another feather in her cap," exultantly wrote a Boston editor. "In no part of the globe," soberly wrote John Marshall, "was this revolution hailed with more joy than in America.... But one sentiment existed." The main key to the Bastille, sent to Washington as a memento, was accepted as "a token of the victory gained by liberty." Thomas Paine saw in the great event "the first ripe fruits of American principles transplanted into Europe." Federalists and Anti-Federalists regarded the new constitution of France as another vindication of American ideals.

The Reign of Terror.—While profuse congratulations were being exchanged, rumors began to come that all was not well in France. Many noblemen, enraged at the loss of their special privileges, fled into Germany and plotted an invasion of France to overthrow the new system of government. Louis XVI entered into negotiations with his brother monarchs on the continent to secure their help in the same enterprise, and he finally betrayed to the French people his true sentiments by attempting to escape from his kingdom, only to be captured and taken back to Paris in disgrace.

A new phase of the revolution now opened. The working people, excluded from all share in the government by the first French constitution, became restless, especially in Paris. Assembling on the Champs de Mars, a great open field, they signed a petition calling for another constitution giving them the suffrage. When told to disperse, they refused and were fired upon by the national guard. This "massacre," as it was called, enraged the populace. A radical party, known as "Jacobins," then sprang up, taking its name from a Jacobin monastery in which it held its sessions. In a little while it became the master of the popular convention convoked in September, 1792. The monarchy was immediately abolished and a republic established. On January 21, 1793, Louis was sent to the scaffold. To the war on Austria, already raging, was added a war on England. Then came the Reign of Terror, during which radicals in possession of the convention executed in large numbers counter-revolutionists and those suspected of sympathy with the monarchy. They shot down peasants who rose in insurrection against their rule and established a relentless dictatorship. Civil war followed. Terrible atrocities were committed on both sides in the name of liberty, and in the name of monarchy. To Americans of conservative temper it now seemed that the Revolution, so auspiciously begun, had degenerated into anarchy and mere bloodthirsty strife.

Burke Summons the World to War on France.—In England, Edmund Burke led the fight against the new French principles which he feared might spread to all Europe. In his *Reflections on the French Revolution*, written in 1790, he attacked with terrible wrath the whole program of popular government; he called for war, relentless war, upon the French as monsters and outlaws; he demanded that they be reduced to order by the restoration of the king to full power under the protection of the arms of European nations.

Paine's Defense of the French Revolution.—To counteract the campaign of hate against the French, Thomas Paine replied to Burke in another of his famous tracts, *The Rights of Man*, which was given to the American public in an edition containing a letter of approval from Jefferson. Burke, said Paine, had been mourning about the glories of the French monarchy and aristocracy but had forgotten the starving peasants and the oppressed people; had wept over the plumage and neglected the dying bird. Burke had denied the right of the French people to choose their own governors, blandly forgetting that the English government in which he saw final perfection itself rested on two revolutions. He had boasted that the king of England held his crown in contempt of the democratic societies. Paine answered: "If I ask a man in America if he wants a king, he retorts and asks me if I take him for an idiot." To the charge that the doctrines of the rights of man were "new fangled," Paine replied that the question was not whether they were new or old but whether they were right or wrong. As to the French disorders and difficulties, he bade the world wait to see what would be brought forth in due time.

The Effect of the French Revolution on American Politics.—The course of the French Revolution and the controversies accompanying it, exercised a profound influence on the formation of the first political parties in America. The followers of Hamilton, now proud of the name "Federalists," drew back in fright as they heard of the cruel deeds committed during the Reign of Terror. They turned savagely upon the revolutionists and their friends in America, denouncing as "Jacobin" everybody who did not condemn loudly enough the proceedings of the French Republic. A Massachusetts preacher roundly assailed "the atheistical, anarchical, and in other respects immoral principles of the French Republicans"; he then proceeded with equal passion to attack Jefferson and the Anti-Federalists, whom he charged with spreading false French propaganda and betraying America. "The editors, patrons, and abettors of these vehicles of slander," he exclaimed, "ought to be considered and treated as enemies to their country.... Of all traitors they are the most aggravatedly criminal; of all villains, they are the most infamous and detestable."

The Anti-Federalists, as a matter of fact, were generally favorable to the Revolution although they deplored many of the events associated with it. Paine's pamphlet, indorsed by Jefferson, was widely read. Democratic societies, after the fashion of French political clubs, arose in the cities; the coalition of European monarchs against France was denounced as a coalition against the very principles of republicanism; and the execution of Louis XVI was openly celebrated at a banquet in Philadelphia. Harmless titles, such as "Sir," "the Honorable," and "His Excellency," were decried as aristocratic and some of the more excited insisted on adopting the French title, "Citizen," speaking, for example, of "Citizen Judge" and "Citizen Toastmaster." Pamphlets in defense of the French streamed from the press, while subsidized newspapers kept the propaganda in full swing.

The European War Disturbs American Commerce.—This battle of wits, or rather contest in calumny, might have gone on indefinitely in America without producing any serious results, had it not been for the war between England and France, then raging. The English, having command of the seas, claimed the right to seize American produce bound for French ports and to confiscate American ships engaged in carrying French goods. Adding fuel to a fire already hot enough, they began to search American ships and to carry off British-born sailors found on board American vessels.

The French Appeal for Help.—At the same time the French Republic turned to the United States for aid in its war on England and sent over as its diplomatic representative "Citizen" Genêt, an ardent supporter of the new order. On his arrival at Charleston, he was greeted with fervor by the Anti-Federalists. As he made his way North, he was wined and dined and given popular ovations that turned his head. He thought the whole country was ready to join the French Republic in its contest with England. Genêt therefore attempted to use the American ports as the base of operations for French privateers preying on British merchant ships; and he insisted that the United States was in honor bound to help France under the treaty of 1778.

The Proclamation of Neutrality and the Jay Treaty.—Unmoved by the rising tide of popular sympathy for France, Washington took a firm course. He received Genêt coldly. The demand that the United States aid France under the old treaty of alliance he answered by proclaiming the neutrality of America and warning American citizens against hostile acts toward either France or England. When Genêt continued to hold meetings, issue manifestoes, and stir up the people against England, Washington asked the French government to recall him. This act he followed up by sending the Chief Justice, John Jay, on a pacific mission to England.

The result was the celebrated Jay treaty of 1794. By its terms Great Britain agreed to withdraw her troops from the western forts where they had been since the war for independence and to grant certain slight trade concessions. The chief sources of bitterness—the failure of the British to return slaves carried off during the Revolution, the seizure of American ships, and the impressment of sailors—were not touched, much to the distress of everybody in America, including loyal Federalists. Nevertheless, Washington, dreading an armed conflict with England, urged the Senate to ratify the treaty. The weight of his influence carried the day.

At this, the hostility of the Anti-Federalists knew no bounds. Jefferson declared the Jay treaty "an infamous act which is really nothing more than an alliance between England and the Anglo-men of this country, against the legislature and the people of the United States." Hamilton, defending it with his usual courage, was stoned by a mob in New York and driven from the platform with blood streaming from his face. Jay was burned in effigy. Even Washington was not spared. The House of Representatives was openly hostile. To display its feelings, it called upon the President for the papers relative to the treaty negotiations, only to be more highly incensed by his flat refusal to present them, on the ground that the House did not share in the treaty-making power.

Washington Retires from Politics.—Such angry contests confirmed the President in his slowly maturing determination to retire at the end of his second term in office. He did not believe that a third term was unconstitutional or improper; but, worn out by his long and arduous labors in war and in peace and wounded by harsh attacks from former friends, he longed for the quiet of his beautiful estate at Mount Vernon.

In September, 1796, on the eve of the presidential election, Washington issued his Farewell Address, another state paper to be treasured and read by generations of Americans to come. In this address he directed the attention of the people to three subjects of lasting interest. He warned them against sectional jealousies. He remonstrated against the spirit of partisanship, saying that in government "of the popular character, in government purely elective, it is a spirit not to be encouraged." He likewise cautioned the people against "the insidious wiles of foreign influence," saying: "Europe has a set of primary interests which to us have none or a very remote relation. Hence she must be engaged in frequent controversies, the causes of which are essentially foreign to our concerns. Hence, therefore, it would be unwise in us to implicate ourselves, by artificial ties, in the ordinary vicissitudes of her politics or the ordinary combinations and collisions of her friendships or enmities.... Why forego the advantages of so peculiar a situation?... It is our true policy to steer clear of permanent alliances with any portion of the foreign world.... Taking care always to keep ourselves, by suitable establishments, on a respectable defensive posture, we may safely trust to temporary alliances for extraordinary emergencies."

The Campaign of 1796—Adams Elected.—On hearing of the retirement of Washington, the Anti-Federalists cast off all restraints. In honor of France and in opposition to what they were pleased to call the monarchical tendencies of the Federalists, they boldly assumed the name "Republican"; the term "Democrat," then applied only to obscure and despised radicals, had not come into general use. They selected Jefferson as their candidate for President against John Adams, the Federalist nominee, and carried on such a spirited campaign that they came within four votes of electing him.

The successful candidate, Adams, was not fitted by training or opinion for conciliating a determined opposition. He was a reserved and studious man. He was neither a good speaker nor a skillful negotiator. In one of his books he had declared himself in favor of "government by an aristocracy of talents and wealth"—an offense which the Republicans never forgave. While John Marshall found him "a sensible, plain, candid, good-tempered man," Jefferson could see in him nothing but a "monocrat" and "Anglo-man." Had it not been for the conduct of the French government, Adams would hardly have enjoyed a moment's genuine popularity during his administration.

The Quarrel with France.—The French Directory, the executive department established under the constitution of 1795, managed, however, to stir the anger of Republicans and Federalists alike. It regarded the Jay treaty as a rebuke to France and a flagrant violation of obligations solemnly registered in the treaty of 1778. Accordingly it refused to receive the American minister, treated him in a humiliating way, and finally told him to leave the country. Overlooking this affront in his anxiety to maintain peace, Adams dispatched to France a commission of eminent men with instructions to reach an understanding with the French Republic. On their arrival, they were chagrined to find, instead of a decent reception, an indirect demand for an apology respecting the past conduct of the American government, a payment in cash, and an annual tribute as the price of continued friendship. When the news of this affair reached President Adams, he promptly laid it before Congress, referring to the Frenchmen who had made the demands as "Mr. X, Mr. Y, and Mr. Z."

This insult, coupled with the fact that French privateers, like the British, were preying upon American commerce, enraged even the Republicans who had been loudest in the profession of their French sympathies. They forgot their wrath over the Jay treaty and joined with the Federalists in shouting: "Millions for defense, not a cent for tribute!" Preparations for war were made on every hand. Washington was once more called from Mount Vernon to take his old position at the head of the army. Indeed, fighting actually began upon the high seas and went on without a formal declaration of war until the year 1800. By that time the Directory had been overthrown. A treaty was readily made with Napoleon, the First Consul, who was beginning his remarkable career as chief of the French Republic, soon to be turned into an empire.

Alien and Sedition Laws.—Flushed with success, the Federalists determined, if possible, to put an end to radical French influence in America and to silence Republican opposition. They therefore passed two drastic laws in the summer of 1798: the Alien and Sedition Acts.

The first of these measures empowered the President to expel from the country or to imprison any alien whom he regarded as "dangerous" or "had reasonable grounds to suspect" of "any treasonable or secret machinations against the government."

The second of the measures, the Sedition Act, penalized not only those who attempted to stir up unlawful combinations against the government but also every one who wrote, uttered, or published "any false, scandalous, and malicious writing ... against the government of the United States or either House of Congress, or the President of the United States, with intent to defame said government ... or to bring them or either of them into contempt or disrepute." This measure was hurried through Congress in spite of the opposition and the clear provision in the Constitution that Congress shall make no law abridging the freedom of speech or of the press. Even many Federalists feared the consequences of the action.

Hamilton was alarmed when he read the bill, exclaiming: "Let us not establish a tyranny. Energy is a very different thing from violence." John Marshall told his friends in Virginia that, had he been in Congress, he would have opposed the two bills because he thought them "useless" and "calculated to create unnecessary discontents and jealousies."

The Alien law was not enforced; but it gave great offense to the Irish and French whose activities against the American government's policy respecting Great Britain put them in danger of prison. The Sedition law, on the other hand, was vigorously applied. Several editors of Republican newspapers soon found themselves in jail or broken by ruinous fines for their caustic criticisms of the Federalist President and his policies. Bystanders at political meetings, who uttered sentiments which, though ungenerous and severe, seem harmless enough now, were hurried before Federalist judges and promptly fined and imprisoned. Although the prosecutions were notnumerous, they aroused a keen resentment. The Republicans were convinced that their political opponents, having saddled upon the country Hamilton's fiscal system and the British treaty, were bent on silencing all censure. The measures therefore had exactly the opposite effect from that which their authors intended. Instead of helping the Federalist party, they made criticism of it more bitter than ever.

The Kentucky and Virginia Resolutions.—Jefferson was quick to take advantage of the discontent. He drafted a set of resolutions declaring the Sedition law null and void, as violating the federal Constitution. His resolutions were passed by the Kentucky legislature late in 1798, signed by the governor, and transmitted to the other states for their consideration. Though receiving unfavorable replies from a number of Northern states, Kentucky the following year reaffirmed its position and declared that the nullification of all unconstitutional acts of Congress was the rightful remedy to be used by the states in the redress of grievances. It thus defied the federal government and announced a doctrine hostile to nationality and fraught with terrible meaning for the future. In the neighboring state of Virginia, Madison led a movement against the Alien and Sedition laws. He induced the legislature to pass resolutions condemning the acts as unconstitutional and calling upon the other states to take proper means to preserve their rights and the rights of the people.

The Republican Triumph in 1800.—Thus the way was prepared for the election of 1800. The Republicans left no stone unturned in their efforts to place on the Federalist candidate, President Adams, all the odium of the Alien and Sedition laws, in addition to responsibility for approving Hamilton's measures and policies. The Federalists, divided in councils and cold in their affection for Adams, made a poor campaign. They tried to discredit their opponents with epithets of "Jacobins" and "Anarchists"— terms which had been weakened by excessive use. When the vote was counted, it was found that Adams had been defeated; while the Republicans had carried the entire South and New York also and secured eight of the fifteen electoral votes cast by Pennsylvania. "Our beloved Adams will now close his bright career," lamented a Federalist newspaper. "Sons of faction, demagogues and high priests of anarchy, now you have cause to triumph!"

Jefferson's election, however, was still uncertain. By a curious provision in the Constitution, presidential electors were required to vote for two persons without indicating which office each was to fill, the one receiving the highest number of votes to be President and the candidate standing next to be Vice President. It so happened that Aaron Burr, the Republican candidate for Vice President, had received the same number of votes as Jefferson; as neither had a majority the election was thrown into the House of Representatives, where the Federalists held the balance of power. Although it was well known that Burr was not even a candidate for President, his friends and many Federalists began intriguing for his election to that high office. Had it not been for the vigorous action of Hamilton the prize might have been snatched out of Jefferson's hands. Not until the thirty-sixth ballot on February 17, 1801, was the great issue decided in his favor.[2]

References

J.S. Bassett, *The Federalist System* (American Nation Series).

C.A. Beard, *Economic Origins of Jeffersonian Democracy*.

H. Lodge, *Alexander Hamilton*.

J.T. Morse, *Thomas Jefferson*.

Questions

1. Who were the leaders in the first administration under the Constitution?

2. What step was taken to appease the opposition?

3. Enumerate Hamilton's great measures and explain each in detail.

4. Show the connection between the parts of Hamilton's system.

5. Contrast the general political views of Hamilton and Jefferson.

6. What were the important results of the "peaceful" French Revolution (1789-92)?

7. Explain the interaction of opinion between France and the United States.

8. How did the "Reign of Terror" change American opinion?

9. What was the Burke-Paine controversy?

10. Show how the war in Europe affected American commerce and involved America with England and France.

11. What were American policies with regard to each of those countries?

12. What was the outcome of the Alien and Sedition Acts?

Research Topics

Early Federal Legislation.—Coman, *Industrial History of the United States*, pp. 133-156; Elson, *History of the United States*, pp. 341-348.

Hamilton's Report on Public Credit.—Macdonald, *Documentary Source Book*, pp. 233-243.

The French Revolution.—Robinson and Beard, *Development of Modern Europe*, Vol. I, pp. 224-282; Elson, pp. 351-354.

The Burke-Paine Controversy.—Make an analysis of Burke's *Reflections on the French Revolution* and Paine's *Rights of Man*.

The Alien and Sedition Acts.—Macdonald, *Documentary Source Book*, pp. 259-267; Elson, pp. 367-375.

Kentucky and Virginia Resolutions.—Macdonald, pp. 267-278.

Source Studies.—Materials in Hart, *American History Told by Contemporaries*, Vol. III, pp. 255-343.

Biographical Studies.—Alexander Hamilton, John Adams, Thomas Jefferson, and Albert Gallatin.

The Twelfth Amendment.—Contrast the provision in the original Constitution with the terms of the Amendment. *See* Appendix.

CHAPTER IX

THE JEFFERSONIAN REPUBLICANS IN POWER

REPUBLICAN PRINCIPLES AND POLICIES

Opposition to Strong Central Government.—Cherishing especially the agricultural interest, as Jefferson said, the Republicans were in the beginning provincial in their concern and outlook. Their attachment to America was, certainly, as strong as that of Hamilton; but they regarded the state, rather than the national government, as the proper center of power and affection. Indeed, a large part of the rank and file had been among the opponents of the Constitution in the days of its adoption. Jefferson had entertained doubts about it and Monroe, destined to be the fifth President, had been one of the bitter foes of ratification. The former went so far in the direction of local autonomy that he exalted the state above the nation in the Kentucky resolutions of 1798, declaring the Constitution to be a mere compact and the states competent to interpret and nullify federal law. This was provincialism with a vengeance. "It is jealousy, not confidence, which prescribes limited constitutions," wrote Jefferson for the Kentucky legislature. Jealousy of the national government, not confidence in it—this is the ideal that reflected the provincial and agricultural interest.

Republican Simplicity.—Every act of the Jeffersonian party during its early days of power was in accord with the ideals of government which it professed. It had opposed all pomp and ceremony, calculated to give weight and dignity to the chief executive of the nation, as symbols of monarchy and high prerogative. Appropriately, therefore, Jefferson's inauguration on March 4, 1801, the first at the new capital at Washington, was marked by extreme simplicity. In keeping with this procedure he quit the practice, followed by Washington and Adams, of reading presidential addresses to Congress in joint assembly and adopted in its stead the plan of sending his messages in writing—a custom that was continued unbroken until 1913 when President Wilson returned to the example set by the first chief magistrate.

Republican Measures.—The Republicans had complained of a great national debt as the source of a dangerous "money power," giving strength to the federal government; accordingly they began to pay it off as rapidly as possible. They had held commerce in low esteem and looked upon a large navy as a mere device to protect it; consequently they reduced the number of warships. They had objected to excise taxes, particularly on whisky; these they quickly abolished, to the intense satisfaction of the farmers. They had protested against the heavy cost of the federal government; they reduced expenses by discharging hundreds of men from the army and abolishing many offices.

They had savagely criticized the Sedition law and Jefferson refused to enforce it. They had been deeply offended by the assault on freedom of speech and press and they promptly impeached Samuel Chase, a justice of the Supreme Court, who had been especially severe in his attacks upon offenders under the Sedition Act. Their failure to convict Justice Chase by a narrow margin was due to no lack of zeal on their part but to the Federalist strength in the Senate where the trial was held. They had regarded the appointment of a large number of federal judges during the last hours of Adams' administration as an attempt to intrench Federalists in the judiciary and to enlarge the sphere of the national government. Accordingly, they at once repealed the act creating the new judgeships, thus depriving the "midnight appointees" of their posts. They had considered the federal offices, civil and military, as sources of great strength to the Federalists and Jefferson, though committed to the principle that offices should be open to all and distributed according to merit, was careful to fill most of the vacancies as they occurred with trusted Republicans. To his credit, however, it must be said that he did not make wholesale removals to find room for party workers.

The Republicans thus hewed to the line of their general policy of restricting the weight, dignity, and activity of the national government. Yet there were no Republicans, as the Federalists asserted, prepared to urge serious modifications in the Constitution. "If there be any among us who wish to dissolve this union or to change its republican form," wrote Jefferson in his first inaugural, "let them stand undisturbed as monuments of the safety with which error of opinion may be tolerated where reason is left free to combat it." After reciting the fortunate circumstances of climate, soil, and isolation which made the future of America so full of promise, Jefferson concluded: "A wise and frugal government which shall restrain men from injuring one another, shall leave them otherwise free to regulate their own pursuits of industry and improvement and shall not take from the mouth of labour the bread it has earned. This is the sum of good government; and this is necessary to close the circle of our felicities."

In all this the Republicans had not reckoned with destiny. In a few short years that lay ahead it was their fate to double the territory of the country, making inevitable a continental nation; to give the Constitution a generous interpretation that shocked many a Federalist; to wage war on behalf of American commerce; to reëstablish the hated United States Bank; to enact a high protective tariff; to see their Federalist opponents in their turn discredited as nullifiers and provincials; to announce high national doctrines in foreign affairs; and to behold the Constitution exalted and defended against the pretensions of states by a son of old Virginia, John Marshall, Chief Justice of the Supreme Court of the United States.

The Republicans and the Great West

Expansion and Land Hunger.—The first of the great measures which drove the Republicans out upon this new national course—the purchase of the Louisiana territory—was the product of circumstances rather than of their deliberate choosing. It was not the lack of land for his cherished farmers that led Jefferson to add such an immense domain to the original possessions of the United States. In the Northwest territory, now embracing Ohio, Indiana, Illinois, Michigan, Wisconsin, and a portion of Minnesota, settlements were mainly confined to the north bank of the Ohio River. To the south, in Kentucky and Tennessee, where there were more than one hundred thousand white people who had pushed over the mountains from Virginia and the Carolinas, there were still wide reaches of untilled soil. The Alabama and Mississippi regions were vast Indian frontiers of the state of Georgia, unsettled and almost unexplored. Even to the wildest imagination there seemed to be territory enough to satisfy the land hunger of the American people for a century to come.

The Significance of the Mississippi River.—At all events the East, then the center of power, saw no good reason for expansion. The planters of the Carolinas, the manufacturers of Pennsylvania, the importers of New York, the shipbuilders of New England, looking to the seaboard and to Europe for trade, refinements, and sometimes their ideas of government, were slow to appreciate the place of the West in national economy. The better educated the Easterners were, the less, it seems, they comprehended the destiny of the nation. Sons of Federalist fathers at Williams College, after a long debate decided by a vote of fifteen to one that the purchase of Louisiana was undesirable.

On the other hand, the pioneers of Kentucky, Ohio, and Tennessee, unlearned in books, saw with their own eyes the resources of the wilderness. Many of them had been across the Mississippi and had beheld the rich lands awaiting the plow of the white man. Down the great river they floated their wheat, corn, and bacon to ocean-going ships bound for the ports of the seaboard or for Europe. The land journeys over the mountain barriers with bulky farm produce, they knew from experience, were almost impossible, and costly at best. Nails, bolts of cloth, tea, and coffee could go or come that way, but not corn and bacon. A free outlet to the sea by the Mississippi was as essential to the pioneers of the Kentucky region as the harbor of Boston to the merchant princes of that metropolis.

Louisiana under Spanish Rule.—For this reason they watched with deep solicitude the fortunes of the Spanish king to whom, at the close of the Seven Years' War, had fallen the Louisiana territory stretching from New Orleans to the Rocky Mountains. While he controlled the mouth of the Mississippi there was little to fear, for he had neither the army nor the navy necessary to resist any invasion of American trade. Moreover, Washington had been able, by the exercise of great tact, to secure from Spain in 1795 a trading privilege through New Orleans which satisfied the present requirements of the frontiersmen even if it did not allay their fears for the future. So things stood when a swift succession of events altered the whole situation.

Louisiana Transferred to France.—In July, 1802, a royal order from Spain instructed the officials at New Orleans to close the port to American produce. About the same time a disturbing rumor, long current, was confirmed—Napoleon had coerced Spain into returning Louisiana to France by a secret treaty signed in 1800. "The scalers of the Alps and conquerors of Venice" now looked across the sea for new scenes of adventure. The West was ablaze with excitement. A call for war ran through the frontier; expeditions were organized to prevent the landing of the French; and petitions for instant action flooded in upon Jefferson.

Jefferson Sees the Danger.—Jefferson, the friend of France and sworn enemy of England, compelled to choose in the interest of America, never winced. "The cession of Louisiana and the Floridas by Spain to France," he wrote to Livingston, the American minister in Paris, "works sorely on the United States. It completely reverses all the political relations of the United States and will form a new epoch in our political course.... There is on the globe one single spot, the possessor of which is our natural and habitual enemy. It is New Orleans through which the produce of three-eighths of our territory must pass to market.... France, placing herself in that door, assumes to us an attitude of defiance. Spain might have retained it quietly for years. Her pacific dispositions, her feeble state would induce her to increase our facilities there.... Not so can it ever be in the hands of France.... The day that France takes possession of New Orleans fixes the sentence which is to restrain her forever within her low water mark.... It seals the union of the two nations who in conjunction can maintain exclusive possession of the ocean. From that moment we must marry ourselves to the British fleet and nation.... This is not a state of things we seek or desire. It is one which this measure, if adopted by France, forces on us as necessarily as any other cause by the laws of nature brings on its necessary effect."

Louisiana Purchased.—Acting on this belief, but apparently seeing only the Mississippi outlet at stake, Jefferson sent his friend, James Monroe, to France with the power to buy New Orleans and West Florida. Before Monroe arrived, the regular minister, Livingston, had already convinced Napoleon that it would be well to sell territory which might be wrested from him at any moment by the British sea power, especially as the war, temporarily stopped by the peace of Amiens, was once more raging in Europe. Wise as he was in his day, Livingston had at first no thought of buying the whole Louisiana country. He was simply dazed when Napoleon offered to sell the entire domain and get rid of the business altogether. Though staggered by the proposal, he and Monroe decided to accept. On April 30, they signed the treaty of cession, agreeing to pay $11,250,000 in six per cent bonds and to discharge certain debts due French citizens, making in all approximately fifteen millions. Spain protested, Napoleon's brother fumed, French newspapers objected; but the deed was done.

Jefferson and His Constitutional Scruples.—When the news of this extraordinary event reached the United States, the people were filled with astonishment, and no one was more surprised than Jefferson himself. He had thought of buying New Orleans and West Florida for a small sum, and now a vast domain had been dumped into the lap of the nation. He was puzzled. On looking into the Constitution he found not a line authorizing the purchase of more territory and so he drafted an amendment declaring "Louisiana, as ceded by France,—a part of the United States." He had belabored the Federalists for piling up a big national debt and he could hardly endure the thought of issuing more bonds himself.

In the midst of his doubts came the news that Napoleon might withdraw from the bargain. Thoroughly alarmed by that, Jefferson pressed the Senate for a ratification of the treaty. He still clung to his original idea that the Constitution did not warrant the purchase; but he lamely concluded: "If our friends shall think differently, I shall certainly acquiesce with satisfaction; confident that the good sense of our country will correct the evil of construction when it shall produce ill effects." Thus the stanch advocate of "strict interpretation" cut loose from his own doctrine and intrusted the construction of the Constitution to "the good sense" of his countrymen.

The Treaty Ratified.—This unusual transaction, so favorable to the West, aroused the ire of the seaboard Federalists. Some denounced it as unconstitutional, easily forgetting Hamilton's masterly defense of the bank, also not mentioned in the Constitution. Others urged that, if "the howling wilderness" ever should be settled, it would turn against the East, form new commercial connections, and escape from federal control. Still others protested that the purchase would lead inevitably to the dominance of a "hotch potch of wild men from the Far West." Federalists, who thought "the broad back of America" could readily bear Hamilton's consolidated debt, now went into agonies over a bond issue of less than one-sixth of that amount. But in vain. Jefferson's party with a high hand carried the day. The Senate, after hearing the Federalist protest, ratified the treaty. In December, 1803, the French flag was hauled down from the old government buildings in New Orleans and the Stars and Stripes were hoisted as a sign that the land of Coronado, De Soto, Marquette, and La Salle had passed forever to the United States.

By a single stroke, the original territory of the United States was more than doubled. While the boundaries of the purchase were uncertain, it is safe to say that the Louisiana territory included what is now Arkansas, Missouri, Iowa, Oklahoma, Kansas, Nebraska, South Dakota, and large portions of Louisiana, Minnesota, North Dakota, Colorado, Montana, and Wyoming. The farm lands that the friends of "a little America" on the seacoast declared a hopeless wilderness were, within a hundred years, fully occupied and valued at nearly seven billion dollars—almost five hundred times the price paid to Napoleon.

Western Explorations.—Having taken the fateful step, Jefferson wisely began to make the most of it. He prepared for the opening of the new country by sending the Lewis and Clark expedition to explore it, discover its resources, and lay out an overland route through the Missouri Valley and across the Great Divide to the Pacific. The story of this mighty exploit, which began in the spring of 1804 and ended in the autumn of 1806, was set down with skill and pains in the journal of Lewis and Clark; when published even in a short form, it invited the forward-looking men of the East to take thought about the western empire. At the same time Zebulon Pike, in a series of journeys, explored the sources of the Mississippi River and penetrated the Spanish territories of the far Southwest. Thus scouts and pioneers continued the work of diplomats.

THE REPUBLICAN WAR FOR COMMERCIAL INDEPENDENCE

The English and French Blockades.—In addition to bringing Louisiana to the United States, the reopening of the European War in 1803, after a short lull, renewed in an acute form the commercial difficulties that had plagued the country all during the administrations of Washington and Adams. The Republicans were now plunged into the hornets' nest. The party whose ardent spirits had burned Jay in effigy, stoned Hamilton for defending his treaty, jeered Washington's proclamation of neutrality, and spoken bitterly of "timid traders," could no longer take refuge in criticism. It had to act.

Its troubles took a serious turn in 1806. England, in a determined effort to bring France to her knees by starvation, declared the coast of Europe blockaded from Brest to the mouth of the Elbe River. Napoleon retaliated by his Berlin Decree of November, 1806, blockading the British Isles—a measure terrifying to American ship owners whose vessels were liable to seizure by any French rover, though Napoleon had no navy to make good his proclamation. Great Britain countered with a still more irritating decree—the Orders in Council of 1807. It modified its blockade, but in so doing merely authorized American ships not carrying munitions of war to complete their voyage to the Continent, on condition of their stopping at a British port, securing a license, and paying a tax. This, responded Napoleon, was the height of insolence, and he denounced it as a gross violation of international law. He then closed the circle of American troubles by issuing his Milan Decree of December, 1807. This order declared that any ship which complied with the British rules would be subject to seizure and confiscation by French authorities.

The Impressment of Seamen.—That was not all. Great Britain, in dire need of men for her navy, adopted the practice of stopping American ships, searching them, and carrying away British-born sailors found on board. British sailors were so badly treated, so cruelly flogged for trivial causes, and so meanly fed that they fled in crowds to the American marine. In many cases it was difficult to tell whether seamen were English or American. They spoke the same language, so that language was no test. Rovers on the deep and stragglers in the ports of both countries, they frequently had no papers to show their nativity. Moreover, Great Britain held to the old rule—"Once an Englishman, always an Englishman"—a doctrine rejected by the United States in favor of the principle that a man could choose the nation to which he would give allegiance. British sea captains, sometimes by mistake, and often enough with reckless indifference, carried away into servitude in their own navy genuine American citizens. The process itself, even when executed with all the civilities of law, was painful enough, for it meant that American ships were forced to "come to," and compelled to rest submissively under British guns until the searching party had pried into records, questioned seamen, seized and handcuffed victims. Saints could not have done this work without raising angry passions, and only saints could have endured it with patience and fortitude.

Had the enactment of the scenes been confined to the high seas and knowledge of them to rumors and newspaper stories, American resentment might not have been so intense; but many a search and seizure was made in sight of land. British and French vessels patrolled the coasts, firing on one another and chasing one another in American waters within the three-mile limit. When, in the summer of 1807, the American frigate *Chesapeake* refused to surrender men alleged to be deserters from King George's navy, the British warship *Leopard* opened fire, killing three men and wounding eighteen more—an act which even the British ministry could hardly excuse. If the French were less frequently the offenders, it was not because of their tenderness about American rights but because so few of their ships escaped the hawk-eyed British navy to operate in American waters.

The Losses in American Commerce.—This high-handed conduct on the part of European belligerents was very injurious to American trade. By their enterprise, American shippers had become the foremost carriers on the Atlantic Ocean. In a decade they had doubled the tonnage of American merchant ships under the American flag, taking the place of the French marine when Britain swept that from the seas, and supplying Britain with the sinews of war for the contest with the Napoleonic empire. The American shipping engaged in foreign trade embraced 363,110 tons in 1791; 669,921 tons in 1800; and almost 1,000,000 tons in 1810. Such was the enterprise attacked by the British and French decrees. American ships bound for Great Britain were liable to be captured by French privateers which, in spite of the disasters of the Nile and Trafalgar, ranged the seas. American ships destined for the Continent, if they failed to stop at British ports and pay tribute, were in great danger of capture by the sleepless British navy and its swarm of auxiliaries. American sea captains who, in fear of British vengeance, heeded the Orders in Council and paid the tax were almost certain to fall a prey to French vengeance, for the French were vigorous in executing the Milan Decree.

Jefferson's Policy.—The President's dilemma was distressing. Both the belligerents in Europe were guilty of depredations on American commerce. War on both of them was out of the question. War on France was impossible because she had no territory on this side of the water which could be reached by American troops and her naval forces had been shattered at the battles of the Nile and Trafalgar. War on Great Britain, a power which Jefferson's followers feared and distrusted, was possible but not inviting. Jefferson shrank from it. A man of peace, he disliked war's brazen clamor; a man of kindly spirit, he was startled at the death and destruction which it brought in its train. So for the eight years Jefferson steered an even course, suggesting measure after measure with a view to avoiding bloodshed. He sent, it is true, Commodore Preble in 1803 to punish Mediterranean pirates preying upon American commerce; but a great war he evaded with passionate earnestness, trying in its place every other expedient to protect American rights.

The Embargo and Non-intercourse Acts.—In 1806, Congress passed and Jefferson approved a non-importation act closing American ports to certain products from British dominions—a measure intended as a club over the British government's head. This law, failing in its purpose, Jefferson proposed and Congress adopted in December, 1807, the Embargo Act forbidding all vessels to leave American harbors for foreign ports. France and England were to be brought to terms by cutting off their supplies.

The result of the embargo was pathetic. England and France refused to give up search and seizure. American ship owners who, lured by huge profits, had formerly been willing to take the risk were now restrained by law to their home ports. Every section suffered. The South and West found their markets for cotton, rice, tobacco, corn, and bacon curtailed. Thus they learned by bitter experience the national significance of commerce. Ship masters, ship builders, longshoremen, and sailors were thrown out of employment while the prices of foreign goods doubled. Those who obeyed the law were ruined; violators of the law smuggled goods into Canada and Florida for shipment abroad.

Jefferson's friends accepted the medicine with a wry face as the only alternative to supine submission or open war. His opponents, without offering any solution of their own, denounced it as a contemptible plan that brought neither relief nor honor. Beset by the clamor that arose on all sides, Congress, in the closing days of Jefferson's administration, repealed the Embargo law and substituted a Non-intercourse act forbidding trade with England and France while permitting it with other countries—a measure equally futile in staying the depredations on American shipping.

Jefferson Retires in Favor of Madison.—Jefferson, exhausted by endless wrangling and wounded, as Washington had been, by savage criticism, welcomed March 4, 1809. His friends urged him to "stay by the ship" and accept a third term. He declined, saying that election for life might result from repeated reëlection. In following Washington's course and defending it on principle, he set an example to all his successors, making the "third term doctrine" a part of American unwritten law.

His intimate friend, James Madison, to whom he turned over the burdens of his high office was, like himself, a man of peace. Madison had been a leader since the days of the Revolution, but in legislative halls and council chambers, not on the field of battle. Small in stature, sensitive in feelings, studious in habits, he was no man for the rough and tumble of practical politics. He had taken a prominent and distinguished part in the framing and the adoption of the Constitution. He had served in the first Congress as a friend of Hamilton's measures. Later he attached himself to Jefferson's fortunes and served for eight years as his first counselor, the Secretary of State. The principles of the Constitution, which he had helped to make and interpret, he was now as President called upon to apply in one of the most perplexing moments in all American history. In keeping with his own traditions and following in the footsteps of Jefferson, he vainly tried to solve the foreign problem by negotiation.

The Trend of Events.—Whatever difficulties Madison had in making up his mind on war and peace were settled by events beyond his own control. In the spring of 1811, a British frigate held up an American ship near the harbor of New York and impressed a seaman alleged to be an American citizen. Burning with resentment, the captain of the *President*, an American warship, acting under orders, poured several broadsides into the *Little Belt*, a British sloop, suspected of being the guilty party. The British also encouraged the Indian chief Tecumseh, who welded together the Indians of the Northwest under British protection and gave signs of restlessness presaging a revolt. This sent a note of alarm along the frontier that was not checked even when, in November, Tecumseh's men were badly beaten at Tippecanoe by William Henry Harrison. The Indians stood in the way of the advancing frontier, and it seemed to the pioneers that, without support from the British in Canada, the Red Men would soon be subdued.

Clay and Calhoun.—While events were moving swiftly and rumors were flying thick and fast, the mastery of the government passed from the uncertain hands of Madison to a party of ardent young men in Congress, dubbed "Young Republicans," under the leadership of two members destined to be mighty figures in American history: Henry Clay of Kentucky and John C. Calhoun of South Carolina. The former contended, in a flair of folly, that "the militia of Kentucky alone are competent to place Montreal and Upper Canada at your feet." The latter with a light heart spoke of conquering Canada in a four weeks' campaign. "It must not be inferred," says Channing, "that in advocating conquest, the Westerners were actuated merely by desire for land; they welcomed war because they thought it would be the easiest way to abate Indian troubles. The savages were supported by the fur-trading interests that centred at Quebec and London.... The Southerners on their part wished for Florida and they thought that the conquest of Canada would obviate some Northern opposition to this acquisition of slave territory." While Clay and Calhoun, spokesmen of the West and South, were not unmindful of what Napoleon had done to American commerce, they knew that their followers still remembered with deep gratitude the aid of the French in the war for independence and that the embers of the old hatred for George III, still on the throne, could be readily blown into flame.

Madison Accepts War as Inevitable.—The conduct of the British ministers with whom Madison had to deal did little to encourage him in adhering to the policy of "watchful waiting." One of them, a high Tory, believed that all Americans were alike "except that a few are less knaves than others" and his methods were colored by his belief. On the recall of this minister the British government selected another no less high and mighty in his principles and opinions. So Madison became thoroughly discouraged about the outcome of pacific measures. When the pressure from Congress upon him became too heavy, he gave way, signing on June 18, 1812, the declaration of war on Great Britain. In proclaiming hostilities, the administration set forth the causes which justified the declaration; namely, the British had been encouraging the Indians to attack American citizens on the frontier; they had ruined American trade by blockades; they had insulted the American flag by stopping and searching our ships; they had illegally seized American sailors and driven them into the British navy.

The Course of the War.—The war lasted for nearly three years without bringing victory to either side. The surrender of Detroit by General Hull to the British and the failure of the American invasion of Canada were offset by Perry's victory on Lake Erie and a decisive blow administered to British designs for an invasion of New York by way of Plattsburgh. The triumph of Jackson at New Orleans helped to atone for the humiliation suffered in the burning of the Capitol by the British. The stirring deeds of the *Constitution*, the *United States*, and the *Argus* on the seas, the heroic death of Lawrence and the victories of a hundred privateers furnished consolation for those who suffered from the iron blockade finally established by the British government when it came to appreciate the gravity of the situation. While men love the annals of the sea, they will turn to the running battles, the narrow escapes, and the reckless daring of American sailors in that naval contest with Great Britain.

All this was exciting but it was inconclusive. In fact, never was a government less prepared than was that of the United States in 1812. It had neither the disciplined troops, the ships of war, nor the supplies required by the magnitude of the military task. It was fortune that favored the American cause. Great Britain, harassed, worn, and financially embarrassed by nearly twenty years of fighting in Europe, was in no mood to gather her forces for a titanic effort in America even after Napoleon was overthrown and sent into exile at Elba in the spring of 1814. War clouds still hung on the European horizon and the conflict temporarily halted did again break out. To be rid of American anxieties and free for European eventualities, England was ready to settle with the United States, especially as that could be done without conceding anything or surrendering any claims.

The Treaty of Peace.—Both countries were in truth sick of a war that offered neither glory nor profit. Having indulged in the usual diplomatic skirmishing, they sent representatives to Ghent to discuss terms of peace. After long negotiations an agreement was reached on Christmas eve, 1814, a few days before Jackson's victory at New Orleans. When the treaty reached America the people were surprised to find that it said nothing about the seizure of American sailors, the destruction of American trade, the searching of American ships, or the support of Indians on the frontier. Nevertheless, we are told, the people "passed from gloom to glory" when the news of peace arrived. The bells were rung; schools were closed; flags were displayed; and many a rousing toast was drunk in tavern and private home. The rejoicing could continue. With Napoleon definitely beaten at Waterloo in June, 1815, Great Britain had no need to impress sailors, search ships, and confiscate American goods bound to the Continent. Once more the terrible sea power sank into the background and the ocean was again white with the sails of merchantmen.

THE REPUBLICANS NATIONALIZED

The Federalists Discredited.—By a strange turn of fortune's wheel, the party of Hamilton, Washington, Adams, the party of the grand nation, became the party of provincialism and nullification. New England, finding its shipping interests crippled in the European conflict and then penalized by embargoes, opposed the declaration of war on Great Britain, which meant the completion of the ruin already begun. In the course of the struggle, the Federalist leaders came perilously near to treason in their efforts to hamper the government of the United States; and in their desperation they fell back upon the doctrine of nullification so recently condemned by them when it came from Kentucky. The Senate of Massachusetts, while the war was in progress, resolved that it was waged "without justifiable cause," and refused to approve military and naval projects not connected with "the defense of our seacoast and soil." A Boston newspaper declared that the union was nothing but a treaty among sovereign states, that states could decide for themselves the question of obeying federal law, and that armed resistance under the banner of a state would not be rebellion or treason. The general assembly of Connecticut reminded the administration at Washington that "the state of Connecticut is a free, sovereign, and independent state." Gouverneur Morris, a member of the convention which had drafted the Constitution, suggested the holding of another conference to consider whether the Northern states should remain in the union.

In October, 1814, a convention of delegates from Connecticut, Massachusetts, Rhode Island, and certain counties of New Hampshire and Vermont was held at Hartford, on the call of Massachusetts. The counsels of the extremists were rejected but the convention solemnly went on record to the effect that acts of Congress in violation of the Constitution are void; that in cases of deliberate, dangerous, and palpable infractions the state is duty bound to interpose its authority for the protection of its citizens; and that when emergencies occur the states must be their own judges and execute their own decisions. Thus New England answered the challenge of Calhoun and Clay. Fortunately its actions were not as rash as its words. The Hartford convention merely proposed certain amendments to the Constitution and adjourned. At the close of the war, its proposals vanished harmlessly; but the men who made them were hopelessly discredited.

The Second United States Bank.—In driving the Federalists towards nullification and waging a national war themselves, the Republicans lost all their old taint of provincialism. Moreover, in turning to measures of reconstruction called forth by the war, they resorted to the national devices of the Federalists. In 1816, they chartered for a period of twenty years a second United States Bank—the institution which Jefferson and Madison once had condemned as unsound and unconstitutional. The Constitution remained unchanged; times and circumstances had changed. Calhoun dismissed the vexed question of constitutionality with a scant reference to an ancient dispute, while Madison set aside his scruples and signed the bill.

The Protective Tariff of 1816.—The Republicans supplemented the Bank by another Federalist measure—a high protective tariff. Clay viewed it as the beginning of his "American system" of protection. Calhoun defended it on national principles. For this sudden reversal of policy the young Republicans were taunted by some of their older party colleagues with betraying the "agricultural interest" that Jefferson had fostered; but Calhoun refused to listen to their criticisms. "When the seas are open," he said, "the produce of the South may pour anywhere into the markets of the Old World.... What are the effects of a war with a maritime power—with England? Our commerce annihilated ... our agriculture cut off from its accustomed markets, the surplus of the farmer perishes on his hands.... The recent war fell with peculiar pressure on the growers of cotton and tobacco and the other great staples of the country; and the same state of things will recur in the event of another war unless prevented by the foresight of this body.... When our manufactures are grown to a certain perfection, as they soon will be under the fostering care of the government, we shall no longer experience these evils." With the Republicans nationalized, the Federalist party, as an organization, disappeared after a crushing defeat in the presidential campaign of 1816.

Monroe and the Florida Purchase.—To the victor in that political contest, James Monroe of Virginia, fell two tasks of national importance, adding to the prestige of the whole country and deepening the sense of patriotism that weaned men away from mere allegiance to states. The first of these was the purchase of Florida from Spain. The acquisition of Louisiana let the Mississippi flow "unvexed to the sea"; but it left all the states east of the river cut off from the Gulf, affording them ground for discontent akin to that which had moved the pioneers of Kentucky to action a generation earlier. The uncertainty as to the boundaries of Louisiana gave the United States a claim to West Florida, setting on foot a movement for occupation. The Florida swamps were a basis for Indian marauders who periodically swept into the frontier settlements, and hiding places for runaway slaves. Thus the sanction of international law was given to punitive expeditions into alien territory.

The pioneer leaders stood waiting for the signal. It came. President Monroe, on the occasion of an Indian outbreak, ordered General Jackson to seize the offenders, in the Floridas, if necessary. The high-spirited warrior, taking this as a hint that he was to occupy the coveted region, replied that, if possession was the object of the invasion, he could occupy the Floridas within sixty days. Without waiting for an answer to this letter, he launched his expedition, and in the spring of 1818 was master of the Spanish king's domain to the south.

There was nothing for the king to do but to make the best of the inevitable by ceding the Floridas to the United States in return for five million dollars to be paid to American citizens having claims against Spain. On Washington's birthday, 1819, the treaty was signed. It ceded the Floridas to the United States and defined the boundary between Mexico and the United States by drawing a line from the mouth of the Sabine River in a northwesterly direction to the Pacific. On this occasion even Monroe, former opponent of the Constitution, forgot to inquire whether new territory could be constitutionally acquired and incorporated into the American union. The Republicans seemed far away from the days of "strict construction." And Jefferson still lived!

The Monroe Doctrine.—Even more effective in fashioning the national idea was Monroe's enunciation of the famous doctrine that bears his name. The occasion was another European crisis. During the Napoleonic upheaval and the years of dissolution that ensued, the Spanish colonies in America, following the example set by their English neighbors in 1776, declared their independence. Unable to conquer them alone, the king of Spain turned for help to the friendly powers of Europe that looked upon revolution and republics with undisguised horror.

The Holy Alliance.—He found them prepared to view his case with sympathy. Three of them, Austria, Prussia, and Russia, under the leadership of the Czar, Alexander I, in the autumn of 1815, had entered into a Holy Alliance to sustain by reciprocal service the autocratic principle in government. Although the effusive, almost maudlin, language of the treaty did not express their purpose explicitly, the Alliance was later regarded as a mere union of monarchs to prevent the rise and growth of popular government.

The American people thought their worst fears confirmed when, in 1822, a conference of delegates from Russia, Austria, Prussia, and France met at Verona to consider, among other things, revolutions that had just broken out in Spain and Italy. The spirit of the conference is reflected in the first article of the agreement reached by the delegates: "The high contracting powers, being convinced that the system of representative government is equally incompatible with the monarchical principle and the maxim of the sovereignty of the people with the divine right, mutually engage in the most solemn manner to use all their efforts to put an end to the system of representative government in whatever country it may exist in Europe and to prevent its being introduced in those countries where it is not yet known." The Czar, who incidentally coveted the west coast of North America, proposed to send an army to aid the king of Spain in his troubles at home, thus preparing the way for intervention in Spanish America. It was material weakness not want of spirit, that prevented the grand union of monarchs from making open war on popular government.

The Position of England.—Unfortunately, too, for the Holy Alliance, England refused to coöperate. English merchants had built up a large trade with the independent Latin-American colonies and they protested against the restoration of Spanish sovereignty, which meant a renewal of Spain's former trade monopoly. Moreover, divine right doctrines had been laid to rest in England and the representative principle thoroughly established. Already there were signs of the coming democratic flood which was soon to carry the first reform bill of 1832, extending the suffrage, and sweep on to even greater achievements. British statesmen, therefore, had to be cautious. In such circumstances, instead of coöperating with the autocrats of Russia, Austria, and Prussia, they turned to the minister of the United States in London. The British prime minister, Canning, proposed that the two countries join in declaring their unwillingness to see the Spanish colonies transferred to any other power.

Jefferson's Advice.—The proposal was rejected; but President Monroe took up the suggestion with Madison and Jefferson as well as with his Secretary of State, John Quincy Adams. They favored the plan. Jefferson said: "One nation, most of all, could disturb us in this pursuit [of freedom]; she now offers to lead, aid, and accompany us in it. By acceding to her proposition we detach her from the bands, bring her mighty weight into the scale of free government and emancipate a continent at one stroke.... With her on our side we need not fear the whole world. With her then we should most sedulously cherish a cordial friendship."

Monroe's Statement of the Doctrine.—Acting on the advice of trusted friends, President Monroe embodied in his message to Congress, on December 2, 1823, a statement of principles now famous throughout the world as the Monroe Doctrine. To the autocrats of Europe he announced that he would regard "any attempt on their part to extend their system to any portion of this hemisphere as dangerous to our peace and safety." While he did not propose to interfere with existing colonies dependent on European powers, he ranged himself squarely on the side of those that had declared their independence. Any attempt by a European power to oppress them or control their destiny in any manner he characterized as "a manifestation of an unfriendly disposition toward the United States." Referring in another part of his message to a recent claim which the Czar had made to the Pacific coast, President Monroe warned the Old World that "the American continents, by the free and independent condition which they have assumed and maintained, are henceforth not to be considered as subjects for future colonization by any European powers." The effect of this declaration was immediate and profound. Men whose political horizon had been limited to a community or state were led to consider their nation as a great power among the sovereignties of the earth, taking its part in shaping their international relations.

The Missouri Compromise.—Respecting one other important measure of this period, the Republicans also took a broad view of their obligations under the Constitution; namely, the Missouri Compromise. It is true, they insisted on the admission of Missouri as a slave state, balanced against the free state of Maine; but at the same time they assented to the prohibition of slavery in the Louisiana territory north of the line 36° 30'. During the debate on the subject an extreme view had been presented, to the effect that Congress had no constitutional warrant for abolishing slavery in the territories. The precedent of the Northwest Ordinance, ratified by Congress in 1789, seemed a conclusive answer from practice to this contention; but Monroe submitted the issue to his cabinet, which included Calhoun of South Carolina, Crawford of Georgia, and Wirt of Virginia, all presumably adherents to the Jeffersonian principle of strict construction. He received in reply a unanimous verdict to the effect that Congress did have the power to prohibit slavery in the territories governed by it. Acting on this advice he approved, on March 6, 1820, the bill establishing freedom north of the compromise line. This generous interpretation of the powers of Congress stood for nearly forty years, until repudiated by the Supreme Court in the Dred Scott case.

THE NATIONAL DECISIONS OF CHIEF JUSTICE MARSHALL

John Marshall, the Nationalist.—The Republicans in the lower ranges of state politics, who did not catch the grand national style of their leaders charged with responsibilities in the national field, were assisted in their education by a Federalist from the Old Dominion, John Marshall, who, as Chief Justice of the Supreme Court of the United States from 1801 to 1835, lost no occasion to exalt the Constitution above the claims of the provinces. No differences of opinion as to his political views have ever led even his warmest opponents to deny his superb abilities or his sincere devotion to the national idea. All will likewise agree that for talents, native and acquired, he was an ornament to the humble democracy that brought him forth. His whole career was American. Born on the frontier of Virginia, reared in a log cabin, granted only the barest rudiments of education, inured to hardship and rough life, he rose by masterly efforts to the highest judicial honor America can bestow.

On him the bitter experience of the Revolution and of later days made a lasting impression. He was no "summer patriot." He had been a soldier in the Revolutionary army. He had suffered with Washington at Valley Forge. He had seen his comrades in arms starving and freezing because the Continental Congress had neither the power nor the inclination to force the states to do their full duty. To him the Articles of Confederation were the symbol of futility. Into the struggle for the formation of the Constitution and its ratification in Virginia he had thrown himself with the ardor of a soldier. Later, as a member of Congress, a representative to France, and Secretary of State, he had aided the Federalists in establishing the new government. When at length they were driven from power in the executive and legislative branches of the government, he was chosen for their last stronghold, the Supreme Court. By historic irony he administered the oath of office to his bitterest enemy, Thomas Jefferson; and, long after the author of the Declaration of Independence had retired to private life, the stern Chief Justice continued to announce the old Federalist principles from the Supreme Bench.

Marbury *vs.* Madison—An Act of Congress Annulled.—He had been in his high office only two years when he laid down for the first time in the name of the entire Court the doctrine that the judges have the power to declare an act of Congress null and void when in their opinion it violates the Constitution. This power was not expressly conferred on the Court. Though many able men held that the judicial branch of the government enjoyed it, the principle was not positively established until 1803 when the case of Marbury *vs.* Madison was decided. In rendering the opinion of the Court, Marshall cited no precedents. He sought no foundations for his argument in ancient history. He rested it on the general nature of the American system. The Constitution, ran hisreasoning, is the supreme law of the land; it limits and binds all who act in the name of the United States; it limits the powers of Congress and defines the rights of citizens. If Congress can ignore its limitations and trespass upon the rights of citizens, Marshall argued, then the Constitution disappears and Congress is supreme. Since, however, the Constitution is supreme and superior to Congress, it is the duty of judges, under their oath of office, to sustain it against measures which violate it. Therefore, from the nature of the American constitutional system the courts must declare null and void all acts which are not authorized. "A law repugnant to the Constitution," he closed, "is void and the courts as well as other departments are bound by that instrument." From that day to this the practice of federal and state courts in passing upon the constitutionality of laws has remained unshaken.

This doctrine was received by Jefferson and many of his followers with consternation. If the idea was sound, he exclaimed, "then indeed is our Constitution a complete *felo de se* [legally, a suicide]. For, intending to establish three departments, coördinate and independent that they might check and balance one another, it has given, according to this opinion, to one of them alone the right to prescribe rules for the government of the others, and to that one, too, which is unelected by and independent of the nation.... The Constitution, on this hypothesis, is a mere thing of wax in the hands of the judiciary which they may twist and shape into any form they please. It should be remembered, as an axiom of eternal truth in politics, that whatever power in any government is independent, is absolute also.... A judiciary independent of a king or executive alone is a good thing; but independence of the will of the nation is a solecism, at least in a republican government." But Marshall was mighty and his view prevailed, though from time to time other men, clinging to Jefferson's opinion, likewise opposed the exercise by the Courts of the high power of passing upon the constitutionality of acts of Congress.

Acts of State Legislatures Declared Unconstitutional.—Had Marshall stopped with annulling an act of Congress, he would have heard less criticism from Republican quarters; but, with the same firmness, he set aside acts of state legislatures as well, whenever, in his opinion, they violated the federal Constitution. In 1810, in the case of Fletcher *vs.* Peck, he annulled an act of the Georgia legislature, informing the state that it was not sovereign, but "a part of a large empire, ... a member of the American union; and that union has a constitution ... which imposes limits to the legislatures of the several states." In the case of McCulloch *vs.* Maryland, decided in 1819, he declared void an act of the Maryland legislature designed to paralyze the branches of the United States Bank established in that state. In the same year, in the still more memorable Dartmouth College case, he annulled an act of the New Hampshire legislature which infringed upon the charter received by the college from King George long before. That charter, he declared, was a contract between the state and the college, which the legislature under the federal Constitution could not impair. Two years later he stirred the wrath of Virginia by summoning her to the bar of the Supreme Court to answer in a case in which the validity of one of her laws was involved and then justified his action in a powerful opinion rendered in the case of Cohens *vs.* Virginia.

All these decisions aroused the legislatures of the states. They passed sheaves of resolutions protesting and condemning; but Marshall never turned and never stayed. The Constitution of the United States, he fairly thundered at them, is the supreme law of the land; the Supreme Court is the proper tribunal to pass finally upon the validity of the laws of the states; and "those sovereignties," far from possessing the right of review and nullification, are irrevocably bound by the decisions of that Court. This was strong medicine for the authors of the Kentucky and Virginia Resolutions and for the members of the Hartford convention; but they had to take it.

The Doctrine of Implied Powers.—While restraining Congress in the Marbury case and the state legislatures in a score of cases, Marshall also laid the judicial foundation for a broad and liberal view of the Constitution as opposed to narrow and strict construction. In McCulloch *vs.* Maryland, he construed generously the words "necessary and proper" in such a way as to confer upon Congress a wide range of "implied powers" in addition to their express powers. That case involved, among other things, the question whether the act establishing the second United States Bank was authorized by the Constitution. Marshall answered in the affirmative. Congress, ran his reasoning, has large powers over taxation and the currency; a bank is of appropriate use in the exercise of these enumerated powers; and therefore, though not absolutely necessary, a bank is entirely proper and constitutional. "With respect to the means by which the powers that the Constitution confers are to be carried into execution," he said, Congress must be allowed the discretion which "will enable that body to perform the high duties assigned to it, in the manner most beneficial to the people." In short, the Constitution of the United States is not a strait jacket but a flexible instrument vesting in Congress the powers necessary to meet national problems as they arise. In delivering this opinion Marshall used language almost identical with that employed by Lincoln when, standing on the battle field of a war waged to preserve the nation, he said that "a government of the people, by the people, for the people shall not perish from the earth."

SUMMARY OF THE UNION AND NATIONAL POLITICS

During the strenuous period between the establishment of American independence and the advent of Jacksonian democracy the great American experiment was under the direction of the men who had launched it. All the Presidents in that period, except John Quincy Adams, had taken part in the Revolution. James Madison, the chief author of the Constitution, lived until 1836. This age, therefore, was the "age of the fathers." It saw the threatened ruin of the country under the Articles of Confederation, the formation of the Constitution, the rise of political parties, the growth of the West, the second war with England, and the apparent triumph of the national spirit over sectionalism.

The new republic had hardly been started in 1783 before its troubles began. The government could not raise money to pay its debts or running expenses; it could not protect American commerce and manufactures against European competition; it could not stop the continual issues of paper money by the states; it could not intervene to put down domestic uprisings that threatened the existence of the state governments. Without money, without an army, without courts of law, the union under the Articles of Confederation was drifting into dissolution. Patriots, who had risked their lives for independence, began to talk of monarchy again. Washington, Hamilton, and Madison insisted that a new constitution alone could save America from disaster.

By dint of much labor the friends of a new form of government induced the Congress to call a national convention to take into account the state of America. In May, 1787, it assembled at Philadelphia and for months it debated and wrangled over plans for a constitution. The small states clamored for equal rights in the union. The large states vowed that they would never grant it. A spirit of conciliation, fair play, and compromise saved the convention from breaking up. In addition, there were jealousies between the planting states and the commercial states. Here, too, compromises had to be worked out. Some of the delegates feared the growth of democracy and others cherished it. These factions also had to be placated. At last a plan of government was drafted—the Constitution of the United States—and submitted to the states for approval. Only after a long and acrimonious debate did enough states ratify the instrument to put it into effect. On April 30, 1789, George Washington was inaugurated first President.

The new government proceeded to fund the old debt of the nation, assume the debts of the states, found a national bank, lay heavy taxes to pay the bills, and enact laws protecting American industry and commerce. Hamilton led the way, but he had not gone far before he encountered opposition. He found a formidable antagonist in Jefferson. In time two political parties appeared full armed upon the scene: the Federalists and the Republicans. For ten years they filled the country with political debate. In 1800 the Federalists were utterly vanquished by the Republicans with Jefferson in the lead.

By their proclamations of faith the Republicans favored the states rather than the new national government, but in practice they added immensely to the prestige and power of the nation. They purchased Louisiana from France, they waged a war for commercial independence against England, they created a second United States Bank, they enacted the protective tariff of 1816, they declared that Congress had power to abolish slavery north of the Missouri Compromise line, and they spread the shield of the Monroe Doctrine between the Western Hemisphere and Europe.

Still America was a part of European civilization. Currents of opinion flowed to and fro across the Atlantic. Friends of popular government in Europe looked to America as the great exemplar of their ideals. Events in Europe reacted upon thought in the United States. The French Revolution exerted a profound influence on the course of political debate. While it was in the stage of mere reform all Americans favored it. When the king was executed and a radical democracy set up, American opinion was divided. When France fell under the military dominion of Napoleon and preyed upon American commerce, the United States made ready for war.

The conduct of England likewise affected American affairs. In 1793 war broke out between England and France and raged with only a slight intermission until 1815. England and France both ravaged American commerce, but England was the more serious offender because she had command of the seas. Though Jefferson and Madison strove for peace, the country was swept into war by the vehemence of the "Young Republicans," headed by Clay and Calhoun.

When the armed conflict was closed, one in diplomacy opened. The autocratic powers of Europe threatened to intervene on behalf of Spain in her attempt to recover possession of her Latin-American colonies. Their challenge to America brought forth the Monroe Doctrine. The powers of Europe were warned not to interfere with the independence or the republican policies of this hemisphere or to attempt any new colonization in it. It seemed that nationalism was to have a peaceful triumph over sectionalism.

References

H. Adams, *History of the United States, 1800-1817* (9 vols.).

K.C. Babcock, *Rise of American Nationality* (American Nation Series).

E. Channing, *The Jeffersonian System* (Same Series).

D.C. Gilman, *James Monroe*.

W. Reddaway, *The Monroe Doctrine*.

T. Roosevelt, *Naval War of 1812*.

Questions

1. What was the leading feature of Jefferson's political theory?

2. Enumerate the chief measures of his administration.

3. Were the Jeffersonians able to apply their theories? Give the reasons.

4. Explain the importance of the Mississippi River to Western farmers.

5. Show how events in Europe forced the Louisiana Purchase.

6. State the constitutional question involved in the Louisiana Purchase.

7. Show how American trade was affected by the European war.

8. Compare the policies of Jefferson and Madison.

9. Why did the United States become involved with England rather than with France?

10. Contrast the causes of the War of 1812 with the results.

11. Give the economic reasons for the attitude of New England.

12. Give five "nationalist" measures of the Republicans. Discuss each in detail.

13. Sketch the career of John Marshall.

14. Discuss the case of Marbury *vs.* Madison.

15. Summarize Marshall's views on: (*a*) states' rights; and (*b*) a liberal interpretation of the Constitution.

Research Topics

The Louisiana Purchase.—Text of Treaty in Macdonald, *Documentary Source Book*, pp. 279-282. Source materials in Hart, *American History Told by Contemporaries*, Vol. III, pp. 363-384. Narrative, Henry Adams, *History of the United States*, Vol. II, pp. 25-115; Elson, *History of the United States*, pp. 383-388.

The Embargo and Non-Intercourse Acts.—Macdonald, pp. 282-288; Adams, Vol. IV, pp. 152-177; Elson, pp. 394-405.

Congress and the War of 1812.—Adams, Vol. VI, pp. 113-198; Elson, pp. 408-450.

Proposals of the Hartford Convention.—Macdonald, pp. 293-302.

Manufactures and the Tariff of 1816.—Coman, *Industrial History of the United States*, pp. 184-194.

The Second United States Bank.—Macdonald, pp. 302-306.

Effect of European War on American Trade.—Callender, *Economic History of the United States*, pp. 240-250.

The Monroe Message.—Macdonald, pp. 318-320.

Lewis and Clark Expedition.—R.G. Thwaites, *Rocky Mountain Explorations*, pp. 92-187. Schafer, *A History of the Pacific Northwest* (rev. ed.), pp. 29-61.

PART IV. THE WEST AND JACKSONIAN DEMOCRACY

CHAPTER X

THE FARMERS BEYOND THE APPALACHIANS

The nationalism of Hamilton was undemocratic. The democracy of Jefferson was, in the beginning, provincial. The historic mission of uniting nationalism and democracy was in the course of time given to new leaders from a region beyond the mountains, peopled by men and women from all sections and free from those state traditions which ran back to the early days of colonization. The voice of the democratic nationalism nourished in the West was heard when Clay of Kentucky advocated his American system of protection for industries; when Jackson of Tennessee condemned nullification in a ringing proclamation that has taken its place among the great American state papers; and when Lincoln of Illinois, in a fateful hour, called upon a bewildered people to meet the supreme test whether this was a nation destined to survive or to perish. And it will be remembered that Lincoln's party chose for its banner that earlier device—Republican—which Jefferson had made a sign of power. The "rail splitter" from Illinois united the nationalism of Hamilton with the democracy of Jefferson, and his appeal was clothed in the simple language of the people, not in the sonorous rhetoric which Webster learned in the schools.

PREPARATION FOR WESTERN SETTLEMENT

The West and the American Revolution.—The excessive attention devoted by historians to the military operations along the coast has obscured the rôle played by the frontier in the American Revolution. The action of Great Britain in closing western land to easy settlement in 1763 was more than an incident in precipitating the war for independence. Americans on the frontier did not forget it; when Indians were employed by England to defend that land, zeal for the patriot cause set the interior aflame. It was the members of the western vanguard, like Daniel Boone, John Sevier, and George Rogers Clark, who first understood the value of the far-away country under the guns of the English forts, where the Red Men still wielded the tomahawk and the scalping knife. It was they who gave the East no rest until their vision was seen by the leaders on the seaboard who directed the course of national policy. It was one of their number, a seasoned Indian fighter, George Rogers Clark, who with aid from Virginia seized Kaskaskia and Vincennes and secured the whole Northwest to the union while the fate of Washington's army was still hanging in the balance.

Western Problems at the End of the Revolution.—The treaty of peace, signed with Great Britain in 1783, brought the definite cession of the coveted territory west to the Mississippi River, but it left unsolved many problems. In the first place, tribes of resentful Indians in the Ohio region, even though British support was withdrawn at last, had to be reckoned with; and it was not until after the establishment of the federal Constitution that a well-equipped army could be provided to guarantee peace on the border. In the second place, British garrisons still occupied forts on Lake Erie pending the execution of the terms of the treaty of 1783—terms which were not fulfilled until after the ratification of the Jay treaty twelve years later. In the third place, Virginia, Connecticut, and Massachusetts had conflicting claims to the land in the Northwest based on old English charters and Indian treaties. It was only after a bitter contest that the states reached an agreement to transfer their rights to the government of the United States, Virginia executing her deed of cession on March 1, 1784. In the fourth place, titles to lands bought by individuals remained uncertain in the absence of official maps and records. To meet this last situation, Congress instituted a systematic survey of the Ohio country, laying it out into townships, sections of 640 acres each, and quarter sections. In every township one section of land was set aside for the support of public schools.

The Northwest Ordinance.—The final problem which had to be solved before settlement on a large scale could be begun was that of governing the territory. Pioneers who looked with hungry eyes on the fertile valley of the Ohio could hardly restrain their impatience. Soldiers of the Revolution, who had been paid for their services in land warrants entitling them to make entries in the West, called for action.

Congress answered by passing in 1787 the famous Northwest Ordinance providing for temporary territorial government to be followed by the creation of a popular assembly as soon as there were five thousand free males in any district. Eventual admission to the union on an equal footing with the original states was promised to the new territories. Religious freedom was guaranteed. The safeguards of trial by jury, regular judicial procedure, and *habeas corpus* were established, in order that the methods of civilized life might take the place of the rough-and-ready justice of lynch law. During the course of the debate on the Ordinance, Congress added the sixth article forbidding slavery and involuntary servitude.

This Charter of the Northwest, so well planned by the Congress under the Articles of Confederation, was continued in force by the first Congress under the Constitution in 1789. The following year its essential provisions, except the ban on slavery, were applied to the territory south of the Ohio, ceded by North Carolina to the national government, and in 1798 to the Mississippi territory, once held by Georgia. Thus it was settled for all time that "the new colonies were not to be exploited for the benefit of the parent states (any more than for the benefit of England) but were to be autonomous and coördinate commonwealths." This outcome, bitterly opposed by some Eastern leaders who feared the triumph of Western states over the seaboard, completed the legal steps necessary by way of preparation for the flood of settlers.

The Land Companies, Speculators, and Western Land Tenure.—As in the original settlement of America, so in the opening of the West, great companies and single proprietors of large grants early figured. In 1787 the Ohio Land Company, a New England concern, acquired a million and a half acres on the Ohio and began operations by planting the town of Marietta. A professional land speculator, J.C. Symmes, secured a million acres lower down where the city of Cincinnati was founded. Other individuals bought up soldiers' claims and so acquired enormous holdings for speculative purposes. Indeed, there was such a rush to make fortunes quickly through the rise in land values that Washington was moved to cry out against the "rage for speculating in and forestalling of land on the North West of the Ohio," protesting that "scarce a valuable spot within any tolerable distance of it is left without a claimant." He therefore urged Congress to fix a reasonable price for the land, not "too exorbitant and burdensome for real occupiers, but high enough to discourage monopolizers."

Congress, however, was not prepared to use the public domain for the sole purpose of developing a body of small freeholders in the West. It still looked upon the sale of public lands as an important source of revenue with which to pay off the public debt; consequently it thought more of instant income than of ultimate results. It placed no limit on the amount which could be bought when it fixed the price at $2 an acre in 1796, and it encouraged the professional land operator by making the first installment only twenty cents an acre in addition to the small registration and survey fee. On such terms a speculator with a few thousand dollars could get possession of an enormous plot of land. If he was fortunate in disposing of it, he could meet the installments, which were spread over a period of four years, and make a handsome profit for himself. Even when the credit or installment feature was abolished in 1821 and the price of the land lowered to a cash price of $1.75 an acre, the opportunity for large speculative purchases continued to attract capital to land ventures.

The Development of the Small Freehold.—The cheapness of land and the scarcity of labor, nevertheless, made impossible the triumph of the huge estate with its semi-servile tenantry. For about $45 a man could get a farm of 160 acres on the installment plan; another payment of $80 was due in forty days; but a four-year term was allowed for the discharge of the balance. With a capital of from two to three hundred dollars a family could embark on a land venture. If it had good crops, it could meet the deferred payments. It was, however, a hard battle at best. Many a man forfeited his land through failure to pay the final installment; yet in the end, in spite of all the handicaps, the small freehold of a few hundred acres at most became the typical unit of Western agriculture, except in the planting states of the Gulf. Even the lands of the great companies were generally broken up and sold in small lots.

The tendency toward moderate holdings, so favored by Western conditions, was also promoted by a clause in the Northwest Ordinance declaring that the land of any person dying intestate—that is, without any will disposing of it—should be divided equally among his descendants. Hildreth says of this provision: "It established the important republican principle, not then introduced into all the states, of the equal distribution of landed as well as personal property." All these forces combined made the wide dispersion of wealth, in the early days of the nineteenth century, an American characteristic, in marked contrast with the European system of family prestige and vast estates based on the law of primogeniture.

THE WESTERN MIGRATION AND NEW STATES

The People.—With government established, federal arms victorious over the Indians, and the lands surveyed for sale, the way was prepared for the immigrants. They came with a rush. Young New Englanders, weary of tilling the stony soil of their native states, poured through New York and Pennsylvania, some settling on the northern bank of the Ohio but most of them in the Lake region. Sons and daughters of German farmers in Pennsylvania and many a redemptioner who had discharged his bond of servitude pressed out into Ohio, Kentucky, Tennessee, or beyond. From the exhausted fields and the clay hills of the Southern states came pioneers of English and Scotch-Irish descent, the latter in great numbers. Indeed one historian of high authority has ventured to say that "the rapid expansion of the United States from a coast strip to a continental area is largely a Scotch-Irish achievement." While native Americans of mixed stocks led the way into the West, it was not long before immigrants direct from Europe, under the stimulus of company enterprise, began to filter into the new settlements in increasing numbers.

The types of people were as various as the nations they represented. Timothy Flint, who published his entertaining *Recollections* in 1826, found the West a strange mixture of all sorts and conditions of people. Some of them, he relates, had been hunters in the upper world of the Mississippi, above the falls of St. Anthony. Some had been still farther north, in Canada. Still others had wandered from the South—the Gulf of Mexico, the Red River, and the Spanish country. French boatmen and trappers, Spanish traders from the Southwest, Virginia planters with their droves of slaves mingled with English, German, and Scotch-Irish farmers. Hunters, forest rangers, restless bordermen, and squatters, like the foaming combers of an advancing tide, went first. Then followed the farmers, masters of the ax and plow, with their wives who shared every burden and hardship and introduced some of the features of civilized life. The hunters and rangers passed on to new scenes; the home makers built for all time.

The Number of Immigrants.—There were no official stations on the frontier to record the number of immigrants who entered the West during the decades following the American Revolution. But travelers of the time record that every road was "crowded" with pioneers and their families, their wagons and cattle; and that they were seldom out of the sound of the snapping whip of the teamster urging forward his horses or the crack of the hunter's rifle as he brought down his evening meal. "During the latter half of 1787," says Coman, "more than nine hundred boats floated down the Ohio carrying eighteen thousand men, women, and children, and twelve thousand horses, sheep, and cattle, and six hundred and fifty wagons." Other lines of travel were also crowded and with the passing years the flooding tide of home seekers rose higher and higher.

The Western Routes.—Four main routes led into the country beyond the Appalachians. The Genesee road, beginning at Albany, ran almost due west to the present site of Buffalo on Lake Erie, through a level country. In the dry season, wagons laden with goods could easily pass along it into northern Ohio. A second route, through Pittsburgh, was fed by three eastern branches, one starting at Philadelphia, one at Baltimore, and another at Alexandria. A third main route wound through the mountains from Alexandria to Boonesboro in Kentucky and then westward across the Ohio to St. Louis. A fourth, the most famous of them all, passed through the Cumberland Gap and by branches extended into the Cumberland valley and the Kentucky country.

Of these four lines of travel, the Pittsburgh route offered the most advantages. Pioneers, no matter from what section they came, when once they were on the headwaters of the Ohio and in possession of a flatboat, could find a quick and easy passage into all parts of the West and Southwest. Whether they wanted to settle in Ohio, Kentucky, or western Tennessee they could find their way down the drifting flood to their destination or at least to some spot near it. Many people from the South as well as the Northern and Middle states chose this route; so it came about that the sons and daughters of Virginia and the Carolinas mingled with those of New York, Pennsylvania, and New England in the settlement of the Northwest territory.

The Methods of Travel into the West.—Many stories giving exact descriptions of methods of travel into the West in the early days have been preserved. The country was hardly opened before visitors from the Old World and from the Eastern states, impelled by curiosity, made their way to the very frontier of civilization and wrote books to inform or amuse the public. One of them, Gilbert Imlay, an English traveler, has given us an account of the Pittsburgh route as he found it in 1791. "If a man ... " he writes, "has a family or goods of any sort to remove, his best way, then, would be to purchase a waggon and team of horses to carry his property to Redstone Old Fort or to Pittsburgh, according as he may come from the Northern or Southern states. A good waggon will cost, at Philadelphia, about £10 ... and the horses about £12 each; they would cost something more both at Baltimore and Alexandria. The waggon may be covered with canvass, and if it is the choice of the people, they may sleep in it of nights with the greatest safety. But if they dislike that, there are inns of accommodation the whole distance on the different roads.... The provisions I would purchase in the same manner [that is, from the farmers along the road]; and by having two or three camp kettles and stopping every evening when the weather is fine upon the brink of some rivulet and by kindling a fire they may soon dress their own food.... This manner of journeying is so far from being disagreeable that in a fine season it is extremely pleasant." The immigrant once at Pittsburgh or Wheeling could then buy a flatboat of a size required for his goods and stock, and drift down the current to his journey's end.

The Admission of Kentucky and Tennessee.—When the eighteenth century drew to a close, Kentucky had a population larger than Delaware, Rhode Island, or New Hampshire. Tennessee claimed 60,000 inhabitants. In 1792 Kentucky took her place as a state beside her none too kindly parent, Virginia. The Eastern Federalists resented her intrusion; but they took some consolation in the admission of Vermont because the balance of Eastern power was still retained.

As if to assert their independence of old homes and conservative ideas the makers of Kentucky's first constitution swept aside the landed qualification on the suffrage and gave the vote to all free white males. Four years later, Kentucky's neighbor to the south, Tennessee, followed this step toward a wider democracy. After encountering fierce opposition from the Federalists, Tennessee was accepted as the sixteenth state.

Ohio.—The door of the union had hardly opened for Tennessee when another appeal was made to Congress, this time from the pioneers in Ohio. The little posts founded at Marietta and Cincinnati had grown into flourishing centers of trade. The stream of immigrants, flowing down the river, added daily to their numbers and the growing settlements all around poured produce into their markets to be exchanged for "store goods." After the Indians were disposed of in 1794 and the last British soldier left the frontier forts under the terms of the Jay treaty of 1795, tiny settlements of families appeared on Lake Erie in the

"Western Reserve," a region that had been retained by Connecticut when she surrendered her other rights in the Northwest.

At the close of the century, Ohio, claiming a population of more than 50,000, grew discontented with its territorial status. Indeed, two years before the enactment of the Northwest Ordinance, squatters in that region had been invited by one John Emerson to hold a convention after the fashion of the men of Hartford, Windsor, and Wethersfield in old Connecticut and draft a frame of government for themselves. This true son of New England declared that men "have an undoubted right to pass into every vacant country and there to form their constitution and that from the confederation of the whole United States Congress is not empowered to forbid them." This grand convention was never held because the heavy hand of the government fell upon the leaders; but the spirit of John Emerson did not perish. In November, 1802, a convention chosen by voters, assembled under the authority of Congress at Chillicothe, drew up a constitution. It went into force after a popular ratification. The roll of the convention bore such names as Abbot, Baldwin, Cutler, Huntington, Putnam, and Sargent, and the list of counties from which they came included Adams, Fairfield, Hamilton, Jefferson, Trumbull, and Washington, showing that the new America in the West was peopled and led by the old stock. In 1803 Ohio was admitted to the union.

Indiana and Illinois.—As in the neighboring state, the frontier in Indiana advanced northward from the Ohio, mainly under the leadership, however, of settlers from the South—restless Kentuckians hoping for better luck in a newer country and pioneers from the far frontiers of Virginia and North Carolina. As soon as a tier of counties swinging upward like the horns of the moon against Ohio on the east and in the Wabash Valley on the west was fairly settled, a clamor went up for statehood. Under the authority of an act of Congress in 1816 the Indianians drafted a constitution and inaugurated their government at Corydon. "The majority of the members of the convention," we are told by a local historian, "were frontier farmers who had a general idea of what they wanted and had sense enough to let their more erudite colleagues put it into shape."

Two years later, the pioneers of Illinois, also settled upward from the Ohio, like Indiana, elected their delegates to draft a constitution. Leadership in the convention, quite properly, was taken by a man born in New York and reared in Tennessee; and the constitution as finally drafted "was in its principal provisions a copy of the then existing constitutions of Kentucky, Ohio, and Indiana.... Many of the articles are exact copies in wording although differently arranged and numbered."

Louisiana, Mississippi, and Alabama.—Across the Mississippi to the far south, clearing and planting had gone on with much bustle and enterprise. The cotton and sugar lands of Louisiana, opened by French and Spanish settlers, were widened in every direction by planters with their armies of slaves from the older states. New Orleans, a good market and a center of culture not despised even by the pioneer, grew apace. In 1810 the population of lower Louisiana was over 75,000. The time had come, said the leaders of the people, to fulfill the promise made to France in the treaty of cession; namely, to grant to the inhabitants of the territory statehood and the rights of American citizens. Federalists from New England still having a voice in Congress, if somewhat weaker, still protested in tones of horror. "I am compelled to declare it as my deliberate opinion," pronounced Josiah Quincy in the House of Representatives, "that if this bill [to admit Louisiana] passes, the bonds of this Union are virtually dissolved ... that as it will be the right of all, so it will be the duty of some [states] to prepare definitely for a separation; amicably if they can, violently if they must.... It is a death blow to the Constitution. It may afterwards linger; but lingering, its fate will, at no very distant period, be consummated." Federalists from New York like those from New England had their doubts about the wisdom of admitting Western states; but the party of Jefferson and Madison, having the necessary majority, granted the coveted statehood to Louisiana in 1812.

When, a few years later, Mississippi and Alabama knocked at the doors of the union, the Federalists had so little influence, on account of their conduct during the second war with England, that spokesmen from the Southwest met a kindlier reception at Washington. Mississippi, in 1817, and Alabama, in 1819, took their places among the United States of America. Both of them, while granting white manhood suffrage, gave their constitutions the tone of the old East by providing landed qualifications for the governor and members of the legislature.

Missouri.—Far to the north in the Louisiana purchase, a new commonwealth was rising to power. It was peopled by immigrants who came down the Ohio in fleets of boats or crossed the Mississippi from Kentucky and Tennessee. Thrifty Germans from Pennsylvania, hardy farmers from Virginia ready to work with their own hands, freemen seeking freemen's homes, planters with their slaves moving on from worn-out fields on the seaboard, came together in the widening settlements of the Missouri country. Peoples from the North and South flowed together, small farmers and big planters mingling in one community. When their numbers had reached sixty thousand or more, they precipitated a contest over their admission to the union, "ringing an alarm bell in the night," as Jefferson phrased it. The favorite expedient of compromise with slavery was brought forth in Congress once more. Maine consequently was brought into the union without slavery and Missouri with slavery. At the same time there was drawn westward through the rest of the Louisiana territory a line separating servitude from slavery.

THE SPIRIT OF THE FRONTIER

Land Tenure and Liberty.—Over an immense western area there developed an unbroken system of freehold farms. In the Gulf states and the lower Mississippi Valley, it is true, the planter with his many slaves even led in the pioneer movement; but through large sections of Tennessee and Kentucky, as well as upper Georgia and Alabama, and all throughout the Northwest territory the small farmer reigned supreme. In this immense dominion there sprang up a civilization without caste or class—a body of people all having about the same amount of this world's goods and deriving their livelihood from one source: the labor of their own hands on the soil. The Northwest territory alone almost equaled in area all the original thirteen states combined, except Georgia, and its system of agricultural economy was unbroken by plantations and feudal estates. "In the subdivision of the soil and the great equality of condition," as Webster said on more than one occasion, "lay the true basis, most certainly, of popular government." There was the undoubted source of Jacksonian democracy.

The Characteristics of the Western People.—Travelers into the Northwest during the early years of the nineteenth century were agreed that the people of that region were almost uniformly marked by the characteristics common to an independent yeomanry. A close observer thus recorded his impressions: "A spirit of adventurous enterprise, a willingness to go through any hardship to accomplish an object.... Independence of thought and action. They have felt the influence of these principles from their childhood. Men who can endure anything; that have lived almost without restraint, free as the mountain air or as the deer and the buffalo of their forests, and who know they are Americans all.... An apparent roughness which some would deem rudeness of manner.... Where there is perfect equality in a neighborhood of people who know little about each other's previous history or ancestry but where each is lord of the soil he cultivates. Where a log cabin is all that the best of families can expect to have for years and of course can possess few of the external decorations which have so much influence in creating a diversity of rank in society. These circumstances have laid the foundation for that equality of intercourse, simplicity of manners, want of deference, want of reserve, great readiness to make acquaintances, freedom of speech, indisposition to brook real or imaginary insults which one witnesses among people of the West."

This equality, this independence, this rudeness so often described by the traveler as marking a new country, were all accentuated by the character of the settlers themselves. Traces of the fierce, unsociable, eagle-eyed, hard-drinking hunter remained. The settlers who followed the hunter were, with some exceptions, soldiers of the Revolutionary army, farmers of the "middling order," and mechanics from the towns,—English, Scotch-Irish, Germans,—poor in possessions and thrown upon the labor of their own hands for support. Sons and daughters from well-to-do Eastern homes sometimes brought softer manners; but the equality of life and the leveling force of labor in forest and field soon made them one in spirit with their struggling neighbors. Even the preachers and teachers, who came when the cabins were raised in the clearings and rude churches and schoolhouses were built, preached sermons and taught lessons that savored of the frontier, as any one may know who reads Peter Cartwright's *A Muscular Christian* or Eggleston's *The Hoosier Schoolmaster*.

THE WEST AND THE EAST MEET

The East Alarmed.—A people so independent as the Westerners and so attached to local self-government gave the conservative East many a rude shock, setting gentlemen in powdered wigs and knee breeches agog with the idea that terrible things might happen in the Mississippi Valley. Not without good grounds did Washington fear that "a touch of a feather would turn" the Western settlers away from the seaboard to the Spaniards; and seriously did he urge the East not to neglect them, lest they be "drawn into the arms of, or be dependent upon foreigners." Taking advantage of the restless spirit in the Southwest, Aaron Burr, having disgraced himself by killing Alexander Hamilton in a duel, laid wild plans, if not to bring about a secession in that region, at least to build a state of some kind out of the Spanish dominions adjoining Louisiana. Frightened at such enterprises and fearing the dominance of the West, the Federalists, with a few conspicuous exceptions, opposed equality between the sections. Had their narrow views prevailed, the West, with its new democracy, would have been held in perpetual tutelage to the seaboard or perhaps been driven into independence as the thirteen colonies had been not long before.

Eastern Friends of the West.—Fortunately for the nation, there were many Eastern leaders, particularly from the South, who understood the West, approved its spirit, and sought to bring the two sections together by common bonds. Washington kept alive and keen the zeal for Western advancement which he acquired in his youth as a surveyor. He never grew tired of urging upon his Eastern friends the importance of the lands beyond the mountains. He pressed upon the governor of Virginia a project for a wagon road connecting the seaboard with the Ohio country and was active in a movement to improve the navigation of the Potomac. He advocated strengthening the ties of commerce. "Smooth the roads," he said, "and make easy the way for them, and then see what an influx of articles will be poured upon us; how amazingly our exports will be increased by them; and how amply we shall be compensated for any trouble and expense we may encounter to effect it." Jefferson, too, was interested in every phase of Western development—the survey of lands, the exploration of waterways, the opening of trade, and even the discovery of the bones of prehistoric animals. Robert Fulton, the inventor of the steamboat, was another man of vision who for many years pressed upon his countrymen the necessity of uniting East and West by a canal which would cement the union, raise the value of the public lands, and extend the principles of confederate and republican government.

The Difficulties of Early Transportation.—Means of communication played an important part in the strategy of all those who sought to bring together the seaboard and the frontier. The produce of the West—wheat, corn, bacon, hemp, cattle, and tobacco—was bulky and the cost of overland transportation was prohibitive. In the Eastern market, "a cow and her calf were given for a bushel of salt, while a suit of 'store clothes' cost as much as a farm." In such circumstances, the inhabitants of the Mississippi Valley were forced to ship their produce over a long route by way of New Orleans and to pay high freight rates for everything that was brought across the mountains. Scows of from five to fifty tons were built at the towns along the rivers and piloted down the stream to the Crescent City. In a few cases small ocean-going vessels were built to transport goods to the West Indies or to the Eastern coast towns. Salt, iron, guns, powder, and the absolute essentials which the pioneers had to buy mainly in Eastern markets were carried over narrow wagon trails that were almost impassable in the rainy season.

The National Road.—To far-sighted men, like Albert Gallatin, "the father of internal improvements," the solution of this problem was the construction of roads and canals. Early in Jefferson's administration, Congress dedicated a part of the proceeds from the sale of lands to building highways from the headwaters of the navigable waters emptying into the Atlantic to the Ohio River and beyond into the Northwest territory. In 1806, after many misgivings, it authorized a great national highway binding the East and the West. The Cumberland Road, as it was called, began in northwestern Maryland, wound through southern Pennsylvania, crossed the narrow neck of Virginia at Wheeling, and then shot almost straight across Ohio, Indiana, and Illinois, into Missouri. By 1817, stagecoaches were running between

Washington and Wheeling; by 1833 contractors had carried their work to Columbus, Ohio, and by 1852, to Vandalia, Illinois. Over this ballasted road mail and passenger coaches could go at high speed, and heavy freight wagons proceed in safety at a steady pace.

Canals and Steamboats.—A second epoch in the economic union of the East and West was reached with the opening of the Erie Canal in 1825, offering an all-water route from New York City to the Great Lakes and the Mississippi Valley. Pennsylvania, alarmed by the advantages conferred on New York by this enterprise, began her system of canals and portages from Philadelphia to Pittsburgh, completing the last link in 1834. In the South, the Chesapeake and Ohio Company, chartered in 1825, was busy with a project to connect Georgetown and Cumberland when railways broke in upon the undertaking before it was half finished. About the same time, Ohio built a canal across the state, affording water communication between Lake Erie and the Ohio River through a rich wheat belt. Passengers could now travel by canal boat into the West with comparative ease and comfort, if not at a rapid speed, and the bulkiest of freight could be easily handled. Moreover, the rate charged for carrying goods was cut by the Erie Canal from $32 a ton per hundred miles to $1. New Orleans was destined to lose her primacy in the Mississippi Valley.

The diversion of traffic to Eastern markets was also stimulated by steamboats which appeared on the Ohio about 1810, three years after Fulton had made his famous trip on the Hudson. It took twenty men to sail and row a five-ton scow up the river at a speed of from ten to twenty miles a day. In 1825, Timothy Flint traveled a hundred miles a day on the new steamer *Grecian* "against the whole weight of the Mississippi current." Three years later the round trip from Louisville to New Orleans was cut to eight days. Heavy produce that once had to float down to New Orleans could be carried upstream and sent to the East by way of the canal systems.

Thus the far country was brought near. The timid no longer hesitated at the thought of the perilous journey. All routes were crowded with Western immigrants. The forests fell before the ax like grain before the sickle. Clearings scattered through the woods spread out into a great mosaic of farms stretching from the Southern Appalachians to Lake Michigan. The national census of 1830 gave 937,000 inhabitants to Ohio; 343,000 to Indiana; 157,000 to Illinois; 687,000 to Kentucky; and 681,000 to Tennessee.

With the increase in population and the growth of agriculture came political influence. People who had once petitioned Congress now sent their own representatives. Men who had hitherto accepted without protests Presidents from the seaboard expressed a new spirit of dissent in 1824 by giving only three electoral votes for John Quincy Adams; and four years later they sent a son of the soil from Tennessee, Andrew Jackson, to take Washington's chair as chief executive of the nation—the first of a long line of Presidents from the Mississippi basin.

References

W.G. Brown, *The Lower South in American History*.

B.A. Hinsdale, *The Old North West* (2 vols.).

A.B. Hulbert, *Great American Canals* and *The Cumberland Road*.

T. Roosevelt, *Thomas H. Benton*.

P.J. Treat, *The National Land System* (1785-1820).

F.J. Turner, *Rise of the New West* (American Nation Series).

J. Winsor, *The Westward Movement*.

Questions

1. How did the West come to play a rôle in the Revolution?

2. What preparations were necessary to settlement?

3. Give the principal provisions of the Northwest Ordinance.

4. Explain how freehold land tenure happened to predominate in the West.

5. Who were the early settlers in the West? What routes did they take? How did they travel?

6. Explain the Eastern opposition to the admission of new Western states. Show how it was overcome.

7. Trace a connection between the economic system of the West and the spirit of the people.

8. Who were among the early friends of Western development?

9. Describe the difficulties of trade between the East and the West.

10. Show how trade was promoted.

Research Topics

Northwest Ordinance.—Analysis of text in Macdonald, *Documentary Source Book.* Roosevelt, *Winning of the West*, Vol. V, pp. 5-57.

The West before the Revolution.—Roosevelt, Vol. I.

The West during the Revolution.—Roosevelt, Vols. II and III.

Tennessee.—Roosevelt, Vol. V, pp. 95-119 and Vol. VI, pp. 9-87.

The Cumberland Road.—A.B. Hulbert, *The Cumberland Road.*

Early Life in the Middle West.—Callender, *Economic History of the United States*, pp. 617-633; 636-641.

Slavery in the Southwest.—Callender, pp. 641-652.

Early Land Policy.—Callender, pp. 668-680.

Westward Movement of Peoples.—Roosevelt, Vol. IV, pp. 7-39.

Lists of books dealing with the early history of Western states are given in Hart, Channing, and Turner, *Guide to the Study and Reading of American History* (rev. ed.), pp. 62-89.

Kentucky.—Roosevelt, Vol. IV, pp. 176-263.

CHAPTER XI

JACKSONIAN DEMOCRACY

The New England Federalists, at the Hartford convention, prophesied that in time the West would dominate the East. "At the adoption of the Constitution," they said, "a certain balance of power among the original states was considered to exist, and there was at that time and yet is among those parties a strong affinity between their great and general interests. By the admission of these [new] states that balance has been materially affected and unless the practice be modified must ultimately be destroyed. The Southern states will first avail themselves of their new confederates to govern the East, and finally the Western states, multiplied in number, and augmented in population, will control the interests of the whole." Strangely enough the fulfillment of this prophecy was being prepared even in Federalist strongholds by the rise of a new urban democracy that was to make common cause with the farmers beyond the mountains.

THE DEMOCRATIC MOVEMENT IN THE EAST

The Aristocratic Features of the Old Order.—The Revolutionary fathers, in setting up their first state constitutions, although they often spoke of government as founded on the consent of the governed, did not think that consistency required giving the vote to all adult males. On the contrary they looked upon property owners as the only safe "depositary" of political power. They went back to the colonial tradition that related taxation and representation. This, they argued, was not only just but a safeguard against the "excesses of democracy."

In carrying their theory into execution they placed taxpaying or property qualifications on the right to vote. Broadly speaking, these limitations fell into three classes. Three states, Pennsylvania (1776), New Hampshire (1784), and Georgia (1798), gave the ballot to all who paid taxes, without reference to the value of their property. Three, Virginia, Delaware, and Rhode Island, clung firmly to the ancient principles that only freeholders could be intrusted with electoral rights. Still other states, while closely restricting the suffrage, accepted the ownership of other things as well as land in fulfillment of the requirements. In Massachusetts, for instance, the vote was granted to all men who held land yielding an annual income of three pounds or possessed other property worth sixty pounds.

The electors thus enfranchised, numerous as they were, owing to the wide distribution of land, often suffered from a very onerous disability. In many states they were able to vote only for persons of wealth because heavy property qualifications were imposed on public officers. In New Hampshire, the governor had to be worth five hundred pounds, one-half in land; in Massachusetts, one thousand pounds, all freehold; in Maryland, five thousand pounds, one thousand of which was freehold; in North Carolina, one thousand pounds freehold; and in South Carolina, ten thousand pounds freehold. A state senator in Massachusetts had to be the owner of a freehold worth three hundred pounds or personal property worth six hundred pounds; in New Jersey, one thousand pounds' worth of property; in North Carolina, three hundred acres of land; in South Carolina, two thousand pounds freehold. For members of the lower house of the legislature lower qualifications were required.

In most of the states the suffrage or office holding or both were further restricted by religious provisions. No single sect was powerful enough to dominate after the Revolution, but, for the most part, Catholics and Jews were either disfranchised or excluded from office. North Carolina and Georgia denied the ballot to any one who was not a Protestant. Delaware withheld it from all who did not believe in the Trinity and the inspiration of the Scriptures. Massachusetts and Maryland limited it to Christians. Virginia and New York, advanced for their day, made no discrimination in government on account of religious opinion.

The Defense of the Old Order.—It must not be supposed that property qualifications were thoughtlessly imposed at the outset or considered of little consequence in practice. In the beginning they were viewed as fundamental. As towns grew in size and the number of landless citizens increased, the restrictions were defended with even more vigor. In Massachusetts, the great Webster upheld the rights of property in government, saying: "It is entirely just that property should have its due weight and consideration in political arrangements.... The disastrous revolutions which the world has witnessed, those political thunderstorms and earthquakes which have shaken the pillars of society to their deepest foundations, have been revolutions against property." In Pennsylvania, a leader in local affairs cried out against a plan to remove the taxpaying limitation on the suffrage: "What does the delegate propose? To place the vicious vagrant, the wandering Arabs, the Tartar hordes of our large cities on the level with the virtuous and good man?" In Virginia, Jefferson himself had first believed in property qualifications and had feared with genuine alarm the "mobs of the great cities." It was near the end of the eighteenth century before he accepted the idea of manhood suffrage. Even then he was unable to convince the constitution-makers of his own state. "It is not an idle chimera of the brain," urged one of them, "that the possession of land furnishes the strongest evidence of permanent, common interest with, and attachment to, the community.... It is upon this foundation I wish to place the right of suffrage. This is the best general standard which can be resorted to for the purpose of determining whether the persons to be invested with the right of suffrage are such persons as could be, consistently with the safety and well-being of the community, intrusted with the exercise of that right."

Attacks on the Restricted Suffrage.—The changing circumstances of American life, however, soon challenged the rule of those with property. Prominent among the new forces were the rising mercantile and business interests. Where the freehold qualification was applied, business men who did not own land were deprived of the vote and excluded from office. In New York, for example, the most illiterate farmer who had one hundred pounds' worth of land could vote for state senator and governor, while the landless banker or merchant could not. It is not surprising, therefore, to find business men taking the lead in breaking down freehold limitations on the suffrage. The professional classes also were interested in removing the barriers which excluded many of them from public affairs. It was a schoolmaster, Thomas Dorr, who led the popular uprising in Rhode Island which brought the exclusive rule by freeholders to an end.

In addition to the business and professional classes, the mechanics of the towns showed a growing hostility to a system of government that generally barred them from voting or holding office. Though not numerous, they had early begun to exercise an influence on the course of public affairs. They had led the riots against the Stamp Act, overturned King George's statue, and "crammed stamps down the throats of collectors." When the state constitutions were framed they took a lively interest, particularly in New York City and Philadelphia. In June, 1776, the "mechanicks in union" in New York protested against putting the new state constitution into effect without their approval, declaring that the right to vote on the acceptance or rejection of a fundamental law "is the birthright of every man to whatever state he may belong." Though their petition was rejected, their spirit remained. When, a few years later, the federal Constitution was being framed, the mechanics watched the process with deep concern; they knew that one of its main objects was to promote trade and commerce, affecting directly their daily bread. During the struggle over ratification, they passed resolutions approving its provisions and they often joined in parades organized to stir up sentiment for the Constitution, even though they could not vote for members of the state conventions and so express their will directly. After the organization of trade unions they collided with the courts of law and thus became interested in the election of judges and lawmakers.

Those who attacked the old system of class rule found a strong moral support in the Declaration of Independence. Was it not said that all men are created equal? Whoever runs may read. Was it not declared that governments derive their just power from the consent of the governed? That doctrine was applied with effect to George III and seemed appropriate for use against the privileged classes of Massachusetts or Virginia. "How do the principles thus proclaimed," asked the non-freeholders of Richmond, in petitioning for the ballot, "accord with the existing regulation of the suffrage? A regulation which, instead of the equality nature ordains, creates an odious distinction between members of the same community ... and vests in a favored class, not in consideration of their public services but of their private possessions, the highest of all privileges."

Abolition of Property Qualifications.—By many minor victories rather than by any spectacular triumphs did the advocates of manhood suffrage carry the day. Slight gains were made even during the Revolution or shortly afterward. In Pennsylvania, the mechanics, by taking an active part in the contest over the Constitution of 1776, were able to force the qualification down to the payment of a small tax. Vermont came into the union in 1792 without any property restrictions. In the same year Delaware gave the vote to all men who paid taxes. Maryland, reckoned one of the most conservative of states, embarked on the experiment of manhood suffrage in 1809; and nine years later, Connecticut, equally conservative, decided that all taxpayers were worthy of the ballot.

Five states, Massachusetts, New York, Virginia, Rhode Island, and North Carolina, remained obdurate while these changes were going on around them; finally they had to yield themselves. The last struggle in Massachusetts took place in the constitutional convention of 1820. There Webster, in the prime of his manhood, and John Adams, in the closing years of his old age, alike protested against such radical innovations as manhood suffrage. Their protests were futile. The property test was abolished and a small tax-paying qualification was substituted. New York surrendered the next year and, after trying some minor restrictions for five years, went completely over to white manhood suffrage in 1826. Rhode Island clung to her freehold qualification through thirty years of agitation. Then Dorr's Rebellion, almost culminating in bloodshed, brought about a reform in 1843 which introduced a slight tax-paying qualification as an alternative to the freehold. Virginia and North Carolina were still unconvinced. The former refused to abandon ownership of land as the test for political rights until 1850 and the latter until 1856. Although religious discriminations and property qualifications for office holders were sometimes retained after the establishment of manhood suffrage, they were usually abolished along with the monopoly of government enjoyed by property owners and taxpayers.

At the end of the first quarter of the nineteenth century, the white male industrial workers and the mechanics of the Northern cities, at least, could lay aside the petition for the ballot and enjoy with the free farmer a voice in the government of their common country. "Universal democracy," sighed Carlyle, who was widely read in the United States, "whatever we may think of it has declared itself the inevitable fact of the days in which we live; and he who has any chance to instruct or lead in these days must begin by admitting that ... Where no government is wanted, save that of the parish constable, as in America with its boundless soil, every man being able to find work and recompense for himself, democracy may subsist; not elsewhere." Amid the grave misgivings of the first generation of statesmen, America was committed to the great adventure, in the populous towns of the East as well as in the forests and fields of the West.

THE NEW DEMOCRACY ENTERS THE ARENA

The spirit of the new order soon had a pronounced effect on the machinery of government and the practice of politics. The enfranchised electors were not long in demanding for themselves a larger share in administration.

The Spoils System and Rotation in Office.—First of all they wanted office for themselves, regardless of their fitness. They therefore extended the system of rewarding party workers with government positions—a system early established in several states, notably New York and Pennsylvania. Closely connected with it was the practice of fixing short terms for officers and making frequent changes in personnel. "Long continuance in office," explained a champion of this idea in Pennsylvania in 1837, "unfits a man for the discharge of its duties, by rendering him arbitrary and aristocratic, and tends to beget, first life office, and then hereditary office, which leads to the destruction of free government." The solution offered was the historic doctrine of "rotation in office." At the same time the principle of popular election was extended to an increasing number of officials who had once been appointed either by the governor or the legislature. Even geologists, veterinarians, surveyors, and other technical officers were declared elective on the theory that their appointment "smacked of monarchy."

Popular Election of Presidential Electors.—In a short time the spirit of democracy, while playing havoc with the old order in state government, made its way upward into the federal system. The framers of the Constitution, bewildered by many proposals and unable to agree on any single plan, had committed the choice of presidential electors to the discretion of the state legislatures. The legislatures, in turn, greedy of power, early adopted the practice of choosing the electors themselves; but they did not enjoy it long undisturbed. Democracy, thundering at their doors, demanded that they surrender the privilege to the people. Reluctantly they yielded, sometimes granting popular election and then withdrawing it. The drift was inevitable, and the climax came with the advent of Jacksonian democracy. In 1824, Vermont, New York, Delaware, South Carolina, Georgia, and Louisiana, though some had experimented with popular election, still left the choice of electors with the legislature. Eight years later South Carolina alone held to the old practice. Popular election had become the final word. The fanciful idea of an electoral college of "good and wise men," selected without passion or partisanship by state legislatures acting as deliberative bodies, was exploded for all time; the election of the nation's chief magistrate was committed to the tempestuous methods of democracy.

The Nominating Convention.—As the suffrage was widened and the popular choice of presidential electors extended, there arose a violent protest against the methods used by the political parties in nominating candidates. After the retirement of Washington, both the Republicans and the Federalists found it necessary to agree upon their favorites before the election, and they adopted a colonial device—the pre-election caucus. The Federalist members of Congress held a conference and selected their candidate, and the Republicans followed the example. In a short time the practice of nominating by a "congressional caucus" became a recognized institution. The election still remained with the people; but the power of picking candidates for their approval passed into the hands of a small body of Senators and Representatives.

A reaction against this was unavoidable. To friends of "the plain people," like Andrew Jackson, it was intolerable, all the more so because the caucus never favored him with the nomination. More conservative men also found grave objections to it. They pointed out that, whereas the Constitution intended the President to be an independent officer, he had now fallen under the control of a caucus of congressmen. The supremacy of the legislative branch had been obtained by an extra-legal political device. To such objections were added practical considerations. In 1824, when personal rivalry had taken the place of party conflicts, the congressional caucus selected as the candidate, William H. Crawford, of Georgia, a man of distinction but no great popularity, passing by such an obvious hero as General Jackson. The followers of the General were enraged and demanded nothing short of the death of "King Caucus." Their clamor was effective. Under their attacks, the caucus came to an ignominious end.

In place of it there arose in 1831 a new device, the national nominating convention, composed of delegates elected by party voters for the sole purpose of nominating candidates. Senators and Representatives were still prominent in the party councils, but they were swamped by hundreds of delegates "fresh from the people," as Jackson was wont to say. In fact, each convention was made up mainly of office holders and office seekers, and the new institution was soon denounced as vigorously as King Caucus had been, particularly by statesmen who failed to obtain a nomination. Still it grew in strength and by 1840 was firmly established.

The End of the Old Generation.—In the election of 1824, the representatives of the "aristocracy" made their last successful stand. Until then the leadership by men of "wealth and talents" had been undisputed. There had been five Presidents—Washington, John Adams, Jefferson, Madison, and Monroe—all Eastern men brought up in prosperous families with the advantages of culture which come from leisure and the possession of life's refinements. None of them had ever been compelled to work with his hands for a livelihood. Four of them had been slaveholders. Jefferson was a philosopher, learned in natural science, a master of foreign languages, a gentleman of dignity and grace of manner, notwithstanding his studied simplicity. Madison, it was said, was armed "with all the culture of his century." Monroe was a graduate of William and Mary, a gentleman of the old school. Jefferson and his three successors called themselves Republicans and professed a genuine faith in the people but they were not "of the people" themselves; they were not sons of the soil or the workshop. They were all men of "the grand old order of society" who gave finish and style even to popular government.

Monroe was the last of the Presidents belonging to the heroic epoch of the Revolution. He had served in the war for independence, in the Congress under the Articles of Confederation, and in official capacity after the adoption of the Constitution. In short, he was of the age that had wrought American independence and set the government afloat. With his passing, leadership went to a new generation; but his successor, John Quincy Adams, formed a bridge between the old and the new in that he combined a high degree of culture with democratic sympathies. Washington had died in 1799, preceded but a few months by Patrick Henry and followed in four years by Samuel Adams. Hamilton had been killed in a duel with Burr in 1804. Thomas Jefferson and John Adams were yet alive in 1824 but they were soon to pass from the scene, reconciled at last, full of years and honors. Madison was in dignified retirement, destined to live long enough to protest against the doctrine of nullification proclaimed by South Carolina before death carried him away at the ripe old age of eighty-five.

The Election of John Quincy Adams (1824).—The campaign of 1824 marked the end of the "era of good feeling" inaugurated by the collapse of the Federalist party after the election of 1816. There were four leading candidates, John Quincy Adams, Andrew Jackson, Henry Clay, and W.H. Crawford. The result of the election was a division of the electoral votes into four parts and no one received a majority. Under the Constitution, therefore, the selection of President passed to the House of Representatives. Clay, who stood at the bottom of the poll, threw his weight to Adams and assured his triumph, much to the chagrin of Jackson's friends. They thought, with a certain justification, that inasmuch as the hero of New Orleans had received the largest electoral vote, the House was morally bound to accept the popular judgment and make him President. Jackson shook hands cordially with Adams on the day of the inauguration, but never forgave him for being elected.

While Adams called himself a Republican in politics and often spoke of "the rule of the people," he was regarded by Jackson's followers as "an aristocrat." He was not a son of the soil. Neither was he acquainted at first hand with the labor of farmers and mechanics. He had been educated at Harvard and in Europe. Like his illustrious father, John Adams, he was a stern and reserved man, little given to seeking popularity. Moreover, he was from the East and the frontiersmen of the West regarded him as a man "born with a silver spoon in his mouth." Jackson's supporters especially disliked him because they thought their hero entitled to the presidency. Their anger was deepened when Adams appointed Clay to the office of Secretary of State; and they set up a cry that there had been a "deal" by which Clay had helped to elect Adams to get office for himself.

Though Adams conducted his administration with great dignity and in a fine spirit of public service, he was unable to overcome the opposition which he encountered on his election to office or to win popularity in the West and South. On the contrary, by advocating government assistance in building roads and canals and public grants in aid of education, arts, and sciences, he ran counter to the current which had set in against appropriations of federal funds for internal improvements. By signing the Tariff Bill of 1828, soon known as the "Tariff of Abominations," he made new enemies without adding to his friends in New York, Pennsylvania, and Ohio where he sorely needed them. Handicapped by the false charge that he had been a party to a "corrupt bargain" with Clay to secure his first election; attacked for his advocacy of a high protective tariff; charged with favoring an "aristocracy of office-holders" in Washington on account of his refusal to discharge government clerks by the wholesale, Adams was retired from the White House after he had served four years.

The Triumph of Jackson in 1828.—Probably no candidate for the presidency ever had such passionate popular support as Andrew Jackson had in 1828. He was truly a man of the people. Born of poor parents in the upland region of South Carolina, schooled in poverty and adversity, without the advantages of education or the refinements of cultivated leisure, he seemed the embodiment of the spirit of the new American democracy. Early in his youth he had gone into the frontier of Tennessee where he soon won a name as a fearless and intrepid Indian fighter. On the march and in camp, he endeared himself to his men by sharing their hardships, sleeping on the ground with them, and eating parched corn when nothing better could be found for the privates. From local prominence he sprang into national fame by his exploit at the battle of New Orleans. His reputation as a military hero was enhanced by the feeling that he had been a martyr to political treachery in 1824. The farmers of the West and South claimed him as their own. The mechanics of the Eastern cities, newly enfranchised, also looked upon him as their friend. Though his views on the tariff, internal improvements, and other issues before the country were either vague or unknown, he was readily elected President.

The returns of the electoral vote in 1828 revealed the sources of Jackson's power. In New England, he received but one ballot, from Maine; he had a majority of the electors in New York and all of them in Pennsylvania; and he carried every state south of Maryland and beyond the Appalachians. Adams did not get a single electoral vote in the South and West. The prophecy of the Hartford convention had been fulfilled.

When Jackson took the oath of office on March 4, 1829, the government of the United States entered into a new era. Until this time the inauguration of a President—even that of Jefferson, the apostle of simplicity—had brought no rude shock to the course of affairs at the capital. Hitherto the installation of a President meant that an old-fashioned gentleman, accompanied by a few servants, had driven to the White House in his own coach, taken the oath with quiet dignity, appointed a few new men to the higher posts, continued in office the long list of regular civil employees, and begun his administration with respectable decorum. Jackson changed all this. When he was inaugurated, men and women journeyed hundreds of miles to witness the ceremony. Great throngs pressed into the White House, "upset the bowls of punch, broke the glasses, and stood with their muddy boots on the satin-covered chairs to see the people's President." If Jefferson's inauguration was, as he called it, the "great revolution," Jackson's inauguration was a cataclysm.

THE NEW DEMOCRACY AT WASHINGTON

The Spoils System.—The staid and respectable society of Washington was disturbed by this influx of farmers and frontiersmen. To speak of politics became "bad form" among fashionable women. The clerks and civil servants of the government who had enjoyed long and secure tenure of office became alarmed at the clamor of new men for their positions. Doubtless the major portion of them had opposed the election of Jackson and looked with feelings akin to contempt upon him and his followers. With a hunter's instinct, Jackson scented his prey. Determined to have none but his friends in office, he made a clean sweep, expelling old employees to make room for men "fresh from the people." This was a new custom. Other Presidents had discharged a few officers for engaging in opposition politics. They had been careful in making appointments not to choose inveterate enemies; but they discharged relatively few men on account of their political views and partisan activities.

By wholesale removals and the frank selection of officers on party grounds—a practice already well intrenched in New York—Jackson established the "spoils system" at Washington. The famous slogan, "to the victor belong the spoils of victory," became the avowed principle of the national government. Statesmen like Calhoun denounced it; poets like James Russell Lowell ridiculed it; faithful servants of the government suffered under it; but it held undisturbed sway for half a century thereafter, each succeeding generation outdoing, if possible, its predecessor in the use of public office for political purposes. If any one remarked that training and experience were necessary qualifications for important public positions, he met Jackson's own profession of faith: "The duties of any public office are so simple or admit of being made so simple that any man can in a short time become master of them."

The Tariff and Nullification.—Jackson had not been installed in power very long before he was compelled to choose between states' rights and nationalism. The immediate occasion of the trouble was the tariff—a matter on which Jackson did not have any very decided views. His mind did not run naturally to abstruse economic questions; and owing to the divided opinion of the country it was "good politics" to be vague and ambiguous in the controversy. Especially was this true, because the tariff issue was threatening to split the country into parties again.

The Development of the Policy of "Protection."—The war of 1812 and the commercial policies of England which followed it had accentuated the need for American economic independence. During that conflict, the United States, cut off from English manufactures as during the Revolution, built up home industries to meet the unusual call for iron, steel, cloth, and other military and naval supplies as well as the demands from ordinary markets. Iron foundries and textile mills sprang up as in the night; hundreds of business men invested fortunes in industrial enterprises so essential to the military needs of the government; and the people at large fell into the habit of buying American-made goods again. As the London *Times* tersely observed of the Americans, "their first war with England made them independent; their second war made them formidable."

In recognition of this state of affairs, the tariff of 1816 was designed: *first*, to prevent England from ruining these "infant industries" by dumping the accumulated stores of years suddenly upon American markets; and, *secondly*, to enlarge in the manufacturing centers the demand for American agricultural produce. It accomplished the purposes of its framers. It kept in operation the mills and furnaces so recently built. It multiplied the number of industrial workers and enhanced the demand for the produce of the soil. It brought about another very important result. It turned the capital and enterprise of New England from shipping to manufacturing, and converted her statesmen, once friends of low tariffs, into ardent advocates of protection.

In the early years of the nineteenth century, the Yankees had bent their energies toward building and operating ships to carry produce from America to Europe and manufactures from Europe to America. For this reason, they had opposed the tariff of 1816 calculated to increase domestic production and cut down the carrying trade. Defeated in their efforts, they accepted the inevitable and turned to manufacturing. Soon they were powerful friends of protection for American enterprise. As the money invested and the labor employed in the favored industries increased, the demand for continued and heavier protection grew apace. Even the farmers who furnished raw materials, like wool, flax, and hemp, began to see eye to eye with the manufacturers. So the textile interests of New England, the iron masters of Connecticut, New Jersey, and Pennsylvania, the wool, hemp, and flax growers of Ohio, Kentucky, and Tennessee, and the sugar planters of Louisiana developed into a formidable combination in support of a high protective tariff.

The Planting States Oppose the Tariff.—In the meantime, the cotton states on the seaboard had forgotten about the havoc wrought during the Napoleonic wars when their produce rotted because there were no ships to carry it to Europe. The seas were now open. The area devoted to cotton had swiftly expanded as Alabama, Mississippi, and Louisiana were opened up. Cotton had in fact become "king" and the planters depended for their prosperity, as they thought, upon the sale of their staple to English manufacturers whose spinning and weaving mills were the wonder of the world. Manufacturing nothing and having to buy nearly everything except farm produce and even much of that for slaves, the planters naturally wanted to purchase manufactures in the cheapest market, England, where they sold most of their cotton. The tariff, they contended, raised the price of the goods they had to buy and was thus in fact a tribute laid on them for the benefit of the Northern mill owners.

The Tariff of Abominations.—They were overborne, however, in 1824 and again in 1828 when Northern manufacturers and Western farmers forced Congress to make an upward revision of the tariff. The Act of 1828 known as "the Tariff of Abominations," though slightly modified in 1832, was "the straw which broke the camel's back." Southern leaders turned in rage against the whole system. The legislatures of Virginia, North Carolina, South Carolina, Georgia, and Alabama denounced it; a general convention of delegates held at Augusta issued a protest of defiance against it; and South Carolina, weary of verbal battles, decided to prevent its enforcement.

South Carolina Nullifies the Tariff.—The legislature of that state, on October 26, 1832, passed a bill calling for a state convention which duly assembled in the following month. In no mood for compromise, it adopted the famous Ordinance of Nullification after a few days' debate. Every line of this document was clear and firm. The tariff, it opened, gives "bounties to classes and individuals ... at the expense and to the injury and oppression of other classes and individuals"; it is a violation of the Constitution of the United States and therefore null and void; its enforcement in South Carolina is unlawful; if the federal government attempts to coerce the state into obeying the law, "the people of this state will thenceforth hold themselves absolved from all further obligations to maintain or preserve their political connection with the people of the other states and will forthwith proceed to organize a separate government and do all other acts and things which sovereign and independent states may of right do."

Southern States Condemn Nullification.—The answer of the country to this note of defiance, couched in the language used in the Kentucky resolutions and by the New England Federalists during the war of 1812, was quick and positive. The legislatures of the Southern states, while condemning the tariff, repudiated the step which South Carolina had taken. Georgia responded: "We abhor the doctrine of nullification as neither a peaceful nor a constitutional remedy." Alabama found it "unsound in theory and dangerous in practice." North Carolina replied that it was "revolutionary in character, subversive of the Constitution of the United States." Mississippi answered: "It is disunion by force—it is civil war." Virginia spoke more softly, condemning the tariff and sustaining the principle of the Virginia resolutions but denying that South Carolina could find in them any sanction for her proceedings.

Jackson Firmly Upholds the Union.—The eyes of the country were turned upon Andrew Jackson. It was known that he looked with no friendly feelings upon nullification, for, at a Jefferson dinner in the spring of 1830 while the subject was in the air, he had with laconic firmness announced a toast: "Our federal union; it must be preserved." When two years later the open challenge came from South Carolina, he replied that he would enforce the law, saying with his frontier directness: "If a single drop of blood shall be shed there in opposition to the laws of the United States, I will hang the first man I can lay my hands on engaged in such conduct upon the first tree that I can reach." He made ready to keep his word by preparing for the use of military and naval forces in sustaining the authority of the federal government. Then in a long and impassioned proclamation to the people of South Carolina he pointed out the national character of the union, and announced his solemn resolve to preserve it by all constitutional means. Nullification he branded as "incompatible with the existence of the union, contradicted expressly by the letter of the Constitution, unauthorized by its spirit, inconsistent with every principle on which it was founded, and destructive of the great objects for which it was formed."

A Compromise.—In his messages to Congress, however, Jackson spoke the language of conciliation. A few days before issuing his proclamation he suggested that protection should be limited to the articles of domestic manufacture indispensable to safety in war time, and shortly afterward he asked for new legislation to aid him in enforcing the laws. With two propositions before it, one to remove the chief grounds for South Carolina's resistance and the other to apply force if it was continued, Congress bent its efforts to avoid a crisis. On February 12, 1833, Henry Clay laid before the Senate a compromise tariff bill providing for the gradual reduction of the duties until by 1842 they would reach the level of the law which Calhoun had supported in 1816. About the same time the "force bill," designed to give the President ample authority in executing the law in South Carolina, was taken up. After a short but acrimonious debate, both measures were passed and signed by President Jackson on the same day, March 2. Looking upon the reduction of the tariff as a complete vindication of her policy and an undoubted victory, South Carolina rescinded her ordinance and enacted another nullifying the force bill.

The Webster-Hayne Debate.—Where the actual victory lay in this quarrel, long the subject of high dispute, need not concern us to-day. Perhaps the chief result of the whole affair was a clarification of the issue between the North and the South—a definite statement of the principles for which men on both sides were years afterward to lay down their lives. On behalf of nationalism and a perpetual union, the stanch old Democrat from Tennessee had, in his proclamation on nullification, spoken a language that admitted of only one meaning. On behalf of nullification, Senator Hayne, of South Carolina, a skilled lawyer and courtly orator, had in a great speech delivered in the Senate in January, 1830, set forth clearly and cogently the doctrine that the union is a compact among sovereign states from which the parties may lawfully withdraw. It was this address that called into the arena Daniel Webster, Senator from Massachusetts, who, spreading the mantle of oblivion over the Hartford convention, delivered a reply to Hayne that has been reckoned among the powerful orations of all time—a plea for the supremacy of the Constitution and the national character of the union.

The War on the United States Bank.—If events forced the issue of nationalism and nullification upon Jackson, the same could not be said of his attack on the bank. That institution, once denounced by every true Jeffersonian, had been reëstablished in 1816 under the administration of Jefferson's disciple, James Madison. It had not been in operation very long, however, before it aroused bitter opposition, especially in the South and the West. Its notes drove out of circulation the paper currency of unsound banks chartered by the states, to the great anger of local financiers. It was accused of favoritism in making loans, of conferring special privileges upon politicians in return for their support at Washington. To all Jackson's followers it was "an insidious money power." One of them openly denounced it as an institution designed "to strengthen the arm of wealth and counterpoise the influence of extended suffrage in the disposition of public affairs."

This sentiment President Jackson fully shared. In his first message to Congress he assailed the bank in vigorous language. He declared that its constitutionality was in doubt and alleged that it had failed to establish a sound and uniform currency. If such an institution was necessary, he continued, it should be a public bank, owned and managed by the government, not a private concern endowed with special privileges by it. In his second and third messages, Jackson came back to the subject, leaving the decision, however, to "an enlightened people and their representatives."

Moved by this frank hostility and anxious for the future, the bank applied to Congress for a renewal of its charter in 1832, four years before the expiration of its life. Clay, with his eye upon the presidency and an issue for the campaign, warmly supported the application. Congress, deeply impressed by his leadership, passed the bill granting the new charter, and sent the open defiance to Jackson. His response was an instant veto. The battle was on and it raged with fury until the close of his second administration, ending in the destruction of the bank, a disordered currency, and a national panic.

In his veto message, Jackson attacked the bank as unconstitutional and even hinted at corruption. He refused to assent to the proposition that the Supreme Court had settled the question of constitutionality by the decision in the McCulloch case. "Each public officer," he argued, "who takes an oath to support the Constitution, swears that he will support it as he understands it, not as it is understood by others."

Not satisfied with his veto and his declaration against the bank, Jackson ordered the Secretary of the Treasury to withdraw the government deposits which formed a large part of the institution's funds. This action he followed up by an open charge that the bank had used money shamefully to secure the return of its supporters to Congress. The Senate, stung by this charge, solemnly resolved that Jackson had "assumed upon himself authority and power not conferred by the Constitution and laws, but in derogation of both."

The effects of the destruction of the bank were widespread. When its charter expired in 1836, banking was once more committed to the control of the states. The state legislatures, under a decision rendered by the Supreme Court after the death of Marshall, began to charter banks under state ownership and control, with full power to issue paper money—this in spite of the provision in the Constitution that states shall not issue bills of credit or make anything but gold and silver coin legal tender in the payment of debts. Once more the country was flooded by paper currency of uncertain value. To make matters worse, Jackson adopted the practice of depositing huge amounts of government funds in these banks, not forgetting to render favors to those institutions which supported him in politics—"pet banks," as they were styled at the time. In 1837, partially, though by no means entirely, as a result of the abolition of the bank, the country was plunged into one of the most disastrous panics which it ever experienced.

Internal Improvements Checked.—The bank had presented to Jackson a very clear problem—one of destruction. Other questions were not so simple, particularly the subject of federal appropriations in aid of roads and other internal improvements. Jefferson had strongly favored government assistance in such matters, but his administration was followed by a reaction. Both Madison and Monroe vetoed acts of Congress appropriating public funds for public roads, advancing as their reason the argument that the Constitution authorized no such laws. Jackson, puzzled by the clamor on both sides, followed their example without making the constitutional bar absolute. Congress, he thought, might lawfully build highways of a national and military value, but he strongly deprecated attacks by local interests on the federal treasury.

The Triumph of the Executive Branch.—Jackson's reëlection in 1832 served to confirm his opinion that he was the chosen leader of the people, freed and instructed to ride rough shod over Congress and even the courts. No President before or since ever entertained in times of peace such lofty notions of executive prerogative. The entire body of federal employees he transformed into obedient servants of his wishes, a sign or a nod from him making and undoing the fortunes of the humble and the mighty. His lawful cabinet of advisers, filling all of the high posts in the government, he treated with scant courtesy, preferring rather to secure his counsel and advice from an unofficial body of friends and dependents who, owing to their secret methods and back stairs arrangements, became known as "the kitchen cabinet." Under the leadership of a silent, astute, and resourceful politician, Amos Kendall, this informal gathering of the faithful both gave and carried out decrees and orders, communicating the President's lightest wish or strictest command to the uttermost part of the country. Resolutely and in the face of bitter opposition Jackson had removed the deposits from the United States Bank. When the Senate protested against this arbitrary conduct, he did not rest until it was forced to expunge the resolution of condemnation; in time one of his lieutenants with his own hands was able to tear the censure from the records. When Chief Justice Marshall issued a decree against Georgia which did not suit him, Jackson, according to tradition, blurted out that Marshall could go ahead and enforce his own orders. To the end he pursued his willful way, finally even choosing his own successor.

THE RISE OF THE WHIGS

Jackson's Measures Arouse Opposition.—Measures so decided, policies so radical, and conduct so high-handed could not fail to arouse against Jackson a deep and exasperated opposition. The truth is the conduct of his entire administration profoundly disturbed the business and finances of the country. It was accompanied by conditions similar to those which existed under the Articles of Confederation. A paper currency, almost as unstable and irritating as the worthless notes of revolutionary days, flooded the country, hindering the easy transaction of business. The use of federal funds for internal improvements, so vital to the exchange of commodities which is the very life of industry, was blocked by executive vetoes. The Supreme Court, which, under Marshall, had held refractory states to their obligations under the Constitution, was flouted; states' rights judges, deliberately selected by Jackson for the bench, began to sap and undermine the rulings of Marshall. The protective tariff, under which the textile industry of New England, the iron mills of Pennsylvania, and the wool, flax, and hemp farms of the West had flourished, had received a severe blow in the compromise of 1833 which promised a steady reduction of duties. To cap the climax, Jackson's party, casting aside the old and reputable name of Republican, boldly chose for its title the term "Democrat," throwing down the gauntlet to every conservative who doubted the omniscience of the people. All these things worked together to evoke an opposition that was sharp and determined.

Clay and the National Republicans.—In this opposition movement, leadership fell to Henry Clay, a son of Kentucky, rather than to Daniel Webster of Massachusetts. Like Jackson, Clay was born in a home haunted by poverty. Left fatherless early and thrown upon his own resources, he went from Virginia into Kentucky where by sheer force of intellect he rose to eminence in the profession of law. Without the martial gifts or the martial spirit of Jackson, he slipped more easily into the social habits of the East at the same time that he retained his hold on the affections of the boisterous West. Farmers of Ohio, Indiana, and Kentucky loved him; financiers of New York and Philadelphia trusted him. He was thus a leader well fitted to gather the forces of opposition into union against Jackson.

Around Clay's standard assembled a motley collection, representing every species of political opinion, united by one tie only—hatred for "Old Hickory." Nullifiers and less strenuous advocates of states' rights were yoked with nationalists of Webster's school; ardent protectionists were bound together with equally ardent free traders, all fraternizing in one grand confusion of ideas under the title of "National Republicans." Thus the ancient and honorable term selected by Jefferson and his party, now abandoned by Jacksonian Democracy, was adroitly adopted to cover the supporters of Clay. The platform of the party, however, embraced all the old Federalist principles: protection for American industry; internal improvements; respect for the Supreme Court; resistance to executive tyranny; and denunciation of the spoils system. Though Jackson was easily victorious in 1832, the popular vote cast for Clay should have given him some doubts about the faith of "the whole people" in the wisdom of his "reign."

Van Buren and the Panic of 1837.—Nothing could shake the General's superb confidence. At the end of his second term he insisted on selecting his own successor; at a national convention, chosen by party voters, but packed with his office holders and friends, he nominated Martin Van Buren of New York. Once more he proved his strength by carrying the country for the Democrats. With a fine flourish, he attended the inauguration of Van Buren and then retired, amid the applause and tears of his devotees, to the Hermitage, his home in Tennessee.

Fortunately for him, Jackson escaped the odium of a disastrous panic which struck the country with terrible force in the following summer. Among the contributory causes of this crisis, no doubt, were the destruction of the bank and the issuance of the "specie circular" of 1836 which required the purchasers of public lands to pay for them in coin, instead of the paper notes of state banks. Whatever the dominating cause, the ruin was widespread. Bank after bank went under; boom towns in the West collapsed; Eastern mills shut down; and working people in the industrial centers, starving from unemployment, begged for relief. Van Buren braved the storm, offering no measure of reform or assistance to the distracted people. He did seek security for government funds by suggesting the removal of deposits from private banks and the establishment of an independent treasury system, with government depositaries for public funds, in several leading cities. This plan was finally accepted by Congress in 1840.

Had Van Buren been a captivating figure he might have lived down the discredit of the panic unjustly laid at his door; but he was far from being a favorite with the populace. Though a man of many talents, he owed his position to the quiet and adept management of Jackson rather than to his own personal qualities. The men of the frontier did not care for him. They suspected that he ate from "gold plate" and they could not forgive him for being an astute politician from New York. Still the Democratic party, remembering Jackson's wishes, renominated him unanimously in 1840 and saw him go down to utter defeat.

The Whigs and General Harrison.—By this time, the National Republicans, now known as Whigs—a title taken from the party of opposition to the Crown in England, had learned many lessons. Taking a leaf out of the Democratic book, they nominated, not Clay of Kentucky, well known for his views on the bank, the tariff, and internal improvements, but a military hero, General William Henry Harrison, a man of uncertain political opinions. Harrison, a son of a Virginia signer of the Declaration of Independence, sprang into public view by winning a battle more famous than important, "Tippecanoe"—a brush with the Indians in Indiana. He added to his laurels by rendering praiseworthy services during the war of 1812. When days of peace returned he was rewarded by a grateful people with a seat in Congress. Then he retired to quiet life in a little village near Cincinnati. Like Jackson he was held to be a son of the South and the West. Like Jackson he was a military hero, a lesser light, but still a light. Like Old Hickory he rode into office on a tide of popular feeling against an Eastern man accused of being something of an aristocrat. His personal popularity was sufficient. The Whigs who nominated him shrewdly refused to adopt a platform or declare their belief in anything. When some Democrat asserted that Harrison was a backwoodsman whose sole wants were a jug of hard cider and a log cabin, the Whigs treated the remark not as an insult but as proof positive that Harrison deserved the votes of Jackson men. The jug and the cabin they proudly transformed into symbols of the campaign, and won for their chieftain 234 electoral votes, while Van Buren got only sixty.

Harrison and Tyler.—The Hero of Tippecanoe was not long to enjoy the fruits of his victory. The hungry horde of Whig office seekers descended upon him like wolves upon the fold. If he went out they waylaid him; if he stayed indoors, he was besieged; not even his bed chamber was spared. He was none too strong at best and he took a deep cold on the day of his inauguration. Between driving out Democrats and appeasing Whigs, he fell mortally ill. Before the end of a month he lay dead at the capitol.

Harrison's successor, John Tyler, the Vice President, whom the Whigs had nominated to catch votes in Virginia, was more of a Democrat than anything else, though he was not partisan enough to please anybody. The Whigs railed at him because he would not approve the founding of another United States Bank. The Democrats stormed at him for refusing, until near the end of his term, to sanction the annexation of Texas, which had declared its independence of Mexico in 1836. His entire administration, marked by unseemly wrangling, produced only two measures of importance. The Whigs, flushed by victory, with the aid of a few protectionist Democrats, enacted, in 1842, a new tariff law destroying the compromise which had brought about the truce between the North and the South, in the days of nullification. The distinguished leader of the Whigs, Daniel Webster, as Secretary of State, in negotiation with Lord Ashburton representing Great Britain, settled the long-standing dispute between the two countries over the Maine boundary. A year after closing this chapter in American diplomacy, Webster withdrew to private life, leaving the President to endure alone the buffets of political fortune.

To the end, the Whigs regarded Tyler as a traitor to their cause; but the judgment of history is that it was a case of the biter bitten. They had nominated him for the vice presidency as a man of views acceptable to Southern Democrats in order to catch their votes, little reckoning with the chances of his becoming President. Tyler had not deceived them and, thoroughly soured, he left the White House in 1845 not to appear in public life again until the days of secession, when he espoused the Southern confederacy. Jacksonian Democracy, with new leadership, serving a new cause—slavery—was returned to power under James K. Polk, a friend of the General from Tennessee. A few grains of sand were to run through the hour glass before the Whig party was to be broken and scattered as the Federalists had been more than a generation before.

THE INTERACTION OF AMERICAN AND EUROPEAN OPINION

Democracy in England and France.—During the period of Jacksonian Democracy, as in all epochs of ferment, there was a close relation between the thought of the New World and the Old. In England, the successes of the American experiment were used as arguments in favor of overthrowing the aristocracy which George III had manipulated with such effect against America half a century before. In the United States, on the other hand, conservatives like Chancellor Kent, the stout opponent of manhood suffrage in New York, cited the riots of the British working classes as a warning against admitting the same classes to a share in the government of the United States. Along with the agitation of opinion went epoch-making events. In 1832, the year of Jackson's second triumph, the British Parliament passed its first reform bill, which conferred the ballot—not on workingmen as yet—but on mill owners and shopkeepers whom the landlords regarded with genuine horror. The initial step was thus taken in breaking down the privileges of the landed aristocracy and the rich merchants of England.

About the same time a popular revolution occurred in France. The Bourbon family, restored to the throne of France by the allied powers after their victory over Napoleon in 1815, had embarked upon a policy of arbitrary government. To use the familiar phrase, they had learned nothing and forgotten nothing. Charles X, who came to the throne in 1824, set to work with zeal to undo the results of the French Revolution, to stifle the press, restrict the suffrage, and restore the clergy and the nobility to their ancient rights. His policy encountered equally zealous opposition and in 1830 he was overthrown. The popular party, under the leadership of Lafayette, established, not a republic as some of the radicals had hoped, but a "liberal" middle-class monarchy under Louis Philippe. This second French Revolution made a profound impression on Americans, convincing them that the whole world was moving toward democracy. The mayor, aldermen, and citizens of New York City joined in a great parade to celebrate the fall of the Bourbons. Mingled with cheers for the new order in France were hurrahs for "the people's own, Andrew Jackson, the Hero of New Orleans and President of the United States!"

European Interest in America.—To the older and more settled Europeans, the democratic experiment in America was either a menace or an inspiration. Conservatives viewed it with anxiety; liberals with optimism. Far-sighted leaders could see that the tide of democracy was rising all over the world and could not be stayed. Naturally the country that had advanced furthest along the new course was the place in which to find arguments for and against proposals that Europe should make experiments of the same character.

De Tocqueville's *Democracy in America*.—In addition to the casual traveler there began to visit the United States the thoughtful observer bent on finding out what manner of nation this was springing up in the wilderness. Those who looked with sympathy upon the growing popular forces of England and France found in the United States, in spite of many blemishes and defects, a guarantee for the future of the people's rule in the Old World. One of these, Alexis de Tocqueville, a French liberal of mildly democratic sympathies, made a journey to this country in 1831; he described in a very remarkable volume, *Democracy in America*, the grand experiment as he saw it. On the whole he was convinced. After examining with a critical eye the life and labor of the American people, as well as the constitutions of the states and the nation, he came to the conclusion that democracy with all its faults was both inevitable and successful. Slavery he thought was a painful contrast to the other features of American life, and he foresaw what proved to be the irrepressible conflict over it. He believed that through blundering the people were destined to learn the highest of all arts, self-government on a grand scale. The absence of a leisure class, devoted to no calling or profession, merely enjoying the refinements of life and adding to its graces—the flaw in American culture that gave deep distress to many a European leader—de Tocqueville thought a necessary virtue in the republic. "Amongst a democratic people where there is no hereditary wealth, every man works to earn a living, or has worked, or is born of parents who have worked. A notion of labor is therefore presented to the mind on every side as the necessary, natural, and honest condition of human existence." It was this notion of a government in the hands of people who labored that struck the French publicist as the most significant fact in the modern world.

Harriet Martineau's Visit to America.—This phase of American life also profoundly impressed the brilliant English writer, Harriet Martineau. She saw all parts of the country, the homes of the rich and the log cabins of the frontier; she traveled in stagecoaches, canal boats, and on horseback; and visited sessions of Congress and auctions at slave markets. She tried to view the country impartially and the thing that left the deepest mark on her mind was the solidarity of the people in one great political body. "However various may be the tribes of inhabitants in those states, whatever part of the world may have been their birthplace, or that of their fathers, however broken may be their language, however servile or noble their employments, however exalted or despised their state, all are declared to be bound together by equal political obligations.... In that self-governing country all are held to have an equal interest in the principles of its institutions and to be bound in equal duty to watch their workings." Miss Martineau was also impressed with the passion of Americans for land ownership and contrasted the United States favorably with England where the tillers of the soil were either tenants or laborers for wages.

Adverse Criticism.—By no means all observers and writers were convinced that America was a success. The fastidious traveler, Mrs. Trollope, who thought the English system of church and state was ideal, saw in the United States only roughness and ignorance. She lamented the "total and universal want of manners both in males and females," adding that while "they appear to have clear heads and active intellects," there was "no charm, no grace in their conversation." She found everywhere a lack of reverence for kings, learning, and rank. Other critics were even more savage. The editor of the *Foreign Quarterly* petulantly exclaimed that the United States was "a brigand confederation." Charles Dickens declared the country to be "so maimed and lame, so full of sores and ulcers that her best friends turn from the loathsome creature in disgust." Sydney Smith, editor of the *Edinburgh Review*, was never tired of trying his caustic wit at the expense of America. "Their Franklins and Washingtons and all the other sages and heroes of their revolution were born and bred subjects of the king of England," he observed in 1820. "During the thirty or forty years of their independence they have done absolutely nothing for the sciences, for the arts, for literature, or even for the statesmanlike studies of politics or political economy.... In the four quarters of the globe who reads an American book? Or goes to an American play? Or looks at an American picture or statue?" To put a sharp sting into his taunt he added, forgetting by whose authority slavery was introduced and fostered: "Under which of the old tyrannical governments of Europe is every sixth man a slave whom his fellow creatures may buy and sell?"

Some Americans, while resenting the hasty and often superficial judgments of European writers, winced under their satire and took thought about certain particulars in the indictments brought against them. The mass of the people, however, bent on the great experiment, gave little heed to carping critics who saw the flaws and not the achievements of our country—critics who were in fact less interested in America than in preventing the rise and growth of democracy in Europe.

References

J.S. Bassett, *Life of Andrew Jackson*.

J.W. Burgess, *The Middle Period*.

H. Lodge, *Daniel Webster*.

W. Macdonald, *Jacksonian Democracy* (American Nation Series).

Ostrogorski, *Democracy and the Organization of Political Parties*, Vol. II.

C.H. Peck, *The Jacksonian Epoch*.

C. Schurz, *Henry Clay*.

Questions

1. By what devices was democracy limited in the first days of our Republic?

2. On what grounds were the limitations defended? Attacked?

3. Outline the rise of political democracy in the United States.

4. Describe three important changes in our political system.

5. Contrast the Presidents of the old and the new generations.

6. Account for the unpopularity of John Adams' administration.

7. What had been the career of Andrew Jackson before 1829?

8. Sketch the history of the protective tariff and explain the theory underlying it.

9. Explain the growth of Southern opposition to the tariff.

10. Relate the leading events connected with nullification in South Carolina.

11. State Jackson's views and tell the outcome of the controversy.

12. Why was Jackson opposed to the bank? How did he finally destroy it?

13. The Whigs complained of Jackson's "executive tyranny." What did they mean?

14. Give some of the leading events in Clay's career.

15. How do you account for the triumph of Harrison in 1840?

16. Why was Europe especially interested in America at this period? Who were some of the European writers on American affairs?

Research Topics

Jackson's Criticisms of the Bank.—Macdonald, *Documentary Source Book*, pp. 320-329.

Financial Aspects of the Bank Controversy.—Dewey, *Financial History of the United States*, Sections 86-87; Elson, *History of the United States*, pp. 492-496.

Jackson's View of the Union.—See his proclamation on nullification in Macdonald, pp. 333-340.

Nullification.—McMaster, *History of the People of the United States*, Vol. VI, pp. 153-182; Elson, pp. 487-492.

The Webster-Hayne Debate.—Analyze the arguments. Extensive extracts are given in Macdonald's larger three-volume work, *Select Documents of United States History, 1776-1761*, pp. 239-260.

The Character of Jackson's Administration.—Woodrow Wilson, *History of the American People*, Vol. IV, pp. 1-87; Elson, pp. 498-501.

The People in 1830.—From contemporary writings in Hart, *American History Told by Contemporaries*, Vol. III, pp. 509-530.

Biographical Studies.—Andrew Jackson, J.Q. Adams, Henry Clay, Daniel Webster, J.C. Calhoun, and W.H. Harrison.

CHAPTER XII

THE MIDDLE BORDER AND THE GREAT WEST

"We shall not send an emigrant beyond the Mississippi in a hundred years," exclaimed Livingston, the principal author of the Louisiana purchase. When he made this astounding declaration, he doubtless had before his mind's eye the great stretches of unoccupied lands between the Appalachians and the Mississippi. He also had before him the history of the English colonies, which told him of the two centuries required to settle the seaboard region. To practical men, his prophecy did not seem far wrong; but before the lapse of half that time there appeared beyond the Mississippi a tier of new states, reaching from the Gulf of Mexico to the southern boundary of Minnesota, and a new commonwealth on the Pacific Ocean where American emigrants had raised the Bear flag of California.

THE ADVANCE OF THE MIDDLE BORDER

Missouri.—When the middle of the nineteenth century had been reached, the Mississippi River, which Daniel Boone, the intrepid hunter, had crossed during Washington's administration "to escape from civilization" in Kentucky, had become the waterway for a vast empire. The center of population of the United States had passed to the Ohio Valley. Missouri, with its wide reaches of rich lands, low-lying, level, and fertile, well adapted to hemp raising, had drawn to its borders thousands of planters from the old Southern states—from Virginia and the Carolinas as well as from Kentucky and Tennessee. When the great compromise of 1820-21 admitted her to the union, wearing "every jewel of sovereignty," as a florid orator announced, migratory slave owners were assured that their property would be safe in Missouri. Along the western shore of the Mississippi and on both banks of the Missouri to the uttermost limits of the state, plantations tilled by bondmen spread out in broad expanses. In the neighborhood of Jefferson City the slaves numbered more than a fourth of the population.

Into this stream of migration from the planting South flowed another current of land-tilling farmers; some from Kentucky, Tennessee, and Mississippi, driven out by the onrush of the planters buying and consolidating small farms into vast estates; and still more from the East and the Old World. To the northwest over against Iowa and to the southwest against Arkansas, these yeomen laid out farms to be tilled by their own labor. In those regions the number of slaves seldom rose above five or six per cent of the population. The old French post, St. Louis, enriched by the fur trade of the Far West and the steamboat traffic of the river, grew into a thriving commercial city, including among its seventy-five thousand inhabitants in 1850 nearly forty thousand foreigners, German immigrants from Pennsylvania and Europe being the largest single element.

Arkansas.—Below Missouri lay the territory of Arkansas, which had long been the paradise of the swarthy hunter and the restless frontiersman fleeing from the advancing borders of farm and town. In search of the life, wild and free, where the rifle supplied the game and a few acres of ground the corn and potatoes, they had filtered into the territory in an unending drift, "squatting" on the land. Without so much as asking the leave of any government, territorial or national, they claimed as their own the soil on which they first planted their feet. Like the Cherokee Indians, whom they had as neighbors, whose very customs and dress they sometimes adopted, the squatters spent their days in the midst of rough plenty, beset by chills, fevers, and the ills of the flesh, but for many years unvexed by political troubles or the restrictions of civilized life.

Unfortunately for them, however, the fertile valleys of the Mississippi and Arkansas were well adapted to the cultivation of cotton and tobacco and their sylvan peace was soon broken by an invasion of planters. The newcomers, with their servile workers, spread upward in the valley toward Missouri and along the southern border westward to the Red River. In time the slaves in the tier of counties against Louisiana ranged from thirty to seventy per cent of the population. This marked the doom of the small farmer, swept

Arkansas into the main current of planting politics, and led to a powerful lobby at Washington in favor of admission to the union, a boon granted in 1836.

Michigan.—In accordance with a well-established custom, a free state was admitted to the union to balance a slave state. In 1833, the people of Michigan, a territory ten times the size of Connecticut, announced that the time had come for them to enjoy the privileges of a commonwealth. All along the southern border the land had been occupied largely by pioneers from New England, who built prim farmhouses and adopted the town-meeting plan of self-government after the fashion of the old home. The famous post of Detroit was growing into a flourishing city as the boats plying on the Great Lakes carried travelers, settlers, and freight through the narrows. In all, according to the census, there were more than ninety thousand inhabitants in the territory; so it was not without warrant that they clamored for statehood. Congress, busy as ever with politics, delayed; and the inhabitants of Michigan, unable to restrain their impatience, called a convention, drew up a constitution, and started a lively quarrel with Ohio over the southern boundary. The hand of Congress was now forced. Objections were made to the new constitution on the ground that it gave the ballot to all free white males, including aliens not yet naturalized; but the protests were overborne in a long debate. The boundary was fixed, and Michigan, though shorn of some of the land she claimed, came into the union in 1837.

Wisconsin.—Across Lake Michigan to the west lay the territory of Wisconsin, which shared with Michigan the interesting history of the Northwest, running back into the heroic days when French hunters and missionaries were planning a French empire for the great monarch, Louis XIV. It will not be forgotten that the French rangers of the woods, the black-robed priests, prepared for sacrifice, even to death, the trappers of the French agencies, and the French explorers—Marquette, Joliet, and Menard— were the first white men to paddle their frail barks through the northern waters. They first blazed their trails into the black forests and left traces of their work in the names of portages and little villages. It was from these forests that Red Men in full war paint journeyed far to fight under the *fleur-de-lis* of France when the soldiers of King Louis made their last stand at Quebec and Montreal against the imperial arms of Britain. It was here that the British flag was planted in 1761 and that the great Pontiac conspiracy was formed two years later to overthrow British dominion.

When, a generation afterward, the Stars and Stripes supplanted the Union Jack, the French were still almost the only white men in the region. They were soon joined by hustling Yankee fur traders who did battle royal against British interlopers. The traders cut their way through forest trails and laid out the routes through lake and stream and over portages for the settlers and their families from the states "back East." It was the forest ranger who discovered the water power later used to turn the busy mills grinding the grain from the spreading farm lands. In the wake of the fur hunters, forest men, and farmers came miners from Kentucky, Tennessee, and Missouri crowding in to exploit the lead ores of the northwest, some of them bringing slaves to work their claims. Had it not been for the gold fever of 1849 that drew the wielders of pick and shovel to the Far West, Wisconsin would early have taken high rank among the mining regions of the country.

From a favorable point of vantage on Lake Michigan, the village of Milwaukee, a center for lumber and grain transport and a place of entry for Eastern goods, grew into a thriving city. It claimed twenty thousand inhabitants, when in 1848 Congress admitted Wisconsin to the union. Already the Germans, Irish, and Scandinavians had found their way into the territory. They joined Americans from the older states in clearing forests, building roads, transforming trails into highways, erecting mills, and connecting streams with canals to make a network of routes for the traffic that poured to and from the Great Lakes.

Iowa and Minnesota.—To the southwest of Wisconsin beyond the Mississippi, where the tall grass of the prairies waved like the sea, farmers from New England, New York, and Ohio had prepared Iowa for statehood. A tide of immigration that might have flowed into Missouri went northward; for freemen, unaccustomed to slavery and slave markets, preferred the open country above the compromise line. With incredible swiftness, they spread farms westward from the Mississippi. With Yankee ingenuity they turned to trading on the river, building before 1836 three prosperous centers of traffic: Dubuque, Davenport, and Burlington. True to their old traditions, they founded colleges and academies that religion and learning might be cherished on the frontier as in the states from which they came. Prepared for self-government, the Iowans laid siege to the door of Congress and were admitted to the union in 1846.

Above Iowa, on the Mississippi, lay the territory of Minnesota—the home of the Dakotas, the Ojibways, and the Sioux. Like Michigan and Wisconsin, it had been explored early by the French scouts, and the first white settlement was the little French village of Mendota. To the people of the United States, the resources of the country were first revealed by the historic journey of Zebulon Pike in 1805 and by American fur traders who were quick to take advantage of the opportunity to ply their arts of hunting and bartering in fresh fields. In 1839 an American settlement was planted at Marina on the St. Croix, the outpost of advancing civilization. Within twenty years, the territory, boasting a population of 150,000, asked for admission to the union. In 1858 the plea was granted and Minnesota showed her gratitude three years later by being first among the states to offer troops to Lincoln in the hour of peril.

ON TO THE PACIFIC—TEXAS AND THE MEXICAN WAR

The Uniformity of the Middle West.—There was a certain monotony about pioneering in the Northwest and on the middle border. As the long stretches of land were cleared or prepared for the plow, they were laid out like checkerboards into squares of forty, eighty, one hundred sixty, or more acres, each the seat of a homestead. There was a striking uniformity also about the endless succession of fertile fields spreading far and wide under the hot summer sun. No majestic mountains relieved the sweep of the prairie. Few monuments of other races and antiquity were there to awaken curiosity about the region. No sonorous bells in old missions rang out the time of day. The chaffering Red Man bartering blankets and furs for powder and whisky had passed farther on. The population was made up of plain farmers and their families engaged in severe and unbroken labor, chopping down trees, draining fever-breeding swamps, breaking new ground, and planting from year to year the same rotation of crops. Nearly all the settlers were of native American stock into whose frugal and industrious lives the later Irish and German immigrants fitted, on the whole, with little friction. Even the Dutch oven fell before the cast-iron cooking stove. Happiness and sorrow, despair and hope were there, but all encompassed by the heavy tedium of prosaic sameness.

A Contrast in the Far West and Southwest.—As George Rogers Clark and Daniel Boone had stirred the snug Americans of the seaboard to seek their fortunes beyond the Appalachians, so now Kit Carson, James Bowie, Sam Houston, Davy Crockett, and John C. Frémont were to lead the way into a new land, only a part of which was under the American flag. The setting for this new scene in the westward movement was thrown out in a wide sweep from the headwaters of the Mississippi to the banks of the Rio Grande; from the valleys of the Sabine and Red rivers to Montana and the Pacific slope. In comparison with the middle border, this region presented such startling diversities that only the eye of faith could foresee the unifying power of nationalism binding its communities with the older sections of the country. What contrasts indeed! The blue grass region of Kentucky or the rich, black soil of Illinois—the painted desert, the home of the sage brush and the coyote! The level prairies of Iowa—the mighty Rockies shouldering themselves high against the horizon! The long bleak winters of Wisconsin—California of endless summer! The log churches of Indiana or Illinois—the quaint missions of San Antonio, Tucson, and Santa Barbara! The little state of Delaware—the empire of Texas, one hundred and twenty times its area! And scattered about through the Southwest were signs of an ancient civilization—fragments of four- and five-story dwellings, ruined dams, aqueducts, and broken canals, which told of once prosperous peoples who, by art and science, had conquered the aridity of the desert and lifted themselves in the scale of culture above the savages of the plain.

The settlers of this vast empire were to be as diverse in their origins and habits as those of the colonies on the coast had been. Americans of English, Irish, and Scotch-Irish descent came as usual from the Eastern states. To them were added the migratory Germans as well. Now for the first time came throngs of Scandinavians. Some were to make their homes on quiet farms as the border advanced against the setting sun. Others were to be Indian scouts, trappers, fur hunters, miners, cowboys, Texas planters, keepers of lonely posts on the plain and the desert, stage drivers, pilots of wagon trains, pony riders, fruit growers, "lumber jacks," and smelter workers. One common bond united them—a passion for the self-government accorded to states. As soon as a few thousand settlers came together in a single territory, there arose a mighty shout for a position beside the staid commonwealths of the East and the South. Statehood meant to the pioneers self-government, dignity, and the right to dispose of land, minerals, and timber in their own way. In the quest for this local autonomy there arose many a wordy contest in Congress, each of the political parties lending a helping hand in the admission of a state when it gave promise of adding new congressmen of the "right political persuasion," to use the current phrase.

Southern Planters and Texas.—While the farmers of the North found the broad acres of the Western prairies stretching on before them apparently in endless expanse, it was far different with the Southern planters. Ever active in their search for new fields as they exhausted the virgin soil of the older states, the restless subjects of King Cotton quickly reached the frontier of Louisiana. There they paused; but only for a moment. The fertile land of Texas just across the boundary lured them on and the Mexican republic to which it belonged extended to them a more than generous welcome. Little realizing the perils lurking in a "peaceful penetration," the authorities at Mexico City opened wide the doors and made large grants of land to American contractors, who agreed to bring a number of families into Texas. The omnipresent Yankee, in the person of Moses Austin of Connecticut, hearing of this good news in the Southwest, obtained a grant in 1820 to settle three hundred Americans near Bexar—a commission finally carried out to the letter by his son and celebrated in the name given to the present capital of the state of Texas. Within a decade some twenty thousand Americans had crossed the border.

Mexico Closes the Door.—The government of Mexico, unaccustomed to such enterprise and thoroughly frightened by its extent, drew back in dismay. Its fears were increased as quarrels broke out between the Americans and the natives in Texas. Fear grew into consternation when efforts were made by President Jackson to buy the territory for the United States. Mexico then sought to close the flood gates. It stopped all American colonization schemes, canceled many of the land grants, put a tariff on farming implements, and abolished slavery. These barriers were raised too late. A call for help ran through the western border of the United States. The sentinels of the frontier answered. Davy Crockett, the noted frontiersman, bear hunter, and backwoods politician; James Bowie, the dexterous wielder of the knife that to this day bears his name; and Sam Houston, warrior and pioneer, rushed to the aid of their countrymen in Texas. Unacquainted with the niceties of diplomacy, impatient at the formalities of international law, they soon made it known that in spite of Mexican sovereignty they would be their own masters.

The Independence of Texas Declared.—Numbering only about one-fourth of the population in Texas, they raised the standard of revolt in 1836 and summoned a convention. Following in the footsteps of their ancestors, they issued a declaration of independence signed mainly by Americans from the slave states. Anticipating that the government of Mexico would not quietly accept their word of defiance as final, they dispatched a force to repel "the invading army," as General Houston called the troops advancing under the command of Santa Ana, the Mexican president. A portion of the Texan soldiers took their stand in the Alamo, an old Spanish mission in the cottonwood trees in the town of San Antonio. Instead of obeying the order to blow up the mission and retire, they held their ground until they were completely surrounded and cut off from all help. Refusing to surrender, they fought to the bitter end, the last man falling a victim to the sword. Vengeance was swift. Within three months General Houston overwhelmed Santa Ana at the San Jacinto, taking him prisoner of war and putting an end to all hopes for the restoration of Mexican sovereignty over Texas.

The Lone Star Republic, with Houston at the head, then sought admission to the United States. This seemed at first an easy matter. All that was required to bring it about appeared to be a treaty annexing Texas to the union. Moreover, President Jackson, at the height of his popularity, had a warm regard for General Houston and, with his usual sympathy for rough and ready ways of doing things, approved the transaction. Through an American representative in Mexico, Jackson had long and anxiously labored, by means none too nice, to wring from the Mexican republic the cession of the coveted territory. When the Texans took matters into their own hands, he was more than pleased; but he could not marshal the approval of two-thirds of the Senators required for a treaty of annexation. Cautious as well as impetuous, Jackson did not press the issue; he went out of office in 1837 with Texas uncertain as to her future.

Northern Opposition to Annexation.—All through the North the opposition to annexation was clear and strong. Anti-slavery agitators could hardly find words savage enough to express their feelings. "Texas," exclaimed Channing in a letter to Clay, "is but the first step of aggression. I trust indeed that Providence will beat back and humble our cupidity and ambition. I now ask whether as a people we are prepared to seize on a neighboring territory for the end of extending slavery? I ask whether as a people we can stand forth in the sight of God, in the sight of nations, and adopt this atrocious policy? Sooner perish! Sooner be our name blotted out from the record of nations!" William Lloyd Garrison called for the secession of the Northern states if Texas was brought into the union with slavery. John Quincy Adams warned his countrymen that they were treading in the path of the imperialism that had brought the nations of antiquity to judgment and destruction. Henry Clay, the Whig candidate for President, taking into account changing public sentiment, blew hot and cold, losing the state of New York and the election of 1844 by giving a qualified approval of annexation. In the same campaign, the Democrats boldly demanded the "Reannexation of Texas," based on claims which the United States once had to Spanish territory beyond the Sabine River.

Annexation.—The politicians were disposed to walk very warily. Van Buren, at heart opposed to slavery extension, refused to press the issue of annexation. Tyler, a pro-slavery Democrat from Virginia, by a strange fling of fortune carried into office as a nominal Whig, kept his mind firmly fixed on the idea of reëlection and let the troublesome matter rest until the end of his administration was in sight. He then listened with favor to the voice of the South. Calhoun stated what seemed to be a convincing argument: All good Americans have their hearts set on the Constitution; the admission of Texas is absolutely essential to the preservation of the union; it will give a balance of power to the South as against the North growing with incredible swiftness in wealth and population. Tyler, impressed by the plea, appointed Calhoun to the office of Secretary of State in 1844, authorizing him to negotiate the treaty of annexation—a commission at once executed. This scheme was blocked in the Senate where the necessary two-thirds vote could not be secured. Balked but not defeated, the advocates of annexation drew up a joint resolution which required only a majority vote in both houses, and in February of the next year, just before Tyler gave way to Polk, they pushed it through Congress. So Texas, amid the groans of Boston and the hurrahs of Charleston, folded up her flag and came into the union.

The Mexican War.—The inevitable war with Mexico, foretold by the abolitionists and feared by Henry Clay, ensued, the ostensible cause being a dispute over the boundaries of the new state. The Texans claimed all the lands down to the Rio Grande. The Mexicans placed the border of Texas at the Nueces River and a line drawn thence in a northerly direction. President Polk, accepting the Texan view of the controversy, ordered General Zachary Taylor to move beyond the Nueces in defense of American sovereignty. This act of power, deemed by the Mexicans an invasion of their territory, was followed by an attack on our troops.

President Polk, not displeased with the turn of events, announced that American blood had been "spilled on American soil" and that war existed "by the act of Mexico." Congress, in a burst of patriotic fervor, brushed aside the protests of those who deplored the conduct of the government as wanton aggression on a weaker nation and granted money and supplies to prosecute the war. The few Whigs in the House of Representatives, who refused to vote in favor of taking up arms, accepted the inevitable with such good grace as they could command. All through the South and the West the war was popular. New England grumbled, but gave loyal, if not enthusiastic, support to a conflict precipitated by policies not of its own choosing. Only a handful of firm objectors held out. James Russell Lowell, in his *Biglow Papers*, flung scorn and sarcasm to the bitter end.

The Outcome of the War.—The foregone conclusion was soon reached. General Taylor might have delivered the fatal thrust from northern Mexico if politics had not intervened. Polk, anxious to avoid raising up another military hero for the Whigs to nominate for President, decided to divide the honors by sending General Scott to strike a blow at the capital, Mexico City. The deed was done with speed and pomp and two heroes were lifted into presidential possibilities. In the Far West a third candidate was made, John C. Frémont, who, in coöperation with Commodores Sloat and Stockton and General Kearney, planted the Stars and Stripes on the Pacific slope.

In February, 1848, the Mexicans came to terms, ceding to the victor California, Arizona, New Mexico, and more—a domain greater in extent than the combined areas of France and Germany. As a salve to the wound, the vanquished received fifteen million dollars in cash and the cancellation of many claims held by American citizens. Five years later, through the negotiations of James Gadsden, a further cession of lands along the southern border of Arizona and New Mexico was secured on payment of ten million dollars.

General Taylor Elected President.—The ink was hardly dry upon the treaty that closed the war before "rough and ready" General Taylor, a slave owner from Louisiana, "a Whig," as he said, "but not an ultra Whig," was put forward as the Whig candidate for President. He himself had not voted for years and he was fairly innocent in matters political. The tariff, the currency, and internal improvements, with a magnificent gesture he referred to the people's representatives in Congress, offering to enforce the laws as made, if elected. Clay's followers mourned. Polk stormed but could not win even a renomination at the hands of the Democrats. So it came about that the hero of Buena Vista, celebrated for his laconic order, "Give 'em a little more grape, Captain Bragg," became President of the United States.

THE PACIFIC COAST AND UTAH

Oregon.—Closely associated in the popular mind with the contest about the affairs of Texas was a dispute with Great Britain over the possession of territory in Oregon. In their presidential campaign of 1844, the Democrats had coupled with the slogan, "The Reannexation of Texas," two other cries, "The Reoccupation of Oregon," and "Fifty-four Forty or Fight." The last two slogans were founded on American discoveries and explorations in the Far Northwest. Their appearance in politics showed that the distant Oregon country, larger in area than New England, New York, and Pennsylvania combined, was at last receiving from the nation the attention which its importance warranted.

Joint Occupation and Settlement.—Both England and the United States had long laid claim to Oregon and in 1818 they had agreed to occupy the territory jointly—a contract which was renewed ten years later for an indefinite period. Under this plan, citizens of both countries were free to hunt and settle anywhere in the region. The vanguard of British fur traders and Canadian priests was enlarged by many new recruits, with Americans not far behind them. John Jacob Astor, the resourceful New York merchant, sent out trappers and hunters who established a trading post at Astoria in 1811. Some twenty years later, American missionaries—among them two very remarkable men, Jason Lee and Marcus Whitman—were preaching the gospel to the Indians.

Through news from the fur traders and missionaries, Eastern farmers heard of the fertile lands awaiting their plows on the Pacific slope; those with the pioneering spirit made ready to take possession of the new country. In 1839 a band went around by Cape Horn. Four years later a great expedition went overland. The way once broken, others followed rapidly. As soon as a few settlements were well established, the pioneers held a mass meeting and agreed upon a plan of government. "We, the people of Oregon territory," runs the preamble to their compact, "for the purposes of mutual protection and to secure peace and prosperity among ourselves, agree to adopt the following laws and regulations until such time as the United States of America extend their jurisdiction over us." Thus self-government made its way across the Rocky Mountains.

The Boundary Dispute with England Adjusted.—By this time it was evident that the boundaries of Oregon must be fixed. Having made the question an issue in his campaign, Polk, after his election in 1844, pressed it upon the attention of the country. In his inaugural address and his first message to Congress he reiterated the claim of the Democratic platform that "our title to the whole territory of Oregon is clear and unquestionable." This pretension Great Britain firmly rejected, leaving the President a choice between war and compromise.

Polk, already having the contest with Mexico on his hands, sought and obtained a compromise. The British government, moved by a hint from the American minister, offered a settlement which would fix the boundary at the forty-ninth parallel instead of "fifty-four forty," and give it Vancouver Island. Polk speedily chose this way out of the dilemma. Instead of making the decision himself, however, and drawing up a treaty, he turned to the Senate for "counsel." As prearranged with party leaders, the advice was favorable to the plan. The treaty, duly drawn in 1846, was ratified by the Senate after an acrimonious debate. "Oh! mountain that was delivered of a mouse," exclaimed Senator Benton, "thy name shall be fifty-four forty!" Thirteen years later, the southern part of the territory was admitted to the union as the state of Oregon, leaving the northern and eastern sections in the status of a territory.

California.—With the growth of the northwestern empire, dedicated by nature to freedom, the planting interests might have been content, had fortune not wrested from them the fair country of California. Upon this huge territory they had set their hearts. The mild climate and fertile soil seemed well suited to slavery and the planters expected to extend their sway to the entire domain. California was a state of more than 155,000 square miles—about seventy times the size of the state of Delaware. It could readily be divided into five or six large states, if that became necessary to preserve the Southern balance of power.

Early American Relations with California.—Time and tide, it seems, were not on the side of the planters. Already Americans of a far different type were invading the Pacific slope. Long before Polk ever dreamed of California, the Yankee with his cargo of notions had been around the Horn. Daring skippers had sailed out of New England harbors with a variety of goods, bent their course around South America to California, on to China and around the world, trading as they went and leaving pots, pans, woolen cloth, guns, boots, shoes, salt fish, naval stores, and rum in their wake. "Home from Californy!" rang the cry in many a New England port as a good captain let go his anchor on his return from the long trading voyage in the Pacific.

The Overland Trails.—Not to be outdone by the mariners of the deep, western scouts searched for overland routes to the Pacific. Zebulon Pike, explorer and pathfinder, by his expedition into the Southwest during Jefferson's administration, had discovered the resources of New Spain and had shown his countrymen how easy it was to reach Santa Fé from the upper waters of the Arkansas River. Not long afterward, traders laid open the route, making Franklin, Missouri, and later Fort Leavenworth the starting point. Along the trail, once surveyed, poured caravans heavily guarded by armed men against marauding Indians. Sand storms often wiped out all signs of the route; hunger and thirst did many a band of wagoners to death; but the lure of the game and the profits at the end kept the business thriving. Huge stocks of cottons, glass, hardware, and ammunition were drawn almost across the continent to be exchanged at Santa Fé for furs, Indian blankets, silver, and mules; and many a fortune was made out of the traffic.

Americans in California.—Why stop at Santa Fé? The question did not long remain unanswered. In 1829, Ewing Young broke the path to Los Angeles. Thirteen years later Frémont made the first of his celebrated expeditions across plain, desert, and mountain, arousing the interest of the entire country in the Far West. In the wake of the pathfinders went adventurers, settlers, and artisans. By 1847, more than one-fifth of the inhabitants in the little post of two thousand on San Francisco Bay were from the United States. The Mexican War, therefore, was not the beginning but the end of the American conquest of California—a conquest initiated by Americans who went to till the soil, to trade, or to follow some mechanical pursuit.

The Discovery of Gold.—As if to clinch the hold on California already secured by the friends of free soil, there came in 1848 the sudden discovery of gold at Sutter's Mill in the Sacramento Valley. When this exciting news reached the East, a mighty rush began to California, over the trails, across the Isthmus of Panama, and around Cape Horn. Before two years had passed, it is estimated that a hundred thousand people, in search of fortunes, had arrived in California—mechanics, teachers, doctors, lawyers, farmers, miners, and laborers from the four corners of the earth.

California a Free State.—With this increase in population there naturally resulted the usual demand for admission to the union. Instead of waiting for authority from Washington, the Californians held a convention in 1849 and framed their constitution. With impatience, the delegates brushed aside the plea that "the balance of power between the North and South" required the admission of their state as a slave commonwealth. Without a dissenting voice, they voted in favor of freedom and boldly made their request for inclusion among the United States. President Taylor, though a Southern man, advised Congress to admit the applicant. Robert Toombs of Georgia vowed to God that he preferred secession. Henry Clay, the great compromiser, came to the rescue and in 1850 California was admitted as a free state.

Utah.—On the long road to California, in the midst of forbidding and barren wastes, a religious sect, the Mormons, had planted a colony destined to a stormy career. Founded in 1830 under the leadership of Joseph Smith of New York, the sect had suffered from many cruel buffets of fortune. From Ohio they had migrated into Missouri where they were set upon and beaten. Some of them were murdered by indignant neighbors. Harried out of Missouri, they went into Illinois only to see their director and prophet, Smith, first imprisoned by the authorities and then shot by a mob. Having raised up a cloud of enemies on account of both their religious faith and their practice of allowing a man to have more than one wife, they fell in heartily with the suggestion of a new leader, Brigham Young, that they go into the Far West beyond the plains of Kansas—into the forlorn desert where the wicked would cease from troubling and the weary could be at rest, as they read in the Bible. In 1847, Young, with a company of picked men, searched far and wide until he found a suitable spot overlooking the Salt Lake Valley. Returning to Illinois, he gathered up his followers, now numbering several thousand, and in one mighty wagon caravan they all went to their distant haven.

Brigham Young and His Economic System.—In Brigham Young the Mormons had a leader of remarkable power who gave direction to the redemption of the arid soil, the management of property, and the upbuilding of industry. He promised them to make the desert blossom as the rose, and verily he did it. He firmly shaped the enterprise of the colony along co-operative lines, holding down the speculator and profiteer with one hand and giving encouragement to the industrious poor with the other. With the shrewdness befitting a good business man, he knew how to draw the line between public and private interest. Land was given outright to each family, but great care was exercised in the distribution so that none should have great advantage over another. The purchase of supplies and the sale of produce were carried on through a coöperative store, the profits of which went to the common good. Encountering for the first time in the history of the Anglo-Saxon race the problem of aridity, the Mormons surmounted the most perplexing obstacles with astounding skill. They built irrigation works by coöperative labor and granted water rights to all families on equitable terms.

The Growth of Industries.—Though farming long remained the major interest of the colony, the Mormons, eager to be self-supporting in every possible way, bent their efforts also to manufacturing and later to mining. Their missionaries, who hunted in the highways and byways of Europe for converts, never failed to stress the economic advantages of the sect. "We want," proclaimed President Young to all the earth, "a company of woolen manufacturers to come with machinery and take the wool from the sheep and convert it into the best clothes. We want a company of potters; we need them; the clay is ready and the dishes wanted.... We want some men to start a furnace forthwith; the iron, coal, and molders are waiting.... We have a printing press and any one who can take good printing and writing paper to the Valley will be a blessing to themselves and the church." Roads and bridges were built; millions were spent in experiments in agriculture and manufacturing; missionaries at a huge cost were maintained in the East and in Europe; an army was kept for defense against the Indians; and colonies were planted in the outlying regions. A historian of Deseret, as the colony was called by the Mormons, estimated in 1895 that by the labor of their hands the people had produced nearly half a billion dollars in wealth since the coming of the vanguard.

Polygamy Forbidden.—The hope of the Mormons that they might forever remain undisturbed by outsiders was soon dashed to earth, for hundreds of farmers and artisans belonging to other religious sects came to settle among them. In 1850 the colony was so populous and prosperous that it was organized into a territory of the United States and brought under the supervision of the federal government. Protests against polygamy were raised in the colony and at the seat of authority three thousand miles away at Washington. The new Republican party in 1856 proclaimed it "the right and duty of Congress to prohibit in the Territories those twin relics of barbarism, polygamy and slavery." In due time the Mormons had to give up their marriage practices which were condemned by the common opinion of all western civilization; but they kept their religious faith. Monuments to their early enterprise are seen in the Temple and the Tabernacle, the irrigation works, and the great wealth of the Church.

SUMMARY OF WESTERN DEVELOPMENT AND NATIONAL POLITICS

While the statesmen of the old generation were solving the problems of their age, hunters, pioneers, and home seekers were preparing new problems beyond the Alleghanies. The West was rising in population and wealth. Between 1783 and 1829, eleven states were added to the original thirteen. All but two were in the West. Two of them were in the Louisiana territory beyond the Mississippi. Here the process of colonization was repeated. Hardy frontier people cut down the forests, built log cabins, laid out farms, and cut roads through the wilderness. They began a new civilization just as the immigrants to Virginia or Massachusetts had done two centuries earlier.

Like the seaboard colonists before them, they too cherished the spirit of independence and power. They had not gone far upon their course before they resented the monopoly of the presidency by the East. In 1829 they actually sent one of their own cherished leaders, Andrew Jackson, to the White House. Again in 1840, in 1844, in 1848, and in 1860, the Mississippi Valley could boast that one of its sons had been chosen for the seat of power at Washington. Its democratic temper evoked a cordial response in the towns of the East where the old aristocracy had been put aside and artisans had been given the ballot.

For three decades the West occupied the interest of the nation. Under Jackson's leadership, it destroyed the second United States Bank. When he smote nullification in South Carolina, it gave him cordial support. It approved his policy of parceling out government offices among party workers—"the spoils system" in all its fullness. On only one point did it really dissent. The West heartily favored internal improvements, the appropriation of federal funds for highways, canals, and railways. Jackson had misgivings on this question and awakened sharp criticism by vetoing a road improvement bill.

From their point of vantage on the frontier, the pioneers pressed on westward. They pushed into Texas, created a state, declared their independence, demanded a place in the union, and precipitated a war with Mexico. They crossed the trackless plain and desert, laying out trails to Santa Fé, to Oregon, and to California. They were upon the scene when the Mexican War brought California under the Stars and Stripes. They had laid out their farms in the Willamette Valley when the slogan "Fifty-Four Forty or Fight" forced a settlement of the Oregon boundary. California and Oregon were already in the union when there arose the Great Civil War testing whether this nation or any nation so conceived and so dedicated could long endure.

References

G.P. Brown, *Westward Expansion* (American Nation Series).

K. Coman, *Economic Beginnings of the Far West* (2 vols.).

F. Parkman, *California and the Oregon Trail*.

R.S. Ripley, *The War with Mexico*.

W.C. Rives, *The United States and Mexico, 1821-48* (2 vols.).

Questions

1. Give some of the special features in the history of Missouri, Arkansas, Michigan, Wisconsin, Iowa, and Minnesota.

2. Contrast the climate and soil of the Middle West and the Far West.

3. How did Mexico at first encourage American immigration?

4. What produced the revolution in Texas? Who led in it?

5. Narrate some of the leading events in the struggle over annexation to the United States.

6. What action by President Polk precipitated war?

7. Give the details of the peace settlement with Mexico.

8. What is meant by the "joint occupation" of Oregon?

9. How was the Oregon boundary dispute finally settled?

10. Compare the American "invasion" of California with the migration into Texas.

11. Explain how California became a free state.

12. Describe the early economic policy of the Mormons.

Research Topics

The Independence of Texas.—McMaster, *History of the People of the United States*, Vol. VI, pp. 251-270. Woodrow Wilson, *History of the American People*, Vol. IV, pp. 102-126.

The Annexation of Texas.—McMaster, Vol. VII. The passages on annexation are scattered through this volume and it is an exercise in ingenuity to make a connected story of them. Source materials in Hart, *American History Told by Contemporaries*, Vol. III, pp. 637-655; Elson, *History of the United States*, pp. 516-521, 526-527.

The War with Mexico.—Elson, pp. 526-538.

The Oregon Boundary Dispute.—Schafer, *History of the Pacific Northwest* (rev. ed.), pp. 88-104; 173-185.

The Migration to Oregon.—Schafer, pp. 105-172. Coman, *Economic Beginnings of the Far West*, Vol. II, pp. 113-166.

The Santa Fé Trail.—Coman, *Economic Beginnings*, Vol. II, pp. 75-93.

The Conquest of California.—Coman, Vol. II, pp. 297-319.

Gold in California.—McMaster, Vol. VII, pp. 585-614.

The Mormon Migration.—Coman, Vol. II, pp. 167-206.

Biographical Studies.—Frémont, Generals Scott and Taylor, Sam Houston, and David Crockett.

The Romance of Western Exploration.—J.G. Neihardt, *The Splendid Wayfaring*. J.G. Neihardt, *The Song of Hugh Glass*.

PART V. SECTIONAL CONFLICT AND RECONSTRUCTION

CHAPTER XIII

THE RISE OF THE INDUSTRIAL SYSTEM

If Jefferson could have lived to see the Stars and Stripes planted on the Pacific Coast, the broad empire of Texas added to the planting states, and the valley of the Willamette waving with wheat sown by farmers from New England, he would have been more than fortified in his faith that the future of America lay in agriculture. Even a stanch old Federalist like Gouverneur Morris or Josiah Quincy would have mournfully conceded both the prophecy and the claim. Manifest destiny never seemed more clearly written in the stars.

As the farmers from the Northwest and planters from the Southwest poured in upon the floor of Congress, the party of Jefferson, christened anew by Jackson, grew stronger year by year. Opponents there were, no doubt, disgruntled critics and Whigs by conviction; but in 1852 Franklin Pierce, the Democratic candidate for President, carried every state in the union except Massachusetts, Vermont, Kentucky, and Tennessee. This victory, a triumph under ordinary circumstances, was all the more significant in that Pierce was pitted against a hero of the Mexican War, General Scott, whom the Whigs, hoping to win by rousing the martial ardor of the voters, had nominated. On looking at the election returns, the new President calmly assured the planters that "the general principle of reduction of duties with a view to revenue may now be regarded as the settled policy of the country." With equal confidence, he waved aside those agitators who devoted themselves "to the supposed interests of the relatively few Africans in the United States." Like a watchman in the night he called to the country: "All's well."

The party of Hamilton and Clay lay in the dust.

THE INDUSTRIAL REVOLUTION

As pride often goeth before a fall, so sanguine expectation is sometimes the symbol of defeat. Jackson destroyed the bank. Polk signed the tariff bill of 1846 striking an effective blow at the principle of protection for manufactures. Pierce promised to silence the abolitionists. His successor was to approve a drastic step in the direction of free trade. Nevertheless all these things left untouched the springs of power that were in due time to make America the greatest industrial nation on the earth; namely, vast national resources, business enterprise, inventive genius, and the free labor supply of Europe. Unseen by the thoughtless, unrecorded in the diaries of wiseacres, rarely mentioned in the speeches of statesmen, there was swiftly rising such a tide in the affairs of America as Jefferson and Hamilton never dreamed of in their little philosophies.

The Inventors.—Watt and Boulton experimenting with steam in England, Whitney combining wood and steel into a cotton gin, Fulton and Fitch applying the steam engine to navigation, Stevens and Peter Cooper trying out the "iron horse" on "iron highways," Slater building spinning mills in Pawtucket, Howe attaching the needle to the flying wheel, Morse spanning a continent with the telegraph, Cyrus Field linking the markets of the new world with the old along the bed of the Atlantic, McCormick breaking the sickle under the reaper—these men and a thousand more were destroying in a mighty revolution of industry the world of the stagecoach and the tallow candle which Washington and Franklin had inherited little changed from the age of Cæsar. Whitney was to make cotton king. Watt and Fulton were to make steel and steam masters of the world. Agriculture was to fall behind in the race for supremacy.

Industry Outstrips Planting.—The story of invention, that tribute to the triumph of mind over matter, fascinating as a romance, need not be treated in detail here. The effects of invention on social and political life, multitudinous and never-ending, form the very warp and woof of American progress from the days of Andrew Jackson to the latest hour. Neither the great civil conflict—the clash of two systems—nor the problems of the modern age can be approached without an understanding of the striking phases of industrialism.

First and foremost among them was the uprush of mills managed by captains of industry and manned by labor drawn from farms, cities, and foreign lands. For every planter who cleared a domain in the Southwest and gathered his army of bondmen about him, there rose in the North a magician of steam and steel who collected under his roof an army of free workers.

In seven league boots this new giant strode ahead of the Southern giant. Between 1850 and 1859, to use dollars and cents as the measure of progress, the value of domestic manufactures including mines and fisheries rose from $1,019,106,616 to $1,900,000,000, an increase of eighty-six per cent in ten years. In this same period the total production of naval stores, rice, sugar, tobacco, and cotton, the staples of the South, went only from $165,000,000, in round figures, to $204,000,000. At the halfway point of the century, the capital invested in industry, commerce, and cities far exceeded the value of all the farm land between the Atlantic and the Pacific; thus the course of economy had been reversed in fifty years. Tested by figures of production, King Cotton had shriveled by 1860 to a petty prince in comparison, for each year the captains of industry turned out goods worth nearly twenty times all the bales of cotton picked on Southern plantations. Iron, boots and shoes, and leather goods pouring from Northern mills surpassed in value the entire cotton output.

The Agrarian West Turns to Industry.—Nor was this vast enterprise confined to the old Northeast where, as Madison had sagely remarked, commerce was early dominant. "Cincinnati," runs an official report in 1854, "appears to be a great central depot for ready-made clothing and its manufacture for the Western markets may be said to be one of the great trades of that city." There, wrote another traveler, "I heard the crack of the cattle driver's whip and the hum of the factory: the West and the East meeting." Louisville and St. Louis were already famous for their clothing trades and the manufacture of cotton bagging. Five hundred of the two thousand woolen mills in the country in 1860 were in the Western states. Of the output of flour and grist mills, which almost reached in value the cotton crop of 1850, the Ohio Valley furnished a rapidly growing share. The old home of Jacksonian democracy, where Federalists had been almost as scarce as monarchists, turned slowly backward, as the needle to the pole, toward the principle of protection for domestic industry, espoused by Hamilton and defended by Clay.

The Extension of Canals and Railways.—As necessary to mechanical industry as steel and steam power was the great market, spread over a wide and diversified area and knit together by efficient means of transportation. This service was supplied to industry by the steamship, which began its career on the Hudson in 1807; by the canals, of which the Erie opened in 1825 was the most noteworthy; and by the railways, which came into practical operation about 1830.

With sure instinct the Eastern manufacturer reached out for the markets of the Northwest territory where free farmers were producing annually staggering crops of corn, wheat, bacon, and wool. The two great canal systems—the Erie connecting New York City with the waterways of the Great Lakes and the Pennsylvania chain linking Philadelphia with the headwaters of the Ohio—gradually turned the tide of trade from New Orleans to the Eastern seaboard. The railways followed the same paths. By 1860, New York had rail connections with Chicago and St. Louis, one of the routes running through the Hudson and Mohawk valleys and along the Great Lakes, the other through Philadelphia and Pennsylvania and across the rich wheat fields of Ohio, Indiana, and Illinois. Baltimore, not to be outdone by her two rivals, reached out over the mountains for the Western trade and in 1857 had trains running into St. Louis.

In railway enterprise the South took more interest than in canals, and the friends of that section came to its aid. To offset the magnet drawing trade away from the Mississippi Valley, lines were built from the Gulf to Chicago, the Illinois Central part of the project being a monument to the zeal and industry of a

Democrat, better known in politics than in business, Stephen A. Douglas. The swift movement of cotton and tobacco to the North or to seaports was of common concern to planters and manufacturers. Accordingly lines were flung down along the Southern coast, linking Richmond, Charleston, and Savannah with the Northern markets. Other lines struck inland from the coast, giving a rail outlet to the sea for Raleigh, Columbia, Atlanta, Chattanooga, Nashville, and Montgomery. Nevertheless, in spite of this enterprise, the mileage of all the Southern states in 1860 did not equal that of Ohio, Indiana, and Illinois combined.

Banking and Finance.—Out of commerce and manufactures and the construction and operation of railways came such an accumulation of capital in the Northern states as merchants of old never imagined. The banks of the four industrial states of Massachusetts, Connecticut, New York, and Pennsylvania in 1860 had funds greater than the banks in all the other states combined. New York City had become the money market of America, the center to which industrial companies, railway promoters, farmers, and planters turned for capital to initiate and carry on their operations. The banks of Louisiana, South Carolina, Georgia, and Virginia, it is true, had capital far in excess of the banks of the Northwest; but still they were relatively small compared with the financial institutions of the East.

The Growth of the Industrial Population.—A revolution of such magnitude in industry, transport, and finance, overturning as it did the agrarian civilization of the old Northwest and reaching out to the very borders of the country, could not fail to bring in its train consequences of a striking character. Some were immediate and obvious. Others require a fullness of time not yet reached to reveal their complete significance. Outstanding among them was the growth of an industrial population, detached from the land, concentrated in cities, and, to use Jefferson's phrase, dependent upon "the caprices and casualties of trade" for a livelihood. This was a result, as the great Virginian had foreseen, which flowed inevitably from public and private efforts to stimulate industry as against agriculture.

It was estimated in 1860, on the basis of the census figures, that mechanical production gave employment to 1,100,000 men and 285,000 women, making, if the average number of dependents upon them be reckoned, nearly six million people or about one-sixth of the population of the country sustained from manufactures. "This," runs the official record, "was exclusive of the number engaged in the production of many of the raw materials and of the food for manufacturers; in the distribution of their products, such as merchants, clerks, draymen, mariners, the employees of railroads, expresses, and steamboats; of capitalists, various artistic and professional classes, as well as carpenters, bricklayers, painters, and the members of other mechanical trades not classed as manufactures. It is safe to assume, then, that one-third of the whole population is supported, directly, or indirectly, by manufacturing industry." Taking, however, the number of persons directly supported by manufactures, namely about six millions, reveals the astounding fact that the white laboring population, divorced from the soil, already exceeded the number of slaves on Southern farms and plantations.

Immigration.—The more carefully the rapid growth of the industrial population is examined, the more surprising is the fact that such an immense body of free laborers could be found, particularly when it is recalled to what desperate straits the colonial leaders were put in securing immigrants,—slavery, indentured servitude, and kidnapping being the fruits of their necessities. The answer to the enigma is to be found partly in European conditions and partly in the cheapness of transportation after the opening of the era of steam navigation. Shrewd observers of the course of events had long foreseen that a flood of cheap labor was bound to come when the way was made easy. Some, among them Chief Justice Ellsworth, went so far as to prophesy that white labor would in time be so abundant that slavery would disappear as the more costly of the two labor systems. The processes of nature were aided by the policies of government in England and Germany.

The Coming of the Irish.—The opposition of the Irish people to the English government, ever furious and irrepressible, was increased in the mid forties by an almost total failure of the potato crop, the main support of the peasants. Catholic in religion, they had been compelled to support a Protestant church. Tillers of the soil by necessity, they were forced to pay enormous tributes to absentee landlords in England whose claim to their estates rested upon the title of conquest and confiscation. Intensely loyal to their race, the Irish were subjected in all things to the Parliament at London, in which their small minority of representatives had little influence save in holding a balance of power between the two contending English parties. To the constant political irritation, the potato famine added physical distress beyond description. In cottages and fields and along the highways the victims of starvation lay dead by the hundreds, the relief which charity afforded only bringing misery more sharply to the foreground. Those who were fortunate enough to secure passage money sought escape to America. In 1844 the total immigration into the United States was less than eighty thousand; in 1850 it had risen by leaps and bounds to more than three hundred thousand. Between 1820 and 1860 the immigrants from the United Kingdom numbered 2,750,000, of whom more than one-half were Irish. It has been said with a touch of exaggeration that the American canals and railways of those days were built by the labor of Irishmen.

The German Migration.—To political discontent and economic distress, such as was responsible for the coming of the Irish, may likewise be traced the source of the Germanic migration. The potato blight that fell upon Ireland visited the Rhine Valley and Southern Germany at the same time with results as pitiful, if less extensive. The calamity inflicted by nature was followed shortly by another inflicted by the despotic conduct of German kings and princes. In 1848 there had occurred throughout Europe a popular uprising in behalf of republics and democratic government. For a time it rode on a full tide of success. Kings were overthrown, or compelled to promise constitutional government, and tyrannical ministers fled from their palaces. Then came reaction. Those who had championed the popular cause were imprisoned, shot, or driven out of the land. Men of attainments and distinction, whose sole offense was opposition to the government of kings and princes, sought an asylum in America, carrying with them to the land of their adoption the spirit of liberty and democracy. In 1847 over fifty thousand Germans came to America, the forerunners of a migration that increased, almost steadily, for many years. The record of 1860 showed that in the previous twenty years nearly a million and a half had found homes in the United States. Far and wide they scattered, from the mills and shops of the seacoast towns to the uttermost frontiers of Wisconsin and Minnesota.

The Labor of Women and Children.—If the industries, canals, and railways of the country were largely manned by foreign labor, still important native sources must not be overlooked; above all, the women and children of the New England textile districts. Spinning and weaving, by a tradition that runs far beyond the written records of mankind, belonged to women. Indeed it was the dexterous housewives, spinsters, and boys and girls that laid the foundations of the textile industry in America, foundations upon which the mechanical revolution was built. As the wheel and loom were taken out of the homes to the factories operated by water power or the steam engine, the women and, to use Hamilton's phrase, "the children of tender years," followed as a matter of course. "The cotton manufacture alone employs six thousand persons in Lowell," wrote a French observer in 1836; "of this number nearly five thousand are young women from seventeen to twenty-four years of age, the daughters of farmers from the different New England states." It was not until after the middle of the century that foreign lands proved to be the chief source from which workers were recruited for the factories of New England. It was then that the daughters of the Puritans, outdone by the competition of foreign labor, both of men and women, left the spinning jenny and the loom to other hands.

The Rise of Organized Labor.—The changing conditions of American life, marked by the spreading mill towns of New England, New York, and Pennsylvania and the growth of cities like Buffalo, Cincinnati, Louisville, St. Louis, Detroit, and Chicago in the West, naturally brought changes, as Jefferson had prophesied, in "manners and morals." A few mechanics, smiths, carpenters, and masons, widely scattered through farming regions and rural villages, raise no such problems as tens of thousands of workers collected in one center in daily intercourse, learning the power of coöperation and union.

Even before the coming of steam and machinery, in the "good old days" of handicrafts, laborers in many trades—printers, shoemakers, carpenters, for example—had begun to draw together in the towns for the advancement of their interests in the form of higher wages, shorter days, and milder laws. The shoemakers of Philadelphia, organized in 1794, conducted a strike in 1799 and held together until indicted seven years later for conspiracy. During the twenties and thirties, local labor unions sprang up in all industrial centers and they led almost immediately to city federations of the several crafts.

As the thousands who were dependent upon their daily labor for their livelihood mounted into the millions and industries spread across the continent, the local unions of craftsmen grew into national craft organizations bound together by the newspapers, the telegraph, and the railways. Before 1860 there were several such national trade unions, including the plumbers, printers, mule spinners, iron molders, and stone cutters. All over the North labor leaders arose—men unknown to general history but forceful and resourceful characters who forged links binding scattered and individual workers into a common brotherhood. An attempt was even made in 1834 to federate all the crafts into a permanent national organization; but it perished within three years through lack of support. Half a century had to elapse before the American Federation of Labor was to accomplish this task.

All the manifestations of the modern labor movement had appeared, in germ at least, by the time the mid-century was reached: unions, labor leaders, strikes, a labor press, a labor political program, and a labor political party. In every great city industrial disputes were a common occurrence. The papers recorded about four hundred in two years, 1853-54, local affairs but forecasting economic struggles in a larger field. The labor press seems to have begun with the founding of the *Mechanics' Free Press* in Philadelphia in 1828 and the establishment of the New York *Workingman's Advocate* shortly afterward. These semi-political papers were in later years followed by regular trade papers designed to weld together and advance the interests of particular crafts. Edited by able leaders, these little sheets with limited circulation wielded an enormous influence in the ranks of the workers.

Labor and Politics.—As for the political program of labor, the main planks were clear and specific: the abolition of imprisonment for debt, manhood suffrage in states where property qualifications still prevailed, free and universal education, laws protecting the safety and health of workers in mills and factories, abolition of lotteries, repeal of laws requiring militia service, and free land in the West.

Into the labor papers and platforms there sometimes crept a note of hostility to the masters of industry, a sign of bitterness that excited little alarm while cheap land in the West was open to the discontented. The Philadelphia workmen, in issuing a call for a local convention, invited "all those of our fellow citizens who live by their own labor and none other." In Newcastle county, Delaware, the association of working people complained in 1830: "The poor have no laws; the laws are made by the rich and of course for the rich." Here and there an extremist went to the length of advocating an equal division of wealth among all the people—the crudest kind of communism.

Agitation of this character produced in labor circles profound distrust of both Whigs and Democrats who talked principally about tariffs and banks; it resulted in attempts to found independent labor parties. In Philadelphia, Albany, New York City, and New England, labor candidates were put up for elections in the early thirties and in a few cases were victorious at the polls. "The balance of power has at length got into the hands of the working people, where it properly belongs," triumphantly exclaimed the *Mechanics' Free Press* of Philadelphia in 1829. But the triumph was illusory. Dissensions appeared in the labor ranks. The old party leaders, particularly of Tammany Hall, the Democratic party organization in New York City, offered concessions to labor in return for votes. Newspapers unsparingly denounced "trade union politicians" as "demagogues," "levellers," and "rag, tag, and bobtail"; and some of them, deeming labor unrest the sour fruit of manhood suffrage, suggested disfranchisement as a remedy. Under the influence of concessions and attacks the political fever quickly died away, and the end of the decade left no remnant of the labor political parties. Labor leaders turned to a task which seemed more substantial and practical, that of organizing workingmen into craft unions for the definite purpose of raising wages and reducing hours.

THE INDUSTRIAL REVOLUTION AND NATIONAL POLITICS

Southern Plans for Union with the West.—It was long the design of Southern statesmen like Calhoun to hold the West and the South together in one political party. The theory on which they based their hope was simple. Both sections were agricultural—the producers of raw materials and the buyers of manufactured goods. The planters were heavy purchasers of Western bacon, pork, mules, and grain. The Mississippi River and its tributaries formed the natural channel for the transportation of heavy produce southward to the plantations and outward to Europe. Therefore, ran their political reasoning, the interests of the two sections were one. By standing together in favor of low tariffs, they could buy their manufactures cheaply in Europe and pay for them in cotton, tobacco, and grain. The union of the two sections under Jackson's management seemed perfect.

The East Forms Ties with the West.—Eastern leaders were not blind to the ambitions of Southern statesmen. On the contrary, they also recognized the importance of forming strong ties with the agrarian West and drawing the produce of the Ohio Valley to Philadelphia and New York. The canals and railways were the physical signs of this economic union, and the results, commercial and political, were soon evident. By the middle of the century, Southern economists noted the change, one of them, De Bow, lamenting that "the great cities of the North have severally penetrated the interior with artificial lines until they have taken from the open and untaxed current of the Mississippi the commerce produced on its borders." To this writer it was an astounding thing to behold "the number of steamers that now descend the upper Mississippi River, loaded to the guards with produce, as far as the mouth of the Illinois River and then turn up that stream with their cargoes to be shipped to New York *via* Chicago. The Illinois canal has not only swept the whole produce along the line of the Illinois River to the East, but it is drawing the products of the upper Mississippi through the same channel; thus depriving New Orleans and St. Louis of a rich portion of their former trade."

If to any shippers the broad current of the great river sweeping down to New Orleans offered easier means of physical communication to the sea than the canals and railways, the difference could be overcome by the credit which Eastern bankers were able to extend to the grain and produce buyers, in the first instance, and through them to the farmers on the soil. The acute Southern observer just quoted, De Bow, admitted with evident regret, in 1852, that "last autumn, the rich regions of Ohio, Indiana, and Illinois were flooded with the local bank notes of the Eastern States, advanced by the New York houses on produce to be shipped by way of the canals in the spring.... These moneyed facilities enable the packer, miller, and speculator to hold on to their produce until the opening of navigation in the spring and they are no longer obliged, as formerly, to hurry off their shipments during the winter by the way of New Orleans in order to realize funds by drafts on their shipments. The banking facilities at the East are doing as much to draw trade from us as the canals and railways which Eastern capital is constructing." Thus canals, railways, and financial credit were swiftly forging bonds of union between the old home of Jacksonian Democracy in the West and the older home of Federalism in the East. The nationalism to which Webster paid eloquent tribute became more and more real with the passing of time. The self-sufficiency of the pioneer was broken down as he began to watch the produce markets of New York and Philadelphia where the prices of corn and hogs fixed his earnings for the year.

The West and Manufactures.—In addition to the commercial bonds between the East and the West there was growing up a common interest in manufactures. As skilled white labor increased in the Ohio Valley, the industries springing up in the new cities made Western life more like that of the industrial East than like that of the planting South. Moreover, the Western states produced some important raw materials for American factories, which called for protection against foreign competition, notably, wool, hemp, and flax. As the South had little or no foreign competition in cotton and tobacco, the East could not offer protection for her raw materials in exchange for protection for industries. With the West, however, it became possible to establish reciprocity in tariffs; that is, for example, to trade a high rate on wool for a high rate on textiles or iron.

The South Dependent on the North.—While East and West were drawing together, the distinctions between North and South were becoming more marked; the latter, having few industries and producing little save raw materials, was being forced into the position of a dependent section. As a result of the protective tariff, Southern planters were compelled to turn more and more to Northern mills for their cloth, shoes, hats, hoes, plows, and machinery. Nearly all the goods which they bought in Europe in exchange for their produce came overseas to Northern ports, whence transshipments were made by rail and water to Southern points of distribution. Their rice, cotton, and tobacco, in as far as they were not carried to Europe in British bottoms, were transported by Northern masters. In these ways, a large part of the financial operations connected with the sale of Southern produce and the purchase of goods in exchange passed into the hands of Northern merchants and bankers who, naturally, made profits from their transactions. Finally, Southern planters who wanted to buy more land and more slaves on credit borrowed heavily in the North where huge accumulations made the rates of interest lower than the smaller banks of the South could afford.

The South Reckons the Cost of Economic Dependence.—As Southern dependence upon Northern capital became more and more marked, Southern leaders began to chafe at what they regarded as restraints laid upon their enterprise. In a word, they came to look upon the planter as a tribute-bearer to the manufacturer and financier. "The South," expostulated De Bow, "stands in the attitude of feeding ... a vast population of [Northern] merchants, shipowners, capitalists, and others who, without claims on her progeny, drink up the life blood of her trade.... Where goes the value of our labor but to those who, taking advantage of our folly, ship for us, buy for us, sell to us, and, after turning our own capital to their profitable account, return laden with our money to enjoy their easily earned opulence at home."

Southern statisticians, not satisfied with generalities, attempted to figure out how great was this tribute in dollars and cents. They estimated that the planters annually lent to Northern merchants the full value of their exports, a hundred millions or more, "to be used in the manipulation of foreign imports." They calculated that no less than forty millions all told had been paid to shipowners in profits. They reckoned that, if the South were to work up her own cotton, she would realize from seventy to one hundred millions a year that otherwise went North. Finally, to cap the climax, they regretted that planters spent some fifteen millions a year pleasure-seeking in the alluring cities and summer resorts of the North.

Southern Opposition to Northern Policies.—Proceeding from these premises, Southern leaders drew the logical conclusion that the entire program of economic measures demanded in the North was without exception adverse to Southern interests and, by a similar chain of reasoning, injurious to the corn and wheat producers of the West. Cheap labor afforded by free immigration, a protective tariff raising prices of manufactures for the tiller of the soil, ship subsidies increasing the tonnage of carrying trade in Northern hands, internal improvements forging new economic bonds between the East and the West, a national banking system giving strict national control over the currency as a safeguard against paper inflation—all these devices were regarded in the South as contrary to the planting interest. They were constantly compared with the restrictive measures by which Great Britain more than half a century before had sought to bind American interests.

As oppression justified a war for independence once, statesmen argued, so it can justify it again. "It is curious as it is melancholy and distressing," came a broad hint from South Carolina, "to see how striking is the analogy between the colonial vassalage to which the manufacturing states have reduced the planting states and that which formerly bound the Anglo-American colonies to the British empire.... England said to her American colonies: 'You shall not trade with the rest of the world for such manufactures as are produced in the mother country.' The manufacturing states say to their Southern colonies: 'You shall not trade with the rest of the world for such manufactures as we produce.'" The conclusion was inexorable: either the South must control the national government and its economic measures, or it must declare, as America had done four score years before, its political and economic independence. As Northern mills multiplied, as railways spun their mighty web over the face of the North, and as accumulated capital rose into the hundreds of millions, the conviction of the planters and their statesmen deepened into desperation.

Efforts to Start Southern Industries Fail.—A few of them, seeing the predominance of the North, made determined efforts to introduce manufactures into the South. To the leaders who were averse to secession and nullification this seemed the only remedy for the growing disparity in the power of the two sections. Societies for the encouragement of mechanical industries were formed, the investment of capital was sought, and indeed a few mills were built on Southern soil. The results were meager. The natural resources, coal and water power, were abundant; but the enterprise for direction and the skilled labor were wanting. The stream of European immigration flowed North and West, not South. The Irish or German laborer, even if he finally made his home in a city, had before him, while in the North, the alternative of a homestead on Western land. To him slavery was a strange, if not a repelling, institution. He did not take to it kindly nor care to fix his home where it flourished. While slavery lasted, the economy of the South was inevitably agricultural. While agriculture predominated, leadership with equal necessity fell to the planting interest. While the planting interest ruled, political opposition to Northern economy was destined to grow in strength.

The Southern Theory of Sectionalism.—In the opinion of the statesmen who frankly represented the planting interest, the industrial system was its deadly enemy. Their entire philosophy of American politics was summed up in a single paragraph by McDuffie, a spokesman for South Carolina: "Owing to the federative character of our government, the great geographical extent of our territory, and the diversity of the pursuits of our citizens in different parts of the union, it has so happened that two great interests have sprung up, standing directly opposed to each other. One of these consists of those manufactures which the Northern and Middle states are capable of producing but which, owing to the high price of labor and the high profits of capital in those states, cannot hold competition with foreign manufactures without the aid of bounties, directly or indirectly given, either by the general government or by the state governments. The other of these interests consists of the great agricultural staples of the Southern states which can find a market only in foreign countries and which can be advantageously sold only in exchange for foreign manufactures which come in competition with those of the Northern and Middle states.... These interests then stand diametrically and irreconcilably opposed to each other. The interest, the pecuniary interest of the Northern manufacturer, is directly promoted by every increase of the taxes imposed upon Southern commerce; and it is unnecessary to add that the interest of the Southern planter is promoted by every diminution of taxes imposed upon the productions of their industry. If, under these circumstances, the manufacturers were clothed with the power of imposing taxes, at their pleasure, upon the foreign imports of the planter, no doubt would exist in the mind of any man that it would have all the characteristics of an absolute and unqualified despotism." The economic soundness of this reasoning, a subject of interesting speculation for the economist, is of little concern to the historian. The historical point is that this opinion was widely held in the South and with the progress of time became the prevailing doctrine of the planting statesmen.

Their antagonism was deepened because they also became convinced, on what grounds it is not necessary to inquire, that the leaders of the industrial interest thus opposed to planting formed a consolidated "aristocracy of wealth," bent upon the pursuit and attainment of political power at Washington. "By the aid of various associated interests," continued McDuffie, "the manufacturing capitalists have obtained a complete and permanent control over the legislation of Congress on this subject [the tariff].... Men confederated together upon selfish and interested principles, whether in pursuit of the offices or the bounties of the government, are ever more active and vigilant than the great majority who act from disinterested and patriotic impulses. Have we not witnessed it on this floor, sir? Who ever knew the tariff men to divide on any question affecting their confederated interests?... The watchword is, stick together, right or wrong upon every question affecting the common cause. Such, sir, is the concert and vigilance and such the combinations by which the manufacturing party, acting upon the interests of some and the prejudices of others, have obtained a decided and permanent control over public opinion in all the tariff states." Thus, as the Southern statesman would have it, the North, in matters affecting national policies, was ruled by a "confederated interest" which menaced the planting interest. As the former grew in magnitude and attached to itself the free farmers of the West through channels of trade and credit, it followed as night the day that in time the planters would be overshadowed and at length overborne in the struggle of giants. Whether the theory was sound or not, Southern statesmen believed it and acted upon it.

References

M. Beard, *Short History of the American Labor Movement*.

E.L. Bogart, *Economic History of the United States*.

J.R. Commons, *History of Labour in the United States* (2 vols.).

E.R. Johnson, *American Railway Transportation*.

C.D. Wright, *Industrial Evolution of the United States*.

Questions

1. What signs pointed to a complete Democratic triumph in 1852?

2. What is the explanation of the extraordinary industrial progress of America?

3. Compare the planting system with the factory system.

4. In what sections did industry flourish before the Civil War? Why?

5. Show why transportation is so vital to modern industry and agriculture.

6. Explain how it was possible to secure so many people to labor in American industries.

7. Trace the steps in the rise of organized labor before 1860.

8. What political and economic reforms did labor demand?

9. Why did the East and the South seek closer ties with the West?

10. Describe the economic forces which were drawing the East and the West together.

11. In what way was the South economically dependent upon the North?

12 State the national policies generally favored in the North and condemned in the South.

13. Show how economic conditions in the South were unfavorable to industry.

14. Give the Southern explanation of the antagonism between the North and the South.

Research Topics

The Inventions.—Assign one to each student. Satisfactory accounts are to be found in any good encyclopedia, especially the Britannica.

River and Lake Commerce.—Callender, *Economic History of the United States*, pp. 313-326.

Railways and Canals.—Callender, pp. 326-344; 359-387. Coman, *Industrial History of the United States*, pp. 216-225.

The Growth of Industry, 1815-1840.—Callender, pp. 459-471. From 1850 to 1860, Callender, pp. 471-486.

Early Labor Conditions.—Callender, pp. 701-718.

Early Immigration.—Callender, pp. 719-732.

Clay's Home Market Theory of the Tariff.—Callender, pp. 498-503.

The New England View of the Tariff.—Callender, pp. 503-514.

CHAPTER XIV

THE PLANTING SYSTEM AND NATIONAL POLITICS

James Madison, the father of the federal Constitution, after he had watched for many days the battle royal in the national convention of 1787, exclaimed that the contest was not between the large and the small states, but between the commercial North and the planting South. From the inauguration of Washington to the election of Lincoln the sectional conflict, discerned by this penetrating thinker, exercised a profound influence on the course of American politics. It was latent during the "era of good feeling" when the Jeffersonian Republicans adopted Federalist policies; it flamed up in the contest between the Democrats and Whigs. Finally it raged in the angry political quarrel which culminated in the Civil War.

SLAVERY—NORTH AND SOUTH

The Decline of Slavery in the North.—At the time of the adoption of the Constitution, slavery was lawful in all the Northern states except Massachusetts. There were almost as many bondmen in New York as in Georgia. New Jersey had more than Delaware or Tennessee, indeed nearly as many as both combined. All told, however, there were only about forty thousand in the North as against nearly seven hundred thousand in the South. Moreover, most of the Northern slaves were domestic servants, not laborers necessary to keep mills going or fields under cultivation.

There was, in the North, a steadily growing moral sentiment against the system. Massachusetts abandoned it in 1780. In the same year, Pennsylvania provided for gradual emancipation. New Hampshire, where there had been only a handful, Connecticut with a few thousand domestics, and New Jersey early followed these examples. New York, in 1799, declared that all children born of slaves after July 4 of that year should be free, though held for a term as apprentices; and in 1827 it swept away the last vestiges of slavery. So with the passing of the generation that had framed the Constitution, chattel servitude disappeared in the commercial states, leaving behind only such discriminations as disfranchisement or high property qualifications on colored voters.

The Growth of Northern Sentiment against Slavery.—In both sections of the country there early existed, among those more or less philosophically inclined, a strong opposition to slavery on moral as well as economic grounds. In the constitutional convention of 1787, Gouverneur Morris had vigorously condemned it and proposed that the whole country should bear the cost of abolishing it. About the same time a society for promoting the abolition of slavery, under the presidency of Benjamin Franklin, laid before Congress a petition that serious attention be given to the emancipation of "those unhappy men who alone in this land of freedom are degraded into perpetual bondage." When Congress, acting on the recommendations of President Jefferson, provided for the abolition of the foreign slave trade on January 1, 1808, several Northern members joined with Southern members in condemning the system as well as the trade. Later, colonization societies were formed to encourage the emancipation of slaves and their return to Africa. James Madison was president and Henry Clay vice president of such an organization.

The anti-slavery sentiment of which these were the signs was nevertheless confined to narrow circles and bore no trace of bitterness. "We consider slavery your calamity, not your crime," wrote a distinguished Boston clergyman to his Southern brethren, "and we will share with you the burden of putting an end to it. We will consent that the public lands shall be appropriated to this object.... I deprecate everything which sows discord and exasperating sectional animosities."

Uncompromising Abolition.—In a little while the spirit of generosity was gone. Just as Jacksonian Democracy rose to power there appeared a new kind of anti-slavery doctrine—the dogmatism of the abolition agitator. For mild speculation on the evils of the system was substituted an imperious and belligerent demand for instant emancipation. If a date must be fixed for its appearance, the year 1831 may be taken when William Lloyd Garrison founded in Boston his anti-slavery paper, *The Liberator*. With singleness of purpose and utter contempt for all opposing opinions and arguments, he pursued his course of passionate denunciation. He apologized for having ever "assented to the popular but pernicious doctrine of gradual abolition." He chose for his motto: "Immediate and unconditional emancipation!" He promised his readers that he would be "harsh as truth and uncompromising as justice"; that he would not "think or speak or write with moderation." Then he flung out his defiant call: "I am in earnest—I will not equivocate—I will not excuse—I will not retreat a single inch—and I will be heard....

'Such is the vow I take, so help me God.'"

Though Garrison complained that "the apathy of the people is enough to make every statue leap from its pedestal," he soon learned how alive the masses were to the meaning of his propaganda. Abolition orators were stoned in the street and hissed from the platform. Their meeting places were often attacked and sometimes burned to the ground. Garrison himself was assaulted in the streets of Boston, finding refuge from the angry mob behind prison bars. Lovejoy, a publisher in Alton, Illinois, for his willingness to give abolition a fair hearing, was brutally murdered; his printing press was broken to pieces as a warning to all those who disturbed the nation's peace of mind. The South, doubly frightened by a slave revolt in 1831 which ended in the murder of a number of men, women, and children, closed all discussion of slavery in that section. "Now," exclaimed Calhoun, "it is a question which admits of neither concession nor compromise."

As the opposition hardened, the anti-slavery agitation gathered in force and intensity. Whittier blew his blast from the New England hills:

"No slave-hunt in our borders—no pirate on our strand;

No fetters in the Bay State—no slave upon our land."

Lowell, looking upon the espousal of a great cause as the noblest aim of his art, ridiculed and excoriated bondage in the South. Those abolitionists, not gifted as speakers or writers, signed petitions against slavery and poured them in upon Congress. The flood of them was so continuous that the House of Representatives, forgetting its traditions, adopted in 1836 a "gag rule" which prevented the reading of appeals and consigned them to the waste basket. Not until the Whigs were in power nearly ten years later was John Quincy Adams able, after a relentless campaign, to carry a motion rescinding the rule.

How deep was the impression made upon the country by this agitation for immediate and unconditional emancipation cannot be measured. If the popular vote for those candidates who opposed not slavery, but its extension to the territories, be taken as a standard, it was slight indeed. In 1844, the Free Soil candidate, Birney, polled 62,000 votes out of over a million and a half; the Free Soil vote of the next campaign went beyond a quarter of a million, but the increase was due to the strength of the leader, Martin Van Buren; four years afterward it receded to 156,000, affording all the outward signs for the belief that the pleas of the abolitionist found no widespread response among the people. Yet the agitation undoubtedly ran deeper than the ballot box. Young statesmen of the North, in whose hands the destiny of frightful years was to lie, found their indifference to slavery broken and their consciences stirred by the unending appeal and the tireless reiteration. Charles Sumner afterward boasted that he read the *Liberator* two years before Wendell Phillips, the young Boston lawyer who cast aside his profession to take up the dangerous cause.

Early Southern Opposition to Slavery.—In the South, the sentiment against slavery was strong; it led some to believe that it would also come to an end there in due time. Washington disliked it and directed in his will that his own slaves should be set free after the death of his wife. Jefferson, looking into the future, condemned the system by which he also lived, saying: "Can the liberties of a nation be thought secure when we have removed their only firm basis, a conviction in the minds of the people that their liberties are the gift of God? Are they not to be violated but with His wrath? Indeed I tremble for my country when I reflect that God is just; that His justice cannot sleep forever." Nor did Southern men confine their sentiments to expressions of academic opinion. They accepted in 1787 the Ordinance which excluded slavery from the Northwest territory forever and also the Missouri Compromise, which shut it out of a vast section of the Louisiana territory.

The Revolution in the Slave System.—Among the representatives of South Carolina and Georgia, however, the anti-slavery views of Washington and Jefferson were by no means approved; and the drift of Southern economy was decidedly in favor of extending and perpetuating, rather than abolishing, the system of chattel servitude. The invention of the cotton gin and textile machinery created a market for cotton which the planters, with all their skill and energy, could hardly supply. Almost every available acre was brought under cotton culture as the small farmers were driven steadily from the seaboard into the uplands or to the Northwest.

The demand for slaves to till the swiftly expanding fields was enormous. The number of bondmen rose from 700,000 in Washington's day to more than three millions in 1850. At the same time slavery itself was transformed. Instead of the homestead where the same family of masters kept the same families of slaves from generation to generation, came the plantation system of the Far South and Southwest where masters were ever moving and ever extending their holdings of lands and slaves. This in turn reacted on the older South where the raising of slaves for the market became a regular and highly profitable business.

Slavery Defended as a Positive Good.—As the abolition agitation increased and the planting system expanded, apologies for slavery became fainter and fainter in the South. Then apologies were superseded by claims that slavery was a beneficial scheme of labor control. Calhoun, in a famous speech in the Senate in 1837, sounded the new note by declaring slavery "instead of an evil, a good—a positive good." His reasoning was as follows: in every civilized society one portion of the community must live on the labor of another; learning, science, and the arts are built upon leisure; the African slave, kindly treated by his master and mistress and looked after in his old age, is better off than the free laborers of Europe; and under the slave system conflicts between capital and labor are avoided. The advantages of slavery in this respect, he concluded, "will become more and more manifest, if left undisturbed by interference from without, as the country advances in wealth and numbers."

Slave Owners Dominate Politics.—The new doctrine of Calhoun was eagerly seized by the planters as they came more and more to overshadow the small farmers of the South and as they beheld the menace of abolition growing upon the horizon. It formed, as they viewed matters, a moral defense for their labor system—sound, logical, invincible. It warranted them in drawing together for the protection of an institution so necessary, so inevitable, so beneficent.

Though in 1850 the slave owners were only about three hundred and fifty thousand in a national population of nearly twenty million whites, they had an influence all out of proportion to their numbers. They were knit together by the bonds of a common interest. They had leisure and wealth. They could travel and attend conferences and conventions. Throughout the South and largely in the North, they had the press, the schools, and the pulpits on their side. They formed, as it were, a mighty union for the protection and advancement of their common cause. Aided by those mechanics and farmers of the North who stuck by Jacksonian Democracy through thick and thin, the planters became a power in the federal government. "We nominate Presidents," exultantly boasted a Richmond newspaper; "the North elects them."

This jubilant Southern claim was conceded by William H. Seward, a Republican Senator from New York, in a speech describing the power of slavery in the national government. "A party," he said, "is in one sense a joint stock association, in which those who contribute most direct the action and management of the concern.... The slaveholders, contributing in an overwhelming proportion to the strength of the Democratic party, necessarily dictate and prescribe its policy." He went on: "The slaveholding class has become the governing power in each of the slaveholding states and it practically chooses thirty of the sixty-two members of the Senate, ninety of the two hundred and thirty-three members of the House of Representatives, and one hundred and five of the two hundred and ninety-five electors of President and Vice-President of the United States." Then he considered the slave power in the Supreme Court. "That tribunal," he exclaimed, "consists of a chief justice and eight associate justices. Of these, five were called from slave states and four from free states. The opinions and bias of each of them were carefully considered by the President and Senate when he was appointed. Not one of them was found wanting in soundness of politics, according to the slaveholder's exposition of the Constitution." Such was the Northern view of the planting interest that, from the arena of national politics, challenged the whole country in 1860.

SLAVERY IN NATIONAL POLITICS

National Aspects of Slavery.—It may be asked why it was that slavery, founded originally on state law and subject to state government, was drawn into the current of national affairs. The answer is simple. There were, in the first place, constitutional reasons. The Congress of the United States had to make all needful rules for the government of the territories, the District of Columbia, the forts and other property under national authority; so it was compelled to determine whether slavery should exist in the places subject to its jurisdiction. Upon Congress was also conferred the power of admitting new states; whenever a territory asked for admission, the issue could be raised as to whether slavery should be sanctioned or excluded. Under the Constitution, provision was made for the return of runaway slaves; Congress had the power to enforce this clause by appropriate legislation. Since the control of the post office was vested in the federal government, it had to face the problem raised by the transmission of abolition literature through the mails. Finally citizens had the right of petition; it inheres in all free government and it is expressly guaranteed by the first amendment to the Constitution. It was therefore legal for abolitionists to present to Congress their petitions, even if they asked for something which it had no right to grant. It was thus impossible, constitutionally, to draw a cordon around the slavery issue and confine the discussion of it to state politics.

There were, in the second place, economic reasons why slavery was inevitably drawn into the national sphere. It was the basis of the planting system which had direct commercial relations with the North and European countries; it was affected by federal laws respecting tariffs, bounties, ship subsidies, banking, and kindred matters. The planters of the South, almost without exception, looked upon the protective tariff as a tribute laid upon them for the benefit of Northern industries. As heavy borrowers of money in the North, they were generally in favor of "easy money," if not paper currency, as an aid in the repayment of their debts. This threw most of them into opposition to the Whig program for a United States Bank. All financial aids to American shipping they stoutly resisted, preferring to rely upon the cheaper service rendered by English shippers. Internal improvements, those substantial ties that were binding the West to the East and turning the traffic from New Orleans to Philadelphia and New York, they viewed with alarm. Free homesteads from the public lands, which tended to overbalance the South by building free states, became to them a measure dangerous to their interests. Thus national economic policies, which could not by any twist or turn be confined to state control, drew the slave system and its defenders into the political conflict that centered at Washington.

Slavery and the Territories—the Missouri Compromise (1820).—Though men continually talked about "taking slavery out of politics," it could not be done. By 1818 slavery had become so entrenched and the anti-slavery sentiment so strong, that Missouri's quest for admission brought both houses of Congress into a deadlock that was broken only by compromise. The South, having half the Senators, could prevent the admission of Missouri stripped of slavery; and the North, powerful in the House of Representatives, could keep Missouri with slavery out of the union indefinitely. An adjustment of pretensions was the last resort. Maine, separated from the parent state of Massachusetts, was brought into the union with freedom and Missouri with bondage. At the same time it was agreed that the remainder of the vast Louisiana territory north of the parallel of 36° 30' should be, like the old Northwest, forever free; while the southern portion was left to slavery. In reality this was an immense gain for liberty. The area dedicated to free farmers was many times greater than that left to the planters. The principle was once more asserted that Congress had full power to prevent slavery in the territories.

The Territorial Question Reopened by the Wilmot Proviso.—To the Southern leaders, the annexation of Texas and the conquest of Mexico meant renewed security to the planting interest against the increasing wealth and population of the North. Texas, it was said, could be divided into four slave states. The new territories secured by the treaty of peace with Mexico contained the promise of at least three more. Thus, as each new free soil state knocked for admission into the union, theSouth could demand as the price of its consent a new slave state. No wonder Southern statesmen saw, in the annexation of Texas and the conquest of Mexico, slavery and King Cotton triumphant—secure for all time against adverse legislation. Northern leaders were equally convinced that the Southern prophecy was true. Abolitionists and moderate opponents of slavery alike were in despair. Texas, they lamented, would fasten slavery upon the country forevermore. "No living man," cried one, "will see the end of slavery in the United States!"

It so happened, however, that the events which, it was thought, would secure slavery let loose a storm against it. A sign appeared first on August 6, 1846, only a few months after war was declared on Mexico. On that day, David Wilmot, a Democrat from Pennsylvania, introduced into the House of Representatives a resolution to the effect that, as an express and fundamental condition to the acquisition of any territory from the republic of Mexico, slavery should be forever excluded from every part of it. "The Wilmot Proviso," as the resolution was popularly called, though defeated on that occasion, was a challenge to the South.

The South answered the challenge. Speaking in the House of Representatives, Robert Toombs of Georgia boldly declared: "In the presence of the living God, if by your legislation you seek to drive us from the territories of California and New Mexico ... I am for disunion." South Carolina announced that the day for talk had passed and the time had come to join her sister states "in resisting the application of the Wilmot Proviso at any and all hazards." A conference, assembled at Jackson, Mississippi, in the autumn of 1849, called a general convention of Southern states to meet at Nashville the following summer. The avowed purpose was to arrest "the course of aggression" and, if that was not possible, to provide "in the last resort for their separate welfare by the formation of a compact and union that will afford protection to their liberties and rights." States that had spurned South Carolina's plea for nullification in 1832 responded to this new appeal with alacrity—an augury of the secession to come.

The Great Debate of 1850.—The temper of the country was white hot when Congress convened in December, 1849. It was a memorable session, memorable for the great men who took part in the debates and memorable for the grand Compromise of 1850 which it produced. In the Senate sat for the last time three heroic figures: Webster from the North, Calhoun from the South, and Clay from a border state. For nearly forty years these three had been leaders of men. All had grown old and gray in service. Calhoun was already broken in health and in a few months was to be borne from the political arena forever. Clay and Webster had but two more years in their allotted span.

Experience, learning, statecraft—all these things they now marshaled in a mighty effort to solve the slavery problem. On January 29, 1850, Clay offered to the Senate a compromise granting concessions to both sides; and a few days later, in a powerful oration, he made a passionate appeal for a union of hearts through mutual sacrifices. Calhoun relentlessly demanded the full measure of justice for the South: equal rights in the territories bought by common blood; the return of runaway slaves as required by the Constitution; the suppression of the abolitionists; and the restoration of the balance of power between the North and the South. Webster, in his notable "Seventh of March speech," condemned the Wilmot Proviso, advocated a strict enforcement of the fugitive slave law, denounced the abolitionists, and made a final plea for the Constitution, union, and liberty. This was the address which called forth from Whittier the poem, "Ichabod," deploring the fall of the mighty one whom he thought lost to all sense of faith and honor.

The Terms of the Compromise of 1850.—When the debates were closed, the results were totaled in a series of compromise measures, all of which were signed in September, 1850, by the new President, Millard Fillmore, who had taken office two months before on the death of Zachary Taylor. By these acts the boundaries of Texas were adjusted and the territory of New Mexico created, subject to the provision that all or any part of it might be admitted to the union "with or without slavery as their constitution may provide at the time of their admission." The Territory of Utah was similarly organized with the same conditions as to slavery, thus repudiating the Wilmot Proviso without guaranteeing slavery to the planters. California was admitted as a free state under a constitution in which the people of the territory had themselves prohibited slavery.

The slave trade was abolished in the District of Columbia, but slavery itself existed as before at the capital of the nation. This concession to anti-slavery sentiment was more than offset by a fugitive slave law, drastic in spirit and in letter. It placed the enforcement of its terms in the hands of federal officers appointed from Washington and so removed it from the control of authorities locally elected. It provided that masters or their agents, on filing claims in due form, might summarily remove their escaped slaves without affording their "alleged fugitives" the right of trial by jury, the right to witness, the right to offer any testimony in evidence. Finally, to "put teeth" into the act, heavy penalties were prescribed for all who obstructed or assisted in obstructing the enforcement of the law. Such was the Great Compromise of 1850.

The Pro-slavery Triumph in the Election of 1852.—The results of the election of 1852 seemed to show conclusively that the nation was weary of slavery agitation and wanted peace. Both parties, Whigs and Democrats, endorsed the fugitive slave law and approved the Great Compromise. The Democrats, with Franklin Pierce as their leader, swept the country against the war hero, General Winfield Scott, on whom the Whigs had staked their hopes. Even Webster, broken with grief at his failure to receive the nomination, advised his friends to vote for Pierce and turned away from politics to meditate upon approaching death. The verdict of the voters would seem to indicate that for the time everybody, save a handful of disgruntled agitators, looked upon Clay's settlement as the last word. "The people, especially the business men of the country," says Elson, "were utterly weary of the agitation and they gave their suffrages to the party that promised them rest." The Free Soil party, condemning slavery as "a sin against God and a crime against man," and advocating freedom for the territories, failed to carry a single state. In fact it polled fewer votes than it had four years earlier—156,000 as against nearly 3,000,000, the combined vote of the Whigs and Democrats. It is not surprising, therefore, that President Pierce, surrounded in his cabinet by strong Southern sympathizers, could promise to put an end to slavery agitation and to crush the abolition movement in the bud.

Anti-slavery Agitation Continued.—The promise was more difficult to fulfill than to utter. In fact, the vigorous execution of one measure included in the Compromise—the fugitive slave law—only made matters worse. Designed as security for the planters, it proved a powerful instrument in their undoing. Slavery five hundred miles away on a Louisiana plantation was so remote from the North that only the strongest imagination could maintain a constant rage against it. "Slave catching," "man hunting" by federal officers on the streets of Philadelphia, New York, Boston, Chicago, or Milwaukee and in the hamlets and villages of the wide-stretching farm lands of the North was another matter. It brought the most odious aspects of slavery home to thousands of men and women who would otherwise have been indifferent to the system. Law-abiding business men, mechanics, farmers, and women, when they saw peaceful negroes, who had resided in their neighborhoods perhaps for years, torn away by federal officers and carried back to bondage, were transformed into enemies of the law. They helped slaves to escape; they snatched them away from officers who had captured them; they broke open jails and carried fugitives off to Canada.

Assistance to runaway slaves, always more or less common in the North, was by this time organized into a system. Regular routes, known as "underground railways," were laid out across the free states into Canada, and trusted friends of freedom maintained "underground stations" where fugitives were concealed in the daytime between their long night journeys. Funds were raised and secret agents sent into the South to help negroes to flee. One negro woman, Harriet Tubman, "the Moses of her people," with headquarters at Philadelphia, is accredited with nineteen invasions into slave territory and the emancipation of three hundred negroes. Those who worked at this business were in constant peril. One underground operator, Calvin Fairbank, spent nearly twenty years in prison for aiding fugitives from justice. Yet perils and prisons did not stay those determined men and women who, in obedience to their consciences, set themselves to this lawless work.

From thrilling stories of adventure along the underground railways came some of the scenes and themes of the novel by Harriet Beecher Stowe, "Uncle Tom's Cabin," published two years after the Compromise of 1850. Her stirring tale set forth the worst features of slavery in vivid word pictures that caught and held the attention of millions of readers. Though the book was unfair to the South and was denounced as a hideous distortion of the truth, it was quickly dramatized and played in every city and town throughout the North. Topsy, Little Eva, Uncle Tom, the fleeing slave, Eliza Harris, and the cruel slave driver, Simon Legree, with his baying blood hounds, became living specters in many a home that sought to bar the door to the "unpleasant and irritating business of slavery agitation."

THE DRIFT OF EVENTS TOWARD THE IRREPRESSIBLE CONFLICT

Repeal of the Missouri Compromise.—To practical men, after all, the "rub-a-dub" agitation of a few abolitionists, an occasional riot over fugitive slaves, and the vogue of a popular novel seemed of slight or transient importance. They could point with satisfaction to the election returns of 1852; but their very security was founded upon shifting sands. The magnificent triumph of the pro-slavery Democrats in 1852 brought a turn in affairs that destroyed the foundations under their feet. Emboldened by their own strength and the weakness of their opponents, they now dared to repeal the Missouri Compromise. The leader in this fateful enterprise was Stephen A. Douglas, Senator from Illinois, and the occasion for the deed was the demand for the organization of territorial government in the regions west of Iowa and Missouri.

Douglas, like Clay and Webster before him, was consumed by a strong passion for the presidency, and, to reach his goal, it was necessary to win the support of the South. This he undoubtedly sought to do when he introduced on January 4, 1854, a bill organizing the Nebraska territory on the principle of the Compromise of 1850; namely, that the people in the territory might themselves decide whether they would have slavery or not. Unwittingly the avalanche was started.

After a stormy debate, in which important amendments were forced on Douglas, the Kansas-Nebraska Bill became a law on May 30, 1854. The measure created two territories, Kansas and Nebraska, and provided that they, or territories organized out of them, could come into the union as states "with or without slavery as their constitutions may prescribe at the time of their admission." Not content with this, the law went on to declare the Missouri Compromise null and void as being inconsistent with the principle of non-intervention by Congress with slavery in the states and territories. Thus by a single blow the very heart of the continent, dedicated to freedom by solemn agreement, was thrown open to slavery. A desperate struggle between slave owners and the advocates of freedom was the outcome in Kansas.

If Douglas fancied that the North would receive the overthrow of the Missouri Compromise in the same temper that it greeted Clay's settlement, he was rapidly disillusioned. A blast of rage, terrific in its fury, swept from Maine to Iowa. Staid old Boston hanged him in effigy with an inscription—"Stephen A. Douglas, author of the infamous Nebraska bill: the Benedict Arnold of 1854." City after city burned him in effigy until, as he himself said, he could travel from the Atlantic coast to Chicago in the light of the fires. Thousands of Whigs and Free-soil Democrats deserted their parties which had sanctioned or at least tolerated the Kansas-Nebraska Bill, declaring that the startling measure showed an evident resolve on the part of the planters to rule the whole country. A gage of defiance was thrown down to the abolitionists. An issue was set even for the moderate and timid who had been unmoved by the agitation over slavery in the Far South. That issue was whether slavery was to be confined within its existing boundaries or be allowed to spread without interference, thereby placing the free states in the minority and surrendering the federal government wholly to the slave power.

The Rise of the Republican Party.—Events of terrible significance, swiftly following, drove the country like a ship before a gale straight into civil war. The Kansas-Nebraska Bill rent the old parties asunder and called into being the Republican party. While that bill was pending in Congress, many Northern Whigs and Democrats had come to the conclusion that a new party dedicated to freedom in the territories must follow the repeal of the Missouri Compromise. Several places claim to be the original home of the Republican party; but historians generally yield it to Wisconsin. At Ripon in that state, a mass meeting of Whigs and Democrats assembled in February, 1854, and resolved to form a new party if the Kansas-Nebraska Bill should pass. At a second meeting a fusion committee representing Whigs, Free Soilers, and Democrats was formed and the name Republican—the name of Jefferson's old party—was selected. All over the country similar meetings were held and political committees were organized.

When the presidential campaign of 1856 began the Republicans entered the contest. After a preliminary conference in Pittsburgh in February, they held a convention in Philadelphia at which was drawn up a platform opposing the extension of slavery to the territories. John C. Frémont, the distinguished explorer, was named for the presidency. The results of the election were astounding as compared with the Free-soil failure of the preceding election. Prominent men like Longfellow, Washington Irving, William Cullen Bryant, Ralph Waldo Emerson, and George William Curtis went over to the new party and 1,341,264 votes were rolled up for "free labor, free speech, free men, free Kansas, and Frémont." Nevertheless the victory of the Democrats was decisive. Their candidate, James Buchanan of Pennsylvania, was elected by a majority of 174 to 114 electoral votes.

The Dred Scott Decision (1857).—In his inaugural, Buchanan vaguely hinted that in a forthcoming decision the Supreme Court would settle one of the vital questions of the day. This was a reference to the Dred Scott case then pending. Scott was a slave who had been taken by his master into the upper Louisiana territory, where freedom had been established by the Missouri Compromise, and then carried back into his old state of Missouri. He brought suit for his liberty on the ground that his residence in the free territory made him free. This raised the question whether the law of Congress prohibiting slavery north of 36° 30' was authorized by the federal Constitution or not. The Court might have avoided answering it by saying that even though Scott was free in the territory, he became a slave again in Missouri by virtue of the law of that state. The Court, however, faced the issue squarely. It held that Scott had not been free anywhere and that, besides, the Missouri Compromise violated the Constitution and was null and void.

The decision was a triumph for the South. It meant that Congress after all had no power to abolish slavery in the territories. Under the decree of the highest court in the land, that could be done only by an amendment to the Constitution which required a two-thirds vote in Congress and the approval of three-fourths of the states. Such an amendment was obviously impossible—the Southern states were too numerous; but the Republicans were not daunted. "We know," said Lincoln, "the Court that made it has often overruled its own decisions and we shall do what we can to have it overrule this." Legislatures of Northern states passed resolutions condemning the decision and the Republican platform of 1860 characterized the dogma that the Constitution carried slavery into the territories as "a dangerous political heresy at variance with the explicit provisions of that instrument itself ... with legislative and judicial precedent ... revolutionary in tendency and subversive of the peace and harmony of the country."

The Panic of 1857.—In the midst of the acrimonious dispute over the Dred Scott decision, came one of the worst business panics which ever afflicted the country. In the spring and summer of 1857, fourteen railroad corporations, including the Erie, Michigan Central, and the Illinois Central, failed to meet their obligations; banks and insurance companies, some of them the largest and strongest institutions in the North, closed their doors; stocks and bonds came down in a crash on the markets; manufacturing was paralyzed; tens of thousands of working people were thrown out of employment; "hunger meetings" of idle men were held in the cities and bannersbearing the inscription, "We want bread," were flung out. In New York, working men threatened to invade the Council Chamber to demand "work or bread," and the frightened mayor called for the police and soldiers. For this distressing state of affairs many remedies were offered; none with more zeal and persistence than the proposal for a higher tariff to take the place of the law of March, 1857, a Democratic measure making drastic reductions in the rates of duty. In the manufacturing districts of the North, the panic was ascribed to the "Democratic assault on business." So an old issue was again vigorously advanced, preparatory to the next presidential campaign.

The Lincoln-Douglas Debates.—The following year the interest of the whole country was drawn to a series of debates held in Illinois by Lincoln and Douglas, both candidates for the United States Senate. In the course of his campaign Lincoln had uttered his trenchant saying that "a house divided against itself cannot stand. I believe this government cannot endure permanently half slave and half free." At the same time he had accused Douglas, Buchanan, and the Supreme Court of acting in concert to make slavery national. This daring statement arrested the attention of Douglas, who was making his campaign on the doctrine of "squatter sovereignty;" that is, the right of the people of each territory "to vote slavery up or down." After a few long-distance shots at each other, the candidates agreed to meet face to face and discuss the issues of the day. Never had such crowds been seen at political meetings in Illinois. Farmers deserted their plows, smiths their forges, and housewives their baking to hear "Honest Abe" and "the Little Giant."

The results of the series of debates were momentous. Lincoln clearly defined his position. The South, he admitted, was entitled under the Constitution to a fair, fugitive slave law. He hoped that there might be no new slave states; but he did not see how Congress could exclude the people of a territory from admission as a state if they saw fit to adopt a constitution legalizing the ownership of slaves. He favored the gradual abolition of slavery in the District of Columbia and the total exclusion of it from the territories of the United States by act of Congress.

Moreover, he drove Douglas into a hole by asking how he squared "squatter sovereignty" with the Dred Scott decision; how, in other words, the people of a territory could abolish slavery when the Court had declared that Congress, the superior power, could not do it under the Constitution? To this baffling question Douglas lamely replied that the inhabitants of a territory, by "unfriendly legislation," might make property in slaves insecure and thus destroy the institution. This answer to Lincoln's query alienated many Southern Democrats who believed that the Dred Scott decision settled the question of slavery in the territories for all time. Douglas won the election to the Senate; but Lincoln, lifted into national fame by the debates, beat him in the campaign for President two years later.

John Brown's Raid.—To the abolitionists the line of argument pursued by Lincoln, including his proposal to leave slavery untouched in the states where it existed, was wholly unsatisfactory. One of them, a grim and resolute man, inflamed by a hatred for slavery in itself, turned from agitation to violence. "These men are all talk; what is needed is action—action!" So spoke John Brown of New York. During the sanguinary struggle in Kansas he hurried to the frontier, gun and dagger in hand, to help drive slave owners from the free soil of the West. There he committed deeds of such daring and cruelty that he was outlawed and a price put upon his head. Still he kept on the path of "action." Aided by funds from Northern friends, he gathered a small band of his followers around him, saying to them: "If God be for us, who can be against us?" He went into Virginia in the autumn of 1859, hoping, as he explained, "to effect a mighty conquest even though it be like the last victory of Samson." He seized the government armory at Harper's Ferry, declared free the slaves whom he found, and called upon them to take up arms in defense of their liberty. His was a hope as forlorn as it was desperate. Armed forces came down upon him and, after a hard battle, captured him. Tried for treason, Brown was condemned to death. The governor of Virginia turned a deaf ear to pleas for clemency based on the ground that the prisoner was simply a lunatic. "This is a beautiful country," said the stern old Brown glancing upward to the eternal hills on his way to the gallows, as calmly as if he were returning home from a long journey. "So perish all such enemies of Virginia. All such enemies of the Union. All such foes of the human race," solemnly announced the executioner as he fulfilled the judgment of the law.

The raid and its grim ending deeply moved the country. Abolitionists looked upon Brown as a martyr and tolled funeral bells on the day of his execution. Longfellow wrote in his diary: "This will be a great day in our history; the date of a new revolution as much needed as the old one." Jefferson Davis saw in the affair "the invasion of a state by a murderous gang of abolitionists bent on inciting slaves to murder helpless women and children"—a crime for which the leader had met a felon's death. Lincoln spoke of the raid as absurd, the deed of an enthusiast who had brooded over the oppression of a people until he fancied himself commissioned by heaven to liberate them—an attempt which ended in "little else than his own execution." To Republican leaders as a whole, the event was very embarrassing. They were taunted by the Democrats with responsibility for the deed. Douglas declared his "firm and deliberate conviction that the Harper's Ferry crime was the natural, logical, inevitable result of the doctrines and teachings of the

Republican party." So persistent were such attacks that the Republicans felt called upon in 1860 to denounce Brown's raid "as among the gravest of crimes."

The Democrats Divided.—When the Democratic convention met at Charleston in the spring of 1860, a few months after Brown's execution, it soon became clear that there was danger ahead. Between the extreme slavery advocates of the Far South and the so-called pro-slavery Democrats of the Douglas type, there was a chasm which no appeals to party loyalty could bridge. As the spokesman of the West, Douglas knew that, while the North was not abolitionist, it was passionately set against an extension of slavery into the territories by act of Congress; that squatter sovereignty was the mildest kind of compromise acceptable to the farmers whose votes would determine the fate of the election. Southern leaders would not accept his opinion. Yancey, speaking for Alabama, refused to palter with any plan not built on the proposition that slavery was in itself right. He taunted the Northern Democrats with taking the view that slavery was wrong, but that they could not do anything about it. That, he said, was the fatal error—the cause of all discord, the source of "Black Republicanism," as well as squatter sovereignty. The gauntlet was thus thrown down at the feet of the Northern delegates: "You must not apologize for slavery; you must declare it right; you must advocate its extension." The challenge, so bluntly put, was as bluntly answered. "Gentlemen of the South," responded a delegate from Ohio, "you mistake us. You mistake us. We will not do it."

For ten days the Charleston convention wrangled over the platform and balloted for the nomination of a candidate. Douglas, though in the lead, could not get the two-thirds vote required for victory. For more than fifty times the roll of the convention was called without a decision. Then in sheer desperation the convention adjourned to meet later at Baltimore. When the delegates again assembled, their passions ran as high as ever. The division into two irreconcilable factions was unchanged. Uncompromising delegates from the South withdrew to Richmond, nominated John C. Breckinridge of Kentucky for President, and put forth a platform asserting the rights of slave owners in the territories and the duty of the federal government to protect them. The delegates who remained at Baltimore nominated Douglas and endorsed his doctrine of squatter sovereignty.

The Constitutional Union Party.—While the Democratic party was being disrupted, a fragment of the former Whig party, known as the Constitutional Unionists, held a convention at Baltimore and selected national candidates: John Bell from Tennessee and Edward Everett from Massachusetts. A melancholy interest attached to this assembly. It was mainly composed of old men whose political views were those of Clay and Webster, cherished leaders now dead and gone. In their platform they sought to exorcise the evil spirit of partisanship by inviting their fellow citizens to "support the Constitution of the country, the union of the states, and the enforcement of the laws." The party that campaigned on this grand sentiment only drew laughter from the Democrats and derision from the Republicans and polled less than one-fourth the votes.

The Republican Convention.—With the Whigs definitely forced into a separate group, the Republican convention at Chicago was fated to be sectional in character, although five slave states did send delegates. As the Democrats were split, the party that had led a forlorn hope four years before was on the high road to success at last. New and powerful recruits were found. The advocates of a high protective tariff and the friends of free homesteads for farmers and workingmen mingled with enthusiastic foes of slavery. While still firm in their opposition to slavery in the territories, the Republicans went on record in favor of a homestead law granting free lands to settlers and approved customs duties designed "to encourage the development of the industrial interests of the whole country." The platform was greeted with cheers which, according to the stenographic report of the convention, became loud and prolonged as the protective tariff and homestead planks were read.

Having skillfully drawn a platform to unite the North in opposition to slavery and the planting system, the Republicans were also adroit in their selection of a candidate. The tariff plank might carry Pennsylvania, a Democratic state; but Ohio, Indiana, and Illinois were equally essential to success at the polls. The southern counties of these states were filled with settlers from Virginia, North Carolina, and Kentucky who, even if they had no love for slavery, were no friends of abolition. Moreover, remembering the old fight on the United States Bank in Andrew Jackson's day, they were suspicious of men from the East. Accordingly, they did not favor the candidacy of Seward, the leading Republican statesman and "favorite son" of New York.

After much trading and discussing, the convention came to the conclusion that Abraham Lincoln of Illinois was the most "available" candidate. He was of Southern origin, born in Kentucky in 1809, a fact that told heavily in the campaign in the Ohio Valley. He was a man of the soil, the son of poor frontier parents, a pioneer who in his youth had labored in the fields and forests, celebrated far and wide as "honest Abe, the rail-splitter." It was well-known that he disliked slavery, but was no abolitionist. He had come dangerously near to Seward's radicalism in his "house-divided-against-itself" speech but he had never committed himself to the reckless doctrine that there was a "higher law" than the Constitution. Slavery in the South he tolerated as a bitter fact; slavery in the territories he opposed with all his strength. Of his sincerity there could be no doubt. He was a speaker and writer of singular power, commanding, by the use of simple and homely language, the hearts and minds of those who heard him speak or read his printed words. He had gone far enough in his opposition to slavery; but not too far. He was the man of the hour! Amid lusty cheers from ten thousand throats, Lincoln was nominated for the presidency by the Republicans. In the ensuing election, he carried all the free states except New Jersey.

References

P.E. Chadwick, *Causes of the Civil War* (American Nation Series).

W.E. Dodd, *Statesmen of the Old South*.

E. Engle, *Southern Sidelights* (Sympathetic account of the Old South).

A.B. Hart, *Slavery and Abolition* (American Nation Series).

J.F. Rhodes, *History of the United States*, Vols. I and II.

T.C. Smith, *Parties and Slavery* (American Nation Series).

Questions

1. Trace the decline of slavery in the North and explain it.

2. Describe the character of early opposition to slavery.

3. What was the effect of abolition agitation?

4. Why did anti-slavery sentiment practically disappear in the South?

5. On what grounds did Calhoun defend slavery?

6. Explain how slave owners became powerful in politics.

7. Why was it impossible to keep the slavery issue out of national politics?

8. Give the leading steps in the long controversy over slavery in the territories.

9. State the terms of the Compromise of 1850 and explain its failure.

10. What were the startling events between 1850 and 1860?

11. Account for the rise of the Republican party. What party had used the title before?

12. How did the Dred Scott decision become a political issue?

13. What were some of the points brought out in the Lincoln-Douglas debates?

14. Describe the party division in 1860.

15. What were the main planks in the Republican platform?

Research Topics

The Extension of Cotton Planting.—Callender, *Economic History of the United States*, pp. 760-768.

Abolition Agitation.—McMaster, *History of the People of the United States*, Vol. VI, pp. 271-298.

Calhoun's Defense of Slavery.—Harding, *Select Orations Illustrating American History*, pp. 247-257.

The Compromise of 1850.—Clay's speech in Harding, *Select Orations*, pp. 267-289. The compromise laws in Macdonald, *Documentary Source Book of American History*, pp. 383-394. Narrative account in McMaster, Vol. VIII, pp. 1-55; Elson, *History of the United States*, pp. 540-548.

The Repeal of the Missouri Compromise.—McMaster, Vol. VIII, pp. 192-231; Elson, pp. 571-582.

The Dred Scott Case.—McMaster, Vol. VIII, pp. 278-282. Compare the opinion of Taney and the dissent of Curtis in Macdonald, *Documentary Source Book*, pp. 405-420; Elson, pp. 595-598.

The Lincoln-Douglas Debates.—Analysis of original speeches in Harding, *Select Orations* pp. 309-341; Elson, pp. 598-604.

Biographical Studies.—Calhoun, Clay, Webster, A.H. Stephens, Douglas, W.H. Seward, William Lloyd Garrison, Wendell Phillips, and Harriet Beecher Stowe.

CHAPTER XV

THE CIVIL WAR AND RECONSTRUCTION

"The irrepressible conflict is about to be visited upon us through the Black Republican nominee and his fanatical, diabolical Republican party," ran an appeal to the voters of South Carolina during the campaign of 1860. If that calamity comes to pass, responded the governor of the state, the answer should be a declaration of independence. In a few days the suspense was over. The news of Lincoln's election came speeding along the wires. Prepared for the event, the editor of the Charleston *Mercury* unfurled the flag of his state amid wild cheers from an excited throng in the streets. Then he seized his pen and wrote: "The tea has been thrown overboard; the revolution of 1860 has been initiated." The issue was submitted to the voters in the choice of delegates to a state convention called to cast off the yoke of the Constitution.

THE SOUTHERN CONFEDERACY

Secession.—As arranged, the convention of South Carolina assembled in December and without a dissenting voice passed the ordinance of secession withdrawing from the union. Bells were rung exultantly, the roar of cannon carried the news to outlying counties, fireworks lighted up the heavens, and champagne flowed. The crisis so long expected had come at last; even the conservatives who had prayed that they might escape the dreadful crash greeted it with a sigh of relief.

South Carolina now sent forth an appeal to her sister states—states that had in Jackson's day repudiated nullification as leading to "the dissolution of the union." The answer that came this time was in a different vein. A month had hardly elapsed before five other states—Florida, Georgia, Alabama, Mississippi, and Louisiana—had withdrawn from the union. In February, Texas followed. Virginia, hesitating until the bombardment of Fort Sumter forced a conclusion, seceded in April; but fifty-five of the one hundred and forty-three delegates dissented, foreshadowing the creation of the new state of West Virginia which Congress admitted to the union in 1863. In May, North Carolina, Arkansas, and Tennessee announced their independence.

Secession and the Theories of the Union.—In severing their relations with the union, the seceding states denied every point in the Northern theory of the Constitution. That theory, as every one knows, was carefully formulated by Webster and elaborated by Lincoln. According to it, the union was older than the states; it was created before the Declaration of Independence for the purpose of common defense. The Articles of Confederation did but strengthen this national bond and the Constitution sealed it forever. The federal government was not a creature of state governments. It was erected by the people and derived its powers directly from them. "It is," said Webster, "the people's Constitution, the people's government; made for the people; made by the people; and answerable to the people. The people of the United States have declared that this Constitution shall be the supreme law." When a state questions the lawfulness of any act of the federal government, it cannot nullify that act or withdraw from the union; it must abide by the decision of the Supreme Court of the United States. The union of these states is perpetual, ran Lincoln's simple argument in the first inaugural; the federal Constitution has no provision for its own termination; it can be destroyed only by some action not provided for in the instrument itself; even if it is a compact among all the states the consent of all must be necessary to its dissolution; therefore no state can lawfully get out of the union and acts of violence against the United States are insurrectionary or revolutionary. This was the system which he believed himself bound to defend by his oath of office "registered in heaven."

All this reasoning Southern statesmen utterly rejected. In their opinion the thirteen original states won their independence as separate and sovereign powers. The treaty of peace with Great Britain named them all and acknowledged them "to be free, sovereign, and independent states." The Articles of Confederation very explicitly declared that "each state retains its sovereignty, freedom, and independence." The Constitution was a "league of nations" formed by an alliance of thirteen separate powers, each one of which ratified the instrument before it was put into effect. They voluntarily entered the union under the Constitution and voluntarily they could leave it. Such was the constitutional doctrine of Hayne, Calhoun, and Jefferson Davis. In seceding, the Southern states had only to follow legal methods, and the transaction would be correct in every particular. So conventions were summoned, elections were held, and "sovereign assemblies of the people" set aside the Constitution in the same manner as it had been ratified nearly four score years before. Thus, said the Southern people, the moral judgment was fulfilled and the letter of the law carried into effect.

The Formation of the Confederacy.—Acting on the call of Mississippi, a congress of delegates from the seceded states met at Montgomery, Alabama, and on February 8, 1861, adopted a temporary plan of union. It selected, as provisional president, Jefferson Davis of Mississippi, a man well fitted by experience and moderation for leadership, a graduate of West Point, who had rendered distinguished service on the field of battle in the Mexican War, in public office, and as a member of Congress.

In March, a permanent constitution of the Confederate states was drafted. It was quickly ratified by the states; elections were held in November; and the government under it went into effect the next year. This new constitution, in form, was very much like the famous instrument drafted at Philadelphia in 1787. It provided for a President, a Senate, and a House of Representatives along almost identical lines. In the powers conferred upon them, however, there were striking differences. The right to appropriate money for internal improvements was expressly withheld; bounties were not to be granted from the treasury nor import duties so laid as to promote or foster any branch of industry. The dignity of the state, if any might be bold enough to question it, was safeguarded in the opening line by the declaration that each acted "in its sovereign and independent character" in forming the Southern union.

Financing the Confederacy.—No government ever set out upon its career with more perplexing tasks in front of it. The North had a monetary system; the South had to create one. The North had a scheme of taxation that produced large revenues from numerous sources; the South had to formulate and carry out a financial plan. Like the North, the Confederacy expected to secure a large revenue from customs duties, easily collected and little felt among the masses. To this expectation the blockade of Southern ports inaugurated by Lincoln in April, 1861, soon put an end. Following the precedent set by Congress under the Articles of Confederation, the Southern Congress resorted to a direct property tax apportioned among the states, only to meet the failure that might have been foretold.

The Confederacy also sold bonds, the first issue bringing into the treasury nearly all the specie available in the Southern banks. This specie by unhappy management was early sent abroad to pay for supplies, sapping the foundations of a sound currency system. Large amounts of bonds were sold overseas, commanding at first better terms than those of the North in the markets of London, Paris, and Amsterdam, many an English lord and statesman buying with enthusiasm and confidence to lament within a few years the proofs of his folly. The difficulties of bringing through the blockade any supplies purchased by foreign bond issues, however, nullified the effect of foreign credit and forced the Confederacy back upon the device of paper money. In all approximately one billion dollars streamed from the printing presses, to fall in value at an alarming rate, reaching in January, 1863, the astounding figure of fifty dollars in paper money for one in gold. Every known device was used to prevent its depreciation, without result. To the issues of the Confederate Congress were added untold millions poured out by the states and by private banks.

Human and Material Resources.—When we measure strength for strength in those signs of power—men, money, and supplies—it is difficult to see how the South was able to embark on secession and war with such confidence in the outcome. In the Confederacy at the final reckoning there were eleven states in all, to be pitted against twenty-two; a population of nine millions, nearly one-half servile, to be pitted against twenty-two millions; a land without great industries to produce war supplies and without vast capital to furnish war finances, joined in battle with a nation already industrial and fortified by property worth eleven billion dollars. Even after the Confederate Congress authorized conscription in 1862, Southern man power, measured in numbers, was wholly inadequate to uphold the independence which had been declared. How, therefore, could the Confederacy hope to sustain itself against such a combination of men, money, and materials as the North could marshal?

Southern Expectations.—The answer to this question is to be found in the ideas that prevailed among Southern leaders. First of all, they hoped, in vain, to carry the Confederacy up to the Ohio River; and, with the aid of Missouri, to gain possession of the Mississippi Valley, the granary of the nation. In the second place, they reckoned upon a large and continuous trade with Great Britain—the exchange of cotton for war materials. They likewise expected to receive recognition and open aid from European powers that looked with satisfaction upon the breakup of the great American republic. In the third place, they believed that their control over several staples so essential to Northern industry would enable them to bring on an industrial crisis in the manufacturing states. "I firmly believe," wrote Senator Hammond, of South Carolina, in 1860, "that the slave-holding South is now the controlling power of the world; that no other power would face us in hostility. Cotton, rice, tobacco, and naval stores command the world; and we have the sense to know it and are sufficiently Teutonic to carry it out successfully. The North without us would be a motherless calf, bleating about, and die of mange and starvation."

There were other grounds for confidence. Having seized all of the federal military and naval supplies in the South, and having left the national government weak in armed power during their possession of the presidency, Southern leaders looked to a swift war, if it came at all, to put the finishing stroke to independence. "The greasy mechanics of the North," it was repeatedly said, "will not fight." As to disparity in numbers they drew historic parallels. "Our fathers, a mere handful, overcame the enormous power of Great Britain," a saying of ex-President Tyler, ran current to reassure the doubtful. Finally, and this point cannot be too strongly emphasized, the South expected to see a weakened and divided North. It knew that the abolitionists and the Southern sympathizers were ready to let the Confederate states go in peace; that Lincoln represented only a little more than one-third the voters of the country; and that the vote for Douglas, Bell, and Breckinridge meant a decided opposition to the Republicans and their policies.

Efforts at Compromise.—Republican leaders, on reviewing the same facts, were themselves uncertain as to the outcome of a civil war and made many efforts to avoid a crisis. Thurlow Weed, an Albany journalist and politician who had done much to carry New York for Lincoln, proposed a plan for extending the Missouri Compromise line to the Pacific. Jefferson Davis, warning his followers that a war if it came would be terrible, was prepared to accept the offer; but Lincoln, remembering his campaign pledges, stood firm as a rock against it. His followers in Congress took the same position with regard to a similar settlement suggested by Senator Crittenden of Kentucky.

Though unwilling to surrender his solemn promises respecting slavery in the territories, Lincoln was prepared to give to Southern leaders a strong guarantee that his administration would not interfere directly or indirectly with slavery in the states. Anxious to reassure the South on this point, the Republicans in Congress proposed to write into the Constitution a declaration that no amendment should ever be made authorizing the abolition of or interference with slavery in any state. The resolution, duly passed, was sent forth on March 4, 1861, with the approval of Lincoln; it was actually ratified by three states before the storm of war destroyed it. By the irony of fate the thirteenth amendment was to abolish, not guarantee, slavery.

THE WAR MEASURES OF THE FEDERAL GOVERNMENT

Raising the Armies.—The crisis at Fort Sumter, on April 12-14, 1861, forced the President and Congress to turn from negotiations to problems of warfare. Little did they realize the magnitude of the task before them. Lincoln's first call for volunteers, issued on April 15, 1861, limited the number to 75,000, put their term of service at three months, and prescribed their duty as the enforcement of the law against combinations too powerful to be overcome by ordinary judicial process. Disillusionment swiftly followed.

The terrible defeat of the Federals at Bull Run on July 21 revealed the serious character of the task before them; and by a series of measures Congress put the entire man power of the country at the President's command. Under these acts, he issued new calls for volunteers. Early in August, 1862, he ordered a draft of militiamen numbering 300,000 for nine months' service. The results were disappointing—ominous—for only about 87,000 soldiers were added to the army. Something more drastic was clearly necessary.

In March, 1863, Lincoln signed the inevitable draft law; it enrolled in the national forces liable to military duty all able-bodied male citizens and persons of foreign birth who had declared their intention to become citizens, between the ages of twenty and forty-five years—with exemptions on grounds of physical weakness and dependency. From the men enrolled were drawn by lot those destined to active service. Unhappily the measure struck a mortal blow at the principle of universal liability by excusing any person who found a substitute for himself or paid into the war office a sum, not exceeding three hundred dollars, to be fixed by general order. This provision, so crass and so obviously favoring the well-to-do, sowed seeds of bitterness which sprang up a hundredfold in the North.

The beginning of the drawings under the draft act in New York City, on Monday, July 13, 1863, was the signal for four days of rioting. In the course of this uprising, draft headquarters were destroyed; the office of the *Tribune* was gutted; negroes were seized, hanged, and shot; the homes of obnoxious Unionists were burned down; the residence of the mayor of the city was attacked; and regular battles were fought in the streets between the rioters and the police. Business stopped and a large part of the city passed absolutely into the control of the mob. Not until late the following Wednesday did enough troops arrive to restore order and enable the residents of the city to resume their daily activities. At least a thousand people had been killed or wounded and more than a million dollars' worth of damage done to property. The draft temporarily interrupted by this outbreak was then resumed and carried out without further trouble.

The results of the draft were in the end distinctly disappointing to the government. The exemptions were numerous and the number who preferred and were able to pay $300 rather than serve exceeded all expectations. Volunteering, it is true, was stimulated, but even that resource could hardly keep the thinning ranks of the army filled. With reluctance Congress struck out the $300 exemption clause, but still favored the well-to-do by allowing them to hire substitutes if they could find them. With all this power in its hands the administration was able by January, 1865, to construct a union army that outnumbered the Confederates two to one.

War Finance.—In the financial sphere the North faced immense difficulties. The surplus in the treasury had been dissipated by 1861 and the tariff of 1857 had failed to produce an income sufficient to meet the ordinary expenses of the government. Confronted by military and naval expenditures of appalling magnitude, rising from $35,000,000 in the first year of the war to $1,153,000,000 in the last year, the administration had to tap every available source of income. The duties on imports were increased, not once but many times, producing huge revenues and also meeting the most extravagant demands of the manufacturers for protection. Direct taxes were imposed on the states according to their respective populations, but the returns were meager—all out of proportion to the irritation involved. Stamp taxes and taxes on luxuries, occupations, and the earnings of corporations were laid with a weight that, in ordinary times, would have drawn forth opposition of ominous strength. The whole gamut of taxation was run. Even a tax on incomes and gains by the year, the first in the history of the federal government, was included in the long list.

Revenues were supplemented by bond issues, mounting in size and interest rate, until in October, at the end of the war, the debt stood at $2,208,000,000. The total cost of the war was many times the money value of all the slaves in the Southern states. To the debt must be added nearly half a billion dollars in "greenbacks"—paper money issued by Congress in desperation as bond sales and revenues from taxes failed to meet the rising expenditures. This currency issued at par on questionable warrant from the Constitution, like all such paper, quickly began to decline until in the worst fortunes of 1864 one dollar in gold was worth nearly three in greenbacks.

The Blockade of Southern Ports.—Four days after his call for volunteers, April 19, 1861, President Lincoln issued a proclamation blockading the ports of the Southern Confederacy. Later the blockade was extended to Virginia and North Carolina, as they withdrew from the union. Vessels attempting to enter or leave these ports, if they disregarded the warnings of a blockading ship, were to be captured and brought as prizes to the nearest convenient port. To make the order effective, immediate steps were taken to increase the naval forces, depleted by neglect, until the entire coast line was patrolled with such a number of ships that it was a rare captain who ventured to run the gantlet. The collision between the *Merrimac* and the *Monitor* in March, 1862, sealed the fate of the Confederacy. The exploits of the union navy are recorded in the falling export of cotton: $202,000,000 in 1860; $42,000,000 in 1861; and $4,000,000 in 1862.

The deadly effect of this paralysis of trade upon Southern war power may be readily imagined. Foreign loans, payable in cotton, could be negotiated but not paid off. Supplies could be purchased on credit but not brought through the drag net. With extreme difficulty could the Confederate government secure even paper for the issue of money and bonds. Publishers, in despair at the loss of supplies, were finally driven to the use of brown wrapping paper and wall paper. As the railways and rolling stock wore out, it became impossible to renew them from England or France. Unable to export their cotton, planters on the seaboard burned it in what were called "fires of patriotism." In their lurid light the fatal weakness of Southern economy stood revealed.

Diplomacy.—The war had not advanced far before the federal government became involved in many perplexing problems of diplomacy in Europe. The Confederacy early turned to England and France for financial aid and for recognition as an independent power. Davis believed that the industrial crisis created by the cotton blockade would in time literally compel Europe to intervene in order to get this essential staple. The crisis came as he expected but not the result. Thousands of English textile workers were thrown out of employment; and yet, while on the point of starvation, they adopted resolutions favoring the North instead of petitioning their government to aid the South by breaking the blockade.

With the ruling classes it was far otherwise. Napoleon III, the Emperor of the French, was eager to help in disrupting the American republic; if he could have won England's support, he would have carried out his designs. As it turned out he found plenty of sympathy across the Channel but not open and official coöperation. According to the eminent historian, Rhodes, "four-fifths of the British House of Lords and most members of the House of Commons were favorable to the Confederacy and anxious for its triumph." Late in 1862 the British ministers, thus sustained, were on the point of recognizing the independence of the Confederacy. Had it not been for their extreme caution, for the constant and harassing criticism by English friends of the United States—like John Bright—and for the victories of Vicksburg and Gettysburg, both England and France would have doubtless declared the Confederacy to be one of the independent powers of the earth.

While stopping short of recognizing its independence, England and France took several steps that were in favor of the South. In proclaiming neutrality, they early accepted the Confederates as "belligerents" and accorded them the rights of people at war—a measure which aroused anger in the North at first but was later admitted to be sound. Otherwise Confederates taken in battle would have been regarded as "rebels" or "traitors" to be hanged or shot. Napoleon III proposed to Russia in 1861 a coalition of powers against the North, only to meet a firm refusal. The next year he suggested intervention to Great Britain, encountering this time a conditional rejection of his plans. In 1863, not daunted by rebuffs, he offered his services to Lincoln as a mediator, receiving in reply a polite letter declining his proposal and a sharp resolution from Congress suggesting that he attend to his own affairs.

In both England and France the governments pursued a policy of friendliness to the Confederate agents. The British ministry, with indifference if not connivance, permitted rams and ships to be built in British docks and allowed them to escape to play havoc under the Confederate flag with American commerce. One of them, the *Alabama*, built in Liverpool by a British firm and paid for by bonds sold in England, ran an extraordinary career and threatened to break the blockade. The course followed by the British government, against the protests of the American minister in London, was later regretted. By an award of a tribunal of arbitration at Geneva in 1872, Great Britain was required to pay the huge sum of $15,500,000 to cover the damages wrought by Confederate cruisers fitted out in England.

In all fairness it should be said that the conduct of the North contributed to the irritation between the two countries. Seward, the Secretary of State, was vindictive in dealing with Great Britain; had it not been for the moderation of Lincoln, he would have pursued a course verging in the direction of open war. The New York and Boston papers were severe in their attacks on England. Words were, on one occasion at least, accompanied by an act savoring of open hostility. In November, 1861, Captain Wilkes, commanding a union vessel, overhauled the British steamer *Trent*, and carried off by force two Confederate agents, Mason and Slidell, sent by President Davis to represent the Confederacy at London and Paris respectively. This was a clear violation of the right of merchant vessels to be immune from search and impressment; and, in answer to the demand of Great Britain for the release of the two men, the United States conceded that it was in the wrong. It surrendered the two Confederate agents to a British vessel for safe conduct abroad, and made appropriate apologies.

Emancipation.—Among the extreme war measures adopted by the Northern government must be counted the emancipation of the slaves in the states in arms against the union. This step was early and repeatedly suggested to Lincoln by the abolitionists; but was steadily put aside. He knew that the abolitionists were a mere handful, that emancipation might drive the border states into secession, and that the Northern soldiers had enlisted to save the union. Moreover, he had before him a solemn resolution passed by Congress on July 22, 1861, declaring the sole purpose of the war to be the salvation of the union and disavowing any intention of interfering with slavery.

The federal government, though pledged to the preservation of slavery, soon found itself beaten back upon its course and out upon a new tack. Before a year had elapsed, namely on April 10, 1862, Congress resolved that financial aid should be given to any state that might adopt gradual emancipation. Six days later it abolished slavery in the District of Columbia. Two short months elapsed. On June 19, 1862, it swept slavery forever from the territories of the United States. Chief Justice Taney still lived, the Dred Scott decision stood as written in the book, but the Constitution had been re-read in the light of the Civil War. The drift of public sentiment in the North was being revealed.

While these measures were pending in Congress, Lincoln was slowly making up his mind. By July of that year he had come to his great decision. Near the end of that month he read to his cabinet the draft of a proclamation of emancipation; but he laid it aside until a military achievement would make it something more than an idle gesture. In September, the severe check administered to Lee at Antietam seemed to offer the golden opportunity. On the 22d, the immortal document was given to the world announcing that, unless the states in arms returned to the union by January 1, 1863, the fatal blow at their "peculiar institution" would be delivered. Southern leaders treated it with slight regard, and so on the date set the promise was fulfilled. The proclamation was issued as a war measure, adopted by the President as commander-in-chief of the armed forces, on grounds of military necessity. It did not abolish slavery. It simply emancipated slaves in places then in arms against federal authority. Everywhere else slavery, as far as the Proclamation was concerned, remained lawful.

To seal forever the proclamation of emancipation, and to extend freedom to the whole country, Congress, in January, 1865, on the urgent recommendation of Lincoln, transmitted to the states the thirteenth amendment, abolishing slavery throughout the United States. By the end of 1865 the amendment was ratified. The house was not divided against itself; it did not fall; it was all free.

The Restraint of Civil Liberty.—As in all great wars, particularly those in the nature of a civil strife, it was found necessary to use strong measures to sustain opinion favorable to the administration's military policies and to frustrate the designs of those who sought to hamper its action. Within two weeks of his first call for volunteers, Lincoln empowered General Scott to suspend the writ of *habeas corpus* along the line of march between Philadelphia and Washington and thus to arrest and hold without interference from civil courts any one whom he deemed a menace to the union. At a later date the area thus ruled by military officers was extended by executive proclamation. By an act of March 3, 1863, Congress, desiring to lay all doubts about the President's power, authorized him to suspend the writ throughout the United States or in any part thereof. It also freed military officers from the necessity of surrendering to civil courts persons arrested under their orders, or even making answers to writs issued from such courts. In the autumn of that year the President, acting under the terms of this law, declared this ancient and honorable instrument for the protection of civil liberties, the *habeas corpus*, suspended throughout the length and breadth of the land. The power of the government was also strengthened by an act defining and punishing certain conspiracies, passed on July 31, 1861—a measure which imposed heavy penalties on those who by force, intimidation, or threat interfered with the execution of the law.

Thus doubly armed, the military authorities spared no one suspected of active sympathy with the Southern cause. Editors were arrested and imprisoned, their papers suspended, and their newsboys locked up. Those who organized "peace meetings" soon found themselves in the toils of the law. Members of the Maryland legislature, the mayor of Baltimore, and local editors suspected of entertaining secessionist opinions, were imprisoned on military orders although charged with no offense, and were denied the privilege of examination before a civil magistrate. A Vermont farmer, too outspoken in his criticism of the government, found himself behind the bars until the government, in its good pleasure, saw fit to release him. These measures were not confined to the theater of war nor to the border states where the spirit of secession was strong enough to endanger the cause of union. They were applied all through the Northern states up to the very boundaries of Canada. Zeal for the national cause, too often supplemented by a zeal for persecution, spread terror among those who wavered in the singleness of their devotion to the union.

These drastic operations on the part of military authorities, so foreign to the normal course of civilized life, naturally aroused intense and bitter hostility. Meetings of protest were held throughout the country. Thirty-six members of the House of Representatives sought to put on record their condemnation of the suspension of the *habeas corpus* act, only to meet a firm denial by the supporters of the act. Chief Justice Taney, before whom the case of a man arrested under the President's military authority was brought, emphatically declared, in a long and learned opinion bristling with historical examples, that the President had no power to suspend the writ of *habeas corpus*. In Congress and out, Democrats, abolitionists, and champions of civil liberty denounced Lincoln and his Cabinet in unsparing terms. Vallandigham, a Democratic leader of Ohio, afterward banished to the South for his opposition to the war, constantly applied to Lincoln the epithet of "Cæsar." Wendell Phillips saw in him "a more unlimited despot than the world knows this side of China."

Sensitive to such stinging thrusts and no friend of wanton persecution, Lincoln attempted to mitigate the rigors of the law by paroling many political prisoners. The general policy, however, he defended in homely language, very different in tone and meaning from the involved reasoning of the lawyers. "Must I shoot a simple-minded soldier boy who deserts, while I must not touch a hair of the wily agitator who induces him to desert?" he asked in a quiet way of some spokesmen for those who protested against arresting people for "talking against the war." This summed up his philosophy. He was engaged in a war to save the union, and all measures necessary and proper to accomplish that purpose were warranted by the Constitution which he had sworn to uphold.

Military Strategy—North and South.—The broad outlines of military strategy followed by the commanders of the opposing forces are clear even to the layman who cannot be expected to master the details of a campaign or, for that matter, the maneuvers of a single great battle. The problem for the South was one of defense mainly, though even for defense swift and paralyzing strokes at the North were later deemed imperative measures. The problem of the North was, to put it baldly, one of invasion and conquest. Southern territory had to be invaded and Southern armies beaten on their own ground or worn down to exhaustion there.

In the execution of this undertaking, geography, as usual, played a significant part in the disposition of forces. The Appalachian ranges, stretching through the Confederacy to Northern Alabama, divided the campaigns into Eastern and Western enterprises. Both were of signal importance. Victory in the East promised the capture of the Confederate capital of Richmond, a stroke of moral worth, hardly to be overestimated. Victory in the West meant severing the Confederacy and opening the Mississippi Valley down to the Gulf.

As it turned out, the Western forces accomplished their task first, vindicating the military powers of union soldiers and shaking the confidence of opposing commanders. In February, 1862, Grant captured Fort Donelson on the Tennessee River, rallied wavering unionists in Kentucky, forced the evacuation of Nashville, and opened the way for two hundred miles into the Confederacy. At Shiloh, Murfreesboro, Vicksburg, Chickamauga, Chattanooga, desperate fighting followed and, in spite of varying fortunes, it resulted in the discomfiture and retirement of Confederate forces to the Southeast into Georgia. By the middle of 1863, the Mississippi Valley was open to the Gulf, the initiative taken out of the hands of Southern commanders in the West, and the way prepared for Sherman's final stroke—the march from Atlanta to the sea—a maneuver executed with needless severity in the autumn of 1864.

For the almost unbroken succession of achievements in the West by Generals Grant, Sherman, Thomas, and Hooker against Albert Sidney Johnston, Bragg, Pemberton, and Hood, the union forces in the East offered at first an almost equally unbroken series of misfortunes and disasters. Far from capturing Richmond, they had been thrown on the defensive. General after general—McClellan, Pope, Burnside, Hooker, and Meade—was tried and found wanting. None of them could administer a crushing defeat to the Confederate troops and more than once the union soldiers were beaten in a fair battle. They did succeed, however, in delivering a severe check to advancing Confederates under General Robert E. Lee, first at Antietam in September, 1862, and then at Gettysburg in July, 1863—checks reckoned as victories though in each instance the Confederates escaped without demoralization. Not until the beginning of the next year, when General Grant, supplied with almost unlimited men and munitions, began his irresistible hammering at Lee's army, did the final phase of the war commence. The pitiless drive told at last. General Lee, on April 9, 1865, seeing the futility of further conflict, surrendered an army still capable of hard fighting, at Appomattox, not far from the capital of the Confederacy.

Abraham Lincoln.—The services of Lincoln to the cause of union defy description. A judicial scrutiny of the war reveals his thought and planning in every part of the varied activity that finally crowned Northern arms with victory. Is it in the field of diplomacy? Does Seward, the Secretary of State, propose harsh and caustic measures likely to draw England's sword into the scale? Lincoln counsels moderation. He takes the irritating message and with his own hand strikes out, erases, tones down, and interlines, exchanging for words that sting and burn the language of prudence and caution. Is it a matter of compromise with the South, so often proposed by men on both sides sick of carnage? Lincoln is always ready to listen and turns away only when he is invited to surrender principles essential to the safety of the union. Is it high strategy of war, a question of the general best fitted to win Gettysburg—Hooker, Sedgwick, or Meade? Lincoln goes in person to the War Department in the dead of night to take counsel with his Secretary and to make the fateful choice.

Is it a complaint from a citizen, deprived, as he believes, of his civil liberties unjustly or in violation of the Constitution? Lincoln is ready to hear it and anxious to afford relief, if warrant can be found for it. Is a mother begging for the life of a son sentenced to be shot as a deserter? Lincoln hears her petition, and grants it even against the protests made by his generals in the name of military discipline. Do politicians sow dissensions in the army and among civilians? Lincoln grandly waves aside their petty personalities and invites them to think of the greater cause. Is it a question of securing votes to ratify the thirteenth amendment abolishing slavery? Lincoln thinks it not beneath his dignity to traffic and huckster with politicians over the trifling jobs asked in return by the members who hold out against him. Does a New York newspaper call him an ignorant Western boor? Lincoln's reply is a letter to a mother who has given her all—her sons on the field of battle—and an address at Gettysburg, both of which will live as long as the tongue in which they were written. These are tributes not only to his mastery of the English language but also to his mastery of all those sentiments of sweetness and strength which are the finest flowers of culture.

Throughout the entire span of service, however, Lincoln was beset by merciless critics. The fiery apostles of abolition accused him of cowardice when he delayed the bold stroke at slavery. Anti-war Democrats lashed out at every step he took. Even in his own party he found no peace. Charles Sumner complained: "Our President is now dictator, *imperator*—whichever you like; but how vain to have the power of a god and not to use it godlike." Leaders among the Republicans sought to put him aside in 1864 and place Chase in his chair. "I hope we may never have a worse man," was Lincoln's quiet answer.

Wide were the dissensions in the North during that year and the Republicans, while selecting Lincoln as their candidate again, cast off their old name and chose the simple title of the "Union party." Moreover, they selected a Southern man, Andrew Johnson, of Tennessee, to be associated with him as candidate for Vice President. This combination the Northern Democrats boldly confronted with a platform declaring that "after four years of failure to restore the union by the experiment of war, during which, under the pretence of military necessity or war power higher than the Constitution, the Constitution itself has been disregarded in every part and public liberty and private right alike trodden down ... justice, humanity, liberty, and public welfare demand that immediate efforts be made for a cessation of hostilities, to the end that peace may be restored on the basis of the federal union of the states." It is true that the Democratic candidate, General McClellan, sought to break the yoke imposed upon him by the platform, saying that he could not look his old comrades in the face and pronounce their efforts vain; but the party call to the nation to repudiate Lincoln and his works had gone forth. The response came, giving Lincoln 2,200,000 votes against 1,800,000 for his opponent. The bitter things said about him during the campaign, he forgot and forgave. When in April, 1865, he was struck down by the assassin's hand, he above all others in Washington was planning measures of moderation and healing.

THE RESULTS OF THE CIVIL WAR

There is a strong and natural tendency on the part of writers to stress the dramatic and heroic aspects of war; but the long judgment of history requires us to include all other significant phases as well. Like every great armed conflict, the Civil War outran the purposes of those who took part in it. Waged over the nature of the union, it made a revolution in the union, changing public policies and constitutional principles and giving a new direction to agriculture and industry.

The Supremacy of the Union.—First and foremost, the war settled for all time the long dispute as to the nature of the federal system. The doctrine of state sovereignty was laid to rest. Men might still speak of the rights of states and think of their commonwealths with affection, but nullification and secession were destroyed. The nation was supreme.

The Destruction of the Slave Power.—Next to the vindication of national supremacy was the destruction of the planting aristocracy of the South—that great power which had furnished leadership of undoubted ability and had so long contested with the industrial and commercial interests of the North. The first paralyzing blow at the planters was struck by the abolition of slavery. The second and third came with the fourteenth (1868) and fifteenth (1870) amendments, giving the ballot to freedmen and excluding from public office the Confederate leaders—driving from the work of reconstruction the finest talents of the South. As if to add bitterness to gall and wormwood, the fourteenth amendment forbade the United States or any state to pay any debts incurred in aid of the Confederacy or in the emancipation of the slaves—plunging into utter bankruptcy the Southern financiers who had stripped their section of capital to support their cause. So the Southern planters found themselves excluded from public office and ruled over by their former bondmen under the tutelage of Republican leaders. Their labor system was wrecked and their money and bonds were as worthless as waste paper. The South was subject to the North. That which neither the Federalists nor the Whigs had been able to accomplish in the realm of statecraft was accomplished on the field of battle.

The Triumph of Industry.—The wreck of the planting system was accompanied by a mighty upswing of Northern industry which made the old Whigs of Massachusetts and Pennsylvania stare in wonderment. The demands of the federal government for manufactured goods at unrestricted prices gave a stimulus to business which more than replaced the lost markets of the South. Between 1860 and 1870 the number of manufacturing establishments increased 79.6 per cent as against 14.2 for the previous decade; while the number of persons employed almost doubled. There was no doubt about the future of American industry.

The Victory for the Protective Tariff.—Moreover, it was henceforth to be well protected. For many years before the war the friends of protection had been on the defensive. The tariff act of 1857 imposed duties so low as to presage a tariff for revenue only. The war changed all that. The extraordinary military expenditures, requiring heavy taxes on all sources, justified tariffs so high that a follower of Clay or Webster might well have gasped with astonishment. After the war was over the debt remained and both interest and principal had to be paid. Protective arguments based on economic reasoning were supported by a plain necessity for revenue which admitted no dispute.

A Liberal Immigration Policy.—Linked with industry was the labor supply. The problem of manning industries became a pressing matter, and Republican leaders grappled with it. In the platform of the Union party adopted in 1864 it was declared "that foreign immigration, which in the past has added so much to the wealth, the development of resources, and the increase of power to this nation—the asylum of the oppressed of all nations—should be fostered and encouraged by a liberal and just policy." In that very year Congress, recognizing the importance of the problem, passed a measure of high significance, creating a bureau of immigration, and authorizing a modified form of indentured labor, by making it legal for immigrants to pledge their wages in advance to pay their passage over. Though the bill was soon repealed, the practice authorized by it was long continued. The cheapness of the passage shortened the term of service; but the principle was older than the days of William Penn.

The Homestead Act of 1862.—In the immigration measure guaranteeing a continuous and adequate labor supply, the manufacturers saw an offset to the Homestead Act of 1862 granting free lands to settlers. The Homestead law they had resisted in a long and bitter congressional battle. Naturally, they had not taken kindly to a scheme which lured men away from the factories or enabled them to make unlimited demands for higher wages as the price of remaining. Southern planters likewise had feared free homesteads for the very good reason that they only promised to add to the overbalancing power of the North.

In spite of the opposition, supporters of a liberal land policy made steady gains. Free-soil Democrats,—Jacksonian farmers and mechanics,—labor reformers, and political leaders, like Stephen A. Douglas of Illinois and Andrew Johnson of Tennessee, kept up the agitation in season and out. More than once were they able to force a homestead bill through the House of Representatives only to have it blocked in the Senate where Southern interests were intrenched. Then, after the Senate was won over, a Democratic President, James Buchanan, vetoed the bill. Still the issue lived. The Republicans, strong among the farmers of the Northwest, favored it from the beginning and pressed it upon the attention of the country. Finally the manufacturers yielded; they received their compensation in the contract labor law. In 1862 Congress provided for the free distribution of land in 160-acre lots among men and women of strong arms and willing hearts ready to build their serried lines of homesteads to the Rockies and beyond.

Internal Improvements.—If farmers and manufacturers were early divided on the matter of free homesteads, the same could hardly be said of internal improvements. The Western tiller of the soil was as eager for some easy way of sending his produce to market as the manufacturer was for the same means to transport his goods to the consumer on the farm. While the Confederate leaders were writing into their constitution a clause forbidding all appropriations for internal improvements, the Republican leaders at Washington were planning such expenditures from the treasury in the form of public land grants to railways as would have dazed the authors of the national road bill half a century earlier.

Sound Finance—National Banking.—From Hamilton's day to Lincoln's, business men in the East had contended for a sound system of national currency. The experience of the states with paper money, painfully impressive in the years before the framing of the Constitution, had been convincing to those who understood the economy of business. The Constitution, as we have seen, bore the signs of this experience. States were forbidden to emit bills of credit: paper money, in short. This provision stood clear in the document; but judicial ingenuity had circumvented it in the age of Jacksonian Democracy. The states had enacted and the Supreme Court, after the death of John Marshall, had sustained laws chartering banking companies and authorizing them to issue paper money. So the country was beset by the old curse, the banks of Western and Southern states issuing reams of paper notes to help borrowers pay their debts.

In dealing with war finances, the Republicans attacked this ancient evil. By act of Congress in 1864, they authorized a series of national banks founded on the credit of government bonds and empowered to issue notes. The next year they stopped all bank paper sent forth under the authority of the states by means of a prohibitive tax. In this way, by two measures Congress restored federal control over the monetary system although it did not reëstablish the United States Bank so hated by Jacksonian Democracy.

Destruction of States' Rights by Fourteenth Amendment.—These acts and others not cited here were measures of centralization and consolidation at the expense of the powers and dignity of the states. They were all of high import, but the crowning act of nationalism was the fourteenth amendment which, among other things, forbade states to "deprive any person of life, liberty or property without due process of law." The immediate occasion, though not the actual cause of this provision, was the need for protecting the rights of freedmen against hostile legislatures in the South. The result of the amendment, as was prophesied in protests loud and long from every quarter of the Democratic party, was the subjection of every act of state, municipal, and county authorities to possible annulment by the Supreme Court at Washington. The expected happened.

Few negroes ever brought cases under the fourteenth amendment to the attention of the courts; but thousands of state laws, municipal ordinances, and acts of local authorities were set aside as null and void under it. Laws of states regulating railway rates, fixing hours of labor in bakeshops, and taxing corporations were in due time to be annulled as conflicting with an amendment erroneously supposed to be designed solely for the protection of negroes. As centralized power over tariffs, railways, public lands, and other national concerns went to Congress, so centralized power over the acts of state and local authorities involving an infringement of personal and property rights was conferred on the federal judiciary, the apex of which was the Supreme Court at Washington. Thus the old federation of "independent states," all equal in rights and dignity, each wearing the "jewel of sovereignty" so celebrated in Southern oratory, had gone the way of all flesh under the withering blasts of Civil War.

Reconstruction in the South

Theories about the Position of the Seceded States.—On the morning of April 9, 1865, when General Lee surrendered his army to General Grant, eleven states stood in a peculiar relation to the union now declared perpetual. Lawyers and political philosophers were much perturbed and had been for some time as to what should be done with the members of the former Confederacy. Radical Republicans held that they were "conquered provinces" at the mercy of Congress, to be governed under such laws as it saw fit to enact and until in its wisdom it decided to readmit any or all of them to the union. Men of more conservative views held that, as the war had been waged by the North on the theory that no state could secede from the union, the Confederate states had merely attempted to withdraw and had failed. The corollary of this latter line of argument was simple: "The Southern states are still in the union and it is the duty of the President, as commander-in-chief, to remove the federal troops as soon as order is restored and the state governments ready to function once more as usual."

Lincoln's Proposal.—Some such simple and conservative form of reconstruction had been suggested by Lincoln in a proclamation of December 8, 1863. He proposed pardon and a restoration of property, except in slaves, to nearly all who had "directly or by implication participated in the existing rebellion," on condition that they take an oath of loyalty to the union. He then announced that when, in any of the states named, a body of voters, qualified under the law as it stood before secession and equal in number to one-tenth the votes cast in 1860, took the oath of allegiance, they should be permitted to reëstablish a state government. Such a government, he added, should be recognized as a lawful authority and entitled to protection under the federal Constitution. With reference to the status of the former slaves Lincoln made it clear that, while their freedom must be recognized, he would not object to any legislation "which may yet be consistent as a temporary arrangement with their present condition as a laboring, landless, and homeless class."

Andrew Johnson's Plan—His Impeachment.—Lincoln's successor, Andrew Johnson, the Vice President, soon after taking office, proposed to pursue a somewhat similar course. In a number of states he appointed military governors, instructing them at the earliest possible moment to assemble conventions, chosen "by that portion of the people of the said states who are loyal to the United States," and proceed to the organization of regular civil government. Johnson, a Southern man and a Democrat, was immediately charged by the Republicans with being too ready to restore the Southern states. As the months went by, the opposition to his measures and policies in Congress grew in size and bitterness. The contest resulted in the impeachment of Johnson by the House of Representatives in March, 1868, and his acquittal by the Senate merely because his opponents lacked one vote of the two-thirds required for conviction.

Congress Enacts "Reconstruction Laws."—In fact, Congress was in a strategic position. It was the law-making body, and it could, moreover, determine the conditions under which Senators and Representatives from the South were to be readmitted. It therefore proceeded to pass a series of reconstruction acts—carrying all of them over Johnson's veto. These measures, the first of which became a law on March 2, 1867, betrayed an animus not found anywhere in Lincoln's plans or Johnson's proclamations.

They laid off the ten states—the whole Confederacy with the exception of Tennessee—still outside the pale, into five military districts, each commanded by a military officer appointed by the President. They ordered the commanding general to prepare a register of voters for the election of delegates to conventions chosen for the purpose of drafting new constitutions. Such voters, however, were not to be, as Lincoln had suggested, loyal persons duly qualified under the law existing before secession but "the male citizens of said state, twenty-one years old and upward, of whatever race, color, or previous condition, ... except such as may be disfranchised for participation in the rebellion or for felony at common law." This was the death knell to the idea that the leaders of the Confederacy and their white supporters might be permitted to share in the establishment of the new order. Power was thus arbitrarily thrust into the hands of the newly emancipated male negroes and the handful of whites who could show a record of loyalty. That was not all. Each state was, under the reconstruction acts, compelled to ratify the fourteenth amendment to the federal Constitution as a price of restoration to the union.

The composition of the conventions thus authorized may be imagined. Bondmen without the asking and without preparation found themselves the governing power. An army of adventurers from the North, "carpet baggers" as they were called, poured in upon the scene to aid in "reconstruction." Undoubtedly many men of honor and fine intentions gave unstinted service, but the results of their deliberations only aggravated the open wound left by the war. Any number of political doctors offered their prescriptions; but no effective remedy could be found. Under measures admittedly open to grave objections, the Southern states were one after another restored to the union by the grace of Congress, the last one in 1870. Even this grudging concession of the formalities of statehood did not mean a full restoration of honors and privileges. The last soldier was not withdrawn from the last Southern capital until 1877, and federal control over elections long remained as a sign of congressional supremacy.

The Status of the Freedmen.—Even more intricate than the issues involved in restoring the seceded states to the union was the question of what to do with the newly emancipated slaves. That problem, often put to abolitionists before the war, had become at last a real concern. The thirteenth amendment abolishing slavery had not touched it at all. It declared bondmen free, but did nothing to provide them with work or homes and did not mention the subject of political rights. All these matters were left to the states, and the legislatures of some of them, by their famous "black codes," restored a form of servitude under the guise of vagrancy and apprentice laws. Such methods were in fact partly responsible for the reaction that led Congress to abandon Lincoln's policies and undertake its own program of reconstruction.

Still no extensive effort was made to solve by law the economic problems of the bondmen. Radical abolitionists had advocated that the slaves when emancipated should be given outright the fields of their former masters; but Congress steadily rejected the very idea of confiscation. The necessity of immediate assistance it recognized by creating in 1865 the Freedmen's Bureau to take care of refugees. It authorized the issue of food and clothing to the destitute and the renting of abandoned and certain other lands under federal control to former slaves at reasonable rates. But the larger problem of the relation of the freedmen to the land, it left to the slow working of time.

Against sharp protests from conservative men, particularly among the Democrats, Congress did insist, however, on conferring upon the freedmen certain rights by national law. These rights fell into broad divisions, civil and political. By an act passed in 1866, Congress gave to former slaves the rights of white citizens in the matter of making contracts, giving testimony in courts, and purchasing, selling, and leasing property. As it was doubtful whether Congress had the power to enact this law, there was passed and submitted to the states the fourteenth amendment which gave citizenship to the freedmen, assured them of the privileges and immunities of citizens of the United States, and declared that no state should deprive any person of his life, liberty, or property without due process of law. Not yet satisfied, Congress attempted to give social equality to negroes by the second civil rights bill of 1875 which promised to them, among other things, the full and equal enjoyment of inns, theaters, public conveyances, and places of amusement—a law later declared unconstitutional by the Supreme Court.

The matter of political rights was even more hotly contested; but the radical Republicans, like Charles Sumner, asserted that civil rights were not secure unless supported by the suffrage. In this same fourteenth amendment they attempted to guarantee the ballot to all negro men, leaving the women to take care of themselves. The amendment declared in effect that when any state deprived adult male citizens of the right to vote, its representation in Congress should be reduced in the proportion such persons bore to the voting population.

This provision having failed to accomplish its purpose, the fifteenth amendment was passed and ratified, expressly declaring that no citizen should be deprived of the right to vote "on account of race, color, or previous condition of servitude." To make assurance doubly secure, Congress enacted in 1870, 1872, and 1873 three drastic laws, sometimes known as "force bills," providing for the use of federal authorities, civil and military, in supervising elections in all parts of the Union. So the federal government, having destroyed chattel slavery, sought by legal decree to sweep away all its signs and badges, civil, social, and political. Never, save perhaps in some of the civil conflicts of Greece or Rome, had there occurred in the affairs of a nation a social revolution so complete, so drastic, and far-reaching in its results.

SUMMARY OF THE SECTIONAL CONFLICT

Just as the United States, under the impetus of Western enterprise, rounded out the continental domain, its very existence as a nation was challenged by a fratricidal conflict between two sections. This storm had been long gathering upon the horizon. From the very beginning in colonial times there had been a marked difference between the South and the North. The former by climate and soil was dedicated to a planting system—the cultivation of tobacco, rice, cotton, and sugar cane—and in the course of time slave labor became the foundation of the system. The North, on the other hand, supplemented agriculture by commerce, trade, and manufacturing. Slavery, though lawful, did not flourish there. An abundant supply of free labor kept the Northern wheels turning.

This difference between the two sections, early noted by close observers, was increased with the advent of the steam engine and the factory system. Between 1815 and 1860 an industrial revolution took place in the North. Its signs were gigantic factories, huge aggregations of industrial workers, immense cities, a flourishing commerce, and prosperous banks. Finding an unfavorable reception in the South, the new industrial system was confined mainly to the North. By canals and railways New York, Boston, and Philadelphia were linked with the wheatfields of Ohio, Indiana, and Illinois. A steel net wove North and Northwest together. A commercial net supplemented it. Western trade was diverted from New Orleans to the East and Eastern credit sustained Western enterprise.

In time, the industrial North and the planting South evolved different ideas of political policy. The former looked with favor on protective tariffs, ship subsidies, a sound national banking system, and internal improvements. The farmers of the West demanded that the public domain be divided up into free homesteads for farmers. The South steadily swung around to the opposite view. Its spokesmen came to regard most of these policies as injurious to the planting interests.

The economic questions were all involved in a moral issue. The Northern states, in which slavery was of slight consequence, had early abolished the institution. In the course of a few years there appeared uncompromising advocates of universal emancipation. Far and wide the agitation spread. The South was thoroughly frightened. It demanded protection against the agitators, the enforcement of its rights in the case of runaway slaves, and equal privileges for slavery in the new territories.

With the passing years the conflict between the two sections increased in bitterness. It flamed up in 1820 and was allayed by the Missouri compromise. It took on the form of a tariff controversy and nullification in 1832. It appeared again after the Mexican war when the question of slavery in the new territories was raised. Again compromise—the great settlement of 1850—seemed to restore peace, only to prove an illusion. A series of startling events swept the country into war: the repeal of the Missouri compromise in 1854, the rise of the Republican party pledged to the prohibition of slavery in the territories, the Dred Scott decision of 1857, the Lincoln-Douglas debates, John Brown's raid, the election of Lincoln, and secession.

The Civil War, lasting for four years, tested the strength of both North and South, in leadership, in finance, in diplomatic skill, in material resources, in industry, and in armed forces. By the blockade of Southern ports, by an overwhelming weight of men and materials, and by relentless hammering on the field of battle, the North was victorious.

The results of the war were revolutionary in character. Slavery was abolished and the freedmen given the ballot. The Southern planters who had been the leaders of their section were ruined financially and almost to a man excluded from taking part in political affairs. The union was declared to be perpetual and the right of a state to secede settled by the judgment of battle. Federal control over the affairs of states, counties, and cities was established by the fourteenth amendment. The power and prestige of the federal government were enhanced beyond imagination. The North was now free to pursue its economic policies: a protective tariff, a national banking system, land grants for railways, free lands for farmers. Planting had dominated the country for nearly a generation. Business enterprise was to take its place.

References

NORTHERN ACCOUNTS

J.K. Hosmer, *The Appeal to Arms* and *The Outcome of the Civil War* (American Nation Series).

J. Ropes, *History of the Civil War* (best account of military campaigns).

J.F. Rhodes, *History of the United States*, Vols. III, IV, and V.

J.T. Morse, *Abraham Lincoln* (2 vols.).

SOUTHERN ACCOUNTS

W.E. Dodd, *Jefferson Davis*.

Jefferson Davis, *Rise and Fall of the Confederate Government*.

E. Pollard, *The Lost Cause*.

A.H. Stephens, *The War between the States*.

Questions

1. Contrast the reception of secession in 1860 with that given to nullification in 1832.

2. Compare the Northern and Southern views of the union.

3. What were the peculiar features of the Confederate constitution?

4. How was the Confederacy financed?

5. Compare the resources of the two sections.

6. On what foundations did Southern hopes rest?

7. Describe the attempts at a peaceful settlement.

8. Compare the raising of armies for the Civil War with the methods employed in the World War. (See below, chapter XXV.)

9. Compare the financial methods of the government in the two wars.

10. Explain why the blockade was such a deadly weapon.

11. Give the leading diplomatic events of the war.

12. Trace the growth of anti-slavery sentiment.

13. What measures were taken to restrain criticism of the government?

14. What part did Lincoln play in all phases of the war?

15. State the principal results of the war.

16. Compare Lincoln's plan of reconstruction with that adopted by Congress.

17. What rights did Congress attempt to confer upon the former slaves?

Research Topics

Was Secession Lawful?—The Southern view by Jefferson Davis in Harding, *Select Orations Illustrating American History*, pp. 364-369. Lincoln's view, Harding, pp. 371-381.

The Confederate Constitution.—Compare with the federal Constitution in Macdonald, *Documentary Source Book*, pp. 424-433 and pp. 271-279.

Federal Legislative Measures.—Prepare a table and brief digest of the important laws relating to the war. Macdonald, pp. 433-482.

Economic Aspects of the War.—Coman, *Industrial History of the United States*, pp. 279-301. Dewey, *Financial History of the United States*, Chaps. XII and XIII. Tabulate the economic measures of Congress in Macdonald.

Military Campaigns.—The great battles are fully treated in Rhodes, *History of the Civil War*, and teachers desiring to emphasize military affairs may assign campaigns to members of the class for study and report. A briefer treatment in Elson, *History of the United States*, pp. 641-785.

Biographical Studies.—Lincoln, Davis, Lee, Grant, Sherman, and other leaders in civil and military affairs, with reference to local "war governors."

English and French Opinion of the War.—Rhodes, *History of the United States*, Vol. IV, pp. 337-394.

The South during the War.—Rhodes, Vol. V, pp. 343-382.

The North during the War.—Rhodes, Vol. V, pp. 189-342.

Reconstruction Measures.—Macdonald, *Source Book*, pp. 500-511; 514-518; 529-530; Elson, pp. 786-799.

The Force Bills.—Macdonald, pp. 547-551; 554-564.

PART VI. NATIONAL GROWTH AND WORLD POLITICS

CHAPTER XVI

THE POLITICAL AND ECONOMIC EVOLUTION OF THE SOUTH

The outcome of the Civil War in the South was nothing short of a revolution. The ruling class, the law, and the government of the old order had been subverted. To political chaos was added the havoc wrought in agriculture, business, and transportation by military operations. And as if to fill the cup to the brim, the task of reconstruction was committed to political leaders from another section of the country, strangers to the life and traditions of the South.

THE SOUTH AT THE CLOSE OF THE WAR

A Ruling Class Disfranchised.—As the sovereignty of the planters had been the striking feature of the old régime, so their ruin was the outstanding fact of the new. The situation was extraordinary. The American Revolution was carried out by people experienced in the arts of self-government, and at its close they were free to follow the general course to which they had long been accustomed. The French Revolution witnessed the overthrow of the clergy and the nobility; but middle classes who took their places had been steadily rising in intelligence and wealth.

The Southern Revolution was unlike either of these cataclysms. It was not brought about by a social upheaval, but by an external crisis. It did not enfranchise a class that sought and understood power, but bondmen who had played no part in the struggle. Moreover it struck down a class equipped to rule. The leading planters were almost to a man excluded from state and federal offices, and the fourteenth amendment was a bar to their return. All civil and military places under the authority of the United States and of the states were closed to every man who had taken an oath to support the Constitution as a member of Congress, as a state legislator, or as a state or federal officer, and afterward engaged in "insurrection or rebellion," or "given aid and comfort to the enemies" of the United States. This sweeping provision, supplemented by the reconstruction acts, laid under the ban most of the talent, energy, and spirit of the South.

The Condition of the State Governments.—The legislative, executive, and judicial branches of the state governments thus passed into the control of former slaves, led principally by Northern adventurers or Southern novices, known as "Scalawags." The result was a carnival of waste, folly, and corruption. The "reconstruction" assembly of South Carolina bought clocks at $480 apiece and chandeliers at $650. To purchase land for former bondmen the sum of $800,000 was appropriated; and swamps bought at seventy-five cents an acre were sold to the state at five times the cost. In the years between 1868 and 1873, the debt of the state rose from about $5,800,000 to $24,000,000, and millions of the increase could not be accounted for by the authorities responsible for it.

Economic Ruin—Urban and Rural.—No matter where Southern men turned in 1865 they found devastation—in the towns, in the country, and along the highways. Atlanta, the city to which Sherman applied the torch, lay in ashes; Nashville and Chattanooga had been partially wrecked; Richmond and Augusta had suffered severely from fires. Charleston was described by a visitor as "a city of ruins, of desolation, of vacant houses, of rotten wharves, of deserted warehouses, of weed gardens, of miles of grass-grown streets.... How few young men there are, how generally the young women are dressed in black! The flower of their proud aristocracy is buried on scores of battle fields."

Those who journeyed through the country about the same time reported desolation equally widespread and equally pathetic. An English traveler who made his way along the course of the Tennessee River in 1870 wrote: "The trail of war is visible throughout the valley in burnt-up gin houses, ruined bridges, mills, and factories ... and large tracts of once cultivated land are stripped of every vestige of fencing. The roads, long neglected, are in disorder and, having in many places become impassable, new tracks have been made through the woods and fields without much respect to boundaries." Many a great plantation had been confiscated by the federal authorities while the owner was in Confederate service. Many more lay in waste. In the wake of the armies the homes of rich and poor alike, if spared the torch, had been despoiled of the stock and seeds necessary to renew agriculture.

Railways Dilapidated.—Transportation was still more demoralized. This is revealed in the pages of congressional reports based upon first-hand investigations. One eloquent passage illustrates all the rest. From Pocahontas to Decatur, Alabama, a distance of 114 miles, we are told, the railroad was "almost entirely destroyed, except the road bed and iron rails, and they were in a very bad condition—every bridge and trestle destroyed, cross-ties rotten, buildings burned, water tanks gone, tracks grown up in weeds and bushes, not a saw mill near the line and the labor system of the country gone. About forty miles of the track were burned, the cross-ties entirely destroyed, and the rails bent and twisted in such a manner as to require great labor to straighten and a large portion of them requiring renewal."

Capital and Credit Destroyed.—The fluid capital of the South, money and credit, was in the same prostrate condition as the material capital. The Confederate currency, inflated to the bursting point, had utterly collapsed and was as worthless as waste paper. The bonds of the Confederate government were equally valueless. Specie had nearly disappeared from circulation. The fourteenth amendment to the federal Constitution had made all "debts, obligations, and claims" incurred in aid of the Confederate cause "illegal and void." Millions of dollars owed to Northern creditors before the war were overdue and payment was pressed upon the debtors. Where such debts were secured by mortgages on land, executions against the property could be obtained in federal courts.

THE RESTORATION OF WHITE SUPREMACY

Intimidation.—In both politics and economics, the process of reconstruction in the South was slow and arduous. The first battle in the political contest for white supremacy was won outside the halls of legislatures and the courts of law. It was waged, in the main, by secret organizations, among which the Ku Klux Klan and the White Camelia were the most prominent. The first of these societies appeared in Tennessee in 1866 and held its first national convention the following year. It was in origin a social club. According to its announcement, its objects were "to protect the weak, the innocent, and the defenceless from the indignities, wrongs, and outrages of the lawless, the violent, and the brutal; and to succor the suffering, especially the widows and orphans of the Confederate soldiers." The whole South was called "the Empire" and was ruled by a "Grand Wizard." Each state was a realm and each county a province. In the secret orders there were enrolled over half a million men.

The methods of the Ku Klux and the White Camelia were similar. Solemn parades of masked men on horses decked in long robes were held, sometimes in the daytime and sometimes at the dead of night. Notices were sent to obnoxious persons warning them to stop certain practices. If warning failed, something more convincing was tried. Fright was the emotion most commonly stirred. A horseman, at the witching hour of midnight, would ride up to the house of some offender, lift his head gear, take off a skull, and hand it to the trembling victim with the request that he hold it for a few minutes. Frequently violence was employed either officially or unofficially by members of the Klan. Tar and feathers were freely applied; the whip was sometimes laid on unmercifully, and occasionally a brutal murder was committed. Often the members were fired upon from bushes or behind trees, and swift retaliation followed. So alarming did the clashes become that in 1870 Congress forbade interference with electors or going in disguise for the purpose of obstructing the exercise of the rights enjoyed under federal law.

In anticipation of such a step on the part of the federal government, the Ku Klux was officially dissolved by the "Grand Wizard" in 1869. Nevertheless, the local societies continued their organization and methods. The spirit survived the national association. "On the whole," says a Southern writer, "it is not easy to see what other course was open to the South.... Armed resistance was out of the question. And yet there must be some control had of the situation.... If force was denied, craft was inevitable."

The Struggle for the Ballot Box.—The effects of intimidation were soon seen at elections. The freedman, into whose inexperienced hand the ballot had been thrust, was ordinarily loath to risk his head by the exercise of his new rights. He had not attained them by a long and laborious contest of his own and he saw no urgent reason why he should battle for the privilege of using them. The mere show of force, the mere existence of a threat, deterred thousands of ex-slaves from appearing at the polls. Thus the whites steadily recovered their dominance. Nothing could prevent it. Congress enacted force bills establishing federal supervision of elections and the Northern politicians protested against the return of former Confederates to practical, if not official, power; but all such opposition was like resistance to the course of nature.

Amnesty for Southerners.—The recovery of white supremacy in this way was quickly felt in national councils. The Democratic party in the North welcomed it as a sign of its return to power. The more moderate Republicans, anxious to heal the breach in American unity, sought to encourage rather than to repress it. So it came about that amnesty for Confederates was widely advocated. Yet it must be said that the struggle for the removal of disabilities was stubborn and bitter. Lincoln, with characteristic generosity, in the midst of the war had issued a general proclamation of amnesty to nearly all who had been in arms against the Union, on condition that they take an oath of loyalty; but Johnson, vindictive toward Southern leaders and determined to make "treason infamous," had extended the list of exceptions. Congress, even more relentless in its pursuit of Confederates, pushed through the fourteenth amendment which worked the sweeping disabilities we have just described.

To appeals for comprehensive clemency, Congress was at first adamant. In vain did men like Carl Schurz exhort their colleagues to crown their victory in battle with a noble act of universal pardon and oblivion. Congress would not yield. It would grant amnesty in individual cases; for the principle of proscription it stood fast. When finally in 1872, seven years after the surrender at Appomattox, it did pass the general amnesty bill, it insisted on certain exceptions. Confederates who had been members of Congress just before the war, or had served in other high posts, civil or military, under the federal government, were still excluded from important offices. Not until the summer of 1898, when the war with Spain produced once more a union of hearts, did Congress relent and abolish the last of the disabilities imposed on the Confederates.

The Force Bills Attacked and Nullified.—The granting of amnesty encouraged the Democrats to redouble their efforts all along the line. In 1874 they captured the House of Representatives and declared war on the "force bills." As a Republican Senate blocked immediate repeal, they resorted to an ingenious parliamentary trick. To the appropriation bill for the support of the army they attached a "rider," or condition, to the effect that no troops should be used to sustain the Republican government in Louisiana. The Senate rejected the proposal. A deadlock ensued and Congress adjourned without making provision for the army. Satisfied with the technical victory, the Democrats let the army bill pass the next session, but kept up their fight on the force laws until they wrung from President Hayes a measure forbidding the use of United States troops in supervising elections. The following year they again had recourse to a rider on the army bill and carried it through, putting an end to the use of money for military control of elections. The reconstruction program was clearly going to pieces, and the Supreme Court helped along the process of dissolution by declaring parts of the laws invalid. In 1878 the Democrats even won a majority in the Senate and returned to power a large number of men once prominent in the Confederate cause.

The passions of the war by this time were evidently cooling. A new generation of men was coming on the scene. The supremacy of the whites in the South, if not yet complete, was at least assured. Federal marshals, their deputies, and supervisors of elections still possessed authority over the polls, but their strength had been shorn by the withdrawal of United States troops. The war on the remaining remnants of the "force bills" lapsed into desultory skirmishing. When in 1894 the last fragment was swept away, the country took little note of the fact. The only task that lay before the Southern leaders was to write in the constitutions of their respective states theprovisions of law which would clinch the gains so far secured and establish white supremacy beyond the reach of outside intervention.

White Supremacy Sealed by New State Constitutions.—The impetus to this final step was given by the rise of the Populist movement in the South, which sharply divided the whites and in many communities threw the balance of power into the hands of the few colored voters who survived the process of intimidation. Southern leaders now devised new constitutions so constructed as to deprive negroes of the ballot by law. Mississippi took the lead in 1890; South Carolina followed five years later; Louisiana, in 1898; North Carolina, in 1900; Alabama and Maryland, in 1901; and Virginia, in 1902.

The authors of these measures made no attempt to conceal their purposes. "The intelligent white men of the South," said Governor Tillman, "intend to govern here." The fifteenth amendment to the federal Constitution, however, forbade them to deprive any citizen of the right to vote on account of race, color, or previous condition of servitude. This made necessary the devices of indirection. They were few, simple, and effective. The first and most easily administered was the ingenious provision requiring each prospective voter to read a section of the state constitution or "understand and explain it" when read to him by the election officers. As an alternative, the payment of taxes or the ownership of a small amount of property was accepted as a qualification for voting. Southern leaders, unwilling to disfranchise any of the poor white men who had stood side by side with them "in the dark days of reconstruction," also resorted to a famous provision known as "the grandfather clause." This plan admitted to the suffrage any man who did not have either property or educational qualifications, provided he had voted on or before 1867 or was the son or grandson of any such person.

The devices worked effectively. Of the 147,000 negroes in Mississippi above the age of twenty-one, only about 8600 registered under the constitution of 1890. Louisiana had 127,000 colored voters enrolled in 1896; under the constitution drafted two years later the registration fell to 5300. An analysis of the figures for South Carolina in 1900 indicates that only about one negro out of every hundred adult males of that race took part in elections. Thus was closed this chapter of reconstruction.

The Supreme Court Refuses to Intervene.—Numerous efforts were made to prevail upon the Supreme Court of the United States to declare such laws unconstitutional; but the Court, usually on technical grounds, avoided coming to a direct decision on the merits of the matter. In one case the Court remarked that it could not take charge of and operate the election machinery of Alabama; it concluded that "relief from a great political wrong, if done as alleged, by the people of a state and by the state itself, must be given by them, or by the legislative and executive departments of the government of the United States." Only one of the several schemes employed, namely, the "grandfather clause," was held to be a violation of the federal Constitution. This blow, effected in 1915 by the decision in the Oklahoma and Maryland cases, left, however, the main structure of disfranchisement unimpaired.

Proposals to Reduce Southern Representation in Congress.—These provisions excluding thousands of male citizens from the ballot did not, in express terms, deprive any one of the vote on account of race or color. They did not, therefore, run counter to the letter of the fifteenth amendment; but they did unquestionably make the states which adopted them liable to the operations of the fourteenth amendment. The latter very explicitly provides that whenever any state deprives adult male citizens of the right to vote (except in certain minor cases) the representation of the state in Congress shall be reduced in the proportion which such number of disfranchised citizens bears to the whole number of male citizens over twenty-one years of age.

Mindful of this provision, those who protested against disfranchisement in the South turned to the Republican party for relief, asking for action by the political branches of the federal government as the Supreme Court had suggested. The Republicans responded in their platform of 1908 by condemning all devices designed to deprive any one of the ballot for reasons of color alone; they demanded the enforcement in letter and spirit of the fourteenth as well as all other amendments. Though victorious in the election, the Republicans refrained from reopening the ancient contest; they made no attempt to reduce Southern representation in the House. Southern leaders, while protesting against the declarations of their opponents, were able to view them as idle threats in no way endangering the security of the measures by which political reconstruction had been undone.

The Solid South.—Out of the thirty-year conflict against "carpet-bag rule" there emerged what was long known as the "solid South"—a South that, except occasionally in the border states, never gave an electoral vote to a Republican candidate for President. Before the Civil War, the Southern people had been divided on political questions. Take, for example, the election of 1860. In all the fifteen slave states the variety of opinion was marked. In nine of them—Delaware, Virginia, Tennessee, Missouri, Maryland, Louisiana, Kentucky, Georgia, and Arkansas—the combined vote against the representative of the extreme Southern point of view, Breckinridge, constituted a safe majority. In each of the six states which were carried by Breckinridge, there was a large and powerful minority. In North Carolina Breckinridge's majority over Bell and Douglas was only 849 votes. Equally astounding to those who imagine the South united in defense of extreme views in 1860 was the vote for Bell, the Unionist candidate, who stood firmly for the Constitution and silence on slavery. In every Southern state Bell's vote was large. In Virginia, Kentucky, Missouri, and Tennessee it was greater than that received by Breckinridge; in Georgia, it was 42,000 against 51,000; in Louisiana, 20,000 against 22,000; in Mississippi, 25,000 against 40,000.

The effect of the Civil War upon these divisions was immediate and decisive, save in the border states where thousands of men continued to adhere to the cause of Union. In the Confederacy itself nearly all dissent was silenced by war. Men who had been bitter opponents joined hands in defense of their homes; when the armed conflict was over they remained side by side working against "Republican misrule and negro domination." By 1890, after Northern supremacy was definitely broken, they boasted that there were at least twelve Southern states in which no Republican candidate for President could win a single electoral vote.

Dissent in the Solid South.—Though every one grew accustomed to speak of the South as "solid," it did not escape close observers that in a number of Southern states there appeared from time to time a fairly large body of dissenters. In 1892 the Populists made heavy inroads upon the Democratic ranks. On other occasions, the contests between factions within the Democratic party over the nomination of candidates revealed sharp differences of opinion. In some places, moreover, there grew up a Republican minority of respectable size. For example, in Georgia, Mr. Taft in 1908 polled 41,000 votes against 72,000 for Mr. Bryan; in North Carolina, 114,000 against 136,000; in Tennessee, 118,000 against 135,000; in Kentucky, 235,000 against 244,000. In 1920, Senator Harding, the Republican candidate, broke the record by carrying Tennessee as well as Kentucky, Oklahoma, and Maryland.

THE ECONOMIC ADVANCE OF THE SOUTH

The Break-up of the Great Estates.—In the dissolution of chattel slavery it was inevitable that the great estate should give way before the small farm. The plantation was in fact founded on slavery. It was continued and expanded by slavery. Before the war the prosperous planter, either by inclination or necessity, invested his surplus in more land to add to his original domain. As his slaves increased in number, he was forced to increase his acreage or sell them, and he usually preferred the former, especially in the Far South. Still another element favored the large estate. Slave labor quickly exhausted the soil and of its own force compelled the cutting of the forests and the extension of the area under cultivation.

Finally, the planter took a natural pride in his great estate; it was a sign of his prowess and his social prestige.

In 1865 the foundations of the planting system were gone. It was difficult to get efficient labor to till the vast plantations. The planters themselves were burdened with debts and handicapped by lack of capital. Negroes commonly preferred tilling plots of their own, rented or bought under mortgage, to the more irksome wage labor under white supervision. The land hunger of the white farmer, once checked by the planting system, reasserted itself. Before these forces the plantation broke up. The small farm became the unit of cultivation in the South as in the North. Between 1870 and 1900 the number of farms doubled in every state south of the line of the Potomac and Ohio rivers, except in Arkansas and Louisiana. From year to year the process of breaking up continued, with all that it implied in the creation of land-owning farmers.

The Diversification of Crops.—No less significant was the concurrent diversification of crops. Under slavery, tobacco, rice, and sugar were staples and "cotton was king." These were standard crops. The methods of cultivation were simple and easily learned. They tested neither the skill nor the ingenuity of the slaves. As the returns were quick, they did not call for long-time investments of capital. After slavery was abolished, they still remained the staples, but far-sighted agriculturists saw the dangers of depending upon a few crops. The mild climate all the way around the coast from Virginia to Texas and the character of the alluvial soil invited the exercise of more imagination. Peaches, oranges, peanuts, and other fruits and vegetables were found to grow luxuriantly. Refrigeration for steamships and freight cars put the markets of great cities at the doors of Southern fruit and vegetable gardeners. The South, which in planting days had relied so heavily upon the Northwest for its foodstuffs, began to battle for independence. Between 1880 and the close of the century the value of its farm crops increased from $660,000,000 to $1,270,000,000.

The Industrial and Commercial Revolution.—On top of the radical changes in agriculture came an industrial and commercial revolution. The South had long been rich in natural resources, but the slave system had been unfavorable to their development. Rivers that would have turned millions of spindles tumbled unheeded to the seas. Coal and iron beds lay unopened. Timber was largely sacrificed in clearing lands for planting, or fell to earth in decay. Southern enterprise was consumed in planting. Slavery kept out the white immigrants who might have supplied the skilled labor for industry.

After 1865, achievement and fortune no longer lay on the land alone. As soon as the paralysis of the war was over, the South caught the industrial spirit that had conquered feudal Europe and the agricultural North. In the development of mineral wealth, enormous strides were taken. Iron ore of every quality was found, the chief beds being in Virginia, West Virginia, Tennessee, Kentucky, North Carolina, Georgia, Alabama, Arkansas, and Texas. Five important coal basins were uncovered: in Virginia, North Carolina, the Appalachian chain from Maryland to Northern Alabama, Kentucky, Arkansas, and Texas. Oil pools were found in Kentucky, Tennessee, and Texas. Within two decades, 1880 to 1900, the output of mineral wealth multiplied tenfold: from ten millions a year to one hundred millions. The iron industries of West Virginia and Alabama began to rival those of Pennsylvania. Birmingham became the Pittsburgh and Atlanta the Chicago of the South.

In other lines of industry, lumbering and cotton manufacturing took a high rank. The development of Southern timber resources was in every respect remarkable, particularly in Louisiana, Arkansas, and Mississippi. At the end of the first decade of the twentieth century, primacy in lumber had passed from the Great Lakes region to the South. In 1913 eight Southern states produced nearly four times as much lumber as the Lake states and twice as much as the vast forests of Washington and Oregon.

The development of the cotton industry, in the meantime, was similarly astounding. In 1865 cotton spinning was a negligible matter in the Southern states. In 1880 they had one-fourth of the mills of the country. At the end of the century they had one-half the mills, the two Carolinas taking the lead by consuming more than one-third of their entire cotton crop. Having both the raw materials and the power at hand, they enjoyed many advantages over the New England rivals, and at the opening of the new century were outstripping the latter in the proportion of spindles annually put into operation. Moreover, the cotton planters, finding a market at the neighboring mills, began to look forward to a day when they would be somewhat emancipated from absolute dependence upon the cotton exchanges of New York, New Orleans, and Liverpool.

Transportation kept pace with industry. In 1860, the South had about ten thousand miles of railway. By 1880 the figure had doubled. During the next twenty years over thirty thousand miles were added, most of the increase being in Texas. About 1898 there opened a period of consolidation in which scores of short lines were united, mainly under the leadership of Northern capitalists, and new through service opened to the North and West. Thus Southern industries were given easy outlets to the markets of the nation and brought within the main currents of national business enterprise.

The Social Effects of the Economic Changes.—As long as the slave system lasted and planting was the major interest, the South was bound to be sectional in character. With slavery gone, crops diversified, natural resources developed, and industries promoted, the social order of the ante-bellum days inevitably dissolved; the South became more and more assimilated to the system of the North. In this process several lines of development are evident.

In the first place we see the steady rise of the small farmer. Even in the old days there had been a large class of white yeomen who owned no slaves and tilled the soil with their own hands, but they labored under severe handicaps. They found the fertile lands of the coast and river valleys nearly all monopolized by planters, and they were by the force of circumstances driven into the uplands where the soil was thin and the crops were light. Still they increased in numbers and zealously worked their freeholds.

The war proved to be their opportunity. With the break-up of the plantations, they managed to buy land more worthy of their plows. By intelligent labor and intensive cultivation they were able to restore much of the worn-out soil to its original fertility. In the meantime they rose with their prosperity in the social and political scale. It became common for the sons of white farmers to enter the professions, while their daughters went away to college and prepared for teaching. Thus a more democratic tone was given to the white society of the South. Moreover the migration to the North and West, which had formerly carried thousands of energetic sons and daughters to search for new homesteads, was materially reduced. The energy of the agricultural population went into rehabilitation.

The increase in the number of independent farmers was accompanied by the rise of small towns and villages which gave diversity to the life of the South. Before 1860 it was possible to travel through endless stretches of cotton and tobacco. The social affairs of the planter's family centered in the homestead even if they were occasionally interrupted by trips to distant cities or abroad. Carpentry, bricklaying, and blacksmithing were usually done by slaves skilled in simple handicrafts. Supplies were bought wholesale. In this way there was little place in plantation economy for villages and towns with their stores and mechanics.

The abolition of slavery altered this. Small farms spread out where plantations had once stood. The skilled freedmen turned to agriculture rather than to handicrafts; white men of a business or mechanical bent found an opportunity to serve the needs of their communities. So local merchants and mechanics became an important element in the social system. In the county seats, once dominated by the planters, business and professional men assumed the leadership.

Another vital outcome of this revolution was the transference of a large part of planting enterprise to business. Mr. Bruce, a Southern historian of fine scholarship, has summed up this process in a single telling paragraph: "The higher planting class that under the old system gave so much distinction to rural life has, so far as it has survived at all, been concentrated in the cities. The families that in the time of slavery would have been found only in the country are now found, with a few exceptions, in the towns. The transplantation has been practically universal. The talent, the energy, the ambition that formerly sought expression in the management of great estates and the control of hosts of slaves, now seek a field of action in trade, in manufacturing enterprises, or in the general enterprises of development. This was for the ruling class of the South the natural outcome of the great economic revolution that followed the war."

As in all other parts of the world, the mechanical revolution was attended by the growth of a population of industrial workers dependent not upon the soil but upon wages for their livelihood. When Jefferson Davis was inaugurated President of the Southern Confederacy, there were approximately only one hundred thousand persons employed in Southern manufactures as against more than a million in Northern mills. Fifty years later, Georgia and Alabama alone had more than one hundred and fifty thousand wage-earners. Necessarily this meant also a material increase in urban population, although the wide dispersion of cotton spinning among small centers prevented the congestion that had accompanied the rise of the textile industry in New England. In 1910, New Orleans, Atlanta, Memphis, Nashville, and Houston stood in the same relation to the New South that Cincinnati, Chicago, Cleveland, and Detroit had stood to the New West fifty years before. The problems of labor and capital and municipal administration, which the earlier writers boasted would never perplex the planting South, had come in full force.

The Revolution in the Status of the Slaves.—No part of Southern society was so profoundly affected by the Civil War and economic reconstruction as the former slaves. On the day of emancipation, they stood free, but empty-handed, the owners of no tools or property, the masters of no trade and wholly inexperienced in the arts of self-help that characterized the whites in general. They had never been accustomed to looking out for themselves. The plantation bell had called them to labor and released them. Doles of food and clothing had been regularly made in given quantities. They did not understand wages, ownership, renting, contracts, mortgages, leases, bills, or accounts.

When they were emancipated, four courses were open to them. They could flee from the plantation to the nearest town or city, or to the distant North, to seek a livelihood. Thousands of them chose this way, overcrowding cities where disease mowed them down. They could remain where they, were in their cabins and work for daily wages instead of food, clothing, and shelter. This second course the major portion of them chose; but, as few masters had cash to dispense, the new relation was much like the old, in fact. It was still one of barter. The planter offered food, clothing, and shelter; the former slaves gave their labor in return. That was the best that many of them could do.

A third course open to freedmen was that of renting from the former master, paying him usually with a share of the produce of the land. This way a large number of them chose. It offered them a chance to become land owners in time and it afforded an easier life, the renter being, to a certain extent at least, master of his own hours of labor. The final and most difficult path was that to ownership of land. Many a master helped his former slaves to acquire small holdings by offering easy terms. The more enterprising and the more fortunate who started life as renters or wage-earners made their way upward to ownership in so many cases that by the end of the century, one-fourth of the colored laborers on the land owned the soil they tilled.

In the meantime, the South, though relatively poor, made relatively large expenditures for the education of the colored population. By the opening of the twentieth century, facilities were provided for more than one-half of the colored children of school age. While in many respects this progress was disappointing, its significance, to be appreciated, must be derived from a comparison with the total illiteracy which prevailed under slavery.

In spite of all that happened, however, the status of the negroes in the South continued to give a peculiar character to that section of the country. They were almost entirely excluded from the exercise of the suffrage, especially in the Far South. Special rooms were set aside for them at the railway stations and special cars on the railway lines. In the field of industry calling for technical skill, it appears, from the census figures, that they lost ground between 1890 and 1900—a condition which their friends ascribed to discriminations against them in law and in labor organizations and their critics ascribed to their lack of aptitude. Whatever may be the truth, the fact remained that at the opening of the twentieth century neither the hopes of the emancipators nor the fears of their opponents were realized. The marks of the "peculiar institution" were still largely impressed upon Southern society.

The situation, however, was by no means unchanging. On the contrary there was a decided drift in affairs. For one thing, the proportion of negroes in the South had slowly declined. By 1900 they were in a majority in only two states, South Carolina and Mississippi. In Arkansas, Virginia, West Virginia, and North Carolina the proportion of the white population was steadily growing. The colored migration northward increased while the westward movement of white farmers which characterized pioneer days declined. At the same time a part of the foreign immigration into the United States was diverted southward. As the years passed these tendencies gained momentum. The already huge colored quarters in some Northern cities were widely expanded, as whole counties in the South were stripped of their colored laborers. The race question, in its political and economic aspects, became less and less sectional, more and more national. The South was drawn into the main stream of national life. The separatist forces which produced the cataclysm of 1861 sank irresistibly into the background.

References

H.W. Grady, *The New South* (1890).

H.A. Herbert, *Why the Solid South*.

W.G. Brown, *The Lower South*.

E.G. Murphy, *Problems of the Present South*.

B.T. Washington, *The Negro Problem*; *The Story of the Negro*; *The Future of the Negro*.

A.B. Hart, *The Southern South* and R.S. Baker, *Following the Color Line* (two works by Northern writers).

T.N. Page, *The Negro, the Southerner's Problem*.

Questions

1. Give the three main subdivisions of the chapter.

2. Compare the condition of the South in 1865 with that of the North. Compare with the condition of the United States at the close of the Revolutionary War. At the close of the World War in 1918.

3. Contrast the enfranchisement of the slaves with the enfranchisement of white men fifty years earlier.

4. What was the condition of the planters as compared with that of the Northern manufacturers?

5. How does money capital contribute to prosperity? Describe the plight of Southern finance.

6. Give the chief steps in the restoration of white supremacy.

7. Do you know of any other societies to compare with the Ku Klux Klan?

8. Give Lincoln's plan for amnesty. What principles do you think should govern the granting of amnesty?

9. How were the "Force bills" overcome?

10. Compare the fourteenth and fifteenth amendments with regard to the suffrage provisions.

11. Explain how they may be circumvented.

12. Account for the Solid South. What was the situation before 1860?

13. In what ways did Southern agriculture tend to become like that of the North? What were the social results?

14. Name the chief results of an "industrial revolution" in general. In the South, in particular.

15. What courses were open to freedmen in 1865?

16. Give the main features in the economic and social status of the colored population in the South.

17. Explain why the race question is national now, rather than sectional.

Research Topics

Amnesty for Confederates.—Study carefully the provisions of the fourteenth amendment in the Appendix. Macdonald, *Documentary Source Book of American History*, pp. 470 and 564. A plea for amnesty in Harding, *Select Orations Illustrating American History*, pp. 467-488.

Political Conditions in the South in 1868.—Dunning, *Reconstruction, Political and Economic* (American Nation Series), pp. 109-123; Hart, *American History Told by Contemporaries*, Vol. IV, pp. 445-458, 497-500; Elson, *History of the United States*, pp. 799-805.

Movement for White Supremacy.—Dunning, *Reconstruction*, pp. 266-280; Paxson, *The New Nation* (Riverside Series), pp. 39-58; Beard, *American Government and Politics*, pp. 454-457.

The Withdrawal of Federal Troops from the South.—Sparks, *National Development* (American Nation Series), pp. 84-102; Rhodes, *History of the United States*, Vol. VIII, pp. 1-12.

Southern Industry.—Paxson, *The New Nation*, pp. 192-207; T.M. Young, *The American Cotton Industry*, pp. 54-99.

The Race Question.—B.T. Washington, *Up From Slavery* (sympathetic presentation); A.H. Stone, *Studies in the American Race Problem* (coldly analytical); Hart, *Contemporaries*, Vol. IV, pp. 647-649, 652-654, 663-669.

CHAPTER XVII

BUSINESS ENTERPRISE AND THE REPUBLICAN PARTY

If a single phrase be chosen to characterize American life during the generation that followed the age of Douglas and Lincoln, it must be "business enterprise"—the tremendous, irresistible energy of a virile people, mounting in numbers toward a hundred million and applied without let or hindrance to the developing of natural resources of unparalleled richness. The chief goal of this effort was high profits for the captains of industry, on the one hand; and high wages for the workers, on the other. Its signs, to use the language of a Republican orator in 1876, were golden harvest fields, whirling spindles, turning wheels, open furnace doors, flaming forges, and chimneys filled with eager fire. The device blazoned on its shield and written over its factory doors was "prosperity." A Republican President was its "advance agent." Released from the hampering interference of the Southern planters and the confusing issues of the slavery controversy, business enterprise sprang forward to the task of winning the entire country. Then it flung its outposts to the uttermost parts of the earth—Europe, Africa, and the Orient—where were to be found markets for American goods and natural resources for American capital to develop.

RAILWAYS AND INDUSTRY

The Outward Signs of Enterprise.—It is difficult to comprehend all the multitudinous activities of American business energy or to appraise its effects upon the life and destiny of the American people; for beyond the horizon of the twentieth century lie consequences as yet undreamed of in our poor philosophy. Statisticians attempt to record its achievements in terms of miles of railways built, factories opened, men and women employed, fortunes made, wages paid, cities founded, rivers spanned, boxes, bales, and tons produced. Historians apply standards of comparison with the past. Against the slow and leisurely stagecoach, they set the swift express, rushing from New York to San Francisco in less time than Washington consumed in his triumphal tour from Mt. Vernon to New York for his first inaugural. Against the lazy sailing vessel drifting before a genial breeze, they place the turbine steamer crossing the Atlantic in five days or the still swifter airplane, in fifteen hours. For the old workshop where a master and a dozen workmen and apprentices wrought by hand, they offer the giant factory where ten thousand persons attend the whirling wheels driven by steam. They write of the "romance of invention" and the "captains of industry."

The Service of the Railway.—All this is fitting in its way. Figures and contrasts cannot, however, tell the whole story. Take, for example, the extension of railways. It is easy to relate that there were 30,000 miles in 1860; 166,000 in 1890; and 242,000 in 1910. It is easy to show upon the map how a few straggling lines became a perfect mesh of closely knitted railways; or how, like the tentacles of a great monster, the few roads ending in the Mississippi Valley in 1860 were extended and multiplied until they tapped every wheat field, mine, and forest beyond the valley. All this, eloquent of enterprise as it truly is, does not reveal the significance of railways for American life. It does not indicate how railways made a continental market for American goods; nor how they standardized the whole country, giving to cities on the advancing frontier the leading features of cities in the old East; nor how they carried to the pioneer the comforts of civilization; nor yet how in the West they were the forerunners of civilization, the makers of homesteads, the builders of states.

Government Aid for Railways.—Still the story is not ended. The significant relation between railways and politics must not be overlooked. The bounty of a lavish government, for example, made possible the work of railway promoters. By the year 1872 the Federal government had granted in aid of railways 155,000,000 acres of land—an area estimated as almost equal to Pennsylvania, New York,

Connecticut, Rhode Island, Massachusetts, Maine, New Hampshire, and Vermont. The Union Pacific Company alone secured from the federal government a free right of way through the public domain, twenty sections of land with each mile of railway, and a loan up to fifty millions of dollars secured by a second mortgage on the company's property. More than half of the northern tier of states lying against Canada from Lake Michigan to the Pacific was granted to private companies in aid of railways and wagon roads. About half of New Mexico, Arizona, and California was also given outright to railway companies. These vast grants from the federal government were supplemented by gifts from the states in land and by subscriptions amounting to more than two hundred million dollars. The history of these gifts and their relation to the political leaders that engineered them would alone fill a large and interesting volume.

Railway Fortunes and Capital.—Out of this gigantic railway promotion, the first really immense American fortunes were made. Henry Adams, the grandson of John Quincy Adams, related that his grandfather on his mother's side, Peter Brooks, on his death in 1849, left a fortune of two million dollars, "supposed to be the largest estate in Boston," then one of the few centers of great riches. Compared with the opulence that sprang out of the Union Pacific, the Northern Pacific, the Southern Pacific, with their subsidiary and component lines, the estate of Peter Brooks was a poor man's heritage.

The capital invested in these railways was enormous beyond the imagination of the men of the stagecoach generation. The total debt of the United States incurred in the Revolutionary War—a debt which those of little faith thought the country could never pay—was reckoned at a figure well under $75,000,000. When the Union Pacific Railroad was completed, there were outstanding against it $27,000,000 in first mortgage bonds, $27,000,000 in second mortgage bonds held by the government, $10,000,000 in income bonds, $10,000,000 in land grant bonds, and, on top of that huge bonded indebtedness, $36,000,000 in stock—making $110,000,000 in all. If the amount due the United States government be subtracted, still there remained, in private hands, stocks and bonds exceeding in value the whole national debt of Hamilton's day—a debt that strained all the resources of the Federal government in 1790. Such was the financial significance of the railways.

Growth and Extension of Industry.—In the field of manufacturing, mining, and metal working, the results of business enterprise far outstripped, if measured in mere dollars, the results of railway construction. By the end of the century there were about ten billion dollars invested in factories alone and five million wage-earners employed in them; while the total value of the output, fourteen billion dollars, was fifteen times the figure for 1860. In the Eastern states industries multiplied. In the Northwest territory, the old home of Jacksonian Democracy, they overtopped agriculture. By the end of the century, Ohio had almost reached and Illinois had surpassed Massachusetts in the annual value of manufacturing output.

That was not all. Untold wealth in the form of natural resources was discovered in the South and West. Coal deposits were found in the Appalachians stretching from Pennsylvania down to Alabama, in Michigan, in the Mississippi Valley, and in the Western mountains from North Dakota to New Mexico. In nearly every coal-bearing region, iron was also discovered and the great fields of Michigan, Wisconsin, and Minnesota soon rivaled those of the Appalachian area. Copper, lead, gold, and silver in fabulous quantities were unearthed by the restless prospectors who left no plain or mountain fastness unexplored. Petroleum, first pumped from the wells of Pennsylvania in the summer of 1859, made new fortunes equaling those of trade, railways, and land speculation. It scattered its riches with an especially lavish hand through Oklahoma, Texas, and California.

The Trust—an Instrument of Industrial Progress.—Business enterprise, under the direction of powerful men working single-handed, or of small groups of men pooling their capital for one or more undertakings, had not advanced far before there appeared upon the scene still mightier leaders of even greater imagination. New constructive genius now brought together and combined under one management hundreds of concerns or thousands of miles of railways, revealing the magic strength of coöperation on a national scale. Price-cutting in oil, threatening ruin to those engaged in the industry, as early as 1879, led a number of companies in Cleveland, Pittsburgh, and Philadelphia to unite in price-fixing. Three years later a group of oil interests formed a close organization, placing all their stocks in the hands of trustees, among whom was John D. Rockefeller. The trustees, in turn, issued certificates representing the share to which each participant was entitled; and took over the management of the entire business. Such was the nature of the "trust," which was to play such an unique rôle in the progress of America.

The idea of combination was applied in time to iron and steel, copper, lead, sugar, cordage, coal, and other commodities, until in each field there loomed a giant trust or corporation, controlling, if not most of the output, at least enough to determine in a large measure the prices charged to consumers. With the passing years, the railways, mills, mines, and other business concerns were transferred from individual owners to corporations. At the end of the nineteenth century, the whole face of American business was changed. Three-fourths of the output from industries came from factories under corporate management and only one-fourth from individual and partnership undertakings.

The Banking Corporation.—Very closely related to the growth of business enterprise on a large scale was the system of banking. In the old days before banks, a person with savings either employed them in his own undertakings, lent them to a neighbor, or hid them away where they set no industry in motion. Even in the early stages of modern business, it was common for a manufacturer to rise from small beginnings by financing extensions out of his own earnings and profits. This state of affairs was profoundly altered by the growth of the huge corporations requiring millions and even billions of capital. The banks, once an adjunct to business, became the leaders in business.

It was the banks that undertook to sell the stocks and bonds issued by new corporations and trusts and to supply them with credit to carry on their operations. Indeed, many of the great mergers or combinations in business were initiated by magnates in the banking world with millions and billions under their control. Through their connections with one another, the banks formed a perfect network of agencies gathering up the pennies and dollars of the masses as well as the thousands of the richand pouring them all into the channels of business and manufacturing. In this growth of banking on a national scale, it was inevitable that a few great centers, like Wall Street in New York or State Street in Boston, should rise to a position of dominance both in concentrating the savings and profits of the nation and in financing new as well as old corporations.

The Significance of the Corporation.—The corporation, in fact, became the striking feature of American business life, one of the most marvelous institutions of all time, comparable in wealth and power and the number of its servants with kingdoms and states of old. The effect of its rise and growth cannot be summarily estimated; but some special facts are obvious. It made possible gigantic enterprises once entirely beyond the reach of any individual, no matter how rich. It eliminated many of the futile and costly wastes of competition in connection with manufacture, advertising, and selling. It studied the cheapest methods of production and shut down mills that were poorly equipped or disadvantageously located. It established laboratories for research in industry, chemistry, and mechanical inventions. Through the sale of stocks and bonds, it enabled tens of thousands of people to become capitalists, if only in a small way. The corporation made it possible for one person to own, for instance, a $50 share in a million dollar business concern—a thing entirely impossible under a régime of individual owners and partnerships.

There was, of course, another side to the picture. Many of the corporations sought to become monopolies and to make profits, not by economies and good management, but by extortion from purchasers. Sometimes they mercilessly crushed small business men, their competitors, bribed members of legislatures to secure favorable laws, and contributed to the campaign funds of both leading parties. Wherever a trust approached the position of a monopoly, it acquired a dominion over the labor market which enabled it to break even the strongest trade unions. In short, the power of the trust in finance, in manufacturing, in politics, and in the field of labor control can hardly be measured.

The Corporation and Labor.—In the development of the corporation there was to be observed a distinct severing of the old ties between master and workmen, which existed in the days of small industries. For the personal bond between the owner and the employees was substituted a new relation.

"In most parts of our country," as President Wilson once said, "men work, not for themselves, not as partners in the old way in which they used to work, but generally as employees—in a higher or lower grade—of great corporations." The owner disappeared from the factory and in his place came the manager, representing the usually invisible stockholders and dependent for his success upon his ability to make profits for the owners. Hence the term "soulless corporation," which was to exert such a deep influence on American thinking about industrial relations.

Cities and Immigration.—Expressed in terms of human life, this era of unprecedented enterprise meant huge industrial cities and an immense labor supply, derived mainly from European immigration. Here, too, figures tell only a part of the story. In Washington's day nine-tenths of the American people were engaged in agriculture and lived in the country; in 1890 more than one-third of the population dwelt in towns of 2500 and over; in 1920 more than half of the population lived in towns of over 2500. In forty years, between 1860 and 1900, Greater New York had grown from 1,174,000 to 3,437,000; San Francisco from 56,000 to 342,000; Chicago from 109,000 to 1,698,000. The miles of city tenements began to rival, in the number of their residents, the farm homesteads of the West. The time so dreaded by Jefferson had arrived. People were "piled upon one another in great cities" and the republic of small farmers had passed away.

To these industrial centers flowed annually an ever-increasing tide of immigration, reaching the half million point in 1880; rising to three-quarters of a million three years later; and passing the million mark in a single year at the opening of the new century. Immigration was as old as America but new elements now entered the situation. In the first place, there were radical changes in the nationality of the newcomers. The migration from Northern Europe—England, Ireland, Germany, and Scandinavia—diminished; that from Italy, Russia, and Austria-Hungary increased, more than three-fourths of the entire number coming from these three lands between the years 1900 and 1910. These later immigrants were Italians, Poles, Magyars, Czechs, Slovaks, Russians, and Jews, who came from countries far removed from the language and the traditions of England whence came the founders of America.

In the second place, the reception accorded the newcomers differed from that given to the immigrants in the early days. By 1890 all the free land was gone. They could not, therefore, be dispersed widely among the native Americans to assimilate quickly and unconsciously the habits and ideas of American life. On the contrary, they were diverted mainly to the industrial centers. There they crowded—nay, overcrowded—into colonies of their own where they preserved their languages, their newspapers, and their old-world customs and views.

So eager were American business men to get an enormous labor supply that they asked few questions about the effect of this "alien invasion" upon the old America inherited from the fathers. They even stimulated the invasion artificially by importing huge armies of foreigners under contract to work in specified mines and mills. There seemed to be no limit to the factories, forges, refineries, and railways that could be built, to the multitudes that could be employed in conquering a continent. As for the future, that was in the hands of Providence!

Business Theories of Politics.—As the statesmen of Hamilton's school and the planters of Calhoun's had their theories of government and politics, so the leaders in business enterprise had theirs. It was simple and easily stated. "It is the duty of the government," they urged, "to protect American industry against foreign competition by means of high tariffs on imported goods, to aid railways by generous grants of land, to sell mineral and timber lands at low prices to energetic men ready to develop them, and then to leave the rest to the initiative and drive of individuals and companies." All government interference with the management, prices, rates, charges, and conduct of private business they held to be either wholly pernicious or intolerably impertinent. Judging from their speeches and writings, they conceived the nation as a great collection of individuals, companies, and labor unions all struggling for profits or high wages and held together by a government whose principal duty was to keep the peace among them and protect industry against the foreign manufacturer. Such was the political theory of business during the generation that followed the Civil War.

THE SUPREMACY OF THE REPUBLICAN PARTY (1861-85)

Business Men and Republican Policies.—Most of the leaders in industry gravitated to the Republican ranks. They worked in the North and the Republican party was essentially Northern. It was moreover—at least so far as the majority of its members were concerned—committed to protective tariffs, a sound monetary and banking system, the promotion of railways and industry by land grants, and the development of internal improvements. It was furthermore generous in its immigration policy. It proclaimed America to be an asylum for the oppressed of all countries and flung wide the doors for immigrants eager to fill the factories, man the mines, and settle upon Western lands. In a word the Republicans stood for all those specific measures which favored the enlargement and prosperity of business. At the same time they resisted government interference with private enterprise. They did not regulate railway rates, prosecute trusts for forming combinations, or prevent railway companies from giving lower rates to some shippers than to others. To sum it up, the political theories of the Republican party for three decades after the Civil War were the theories of American business—prosperous and profitable industries for the owners and "the full dinner pail" for the workmen. Naturally a large portion of those who flourished under its policies gave their support to it, voted for its candidates, and subscribed to its campaign funds.

Sources of Republican Strength in the North.—The Republican party was in fact a political organization of singular power. It originated in a wave of moral enthusiasm, having attracted to itself, if not the abolitionists, certainly all those idealists, like James Russell Lowell and George William Curtis, who had opposed slavery when opposition was neither safe nor popular. To moral principles it added practical considerations. Business men had confidence in it. Workingmen, who longed for the independence of the farmer, owed to its indulgent land policy the opportunity of securing free homesteads in the West. The immigrant, landing penniless on these shores, as a result of the same beneficent system, often found himself in a little while with an estate as large as many a baronial domain in the Old World. Under a Republican administration, the union had been saved. To it the veterans of the war could turn with confidence for those rewards of service which the government could bestow: pensions surpassing in liberality anything that the world had ever seen. Under a Republican administration also the great debt had been created in the defense of the union, and to the Republican party every investor in government bonds could look for the full and honorable discharge of the interest and principal. The spoils system, inaugurated by Jacksonian Democracy, in turn placed all the federal offices in Republican hands, furnishing an army of party workers to be counted on for loyal service in every campaign.

Of all these things Republican leaders made full and vigorous use, sometimes ascribing to the party, in accordance with ancient political usage, merits and achievements not wholly its own. Particularly was this true in the case of saving the union. "When in the economy of Providence, this land was to be purged of human slavery ... the Republican party came into power," ran a declaration in one platform. "The Republican party suppressed a gigantic rebellion, emancipated four million slaves, decreed the equal citizenship of all, and established universal suffrage," ran another. As for the aid rendered by the millions of Northern Democrats who stood by the union and the tens of thousands of them who actually fought in the union army, the Republicans in their zeal were inclined to be oblivious. They repeatedly charged the Democratic party "with being the same in character and spirit as when it sympathized with treason."

Republican Control of the South.—To the strength enjoyed in the North, the Republicans for a long time added the advantages that came from control over the former Confederate states where the newly enfranchised negroes, under white leadership, gave a grateful support to the party responsible for their freedom. In this branch of politics, motives were so mixed that no historian can hope to appraise them all at their proper values. On the one side of the ledger must be set the vigorous efforts of the honest and sincere friends of the freedmen to win for them complete civil and political equality, wiping out not only slavery but all its badges of misery and servitude. On the same side must be placed the labor of those who had valiantly fought in forum and field to save the union and who regarded continued Republican supremacy after the war as absolutely necessary to prevent the former leaders in secession from coming back to power. At the same time there were undoubtedly some men of the baser sort who looked on politics as a game and who made use of "carpet-bagging" in the South to win the spoils that might result from it. At all events, both by laws and presidential acts, the Republicans for many years kept a keen eye upon the maintenance of their dominion in the South. Their declaration that neither the law nor its administration should admit any discrimination in respect of citizens by reason of race, color, or previous condition of servitude appealed to idealists and brought results in elections. Even South Carolina, where reposed the ashes of John C. Calhoun, went Republican in 1872 by a vote of three to one!

Republican control was made easy by the force bills described in a previous chapter—measures which vested the supervision of elections in federal officers appointed by Republican Presidents. These drastic measures, departing from American tradition, the Republican authors urged, were necessary to safeguard the purity of the ballot, not merely in the South where the timid freedman might readily be frightened from using it; but also in the North, particularly in New York City, where it was claimed that fraud was regularly practiced by Democratic leaders.

The Democrats, on their side, indignantly denied the charges, replying that the force bills were nothing but devices created by the Republicans for the purpose of securing their continued rule through systematic interference with elections. Even the measures of reconstruction were deemed by Democratic leaders as thinly veiled schemes to establish Republican power throughout the country. "Nor is there the slightest doubt," exclaimed Samuel J. Tilden, spokesman of the Democrats in New York and candidate for President in 1876, "that the paramount object and motive of the Republican party is by these means to secure itself against a reaction of opinion adverse to it in our great populous Northern commonwealths.... When the Republican party resolved to establish negro supremacy in the ten states in order to gain to itself the representation of those states in Congress, it had to begin by governing the people of those states by the sword.... The next was the creation of new electoral bodies for those ten states, in which, by exclusions, by disfranchisements and proscriptions, by control over registration, by applying test oaths ... by intimidation and by every form of influence, three million negroes are made to predominate over four and a half million whites."

The War as a Campaign Issue.—Even the repeal of force bills could not allay the sectional feelings engendered by the war. The Republicans could not forgive the men who had so recently been in arms against the union and insisted on calling them "traitors" and "rebels." The Southerners, smarting under the reconstruction acts, could regard the Republicans only as political oppressors. The passions of the war had been too strong; the distress too deep to be soon forgotten. The generation that went through it all remembered it all. For twenty years, the Republicans, in their speeches and platforms, made "a straight appeal to the patriotism of the Northern voters." They maintained that their party, which had saved the union and emancipated the slaves, was alone worthy of protecting the union and uplifting the freedmen.

Though the Democrats, especially in the North, resented this policy and dubbed it with the expressive but inelegant phrase, "waving the bloody shirt," the Republicans refused to surrender a slogan which made such a ready popular appeal. As late as 1884, a leader expressed the hope that they might "wring one more President from the bloody shirt." They refused to let the country forget that the Democratic candidate, Grover Cleveland, had escaped military service by hiring a substitute; and they made political capital out of the fact that he had "insulted the veterans of the Grand Army of the Republic" by going fishing on Decoration Day.

Three Republican Presidents.—Fortified by all these elements of strength, the Republicans held the presidency from 1869 to 1885. The three Presidents elected in this period, Grant, Hayes, and Garfield, had certain striking characteristics in common. They were all of origin humble enough to please the most exacting Jacksonian Democrat. They had been generals in the union army. Grant, next to Lincoln, was regarded as the savior of the Constitution. Hayes and Garfield, though lesser lights in the military firmament, had honorable records duly appreciated by veterans of the war, now thoroughly organized into the Grand Army of the Republic. It is true that Grant was not a politician and had never voted the Republican ticket; but this was readily overlooked. Hayes and Garfield on the other hand were loyal party men. The former had served in Congress and for three terms as governor of his state. The latter had long been a member of the House of Representatives and was Senator-elect when he received the nomination for President.

All of them possessed, moreover, another important asset, which was not forgotten by the astute managers who led in selecting candidates. All of them were from Ohio—though Grant had been in Illinois when the summons to military duties came—and Ohio was a strategic state. It lay between the manufacturing East and the agrarian country to the West. Having growing industries and wool to sell it benefited from the protective tariff. Yet being mainly agricultural still, it was not without sympathy for the farmers who showed low tariff or free trade tendencies. Whatever share the East had in shaping laws and framing policies, it was clear that the West was to have the candidates. This division in privileges—not uncommon in political management—was always accompanied by a judicious selection of the candidate for Vice President. With Garfield, for example, was associated a prominent New York politician, Chester A. Arthur, who, as fate decreed, was destined to more than three years' service as chief magistrate, on the assassination of his superior in office.

The Disputed Election of 1876.—While taking note of the long years of Republican supremacy, it must be recorded that grave doubts exist in the minds of many historians as to whether one of the three Presidents, Hayes, was actually the victor in 1876 or not. His Democratic opponent, Samuel J. Tilden, received a popular plurality of a quarter of a million and had a plausible claim to a majority of the electoral vote. At all events, four states sent in double returns, one set for Tilden and another for Hayes; and a deadlock ensued. Both parties vehemently claimed the election and the passions ran so high that sober men did not shrink from speaking of civil war again. Fortunately, in the end, the counsels of peace prevailed. Congress provided for an electoral commission of fifteen men to review the contested returns. The Democrats, inspired by Tilden's moderation, accepted the judgment in favor of Hayes even though they were not convinced that he was really entitled to the office.

THE GROWTH OF OPPOSITION TO REPUBLICAN RULE

Abuses in American Political Life.—During their long tenure of office, the Republicans could not escape the inevitable consequences of power; that is, evil practices and corrupt conduct on the part of some who found shelter within the party. For that matter neither did the Democrats manage to avoid such difficulties in those states and cities where they had the majority. In New York City, for instance, the local Democratic organization, known as Tammany Hall, passed under the sway of a group of politicians headed by "Boss" Tweed. He plundered the city treasury until public-spirited citizens, supported by Samuel J. Tilden, the Democratic leader of the state, rose in revolt, drove the ringleader from power, and sent him to jail. In Philadelphia, the local Republican bosses were guilty of offenses as odious as those committed by New York politicians. Indeed, the decade that followed the Civil War was marred by so many scandals in public life that one acute editor was moved to inquire: "Are not all the great communities of the Western World growing more corrupt as they grow in wealth?"

In the sphere of national politics, where the opportunities were greater, betrayals of public trust were even more flagrant. One revelation after another showed officers, high and low, possessed with the spirit of peculation. Members of Congress, it was found, accepted railway stock in exchange for votes in favor of land grants and other concessions to the companies. In the administration as well as the legislature the disease was rife. Revenue officers permitted whisky distillers to evade their taxes and received heavy bribes in return. A probe into the post-office department revealed the malodorous "star route frauds"—the deliberate overpayment of certain mail carriers whose lines were indicated in the official record by asterisks or stars. Even cabinet officers did not escape suspicion, for the trail of the serpent led straight to the door of one of them.

In the lower ranges of official life, the spoils system became more virulent as the number of federal employees increased. The holders of offices and the seekers after them constituted a veritable political army. They crowded into Republican councils, for the Republicans, being in power, could alone dispense federal favors. They filled positions in the party ranging from the lowest township committee to the national convention. They helped to nominate candidates and draft platforms and elbowed to one side the busy citizen, not conversant with party intrigues, who could only give an occasional day to political matters. Even the Civil Service Act of 1883, wrung from a reluctant Congress two years after the assassination of Garfield, made little change for a long time. It took away from the spoilsmen a few thousand government positions, but it formed no check on the practice of rewarding party workers from the public treasury.

On viewing this state of affairs, many a distinguished citizen became profoundly discouraged. James Russell Lowell, for example, thought he saw a steady decline in public morals. In 1865, hearing of Lee's surrender, he had exclaimed: "There is something magnificent in having a country to love!" Ten years later, when asked to write an ode for the centennial at Philadelphia in 1876, he could think only of a biting satire on the nation:

"Show your state legislatures; show your Rings;And challenge Europe to produce such thingsAs high officials sitting half in sightTo share the plunder and fix things right.If that don't fetch her, why, you need onlyTo show your latest style in martyrs,—Tweed:She'll find it hard to hide her spiteful tearsAt such advance in one poor hundred years."

When his critics condemned him for this "attack upon his native land," Lowell replied in sadness: "These fellows have no notion of what love of country means. It was in my very blood and bones. If I am not an American who ever was?... What fills me with doubt and dismay is the degradation of the moral tone. Is it or is it not a result of democracy? Is ours a 'government of the people, by the people, for the people,' or a Kakistocracy [a government of the worst], rather for the benefit of knaves at the cost of fools?"

The Reform Movement in Republican Ranks.—The sentiments expressed by Lowell, himself a Republican and for a time American ambassador to England, were shared by many men in his party. Very soon after the close of the Civil War some of them began to protest vigorously against the policies and conduct of their leaders. In 1872, the dissenters, calling themselves Liberal Republicans, broke away altogether, nominated a candidate of their own, Horace Greeley, and put forward a platform indicting the Republican President fiercely enough to please the most uncompromising Democrat. They accused Grant of using "the powers and opportunities of his high office for the promotion of personal ends." They charged him with retaining "notoriously corrupt and unworthy men in places of power and responsibility." They alleged that the Republican party kept "alive the passions and resentments of the late civil war to use them for their own advantages," and employed the "public service of the government as a machinery of corruption and personal influence."

It was not apparent, however, from the ensuing election that any considerable number of Republicans accepted the views of the Liberals. Greeley, though indorsed by the Democrats, was utterly routed and died of a broken heart. The lesson of his discomfiture seemed to be that independent action was futile. So, at least, it was regarded by most men of the rising generation like Henry Cabot Lodge, of Massachusetts, and Theodore Roosevelt, of New York. Profiting by the experience of Greeley they insisted in season and out that reformers who desired to rid the party of abuses should remain loyal to it and do their work "on the inside."

The Mugwumps and Cleveland Democracy in 1884.—Though aided by Republican dissensions, the Democrats were slow in making headway against the political current. They were deprived of the energetic and capable leadership once afforded by the planters, like Calhoun, Davis, and Toombs; they were saddled by their opponents with responsibility for secession; and they were stripped of the support of the prostrate South. Not until the last Southern state was restored to the union, not until a general amnesty was wrung from Congress, not until white supremacy was established at the polls, and the last federal soldier withdrawn from Southern capitals did they succeed in capturing the presidency.

The opportune moment for them came in 1884 when a number of circumstances favored their aspirations. The Republicans, leaving the Ohio Valley in their search for a candidate, nominated James G. Blaine of Maine, a vigorous and popular leader but a man under fire from the reformers in his own party. The Democrats on their side were able to find at this juncture an able candidate who had no political enemies in the sphere of national politics, Grover Cleveland, then governor of New York and widely celebrated as a man of "sterling honesty." At the same time a number of dissatisfied Republicans openly espoused the Democratic cause,—among them Carl Schurz, George William Curtis, Henry Ward Beecher, and William Everett, men of fine ideals and undoubted integrity. Though the "regular" Republicans called them "Mugwumps" and laughed at them as the "men milliners, the dilettanti, and carpet knights of politics," they had a following that was not to be despised.

The campaign which took place that year was one of the most savage in American history. Issues were thrust into the background. The tariff, though mentioned, was not taken seriously. Abuse of the opposition was the favorite resource of party orators. The Democrats insisted that "the Republican party so far as principle is concerned is a reminiscence. In practice it is an organization for enriching those who control its machinery." For the Republican candidate, Blaine, they could hardly find words to express their contempt. The Republicans retaliated in kind. They praised their own good works, as of old, in saving the union, and denounced the "fraud and violence practiced by the Democracy in the Southern states." Seeing little objectionable in the public record of Cleveland as mayor of Buffalo and governor of New York, they attacked his personal character. Perhaps never in the history of political campaigns did the discussions on the platform and in the press sink to so low a level. Decent people were sickened. Even hot partisans shrank from their own words when, after the election, they had time to reflect on their heedless passions. Moreover, nothing was decided by the balloting. Cleveland was elected, but his victory was a narrow one. A change of a few hundred votes in New York would have sent his opponent to the White House instead.

Changing Political Fortunes (1888-96).—After the Democrats had settled down to the enjoyment of their hard-earned victory, President Cleveland in his message of 1887 attacked the tariff as "vicious, inequitable, and illogical"; as a system of taxation that laid a burden upon "every consumer in the land for the benefit of our manufacturers." Business enterprise was thoroughly alarmed. The Republicans characterized the tariff message as a free-trade assault upon the industries of the country. Mainly on that issue they elected in 1888 Benjamin Harrison of Indiana, a shrewd lawyer, a reticent politician, a descendant of the hero of Tippecanoe, and a son of the old Northwest. Accepting the outcome of the election as a vindication of their principles, the Republicans, under the leadership of William McKinley in the House of Representatives, enacted in 1890 a tariff law imposing the highest duties yet laid in our history. To their utter surprise, however, they were instantly informed by the country that their program was not approved. That very autumn they lost in the congressional elections, and two years later they were decisively beaten in the presidential campaign, Cleveland once more leading his party to victory.

References

L.H. Haney, *Congressional History of Railways* (2 vols.).

J.P. Davis, *Union Pacific Railway*.

J.M. Swank, *History of the Manufacture of Iron*.

M.T. Copeland, *The Cotton Manufacturing Industry in the United States* (Harvard Studies).

E.W. Bryce, *Progress of Invention in the Nineteenth Century*.

Ida Tarbell, *History of the Standard Oil Company* (Critical).

G.H. Montague, *Rise and Progress of the Standard Oil Company* (Friendly).

H.P. Fairchild, *Immigration*, and F.J. Warne, *The Immigrant Invasion* (Both works favor exclusion).

I.A. Hourwich, *Immigration* (Against exclusionist policies).

J.F. Rhodes, *History of the United States, 1877-1896*, Vol. VIII.

Edward Stanwood, *A History of the Presidency*, Vol. I, for the presidential elections of the period.

Questions

1. Contrast the state of industry and commerce at the close of the Civil War with its condition at the close of the Revolutionary War.

2. Enumerate the services rendered to the nation by the railways.

3. Explain the peculiar relation of railways to government.

4. What sections of the country have been industrialized?

5. How do you account for the rise and growth of the trusts? Explain some of the economic advantages of the trust.

6. Are the people in cities more or less independent than the farmers? What was Jefferson's view?

7. State some of the problems raised by unrestricted immigration.

8. What was the theory of the relation of government to business in this period? Has it changed in recent times?

9. State the leading economic policies sponsored by the Republican party.

10. Why were the Republicans especially strong immediately after the Civil War?

11. What illustrations can you give showing the influence of war in American political campaigns?

12. Account for the strength of middle-western candidates.

13. Enumerate some of the abuses that appeared in American political life after 1865.

14. Sketch the rise and growth of the reform movement.

15. How is the fluctuating state of public opinion reflected in the elections from 1880 to 1896?

Research Topics

Invention, Discovery, and Transportation.—Sparks, *National Development* (American Nation Series), pp. 37-67; Bogart, *Economic History of the United States*, Chaps. XXI, XXII, and XXIII.

Business and Politics.—Paxson, *The New Nation* (Riverside Series), pp. 92-107; Rhodes, *History of the United States*, Vol. VII, pp. 1-29, 64-73, 175-206; Wilson, *History of the American People*, Vol. IV, pp. 78-96.

Immigration.—Coman, *Industrial History of the United States* (2d ed.), pp. 369-374; E.L. Bogart, *Economic History of the United States*, pp. 420-422, 434-437; Jenks and Lauck, *Immigration Problems*, Commons, *Races and Immigrants*.

The Disputed Election of 1876.—Haworth, *The United States in Our Own Time*, pp. 82-94; Dunning, *Reconstruction, Political and Economic* (American Nation Series), pp. 294-341; Elson, *History of the United States*, pp. 835-841.

Abuses in Political Life.—Dunning, *Reconstruction*, pp. 281-293; see criticisms in party platforms in Stanwood, *History of the Presidency*, Vol. I; Bryce, *American Commonwealth* (1910 ed.), Vol. II, pp. 379-448; 136-167.

Studies of Presidential Administrations.—(*a*) Grant, (*b*) Hayes, (*c*) Garfield-Arthur, (*d*) Cleveland, and (*e*) Harrison, in Haworth, *The United States in Our Own Time*, or in Paxson, *The New Nation* (Riverside Series), or still more briefly in Elson.

Cleveland Democracy.—Haworth, *The United States*, pp. 164-183; Rhodes, *History of the United States*, Vol. VIII, pp. 240-327; Elson, pp. 857-887.

Analysis of Modern Immigration Problems.—*Syllabus in History* (New York State, 1919), pp. 110-112.

CHAPTER XVIII

THE DEVELOPMENT OF THE GREAT WEST

At the close of the Civil War, Kansas and Texas were sentinel states on the middle border. Beyond the Rockies, California, Oregon, and Nevada stood guard, the last of them having been just admitted to furnish another vote for the fifteenth amendment abolishing slavery. Between the near and far frontiers lay a vast reach of plain, desert, plateau, and mountain, almost wholly undeveloped. A broad domain, extending from Canada to Mexico, and embracing the regions now included in Washington, Idaho, Wyoming, Montana, Utah, Arizona, New Mexico, the Dakotas, and Oklahoma, had fewer than half a million inhabitants. It was laid out into territories, each administered under a governor appointed by the President and Senate and, as soon as there was the requisite number of inhabitants, a legislature elected by the voters. No railway line stretched across the desert. St. Joseph on the Missouri was the terminus of the Eastern lines. It required twenty-five days for a passenger to make the overland journey to California by the stagecoach system, established in 1858, and more than ten days for the swift pony express, organized in 1860, to carry a letter to San Francisco. Indians still roamed the plain and desert and more than one powerful tribe disputed the white man's title to the soil.

THE RAILWAYS AS TRAIL BLAZERS

Opening Railways to the Pacific.—A decade before the Civil War the importance of rail connection between the East and the Pacific Coast had been recognized. Pressure had already been brought to bear on Congress to authorize the construction of a line and to grant land and money in its aid. Both the Democrats and Republicans approved the idea, but it was involved in the slavery controversy. Indeed it was submerged in it. Southern statesmen wanted connections between the Gulf and the Pacific through Texas, while Northerners stood out for a central route.

The North had its way during the war. Congress, by legislation initiated in 1862, provided for the immediate organization of companies to build a line from the Missouri River to California and made grants of land and loans of money to aid in the enterprise. The Western end, the Central Pacific, was laid out under the supervision of Leland Stanford. It was heavily financed by the Mormons of Utah and also by the state government, the ranchmen, miners, and business men of California; and it was built principally by Chinese labor. The Eastern end, the Union Pacific, starting at Omaha, was constructed mainly by veterans of the Civil War and immigrants from Ireland and Germany. In 1869 the two companies met near Ogden in Utah and the driving of the last spike, uniting the Atlantic and the Pacific, was the occasion of a great demonstration.

Other lines to the Pacific were projected at the same time; but the panic of 1873 checked railway enterprise for a while. With the revival of prosperity at the end of that decade, construction was renewed with vigor and the year 1883 marked a series of railway triumphs. In February trains were running from New Orleans through Houston, San Antonio, and Yuma to San Francisco, as a result of a union of the Texas Pacific with the Southern Pacific and its subsidiary corporations. In September the last spike was driven in the Northern Pacific at Helena, Montana. Lake Superior was connected with Puget Sound. The waters explored by Joliet and Marquette were joined to the waters plowed by Sir Francis Drake while he was searching for a route around the world. That same year also a third line was opened to the Pacific by way of the Atchison, Topeka and Santa Fé, making connections through Albuquerque and Needles with San Francisco. The fondest hopes of railway promoters seemed to be realized.

Western Railways Precede Settlement.—In the Old World and on our Atlantic seaboard, railways followed population and markets. In the Far West, railways usually preceded the people. Railway builders planned cities on paper before they laid tracks connecting them. They sent missionaries to spread the gospel of "Western opportunity" to people in the Middle West, in the Eastern cities, and in Southern states. Then they carried their enthusiastic converts bag and baggage in long trains to the distant Dakotas and still farther afield. So the development of the Far West was not left to the tedious processes of time. It was pushed by men of imagination—adventurers who made a romance of money-making and who had dreams of empire unequaled by many kings of the past.

These empire builders bought railway lands in huge tracts; they got more from the government; they overcame every obstacle of cañon, mountain, and stream with the aid of science; they built cities according to the plans made by the engineers. Having the towns ready and railway and steamboat connections formed with the rest of the world, they carried out the people to use the railways, the steamships, the houses, and the land. It was in this way that "the frontier speculator paved the way for the frontier agriculturalist who had to be near a market before he could farm." The spirit of this imaginative enterprise, which laid out railways and towns in advance of the people, is seen in an advertisement of that day: "This extension will run 42 miles from York, northeast through the Island Lake country, and will have five good North Dakota towns. The stations on the line will be well equipped with elevators and will be constructed and ready for operation at the commencement of the grain season. Prospective merchants have been active in securing desirable locations at the different towns on the line. There are still opportunities for hotels, general merchandise, hardware, furniture, and drug stores, etc."

Among the railway promoters and builders in the West, James J. Hill, of the Great Northern and allied lines, was one of the most forceful figures. He knew that tracks and trains were useless without passengers and freight; without a population of farmers and town dwellers. He therefore organized publicity in the Virginias, Iowa, Ohio, Indiana, Illinois, Wisconsin, and Nebraska especially. He sent out agents to tell the story of Western opportunity in this vein: "You see your children come out of school with no chance to get farms of their own because the cost of land in your older part of the country is so high that you can't afford to buy land to start your sons out in life around you. They have to go to the cities to make a living or become laborers in the mills or hire out as farm hands. There is no future for them there. If you are doing well where you are and can safeguard the future of your children and see them prosper around you, don't leave here. But if you want independence, if you are renting your land, if the money-lender is carrying you along and you are running behind year after year, you can do no worse by moving.... You farmers talk of free trade and protection and what this or that political party will do for you. Why don't you vote a homestead for yourself? That is the only thing Uncle Sam will ever give you. Jim Hill hasn't an acre of land to sell you. We are not in the real estate business. We don't want you to go out West and make a failure of it because the rates at which we haul you and your goods make the first transaction a loss.... We must have landless men for a manless land."

Unlike steamship companies stimulating immigration to get the fares, Hill was seeking permanent settlers who would produce, manufacture, and use the railways as the means of exchange. Consequently he fixed low rates and let his passengers take a good deal of live stock and household furniture free. By doing this he made an appeal that was answered by eager families. In 1894 the vanguard of home seekers left Indiana in fourteen passenger coaches, filled with men, women, and children, and forty-eight freight cars carrying their household goods and live stock. In the ten years that followed, 100,000 people from the Middle West and the South, responding to his call, went to the Western country where they brought eight million acres of prairie land under cultivation.

When Hill got his people on the land, he took an interest in everything that increased the productivity of their labor. Was the output of food for his freight cars limited by bad drainage on the farms? Hill then interested himself in practical ways of ditching and tiling. Were farmers hampered in hauling their goods to his trains by bad roads? In that case, he urged upon the states the improvement of highways. Did the traffic slacken because the food shipped was not of the best quality? Then live stock must be improved and scientific farming promoted. Did the farmers need credit? Banks must be established close at hand to advance it. In all conferences on scientific farm management, conservation of natural resources, banking and credit in relation to agriculture and industry, Hill was an active participant. His was the long vision, seeing in conservation and permanent improvements the foundation of prosperity for the railways and the people.

Indeed, he neglected no opportunity to increase the traffic on the lines. He wanted no empty cars running in either direction and no wheat stored in warehouses for the lack of markets. So he looked to the Orient as well as to Europe as an outlet for the surplus of the farms. He sent agents to China and Japan to discover what American goods and produce those countries would consume and what manufactures they had to offer to Americans in exchange. To open the Pacific trade he bought two ocean monsters, the *Minnesota* and the *Dakota*, thus preparing for emergencies West as well as East. When some Japanese came to the United States on their way to Europe to buy steel rails, Hill showed them how easy it was for them to make their purchase in this country and ship by way of American railways and American vessels. So the railway builder and promoter, who helped to break the virgin soil of the prairies, lived through the pioneer epoch and into the age of great finance. Before he died he saw the wheat fields of North Dakota linked with the spinning jennies of Manchester and the docks of Yokohama.

THE EVOLUTION OF GRAZING AND AGRICULTURE

The Removal of the Indians.—Unlike the frontier of New England in colonial days or that of Kentucky later, the advancing lines of home builders in the Far West had little difficulty with warlike natives. Indian attacks were made on the railway construction gangs; General Custer had his fatal battle with the Sioux in 1876 and there were minor brushes; but they were all of relatively slight consequence. The former practice of treating with the Indians as independent nations was abandoned in 1871 and most of them were concentrated in reservations where they were mainly supported by the government. The supervision of their affairs was vested in a board of commissioners created in 1869 and instructed to treat them as wards of the nation—a trust which unfortunately was often betrayed. A further step in Indian policy was taken in 1887 when provision was made for issuing lands to individual Indians, thus permitting them to become citizens and settle down among their white neighbors as farmers or cattle raisers. The disappearance of the buffalo, the main food supply of the wild Indians, had made them more tractable and more willing to surrender the freedom of the hunter for the routine of the reservation, ranch, or wheat field.

The Cowboy and Cattle Ranger.—Between the frontier of farms and the mountains were plains and semi-arid regions in vast reaches suitable for grazing. As soon as the railways were open into the Missouri Valley, affording an outlet for stock, there sprang up to the westward cattle and sheep raising on an immense scale. The far-famed American cowboy was the hero in this scene. Great herds of cattle were bred in Texas; with the advancing spring and summer seasons, they were driven northward across the plains and over the buffalo trails. In a single year, 1884, it is estimated that nearly one million head of cattle were moved out of Texas to the North by four thousand cowboys, supplied with 30,000 horses and ponies.

During the two decades from 1870 to 1890 both the cattle men and the sheep raisers had an almost free run of the plains, using public lands without paying for the privilege and waging war on one another over the possession of ranges. At length, however, both had to go, as the homesteaders and land companies came and fenced in the plain and desert with endless lines of barbed wire. Already in 1893 a writer familiar with the frontier lamented the passing of the picturesque days: "The unique position of the cowboys among the Americans is jeopardized in a thousand ways. Towns are growing up on their pasture lands; irrigation schemes of a dozen sorts threaten to turn bunch-grass scenery into farm-land views; farmers are pre-empting valleys and the sides of waterways; and the day is not far distant when stock-raising must be done mainly in small herds, with winter corrals, and then the cowboy's days will end. Even now his condition disappoints those who knew him only half a dozen years ago. His breed seems to have deteriorated and his ranks are filling with men who work for wages rather than for the love of the free life and bold companionship that once tempted men into that calling. Splendid Cheyenne saddles are less and less numerous in the outfits; the distinctive hat that made its way up from Mexico may or may not be worn; all the civil authorities in nearly all towns in the grazing country forbid the wearing of side arms; nobody shoots up these towns any more. The fact is the old simon-pure cowboy days are gone already."

Settlement under the Homestead Act of 1862.—Two factors gave a special stimulus to the rapid settlement of Western lands which swept away the Indians and the cattle rangers. The first was the policy of the railway companies in selling large blocks of land received from the government at low prices to induce immigration. The second was the operation of the Homestead law passed in 1862. This measure practically closed the long controversy over the disposition of the public domain that was suitable for agriculture. It provided for granting, without any cost save a small registration fee, public lands in lots of 160 acres each to citizens and aliens who declared their intention of becoming citizens. The one important condition attached was that the settler should occupy the farm for five years before his title was finally confirmed. Even this stipulation was waived in the case of the Civil War veterans who were allowed to count their term of military service as a part of the five years' occupancy required. As the soldiers of the Revolutionary and Mexican wars had advanced in great numbers to the frontier in earlier days, so now veterans led in the settlement of the middle border. Along with them went thousands of German, Irish, and Scandinavian immigrants, fresh from the Old World. Between 1867 and 1874, 27,000,000 acres were staked out in quarter-section farms. In twenty years (1860-80), the population of Nebraska leaped from 28,000 to almost half a million; Kansas from 100,000 to a million; Iowa from 600,000 to 1,600,000; and the Dakotas from 5000 to 140,000.

The Diversity of Western Agriculture.—In soil, produce, and management, Western agriculture presented many contrasts to that of the East and South. In the region of arable and watered lands the typical American unit—the small farm tilled by the owner—appeared as usual; but by the side of it many a huge domain owned by foreign or Eastern companies and tilled by hired labor. Sometimes the great estate took the shape of the "bonanza farm" devoted mainly to wheat and corn and cultivated on a large scale by machinery. Again it assumed the form of the cattle ranch embracing tens of thousands of acres. Again it was a vast holding of diversified interest, such as the Santa Anita ranch near Los Angeles, a domain of 60,000 acres "cultivated in a glorious sweep of vineyards and orange and olive orchards, rich sheep and cattle pastures and horse ranches, their life and customs handed down from the Spanish owners of the various ranches which were swept into one estate."

Irrigation.—In one respect agriculture in the Far West was unique. In a large area spreading through eight states, Montana, Idaho, Wyoming, Utah, Colorado, Nevada, Arizona, New Mexico, and parts of adjoining states, the rainfall was so slight that the ordinary crops to which the American farmer was accustomed could not be grown at all. The Mormons were the first Anglo-Saxons to encounter aridity, and they were baffled at first; but they studied it and mastered it by magnificent irrigation systems. As other settlers poured into the West the problem of the desert was attacked with a will, some of them replying to the commiseration of Eastern farmers by saying that it was easier to scoop out an irrigation ditch than to cut forests and wrestle with stumps and stones. Private companies bought immense areas at low prices, built irrigation works, and disposed of their lands in small plots. Some ranchers with an instinct for water, like that of the miner for metal, sank wells into the dry sand and were rewarded with gushers that "soused the thirsty desert and turned its good-for-nothing sand into good-for-anything loam." The federal government came to the aid of the arid regions in 1894 by granting lands to the states to be used for irrigation purposes. In this work Wyoming took the lead with a law which induced capitalists to invest in irrigation and at the same time provided for the sale of the redeemed lands to actual settlers. Finally in 1902 the federal government by its liberal Reclamation Act added its strength to that of individuals, companies, and states in conquering "arid America."

"Nowhere," writes Powell, a historian of the West, in his picturesque *End of the Trail*, "has the white man fought a more courageous fight or won a more brilliant victory than in Arizona. His weapons have been the transit and the level, the drill and the dredge, the pick and the spade; and the enemy which he has conquered has been the most stubborn of all foes—the hostile forces of Nature.... The story of how the white man within the space of less than thirty years penetrated, explored, and mapped this almost unknown region; of how he carried law, order, and justice into a section which had never had so much as a speaking acquaintance with any one of the three before; of how, realizing the necessity for means of communication, he built highways of steel across this territory from east to west and from north to south; of how, undismayed by the savageness of the countenance which the desert turned upon him, he laughed and rolled up his sleeves, and spat upon his hands, and slashed the face of the desert with canals and irrigating ditches, and filled those ditches with water brought from deep in the earth or high in the mountains; and of how, in the conquered and submissive soil, he replaced the aloe with alfalfa, the mesquite with maize, the cactus with cotton, forms one of the most inspiring chapters in our history. It is one of the epics of civilization, this reclamation of the Southwest, and its heroes, thank God, are Americans.

"Other desert regions have been redeemed by irrigation—Egypt, for example, and Mesopotamia and parts of the Sudan—but the people of all those regions lay stretched out in the shade of a convenient palm, metaphorically speaking, and waited for some one with more energy than themselves to come along and do the work. But the Arizonians, mindful of the fact that God, the government, and Carnegie help those who help themselves, spent their days wielding the pick and shovel, and their evenings in writing letters to Washington with toil-hardened hands. After a time the government was prodded into action and the great dams at Laguna and Roosevelt are the result. Then the people, organizing themselves into coöperative leagues and water-users' associations, took up the work of reclamation where the government left off; it is to these energetic, persevering men who have drilled wells, plowed fields, and dug ditches through the length and breadth of that great region which stretches from Yuma to Tucson, that the metamorphosis of Arizona is due."

The effect of irrigation wherever introduced was amazing. Stretches of sand and sagebrush gave way to fertile fields bearing crops of wheat, corn, fruits, vegetables, and grass. Huge ranches grazed by browsing sheep were broken up into small plots. The cowboy and ranchman vanished. In their place rose the prosperous community—a community unlike the township of Iowa or the industrial center of the East. Its intensive tillage left little room for hired labor. Its small holdings drew families together in village life rather than dispersing them on the lonely plain. Often the development of water power in connection with irrigation afforded electricity for labor-saving devices and lifted many a burden that in other days fell heavily upon the shoulders of the farmer and his family.

MINING AND MANUFACTURING IN THE WEST

Mineral Resources.—In another important particular the Far West differed from the Mississippi Valley states. That was in the predominance of mining over agriculture throughout a vast section. Indeed it was the minerals rather than the land that attracted the pioneers who first opened the country. The discovery of gold in California in 1848 was the signal for the great rush of prospectors, miners, and promoters who explored the valleys, climbed the hills, washed the sands, and dug up the soil in their feverish search for gold, silver, copper, coal, and other minerals. In Nevada and Montana the development of mineral resources went on all during the Civil War. Alder Gulch became Virginia City in 1863; Last Chance Gulch was named Helena in 1864; and Confederate Gulch was christened Diamond City in 1865. At Butte the miners began operations in 1864 and within five years had washed out eight million dollars' worth of gold. Under the gold they found silver; under silver they found copper.

Even at the end of the nineteenth century, after agriculture was well advanced and stock and sheep raising introduced on a large scale, minerals continued to be the chief source of wealth in a number of states. This was revealed by the figures for 1910. The gold, silver, iron, and copper of Colorado were worth more than the wheat, corn, and oats combined; the copper of Montana sold for more than all the cereals and four times the price of the wheat. The interest of Nevada was also mainly mining, the receipts from the mineral output being $43,000,000 or more than one-half the national debt of Hamilton's day. The yield of the mines of Utah was worth four or five times the wheat crop; the coal of Wyoming brought twice as much as the great wool clip; the minerals of Arizona were totaled at $43,000,000 as against a wool clip reckoned at $1,200,000; while in Idaho alone of this group of states did the wheat crop exceed in value the output of the mines.

Timber Resources.—The forests of the great West, unlike those of the Ohio Valley, proved a boon to the pioneers rather than a foe to be attacked. In Ohio and Indiana, for example, the frontier line of homemakers had to cut, roll, and burn thousands of trees before they could put out a crop of any size. Beyond the Mississippi, however, there were all ready for the breaking plow great reaches of almost treeless prairie, where every stick of timber was precious. In the other parts, often rough and mountainous, where stood primeval forests of the finest woods, the railroads made good use of the timber. They consumed acres of forests themselves in making ties, bridge timbers, and telegraph poles, and they laid a heavy tribute upon the forests for their annual upkeep. The surplus trees, such as had burdened the pioneers of the Northwest Territory a hundred years before, they carried off to markets on the east and west coasts.

Western Industries.—The peculiar conditions of the Far West stimulated a rise of industries more rapid than is usual in new country. The mining activities which in many sections preceded agriculture called for sawmills to furnish timber for the mines and smelters to reduce and refine ores. The ranches supplied sheep and cattle for the packing houses of Kansas City as well as Chicago. The waters of the Northwest afforded salmon for 4000 cases in 1866 and for 1,400,000 cases in 1916. The fruits and vegetables of California brought into existence innumerable canneries. The lumber industry, starting with crude sawmills to furnish rough timbers for railways and mines, ended in specialized factories for paper, boxes, and furniture. As the railways preceded settlement and furnished a ready outlet for local manufactures, so they encouraged the early establishment of varied industries, thus creating a state of affairs quite unlike that which obtained in the Ohio Valley in the early days before the opening of the Erie Canal.

Social Effects of Economic Activities.—In many respects the social life of the Far West also differed from that of the Ohio Valley. The treeless prairies, though open to homesteads, favored the great estate tilled in part by tenant labor and in part by migratory seasonal labor, summoned from all sections of the country for the harvests. The mineral resources created hundreds of huge fortunes which made the accumulations of eastern mercantile families look trivial by comparison. Othermillionaires won their fortunes in the railway business and still more from the cattle and sheep ranges. In many sections the "cattle king," as he was called, was as dominant as the planter had been in the old South. Everywhere in the grazing country he was a conspicuous and important person. He "sometimes invested money in banks, in railroad stocks, or in city property.... He had his rating in the commercial reviews and could hobnob with bankers, railroad presidents, and metropolitan merchants.... He attended party caucuses and conventions, ran for the state legislature, and sometimes defeated a lawyer or metropolitan 'business man' in the race for a seat in Congress. In proportion to their numbers, the ranchers ... have constituted a highly impressive class."

Although many of the early capitalists of the great West, especially from Nevada, spent their money principally in the East, others took leadership in promoting the sections in which they had made their fortunes. A railroad pioneer, General Palmer, built his home at Colorado Springs, founded the town, and encouraged local improvements. Denver owed its first impressive buildings to the civic patriotism of Horace Tabor, a wealthy mine owner. Leland Stanford paid his tribute to California in the endowment of a large university. Colonel W.F. Cody, better known as "Buffalo Bill," started his career by building a "boom town" which collapsed, and made a large sum of money supplying buffalo meat to construction hands (hence his popular name). By his famous Wild West Show, he increased it to a fortune which he devoted mainly to the promotion of a western reclamation scheme.

While the Far West was developing this vigorous, aggressive leadership in business, a considerable industrial population was springing up. Even the cattle ranges and hundreds of farms were conducted like factories in that they were managed through overseers who hired plowmen, harvesters, and cattlemen at regular wages. At the same time there appeared other peculiar features which made a lasting impression on western economic life. Mining, lumbering, and fruit growing, for instance, employed thousands of workers during the rush months and turned them out at other times. The inevitable result was an army of migratory laborers wandering from camp to camp, from town to town, and from ranch to ranch, without fixed homes or established habits of life. From this extraordinary condition there issued many a long and lawless conflict between capital and labor, giving a distinct color to the labor movement in whole sections of the mountain and coast states.

The Admission of New States

The Spirit of Self-Government.—The instinct of self-government was strong in the western communities. In the very beginning, it led to the organization of volunteer committees, known as "vigilantes," to suppress crime and punish criminals. As soon as enough people were settled permanently in a region, they took care to form a more stable kind of government. An illustration of this process is found in the Oregon compact made by the pioneers in 1843, the spirit of which is reflected in an editorial in an old copy of the *Rocky Mountain News*: "We claim that any body or community of American citizens which from any cause or under any circumstances is cut off from or from isolation is so situated as not to be under any active and protecting branch of the central government, have a right, if on American soil, to frame a government and enact such laws and regulations as may be necessary for their own safety, protection, and happiness, always with the condition precedent, that they shall, at the earliest moment when the central government shall extend an effective organization and laws over them, give it their unqualified support and obedience."

People who turned so naturally to the organization of local administration were equally eager for admission to the union as soon as any shadow of a claim to statehood could be advanced. As long as a region was merely one of the territories of the United States, the appointment of the governor and other officers was controlled by politics at Washington. Moreover the disposition of land, mineral rights, forests, and water power was also in the hands of national leaders. Thus practical considerations were united with the spirit of independence in the quest for local autonomy.

Nebraska and Colorado.—Two states, Nebraska and Colorado, had little difficulty in securing admission to the union. The first, Nebraska, had been organized as a territory by the famous Kansas-Nebraska bill which did so much to precipitate the Civil War. Lying to the north of Kansas, which had been admitted in 1861, it escaped the invasion of slave owners from Missouri and was settled mainly by farmers from the North. Though it claimed a population of only 67,000, it was regarded with kindly interest by the Republican Congress at Washington and, reduced to its present boundaries, it received the coveted statehood in 1867.

This was hardly accomplished before the people of Colorado to the southwest began to make known their demands. They had been organized under territorial government in 1861 when they numbered only a handful; but within ten years the aspect of their affairs had completely changed. The silver and gold deposits of the Leadville and Cripple Creek regions had attracted an army of miners and prospectors. The city of Denver, founded in 1858 and named after the governor of Kansas whence came many of the early settlers, had grown from a straggling camp of log huts into a prosperous center of trade. By 1875 it was reckoned that the population of the territory was not less than one hundred thousand; the following year Congress, yielding to the popular appeal, made Colorado a member of the American union.

Six New States (1889-1890).—For many years there was a deadlock in Congress over the admission of new states. The spell was broken in 1889 under the leadership of the Dakotas. For a long time the Dakota territory, organized in 1861, had been looked upon as the home of the powerful Sioux Indians whose enormous reservation blocked the advance of the frontier. The discovery of gold in the Black Hills, however, marked their doom. Even before Congress could open their lands to prospectors, pioneers were swarming over the country. Farmers from the adjoining Minnesota and the Eastern states, Scandinavians, Germans, and Canadians, came in swelling waves to occupy the fertile Dakota lands, now famous even as far away as the fjords of Norway. Seldom had the plow of man cut through richer soil than was found in the bottoms of the Red River Valley, and it became all the more precious when the opening of the Northern Pacific in 1883 afforded a means of transportation east and west. The population, which had numbered 135,000 in 1880, passed the half million mark before ten years had elapsed.

Remembering that Nebraska had been admitted with only 67,000 inhabitants, the Dakotans could not see why they should be kept under federal tutelage. At the same time Washington, far away on the Pacific Coast, Montana, Idaho, and Wyoming, boasting of their populations and their riches, put in their own eloquent pleas. But the members of Congress were busy with politics. The Democrats saw no good reason for admitting new Republican states until after their defeat in 1888. Near the end of their term the next year they opened the door for North and South Dakota, Washington, and Montana. In 1890, a Republican Congress brought Idaho and Wyoming into the union, the latter with woman suffrage, which had been granted twenty-one years before.

Utah.—Although Utah had long presented all the elements of a well-settled and industrious community, its admission to the union was delayed on account of popular hostility to the practice of polygamy. The custom, it is true, had been prohibited by act of Congress in 1862; but the law had been systematically evaded. In 1882 Congress made another and more effective effort to stamp out polygamy. Five years later it even went so far as to authorize the confiscation of the property of the Mormon Church in case the practice of plural marriages was not stopped. Meanwhile the Gentile or non-Mormon population was steadily increasing and the leaders inthe Church became convinced that the battle against the sentiment of the country was futile. At last in 1896 Utah was admitted as a state under a constitution which forbade plural marriages absolutely and forever. Horace Greeley, who visited Utah in 1859, had prophesied that the Pacific Railroad would work a revolution in the land of Brigham Young. His prophecy had come true.

Rounding out the Continent.—Three more territories now remained out of the Union. Oklahoma, long an Indian reservation, had been opened for settlement to white men in 1889. The rush upon the fertile lands of this region, the last in the history of America, was marked by all the frenzy of the final, desperate chance. At a signal from a bugle an army of men with families in wagons, men and women on horseback and on foot, burst into the territory. During the first night a city of tents was raised at Guthrie and Oklahoma City. In ten days wooden houses rose on the plains. In a single year there were schools, churches, business blocks, and newspapers. Within fifteen years there was a population of more than half a million. To the west, Arizona with a population of about 125,000 and New Mexico with 200,000 inhabitants joined Oklahoma in asking for statehood. Congress, then Republican, looked with reluctance upon the addition of more Democratic states; but in 1907 it was literally compelled by public sentiment and a sense of justice to admit Oklahoma. In 1910 the House of Representatives went to the Democrats and within two years Arizona and New Mexico were "under the roof." So the continental domain was rounded out.

THE INFLUENCE OF THE FAR WEST ON NATIONAL LIFE

The Last of the Frontier.—When Horace Greeley made his trip west in 1859 he thus recorded the progress of civilization in his journal:

"May 12th, Chicago.—Chocolate and morning journals last seen on the hotel breakfast table.

23rd, Leavenworth (Kansas).—Room bells and bath tubs make their final appearance.

26th, Manhattan.—Potatoes and eggs last recognized among the blessings that 'brighten as they take their flight.'

27th, Junction City.—Last visitation of a boot-black, with dissolving views of a board bedroom. Beds bid us good-by."

Within thirty years travelers were riding across that country in Pullman cars and enjoying at the hotels all the comforts of a standardized civilization. The "wild west" was gone, and with it that frontier of pioneers and settlers who had long given such a bent and tone to American life and had "poured in upon the floor of Congress" such a long line of "backwoods politicians," as they were scornfully styled.

Free Land and Eastern Labor.—It was not only the picturesque features of the frontier that were gone. Of far more consequence was the disappearance of free lands with all that meant for American labor. For more than a hundred years, any man of even moderate means had been able to secure a homestead of his own and an independent livelihood. For a hundred years America had been able to supply farms to as many immigrants as cared to till the soil. Every new pair of strong arms meant more farms and more wealth. Workmen in Eastern factories, mines, or mills who did not like their hours, wages, or conditions of labor, could readily find an outlet to the land. Now all that was over. By about 1890 most of the desirable land available under the Homestead act had disappeared. American industrial workers confronted a new situation.

Grain Supplants King Cotton.—In the meantime a revolution was taking place in agriculture. Until 1860 the chief staples sold by America were cotton and tobacco. With the advance of the frontier, corn and wheat supplanted them both in agrarian economy. The West became the granary of the East and of Western Europe. The scoop shovel once used to handle grain was superseded by the towering elevator, loading and unloading thousands of bushels every hour. The refrigerator car and ship made the packing industry as stable as the production of cotton or corn, and gave an immense impetus to cattle raising and sheep farming. So the meat of the West took its place on the English dinner table by the side of bread baked from Dakotan wheat.

Aid in American Economic Independence.—The effects of this economic movement were manifold and striking. Billions of dollars' worth of American grain, dairy produce, and meat were poured into European markets where they paid off debts due money lenders and acquired capital to develop American resources. Thus they accelerated the progress of American financiers toward national independence. The country, which had timidly turned to the Old World for capital in Hamilton's day and had borrowed at high rates of interest in London in Lincoln's day, moved swiftly toward the time when it would be among the world's first bankers and money lenders itself. Every grain of wheat and corn pulled the balance down on the American side of the scale.

Eastern Agriculture Affected.—In the East as well as abroad the opening of the western granary produced momentous results. The agricultural economy of that part of the country was changed in many respects. Whole sections of the poorest land went almost out of cultivation, the abandoned farms of the New England hills bearing solemn witness to the competing power of western wheat fields. Sheep and cattle raising, as well as wheat and corn production, suffered at least a relative decline. Thousands of farmers cultivating land of the lower grade were forced to go West or were driven to the margin of subsistence. Even the herds that supplied Eastern cities with milk were fed upon grain brought halfway across the continent.

The Expansion of the American Market.—Upon industry as well as agriculture, the opening of vast food-producing regions told in a thousand ways. The demand for farm machinery, clothing, boots, shoes, and other manufactures gave to American industries such a market as even Hamilton had never foreseen. Moreover it helped to expand far into the Mississippi Valley the industrial area once confined to the Northern seaboard states and to transform the region of the Great Lakes into an industrial empire. Herein lies the explanation of the growth of mid-western cities after 1865. Chicago, with its thirty-five railways, tapped every locality of the West and South. To the railways were added the water routes of the Lakes, thus creating a strategic center for industries. Long foresight carried the McCormick reaper works to Chicago before 1860. From Troy, New York, went a large stove plant. That was followed by a shoe factory from Massachusetts. The packing industry rose as a matter of course at a point so advantageous for cattle raisers and shippers and so well connected with Eastern markets.

To the opening of the Far West also the Lake region was indebted for a large part of that water-borne traffic which made it "the Mediterranean basin of North America." The produce of the West and the manufactures of the East poured through it in an endless stream. The swift growth of shipbuilding on the Great Lakes helped to compensate for the decline of the American marine on the high seas. In response to this stimulus Detroit could boast that her shipwrights were able to turn out a ten thousand ton Leviathan for ore or grain about "as quickly as carpenters could put up an eight-room house." Thus in relation to the Far West the old Northwest territory—the wilderness of Jefferson's time—had taken the position formerly occupied by New England alone. It was supplying capital and manufactures for a vast agricultural empire West and South.

America on the Pacific.—It has been said that the Mediterranean Sea was the center of ancient civilization; that modern civilization has developed on the shores of the Atlantic; and that the future belongs to the Pacific. At any rate, the sweep of the United States to the shores of the Pacific quickly exercised a powerful influence on world affairs and it undoubtedly has a still greater significance for the future.

Very early regular traffic sprang up between the Pacific ports and the Hawaiian Islands, China, and Japan. Two years before the adjustment of the Oregon controversy with England, namely in 1844, the United States had established official and trading relations with China. Ten years later, four years after the admission of California to the union, the barred door of Japan was forced open by Commodore Perry. The commerce which had long before developed between the Pacific ports and Hawaii, China, and Japan now flourished under official care. In 1865 a ship from Honolulu carried sugar, molasses, and fruits from Hawaii to the Oregon port of Astoria. The next year a vessel from Hongkong brought rice, mats, and tea from China. An era of lucrative trade was opened. The annexation of Hawaii in 1898, the addition of the Philippines at the same time, and the participation of American troops in the suppression of the Boxer rebellion in Peking in 1900, were but signs and symbols of American power on the Pacific.

Conservation and the Land Problem.—The disappearance of the frontier also brought new and serious problems to the governments of the states and the nation. The people of the whole United States suddenly were forced to realize that there was a limit to the rich, new land to exploit and to the forests and minerals awaiting the ax and the pick. Then arose in America the questions which had long perplexed the countries of the Old World—the scientific use of the soils and conservation of natural resources. Hitherto the government had followed the easy path of giving away arable land and selling forest and mineral lands at low prices. Now it had to face far more difficult and complex problems. It also had to consider questions of land tenure again, especially if the ideal of a nation of home-owning farmers was to be maintained. While there was plenty of land for every man or woman who wanted a home on the soil, it made little difference if single landlords or companies got possession of millions of acres, if a hundred men in one western river valley owned 17,000,000 acres; but when the good land for small homesteads was all gone, then was raised the real issue. At the opening of the twentieth century the nation, which a hundred years before had land and natural resources apparently without limit, was compelled to enact law after law conserving its forests and minerals. Then it was that the great state of California, on the very border of the continent, felt constrained to enact a land settlement measure providing government assistance in an effort to break up large holdings into small lots and to make it easy for actual settlers to acquire small farms. America was passing into a new epoch.

References

Henry Inman, *The Old Santa Fé Trail*.

R.I. Dodge, *The Plains of the Great West* (1877).

C.H. Shinn, *The Story of the Mine*.

Cy Warman, *The Story of the Railroad*.

Emerson Hough, *The Story of the Cowboy*.

H.H. Bancroft is the author of many works on the West but his writings will be found only in the larger libraries.

Joseph Schafer, *History of the Pacific Northwest* (ed. 1918).

T.H. Hittel, *History of California* (4 vols.).

W.H. Olin, *American Irrigation Farming*.

W.E. Smythe, *The Conquest of Arid America*.

H.A. Millis, *The American-Japanese Problem*.

E.S. Meany, *History of the State of Washington*.

H.K. Norton, *The Story of California*.

Questions

1. Name the states west of the Mississippi in 1865.

2. In what manner was the rest of the western region governed?

3. How far had settlement been carried?

4. What were the striking physical features of the West?

5. How was settlement promoted after 1865?

6. Why was admission to the union so eagerly sought?

7. Explain how politics became involved in the creation of new states.

8. Did the West rapidly become like the older sections of the country?

9. What economic peculiarities did it retain or develop?

10. How did the federal government aid in western agriculture?

11. How did the development of the West affect the East? The South?

12. What relation did the opening of the great grain areas of the West bear to the growth of America's commercial and financial power?

13. State some of the new problems of the West.

14. Discuss the significance of American expansion to the Pacific Ocean.

Research Topics

The Passing of the Wild West.—Haworth, *The United States in Our Own Times*, pp. 100-124.

The Indian Question.—Sparks, *National Development* (American Nation Series), pp. 265-281.

The Chinese Question.—Sparks, *National Development*, pp. 229-250; Rhodes, *History of the United States*, Vol. VIII, pp. 180-196.

The Railway Age.—Schafer, *History of the Pacific Northwest*, pp. 230-245; E.V. Smalley, *The Northern Pacific Railroad*; Paxson, *The New Nation* (Riverside Series), pp. 20-26, especially the map on p. 23, and pp. 142-148.

Agriculture and Business.—Schafer, *Pacific Northwest*, pp. 246-289.

Ranching in the Northwest.—Theodore Roosevelt, *Ranch Life*, and *Autobiography*, pp. 103-143.

The Conquest of the Desert.—W.E. Smythe, *The Conquest of Arid America*.

Studies of Individual Western States.—Consult any good encyclopedia.

CHAPTER XIX

DOMESTIC ISSUES BEFORE THE COUNTRY (1865-1897)

For thirty years after the Civil War the leading political parties, although they engaged in heated presidential campaigns, were not sharply and clearly opposed on many matters of vital significance. During none of that time was there a clash of opinion over specific issues such as rent the country in 1800 when Jefferson rode a popular wave to victory, or again in 1828 when Jackson's western hordes came sweeping into power. The Democrats, who before 1860 definitely opposed protective tariffs, federal banking, internal improvements, and heavy taxes, now spoke cautiously on all these points. The Republicans, conscious of the fact that they had been a minority of the voters in 1860 and warned by the early loss of the House of Representatives in 1874, also moved with considerable prudence among the perplexing problems of the day. Again and again the votes in Congress showed that no clear line separated all the Democrats from all the Republicans. There were Republicans who favored tariff reductions and "cheap money." There were Democrats who looked with partiality upon high protection or with indulgence upon the contraction of the currency. Only on matters relating to the coercion of the South was the division between the parties fairly definite; this could be readily accounted for on practical as well as sentimental grounds.

After all, the vague criticisms and proposals that found their way into the political platforms did but reflect the confusion of mind prevailing in the country. The fact that, out of the eighteen years between 1875 and 1893, the Democrats held the House of Representatives for fourteen years while the Republicans had every President but one showed that the voters, like the politicians, were in a state of indecision. Hayes had a Democratic House during his entire term and a Democratic Senate for two years of the four. Cleveland was confronted by a belligerent Republican majority in the Senate during his first administration; and at the same time was supported by a Democratic majority in the House. Harrison was sustained by continuous Republican successes in Senatorial elections; but in the House he had the barest majority from 1889 to 1891 and lost that altogether at the election held in the middle of his term. The opinion of the country was evidently unsettled and fluctuating. It was still distracted by memories of the dead past and uncertain as to the trend of the future.

THE CURRENCY QUESTION

Nevertheless these years of muddled politics and nebulous issues proved to be a period in which social forces were gathering for the great campaign of 1896. Except for three new features—the railways, the trusts, and the trade unions—the subjects of debate among the people were the same as those that had engaged their attention since the foundation of the republic: the currency, the national debt, banking, the tariff, and taxation.

Debtors and the Fall in Prices.—For many reasons the currency question occupied the center of interest. As of old, the farmers and planters of the West and South were heavily in debt to the East for borrowed money secured by farm mortgages; and they counted upon the sale of cotton, corn, wheat, and hogs to meet interest and principal when due. During the war, the Western farmers had been able to dispose of their produce at high prices and thus discharge their debts with comparative ease; but after the war prices declined. Wheat that sold at two dollars a bushel in 1865 brought sixty-four cents twenty years later. The meaning of this for the farmers in debt—and nearly three-fourths of them were in that class—can be shown by a single illustration. A thousand-dollar mortgage on a Western farm could be paid off by five hundred bushels of wheat when prices were high; whereas it took about fifteen hundred bushels to pay the same debt when wheat was at the bottom of the scale. For the farmer, it must be remembered, wheat was the measure of his labor, the product of his toil under the summer sun; and in its price he found the test of his prosperity.

Creditors and Falling Prices.—To the bondholders or creditors, on the other hand, falling prices were clear gain. If a fifty-dollar coupon on a bond bought seventy or eighty bushels of wheat instead of twenty or thirty, the advantage to the owner of the coupon was obvious. Moreover the advantage seemed to him entirely just. Creditors had suffered heavy losses when the Civil War carried prices skyward while the interest rates on their old bonds remained stationary. For example, if a man had a $1000 bond issued before 1860 and paying interest at five per cent, he received fifty dollars a year from it. Before the war each dollar would buy a bushel of wheat; in 1865 it would only buy half a bushel. When prices—that is, the cost of living—began to go down, creditors therefore generally regarded the change with satisfaction as a return to normal conditions.

The Cause of Falling Prices.—The fall in prices was due, no doubt, to many factors. Among them must be reckoned the discontinuance of government buying for war purposes, labor-saving farm machinery, immigration, and the opening of new wheat-growing regions. The currency, too, was an element in the situation. Whatever the cause, the discontented farmers believed that the way to raise prices was to issue more money. They viewed it as a case of supply and demand. If there was a small volume of currency in circulation, prices would be low; if there was a large volume, prices would be high. Hence they looked with favor upon all plans to increase the amount of money in circulation. First they advocated more paper notes—greenbacks—and then they turned to silver as the remedy. The creditors, on the other hand, naturally approved the reduction of the volume of currency. They wished to see the greenbacks withdrawn from circulation and gold—a metal more limited in volume than silver—made the sole basis of the national monetary system.

The Battle over the Greenbacks.—The contest between these factions began as early as 1866. In that year, Congress enacted a law authorizing the Treasury to withdraw the greenbacks from circulation. The paper money party set up a shrill cry of protest, and kept up the fight until, in 1878, it forced Congress to provide for the continuous re-issue of the legal tender notes as they came into the Treasury in payment of taxes and other dues. Then could the friends of easy money rejoice:

"Thou, Greenback, 'tis of thee

Fair money of the free,

Of thee we sing."

Resumption of Specie Payment.—There was, however, another side to this victory. The opponents of the greenbacks, unable to stop the circulation of paper, induced Congress to pass a law in 1875 providing that on and after January 1, 1879, "the Secretary of the Treasury shall redeem in coin the United States legal tender notes then outstanding on their presentation at the office of the Assistant Treasurer of the United States in the City of New York in sums of not less than fifty dollars." "The way to resume," John Sherman had said, "is to resume." When the hour for redemption arrived, the Treasury was prepared with a large hoard of gold. "On the appointed day," wrote the assistant secretary, "anxiety reigned in the office of the Treasury. Hour after hour passed; no news from New York. Inquiry by wire showed that all was quiet. At the close of the day this message came: '$135,000 of notes presented for coin—$400,000 of gold for notes.' That was all. Resumption was accomplished with no disturbance. By five o'clock the news was all over the land, and the New York bankers were sipping their tea in absolute safety."

The Specie Problem—the Parity of Gold and Silver.—Defeated in their efforts to stop "the present suicidal and destructive policy of contraction," the advocates of an abundant currency demanded an increase in the volume of silver in circulation. This precipitated one of the sharpest political battles in American history. The issue turned on legal as well as economic points. The Constitution gave Congress the power to coin money and it forbade the states to make anything but gold and silver legal tender in the payment of debts. It evidently contemplated the use of both metals in the currency system. Such, at least, was the view of many eminent statesmen, including no less a personage than James G. Blaine. The difficulty, however, lay in maintaining gold and silver coins on a level which would permit them to circulate with equal facility. Obviously, if the gold in a gold dollar exceeds the value of the silver in a silver dollar on the open market, men will hoard gold money and leave silver money in circulation. When, for example, Congress in 1792 fixed the ratio of the two metals at one to fifteen—one ounce of gold declared worth fifteen of silver—it was soon found that gold had been undervalued. When again in 1834 the ratio was put at one to sixteen, it was found that silver was undervalued. Consequently the latter metal was not brought in for coinage and silver almost dropped out of circulation. Many a silver dollar was melted down by silverware factories.

Silver Demonetized in 1873.—So things stood in 1873. At that time, Congress, in enacting a mintage law, discontinued the coinage of the standard silver dollar, then practically out of circulation. This act was denounced later by the friends of silver as "the crime of '73," a conspiracy devised by the money power and secretly carried out. This contention the debates in Congress do not seem to sustain. In the course of the argument on the mint law it was distinctly said by one speaker at least: "This bill provides for the making of changes in the legal tender coin of the country and for substituting as legal tender, coin of only one metal instead of two as heretofore."

The Decline in the Value of Silver.—Absorbed in the greenback controversy, the people apparently did not appreciate, at the time, the significance of the "demonetization" of silver; but within a few years several events united in making it the center of a political storm. Germany, having abandoned silver in 1871, steadily increased her demand for gold. Three years later, the countries of the Latin Union followed this example, thus helping to enhance the price of the yellow metal. All the while, new silver lodes, discovered in the Far West, were pouring into the market great streams of the white metal, bearing down the price. Then came the resumption of specie payment, which, in effect, placed the paper money on a gold basis. Within twenty years silver was worth in gold only about half the price of 1870.

That there had been a real decline in silver was denied by the friends of that metal. They alleged that gold had gone up because it had been given a monopoly in the coinage markets of civilized governments. This monopoly, they continued, was the fruit of a conspiracy against the people conceived by the bankers of the world. Moreover, they went on, the placing of the greenbacks on a gold basis had itself worked a contraction of the currency; it lowered the prices of labor and produce to the advantage of the holders of long-term investments bearing a fixed rate of interest. When wheat sold at sixty-four cents a bushel, their search for relief became desperate, and they at last concentrated their efforts on opening the mints of the government for the free coinage of silver at the ratio of sixteen to one.

Republicans and Democrats Divided.—On this question both Republicans and Democrats were divided, the line being drawn between the East on the one hand and the South and West on the other, rather than between the two leading parties. So trusted a leader as James G. Blaine avowed, in a speech delivered in the Senate in 1878, that, as the Constitution required Congress to make both gold and silver the money of the land, the only question left was that of fixing the ratio between them. He affirmed, moreover, the main contention of the silver faction that a reopening of the government mints of the world to silver would bring it up to its old relation with gold. He admitted also that their most ominous warnings were well founded, saying: "I believe the struggle now going on in this country and in other countries for a single gold standard would, if successful, produce widespread disaster throughout the commercial world. The destruction of silver as money and the establishment of gold as the sole unit of value must have a ruinous effect on all forms of property, except those investments which yield a fixed return."

This was exactly the concession that the silver party wanted. "Three-fourths of the business enterprises of this country are conducted on borrowed capital," said Senator Jones, of Nevada. "Three-fourths of the homes and farms that stand in the names of the actual occupants have been bought on time and a very large proportion of them are mortgaged for the payment of some part of the purchase money. Under the operation of a shrinkage in the volume of money, this enormous mass of borrowers, at the maturity of their respective debts, though nominally paying no more than the amount borrowed, with interest, are in reality, in the amount of the principal alone, returning a percentage of value greater than they received— more in equity than they contracted to pay.... In all discussions of the subject the creditors attempt to brush aside the equities involved by sneering at the debtors."

The Silver Purchase Act (1878).—Even before the actual resumption of specie payment, the advocates of free silver were a power to be reckoned with, particularly in the Democratic party. They had a majority in the House of Representatives in 1878 and they carried a silver bill through that chamber. Blocked by the Republican Senate they accepted a compromise in the Bland-Allison bill, which provided for huge monthly purchases of silver by the government for coinage into dollars. So strong was the sentiment that a two-thirds majority was mustered after President Hayes vetoed the measure.

The effect of this act, as some had anticipated, was disappointing. It did not stay silver on its downward course. Thereupon the silver faction pressed through Congress in 1886 a bill providing for the issue of paper certificates based on the silver accumulated in the Treasury. Still silver continued to fall. Then the advocates of inflation declared that they would be content with nothing short of free coinage at the ratio of sixteen to one. If the issue had been squarely presented in 1890, there is good reason for believing that free silver would have received a majority in both houses of Congress; but it was not presented.

The Sherman Silver Purchase Act and the Bond Sales.—Republican leaders, particularly from the East, stemmed the silver tide by a diversion of forces. They passed the Sherman Act of 1890 providing for large monthly purchases of silver and for the issue of notes redeemable in gold or silver at the discretion of the Secretary of the Treasury. In a clause of superb ambiguity they announced that it was "the established policy of the United States to maintain the two metals on a parity with each other upon the present legal ratio or such other ratio as may be provided by law." For a while silver was buoyed up. Then it turned once more on its downward course. In the meantime the Treasury was in a sad plight. To maintain the gold reserve, President Cleveland felt compelled to sell government bonds; and to his dismay he found that as soon as the gold was brought in at the front door of the Treasury, notes were presented for redemption and the gold was quickly carried out at the back door. Alarmed at the vicious circle thus created, he urged upon Congress the repeal of the Sherman Silver Purchase Act. For this he was roundly condemned by many of his own followers who branded his conduct as "treason to the party"; but the Republicans, especially from the East, came to his rescue and in 1893 swept the troublesome sections of the law from the statute book. The anger of the silver faction knew no bounds, and the leaders made ready for the approaching presidential campaign.

THE PROTECTIVE TARIFF AND TAXATION

Fluctuation in Tariff Policy.—As each of the old parties was divided on the currency question, it is not surprising that there was some confusion in their ranks over the tariff. Like the silver issue, the tariff tended to align the manufacturing East against the agricultural West and South rather than to cut directly between the two parties. Still the Republicans on the whole stood firmly by the rates imposed during the Civil War. If we except the reductions of 1872 which were soon offset by increases, we may say that those rates were substantially unchanged for nearly twenty years. When a revision was brought about, however, it was initiated by Republican leaders. Seeing a huge surplus of revenue in the Treasury in 1883, they anticipated popular clamor by revising the tariff on the theory that it ought to be reformed by its friends rather than by its enemies. On the other hand, it was the Republicans also who enacted the McKinley tariff bill of 1890, which carried protection to its highest point up to that time.

The Democrats on their part were not all confirmed free traders or even advocates of tariff for revenue only. In Cleveland's first administration they did attack the protective system in the House, where they had a majority, and in this they were vigorously supported by the President. The assault, however, proved to be a futile gesture for it was blocked by the Republicans in the Senate. When, after the sweeping victory of 1892, the Democrats in the House again attempted to bring down the tariff by the Wilson bill of 1894, they were checkmated by their own party colleagues in the upper chamber. In the end they were driven into a compromise that looked more like a McKinley than a Calhoun tariff. The Republicans taunted them with being "babes in the woods." President Cleveland was so dissatisfied with the bill that he refused to sign it, allowing it to become a law, on the lapse of ten days, without his approval.

The Income Tax of 1894.—The advocates of tariff reduction usually associated with their proposal a tax on incomes. The argument which they advanced in support of their program was simple. Most of the industries, they said, are in the East and the protective tariff which taxes consumers for the benefit of manufacturers is, in effect, a tribute laid upon the rest of the country. As an offset they offered a tax on large incomes; this owing to the heavy concentration of rich people in the East, would fall mainly upon the beneficiaries of protection. "We propose," said one of them, "to place a part of the burden upon the accumulated wealth of the country instead of placing it all upon the consumption of the people." In this spirit the sponsors of the Wilson tariff bill laid a tax upon all incomes of $4000 a year or more.

In taking this step, the Democrats encountered opposition in their own party. Senator Hill, of New York, turned fiercely upon them, exclaiming: "The professors with their books, the socialists with their schemes, the anarchists with their bombs are all instructing the people in the ... principles of taxation." Even the Eastern Republicans were hardly as savage in their denunciation of the tax. But all this labor was wasted. The next year the Supreme Court of the United States declared the income tax to be a direct tax, and therefore null and void because it was laid on incomes wherever found and not apportioned among the states according to population. The fact that four of the nine judges dissented from this decision was also an index to the diversity of opinion that divided both parties.

The Railways and Trusts

The Grangers and State Regulation.—The same uncertainty about the railways and trusts pervaded the ranks of the Republicans and Democrats. As to the railways, the first firm and consistent demand for their regulation came from the West. There the farmers, in the early seventies, having got control in state legislatures, particularly in Iowa, Wisconsin, and Illinois, enacted drastic laws prescribing the maximum charges which companies could make for carrying freight and passengers. The application of these measures, however, was limited because the state could not fix the rates for transporting goods and passengers beyond its own borders. The power of regulating interstate commerce, under the Constitution, belonged to Congress.

The Interstate Commerce Act of 1887.—Within a few years, the movement which had been so effective in western legislatures appeared at Washington in the form of demands for the federal regulation of interstate rates. In 1887, the pressure became so strong that Congress created the interstate commerce commission and forbade many abuses on the part of railways; such as discriminating in charges between one shipper and another and granting secret rebates to favored persons. This law was a significant beginning; but it left the main question of rate-fixing untouched, much to the discontent of farmers and shippers.

The Sherman Anti-Trust Law of 1890.—As in the case of the railways, attacks upon the trusts were first made in state legislatures, where it became the fashion to provide severe penalties for those who formed monopolies and "conspired to enhance prices." Republicans and Democrats united in the promotion of measures of this kind. As in the case of the railways also, the movement to curb the trusts soon had spokesmen at Washington. Though Blaine had declared that "trusts were largely a private affair with which neither the President nor any private citizen had any particular right to interfere," it was a Republican Congress that enacted in 1890 the first measure—the Sherman Anti-Trust Law—directed against great combinations in business. This act declared illegal "every contract, combination in the form of trust or otherwise, or conspiracy in restraint of trade and commerce among the several states or with foreign nations."

The Futility of the Anti-Trust Law.—Whether the Sherman law was directed against all combinations or merely those which placed an "unreasonable restraint" on trade and competition was not apparent. Senator Platt of Connecticut, a careful statesman of the old school, averred: "The questions of whether the bill would be operative, of how it would operate, or whether it was within the power of Congress to enact it, have been whistled down the wind in this Senate as idle talk and the whole effort has been to get some bill headed: 'A bill to punish trusts,' with which to go to the country." Whatever its purpose, its effect upon existing trusts and upon the formation of new combinations was negligible. It was practically unenforced by President Harrison and President Cleveland, in spite of the constant demand for harsh action against "monopolies." It was patent that neither the Republicans nor the Democrats were prepared for a war on the trusts to the bitter end.

THE MINOR PARTIES AND UNREST

The Demands of Dissenting Parties.—From the election of 1872, when Horace Greeley made his ill-fated excursion into politics, onward, there appeared in each presidential campaign one, and sometimes two or more parties, stressing issues that appealed mainly to wage-earners and farmers. Whether they chose to call themselves Labor Reformers, Greenbackers, or Anti-monopolists, their slogans and their platforms all pointed in one direction. Even the Prohibitionists, who in 1872 started on their career with a single issue, the abolition of the liquor traffic, found themselves making declarations of faith on other matters and hopelessly split over the money question in 1896.

A composite view of the platforms put forth by the dissenting parties from the administration of Grant to the close of Cleveland's second term reveals certain notions common to them all. These included among many others: the earliest possible payment of the national debt; regulation of the rates of railways and telegraph companies; repeal of the specie resumption act of 1875; the issue of legal tender notes by the government convertible into interest-bearing obligations on demand; unlimited coinage of silver as well as gold; a graduated inheritance tax; legislation to take from "land, railroad, money, and other gigantic corporate monopolies ... the powers they have so corruptly and unjustly usurped"; popular or direct election of United States Senators; woman suffrage; and a graduated income tax, "placing the burden of government on those who can best afford to pay instead of laying it on the farmers and producers."

Criticism of the Old Parties.—To this long program of measures the reformers added harsh and acrid criticism of the old parties and sometimes, it must be said, of established institutions of government. "We denounce," exclaimed the Labor party in 1888, "the Democratic and Republican parties as hopelessly and shamelessly corrupt and by reason of their affiliation with monopolies equally unworthy of the suffrages of those who do not live upon public plunder." "The United States Senate," insisted the Greenbackers, "is a body composed largely of aristocratic millionaires who according to their own party papers generally purchased their elections in order to protect the great monopolies which they represent." Indeed, if their platforms are to be accepted at face value, the Greenbackers believed that the entire government had passed out of the hands of the people.

The Grangers.—This unsparing, not to say revolutionary, criticism of American political life, appealed, it seems, mainly to farmers in the Middle West. Always active in politics, they had, before the Civil War, cast their lot as a rule with one or the other of the leading parties. In 1867, however, there grew up among them an association known as the "Patrons of Husbandry," which was destined to play a large rôle in the partisan contests of the succeeding decades. This society, which organized local lodges or "granges" on principles of secrecy and fraternity, was originally designed to promote in a general way the interests of the farmers. Its political bearings were apparently not grasped at first by its promoters. Yet, appealing as it did to the most active and independent spirits among the farmers and gathering to itself the strength that always comes from organization, it soon found itself in the hands of leaders more or less involved in politics. Where a few votes are marshaled together in a democracy, there is power.

The Greenback Party.—The first extensive activity of the Grangers was connected with the attack on the railways in the Middle West which forced several state legislatures to reduce freight and passenger rates by law. At the same time, some leaders in the movement, no doubt emboldened by this success, launched in 1876 a new political party, popularly known as the Greenbackers, favoring a continued re-issue of the legal tenders. The beginnings were disappointing; but two years later, in the congressional elections, the Greenbackers swept whole sections of the country. Their candidates polled more than a million votes and fourteen of them were returned to the House of Representatives. To all outward signs a new and formidable party had entered the lists.

The sanguine hopes of the leaders proved to be illusory. The quiet operations of the resumption act the following year, a revival of industry from a severe panic which had set in during 1873, the Silver

Purchase Act, and the re-issue of Greenbacks cut away some of the grounds of agitation. There was also a diversion of forces to the silver faction which had a substantial support in the silver mine owners of the West. At all events the Greenback vote fell to about 300,000 in the election of 1880. A still greater drop came four years later and the party gave up the ghost, its sponsors returning to their former allegiance or sulking in their tents.

The Rise of the Populist Party.—Those leaders of the old parties who now looked for a happy future unvexed by new factions were doomed to disappointment. The funeral of the Greenback party was hardly over before there arose two other political specters in the agrarian sections: the National Farmers' Alliance and Industrial Union, particularly strong in the South and West; and the Farmers' Alliance, operating in the North. By 1890 the two orders claimed over three million members. As in the case of the Grangers many years before, the leaders among them found an easy way into politics. In 1892 they held a convention, nominated a candidate for President, and adopted the name of "People's Party," from which they were known as Populists. Their platform, in every line, breathed a spirit of radicalism. They declared that "the newspapers are largely subsidized or muzzled; public opinion silenced; business prostrate; our homes covered with mortgages; and the land concentrating in the hands of capitalists.... The fruits of the toil of millions are boldly stolen to build up colossal fortunes for a few." Having delivered this sweeping indictment, the Populists put forward their remedies: the free coinage of silver, a graduated income tax, postal savings banks, and government ownership of railways and telegraphs. At the same time they approved the initiative, referendum, and popular election of Senators, and condemned the use of federal troops in labor disputes. On this platform, the Populists polled over a million votes, captured twenty-two presidential electors, and sent a powerful delegation to Congress.

Industrial Distress Augments Unrest.—The four years intervening between the campaign of 1892 and the next presidential election brought forth many events which aggravated the ill-feeling expressed in the portentous platform of Populism. Cleveland, a consistent enemy of free silver, gave his powerful support to the gold standard and insisted on the repeal of the Silver Purchase Act, thus alienating an increasing number of his own party. In 1893 a grave industrial crisis fell upon the land: banks and business houses went into bankruptcy with startling rapidity; factories were closed; idle men thronged the streets hunting for work; and the prices of wheat and corn dropped to a ruinous level. Labor disputes also filled the crowded record. A strike at the Pullman car works in Chicago spread to the railways. Disorders ensued. President Cleveland, against the protests of the governor of Illinois, John P. Altgeld, dispatched troops to the scene of action. The United States district court at Chicago issued an injunction forbidding the president of the Railway Union, Eugene V. Debs, or his assistants to interfere with the transmission of the mails or interstate commerce in any form. For refusing to obey the order, Debs was arrested and imprisoned. With federal troops in possession of the field, with their leader in jail, the strikers gave up the battle, defeated but not subdued. To cap the climax the Supreme Court of the United States, the following year (1895) declared null and void the income tax law just enacted by Congress, thus fanning the flames of Populist discontent all over the West and South.

THE SOUND MONEY BATTLE OF 1896

Conservative Men Alarmed.—Men of conservative thought and leaning in both parties were by this time thoroughly disturbed. They looked upon the rise of Populism and the growth of labor disputes as the signs of a revolutionary spirit, indeed nothing short of a menace to American institutions and ideals. The income tax law of 1894, exclaimed the distinguished New York advocate, Joseph H. Choate, in an impassioned speech before the Supreme Court, "is communistic in its purposes and tendencies and is defended here upon principles as communistic, socialistic—what shall I call them—populistic as ever have been addressed to any political assembly in the world." Mr. Justice Field in the name of the Court replied: "The present assault upon capital is but the beginning. It will be but the stepping stone to others larger and more sweeping till our political conditions will become a war of the poor against the rich." In declaring the income tax unconstitutional, he believed that he was but averting greater evils lurking under its guise. As for free silver, nearly all conservative men were united in calling it a measure of confiscation and repudiation; an effort of the debtors to pay their obligations with money worth fifty cents on the dollar; the climax of villainies openly defended; a challenge to law, order, and honor.

The Republicans Come Out for the Gold Standard.—It was among the Republicans that this opinion was most widely shared and firmly held. It was they who picked up the gauge thrown down by the Populists, though a host of Democrats, like Cleveland and Hill of New York, also battled against the growing Populist defection in Democratic ranks. When the Republican national convention assembled in 1896, the die was soon cast; a declaration of opposition to free silver save by international agreement was carried by a vote of eight to one. The Republican party, to use the vigorous language of Mr. Lodge, arrayed itself against "not only that organized failure, the Democratic party, but all the wandering forces of political chaos and social disorder ... in these bitter times when the forces of disorder are loose and the wreckers with their false lights gather at the shore to lure the ship of state upon the rocks." Yet it is due to historic truth to state that McKinley, whom the Republicans nominated, had voted in Congress for the free coinage of silver, was widely known as a bimetallist, and was only with difficulty persuaded to accept the unequivocal indorsement of the gold standard which was pressed upon him by his counselors. Having accepted it, however, he proved to be a valiant champion, though his major interest was undoubtedly in the protective tariff. To him nothing was more reprehensible than attempts "to array class against class, 'the classes against the masses,' section against section, labor against capital, 'the poor against the rich,' or interest against interest." Such was the language of his acceptance speech. The whole program of Populism he now viewed as a "sudden, dangerous, and revolutionary assault upon law and order."

The Democratic Convention at Chicago.—Never, save at the great disruption on the eve of the Civil War, did a Democratic national convention display more feeling than at Chicago in 1896. From the opening prayer to the last motion before the house, every act, every speech, every scene, every resolution evoked passions and sowed dissensions. Departing from long party custom, it voted down in anger a proposal to praise the administration of the Democratic President, Cleveland. When the platform with its radical planks, including free silver, was reported, a veritable storm broke. Senator Hill, trembling with emotion, protested against the departure from old tests of Democratic allegiance; against principles that must drive out of the party men who had grown gray in its service; against revolutionary, unwise, and unprecedented steps in the history of the party. Senator Vilas of Wisconsin, in great fervor, avowed that there was no difference in principle between the free coinage of silver—"the confiscation of one-half of the credits of the nation for the benefit of debtors"—and communism itself—"a universal distribution of property." In the triumph of that cause he saw the beginning of "the overthrow of all law, all justice, all security and repose in the social order."

The Crown of Thorns Speech.—The champions of free silver replied in strident tones. They accused the gold advocates of being the aggressors who had assailed the labor and the homes of the people. William Jennings Bryan, of Nebraska, voiced their sentiments in a memorable oration. He declared that their cause "was as holy as the cause of liberty—the cause of humanity." He exclaimed that the contest was between the idle holders of idle capital and the toiling millions. Then he named those for whom he spoke—the wage-earner, the country lawyer, the small merchant, the farmer, and the miner. "The man who is employed for wages is as much a business man as his employer. The attorney in a country town is as much a business man as the corporation counsel in a great metropolis. The merchant at the cross roads store is as much a business man as the merchant of New York. The farmer ... is as much a business man as the man who goes upon the board of trade and bets upon the price of grain. The miners who go a thousand feet into the earth or climb two thousand feet upon the cliffs ... are as much business men as the few financial magnates who in a back room corner the money of the world.... It is for these that we speak. We do not come as aggressors. Ours is not a war of conquest. We are fighting in defense of our homes, our families, and our posterity. We have petitioned and our petitions have been scorned. We have entreated and our entreaties have been disregarded. We have begged and they have mocked when our calamity came. We beg no longer; we entreat no more; we petition no more. We defy them.... We shall answer their demands for a gold standard by saying to them, 'You shall not press upon the brow of labor this crown of thorns. You shall not crucify mankind upon a cross of gold.'"

Bryan Nominated.—In all the history of national conventions never had an orator so completely swayed a multitude; not even Yancey in his memorable plea in the Charleston convention of 1860 when, with grave and moving eloquence, he espoused the Southern cause against the impending fates. The delegates, after cheering Mr. Bryan until they could cheer no more, tore the standards from the floor and gathered around the Nebraska delegation to renew the deafening applause. The platform as reported was carried by a vote of two to one and the young orator from the West, hailed as America's Tiberius Gracchus, was nominated as the Democratic candidate for President. The South and West had triumphed over the East. The division was sectional, admittedly sectional—the old combination of power which Calhoun had so anxiously labored to build up a century earlier. The Gold Democrats were repudiated in terms which were clear to all. A few, unable to endure the thought of voting the Republican ticket, held a convention at Indianapolis where, with the sanction of Cleveland, they nominated candidates of their own and endorsed the gold standard in a forlorn hope.

The Democratic Platform.—It was to the call from Chicago that the Democrats gave heed and the Republicans made answer. The platform on which Mr. Bryan stood, unlike most party manifestoes, was explicit in its language and its appeal. It denounced the practice of allowing national banks to issue notes intended to circulate as money on the ground that it was "in derogation of the Constitution," recalling Jackson's famous attack on the Bank in 1832. It declared that tariff duties should be laid "for the purpose of revenue"—Calhoun's doctrine. In demanding the free coinage of silver, it recurred to the practice abandoned in 1873. The income tax came next on the program. The platform alleged that the law of 1894, passed by a Democratic Congress, was "in strict pursuance of the uniform decisions of the Supreme Court for nearly a hundred years," and then hinted that the decision annulling the law might be reversed by the same body "as it may hereafter be constituted."

The appeal to labor voiced by Mr. Bryan in his "crown of thorns" speech was reinforced in the platform. "As labor creates the wealth of the country," ran one plank, "we demand the passage of such laws as may be necessary to protect it in all its rights." Referring to the recent Pullman strike, the passions of which had not yet died away, the platform denounced "arbitrary interference by federal authorities in local affairs as a violation of the Constitution of the United States and a crime against free institutions." A special objection was lodged against "government by injunction as a new and highly dangerous form of oppression by which federal judges, in contempt of the laws of states and rights of citizens, become at once legislators, judges, and executioners." The remedy advanced was a federal law assuring trial by jury in all cases of contempt in labor disputes. Having made this declaration of faith, the Democrats, with Mr. Bryan at the head, raised their standard of battle.

The Heated Campaign.—The campaign which ensued outrivaled in the range of its educational activities and the bitterness of its tone all other political conflicts in American history, not excepting the fateful struggle of 1860. Immense sums of money were contributed to the funds of both parties. Railway, banking, and other corporations gave generously to the Republicans; the silver miners, less lavishly but with the same anxiety, supported the Democrats. The country was flooded with pamphlets, posters, and handbills. Every public forum, from the great auditoriums of the cities to the "red schoolhouses" on the countryside, was occupied by the opposing forces.

Mr. Bryan took the stump himself, visiting all parts of the country in special trains and addressing literally millions of people in the open air. Mr. McKinley chose the older and more formal plan. He received delegations at his home in Canton and discussed the issues of the campaign from his front porch, leaving to an army of well-organized orators the task of reaching the people in their home towns. Parades, processions, and monster demonstrations filled the land with politics. Whole states were polled in advance by the Republicans and the doubtful voters personally visited by men equipped with arguments and literature. Manufacturers, frightened at the possibility of disordered public credit, announced that they would close their doors if the Democrats won the election. Men were dismissed from public and private places on account of their political views, one eminent college president being forced out for advocating free silver. The language employed by impassioned and embittered speakers on both sides roused the public to a state of frenzy, once more showing the lengths to which men could go in personal and political abuse.

The Republican Victory.—The verdict of the nation was decisive. McKinley received 271 of the 447 electoral votes, and 7,111,000 popular votes as against Bryan's 6,509,000. The congressional elections were equally positive although, on account of the composition of the Senate, the "hold-over" Democrats and Populists still enjoyed a power out of proportion to their strength as measured at the polls. Even as it was, the Republicans got full control of both houses—a dominion of theentire government which they were to hold for fourteen years—until the second half of Mr. Taft's administration, when they lost possession of the House of Representatives. The yoke of indecision was broken. The party of sound finance and protective tariffs set out upon its lease of power with untroubled assurance.

REPUBLICAN MEASURES AND RESULTS

The Gold Standard and the Tariff.—Yet strange as it may seem, the Republicans did not at once enact legislation making the gold dollar the standard for the national currency. Not until 1900 did they take that positive step. In his first inaugural President McKinley, as if still uncertain in his own mind or fearing a revival of the contest just closed, placed the tariff, not the money question, in the forefront. "The people have decided," he said, "that such legislation should be had as will give ample protection and encouragement to the industries and development of our country." Protection for American industries, therefore, he urged, is the task before Congress. "With adequate revenue secured, but not until then, we can enter upon changes in our fiscal laws." As the Republicans had only forty-six of the ninety Senators, and at least four of them were known advocates of free silver, the discretion exercised by the President in selecting the tariff for congressional debate was the better part of valor.

Congress gave heed to the warning. Under the direction of Nelson P. Dingley, whose name was given to the bill, a tariff measure levying the highest rates yet laid in the history of American imposts was prepared and driven through the House of Representatives. The opposition encountered in the Senate, especially from the West, was overcome by concessions in favor of that section; but the duties on sugar, tin, steel, lumber, hemp, and in fact all of the essential commodities handled by combinations and trusts, were materially raised.

Growth of Combinations.—The years that followed the enactment of the Dingley law were, whatever the cause, the most prosperous the country had witnessed for many a decade. Industries of every kind were soon running full blast; labor was employed; commerce spread more swiftly than ever to the markets of the world. Coincident with this progress was the organization of the greatest combinations and trusts the world had yet seen. In 1899 the smelters formed a trust with a capital of $65,000,000; in the same year the Standard Oil Company with a capital of over one hundred millions took the place of the old trust; and the Copper Trust was incorporated under the laws of New Jersey, its par value capital being fixed shortly afterward at $175,000,000. A year later the National Sugar Refining Company, of New Jersey, started with a capital of $90,000,000, adopting the policy of issuing to the stockholders no public statement of its earnings or financial condition. Before another twelvemonth had elapsed all previous corporate financing was reduced to small proportions by the flotation of the United States Steel Corporation with a capital of more than a billion dollars, an enterprise set in motion by the famous Morgan banking house of New York.

In nearly all these gigantic undertakings, the same great leaders in finance were more or less intimately associated. To use the language of an eminent authority: "They are all allied and intertwined by their various mutual interests. For instance, the Pennsylvania Railroad interests are on the one hand allied with the Vanderbilts and on the other with the Rockefellers. The Vanderbilts are closely allied with the Morgan group.... Viewed as a whole we find the dominating influences in the trusts to be made up of a network of large and small capitalists, many allied to one another by ties of more or less importance, but all being appendages to or parts of the greater groups which are themselves dependent on and allied with the two mammoth or Rockefeller and Morgan groups. These two mammoth groups jointly ... constitute the heart of the business and commercial life of the nation." Such was the picture of triumphant business enterprise drawn by a financier within a few years after the memorable campaign of 1896.

America had become one of the first workshops of the world. It was, by virtue of the closely knit organization of its business and finance, one of the most powerful and energetic leaders in the struggle of the giants for the business of the earth. The capital of the Steel Corporation alone was more than ten times the total national debt which the apostles of calamity in the days of Washington and Hamilton declared the nation could never pay. American industry, filling domestic markets to overflowing, was ready for new worlds to conquer.

References

F.W. Taussig, *Tariff History of the United States.*

J.L. Laughlin, *Bimetallism in the United States.*

A.B. Hepburn, *History of Coinage and Currency in the United States.*

E.R.A. Seligman, *The Income Tax.*

S.J. Buck, *The Granger Movement* (Harvard Studies).

F.H. Dixon, *State Railroad Control.*

H.R. Meyer, *Government Regulation of Railway Rates.*

W.Z. Ripley (editor), *Trusts, Pools, and Corporations.*

R.T. Ely, *Monopolies and Trusts.*

J.B. Clark, *The Control of Trusts.*

Questions

1. What proof have we that the political parties were not clearly divided over issues between 1865 and 1896?

2. Why is a fall in prices a loss to farmers and a gain to holders of fixed investments?

3. Explain the theory that the quantity of money determines the prices of commodities.

4. Why was it difficult, if not impossible, to keep gold and silver at a parity?

5. What special conditions favored a fall in silver between 1870 and 1896?

6. Describe some of the measures taken to raise the value of silver.

7. Explain the relation between the tariff and the income tax in 1894.

8. How did it happen that the farmers led in regulating railway rates?

9. Give the terms of the Sherman Anti-Trust Act. What was its immediate effect?

10. Name some of the minor parties. Enumerate the reforms they advocated.

11. Describe briefly the experiments of the farmers in politics.

12. How did industrial conditions increase unrest?

13. Why were conservative men disturbed in the early nineties?

14. Explain the Republican position in 1896.

15. Give Mr. Bryan's doctrines in 1896. Enumerate the chief features of the Democratic platform.

16. What were the leading measures adopted by the Republicans after their victory in 1896?

Research Topics

Greenbacks and Resumption.—Dewey, *Financial History of the United States* (6th ed.), Sections 122-125, 154, and 378; MacDonald, *Documentary Source Book of American History*, pp. 446, 566; Hart, *American History Told by Contemporaries*, Vol. IV, pp. 531-533; Rhodes, *History of the United States*, Vol. VIII, pp. 97-101.

Demonetization and Coinage of Silver.—Dewey, *Financial History*, Sections 170-173, 186, 189, 194; MacDonald, *Documentary Source Book*, pp. 174, 573, 593, 595; Hart, *Contemporaries*, Vol. IV, pp. 529-531; Rhodes, *History*, Vol. VIII, pp. 93-97.

Free Silver and the Campaign of 1896.—Dewey, *National Problems* (American Nation Series), pp. 220-237, 314-328; Hart, *Contemporaries*, Vol. IV, pp. 533-538.

Tariff Revision.—Dewey, *Financial History*, Sections 167, 180, 181, 187, 192, 196; Hart, *Contemporaries*, Vol. IV, pp. 518-525; Rhodes, *History*, Vol. VIII, pp. 168-179, 346-351, 418-422.

Federal Regulation of Railways.—Dewey, *National Problems*, pp. 91-111; MacDonald, *Documentary Source Book*, pp. 581-590; Hart, *Contemporaries*, Vol. IV, pp. 521-523; Rhodes, *History*, Vol. VIII, pp. 288-292.

The Rise and Regulation of Trusts.—Dewey, *National Problems*, pp. 188-202; MacDonald, *Documentary Source Book*, pp. 591-593.

The Grangers and Populism.—Paxson, *The New Nation* (Riverside Series), pp. 20-37, 177-191, 208-223.

General Analysis of Domestic Problems.—*Syllabus in History* (New York State, 1920), pp. 137-142.

CHAPTER XX

AMERICA A WORLD POWER (1865-1900)

It has now become a fashion, sanctioned by wide usage and by eminent historians, to speak of America, triumphant over Spain and possessed of new colonies, as entering the twentieth century in the rôle of "a world power," for the first time. Perhaps at this late day, it is useless to protest against the currency of the idea. Nevertheless, the truth is that from the fateful moment in March, 1775, when Edmund Burke unfolded to his colleagues in the British Parliament the resources of an invincible America, down to the settlement at Versailles in 1919 closing the drama of the World War, this nation has been a world power, influencing by its example, by its institutions, by its wealth, trade, and arms the course of international affairs. And it should be said also that neither in the field of commercial enterprise nor in that of diplomacy has it been wanting in spirit or ingenuity.

When John Hay, Secretary of State, heard that an American citizen, Perdicaris, had been seized by Raisuli, a Moroccan bandit, in 1904, he wired his brusque message: "We want Perdicaris alive or Raisuli dead." This was but an echo of Commodore Decatur's equally characteristic answer, "Not a minute," given nearly a hundred years before to the pirates of Algiers begging for time to consider whether they would cease preying upon American merchantmen. Was it not as early as 1844 that the American commissioner, Caleb Cushing, taking advantage of the British Opium War on China, negotiated with the Celestial Empire a successful commercial treaty? Did he not then exultantly exclaim: "The laws of the Union follow its citizens and its banner protects them even within the domain of the Chinese Empire"? Was it not almost half a century before the battle of Manila Bay in 1898, that Commodore Perry with an adequate naval force "gently coerced Japan into friendship with us," leading all the nations of the earth in the opening of that empire to the trade of the Occident? Nor is it inappropriate in this connection to recall the fact that the Monroe Doctrine celebrates in 1923 its hundredth anniversary.

AMERICAN FOREIGN RELATIONS (1865-98)

French Intrigues in Mexico Blocked.—Between the war for the union and the war with Spain, the Department of State had many an occasion to present the rights of America among the powers of the world. Only a little while after the civil conflict came to a close, it was called upon to deal with a dangerous situation created in Mexico by the ambitions of Napoleon III. During the administration of Buchanan, Mexico had fallen into disorder through the strife of the Liberal and the Clerical parties; the President asked for authority to use American troops to bring to a peaceful haven "a wreck upon the ocean, drifting about as she is impelled by different factions." Our own domestic crisis then intervened.

Observing the United States heavily involved in its own problems, the great powers, England, France, and Spain, decided in the autumn of 1861 to take a hand themselves in restoring order in Mexico. They entered into an agreement to enforce the claims of their citizens against Mexico and to protect their subjects residing in that republic. They invited the United States to join them, and, on meeting a polite refusal, they prepared for a combined military and naval demonstration on their own account. In the midst of this action England and Spain, discovering the sinister purposes of Napoleon, withdrew their troops and left the field to him.

The French Emperor, it was well known, looked with jealousy upon the growth of the United States and dreamed of establishing in the Western hemisphere an imperial power to offset the American republic. Intervention to collect debts was only a cloak for his deeper designs. Throwing off that guise in due time, he made the Archduke Maximilian, a brother of the ruler of Austria, emperor in Mexico, and surrounded his throne by French soldiers, in spite of all protests.

This insolent attack upon the Mexican republic, deeply resented in the United States, was allowed to drift in its course until 1865. At that juncture General Sheridan was dispatched to the Mexican border with a large armed force; General Grant urged the use of the American army to expel the French from this continent. The Secretary of State, Seward, counseled negotiation first, and, applying the Monroe Doctrine, was able to prevail upon Napoleon III to withdraw his troops. Without the support of French arms, the sham empire in Mexico collapsed like a house of cards and the unhappy Maximilian, the victim of French ambition and intrigue, met his death at the hands of a Mexican firing squad.

Alaska Purchased.—The Mexican affair had not been brought to a close before the Department of State was busy with negotiations which resulted in the purchase of Alaska from Russia. The treaty of cession, signed on March 30, 1867, added to the United States a domain of nearly six hundred thousand square miles, a territory larger than Texas and nearly three-fourths the size of the Louisiana purchase. Though it was a distant colony separated from our continental domain by a thousand miles of water, no question of "imperialism" or "colonization foreign to American doctrines" seems to have been raised at the time. The treaty was ratified promptly by the Senate. The purchase price, $7,200,000, was voted by the House of Representatives after the display of some resentment against a system that compelled it to appropriate money to fulfill an obligation which it had no part in making. Seward, who formulated the treaty, rejoiced, as he afterwards said, that he had kept Alaska out of the hands of England.

American Interest in the Caribbean.—Having achieved this diplomatic triumph, Seward turned to the increase of American power in another direction. He negotiated, with Denmark, a treaty providing for the purchase of the islands of St. John and St. Thomas in the West Indies, strategic points in the Caribbean for sea power. This project, long afterward brought to fruition by other men, was defeated on this occasion by the refusal of the Senate to ratify the treaty. Evidently it was not yet prepared to exercise colonial dominion over other races.

Undaunted by the misadventure in Caribbean policies, President Grant warmly advocated the acquisition of Santo Domingo. This little republic had long been in a state of general disorder. In 1869 a treaty of annexation was concluded with its president. The document Grant transmitted to the Senate with his cordial approval, only to have it rejected. Not at all changed in his opinion by the outcome of his effort, he continued to urge the subject of annexation. Even in his last message to Congress he referred to it, saying that time had only proved the wisdom of his early course. The addition of Santo Domingo to the American sphere of protection was the work of a later generation. The State Department, temporarily checked, had to bide its time.

The *Alabama* Claims Arbitrated.—Indeed, it had in hand a far more serious matter, a vexing issue that grew out of Civil War diplomacy. The British government, as already pointed out in other connections, had permitted Confederate cruisers, including the famous *Alabama*, built in British ports, to escape and prey upon the commerce of the Northern states. This action, denounced at the time by our government as a grave breach of neutrality as well as a grievous injury to American citizens, led first to remonstrances and finally to repeated claims for damages done to American ships and goods. For a long time Great Britain was firm. Her foreign secretary denied all obligations in the premises, adding somewhat curtly that "he wished to say once for all that Her Majesty's government disclaimed any responsibility for the losses and hoped that they had made their position perfectly clear." Still President Grant was not persuaded that the door of diplomacy, though closed, was barred. Hamilton Fish, his Secretary of State, renewed the demand. Finally he secured from the British government in 1871 the treaty of Washington providing for the arbitration not merely of the *Alabama* and other claims but also all points of serious controversy between the two countries.

The tribunal of arbitration thus authorized sat at Geneva in Switzerland, and after a long and careful review of the arguments on both sides awarded to the United States the lump sum of $15,500,000 to be distributed among the American claimants. The damages thus allowed were large, unquestionably larger than strict justice required and it is not surprising that the decision excited much adverse comment in England. Nevertheless, the prompt payment by the British government swept away at once a great cloud of ill-feeling in America. Moreover, the spectacle of two powerful nations choosing the way of peaceful arbitration to settle an angry dispute seemed a happy, if illusory, omen of a modern method for avoiding the arbitrament of war.

Samoa.—If the Senate had its doubts at first about the wisdom of acquiring strategic points for naval power in distant seas, the same could not be said of the State Department or naval officers. In 1872 Commander Meade, of the United States navy, alive to the importance of coaling stations even in mid-ocean, made a commercial agreement with the chief of Tutuila, one of the Samoan Islands, far below the equator, in the southern Pacific, nearer to Australia than to California. This agreement, providing among other things for our use of the harbor of Pago Pago as a naval base, was six years later changed into a formal treaty ratified by the Senate.

Such enterprise could not escape the vigilant eyes of England and Germany, both mindful of the course of the sea power in history. The German emperor, seizing as a pretext a quarrel between his consul in the islands and a native king, laid claim to an interest in the Samoan group. England, aware of the dangers arising from German outposts in the southern seas so near to Australia, was not content to stand aside. So it happened that all three countries sent battleships to the Samoan waters, threatening a crisis that was fortunately averted by friendly settlement. If, as is alleged, Germany entertained a notion of challenging American sea power then and there, the presence of British ships must have dispelled that dream.

The result of the affair was a tripartite agreement by which the three powers in 1889 undertook a protectorate over the islands. But joint control proved unsatisfactory. There was constant friction between the Germans and the English. The spheres of authority being vague and open to dispute, the plan had to be abandoned at the end of ten years. England withdrew altogether, leaving to Germany all the islands except Tutuila, which was ceded outright to the United States. Thus one of the finest harbors in the Pacific, to the intense delight of the American navy, passed permanently under American dominion. Another triumph in diplomacy was set down to the credit of the State Department.

Cleveland and the Venezuela Affair.—In the relations with South America, as well as in those with the distant Pacific, the diplomacy of the government at Washington was put to the test. For some time it had been watching a dispute between England and Venezuela over the western boundary of British Guiana and, on an appeal from Venezuela, it had taken a lively interest in the contest. In 1895 President Cleveland saw that Great Britain would yield none of her claims. After hearing the arguments of Venezuela, his Secretary of State, Richard T. Olney, in a note none too conciliatory, asked the British government whether it was willing to arbitrate the points in controversy. This inquiry he accompanied by a warning to the effect that the United States could not permit any European power to contest its mastery in this hemisphere. "The United States," said the Secretary, "is practically sovereign on this continent and its fiat is law upon the subjects to which it confines its interposition.... Its infinite resources, combined with its isolated position, render it master of the situation and practically invulnerable against any or all other powers."

The reply evoked from the British government by this strong statement was firm and clear. The Monroe Doctrine, it said, even if not so widely stretched by interpretation, was not binding in international law; the dispute with Venezuela was a matter of interest merely to the parties involved; and arbitration of the question was impossible. This response called forth President Cleveland's startling message of 1895. He asked Congress to create a commission authorized to ascertain by researches the true boundary between Venezuela and British Guiana. He added that it would be the duty of this country "to resist by every means in its power, as a willful aggression upon its rights and interests, the appropriation by Great Britain of any lands or the exercise of governmental jurisdiction over any territory which, after investigation, we have determined of right belongs to Venezuela." The serious character of this statement he thoroughly understood. He declared that he was conscious of his responsibilities, intimating that war, much as it was to be deplored, was not comparable to "a supine submission to wrong and injustice and the consequent loss of national self-respect and honor."

The note of defiance which ran through this message, greeted by shrill cries of enthusiasm in many circles, was viewed in other quarters as a portent of war. Responsible newspapers in both countries spoke of an armed settlement of the dispute as inevitable. Congress created the commission and appropriated money for the investigation; a body of learned men was appointed to determine the merits of the conflicting boundary claims. The British government, deaf to the clamor of the bellicose section of the London press, deplored the incident, courteously replied in the affirmative to a request for assistance in the search for evidence, and finally agreed to the proposition that the issue be submitted to arbitration. The outcome of this somewhat perilous dispute contributed not a little to Cleveland's reputation as "a sterling representative of the true American spirit." This was not diminished when the tribunal of arbitration found that Great Britain was on the whole right in her territorial claims against Venezuela.

The Annexation of Hawaii.—While engaged in the dangerous Venezuela controversy, President Cleveland was compelled by a strange turn in events to consider the annexation of the Hawaiian Islands in the mid-Pacific. For more than half a century American missionaries had been active in converting the natives to the Christian faith and enterprising American business men had been developing the fertile sugar plantations. Both the Department of State and the Navy Department were fully conscious of the strategic relation of the islands to the growth of sea power and watched with anxiety any developments likely to bring them under some other Dominion.

The country at large was indifferent, however, until 1893, when a revolution, headed by Americans, broke out, ending in the overthrow of the native government, the abolition of the primitive monarchy, and the retirement of Queen Liliuokalani to private life. This crisis, a repetition of the Texas affair in a small theater, was immediately followed by a demand from the new Hawaiian government for annexation to the United States. President Harrison looked with favor on the proposal, negotiated the treaty of annexation, and laid it before the Senate for approval. There it still rested when his term of office was brought to a close.

Harrison's successor, Cleveland, it was well known, had doubts about the propriety of American action in Hawaii. For the purpose of making an inquiry into the matter, he sent a special commissioner to the islands. On the basis of the report of his agent, Cleveland came to the conclusion that "the revolution in the island kingdom had been accomplished by the improper use of the armed forces of the United States and that the wrong should be righted by a restoration of the queen to her throne." Such being his matured conviction, though the facts upon which he rested it were warmly controverted, he could do nothing but withdraw the treaty from the Senate and close the incident.

To the Republicans this sharp and cavalier disposal of their plans, carried out in a way that impugned the motives of a Republican President, was nothing less than "a betrayal of American interests." In their platform of 1896 they made clear their position: "Our foreign policy should be at all times firm, vigorous, and dignified and all our interests in the Western hemisphere carefully watched and guarded. The Hawaiian Islands should be controlled by the United States and no foreign power should be permitted to interfere with them." There was no mistaking this view of the issue. As the vote in the election gave popular sanction to Republican policies, Congress by a joint resolution, passed on July 6, 1898, annexed the islands to the United States and later conferred upon them the ordinary territorial form of government.

CUBA AND THE SPANISH WAR

Early American Relations with Cuba.—The year that brought Hawaii finally under the American flag likewise drew to a conclusion another long controversy over a similar outpost in the Atlantic, one of the last remnants of the once glorious Spanish empire—the island of Cuba.

For a century the Department of State had kept an anxious eye upon this base of power, knowing full well that both France and England, already well established in the West Indies, had their attention also fixed upon Cuba. In the administration of President Fillmore they had united in proposing to the United States a tripartite treaty guaranteeing Spain in her none too certain ownership. This proposal, squarely rejected, furnished the occasion for a statement of American policy which stood the test of all the years that followed; namely, that the affair was one between Spain and the United States alone.

In that long contest in the United States for the balance of power between the North and South, leaders in the latter section often thought of bringing Cuba into the union to offset the free states. An opportunity to announce their purposes publicly was afforded in 1854 by a controversy over the seizure of an American ship by Cuban authorities. On that occasion three American ministers abroad, stationed at Madrid, Paris, and London respectively, held a conference and issued the celebrated "Ostend Manifesto." They united in declaring that Cuba, by her geographical position, formed a part of the United States, that possession by a foreign power was inimical to American interests, and that an effort should be made to purchase the island from Spain. In case the owner refused to sell, they concluded, with a menacing flourish, "by every law, human and divine, we shall be justified in wresting it from Spain if we possess the power." This startling proclamation to the world was promptly disowned by the United States government.

Revolutions in Cuba.—For nearly twenty years afterwards the Cuban question rested. Then it was revived in another form during President Grant's administrations, when the natives became engaged in a destructive revolt against Spanish officials. For ten years—1868-78—a guerrilla warfare raged in the island. American citizens, by virtue of their ancient traditions of democracy, naturally sympathized with a war for independence and self-government. Expeditions to help the insurgents were fitted out secretly in American ports. Arms and supplies were smuggled into Cuba. American soldiers of fortune joined their ranks. The enforcement of neutrality against the friends of Cuban independence, no pleasing task for a sympathetic President, the protection of American lives and property in the revolutionary area, and similar matters kept our government busy with Cuba for a whole decade.

A brief lull in Cuban disorders was followed in 1895 by a renewal of the revolutionary movement. The contest between the rebels and the Spanish troops, marked by extreme cruelty and a total disregard for life and property, exceeded all bounds of decency, and once more raised the old questions that had tormented Grant's administration. Gomez, the leader of the revolt, intent upon provoking American interference, laid waste the land with fire and sword. By a proclamation of November 6, 1895, he ordered the destruction of sugar plantations and railway connections and the closure of all sugar factories. The work of ruin was completed by the ruthless Spanish general, Weyler, who concentrated the inhabitants from rural regions into military camps, where they died by the hundreds of disease and starvation. Stories of the atrocities, bad enough in simple form, became lurid when transmuted into American news and deeply moved the sympathies of the American people. Sermons were preached about Spanish misdeeds; orators demanded that the Cubans be sustained "in their heroic struggle for independence"; newspapers, scouting the ordinary forms of diplomatic negotiation, spurned mediation and demanded intervention and war if necessary.

President Cleveland's Policy.—Cleveland chose the way of peace. He ordered the observance of the rule of neutrality. He declined to act on a resolution of Congress in favor of giving to the Cubans the rights of belligerents. Anxious to bring order to the distracted island, he tendered to Spain the good offices of the United States as mediator in the contest—a tender rejected by the Spanish government with the broad hint that President Cleveland might be more vigorous in putting a stop to the unlawful aid in money, arms, and supplies, afforded to the insurgents by American sympathizers. Thereupon the President returned to the course he had marked out for himself, leaving "the public nuisance" to his successor, President McKinley.

Republican Policies.—The Republicans in 1897 found themselves in a position to employ that "firm, vigorous, and dignified" foreign policy which they had approved in their platform. They had declared: "The government of Spain having lost control of Cuba and being unable to protect the property or lives of resident American citizens or to comply with its treaty obligations, we believe that the government of the United States should actively use its influence and good offices to restore peace and give independence to the island." The American property in Cuba to which the Republicans referred in their platform amounted by this time to more than fifty million dollars; the commerce with the island reached more than one hundred millions annually; and the claims of American citizens against Spain for property destroyed totaled sixteen millions. To the pleas of humanity which made such an effective appeal to the hearts of the American people, there were thus added practical considerations of great weight.

President McKinley Negotiates.—In the face of the swelling tide of popular opinion in favor of quick, drastic, and positive action, McKinley chose first the way of diplomacy. A short time after his inauguration he lodged with the Spanish government a dignified protest against its policies in Cuba, thus opening a game of thrust and parry with the suave ministers at Madrid. The results of the exchange of notes were the recall of the obnoxious General Weyler, the appointment of a governor-general less bloodthirsty in his methods, a change in the policy of concentrating civilians in military camps, and finally a promise of "home rule" for Cuba. There is no doubt that the Spanish government was eager to avoid a war that could have but one outcome. The American minister at Madrid, General Woodford, was convinced that firm and patient pressure would have resulted in the final surrender of Cuba by the Spanish government.

The De Lome and the *Maine* Incidents.—Such a policy was defeated by events. In February, 1898, a private letter written by Señor de Lome, the Spanish ambassador at Washington, expressing contempt for the President of the United States, was filched from the mails and passed into the hands of a journalist, William R. Hearst, who published it to the world. In the excited state of American opinion, few gave heed to the grave breach of diplomatic courtesy committed by breaking open private correspondence. The Spanish government was compelled to recall De Lome, thus officially condemning his conduct.

At this point a far more serious crisis put the pacific relations of the two negotiating countries in dire peril. On February 15, the battleship *Maine*, riding in the harbor of Havana, was blown up and sunk, carrying to death two officers and two hundred and fifty-eight members of the crew. This tragedy, ascribed by the American public to the malevolence of Spanish officials, profoundly stirred an already furious nation. When, on March 21, a commission of inquiry reported that the ill-fated ship had been blown up by a submarine mine which had in turn set off some of the ship's magazines, the worst suspicions seemed confirmed. If any one was inclined to be indifferent to the Cuban war for independence, he was now met by the vehement cry: "Remember the *Maine*!"

Spanish Concessions.—Still the State Department, under McKinley's steady hand, pursued the path of negotiation, Spain proving more pliable and more ready with promises of reform in the island. Early in April, however, there came a decided change in the tenor of American diplomacy. On the 4th, McKinley, evidently convinced that promises did not mean performances, instructed our minister at Madrid to warn the Spanish government that as no effective armistice had been offered to the Cubans, he would lay the whole matter before Congress. This decision, every one knew, from the temper of Congress, meant war—a prospect which excited all the European powers. The Pope took an active interest in the crisis. France and Germany, foreseeing from long experience in world politics an increase of American power and prestige through war, sought to prevent it. Spain, hopeless and conscious of her weakness, at last dispatched to the President a note promising to suspend hostilities, to call a Cuban parliament, and to grant all the autonomy that could be reasonably asked.

President McKinley Calls for War.—For reasons of his own—reasons which have never yet been fully explained—McKinley ignored the final program of concessions presented by Spain. At the very moment when his patient negotiations seemed to bear full fruit, he veered sharply from his course and launched the country into the war by sending to Congress his militant message of April 11, 1898. Without making public the last note he had received from Spain, he declared that he was brought to the end of his effort and the cause was in the hands of Congress. Humanity, the protection of American citizens and property, the injuries to American commerce and business, the inability of Spain to bring about permanent peace in the island—these were the grounds for action that induced him to ask for authority to employ military and naval forces in establishing a stable government in Cuba. They were sufficient for a public already straining at the leash.

The Resolution of Congress.—There was no doubt of the outcome when the issue was withdrawn from diplomacy and placed in charge of Congress. Resolutions were soon introduced into the House of Representatives authorizing the President to employ armed force in securing peace and order in the island and "establishing by the free action of the people thereof a stable and independent government of their own." To the form and spirit of this proposal the Democrats and Populists took exception. In the Senate, where they were stronger, their position had to be reckoned with by the narrow Republican majority. As the resolution finally read, the independence of Cuba was recognized; Spain was called upon to relinquish her authority and withdraw from the island; and the President was empowered to use force to the extent necessary to carry the resolutions into effect. Furthermore the United States disclaimed "any disposition or intention to exercise sovereignty, jurisdiction, or control over said island except for the pacification thereof." Final action was taken by Congress on April 19, 1898, and approved by the President on the following day.

War and Victory.—Startling events then followed in swift succession. The navy, as a result in no small measure of the alertness of Theodore Roosevelt, Assistant Secretary of the Department, was ready for the trial by battle. On May 1, Commodore Dewey at Manila Bay shattered the Spanish fleet, marking the doom of Spanish dominion in the Philippines. On July 3, the Spanish fleet under Admiral Cervera, in attempting to escape from Havana, was utterly destroyed by American forces under Commodore Schley. On July 17, Santiago, invested by American troops under General Shafter and shelled by the American ships, gave up the struggle. On July 25 General Miles landed in Porto Rico. On August 13, General Merritt and Admiral Dewey carried Manila by storm. The war was over.

The Peace Protocol.—Spain had already taken cognizance of stern facts. As early as July 26, 1898, acting through the French ambassador, M. Cambon, the Madrid government approached President McKinley for a statement of the terms on which hostilities could be brought to a close. After some skirmishing Spain yielded reluctantly to the ultimatum. On August 12, the preliminary peace protocol was signed, stipulating that Cuba should be free, Porto Rico ceded to the United States, and Manila occupied by American troops pending the formal treaty of peace. On October 1, the commissioners of the two countries met at Paris to bring about the final settlement.

Peace Negotiations.—When the day for the first session of the conference arrived, the government at Washington apparently had not made up its mind on the final disposition of the Philippines. Perhaps, before the battle of Manila Bay, not ten thousand people in the United States knew or cared where the Philippines were. Certainly there was in the autumn of 1898 no decided opinion as to what should be done with the fruits of Dewey's victory. President McKinley doubtless voiced the sentiment of the people when he stated to the peace commissioners on the eve of their departure that there had originally been no thought of conquest in the Pacific.

The march of events, he added, had imposed new duties on the country. "Incidental to our tenure in the Philippines," he said, "is the commercial opportunity to which American statesmanship cannot be indifferent. It is just to use every legitimate means for the enlargement of American trade." On this ground he directed the commissioners to accept not less than the cession of the island of Luzon, the chief of the Philippine group, with its harbor of Manila. It was not until the latter part of October that he definitely instructed them to demand the entire archipelago, on the theory that the occupation of Luzon alone could not be justified "on political, commercial, or humanitarian grounds." This departure from the letter of the peace protocol was bitterly resented by the Spanish agents. It was with heaviness of heart that they surrendered the last sign of Spain's ancient dominion in the far Pacific.

The Final Terms of Peace.—The treaty of peace, as finally agreed upon, embraced the following terms: the independence of Cuba; the cession of Porto Rico, Guam, and the Philippines to the United States; the settlement of claims filed by the citizens of both countries; the payment of twenty million dollars to Spain by the United States for the Philippines; and the determination of the status of the inhabitants of the ceded territories by Congress. The great decision had been made. Its issue was in the hands of the Senate where the Democrats and the Populists held the balance of power under the requirement of the two-thirds vote for ratification.

The Contest in America over the Treaty of Peace.—The publication of the treaty committing the United States to the administration of distant colonies directed the shifting tides of public opinion into two distinct channels: support of the policy and opposition to it. The trend in Republican leadership, long in the direction marked out by the treaty, now came into the open. Perhaps a majority of the men highest in the councils of that party had undergone the change of heart reflected in the letters of John Hay, Secretary of State. In August of 1898 he had hinted, in a friendly letter to Andrew Carnegie, that he sympathized with the latter's opposition to "imperialism"; but he had added quickly: "The only question in my mind is how far it is now possible for us to withdraw from the Philippines." In November of the same year he wrote to Whitelaw Reid, one of the peace commissioners at Paris: "There is a wild and frantic attack now going on in the press against the whole Philippine transaction. Andrew Carnegie really seems to be off his head.... But all this confusion of tongues will go its way. The country will applaud the resolution that has been reached and you will return in the rôle of conquering heroes with your 'brows bound with oak.'"

Senator Beveridge of Indiana and Senator Platt of Connecticut, accepting the verdict of history as the proof of manifest destiny, called for unquestioning support of the administration in its final step. "Every expansion of our territory," said the latter, "has been in accordance with the irresistible law of growth. We could no more resist the successive expansions by which we have grown to be the strongest nation on earth than a tree can resist its growth. The history of territorial expansion is the history of our nation's progress and glory. It is a matter to be proud of, not to lament. We should rejoice that Providence has given us the opportunity to extend our influence, our institutions, and our civilization into regions hitherto closed to us, rather than contrive how we can thwart its designs."

This doctrine was savagely attacked by opponents of McKinley's policy, many a stanch Republican joining with the majority of Democrats in denouncing the treaty as a departure from the ideals of the republic. Senator Vest introduced in the Senate a resolution that "under the Constitution of the United States, no power is given to the federal Government to acquire territory to be held and governed permanently as colonies." Senator Hoar, of Massachusetts, whose long and honorable career gave weight to his lightest words, inveighed against the whole procedure and to the end of his days believed that the new drift into rivalry with European nations as a colonial power was fraught with genuine danger. "Our imperialistic friends," he said, "seem to have forgotten the use of the vocabulary of liberty. They talk about giving good government. 'We shall give them such a government as we think they are fitted for.' 'We shall give them a better government than they had before.' Why, Mr. President, that one phrase conveys to a free man and a free people the most stinging of insults. In that little phrase, as in a seed, is contained the germ of all despotism and of all tyranny. Government is not a gift. Free government is not to be given by all the blended powers of earth and heaven. It is a birthright. It belongs, as our fathers said, and as their children said, as Jefferson said, and as President McKinley said, to human nature itself."

The Senate, more conservative on the question of annexation than the House of Representatives composed of men freshly elected in the stirring campaign of 1896, was deliberate about ratification of the treaty. The Democrats and Populists were especially recalcitrant. Mr. Bryan hurried to Washington and brought his personal influence to bear in favor of speedy action. Patriotism required ratification, it was said in one quarter. The country desires peace and the Senate ought not to delay, it was urged in another. Finally, on February 6, 1899, the requisite majority of two-thirds was mustered, many a Senator who voted for the treaty, however, sharing the misgivings of Senator Hoar as to the "dangers of imperialism." Indeed at the time, the Senators passed a resolution declaring that the policy to be adopted in the Philippines was still an open question, leaving to the future, in this way, the possibility of retracing their steps.

The Attitude of England.—The Spanish war, while accomplishing the simple objects of those who launched the nation on that course, like all other wars, produced results wholly unforeseen. In the first place, it exercised a profound influence on the drift of opinion among European powers. In England, sympathy with the United States was from the first positive and outspoken. "The state of feeling here," wrote Mr. Hay, then ambassador in London, "is the best I have ever known. From every quarter the evidences of it come to me. The royal family by habit and tradition are most careful not to break the rules of strict neutrality, but even among them I find nothing but hearty kindness and—so far as is consistent with propriety—sympathy. Among the political leaders on both sides I find not only sympathy but a somewhat eager desire that 'the other fellows' shall not seem more friendly."

Joseph Chamberlain, the distinguished Liberal statesman, thinking no doubt of the continental situation, said in a political address at the very opening of the war that the next duty of Englishmen "is to establish and maintain bonds of permanent unity with our kinsmen across the Atlantic.... I even go so far as to say that, terrible as war may be, even war would be cheaply purchased if, in a great and noble cause, the Stars and Stripes and the Union Jack should wave together over an Anglo-Saxon alliance." To the American ambassador he added significantly that he did not "care a hang what they say about it on the continent," which was another way of expressing the hope that the warning to Germany and France was sufficient. This friendly English opinion, so useful to the United States when a combination of powers to support Spain was more than possible, removed all fears as to the consequences of the war. Henry Adams, recalling days of humiliation in London during the Civil War, when his father was the American ambassador, coolly remarked that it was "the sudden appearance of Germany as the grizzly terror" that "frightened England into America's arms"; but the net result in keeping the field free for an easy triumph of American arms was none the less appreciated in Washington where, despite outward calm, fears of European complications were never absent.

AMERICAN POLICIES IN THE PHILIPPINES AND THE ORIENT

The Filipino Revolt against American Rule.—In the sphere of domestic politics, as well as in the field of foreign relations, the outcome of the Spanish war exercised a marked influence. It introduced at once problems of colonial administration and difficulties in adjusting trade relations with the outlying dominions. These were furthermore complicated in the very beginning by the outbreak of an insurrection against American sovereignty in the Philippines. The leader of the revolt, Aguinaldo, had been invited to join the American forces in overthrowing Spanish dominion, and he had assumed, apparently without warrant, that independence would be the result of the joint operations. When the news reached him that the American flag had been substituted for the Spanish flag, his resentment was keen. In February, 1899, there occurred a slight collision between his men and some American soldiers. The conflict thus begun was followed by serious fighting which finally dwindled into a vexatious guerrilla warfare lasting three years and costing heavily in men and money. Atrocities were committed by the native insurrectionists and, sad to relate, they were repaid in kind; it was argued in defense of the army that the ordinary rules of warfare were without terror to men accustomed to fighting like savages. In vain did McKinley assure the Filipinos that the institutions and laws established in the islands would be designed "not for our satisfaction or for the expression of our theoretical views, but for the happiness, peace, and prosperity of the people of the Philippine Islands." Nothing short of military pressure could bring the warring revolutionists to terms.

Attacks on Republican "Imperialism."—The Filipino insurrection, following so quickly upon the ratification of the treaty with Spain, moved the American opponents of McKinley's colonial policies to redouble their denunciation of what they were pleased to call "imperialism." Senator Hoar was more than usually caustic in his indictment of the new course. The revolt against American rule did but convince him of the folly hidden in the first fateful measures. Everywhere he saw a conspiracy of silence and injustice. "I have failed to discover in the speeches, public or private, of the advocates of this war," he contended in the Senate, "or in the press which supports it and them, a single expression anywhere of a desire to do justice to the people of the Philippine Islands, or of a desire to make known to the people of the United States the truth of the case.... The catchwords, the cries, the pithy and pregnant phrases of which their speech is full, all mean dominion. They mean perpetual dominion.... There is not one of these gentlemen who will rise in his place and affirm that if he were a Filipino he would not do exactly as the Filipinos are doing; that he would not despise them if they were to do otherwise. So much at least they owe of respect to the dead and buried history—the dead and buried history so far as they can slay and bury it—of their country." In the way of practical suggestions, the Senator offered as a solution of the problem: the recognition of independence, assistance in establishing self-government, and an invitation to all powers to join in a guarantee of freedom to the islands.

The Republican Answer.—To McKinley and his supporters, engaged in a sanguinary struggle to maintain American supremacy, such talk was more than quixotic; it was scarcely short of treasonable.

They pointed out the practical obstacles in the way of uniform self-government for a collection of seven million people ranging in civilization from the most ignorant hill men to the highly cultivated inhabitants of Manila. The incidents of the revolt and its repression, they admitted, were painful enough; but still nothing as compared with the chaos that would follow the attempt of a people who had never had experience in such matters to set up and sustain democratic institutions. They preferred rather the gradual process of fitting the inhabitants of the islands for self-government. This course, in their eyes, though less poetic, was more in harmony with the ideals of humanity. Having set out upon it, they pursued it steadfastly to the end. First, they applied force without stint to the suppression of the revolt. Then they devoted such genius for colonial administration as they could command to the development of civil government, commerce, and industry.

The Boxer Rebellion in China.—For a nation with a world-wide trade, steadily growing, as the progress of home industries redoubled the zeal for new markets, isolation was obviously impossible. Never was this clearer than in 1900 when a native revolt against foreigners in China, known as the Boxer uprising, compelled the United States to join with the powers of Europe in a military expedition and a diplomatic settlement. The Boxers, a Chinese association, had for some time carried on a campaign of hatred against all aliens in the Celestial empire, calling upon the natives to rise in patriotic wrath and drive out the foreigners who, they said, "were lacerating China like tigers." In the summer of 1900 the revolt flamed up in deeds of cruelty. Missionaries and traders were murdered in the provinces; foreign legations were stoned; the German ambassador, one of the most cordially despised foreigners, was killed in the streets of Peking; and to all appearances a frightful war of extermination had begun. In the month of June nearly five hundred men, women, and children, representing all nations, were besieged in the British quarters in Peking under constant fire of Chinese guns and in peril of a terrible death.

Intervention in China.—Nothing but the arrival of armed forces, made up of Japanese, Russian, British, American, French, and German soldiers and marines, prevented the destruction of the beleaguered aliens. When once the foreign troops were in possession of the Chinese capital, diplomatic questions of the most delicate character arose. For more than half a century, the imperial powers of Europe had been carving up the Chinese empire, taking to themselves territory, railway concessions, mining rights, ports, and commercial privileges at the expense of the huge but helpless victim. The United States alone among the great nations, while as zealous as any in the pursuit of peaceful trade, had refrained from seizing Chinese territory or ports. Moreover, the Department of State had been urging European countries to treat China with fairness, to respect her territorial integrity, and to give her equal trading privileges with all nations.

The American Policy of the "Open Door."—In the autumn of 1899, Secretary Hay had addressed to London, Berlin, Rome, Paris, Tokyo, and St. Petersburg his famous note on the "open door" policy in China. In this document he proposed that existing treaty ports and vested interests of the several foreign countries should be respected; that the Chinese government should be permitted to extend its tariffs to all ports held by alien powers except the few free ports; and that there should be no discrimination in railway and port charges among the citizens of foreign countries operating in the empire. To these principles the governments addressed by Mr. Hay, finally acceded with evident reluctance.

On this basis he then proposed the settlement that had to follow the Boxer uprising. "The policy of the Government of the United States," he said to the great powers, in the summer of 1900, "is to seek a solution which may bring about permanent safety and peace to China, preserve Chinese territorial and administrative entity, protect all rights guaranteed to friendly powers by treaty and international law, and safeguard for the world the principle of equal and impartial trade with all parts of the Chinese empire." This was a friendly warning to the world that the United States would not join in a scramble to punish the Chinese by carving out more territory. "The moment we acted," said Mr. Hay, "the rest of the world paused and finally came over to our ground; and the German government, which is generally brutal but seldom silly, recovered its senses, and climbed down off its perch."

In taking this position, the Secretary of State did but reflect the common sense of America. "We are, of course," he explained, "opposed to the dismemberment of that empire and we do not think that the public opinion of the United States would justify this government in taking part in the great game of spoliation now going on." Heavy damages were collected by the European powers from China for the injuries inflicted upon their citizens by the Boxers; but the United States, finding the sum awarded in excess of the legitimate claims, returned the balance in the form of a fund to be applied to the education of Chinese students in American universities. "I would rather be, I think," said Mr. Hay, "the dupe of China than the chum of the Kaiser." By pursuing a liberal policy, he strengthened the hold of the United States upon the affections of the Chinese people and, in the long run, as he remarked himself, safeguarded "our great commercial interests in that Empire."

Imperialism in the Presidential Campaign of 1900.—It is not strange that the policy pursued by the Republican administration in disposing of the questions raised by the Spanish War became one of the first issues in the presidential campaign of 1900. Anticipating attacks from every quarter, the Republicans, in renominating McKinley, set forth their position in clear and ringing phrases: "In accepting by the treaty of Paris the just responsibility of our victories in the Spanish War the President and Senate won the undoubted approval of the American people. No other course was possible than to destroy Spain's sovereignty throughout the West Indies and in the Philippine Islands. That course created our responsibility, before the world and with the unorganized population whom our intervention had freed from Spain, to provide for the maintenance of law and order, and for the establishment of good government and for the performance of international obligations. Our authority could not be less than our responsibility, and wherever sovereign rights were extended it became the high duty of the government to maintain its authority, to put down armed insurrection, and to confer the blessings of liberty and civilization upon all the rescued peoples. The largest measure of self-government consistent with their welfare and our duties shall be secured to them by law." To give more strength to their ticket, the Republican convention, in a whirlwind of enthusiasm, nominated for the vice presidency, against his protest, Theodore Roosevelt, the governor of New York and the hero of the Rough Riders, so popular on account of their Cuban campaign.

The Democrats, as expected, picked up the gauntlet thrown down with such defiance by the Republicans. Mr. Bryan, whom they selected as their candidate, still clung to the currency issue; but the main emphasis, both of the platform and the appeal for votes, was on the "imperialistic program" of the Republican administration. The Democrats denounced the treatment of Cuba and Porto Rico and condemned the Philippine policy in sharp and vigorous terms. "As we are not willing," ran the platform, "to surrender our civilization or to convert the Republic into an empire, we favor an immediate declaration of the Nation's purpose to give to the Filipinos, first, a stable form of government; second, independence; third, protection from outside interference.... The greedy commercialism which dictated the Philippine policy of the Republican administration attempts to justify it with the plea that it will pay, but even this sordid and unworthy plea fails when brought to the test of facts. The war of 'criminal aggression' against the Filipinos entailing an annual expense of many millions has already cost more than any possible profit that could accrue from the entire Philippine trade for years to come.... We oppose militarism. It means conquest abroad and intimidation and oppression at home. It means the strong arm which has ever been fatal to free institutions. It is what millions of our citizens have fled from in Europe. It will impose upon our peace-loving people a large standing army, an unnecessary burden of taxation, and would be a constant menace to their liberties." Such was the tenor of their appeal to the voters.

With the issues clearly joined, the country rejected the Democratic candidate even more positively than four years before. The popular vote cast for McKinley was larger and that cast for Bryan smaller than in the silver election. Thus vindicated at the polls, McKinley turned with renewed confidence to the development of the policies he had so far advanced. But fate cut short his designs. In the September following his second inauguration, he was shot by an anarchist while attending the Buffalo exposition. "What a strange and tragic fate it has been of mine," wrote the Secretary of State, John Hay, on the day of the President's death, "to stand by the bier of three of my dearest friends, Lincoln, Garfield, and McKinley, three of the gentlest of men, all risen to the head of the state and all done to death by assassins." On September 14, 1901, the Vice President, Theodore Roosevelt, took up the lines of power that had fallen from the hands of his distinguished chief, promising to continue "absolutely unbroken" the policies he had inherited.

SUMMARY OF NATIONAL GROWTH AND WORLD POLITICS

The economic aspects of the period between 1865 and 1900 may be readily summed up: the recovery of the South from the ruin of the Civil War, the extension of the railways, the development of the Great West, and the triumph of industry and business enterprise. In the South many of the great plantations were broken up and sold in small farms, crops were diversified, the small farming class was raised in the scale of social importance, the cotton industry was launched, and the coal, iron, timber, and other resources were brought into use. In the West the free arable land was practically exhausted by 1890 under the terms of the Homestead Act; gold, silver, copper, coal and other minerals were discovered in abundance; numerous rail connections were formed with the Atlantic seaboard; the cowboy and the Indian were swept away before a standardized civilization of electric lights and bathtubs. By the end of the century the American frontier had disappeared. The wild, primitive life so long associated with America was gone. The unity of the nation was established.

In the field of business enterprise, progress was most marked. The industrial system, which had risen and flourished before the Civil War, grew into immense proportions and the industrial area was extended from the Northeast into all parts of the country. Small business concerns were transformed into huge corporations. Individual plants were merged under the management of gigantic trusts. Short railway lines were consolidated into national systems. The industrial population of wage-earners rose into the tens of millions. The immigration of aliens increased by leaps and bounds. The cities overshadowed the country. The nation that had once depended upon Europe for most of its manufactured goods became a competitor of Europe in the markets of the earth.

In the sphere of politics, the period witnessed the recovery of white supremacy in the South; the continued discussion of the old questions, such as the currency, the tariff, and national banking; and the injection of new issues like the trusts and labor problems. As of old, foreign affairs were kept well at the front. Alaska was purchased from Russia; attempts were made to extend American influence in the Caribbean region; a Samoan island was brought under the flag; and the Hawaiian islands were annexed. The Monroe Doctrine was applied with vigor in the dispute between Venezuela and Great Britain.

Assistance was given to the Cubans in their revolutionary struggle against Spain and thus there was precipitated a war which ended in the annexation of Porto Rico and the Philippines. American influence in the Pacific and the Orient was so enlarged as to be a factor of great weight in world affairs. Thus questions connected with foreign and "imperial" policies were united with domestic issues to make up the warp and woof of politics. In the direction of affairs, the Republicans took the leadership, for they held the presidency during all the years, except eight, between 1865 and 1900.

References

J.W. Foster, *A Century of American Diplomacy; American Diplomacy in the Orient.*

W.F. Reddaway, *The Monroe Doctrine.*

J.H. Latané, *The United States and Spanish America.*

A.C. Coolidge, *United States as a World Power.*

A.T. Mahan, *Interest of the United States in the Sea Power.*

F.E. Chadwick, *Spanish-American War.*

D.C. Worcester, *The Philippine Islands and Their People.*

M.M. Kalaw, *Self-Government in the Philippines*.

L.S. Rowe, *The United States and Porto Rico*.

F.E. Chadwick, *The Relations of the United States and Spain*.

W.R. Shepherd, *Latin America; Central and South America*.

Questions

1. Tell the story of the international crisis that developed soon after the Civil War with regard to Mexico.

2. Give the essential facts relating to the purchase of Alaska.

3. Review the early history of our interest in the Caribbean.

4. Amid what circumstances was the Monroe Doctrine applied in Cleveland's administration?

5. Give the causes that led to the war with Spain.

6. Tell the leading events in that war.

7. What was the outcome as far as Cuba was concerned? The outcome for the United States?

8. Discuss the attitude of the Filipinos toward American sovereignty in the islands.

9. Describe McKinley's colonial policy.

10. How was the Spanish War viewed in England? On the Continent?

11. Was there a unified American opinion on American expansion?

12. Was this expansion a departure from our traditions?

13. What events led to foreign intervention in China?

14. Explain the policy of the "open door."

Research Topics

Hawaii and Venezuela.—Dewey, *National Problems* (American Nation Series), pp. 279-313; Macdonald, *Documentary Source Book*, pp. 600-602; Hart, *American History Told by Contemporaries*, Vol. IV, pp. 612-616.

Intervention in Cuba.—Latané, *America as a World Power* (American Nation Series), pp. 3-28; Macdonald, *Documentary Source Book*, pp. 597-598; Roosevelt, *Autobiography*, pp. 223-277; Haworth, *The United States in Our Own Time*, pp. 232-256; Hart, *Contemporaries*, Vol. IV, pp. 573-578.

The War with Spain.—Elson, *History of the United States*, pp. 889-896.

Terms of Peace with Spain.—Latané, pp. 63-81; Macdonald, pp. 602-608; Hart, *Contemporaries*, Vol. IV, pp. 588-590.

The Philippine Insurrection.—Latané, pp. 82-99.

Imperialism as a Campaign Issue.—Latané, pp. 120-132; Haworth, pp. 257-277; Hart, *Contemporaries*, Vol. IV, pp. 604-611.

Biographical Studies.—William McKinley, M.A. Hanna, John Hay; Admirals, George Dewey, W.T. Sampson, and W.S. Schley; and Generals, W.R. Shafter, Joseph Wheeler, and H.W. Lawton.

General Analysis of American Expansion.—*Syllabus in History* (New York State, 1920), pp. 142-147.

PART VII. PROGRESSIVE DEMOCRACY AND THE WORLD WAR

CHAPTER XXI

THE EVOLUTION OF REPUBLICAN POLICIES (1901-13)

The Personality and Early Career of Roosevelt.—On September 14, 1901, when Theodore Roosevelt took the oath of office, the presidency passed to a new generation and a leader of a new type recalling, if comparisons must be made, Andrew Jackson rather than any Republican predecessor. Roosevelt was brusque, hearty, restless, and fond of action—"a young fellow of infinite dash and originality," as John Hay remarked of him; combining the spirit of his old college, Harvard, with the breezy freedom of the plains; interested in everything—a new species of game, a new book, a diplomatic riddle, or a novel theory of history or biology. Though only forty-three years old he was well versed in the art of practical politics. Coming upon the political scene in the early eighties, he had associated himself with the reformers in the Republican party; but he was no Mugwump. From the first he vehemently preached the doctrine of party loyalty; if beaten in the convention, he voted the straight ticket in the election. For twenty years he adhered to this rule and during a considerable portion of that period he held office as a spokesman of his party. He served in the New York legislature, as head of the metropolitan police force, as federal civil service commissioner under President Harrison, as assistant secretary of the navy under President McKinley, and as governor of the Empire state. Political managers of the old school spoke of him as "brilliant but erratic"; they soon found him equal to the shrewdest in negotiation and action.

FOREIGN AFFAIRS

The Panama Canal.—The most important foreign question confronting President Roosevelt on the day of his inauguration, that of the Panama Canal, was a heritage from his predecessor. The idea of a water route across the isthmus, long a dream of navigators, had become a living issue after the historic voyage of the battleship *Oregon* around South America during the Spanish War. But before the United States could act it had to undo the Clayton-Bulwer treaty, made with Great Britain in 1850, providing for the construction of the canal under joint supervision. This was finally effected by the Hay-Pauncefote treaty of 1901 authorizing the United States to proceed alone, on condition that there should be no discriminations against other nations in the matter of rates and charges.

This accomplished, it was necessary to decide just where the canal should be built. One group in Congress favored the route through Nicaragua; in fact, two official commissions had already approved that location. Another group favored cutting the way through Panama after purchasing the rights of the old French company which, under the direction of De Lesseps, the hero of the Suez Canal, had made a costly failure some twenty years before. After a heated argument over the merits of the two plans, preference was given to the Panama route. As the isthmus was then a part of Colombia, President Roosevelt proceeded to negotiate with the government at Bogota a treaty authorizing the United States to cut a canal through its territory. The treaty was easily framed, but it was rejected by the Colombian senate, much to the President's exasperation. "You could no more make an agreement with the Colombian rulers," he exclaimed, "than you could nail jelly to a wall." He was spared the necessity by a timely revolution. On November 3, 1903, Panama renounced its allegiance to Colombia and three days later the United States recognized its independence.

This amazing incident was followed shortly by the signature of a treaty between Panama and the United States in which the latter secured the right to construct the long-discussed canal, in return for a guarantee of independence and certain cash payments. The rights and property of the French concern were then bought, and the final details settled. A lock rather than a sea-level canal was agreed upon. Construction by the government directly instead of by private contractors was adopted. Scientific medicine was summoned to stamp out the tropical diseases that had made Panama a plague spot. Finally, in 1904, as the President said, "the dirt began to fly." After surmounting formidable difficulties—engineering, labor, and sanitary—the American forces in 1913 joined the waters of the Atlantic and the Pacific. Nearly eight thousand miles were cut off the sea voyage from New York to San Francisco. If any were inclined to criticize President Roosevelt for the way in which he snapped off negotiations with Colombia and recognized the Panama revolutionists, their attention was drawn to the magnificent outcome of the affair. Notwithstanding the treaty with Great Britain, Congress passed a tolls bill discriminating in rates in favor of American ships. It was only on the urgent insistence of President Wilson that the measure was later repealed.

The Conclusion of the Russo-Japanese War.—The applause which greeted the President's next diplomatic stroke was unmarred by censure of any kind. In the winter of 1904 there broke out between Japan and Russia a terrible conflict over the division of spoils in Manchuria. The fortunes of war were with the agile forces of Nippon. In this struggle, it seems, President Roosevelt's sympathies were mainly with the Japanese, although he observed the proprieties of neutrality. At all events, Secretary Hay wrote in his diary on New Year's Day, 1905, that the President was "quite firm in his view that we cannot permit Japan to be robbed a second time of her victory," referring to the fact that Japan, ten years before, after defeating China on the field of battle, had been forced by Russia, Germany, and France to forego the fruits of conquest.

Whatever the President's personal feelings may have been, he was aware that Japan, despite her triumphs over Russia, was staggering under a heavy burden of debt. At a suggestion from Tokyo, he invited both belligerents in the summer of 1905 to join in a peace conference. The celerity of their reply was aided by the pressure of European bankers, who had already come to a substantial agreement that the war must stop. After some delay, Portsmouth, New Hampshire, was chosen as the meeting place for the spokesmen of the two warring powers. Roosevelt presided over the opening ceremonies with fine urbanity, thoroughly enjoying the justly earned honor of being for the moment at the center of the world's interest. He had the satisfaction of seeing the conference end in a treaty of peace and amity.

The Monroe Doctrine Applied to Germany.—Less spectacular than the Russo-Japanese settlement but not less important was a diplomatic passage-at-arms with Germany over the Monroe Doctrine. This clash grew out of the inability or unwillingness of the Venezuelan government to pay debts due foreign creditors. Having exhausted their patience in negotiations, England and Germany, in December 1901, sent battleships to establish what they characterized as "a peaceful blockade" of Venezuelan ports. Their action was followed by the rupture of diplomatic relations; there was a possibility that war and the occupation of Venezuelan territory might result.

While unwilling to stand between a Latin-American country and its creditors, President Roosevelt was determined that debt collecting should not be made an excuse for European countries to seize territory. He therefore urged arbitration of the dispute, winning the assent of England and Italy. Germany, with a somewhat haughty air, refused to take the milder course. The President, learning of this refusal, called the German ambassador to the White House and informed him in very precise terms that, unless the Imperial German Government consented to arbitrate, Admiral Dewey would be ordered to the scene with instructions to prevent Germany from seizing any Venezuelan territory. A week passed and no answer came from Berlin. Not baffled, the President again took the matter up with the ambassador, this time with even more firmness; he stated in language admitting of but one meaning that, unless within forty-eight hours the Emperor consented to arbitration, American battleships, already coaled and cleared, would sail for Venezuelan waters. The hint was sufficient. The Kaiser accepted the proposal and the President, with the fine irony of diplomacy, complimented him publicly on "being so stanch an advocate of arbitration." In terms of the Monroe Doctrine this action meant that the United States, while not denying the obligations of debtors, would not permit any move on the part of European powers that might easily lead to the temporary or permanent occupation of Latin-American territory.

The Santo Domingo Affair.—The same issue was involved in a controversy over Santo Domingo which arose in 1904. The Dominican republic, like Venezuela, was heavily in debt, and certain European countries declared that, unless the United States undertook to look after the finances of the embarrassed debtor, they would resort to armed coercion. What was the United States to do? The danger of having some European power strongly intrenched in Santo Domingo was too imminent to be denied. President Roosevelt acted with characteristic speed, and notwithstanding strong opposition in the Senate was able, in 1907, to effect a treaty arrangement which placed Dominican finances under American supervision.

In the course of the debate over this settlement, a number of interesting questions arose. It was pertinently asked whether the American navy should be used to help creditors collect their debts anywhere in Latin-America. It was suggested also that no sanction should be given to the practice among European governments of using armed force to collect private claims. Opponents of President Roosevelt's policy, and they were neither few nor insignificant, urged that such matters should be referred to the Hague Court or to special international commissions for arbitration. To this the answer was made that the United States could not surrender any question coming under the terms of the Monroe Doctrine to the decision of an international tribunal. The position of the administration was very clearly stated by President Roosevelt himself. "The country," he said, "would certainly decline to go to war to prevent a foreign government from collecting a just debt; on the other hand, it is very inadvisable to permit any foreign power to take possession, even temporarily, of the customs houses of an American republic in order to enforce the payment of its obligations; for such a temporary occupation might turn into a permanent occupation. The only escape from these alternatives may at any time be that we must ourselves undertake to bring about some arrangement by which so much as possible of a just obligation shall be paid." The Monroe Doctrine was negative. It denied to European powers a certain liberty of operation in this hemisphere. The positive obligations resulting from its application by the United States were points now emphasized and developed.

The Hague Conference.—The controversies over Latin-American relations and his part in bringing the Russo-Japanese War to a close naturally made a deep impression upon Roosevelt, turning his mind in the direction of the peaceful settlement of international disputes. The subject was moreover in the air. As if conscious of impending calamity, the statesmen of the Old World, to all outward signs at least, seemed searching for a way to reduce armaments and avoid the bloody and costly trial of international causes by the ancient process of battle. It was the Czar, Nicholas II, fated to die in one of the terrible holocausts which he helped to bring upon mankind, who summoned the delegates of the nations in the first Hague Peace Conference in 1899. The conference did nothing to reduce military burdens or avoid wars but it did recognize the right of friendly nations to offer the services of mediation to countries at war and did establish a Court at the Hague for the arbitration of international disputes.

Encouraged by this experiment, feeble as it was, President Roosevelt in 1904 proposed a second conference, yielding to the Czar the honor of issuing the call. At this great international assembly, held at the Hague in 1907, the representatives of the United States proposed a plan for the compulsory arbitration of certain matters of international dispute. This was rejected with contempt by Germany. Reduction of armaments, likewise proposed in the conference, was again deferred. In fact, nothing was accomplished beyond agreement upon certain rules for the conduct of "civilized warfare," casting a somewhat lurid light upon the "pacific" intentions of most of the powers assembled.

The World Tour of the Fleet.—As if to assure the world then that the United States placed little reliance upon the frail reed of peace conferences, Roosevelt the following year (1908) made an imposing display of American naval power by sending a fleet of sixteen battleships on a tour around the globe. On his own authority, he ordered the ships to sail out of Hampton Roads and circle the earth by way of the Straits of Magellan, San Francisco, Australia, the Philippines, China, Japan, and the Suez Canal. This enterprise was not, as some critics claimed, a "mere boyish flourish." President Roosevelt knew how deep was the influence of sea power on the fate of nations. He was aware that no country could have a wide empire of trade and dominion without force adequate to sustain it. The voyage around the world therefore served a double purpose. It interested his own country in the naval program of the government, and it reminded other powers that the American giant, though quiet, was not sleeping in the midst of international rivalries.

COLONIAL ADMINISTRATION

A Constitutional Question Settled.—In colonial administration, as in foreign policy, President Roosevelt advanced with firm step in a path already marked out. President McKinley had defined the principles that were to control the development of Porto Rico and the Philippines. The Republican party had announced a program of pacification, gradual self-government, and commercial improvement. The only remaining question of importance, to use the popular phrase,—"Does the Constitution follow the flag?"—had been answered by the Supreme Court of the United States. Although it was well known that the Constitution did not contemplate the government of dependencies, such as the Philippines and Porto Rico, the Court, by generous and ingenious interpretations, found a way for Congress to apply any reasonable rules required by the occasion.

Porto Rico.—The government of Porto Rico was a relatively simple matter. It was a single island with a fairly homogeneous population apart from the Spanish upper class. For a time after military occupation in 1898, it was administered under military rule. This was succeeded by the establishment of civil government under the "organic act" passed by Congress in 1900. The law assured to the Porto Ricans American protection but withheld American citizenship—a boon finally granted in 1917. It provided for a governor and six executive secretaries appointed by the President with the approval of the Senate; and for a legislature of two houses—one elected by popular native vote, and an upper chamber composed of the executive secretaries and five other persons appointed in the same manner. Thus the United States turned back to the provincial system maintained by England in Virginia or New York in old colonial days. The natives were given a voice in their government and the power of initiating laws; but the final word both in law-making and administration was vested in officers appointed in Washington. Such was the plan under which the affairs of Porto Rico were conducted by President Roosevelt. It lasted until the new organic act of 1917.

The Philippines.—The administration of the Philippines presented far more difficult questions. The number of islands, the variety of languages and races, the differences in civilization all combined to challenge the skill of the government. Moreover, there was raging in 1901 a stubborn revolt against American authority, which had to be faced. Following the lines laid down by President McKinley, the evolution of American policy fell into three stages. At first the islands were governed directly by the President under his supreme military power. In 1901 a civilian commission, headed by William Howard Taft, was selected by the President and charged with the government of the provinces in which order had been restored. Six years later, under the terms of an organic act, passed by Congress in 1902, the third stage was reached. The local government passed into the hands of a governor and commission, appointed by the President and Senate, and a legislature—one house elected by popular vote and an upper chamber composed of the commission. This scheme, like that obtaining in Porto Rico, remained intact until a Democratic Congress under President Wilson's leadership carried the colonial administration into its fourth phase by making both houses elective. Thus, by the steady pursuit of a liberal policy, self-government was extended to the dependencies; but it encouraged rather than extinguished the vigorous movement among the Philippine natives for independence.

Cuban Relations.—Within the sphere of colonial affairs, Cuba, though nominally independent, also presented problems to the government at Washington. In the fine enthusiasm that accompanied the declaration of war on Spain, Congress, unmindful of practical considerations, recognized the independence of Cuba and disclaimed "any disposition or intention to exercise sovereignty, jurisdiction, or control over said island except for the pacification thereof." In the settlement that followed the war, however, it was deemed undesirable to set the young republic adrift upon the stormy sea of international politics without a guiding hand. Before withdrawing American troops from the island, Congress, in March, 1901, enacted, and required Cuba to approve, a series of restrictions known as the Platt amendment, limiting her power to incur indebtedness, securing the right of the United States to intervene whenever necessary to protect life and property, and reserving to the United States coaling stations at certain points to be agreed upon. The Cubans made strong protests against what they deemed "infringements of their sovereignty"; but finally with good grace accepted their fate. Even when in 1906 President Roosevelt landed American troops in the island to quell a domestic dissension, they acquiesced in the action, evidently regarding it as a distinct warning that they should learn to manage their elections in an orderly manner.

THE ROOSEVELT DOMESTIC POLICIES

Social Questions to the Front.—From the day of his inauguration to the close of his service in 1909, President Roosevelt, in messages, speeches, and interviews, kept up a lively and interesting discussion of trusts, capital, labor, poverty, riches, lawbreaking, good citizenship, and kindred themes. Many a subject previously touched upon only by representatives of the minor and dissenting parties, he dignified by a careful examination. That he did this with any fixed design or policy in mind does not seem to be the case. He admitted himself that when he became President he did not have in hand any settled or far-reaching plan of social betterment. He did have, however, serious convictions on general principles. "I was bent upon making the government," he wrote, "the most efficient possible instrument in helping the people of the United States to better themselves in every way, politically, socially, and industrially. I believed with all my heart in real and thorough-going democracy and I wished to make the democracy industrial as well as political, although I had only partially formulated the method I believed we should follow." It is thus evident at least that he had departed a long way from the old idea of the government as nothing but a great policeman keeping order among the people in a struggle over the distribution of the nation's wealth and resources.

Roosevelt's View of the Constitution.—Equally significant was Roosevelt's attitude toward the Constitution and the office of President. He utterly repudiated the narrow construction of our national charter. He held that the Constitution "should be treated as the greatest document ever devised by the wit of man to aid a people in exercising every power necessary for its own betterment, not as a strait-jacket cunningly fashioned to strangle growth." He viewed the presidency as he did the Constitution. Strict constructionists of the Jeffersonian school, of whom there were many on occasion even in the Republican party, had taken a view that the President could do nothing that he was not specifically authorized by the Constitution to do. Roosevelt took exactly the opposite position. It was his opinion that it was not only the President's right but his duty "to do anything that the needs of the nation demanded unless such action was forbidden by the Constitution or the laws." He went on to say that he acted "for the common well-being of all our people whenever and in whatever manner was necessary, unless prevented by direct constitutional or legislative prohibition."

The Trusts and Railways.—To the trust question, Roosevelt devoted especial attention. This was unavoidable. By far the larger part of the business of the country was done by corporations as distinguished from partnerships and individual owners. The growth of these gigantic aggregations of capital had been the leading feature in American industrial development during the last two decades of the nineteenth century. In the conquest of business by trusts and "the resulting private fortunes of great magnitude," the Populists and the Democrats had seen a grievous danger to the republic. "Plutocracy has taken the place of democracy; the tariff breeds trusts; let us destroy therefore the tariff and the trusts"—such was the battle cry which had been taken up by Bryan and his followers.

President Roosevelt countered vigorously. He rejected the idea that the trusts were the product of the tariff or of governmental action of any kind. He insisted that they were the outcome of "natural economic forces": (1) destructive competition among business men compelling them to avoid ruin by coöperation in fixing prices; (2) the growth of markets on a national scale and even international scale calling for vast accumulations of capital to carry on such business; (3) the possibility of immense savings by the union of many plants under one management. In the corporation he saw a new stage in the development of American industry. Unregulated competition he regarded as "the source of evils which all men concede must be remedied if this civilization of ours is to survive." The notion, therefore, that these immense business concerns should be or could be broken up by a decree of law, Roosevelt considered absurd.

At the same time he proposed that "evil trusts" should be prevented from "wrong-doing of any kind"; that is, punished for plain swindling, for making agreements to limit output, for refusing to sell to customers who dealt with rival firms, and for conspiracies with railways to ruin competitors by charging high freight rates and for similar abuses. Accordingly, he proposed, not the destruction of the trusts, but their regulation by the government. This, he contended, would preserve the advantages of business on a national scale while preventing the evils that accompanied it. The railway company he declared to be a public servant. "Its rates should be just to and open to all shippers alike." So he answered those who thought that trusts and railway combinations were private concerns to be managed solely by their owners without let or hindrance and also those who thought trusts and railway combinations could be abolished by tariff reduction or criminal prosecution.

The Labor Question.—On the labor question, then pressing to the front in public interest, President Roosevelt took advanced ground for his time. He declared that the working-man, single-handed and empty-handed, threatened with starvation if unemployed, was no match for the employer who was able to bargain and wait. This led him, accordingly, to accept the principle of the trade union; namely, that only by collective bargaining can labor be put on a footing to measure its strength equally with capital. While he severely arraigned labor leaders who advocated violence and destructive doctrines, he held that "the organization of labor into trade unions and federations is necessary, is beneficent, and is one of the greatest possible agencies in the attainment of a true industrial, as well as a true political, democracy in the United States." The last resort of trade unions in labor disputes, the strike, he approved in case negotiations failed to secure "a fair deal."

He thought, however, that labor organizations, even if wisely managed, could not solve all the pressing social questions of the time. The aid of the government at many points he believed to be necessary to eliminate undeserved poverty, industrial diseases, unemployment, and the unfortunate consequences of industrial accidents. In his first message of 1901, for instance, he urged that workers injured in industry should have certain and ample compensation. From time to time he advocated other legislation to obtain what he called "a larger measure of social and industrial justice."

Great Riches and Taxation.—Even the challenge of the radicals, such as the Populists, who alleged that "the toil of millions is boldly stolen to build up colossal fortunes for a few"—challenges which his predecessors did not consider worthy of notice—President Roosevelt refused to let pass without an answer. In his first message he denied the truth of the common saying that the rich were growing richer and the poor were growing poorer. He asserted that, on the contrary, the average man, wage worker, farmer, and small business man, was better off than ever before in the history of our country. That there had been abuses in the accumulation of wealth he did not pretend to ignore, but he believed that even immense fortunes, on the whole, represented positive benefits conferred upon the country. Nevertheless he felt that grave dangers to the safety and the happiness of the people lurked in great inequalities of wealth. In 1906 he wrote that he wished it were in his power to prevent the heaping up of enormous fortunes. The next year, to the astonishment of many leaders in his own party, he boldly announced in a message to Congress that he approved both income and inheritance taxes, then generally viewed as Populist or Democratic measures. He even took the stand that such taxes should be laid in order to bring about a more equitable distribution of wealth and greater equality of opportunity among citizens.

Legislative and Executive Activities

Economic Legislation.—When President Roosevelt turned from the field of opinion he found himself in a different sphere. Many of his views were too advanced for the members of his party in Congress, and where results depended upon the making of new laws, his progress was slow. Nevertheless, in his administrations several measures were enacted that bore the stamp of his theories, though it could hardly be said that he dominated Congress to the same degree as did some other Presidents. The Hepburn Railway Act of 1906 enlarged the interstate commerce commission; it extended the commission's power over oil pipe lines, express companies, and other interstate carriers; it gave the commission the right to reduce rates found to be unreasonable and discriminatory; it forbade "midnight tariffs," that is, sudden changes in rates favoring certain shippers; and it prohibited common carriers from transporting goods owned by themselves, especially coal, except for their own proper use. Two important pure food and drug laws, enacted during the same year, were designed to protect the public against diseased meats and deleterious foods and drugs. A significant piece of labor legislation was an act of the same Congress making interstate railways liable to damages for injuries sustained by their employees. When this measure was declared unconstitutional by the Supreme Court it was reënacted with the objectionable clauses removed. A second installment of labor legislation was offered in the law of 1908 limiting the hours of railway employees engaged as trainmen or telegraph operators.

Reclamation and Conservation.—The open country—the deserts, the forests, waterways, and the public lands—interested President Roosevelt no less than railway and industrial questions. Indeed, in his first message to Congress he placed the conservation of natural resources among "the most vital internal problems" of the age, and forcibly emphasized an issue that had been discussed in a casual way since Cleveland's first administration. The suggestion evoked an immediate response in Congress. Under the leadership of Senator Newlands, of Nevada, the Reclamation Act of 1902 was passed, providing for the redemption of the desert areas of the West. The proceeds from the sale of public lands were dedicated to the construction of storage dams and sluiceways to hold water and divert it as needed to the thirsty sands. Furthermore it was stipulated that the rents paid by water users should go into a reclamation fund to continue the good work forever. Construction was started immediately under the terms of the law. Within seventeen years about 1,600,000 acres had been reclaimed and more than a million were actually irrigated. In the single year 1918, the crops of the irrigated districts were valued at approximately $100,000,000.

In his first message, also, President Roosevelt urged the transfer of all control over national forests to trained men in the Bureau of Forestry—a recommendation carried out in 1907 when the Forestry Service was created. In every direction noteworthy advances were made in the administration of the national domain. The science of forestry was improved and knowledge of the subject spread among the people. Lands in the national forest available for agriculture were opened to settlers. Water power sites on the public domain were leased for a term of years to private companies instead of being sold outright. The area of the national forests was enlarged from 43 million acres to 194 million acres by presidential proclamation—more than 43 million acres being added in one year, 1907. The men who turned sheep and cattle to graze on the public lands were compelled to pay a fair rental, much to their dissatisfaction. Fire prevention work was undertaken in the forests on a large scale, reducing the appalling, annual destruction of timber. Millions of acres of coal land, such as the government had been carelessly selling to mining companies at low figures, were withdrawn from sale and held until Congress was prepared to enact laws for the disposition of them in the public interest. Prosecutions were instituted against men who had obtained public lands by fraud and vast tracts were recovered for the national domain. An agitation was begun which bore fruit under the administrations of Taft and Wilson in laws reserving to the federal government the ownership of coal, water power, phosphates, and other natural resources while authorizing corporations to develop them under leases for a period of years.

The Prosecution of the Trusts.—As an executive, President Roosevelt was also a distinct "personality." His discrimination between "good" and "bad" trusts led him to prosecute some of them with vigor. On his initiative, the Northern Securities Company, formed to obtain control of certain great western railways, was dissolved by order of the Supreme Court. Proceedings were instituted against the American Tobacco Company and the Standard Oil Company as monopolies in violation of the Sherman Anti-Trust law. The Sugar Trust was found guilty of cheating the New York customs house and some of the minor officers were sent to prison. Frauds in the Post-office Department were uncovered and the offenders brought to book. In fact hardly a week passed without stirring news of "wrong doers" and "malefactors" haled into federal courts.

The Great Coal Strike.—The Roosevelt theory that the President could do anything for public welfare not forbidden by the Constitution and the laws was put to a severe test in 1902. A strike of the anthracite coal miners, which started in the summer, ran late into the autumn. Industries were paralyzed for the want of coal; cities were threatened with the appalling menace of a winter without heat. Governors and mayors were powerless and appealed for aid. The mine owners rejected the demands of the men and refused to permit the arbitration of the points in dispute, although John Mitchell, the leader of the miners, repeatedly urged it. After observing closely the course affairs, President Roosevelt made up his mind that the situation was intolerable. He arranged to have the federal troops, if necessary, take possession of the mines and operate them until the strike could be settled. He then invited the contestants to the White House and by dint of hard labor induced them to accept, as a substitute or compromise, arbitration by a commission which he appointed. Thus, by stepping outside the Constitution and acting as the first citizen of the land, President Roosevelt averted a crisis of great magnitude.

The Election of 1904.—The views and measures which he advocated with such vigor aroused deep hostility within as well as without his party. There were rumors of a Republican movement to defeat his nomination in 1904 and it was said that the "financial and corporation interests" were in arms against him. A prominent Republican paper in New York City accused him of having "stolen Mr. Bryan's thunder," by harrying the trusts and favoring labor unions. When the Republican convention assembled in Chicago, however, the opposition disappeared and Roosevelt was nominated by acclamation.

This was the signal for a change on the part of Democratic leaders. They denounced the President as erratic, dangerous, and radical and decided to assume the moderate rôle themselves. They put aside Mr. Bryan and selected as their candidate, Judge Alton B. Parker, of New York, a man who repudiated free silver and made a direct appeal for the conservative vote. The outcome of the reversal was astounding. Judge Parker's vote fell more than a million below that cast for Bryan in 1900; of the 476 electoral votes he received only 140. Roosevelt, in addition to sweeping the Republican sections, even invaded Democratic territory, carrying the state of Missouri. Thus vindicated at the polls, he became more outspoken than ever. His leadership in the party was so widely recognized that he virtually selected his own successor.

THE ADMINISTRATION OF PRESIDENT TAFT

The Campaign of 1908.—Long before the end of his elective term, President Roosevelt let it be known that he favored as his successor, William Howard Taft, of Ohio, his Secretary of War. To attain this end he used every shred of his powerful influence. When the Republican convention assembled, Mr. Taft easily won the nomination. Though the party platform was conservative in tone, he gave it a progressive tinge by expressing his personal belief in the popular election of United States Senators, an income tax, and other liberal measures. President Roosevelt announced his faith in the Republican candidate and appealed to the country for his election.

The turn in Republican affairs now convinced Mr. Bryan that the signs were propitious for a third attempt to win the presidency. The disaster to Judge Parker had taught the party that victory did not lie in a conservative policy. With little difficulty, therefore, the veteran leader from Nebraska once more rallied the Democrats around his standard, won the nomination, and wrote a platform vigorously attacking the tariff, trusts, and monopolies. Supported by a loyal following, he entered the lists, only to meet another defeat. Though he polled almost a million and a half more votes than did Judge Parker in 1904, the palm went to Mr. Taft.

The Tariff Revision and Party Dissensions.—At the very beginning of his term, President Taft had to face the tariff issue. He had met it in the campaign. Moved by the Democratic demand for a drastic reduction, he had expressed opinions which were thought to imply a "downward revision." The Democrats made much of the implication and the Republicans from the Middle West rejoiced in it. Pressure was coming from all sides. More than ten years had elapsed since the enactment of the Dingley bill and the position of many industries had been altered with the course of time. Evidently the day for revision—at best a thankless task—had arrived. Taft accepted the inevitable and called Congress in a special session. Until the midsummer of 1909, Republican Senators and Representatives wrangled over tariff schedules, the President making little effort to influence their decisions. When on August 5 the Payne-Aldrich bill became a law, a breach had been made in Republican ranks. Powerful Senators from the Middle West had spoken angrily against many of the high rates imposed by the bill. They had even broken with their party colleagues to vote against the entire scheme of tariff revision.

The Income Tax Amendment.—The rift in party harmony was widened by another serious difference of opinion. During the debate on the tariff bill, there was a concerted movement to include in it an income tax provision—this in spite of the decision of the Supreme Court in 1895 declaring it unconstitutional. Conservative men were alarmed by the evident willingness of some members to flout a solemn decree of that eminent tribunal. At the same time they saw a powerful combination of Republicans and Democrats determined upon shifting some of the burden of taxation to large incomes. In the press of circumstances, a compromise was reached. The income tax bill was dropped for the present; but Congress passed the sixteenth amendment to the Constitution, authorizing taxes upon incomes from whatever source they might be derived, without reference to any apportionment among the states on the basis of population. The states ratified the amendment and early in 1913 it was proclaimed.

President Taft's Policies.—After the enactment of the tariff bill, Taft continued to push forward with his legislative program. He recommended, and Congress created, a special court of commerce with jurisdiction, among other things, over appeals from the interstate commerce commission, thus facilitating judicial review of the railway rates fixed and the orders issued by that body. This measure was quickly followed by an act establishing a system of postal savings banks in connection with the post office—a scheme which had long been opposed by private banks. Two years later, Congress defied the lobby of the express companies and supplemented the savings banks with a parcels post system, thus enabling the American postal service to catch up with that of other progressive nations. With a view to improving the business administration of the federal government, the President obtained from Congress a large appropriation for an economy and efficiency commission charged with the duty of inquiring into wasteful and obsolete methods and recommending improved devices and practices. The chief result of this investigation was a vigorous report in favor of a national budget system, which soon found public backing.

President Taft negotiated with England and France general treaties providing for the arbitration of disputes which were "justiciable" in character even though they might involve questions of "vital interest and national honor." They were coldly received in the Senate and so amended that Taft abandoned them altogether. A tariff reciprocity agreement with Canada, however, he forced through Congress in the face of strong opposition from his own party. After making a serious breach in Republican ranks, he was chagrined to see the whole scheme come to naught by the overthrow of the Liberals in the Canadian elections of 1911.

Prosecution of the Trusts.—The party schism was even enlarged by what appeared to be the successful prosecution of several great combinations. In two important cases, the Supreme Court ordered the dissolution of the Standard Oil Company and the American Tobacco Company on the ground that they violated the Sherman Anti-Trust law. In taking this step Chief Justice White was at some pains to state that the law did not apply to combinations which did not "unduly" restrain trade. His remark, construed to mean that the Court would not interfere with corporations as such, became the subject of a popular outcry against the President and the judges.

Progressive Insurgency and the Election of 1912

Growing Dissensions.—All in all, Taft's administration from the first day had been disturbed by party discord. High words had passed over the tariff bill and disgruntled members of Congress could not forget them. To differences over issues were added quarrels between youth and old age. In the House of Representatives there developed a group of young "insurgent" Republicans who resented the dominance of the Speaker, Joseph G. Cannon, and other members of the "old guard," asthey named the men of long service and conservative minds. In 1910, the insurgents went so far as to join with the Democrats in a movement to break the Speaker's sway by ousting him from the rules committee and depriving him of the power to appoint its members. The storm was brewing. In the autumn of that year the Democrats won a clear majority in the House of Representatives and began an open battle with President Taft by demanding an immediate downward revision of the tariff.

The Rise of the Progressive Republicans.—Preparatory to the campaign of 1912, the dissenters within the Republican party added the prefix "Progressive" to their old title and began to organize a movement to prevent the renomination of Mr. Taft. As early as January 21, 1911, they formed a Progressive Republican League at the home of Senator La Follette of Wisconsin and launched an attack on the Taft measures and policies. In October they indorsed Mr. La Follette as "the logical Republican candidate" and appealed to the party for support. The controversy over the tariff had grown into a formidable revolt against the occupant of the White House.

Roosevelt in the Field.—After looking on for a while, ex-President Roosevelt took a hand in the fray. Soon after his return in 1910 from a hunting trip in Africa and a tour in Europe, he made a series of addresses in which he formulated a progressive program. In a speech in Kansas, he favored regulation of the trusts, a graduated income tax bearing heavily on great fortunes, tariff revision schedule by schedule, conservation of natural resources, labor legislation, the direct primary, and the recall of elective officials. In an address before the Ohio state constitutional convention in February, 1912, he indorsed the initiative and referendum and announced a doctrine known as the "recall of judicial decisions." This was a new and radical note in American politics. An ex-President of the United States proposed that the people at the polls should have the right to reverse the decision of a judge who set aside any act of a state legislature passed in the interests of social welfare. The Progressive Republicans, impressed by these addresses, turned from La Follette to Roosevelt and on February 24, induced him to come out openly as a candidate against Taft for the Republican nomination.

The Split in the Republican Party.—The country then witnessed the strange spectacle of two men who had once been close companions engaged in a bitter rivalry to secure a majority of the delegates to the Republican convention to be held at Chicago. When the convention assembled, about one-fourth of the seats were contested, the delegates for both candidates loudly proclaiming the regularity of their election. In deciding between the contestants the national committee, after the usual hearings, settled the disputes in such a way that Taft received a safe majority. After a week of negotiation, Roosevelt and his followers left the Republican party. Most of his supporters withdrew from the convention and the few who remained behind refused to answer the roll call. Undisturbed by this formidable bolt, the regular Republicans went on with their work. They renominated Mr. Taft and put forth a platform roundly condemning such Progressive doctrines as the recall of judges.

The Formation of the Progressive Party.—The action of the Republicans in seating the Taft delegates was vigorously denounced by Roosevelt. He declared that the convention had no claim to represent the voters of the Republican party; that any candidate named by it would be "the beneficiary of a successful fraud"; and that it would be deeply discreditable to any man to accept the convention's approval under such circumstances. The bitterness of his followers was extreme. On July 8, a call went forth for a "Progressive" convention to be held in Chicago on August 5. The assembly which duly met on that day was a unique political conference. Prominence was given to women delegates, and "politicians" were notably absent. Roosevelt himself, who was cheered as a conquering hero, made an impassioned speech setting forth his "confession of faith." He was nominated by acclamation; Governor Hiram

Johnson of California was selected as his companion candidate for Vice President. The platform endorsed such political reforms as woman suffrage, direct primaries, the initiative, referendum, and recall, popular election of United States Senators, and the short ballot. It favored a program of social legislation, including the prohibition of child labor and minimum wages for women. It approved the regulation, rather than the dissolution, of the trusts. Like apostles in a new and lofty cause, the Progressives entered a vigorous campaign for the election of their distinguished leader.

Woodrow Wilson and the Election of 1912.—With the Republicans divided, victory loomed up before the Democrats. Naturally, a terrific contest over the nomination occurred at their convention in Baltimore. Champ Clark, Speaker of the House of Representatives, and Governor Woodrow Wilson, of New Jersey, were the chief contestants. After tossing to and fro for seven long, hot days, and taking forty-six ballots, the delegates, powerfully influenced by Mr. Bryan, finally decided in favor of the governor. As a professor, a writer on historical and political subjects, and the president of Princeton University, Mr. Wilson had become widely known in public life. As the governor of New Jersey he had attracted the support of the progressives in both parties. With grim determination he had "waged war on the bosses," and pushed through the legislature measures establishing direct primaries, regulating public utilities, and creating a system of workmen's compensation in industries. During the presidential campaign that followed Governor Wilson toured the country and aroused great enthusiasm by a series of addresses later published under the title of *The New Freedom*. He declared that "the government of the United States is at present the foster child of the special interests." He proposed to free the country by breaking the dominance of "the big bankers, the big manufacturers, the big masters of commerce, the heads of railroad corporations and of steamship corporations."

In the election Governor Wilson easily secured a majority of the electoral votes, and his party, while retaining possession of the House of Representatives, captured the Senate as well. The popular verdict, however, indicated a state of confusion in the country. The combined Progressive and Republican vote exceeded that of the Democrats by 1,300,000. The Socialists, with Eugene V. Debs as their candidate again, polled about 900,000 votes, more than double the number received four years before. Thus, as the result of an extraordinary upheaval the Republicans, after holding the office of President for sixteen years, passed out of power, and the government of the country was intrusted to the Democrats under the leadership of a man destined to be one of the outstanding figures of the modern age, Woodrow Wilson.

General References

J.B. Bishop, *Theodore Roosevelt and His Time* (2 vols.).

Theodore Roosevelt, *Autobiography*; *New Nationalism*; *Progressive Principles*.

W.H. Taft, *Popular Government*.

Walter Weyl, *The New Democracy*.

H. Croly, *The Promise of American Life*.

J.B. Bishop, *The Panama Gateway*.

J.B. Scott, *The Hague Peace Conferences*.

W.B. Munro (ed.), *Initiative, Referendum, and Recall*.

C.R. Van Hise, *The Conservation of Natural Resources*.

Gifford Pinchot, *The Fight for Conservation*.

W.F. Willoughby, *Territories and Dependencies of the United States* (1905).

Research Topics

Roosevelt and "Big Business."—Haworth, *The United States in Our Own Time*, pp. 281-289; F.A. Ogg, *National Progress* (American Nation Series), pp. 40-75; Paxson, *The New Nation* (Riverside Series), pp. 293-307.

Our Insular Possessions.—Elson, *History of the United States*, pp. 896-904.

Latin-American Relations.—Haworth, pp. 294-299; Ogg, pp. 254-257.

The Panama Canal.—Haworth, pp. 300-309; Ogg, pp. 266-277; Paxson, pp. 286-292; Elson, pp. 906-911.

Conservation.—Haworth, pp. 331-334; Ogg, pp. 96-115; Beard, *American Government and Politics* (3d ed.), pp. 401-416.

Republican Dissensions under Taft's Administration.—Haworth, pp. 351-360; Ogg, pp. 167-186; Paxson, pp. 324-342; Elson, pp. 916-924.

The Campaign of 1912.—Haworth, pp. 360-379; Ogg, pp. 187-208.

Questions

1. Compare the early career of Roosevelt with that of some other President.

2. Name the chief foreign and domestic questions of the Roosevelt-Taft administrations.

3. What international complications were involved in the Panama Canal problem?

4. Review the Monroe Doctrine. Discuss Roosevelt's applications of it.

5. What is the strategic importance of the Caribbean to the United States?

6. What is meant by the sea power? Trace the voyage of the fleet around the world and mention the significant imperial and commercial points touched.

7. What is meant by the question: "Does the Constitution follow the flag?"

8. Trace the history of self-government in Porto Rico. In the Philippines.

9. What is Cuba's relation to the United States?

10. What was Roosevelt's theory of our Constitution?

11. Give Roosevelt's views on trusts, labor, taxation.

12. Outline the domestic phases of Roosevelt's administrations.

13. Account for the dissensions under Taft.

14. Trace the rise of the Progressive movement.

15. What was Roosevelt's progressive program?

16. Review Wilson's early career and explain the underlying theory of *The New Freedom*.

CHAPTER XXII

THE SPIRIT OF REFORM IN AMERICA

AN AGE OF CRITICISM

Attacks on Abuses in American Life.—The crisis precipitated by the Progressive uprising was not a sudden and unexpected one. It had been long in preparation. The revolt against corruption in politics which produced the Liberal Republican outbreak in the seventies and the Mugwump movement of the eighties was followed by continuous criticism of American political and economic development. From 1880 until his death in 1892, George William Curtis, as president of the Civil Service Reform Association, kept up a running fire upon the abuses of the spoils system. James Bryce, an observant English scholar and man of affairs, in his great work, *The American Commonwealth*, published in 1888, by picturing fearlessly the political rings and machines which dominated the cities, gave the whole country a fresh shock. Six years later Henry D. Lloyd, in a powerful book entitled *Wealth against Commonwealth*, attacked in scathing language certain trusts which had destroyed their rivals and bribed public officials. In 1903 Miss Ida Tarbell, an author of established reputation in the historical field, gave to the public an account of the Standard Oil Company, revealing the ruthless methods of that corporation in crushing competition. About the same time Lincoln Steffens exposed the sordid character of politics in several municipalities in a series of articles bearing the painful heading: *The Shame of the Cities*. The critical spirit appeared in almost every form; in weekly and monthly magazines, in essays and pamphlets, in editorials and news stories, in novels like Churchill's *Coniston* and Sinclair's *The Jungle*. It became so savage and so wanton that the opening years of the twentieth century were well named "the age of the muckrakers."

The Subjects of the Criticism.—In this outburst of invective, nothing was spared. It was charged that each of the political parties had fallen into the hands of professional politicians who devoted their time to managing conventions, making platforms, nominating candidates, and dictating to officials; in return for their "services" they sold offices and privileges. It was alleged that mayors and councils had bargained away for private benefit street railway and other franchises. It was asserted that many powerful labor unions were dominated by men who blackmailed employers. Some critics specialized in descriptions of the poverty, slums, and misery of great cities. Others took up "frenzied finance" and accused financiers of selling worthless stocks and bonds to an innocent public. Still others professed to see in the accumulations of millionaires the downfall of our republic.

The Attack on "Invisible Government."—Some even maintained that the control of public affairs had passed from the people to a sinister minority called "the invisible government." So eminent and conservative a statesman as the Hon. Elihu Root lent the weight of his great name to such an imputation. Speaking of his native state, New York, he said: "What is the government of this state? What has it been during the forty years of my acquaintance with it? The government of the Constitution? Oh, no; not half the time or half way.... From the days of Fenton and Conkling and Arthur and Cornell and Platt, from the days of David B. Hill down to the present time, the government of the state has presented two different lines of activity: one, of the constitutional and statutory officers of the state and the other of the party leaders; they call them party bosses. They call the system—I don't coin the phrase—the system they call 'invisible government.' For I don't know how many years Mr. Conkling was the supreme ruler in this state. The governor did not count, the legislature did not count, comptrollers and secretaries of state and what not did not count. It was what Mr. Conkling said, and in a great outburst of public rage he was pulled down. Then Mr. Platt ruled the state; for nigh upon twenty years he ruled it. It was not the governor; it was not the legislature; it was Mr. Platt. And the capital was not here [in Albany]; it was at 49 Broadway; Mr. Platt and his lieutenants. It makes no difference what name you give, whether you call it Fenton or Conkling or Cornell or Arthur or Platt or by the names of men now living. The ruler of the state during the greater part of the forty years of my acquaintance with the state government has not been any man authorized by the constitution or by law.... The party leader is elected by no one, accountable to no one, bound by no oath of office, removable by no one."

The Nation Aroused.—With the spirit of criticism came also the spirit of reform. The charges were usually exaggerated; often wholly false; but there was enough truth in them to warrant renewed vigilance on the part of American democracy. President Roosevelt doubtless summed up the sentiment of the great majority of citizens when he demanded the punishment of wrong-doers in 1907, saying: "It makes not a particle of difference whether these crimes are committed by a capitalist or by a laborer, by a leading banker or manufacturer or railroad man or by a leading representative of a labor union. Swindling in stocks, corrupting legislatures, making fortunes by the inflation of securities, by wrecking railroads, by destroying competitors through rebates—these forms of wrong-doing in the capitalist are far more infamous than any ordinary form of embezzlement or forgery." The time had come, he added, to stop "muckraking" and proceed to the constructive work of removing the abuses that had grown up.

POLITICAL REFORMS

The Public Service.—It was a wise comprehension of the needs of American democracy that led the friends of reform to launch and to sustain for more than half a century a movement to improve the public service. On the one side they struck at the spoils system; at the right of the politicians to use public offices as mere rewards for partisan work. The federal civil service act of 1883 opened the way to reform by establishing five vital principles in law: (1) admission to office, not on the recommendation of party workers, but on the basis of competitive examinations; (2) promotion for meritorious service of the government rather than of parties; (3) no assessment of office holders for campaign funds; (4) permanent tenure during good behavior; and (5) no dismissals for political reasons. The act itself at first applied to only 14,000 federal offices, but under the constant pressure from the reformers it was extended until in 1916 it covered nearly 300,000 employees out of an executive force of approximately 414,000. While gaining steadily at Washington, civil service reformers carried their agitation into the states and cities. By 1920 they were able to report ten states with civil service commissions and the merit system well intrenched in more than three hundred municipalities.

In excluding spoilsmen from public office, the reformers were, in a sense, engaged in a negative work: that of "keeping the rascals out." But there was a second and larger phase to their movement, one constructive in character: that of getting skilled, loyal, and efficient servants into the places of responsibility. Everywhere on land and sea, in town and country, new burdens were laid upon public officers. They were called upon to supervise the ships sailing to and from our ports; to inspect the water and milk supplies of our cities; to construct and operate great public works, such as the Panama and Erie canals; to regulate the complicated rates of railway companies; to safeguard health and safety in a thousand ways; to climb the mountains to fight forest fires; and to descend into the deeps of the earth to combat the deadly coal gases that assail the miners. In a word, those who labored to master the secrets and the powers of nature were summoned to the aid of the government: chemists, engineers, architects, nurses, surgeons, foresters—the skilled in all the sciences, arts, and crafts.

Keeping rascals out was no task at all compared with the problem of finding competent people for all the technical offices. "Now," said the reformers, "we must make attractive careers in the government work for the best American talent; we must train those applying for admission and increase the skill of those already in positions of trust; we must see to it that those entering at the bottom have a chance to rise to the top; in short, we must work for a government as skilled and efficient as it is strong, one commanding all the wisdom and talent of America that public welfare requires."

The Australian Ballot.—A second line of attack on the political machines was made in connection with the ballot. In the early days elections were frequently held in the open air and the poll was taken by a show of hands or by the enrollment of the voters under names of their favorite candidates. When this ancient practice was abandoned in favor of the printed ballot, there was still no secrecy about elections. Each party prepared its own ballot, often of a distinctive color, containing the names of its candidates. On election day, these papers were handed out to the voters by party workers. Any one could tell from the color of the ballot dropped into the box, or from some mark on the outside of the folded ballot, just how each man voted. Those who bought votes were sure that their purchases were "delivered." Those who intimidated voters could know when their intimidation was effective. In this way the party ballot strengthened the party machine.

As a remedy for such abuses, reformers, learning from the experience of Australia, urged the adoption of the "Australian ballot." That ballot, though it appeared in many forms, had certain constant features. It was official, that is, furnished by the government, not by party workers; it contained the names of all candidates of all parties; it was given out only in the polling places; and it was marked in secret. The first state to introduce it was Massachusetts. The year was 1888. Before the end of the century it had been adopted by nearly all the states in the union. The salutary effect of the reform in reducing the amount of cheating and bribery in elections was beyond all question.

The Direct Primary.—In connection with the uprising against machine politics, came a call for the abolition of the old method of nominating candidates by conventions. These time-honored party assemblies, which had come down from the days of Andrew Jackson, were, it was said, merely conclaves of party workers, sustained by the spoils system, and dominated by an inner circle of bosses. The remedy offered in this case was again "more democracy," namely, the abolition of the party convention and the adoption of the direct primary. Candidates were no longer to be chosen by secret conferences. Any member of a party was to be allowed to run for any office, to present his name to his party by securing signatures to a petition, and to submit his candidacy to his fellow partisans at a direct primary—an election within the party. In this movement Governor La Follette of Wisconsin took the lead and his state was the first in the union to adopt the direct primary for state-wide purposes. The idea spread, rapidly in the West, more slowly in the East. The public, already angered against "the bosses," grasped eagerly at it. Governor Hughes in New York pressed it upon the unwilling legislature. State after state accepted it until by 1918 Rhode Island, Delaware, Connecticut, and New Mexico were the only states that had not bowed to the storm. Still the results were disappointing and at that very time the pendulum was beginning to swing backward.

Popular Election of Federal Senators.—While the movement for direct primaries was still advancing everywhere, a demand for the popular election of Senators, usually associated with it, swept forward to victory. Under the original Constitution, it had been expressly provided that Senators should be chosen by the legislatures of the states. In practice this rule transferred the selection of Senators to secret caucuses of party members in the state legislatures. In connection with these caucuses there had been many scandals, some direct proofs of brazen bribery and corruption, and dark hints besides. The Senate was called by its detractors "a millionaires' club" and it was looked upon as the "citadel of conservatism." The prescription in this case was likewise "more democracy"—direct election of Senators by popular vote.

This reform was not a new idea. It had been proposed in Congress as early as 1826. President Johnson, an ardent advocate, made it the subject of a special message in 1868 Not long afterward it appeared in Congress. At last in 1893, the year after the great Populist upheaval, the House of Representatives by the requisite two-thirds vote incorporated it in an amendment to the federal Constitution. Again and again it passed the House; but the Senate itself was obdurate. Able Senators leveled their batteries against it. Mr. Hoar of Massachusetts declared that it would transfer the seat of power to the "great cities and masses of population"; that it would "overthrow the whole scheme of the Senate and in the end the whole scheme of the national Constitution as designed and established by the framers of the Constitution and the people who adopted it."

Failing in the Senate, advocates of popular election made a rear assault through the states. They induced state legislatures to enact laws requiring the nomination of candidates for the Senate by the direct primary, and then they bound the legislatures to abide by the popular choice. Nevada took the lead in 1899. Shortly afterward Oregon, by the use of the initiative and referendum, practically bound legislators to accept the popular nominee and the country witnessed the spectacle of a Republican legislature "electing" a Democrat to represent the state in the Senate at Washington. By 1910 three-fourths of the states had applied the direct primary in some form to the choice of Senators. Men selected by that method began to pour in upon the floors of Congress; finally in 1912 the two-thirds majority was secured for an amendment to the federal Constitution providing for the popular election of Senators. It was quickly ratified by the states. The following year it was proclaimed in effect.

The Initiative and Referendum.—As a corrective for the evils which had grown up in state legislatures there arose a demand for the introduction of a Swiss device known as the initiative and referendum. The initiative permits any one to draw up a proposed bill; and, on securing a certain number of signatures among the voters, to require the submission of the measure to the people at an election. If the bill thus initiated receives a sufficient majority, it becomes a law. The referendum allows citizens who disapprove any act passed by the legislature to get up a petition against it and thus bring about a reference of the measure to the voters at the polls for approval or rejection. These two practices constitute a form of "direct government."

These devices were prescribed "to restore the government to the people." The Populists favored them in their platform of 1896. Mr. Bryan, two years later, made them a part of his program, and in the same year South Dakota adopted them. In 1902 Oregon, after a strenuous campaign, added a direct legislation amendment to the state constitution. Within ten years all the Southwestern, Mountain, and Pacific states, except Texas and Wyoming, had followed this example. To the east of the Mississippi, however, direct legislation met a chilly reception. By 1920 only five states in this section had accepted it: Maine, Massachusetts, Ohio, Michigan, and Maryland, the last approving the referendum only.

The Recall.—Executive officers and judges, as well as legislatures, had come in for their share of criticism, and it was proposed that they should likewise be subjected to a closer scrutiny by the public. For this purpose there was advanced a scheme known as the recall—which permitted a certain percentage of the voters to compel any officer, at any time during his term, to go before the people at a new election. This feature of direct government, tried out first in the city of Los Angeles, was extended to state-wide uses in Oregon in 1908. It failed, however, to capture popular imagination to the same degree as the initiative and referendum. At the end of ten years' agitation, only ten states, mainly in the West, had adopted it for general purposes, and four of them did not apply it to the judges of the courts. Still it was extensively acclaimed in cities and incorporated into hundreds of municipal laws and charters.

As a general proposition, direct government in all its forms was bitterly opposed by men of a conservative cast of mind. It was denounced by Senator Henry Cabot Lodge as "nothing less than a complete revolution in the fabric of our government and in the fundamental principles upon which that government rests." In his opinion, it promised to break down the representative principle and "undermine and overthrow the bulwarks of ordered liberty and individual freedom." Mr. Taft shared Mr. Lodge's views and spoke of direct government with scorn. "Votes," he exclaimed, "are not bread ... referendums do not pay rent or furnish houses, recalls do not furnish clothes, initiatives do not supply employment or relieve inequalities of condition or of opportunity."

Commission Government for Cities.—In the restless searching out of evils, the management of cities early came under critical scrutiny. City government, Mr. Bryce had remarked, was the one conspicuous failure in America. This sharp thrust, though resented by some, was accepted as a warning by others. Many prescriptions were offered by doctors of the body politic. Chief among them was the idea of simplifying the city government so that the light of public scrutiny could shine through it. "Let us elect only a few men and make them clearly responsible for the city government!" was the new cry in municipal reform. So, many city councils were reduced in size; one of the two houses, which several cities had adopted in imitation of the federal government, was abolished; and in order that the mayor could be held to account, he was given the power to appoint all the chief officials. This made the mayor, in some cases, the only elective city official and gave the voters a "short ballot" containing only a few names—an idea which some proposed to apply also to the state government.

A further step in the concentration of authority was taken in Galveston, Texas, where the people, looking upon the ruin of their city wrought by the devastating storm of 1901, and confronted by the difficult problems of reconstruction, felt the necessity for a more businesslike management of city affairs and instituted a new form of local administration. They abolished the old scheme of mayor and council and vested all power in five commissioners, one of whom, without any special prerogatives, was assigned to the office of "mayor president." In 1908, the commission form of government, as it was soon characterized, was adopted by Des Moines, Iowa. The attention of all municipal reformers was drawn to it and it was hailed as the guarantee of a better day. By 1920, more than four hundred cities, including Memphis, Spokane, Birmingham, Newark, and Buffalo, had adopted it. Still the larger cities like New York and Chicago kept their boards of aldermen.

The City Manager Plan.—A few years' experience with commission government revealed certain patent defects. The division of the work among five men was frequently found to introduce dissensions and irresponsibility. Commissioners were often lacking in the technical ability required to manage such difficult matters as fire and police protection, public health, public works, and public utilities. Some one then proposed to carry over into city government an idea from the business world. In that sphere the stockholders of each corporation elect the directors and the directors, in turn, choose a business manager to conduct the affairs of the company. It was suggested that the city commissioners, instead of attempting to supervise the details of the city administration, should select a manager to do this. The scheme was put into effect in Sumter, South Carolina, in 1912. Like the commission plan, it became popular. Within eight years more than one hundred and fifty towns and cities had adopted it. Among the larger municipalities were Dayton, Springfield (Ohio), Akron, Kalamazoo, and Phoenix. It promised to create a new public service profession, that of city manager.

MEASURES OF ECONOMIC REFORM

The Spirit of American Reform.—The purification of the ballot, the restriction of the spoils system, the enlargement of direct popular control over the organs of government were not the sole answers made by the reformers to the critics of American institutions. Nor were they the most important. In fact, they were regarded not as ends in themselves, but as means to serve a wider purpose. That purpose was the promotion of the "general welfare." The concrete objects covered by that broad term were many and varied; but they included the prevention of extortion by railway and other corporations, the protection of public health, the extension of education, the improvement of living conditions in the cities, the elimination of undeserved poverty, the removal of gross inequalities in wealth, and more equality of opportunity.

All these things involved the use of the powers of government. Although a few clung to the ancient doctrine that the government should not interfere with private business at all, the American people at large rejected that theory as vigorously as they rejected the doctrines of an extreme socialism which exalts the state above the individual. Leaders representing every shade of opinion proclaimed the government an instrument of common welfare to be used in the public interest. "We must abandon definitely," said Roosevelt, "the *laissez-faire* theory of political economy and fearlessly champion a system of increased governmental control, paying no attention to the cries of worthy people who denounce this as socialistic." This view was shared by Mr. Taft, who observed: "Undoubtedly the government can wisely do much more ... to relieve the oppressed, to create greater equality of opportunity, to make reasonable terms for labor in employment, and to furnish vocational education." He was quick to add his caution that "there is a line beyond which the government cannot go with any good practical results in seeking to make men and society better."

The Regulation of Railways.—The first attempts to use the government in a large way to control private enterprise in the public interest were made by the Northwestern states in the decade between 1870 and 1880. Charges were advanced by the farmers, particularly those organized into Granges, that the railways extorted the highest possible rates for freight and passengers, that favoritism was shown to large shippers, that fraudulent stocks and bonds were sold to the innocent public. It was claimed that railways were not like other enterprises, but were "quasi-public" concerns, like the roads and ferries, and thus subject to government control. Accordingly laws were enacted bringing the railroads under state supervision. In some cases the state legislature fixed the maximum rates to be charged by common carriers, and in other cases commissions were created with the power to establish the rates after an investigation. This legislation was at first denounced in the East as nothing less than the "confiscation" of the railways in the interest of the farmers. Attempts to have the Supreme Court of the United States declare it unconstitutional were made without avail; still a principle was finally laid down to the effect that in fixing rates state legislatures and commissions must permit railway companies to earn a "fair" return on the capital invested.

In a few years the Granger spirit appeared in Congress. An investigation revealed a long list of abuses committed by the railways against shippers and travelers. The result was the interstate commerce act of 1887, which created the Interstate Commerce Commission, forbade discriminations in rates, and prohibited other objectionable practices on the part of railways. This measure was loosely enforced and the abuses against which it was directed continued almost unabated. A demand for stricter control grew louder and louder. Congress was forced to heed. In 1903 it enacted the Elkins law, forbidding railways to charge rates other than those published, and laid penalties upon the officers and agents of companies, who granted secret favors to shippers, and upon shippers who accepted them. Three years later a still more drastic step was taken by the passage of the Hepburn act. The Interstate Commerce Commission was authorized, upon complaint of some party aggrieved, and after a public hearing, to determine whether just and reasonable rates had been charged by the companies. In effect, the right to fix freight and passenger rates was taken out of the hands of the owners of the railways engaged in interstate commerce and vested in the hands of the Interstate Commerce Commission. Thus private property to the value of $20,000,000,000 or more was declared to be a matter of public concern and subject to government regulation in the common interest.

Municipal Utilities.—Similar problems arose in connection with the street railways, electric light plants, and other utilities in the great cities. In the beginning the right to construct such undertakings was freely, and often corruptly, granted to private companies by city councils. Distressing abuses arose in connection with such practices. Many grants or franchises were made perpetual, or perhaps for a term of 999 years. The rates charged and services rendered were left largely to the will of the companies holding the franchises. Mergers or unions of companies were common and the public was deluged with stocks and bonds of doubtful value; bankruptcies were frequent. The connection between the utility companies and the politicians was, to say the least, not always in the public interest.

American ingenuity was quick to devise methods for eliminating such evils. Three lines of progress were laid out by the reformers. One group proposed that such utilities should be subject to municipal or state regulation, that the formation of utility companies should be under public control, and that the issue of stocks and bonds must be approved by public authority. In some cases state, and in other cases municipal, commissions were created to exercise this great power over "quasi-public corporations." Wisconsin, by laws enacted in 1907, put all heat, light, water works, telephone, and street railway companies under the supervision of a single railway commission. Other states followed this example rapidly. By 1920 the principle of public control over municipal utilities was accepted in nearly every section of the union.

A second line of reform appeared in the "model franchise" for utility corporations. An illustration of this tendency was afforded by the Chicago street railway settlement of 1906. The total capital of the company was fixed at a definite sum, its earnings were agreed upon, and the city was given the right to buy and operate the system if it desired to do so. In many states, about the same time, it was provided that no franchises to utility companies could run more than twenty-five years.

A third group of reformers were satisfied with nothing short of municipal ownership. They proposed to drive private companies entirely out of the field and vest the ownership and management of municipal plants in the city itself. This idea was extensively applied to electric light and water works plants, but to street railways in only a few cities, including San Francisco and Seattle. In New York the subways are owned by the city but leased for operation.

Tenement House Control.—Among the other pressing problems of the cities was the overcrowding in houses unfit for habitation. An inquiry in New York City made under the authority of the state in 1902 revealed poverty, misery, slums, dirt, and disease almost beyond imagination. The immediate answer was the enactment of a tenement house law prescribing in great detail the size of the rooms, the air space, the light and the sanitary arrangement for all new buildings. An immense improvement followed and the idea was quickly taken up in other states having large industrial centers. In 1920 New York made a further invasion of the rights of landlords by assuring to the public "reasonable rents" for flats and apartments.

Workmen's Compensation.—No small part of the poverty in cities was due to the injury of wage-earners while at their trade. Every year the number of men and women killed or wounded in industry mounted higher. Under the old law, the workman or his family had to bear the loss unless the employer had been guilty of some extraordinary negligence. Even in that case an expensive lawsuit was usually necessary to recover "damages." In short, although employers insured their buildings and machinery against necessary risks from fire and storm, they allowed their employees to assume the heavy losses due to accidents. The injustice of this, though apparent enough now, was once not generally recognized. It was said to be unfair to make the employer pay for injuries for which he was not personally responsible; but the argument was overborne.

About 1910 there set in a decided movement in the direction of lifting the burden of accidents from the unfortunate victims. In the first place, laws were enacted requiring employers to pay damages in certain amounts according to the nature of the case, no matter how the accident occurred, as long as the injured person was not guilty of willful negligence. By 1914 more than one-half the states had such laws. In the second place, there developed schemes of industrial insurance in the form of automatic grants made by state commissions to persons injured in industries, the funds to be provided by the employers or the state or by both. By 1917 thirty-six states had legislation of this type.

Minimum Wages and Mothers' Pensions.—Another source of poverty, especially among women and children, was found to be the low wages paid for their labor. Report after report showed this. In 1912 Massachusetts took a significant step in the direction of declaring the minimum wages which might be paid to women and children. Oregon, the following year, created a commission with power to prescribe minimum wages in certain industries, based on the cost of living, and to enforce the rates fixed. Within a short time one-third of the states had legislation of this character. To cut away some of the evils of poverty and enable widows to keep their homes intact and bring up their children, a device known as mothers' pensions became popular during the second decade of the twentieth century. At the opening of 1913 two states, Colorado and Illinois, had laws authorizing the payment from public funds of definite sums to widows with children. Within four years, thirty-five states had similar legislation.

Taxation and Great Fortunes.—As a part of the campaign waged against poverty by reformers there came a demand for heavy taxes upon great fortunes, particularly taxes upon inheritances or estates passing to heirs on the decease of the owners. Roosevelt was an ardent champion of this type of taxation and dwelt upon it at length in his message to Congress in 1907. "Such a tax," he said, "would help to preserve a measurable equality of opportunity for the people of the generations growing to manhood.... Our aim is to recognize what Lincoln pointed out: the fact that there are some respects in which men are obviously not equal; but also to insist that there should be equality of self-respect and of mutual respect, an equality of rights before the law, and at least an approximate equality in the conditions under which each man obtains the chance to show the stuff that is in him when compared with his fellows."

The spirit of the new age was, therefore, one of reform, not of revolution. It called for no evolutionary or utopian experiments, but for the steady and progressive enactment of measures aimed at admitted abuses and designed to accomplish tangible results in the name of public welfare.

General References

J. Bryce, *The American Commonwealth*.

R.C. Brooks, *Corruption in American Life*.

E.A. Ross, *Changing America*.

P.L. Haworth, *America in Ferment*.

E.R.A. Seligman, *The Income Tax*.

W.Z. Ripley, *Railroads: Rates and Regulation*.

E.S. Bradford, *Commission Government in American Cities*.

H.R. Seager, *A Program of Social Reform*.

C. Zueblin, *American Municipal Progress*.

W.E. Walling, *Progressivism and After*.

The American Year Book (an annual publication which contains reviews of reform legislation).

Research Topics

"The Muckrakers."—Paxson, *The New Nation* (Riverside Series), pp. 309-323.

Civil Service Reform.—Beard, *American Government and Politics* (3d ed.), pp. 222-230; Ogg, *National Progress* (American Nation Series), pp. 135-142.

Direct Government.—Beard, *American Government*, pp. 461-473; Ogg, pp. 160-166.

Popular Election of Senators.—Beard, *American Government*, pp. 241-244; Ogg, pp. 149-150.

Party Methods.—Beard, *American Government*, pp. 656-672.

Ballot Reform.—Beard, *American Government*, pp. 672-705.

Social and Economic Legislation.—Beard, *American Government*, pp. 721-752.

Questions

1. Who were some of the critics of abuses in American life?

2. What particular criticisms were advanced?

3. How did Elihu Root define "invisible government"?

4. Discuss the use of criticism as an aid to progress in a democracy.

5. Explain what is meant by the "merit system" in the civil service. Review the rise of the spoils system.

6. Why is the public service of increasing importance? Give some of its new problems.

7. Describe the Australian ballot and the abuses against which it is directed.

8. What are the elements of direct government? Sketch their progress in the United States.

9. Trace the history of popular election of Senators.

10. Explain the direct primary. Commission government. The city manager plan.

11. How does modern reform involve government action? On what theory is it justified?

12. Enumerate five lines of recent economic reform.

CHAPTER XXIII

THE NEW POLITICAL DEMOCRACY

Women in Public Affairs.—The social legislation enacted in response to the spirit of reform vitally affected women in the home and in industry and was promoted by their organizations. Where they did not lead, they were affiliated with movements for social improvement. No cause escaped their attention; no year passed without widening the range of their interests. They served on committees that inquired into the problems of the day; they appeared before legislative assemblies to advocate remedies for the evils they discovered. By 1912 they were a force to be reckoned with in national politics. In nine states complete and equal suffrage had been established, and a widespread campaign for a national suffrage amendment was in full swing. On every hand lay evidences that their sphere had been broadened to include public affairs. This was the culmination of forces that had long been operating.

A New Emphasis in History.—A movement so deeply affecting important interests could not fail to find a place in time in the written record of human progress. History often began as a chronicle of kings and queens, knights and ladies, written partly to amuse and partly to instruct the classes that appeared in its pages. With the growth of commerce, parliaments, and international relations, politics and diplomacy were added to such chronicles of royal and princely doings. After the rise of democracy, industry, and organized labor, the transactions of everyday life were deemed worthy of a place in the pages of history. In each case history was rewritten and the past rediscovered in the light of the new age. So it will be with the rise and growth of women's political power. The history of their labor, their education, their status in society, their influence on the course of events will be explored and given its place in the general record.

It will be a history of change. The superior position which women enjoy in America to-day is the result of a slow evolution from an almost rightless condition in colonial times. The founders of America brought with them the English common law. Under that law, a married woman's personal property—jewels, money, furniture, and the like—became her husband's property; the management of her lands passed into his control. Even the wages she earned, if she worked for some one else, belonged to him. Custom, if not law, prescribed that women should not take part in town meetings or enter into public discussions of religious questions. Indeed it is a far cry from the banishment of Anne Hutchinson from Massachusetts in 1637, for daring to dispute with the church fathers, to the political conventions of 1920 in which women sat as delegates, made nominating speeches, and served on committees. In the contrast between these two scenes may be measured the change in the privileges of women since the landing of the Pilgrims. The account of this progress is a narrative of individual effort on the part of women, of organizations among them, of generous aid from sympathetic men in the long agitation for the removal of civil and political disabilities. It is in part also a narrative of irresistible economic change which drew women into industry, created a leisure class, gave women wages and incomes, and therewith economic independence.

THE RISE OF THE WOMAN MOVEMENT

Protests of Colonial Women.—The republican spirit which produced American independence was of slow and steady growth. It did not spring up full-armed in a single night. It was, on the contrary, nourished during a long period of time by fireside discussions as well as by debates in the public forum. Women shared that fireside sifting of political principles and passed on the findings of that scrutiny in letters to their friends, newspaper articles, and every form of written word. How widespread was this potent, though not spectacular force, is revealed in the collections of women's letters, articles, songs, dramas, and satirical "skits" on English rule that have come down to us. In this search into the reasons of government, some women began to take thought about laws that excluded them from the ballot. Two women at least left their protests on record. Abigail, the ingenious and witty wife of John Adams, wrote to her husband, in March, 1776, that women objected "to all arbitrary power whether of state or males" and demanded political privileges in the new order then being created. Hannah Lee Corbin, the sister of "Lighthorse" Harry Lee, protested to her brother against the taxation of women without representation.

The Stir among European Women.—Ferment in America, in the case of women as of men, was quickened by events in Europe. In 1792, Mary Wollstonecraft published in England the *Vindication of the Rights of Women*—a book that was destined to serve the cause of liberty among women as the writings of Locke and Paine had served that of men. The specific grievances which stirred English women were men's invasion of women's industries, such as spinning and weaving; the denial of equal educational opportunities; and political disabilities. In France also the great Revolution raised questionings about the status of women. The rights of "citizenesses" as well as the rights of "citizens" were examined by the boldest thinkers. This in turn reacted upon women in the United States.

Leadership in America.—The origins of the American woman movement are to be found in the writings of a few early intellectual leaders. During the first decades of the nineteenth century, books, articles, and pamphlets about women came in increasing numbers from the press. Lydia Maria Child wrote a history of women; Margaret Fuller made a critical examination of the status of women in her time; and Mrs. Elizabeth Ellet supplemented the older histories by showing what an important part women had played in the American Revolution.

The Struggle for Education.—Along with criticism, there was carried on a constructive struggle for better educational facilities for women who had been from the beginning excluded from every college in the country. In this long battle, Emma Willard and Mary Lyon led the way; the former founded a seminary at Troy, New York; and the latter made the beginnings of Mount Holyoke College in Massachusetts. Oberlin College in Ohio, established in 1833, opened its doors to girls and from it were graduated young students to lead in the woman movement. Sarah J. Hale, who in 1827 became the editor of a "Ladies' Magazine," published in Boston, conducted a campaign for equal educational opportunities which helped to bear fruit in the founding of Vassar College shortly after the Civil War.

The Desire to Effect Reforms.—As they came to study their own history and their own part in civilization, women naturally became deeply interested in all the controversies going on around them. The temperance question made a special appeal to them and they organized to demand the right to be heard on it. In 1846 the "Daughters of Temperance" formed a secret society favoring prohibition. They dared to criticize the churches for their indifference and were so bold as to ask that drunkenness be made a ground for divorce.

The slavery issue even more than temperance called women into public life. The Grimké sisters of South Carolina emancipated their bondmen, and one of these sisters, exiled from Charleston for her "Appeal to the Christian Women of the South," went North to work against the slavery system. In 1837 the National Women's Anti-Slavery Convention met in New York; seventy-one women delegates represented eight states. Three years later eight American women, five of them in Quaker costume, attended the World Anti-Slavery Convention in London, much to the horror of the men, who promptly excluded them from the sessions on the ground that it was not fitting for women to take part in such meetings.

In other spheres of activity, especially social service, women steadily enlarged their interest. Nothing human did they consider alien to them. They inveighed against cruel criminal laws and unsanitary prisons. They organized poor relief and led in private philanthropy. Dorothea Dix directed the movement that induced the New York legislature to establish in 1845 a separate asylum for the criminal insane. In the same year Sarah G. Bagley organized the Lowell Female Reform Association for the purpose of reducing the long hours of labor for women, safeguarding "the constitutions of future generations." Mrs. Eliza Woodson Farnham, matron in Sing Sing penitentiary, was known throughout the nation for her social work, especially prison reform. Wherever there were misery and suffering, women were preparing programs of relief.

Freedom of Speech for Women.—In the advancement of their causes, of whatever kind, women of necessity had to make public appeals and take part in open meetings. Here they encountered difficulties. The appearance of women on the platform was new and strange. Naturally it was widely resented. Antoinette Brown, although she had credentials as a delegate, was driven off the platform of a temperance convention in New York City simply because she was a woman. James Russell Lowell, editor of the "Atlantic Monthly," declined a poem from Julia Ward Howe on the theory that no woman could write a poem; but he added on second thought that he might consider an article in prose. Nathaniel Hawthorne, another editor, even objected to something in prose because to him "all ink-stained women were equally detestable." To the natural resentment against their intrusion into new fields was added that aroused by their ideas and methods. As temperance reformers, they criticized in a caustic manner those who would not accept their opinions. As opponents of slavery they were especially bitter. One of their conventions, held at Philadelphia in 1833, passed a resolution calling on all women to leave those churches that would not condemn every form of human bondage. This stirred against them many of the clergy who, accustomed to having women sit silent during services, were in no mood to treat such a revolt leniently. Then came the last straw. Women decided that they would preach—out of the pulpit first, and finally in it.

Women in Industry.—The period of this ferment was also the age of the industrial revolution in America, the rise of the factory system, and the growth of mill towns. The labor of women was transferred from the homes to the factories. Then arose many questions: the hours of labor, the sanitary conditions of the mills, the pressure of foreign immigration on native labor, the wages of women as compared with those of men, and the right of married women to their own earnings. Labor organizations sprang up among working women. The mill girls of Lowell, Massachusetts, mainly the daughters of New England farmers, published a magazine, "The Lowell Offering." So excellent were their writings that the French statesman, Thiers, carried a copy of their paper into the Chamber of Deputies to show what working women could achieve in a republic. As women were now admittedly earning their own way in the world by their own labor, they began to talk of their "economic independence."

The World Shaken by Revolution.—Such was the quickening of women's minds in 1848 when the world was startled once more by a revolution in France which spread to Germany, Poland, Austria, Hungary, and Italy. Once more the people of the earth began to explore the principles of democracy and expound human rights. Women, now better educated and more "advanced" in their ideas, played a rôle of still greater importance in that revolution. They led in agitations and uprisings. They suffered from reaction and persecution. From their prison in France, two of them who had been jailed for too much insistence on women's rights exchanged greetings with American women who were raising the same issue here. By this time the women had more supporters among the men. Horace Greeley, editor of the New York *Tribune*, though he afterwards recanted, used his powerful pen in their behalf. Anti-slavery leaders welcomed their aid and repaid them by urging the enfranchisement of women.

The Woman's Rights Convention of 1848.—The forces, moral and intellectual, which had been stirring among women, crystallized a few months after the outbreak of the European revolution in the first Woman's Rights Convention in the history of America. It met at Seneca Falls, New York, in 1848, on the call of Lucretia Mott, Martha Wright, Elizabeth Cady Stanton, and Mary Ann McClintock, three of them Quakers. Accustomed to take part in church meetings with men, the Quakers naturally suggested that men as well as women be invited to attend the convention. Indeed, a man presided over the conference, for that position seemed too presumptuous even for such stout advocates of woman's rights.

The deliberations of the Seneca Falls convention resulted in a Declaration of Rights modeled after the Declaration of Independence. For example, the preamble began: "When in the course of human events it becomes necessary for one portion of the family of man to assume among the people of the earth a position different from that which they have hitherto occupied...." So also it closed: "Such has been the patient suffering of women under this government and such is now the necessity which constrains them to demand the equal station to which they are entitled." Then followed the list of grievances, the same number which had been exhibited to George III in 1776. Especially did they assail the disabilities imposed upon them by the English common law imported into America—the law which denied married women their property, their wages, and their legal existence as separate persons. All these grievances they recited to "a candid world." The remedies for the evils which they endured were then set forth in detail. They demanded "equal rights" in the colleges, trades, and professions; equal suffrage; the right to share in all political offices, honors, and emoluments; the right to complete equality in marriage, including equal guardianship of the children; and for married women the right to own property, to keep wages, to make contracts, to transact business, and to testify in the courts of justice. In short, they declared women to be persons as men are persons and entitled to all the rights and privileges of human beings. Such was the clarion call which went forth to the world in 1848—to an amused and contemptuous world, it must be admitted—but to a world fated to heed and obey.

The First Gains in Civil Liberty.—The convention of 1848 did not make political enfranchisement the leading issue. Rather did it emphasize the civil disabilities of women which were most seriously under discussion at the time. Indeed, the New York legislature of that very year, as the result of a twelve years' agitation, passed the Married Woman's Property Act setting aside the general principles of the English common law as applied to women and giving them many of the "rights of man." California and Wisconsin followed in 1850; Massachusetts in 1854; and Kansas in 1859. Other states soon fell into line. Women's earnings and inheritances were at last their own in some states at least. In a little while laws were passed granting women rights as equal guardians of their children and permitting them to divorce their husbands on the grounds of cruelty and drunkenness.

By degrees other steps were taken. The Woman's Medical College of Pennsylvania was founded in 1850, and the Philadelphia School of Design for Women three years later. In 1852 the American Women's Educational Association was formed to initiate an agitation for enlarged educational opportunities for women. Other colleges soon emulated the example of Oberlin: the University of Utah in 1850; Hillsdale College in Michigan in 1855; Baker University in Kansas in 1858; and the University of Iowa in 1860. New trades and professions were opened to women and old prejudices against their activities and demands slowly gave way.

THE NATIONAL STRUGGLE FOR WOMAN SUFFRAGE

The Beginnings of Organization.—As women surmounted one obstacle after another, the agitation for equal suffrage came to the front. If any year is to be fixed as the date of its beginning, it may very well be 1850, when the suffragists of Ohio urged the state constitutional convention to confer the vote upon them. With apparent spontaneity there were held in the same year state suffrage conferences in Indiana, Pennsylvania, and Massachusetts; and connections were formed among the leaders of these meetings. At the same time the first national suffrage convention was held in Worcester, Massachusetts, on the call of eighty-nine leading men and women representing six states. Accounts of the convention were widely circulated in this country and abroad. English women,—for instance, Harriet Martineau,— sent words of appreciation for the work thus inaugurated. It inspired a leading article in the "Westminster Review," which deeply interested the distinguished economist, John Stuart Mill. Soon he was the champion of woman suffrage in the British Parliament and the author of a powerful tract *The Subjection of Women*, widely read throughout the English-speaking world. Thus do world movements grow. Strange to relate the women of England were enfranchised before the adoption of the federal suffrage amendment in America.

The national suffrage convention of 1850 was followed by an extraordinary outburst of agitation. Pamphlets streamed from the press. Petitions to legislative bodies were drafted, signed, and presented. There were addresses by favorite orators like Garrison, Phillips, and Curtis, and lectures and poems by men like Emerson, Longfellow, and Whittier. In 1853 the first suffrage paper was founded by the wife of a member of Congress from Rhode Island. By this time the last barrier to white manhood suffrage in the North had been swept away and the woman's movement was gaining momentum every year.

The Suffrage Movement Checked by the Civil War.—Advocates of woman suffrage believed themselves on the high road to success when the Civil War engaged the energies and labors of the nation. Northern women became absorbed in the struggle to preserve the union. They held no suffrage conventions for five years. They transformed their associations into Loyalty Leagues. They banded together to buy only domestic goods when foreign imports threatened to ruin American markets. They rolled up monster petitions in favor of the emancipation of slaves. In hospitals, in military prisons, in agriculture, and in industry they bore their full share of responsibility. Even when the New York legislature took advantage of their unguarded moments and repealed the law giving the mother equal rights with the father in the guardianship of children, they refused to lay aside war work for agitation. As in all other wars, their devotion was unstinted and their sacrifices equal to the necessities of the hour.

The Federal Suffrage Amendment.—Their plans and activities, when the war closed, were shaped by events beyond their control. The emancipation of the slaves and their proposed enfranchisement made prominent the question of a national suffrage for the first time in our history. Friends of the colored man insisted that his civil liberties would not be safe unless he was granted the right to vote. The woman suffragists very pertinently asked why the same principle did not apply to women. The answer which they received was negative. The fourteenth amendment to the federal Constitution, adopted in 1868, definitely put women aside by limiting the scope of its application, so far as the suffrage was concerned, to the male sex. In making manhood suffrage national, however, it nationalized the issue.

This was the signal for the advocates of woman suffrage. In March, 1869, their proposed amendment was introduced in Congress by George W. Julian of Indiana. It provided that no citizen should be deprived of the vote on account of sex, following the language of the fifteenth amendment which forbade disfranchisement on account of race. Support for the amendment, coming from many directions, led the suffragists to believe that their case was hopeful. In their platform of 1872, for example, the Republicans praised the women for their loyal devotion to freedom, welcomed them to spheres of wider usefulness, and declared that the demand of any class of citizens for additional rights deserved "respectful consideration."

Experience soon demonstrated, however, that praise was not the ballot. Indeed the suffragists already had realized that a tedious contest lay before them. They had revived in 1866 their regular national convention. They gave the name of "The Revolution" to their paper, edited by Elizabeth Cady Stanton and Susan B. Anthony. They formed a national suffrage association and organized annual pilgrimages to Congress to present their claims. Such activities bore some results. Many eminent congressmen were converted to their cause and presented it ably to their colleagues of both chambers. Still the subject was ridiculed by the newspapers and looked upon as freakish by the masses.

The State Campaigns.—Discouraged by the outcome of the national campaign, suffragists turned to the voters of the individual states and sought the ballot at their hands. Gains by this process were painfully slow. Wyoming, it is true, while still a territory, granted suffrage to women in 1869 and continued it on becoming a state twenty years later, in spite of strong protests in Congress. In 1893 Colorado established complete political equality. In Utah, the third suffrage state, the cause suffered many vicissitudes. Women were enfranchised by the territorial legislature; they were deprived of the ballot by Congress in 1887; finally in 1896 on the admission of Utah to the union they recovered their former rights. During the same year, 1896, Idaho conferred equal suffrage upon the women. This was the last suffrage victory for more than a decade.

The Suffrage Cause in Congress.—In the midst of the meager gains among the states there were occasional flurries of hope for immediate action on the federal amendment. Between 1878 and 1896 the Senate committee reported the suffrage resolution by a favorable majority on five different occasions. During the same period, however, there were nine unfavorable reports and only once did the subject reach the point of a general debate. At no time could anything like the required two-thirds vote be obtained.

The Changing Status of Women.—While the suffrage movement was lagging, the activities of women in other directions were steadily multiplying. College after college—Vassar, Bryn Mawr, Smith, Wellesley, to mention a few—was founded to give them the advantages of higher education. Other institutions, especially the state universities of the West, opened their doors to women, and women were received into the professions of law and medicine. By the rapid growth of public high schools in which girls enjoyed the same rights as boys, education was extended still more widely. The number of women teachers increased by leaps and bounds.

Meanwhile women were entering nearly every branch of industry and business. How many of them worked at gainful occupations before 1870 we do not know; but from that year forward we have the records of the census. Between 1870 and 1900 the proportion of women in the professions rose from less than two per cent to more than ten per cent; in trade and transportation from 24.8 per cent to 43.2 per cent; and in manufacturing from 13 to 19 per cent. In 1910, there were over 8,000,000 women gainfully employed as compared with 30,000,000 men. When, during the war on Germany, the government established the principle of equal pay for equal work and gave official recognition to the value of their services in industry, it was discovered how far women had traveled along the road forecast by the leaders of 1848.

The Club Movement among Women.—All over the country women's societies and clubs were started to advance this or that reform or merely to study literature, art, and science. In time these women's organizations of all kinds were federated into city, state, and national associations and drawn into the consideration of public questions. Under the leadership of Frances Willard they made temperance reform a vital issue. They took an interest in legislation pertaining to prisons, pure food, public health, and municipal government, among other things. At their sessions and conferences local, state, and national issues were discussed until finally, it seems, everything led to the quest of the franchise. By solemn resolution in 1914 the National Federation of Women's Clubs, representing nearly two million club women, formally endorsed woman suffrage. In the same year the National Education Association, speaking for the public school teachers of the land, added its seal of approval.

State and National Action.—Again the suffrage movement was in full swing in the states. Washington in 1910, California in 1911, Oregon, Kansas, and Arizona in 1912, Nevada and Montana in 1914 by popular vote enfranchised their women. Illinois in 1913 conferred upon them the right to vote for President of the United States. The time had arrived for a new movement. A number of younger suffragists sought to use the votes of women in the equal suffrage states to compel one or both of the national political parties to endorse and carry through Congress the federal suffrage amendment. Pressure then came upon Congress from every direction: from the suffragists who made a straight appeal on the grounds of justice; and from the suffragists who besought the women of the West to vote against candidates for President, who would not approve the federal amendment. In 1916, for the first time, a leading presidential candidate, Mr. Charles E. Hughes, speaking for the Republicans, endorsed the federal amendment and a distinguished ex-President, Roosevelt, exerted a powerful influence to keep it an issue in the campaign.

National Enfranchisement.—After that, events moved rapidly. The great state of New York adopted equal suffrage in 1917. Oklahoma, South Dakota, and Michigan swung into line the following year; several other states, by legislative action, gave women the right to vote for President. In the meantime the suffrage battle at Washington grew intense. Appeals and petitions poured in upon Congress and the President. Militant suffragists held daily demonstrations in Washington. On September 30, 1918, President Wilson, who, two years before, had opposed federal action and endorsed suffrage by state adoption only, went before Congress and urged the passage of the suffrage amendment to the Constitution. In June, 1919, the requisite two-thirds vote was secured; the resolution was carried and transmitted to the states for ratification. On August 28, 1920, the thirty-sixth state, Tennessee, approved the amendment, making three-fourths of the states as required by the Constitution. Thus woman suffrage became the law of the land. A new political democracy had been created. The age of agitation was closed and the epoch of responsible citizenship opened.

General References

Edith Abbott, *Women in Industry*.

C.P. Gilman, *Woman and Economics*.

I.H. Harper, *Life and Work of Susan B. Anthony.*

E.R. Hecker, *Short History of Woman's Rights.*

S.B. Anthony and I.H. Harper, *History of Woman Suffrage* (4 vols.).

J.W. Taylor, *Before Vassar Opened.*

A.H. Shaw, *The Story of a Pioneer.*

Research Topics

The Rise of the Woman Suffrage Movement.—McMaster, *History of the People of the United States*, Vol. VIII, pp. 116-121; K. Porter, *History of Suffrage in the United States*, pp. 135-145.

The Development of the Suffrage Movement.—Porter, pp. 228-254; Ogg, *National Progress* (American Nation Series), pp. 151-156 and p. 382.

Women's Labor in the Colonial Period.—E. Abbott, *Women in Industry*, pp. 10-34.

Women and the Factory System.—Abbott, pp. 35-62.

Early Occupations for Women.—Abbott, pp. 63-85.

Women's Wages.—Abbott, pp. 262-316.

Questions

1. Why were women involved in the reform movements of the new century?

2. What is history? What determines the topics that appear in written history?

3. State the position of women under the old common law.

4. What part did women play in the intellectual movement that preceded the American Revolution?

5. Explain the rise of the discussion of women's rights.

6. What were some of the early writings about women?

7. Why was there a struggle for educational opportunities?

8. How did reform movements draw women into public affairs and what were the chief results?

9. Show how the rise of the factory affected the life and labor of women.

10. Why is the year 1848 an important year in the woman movement? Discuss the work of the Seneca Falls convention.

11. Enumerate some of the early gains in civil liberty for women.

12. Trace the rise of the suffrage movement. Show the effect of the Civil War.

13. Review the history of the federal suffrage amendment.

14. Summarize the history of the suffrage in the states.

CHAPTER XXIV

INDUSTRIAL DEMOCRACY

The New Economic Age.—The spirit of criticism and the measures of reform designed to meet it, which characterized the opening years of the twentieth century, were merely the signs of a new age. The nation had definitely passed into industrialism. The number of city dwellers employed for wages as contrasted with the farmers working on their own land was steadily mounting. The free land, once the refuge of restless workingmen of the East and the immigrants from Europe, was a thing of the past. As President Roosevelt later said in speaking of the great coal strike, "a few generations ago, the American workman could have saved money, gone West, and taken up a homestead. Now the free lands were gone. In earlier days, a man who began with a pick and shovel might come to own a mine. That outlet was now closed as regards the immense majority.... The majority of men who earned wages in the coal industry, if they wished to progress at all, were compelled to progress not by ceasing to be wage-earners but by improving the conditions under which all the wage-earners of the country lived and worked."

The disappearance of the free land, President Roosevelt went on to say, also produced "a crass inequality in the bargaining relation of the employer and the individual employee standing alone. The great coal-mining and coal-carrying companies which employed their tens of thousands could easily dispense with the services of any particular miner. The miner, on the other hand, however expert, could not dispense with the companies. He needed a job; his wife and children would starve if he did not get one.... Individually the miners were impotent when they sought to enter a wage contract with the great companies; they could make fair terms only by uniting into trade unions to bargain collectively." It was of this state of affairs that President Taft spoke when he favored the modification of the common law "so as to put employees of little power and means on a level with their employers in adjusting and agreeing upon their mutual obligations."

John D. Rockefeller, Jr., on the side of the great captains of industry, recognized the same facts. He said: "In the early days of the development of industry, the employer and capital investor were frequently one. Daily contact was had between him and his employees, who were his friends and neighbors.... Because of the proportions which modern industry has attained, employers and employees are too often strangers to each other.... Personal relations can be revived only through adequate representation of the employees. Representation is a principle which is fundamentally just and vital to the successful conduct of industry.... It is not consistent for us as Americans to demand democracy in government and practice autocracy in industry.... With the developments what they are in industry to-day, there is sure to come a progressive evolution from aristocratic single control, whether by capital, labor, or the state, to democratic, coöperative control by all three."

COÖPERATION BETWEEN EMPLOYERS AND EMPLOYEES

Company Unions.—The changed economic life described by the three eminent men just quoted was acknowledged by several great companies and business concerns. All over the country decided efforts were made to bridge the gulf which industry and the corporation had created. Among the devices adopted was that of the "company union." In one of the Western lumber mills, for example, all the employees were invited to join a company organization; they held monthly meetings to discuss matters of common concern; they elected a "shop committee" to confer with the representatives of the company; and periodically the agents of the employers attended the conferences of the men to talk over matters of mutual interest. The function of the shop committee was to consider wages, hours, safety rules, sanitation, recreation and other problems. Whenever any employee had a grievance he took it up with the foreman and, if it was not settled to his satisfaction, he brought it before the shop committee. If the members of the shop committee decided in favor of the man with a grievance, they attempted to settle the matter with the company's agents. All these things failing, the dispute was transferred to a grand meeting of all the employees with the employers' representatives, in common council. A deadlock, if it ensued from such a conference, was broken by calling in impartial arbitrators selected by both sides from among citizens outside the mill. Thus the employees were given a voice in all decisions affecting their work and welfare; rights and grievances were treated as matters of mutual interest rather than individual concern. Representatives of trade unions from outside, however, were rigidly excluded from all negotiations between employers and the employees.

Profit-sharing.—Another proposal for drawing capital and labor together was to supplement the wage system by other ties. Sometimes lump sums were paid to employees who remained in a company's service for a definite period of years. Again they were given a certain percentage of the annual profits. In other instances, employees were allowed to buy stock on easy terms and thus become part owners in the concern. This last plan was carried so far by a large soap manufacturing company that the employees, besides becoming stockholders, secured the right to elect representatives to serve on the board of directors who managed the entire business. So extensive had profit-sharing become by 1914 that the Federal Industrial Relations Committee, appointed by the President, deemed it worthy of a special study. Though opposed by regular trade unions, it was undoubtedly growing in popularity.

Labor Managers and Welfare Work.—Another effort of employers to meet the problems of the new age appeared in the appointment of specialists, known as employment managers, whose task it was to study the relations existing between masters and workers and discover practical methods for dealing with each grievance as it arose. By 1918, hundreds of big companies had recognized this modern "profession" and universities were giving courses of instruction on the subject to young men and women. In that year a national conference of employment managers was held at Rochester, New York. The discussion revealed a wide range of duties assigned to managers, including questions of wages, hours, sanitation, rest rooms, recreational facilities, and welfare work of every kind designed to make the conditions in mills and factories safer and more humane. Thus it was evident that hundreds of employers had abandoned the old idea that they were dealing merely with individual employees and that their obligations ended with the payment of any wages they saw fit to fix. In short, they were seeking to develop a spirit of coöperation to take the place of competition and enmity; and to increase the production of commodities by promoting the efficiency and happiness of the producers.

THE RISE AND GROWTH OF ORGANIZED LABOR

The American Federation of Labor.—Meanwhile a powerful association of workers representing all the leading trades and crafts, organized into unions of their own, had been built up outside the control of employers. This was the American Federation of Labor, a nation-wide union of unions, founded in 1886 on the basis of beginnings made five years before. At the time of its establishment it had approximately 150,000 members. Its growth up to the end of the century was slow, for the total enrollment in 1900 was only 300,000. At that point the increase became marked. The membership reached 1,650,000 in 1904 and more than 3,000,000 in 1919. To be counted in the ranks of organized labor were several strong unions, friendly to the Federation, though not affiliated with it. Such, for example, were the Railway Brotherhoods with more than half a million members. By the opening of 1920 the total strength of organized labor was put at about 4,000,000 members, meaning, if we include their families, that nearly one-fifth of the people of the United States were in some positive way dependent upon the operations of trade unions.

Historical Background.—This was the culmination of a long and significant history. Before the end of the eighteenth century, the skilled workmen—printers, shoemakers, tailors, and carpenters—had, as we have seen, formed local unions in the large cities. Between 1830 and 1860, several aggressive steps were taken in the American labor movement. For one thing, the number of local unions increased by leaps and bounds in all the industrial towns. For another, there was established in every large manufacturing city a central labor body composed of delegates from the unions of the separate trades. In the local union the printers or the cordwainers, for example, considered only their special trade problems. In the central labor union, printers, cordwainers, iron molders, and other craftsmen considered common problems and learned to coöperate with one another in enforcing the demands of each craft. A third step was the federation of the unions of the same craftsmen in different cities. The printers of New York, Philadelphia, Boston, and other towns, for instance, drew together and formed a national trade union of printers built upon the local unions of that craft. By the eve of the Civil War there were four or five powerful national unions of this character. The expansion of the railway made travel and correspondence easier and national conventions possible even for workmen of small means. About 1834 an attempt was made to federate the unions of all the different crafts into a national organization; but the effort was premature.

The National Labor Union.—The plan which failed in 1834 was tried again in the sixties. During the war, industries and railways had flourished as never before; prices had risen rapidly; the demand for labor had increased; wages had mounted slowly, but steadily. Hundreds of new local unions had been founded and eight or ten national trade unions had sprung into being. The time was ripe, it seemed, for a national consolidation of all labor's forces; and in 1866, the year after the surrender of General Lee at Appomattox, the "National Labor Union" was formed at Baltimore under the leadership of an experienced organizer, W.H. Sylvis of the iron molders. The purpose of the National Labor Union was not merely to secure labor's standard demands touching hours, wages, and conditions of work or to maintain the gains already won. It leaned toward political action and radical opinions. Above all, it sought to eliminate the conflict between capital and labor by making workingmen the owners of shops through the formation of coöperative industries. For six years the National Labor Union continued to hold conferences and carry on its propaganda; but most of the coöperative enterprises failed, political dissensions arose, and by 1872 the experiment had come to an end.

The Knights of Labor.—While the National Labor Union was experimenting, there grew up in the industrial world a more radical organization known as the "Noble Order of the Knights of Labor." It was founded in Philadelphia in 1869, first as a secret society with rituals, signs, and pass words; "so that no spy of the boss can find his way into the lodge room to betray his fellows," as the Knights put it. In form the new organization was simple. It sought to bring all laborers, skilled and unskilled, men and women, white and colored, into a mighty body of local and national unions without distinction of trade or craft. By 1885, ten years after the national organization was established, it boasted a membership of over 700,000. In philosophy, the Knights of Labor were socialistic, for they advocated public ownership of the railways and other utilities and the formation of coöperative societies to own and manage stores and factories.

As the Knights were radical in spirit and their strikes, numerous and prolonged, were often accompanied by violence, the organization alarmed employers and the general public, raising up against itself a vigorous opposition. Weaknesses within, as well as foes from without, started the Knights on the path to dissolution. They waged more strikes than they could carry on successfully; their coöperative experiments failed as those of other labor groups before them had failed; and the rank and file could not be kept in line. The majority of the members wanted immediate gains in wages or the reduction of hours; when their hopes were not realized they drifted away from the order. The troubles were increased by the appearance of the American Federation of Labor, a still mightier organization composed mainly of skilled workers who held strategic positions in industry. When they failed to secure the effective support of the Federation in their efforts to organize the unskilled, the employers closed in upon them; then the Knights declined rapidly in power. By 1890 they were a negligible factor and in a short time they passed into the limbo of dead experiments.

The Policies of the American Federation.—Unlike the Knights of Labor, the American Federation of Labor sought, first of all, to be very practical in its objects and methods. It avoided all kinds of socialistic theories and attended strictly to the business of organizing unions for the purpose of increasing wages, shortening hours, and improving working conditions for its members. It did not try to include everybody in one big union but brought together the employees of each particular craft whose interests were clearly the same. To prepare for strikes and periods of unemployment, it raised large funds by imposing heavy dues and created a benefit system to hold men loyally to the union. In order to permit action on a national scale, it gave the superior officers extensive powers over local unions.

While declaring that employers and employees had much in common, the Federation strongly opposed company unions. Employers, it argued, were affiliated with the National Manufacturers' Association or with similar employers' organizations; every important industry was now national in scope; and wages and hours, in view of competition with other shops, could not be determined in a single factory, no matter how amicable might be the relations of the company and its workers in that particular plant. For these reasons, the Federation declared company unions and local shop committees inherently weak; it insisted that hours, wages, and other labor standards should be fixed by general trade agreements applicable to all the plants of a given industry, even if subject to local modifications.

At the same time, the Federation, far from deliberately antagonizing employers, sought to enlist their coöperation and support. It affiliated with the National Civic Federation, an association of business men, financiers, and professional men, founded in 1900 to promote friendly relations in the industrial world. In brief, the American Federation of Labor accepted the modern industrial system and, by organization within it, endeavored to secure certain definite terms and conditions for trade unionists.

THE WIDER RELATIONS OF ORGANIZED LABOR

The Socialists.—The trade unionism "pure and simple," espoused by the American Federation of Labor, seemed to involve at first glance nothing but businesslike negotiations with employers. In practice it did not work out that way. The Federation was only six years old when a new organization, appealing directly for the labor vote—namely, the Socialist Labor Party—nominated a candidate for President, launched into a national campaign, and called upon trade unionists to desert the older parties and enter its fold.

The socialistic idea, introduced into national politics in 1892, had been long in germination. Before the Civil War, a number of reformers, including Nathaniel Hawthorne, Horace Greeley, and Wendell Phillips, deeply moved by the poverty of the great industrial cities, had earnestly sought relief in the establishment of coöperative or communistic colonies. They believed that people should go into the country, secure land and tools, own them in common so that no one could profit from exclusive ownership, and produce by common labor the food and clothing necessary for their support. For a time this movement attracted wide interest, but it had little vitality. Nearly all the colonies failed. Selfishness and indolence usually disrupted the best of them.

In the course of time this "Utopian" idea was abandoned, and another set of socialist doctrines, claiming to be more "scientific," appeared instead. The new school of socialists, adopting the principles of a German writer and agitator, Karl Marx, appealed directly to workingmen. It urged them to unite against the capitalists, to get possession of the machinery of government, and to introduce collective or public ownership of railways, land, mines, mills, and other means of production. The Marxian socialists, therefore, became political. They sought to organize labor and to win elections. Like the other parties they put forward candidates and platforms. The Socialist Labor party in 1892, for example, declared in favor of government ownership of utilities, free school books, woman suffrage, heavy income taxes, and the referendum. The Socialist party, founded in 1900, with Eugene V. Debs, the leader of the Pullman strike, as its candidate, called for public ownership of all trusts, monopolies, mines, railways; and the chief means of production. In the course of time the vote of the latter organization rose to considerable proportions, reaching almost a million in 1912. It declined four years later and then rose in 1920 to about the same figure.

In their appeal for votes, the socialists of every type turned first to labor. At the annual conventions of the American Federation of Labor they besought the delegates to endorse socialism. The president of the Federation, Samuel Gompers, on each occasion took the floor against them. He repudiated socialism and the socialists, on both theoretical and practical grounds. He opposed too much public ownership, declaring that the government was as likely as any private employer to oppress labor. The approval of socialism, he maintained, would split the Federation on the rock of politics, weaken it in its fight for higher wages and shorter hours, and prejudice the public against it. At every turn he was able to vanquish the socialists in the Federation, although he could not prevent it from endorsing public ownership of the railways at the convention of 1920.

The Extreme Radicals.—Some of the socialists, defeated in their efforts to capture organized labor and seeing that the gains in elections were very meager, broke away from both trade unionism and politics. One faction, the Industrial Workers of the World, founded in 1905, declared themselves opposed to all capitalists, the wages system, and craft unions. They asserted that the "working class and the employing class have nothing in common" and that trade unions only pitted one set of workers against another set. They repudiated all government ownership and the government itself, boldly proclaiming their intention to unite all employees into one big union and seize the railways, mines, and mills of the country. This doctrine, so revolutionary in tone, called down upon the extremists the condemnation of the American Federation of Labor as well as of the general public. At its convention in 1919, the Federation went on record as "opposed to Bolshevism, I.W.W.-ism, and the irresponsible leadership that encourages such a policy." It announced its "firm adherence to American ideals."

The Federation and Political Issues.—The hostility of the Federation to the socialists did not mean, however, that it was indifferent to political issues or political parties. On the contrary, from time to time, at its annual conventions, it endorsed political and social reforms, such as the initiative, referendum, and recall, the abolition of child labor, the exclusion of Oriental labor, old-age pensions, and government ownership. Moreover it adopted the policy of "rewarding friends and punishing enemies" by advising members to vote for or against candidates according to their stand on the demands of organized labor.

This policy was pursued with especial zeal in connection with disputes over the use of injunctions in labor controversies. An injunction is a bill or writ issued by a judge ordering some person or corporation to do or to refrain from doing something. For example, a judge may order a trade union to refrain from interfering with non-union men or to continue at work handling goods made by non-union labor; and he may fine or imprison those who disobey his injunction, the penalty being inflicted for "contempt of court." This ancient legal device came into prominence in connection with nation-wide railway strikes in 1877. It was applied with increasing frequency after its effective use against Eugene V. Debs in the Pullman strike of 1894.

Aroused by the extensive use of the writ, organized labor demanded that the power of judges to issue injunctions in labor disputes be limited by law. Representatives of the unions sought support from the Democrats and the Republicans; they received from the former very specific and cordial endorsement. In 1896 the Democratic platform denounced "government by injunction as a new and highly dangerous form of oppression." Mr. Gompers, while refusing to commit the Federation to Democratic politics, privately supported Mr. Bryan. In 1908, he came out openly and boasted that eighty per cent of the votes of the Federation had been cast for the Democratic candidate. Again in 1912 the same policy was pursued. The reward was the enactment in 1914 of a federal law exempting trade unions from prosecution as combinations in restraint of trade, limiting the use of the injunction in labor disputes, and prescribing trial by jury in case of contempt of court. This measure was hailed by Mr. Gompers as the "Magna Carta of Labor" and a vindication of his policy. As a matter of fact, however, it did not prevent the continued use of injunctions against trade unions. Nevertheless Mr. Gompers was unshaken in his conviction that organized labor should not attempt to form an independent political party or endorse socialist or other radical economic theories.

Organized Labor and the Public.—Besides its relations to employers, radicals within its own ranks, and political questions, the Federation had to face responsibilities to the general public. With the passing of time these became heavy and grave. While industries were small and conflicts were local in character, a strike seldom affected anybody but the employer and the employees immediately involved in it. When, however, industries and trade unions became organized on a national scale and a strike could paralyze a basic enterprise like coal mining or railways, the vital interests of all citizens were put in jeopardy. Moreover, as increases in wages and reductions in hours often added directly to the cost of living, the action of the unions affected the well-being of all—the food, clothing, and shelter of the whole people.

For the purpose of meeting the issue raised by this state of affairs, it was suggested that employers and employees should lay their disputes before commissions of arbitration for decision and settlement. President Cleveland, in a message of April 2, 1886, proposed such a method for disposing of industrial controversies, and two years later Congress enacted a voluntary arbitration law applicable to the railways. The principle was extended in 1898 and again in 1913, and under the authority of the federal government many contentions in the railway world were settled by arbitration.

The success of such legislation induced some students of industrial questions to urge that unions and employers should be compelled to submit all disputes to official tribunals of arbitration. Kansas actually passed such a law in 1920. Congress in the Esch-Cummins railway bill of the same year created a federal board of nine members to which all railway controversies, not settled by negotiation, must be submitted. Strikes, however, were not absolutely forbidden. Generally speaking, both employers and employees opposed compulsory adjustments without offering any substitute in case voluntary arbitration should not be accepted by both parties to a dispute.

IMMIGRATION AND AMERICANIZATION

The Problems of Immigration.—From its very inception, the American Federation of Labor, like the Knights of Labor before it, was confronted by numerous questions raised by the ever swelling tide of aliens coming to our shores. In its effort to make each trade union all-inclusive, it had to wrestle with a score or more languages. When it succeeded in thoroughly organizing a craft, it often found its purposes defeated by an influx of foreigners ready to work for lower wages and thus undermine the foundations of the union.

At the same time, persons outside the labor movement began to be apprehensive as they contemplated the undoubted evil, as well as the good, that seemed to be associated with the "alien invasion." They saw whole sections of great cities occupied by people speaking foreign tongues, reading only foreign newspapers, and looking to the Old World alone for their ideas and their customs. They witnessed an expanding army of total illiterates, men and women who could read and write no language at all; while among those aliens who could read few there were who knew anything of American history, traditions, and ideals. Official reports revealed that over twenty per cent of the men of the draft army during the World War could not read a newspaper or write a letter home. Perhaps most alarming of all was the discovery that thousands of alien men are in the United States only on a temporary sojourn, solely to make money and return home with their savings. These men, willing to work for low wages and live in places unfit for human beings, have no stake in this country and do not care what becomes of it.

The Restriction of Immigration.—In all this there was, strictly speaking, no cause for surprise. Since the foundation of our republic the policy of the government had been to encourage the coming of the alien. For nearly one hundred years no restraining act was passed by Congress, while two important laws positively encouraged it; namely, the homestead act of 1862 and the contract immigration law of 1864. Not until American workingmen came into open collision with cheap Chinese labor on the Pacific Coast did the federal government spread the first measure of limitation on the statute books. After the discovery of gold, and particularly after the opening of the railway construction era, a horde of laborers from China descended upon California. Accustomed to starvation wages and indifferent to the conditions of living, they threatened to cut the American standard to the point of subsistence. By 1876 the protest of American labor was loud and long and both the Republicans and the Democrats gave heed to it. In 1882 Congress enacted a law prohibiting the admission of Chinese laborers to the United States for a term of ten years—later extended by legislation. In a little while the demand arose for the exclusion of the Japanese as well. In this case no exclusion law was passed; but an understanding was reached by which Japan agreed not to issue passports to her laborers authorizing them to come to the United States. By act of Congress in 1907 the President was empowered to exclude any laborers who, having passports to Canada, Hawaii, or Mexico, attempted to enter our country.

These laws and agreements, however, did not remove all grounds for the agitation of the subject. They were difficult to enforce and it was claimed by residents of the Coast that in spite of federal authority Oriental laborers were finding their way into American ports. Moreover, several Western states, anxious to preserve the soil for American ownership, enacted laws making it impossible for Chinese and Japanese to buy land outright; and in other ways they discriminated against Orientals. Such proceedings placed the federal government in an embarrassing position. By treaty it had guaranteed specific rights to Japanese citizens in the United States, and the government at Tokyo contended that the state laws just cited violated the terms of the international agreement. The Western states were fixed in their determination to control Oriental residents; Japan was equally persistent in asking that no badge of inferiority be attached to her citizens. Subjected to pressure on both sides, the federal government sought a way out of the deadlock.

Having embarked upon the policy of restriction in 1882, Congress readily extended it. In that same year it barred paupers, criminals, convicts, and the insane. Three years later, mainly owing to the pressure of the Knights of Labor, it forbade any person, company, or association to import aliens under contract. By an act of 1887, the contract labor restriction was made even more severe. In 1903, anarchists were excluded and the bureau of immigration was transferred from the Treasury Department to the Department of Commerce and Labor, in order to provide for a more rigid execution of the law. In 1907 the classes of persons denied admission were widened to embrace those suffering from physical and mental defects and otherwise unfit for effective citizenship. When the Department of Labor was established in 1913 the enforcement of the law was placed in the hands of the Secretary of Labor, W.B. Wilson, who was a former leader in the American Federation of Labor.

The Literacy Test.—Still the advocates of restriction were not satisfied. Still organized labor protested and demanded more protection against the competition of immigrants. In 1917 it won a thirty-year battle in the passage of a bill excluding "all aliens over sixteen years of age, physically capable of reading, who cannot read the English language or some other language or dialect, including Hebrew or Yiddish." Even President Wilson could not block it, for a two-thirds vote to overcome his veto was mustered in Congress.

This act, while it served to exclude illiterates, made no drastic cut in the volume of immigration. Indeed a material reduction was resolutely opposed in many quarters. People of certain nationalities already in the United States objected to every barrier that shut out their own kinsmen. Some Americans of the old stock still held to the idea that the United States should continue to be an asylum for "the oppressed of the earth." Many employers looked upon an increased labor supply as the means of escaping what they called "the domination of trade unions." In the babel of countless voices, the discussion of these vital matters went on in town and country.

Americanization.—Intimately connected with the subject of immigration was a call for the "Americanization" of the alien already within our gates. The revelation of the illiteracy in the army raised the cry and the demand was intensified when it was found that many of the leaders among the extreme radicals were foreign in birth and citizenship. Innumerable programs for assimilating the alien to American life were drawn up, and in 1919 a national conference on the subject was held in Washington under the auspices of the Department of the Interior. All were agreed that the foreigner should be taught to speak and write the language and understand the government of our country. Congress was urged to lend aid in this vast undertaking. America, as ex-President Roosevelt had said, was to find out "whether it was a nation or a boarding-house."

General References

J.R. Commons and Associates, *History of Labor in the United States* (2 vols.).

Samuel Gompers, *Labor and the Common Welfare*.

W.E. Walling, *Socialism as It Is*.

W.E. Walling (and Others), *The Socialism of Today*.

R.T. Ely, *The Labor Movement in America*.

T.S. Adams and H. Sumner, *Labor Problems*.

J.G. Brooks, *American Syndicalism* and *Social Unrest*.

P.F. Hall, *Immigration and Its Effects on the United States*.

Research Topics

The Rise of Trade Unionism.—Mary Beard, *Short History of the American Labor Movement*, pp. 10-18, 47-53, 62-79; Carlton, *Organized Labor in American History*, pp. 11-44.

Labor and Politics.—Beard, *Short History*, pp. 33-46, 54-61, 103-112; Carlton, pp. 169-197; Ogg, *National Progress* (American Nation Series), pp. 76-85.

The Knights of Labor.—Beard, *Short History*, pp. 116-126; Dewey, *National Problems* (American Nation Series), pp. 40-49.

The American Federation of Labor—Organization and Policies.—Beard, *Short History*, pp. 86-112.

Organized Labor and the Socialists.—Beard, *Short History*, pp. 126-149.

Labor and the Great War.—Carlton, pp. 282-306; Beard, *Short History*, pp. 150-170.

Questions

1. What are the striking features of the new economic age?

2. Give Mr. Rockefeller's view of industrial democracy.

3. Outline the efforts made by employers to establish closer relations with their employees.

4. Sketch the rise and growth of the American Federation of Labor.

5. How far back in our history does the labor movement extend?

6. Describe the purposes and outcome of the National Labor Union and the Knights of Labor.

7. State the chief policies of the American Federation of Labor.

8. How does organized labor become involved with outside forces?

9. Outline the rise of the socialist movement. How did it come into contact with the American Federation?

10. What was the relation of the Federation to the extreme radicals? To national politics? To the public?

11. Explain the injunction.

12. Why are labor and immigration closely related?

13. Outline the history of restrictions on immigration.

14. What problems arise in connection with the assimilation of the alien to American life?

CHAPTER XXV

PRESIDENT WILSON AND THE WORLD WAR

"The welfare, the happiness, the energy, and the spirit of the men and women who do the daily work in our mines and factories, on our railroads, in our offices and ports of trade, on our farms, and on the sea are the underlying necessity of all prosperity." Thus spoke Woodrow Wilson during his campaign for election. In this spirit, as President, he gave the signal for work by summoning Congress in a special session on April 7, 1913. He invited the coöperation of all "forward-looking men" and indicated that he would assume the rôle of leadership. As an evidence of his resolve, he appeared before Congress in person to read his first message, reviving the old custom of Washington and Adams. Then he let it be known that he would not give his party any rest until it fulfilled its pledges to the country. When Democratic Senators balked at tariff reductions, they were sharply informed that the party had plighted its word and that no excuses or delays would be tolerated.

DOMESTIC LEGISLATION

Financial Measures.—Under this spirited leadership Congress went to work, passing first the Underwood tariff act of 1913, which made a downward revision in the rates of duty, fixing them on the average about twenty-six per cent lower than the figures of 1907. The protective principle was retained, but an effort was made to permit a moderate element of foreign competition. As a part of the revenue act Congress levied a tax on incomes as authorized by the sixteenth amendment to the Constitution. The tax which roused such party passions twenty years before was now accepted as a matter of course.

Having disposed of the tariff, Congress took up the old and vexatious currency question and offered a new solution in the form of the federal reserve law of December, 1913. This measure, one of the most interesting in the history of federal finance, embraced four leading features. In the first place, it continued the prohibition on the issuance of notes by state banks and provided for a national currency. In the second place, it put the new banking system under the control of a federal reserve board composed entirely of government officials. To prevent the growth of a "central money power," it provided, in the third place, for the creation of twelve federal reserve banks, one in each of twelve great districts into which the country is divided. All local national banks were required and certain other banks permitted to become members of the new system and share in its control. Finally, with a view to expanding the currency, a step which the Democrats had long urged upon the country, the issuance of paper money, under definite safeguards, was authorized.

Mindful of the agricultural interest, ever dear to the heart of Jefferson's followers, the Democrats supplemented the reserve law by the Farm Loan Act of 1916, creating federal agencies to lend money on farm mortgages at moderate rates of interest. Within a year $20,000,000 had been lent to farmers, the heaviest borrowing being in nine Western and Southern states, with Texas in the lead.

Anti-trust Legislation.—The tariff and currency laws were followed by three significant measures relative to trusts. Rejecting utterly the Progressive doctrine of government regulation, President Wilson announced that it was the purpose of the Democrats "to destroy monopoly and maintain competition as the only effective instrument of business liberty." The first step in this direction, the Clayton Anti-trust Act, carried into great detail the Sherman law of 1890 forbidding and penalizing combinations in restraint of interstate and foreign trade. In every line it revealed a determined effort to tear apart the great trusts and to put all business on a competitive basis. Its terms were reinforced in the same year by a law creating a Federal Trade Commission empowered to inquire into the methods of corporations and lodge complaints against concerns "using any unfair method of competition." In only one respect was the severity of the Democratic policy relaxed. An act of 1918 provided that the Sherman law should not apply to companies engaged in export trade, the purpose being to encourage large corporations to enter foreign commerce.

The effect of this whole body of anti-trust legislation, in spite of much labor on it, remained problematical. Very few combinations were dissolved as a result of it. Startling investigations were made into alleged abuses on the part of trusts; but it could hardly be said that huge business concerns had lost any of their predominance in American industry.

Labor Legislation.—By no mere coincidence, the Clayton Anti-trust law of 1914 made many concessions to organized labor. It declared that "the labor of a human being is not a commodity or an article of commerce," and it exempted unions from prosecution as "combinations in restraint of trade." It likewise defined and limited the uses which the federal courts might make of injunctions in labor disputes and guaranteed trial by jury to those guilty of disobedience.

The Clayton law was followed the next year by the Seamen's Act giving greater liberty of contract to American sailors and requiring an improvement of living conditions on shipboard. This was such a drastic law that shipowners declared themselves unable to meet foreign competition under its terms, owing to the low labor standards of other countries.

Still more extraordinary than the Seamen's Act was the Adamson law of 1916 fixing a standard eight-hour work-day for trainmen on railroads—a measure wrung from Congress under a threat of a great strike by the four Railway Brotherhoods. This act, viewed by union leaders as a triumph, called forth a bitter denunciation of "trade union domination," but it was easier to criticize than to find another solution of the problem.

Three other laws enacted during President Wilson's administration were popular in the labor world. One of them provided compensation for federal employees injured in the discharge of their duties. Another prohibited the labor of children under a certain age in the industries of the nation. A third prescribed for coal miners in Alaska an eight-hour day and modern safeguards for life and health. There were positive proofs that organized labor had obtained a large share of power in the councils of the country.

Federal and State Relations.—If the interference of the government with business and labor represented a departure from the old idea of "the less government the better," what can be said of a large body of laws affecting the rights of states? The prohibition of child labor everywhere was one indication of the new tendency. Mr. Wilson had once declared such legislation unconstitutional; the Supreme Court declared it unconstitutional; but Congress, undaunted, carried it into effect under the guise of a tax on goods made by children below the age limit. There were other indications of the drift. Large sums of money were appropriated by Congress in 1916 to assist the states in building and maintaining highways. The same year the Farm Loan Act projected the federal government into the sphere of local money lending. In 1917 millions of dollars were granted to states in aid of vocational education, incidentally imposing uniform standards throughout the country. Evidently the government was no longer limited to the duties of the policeman.

The Prohibition Amendment.—A still more significant form of intervention in state affairs was the passage, in December, 1917, of an amendment to the federal Constitution establishing national prohibition of the manufacture and sale of intoxicating liquors as beverages. This was the climax of a historical movement extending over half a century. In 1872, a National Prohibition party, launched three years before, nominated its first presidential candidate and inaugurated a campaign of agitation. Though its vote was never large, the cause for which it stood found increasing favor among the people. State after state by popular referendum abolished the liquor traffic within its borders. By 1917 at least thirty-two of the forty-eight were "dry." When the federal amendment was submitted for approval, the ratification was surprisingly swift. In a little more than a year, namely, on January 16, 1919, it was proclaimed. Twelve months later the amendment went into effect.

COLONIAL AND FOREIGN POLICIES

The Philippines and Porto Rico.—Independence for the Philippines and larger self-government for Porto Rico had been among the policies of the Democratic party since the campaign of 1900. President Wilson in his annual messages urged upon Congress more autonomy for the Filipinos and a definite promise of final independence. The result was the Jones Organic Act for the Philippines passed in 1916. This measure provided that the upper as well as the lower house of the Philippine legislature should be elected by popular vote, and declared it to be the intention of the United States to grant independence "as soon as a stable government can be established." This, said President Wilson on signing the bill, is "a very satisfactory advance in our policy of extending to them self-government and control of their own affairs." The following year Congress, yielding to President Wilson's insistence, passed a new organic act for Porto Rico, making both houses of the legislature elective and conferring American citizenship upon the inhabitants of the island.

American Power in the Caribbean.—While extending more self-government to its dominions, the United States enlarged its sphere of influence in the Caribbean. The supervision of finances in Santo Domingo, inaugurated in Roosevelt's administration, was transformed into a protectorate under Wilson. In 1914 dissensions in the republic led to the landing of American marines to "supervise" the elections. Two years later, an officer in the American navy, with authority from Washington, placed the entire republic "in a state of military occupation." He proceeded to suspend the government and laws of the country, exile the president, suppress the congress, and substitute American military authority. In 1919 a consulting board of four prominent Dominicans was appointed to aid the American military governor; but it resigned the next year after making a plea for the restoration of independence to the republic. For all practical purposes, it seemed, the sovereignty of Santo Domingo had been transferred to the United States.

In the neighboring republic of Haiti, a similar state of affairs existed. In the summer of 1915 a revolution broke out there—one of a long series beginning in 1804—and our marines were landed to restore order. Elections were held under the supervision of American officers, and a treaty was drawn up placing the management of Haitian finances and the local constabulary under American authority. In taking this action, our Secretary of State was careful to announce: "The United States government has no purpose of aggression and is entirely disinterested in promoting this protectorate." Still it must be said that there were vigorous protests on the part of natives and American citizens against the conduct of our agents in the island. In 1921 President Wilson was considering withdrawal.

In line with American policy in the West Indian waters was the purchase in 1917 of the Danish Islands just off the coast of Porto Rico. The strategic position of the islands, especially in relation to Haiti and Porto Rico, made them an object of American concern as early as 1867, when a treaty of purchase was negotiated only to be rejected by the Senate of the United States. In 1902 a second arrangement was made, but this time it was defeated by the upper house of the Danish parliament. The third treaty brought an end to fifty years of bargaining and the Stars and Stripes were raised over St. Croix, St. Thomas, St. John, and numerous minor islands scattered about in the neighborhood. "It would be suicidal," commented a New York newspaper, "for America, on the threshold of a great commercial expansion in South America, to suffer a Heligoland, or a Gibraltar, or an Aden to be erected by her rivals at the mouth of her Suez." On the mainland American power was strengthened by the establishment of a protectorate over Nicaragua in 1916.

Mexican Relations.—The extension of American enterprise southward into Latin America, of which the operations in the Caribbean regions were merely one phase, naturally carried Americans into Mexico to develop the natural resources of that country. Under the iron rule of General Porfirio Diaz, established in 1876 and maintained with only a short break until 1911, Mexico had become increasingly attractive to our business men. On the invitation of President Diaz, they had invested huge sums in Mexican lands, oil fields, and mines, and had laid the foundations of a new industrial order. The severe régime instituted by Diaz, however, stirred popular discontent. The peons, or serfs, demanded the break-up of the great estates, some of which had come down from the days of Cortez. Their clamor for "the restoration of the land to the people could not be silenced." In 1911 Diaz was forced to resign and left the country.

Mexico now slid down the path to disorder. Revolutions and civil commotions followed in swift succession. A liberal president, Madero, installed as the successor to Diaz, was deposed in 1913 and brutally murdered. Huerta, a military adventurer, hailed for a time as another "strong man," succeeded Madero whose murder he was accused of instigating. Although Great Britain and nearly all the powers of Europe accepted the new government as lawful, the United States steadily withheld recognition. In the meantime Mexico was torn by insurrections under the leadership of Carranza, a friend of Madero, Villa, a bandit of generous pretensions, and Zapata, a radical leader of the peons. Without the support of the United States, Huerta was doomed.

In the summer of 1914, the dictator resigned and fled from the capital, leaving the field to Carranza. For six years the new president, recognized by the United States, held a precarious position which he vigorously strove to strengthen against various revolutionary movements. At length in 1920, he too was deposed and murdered, and another military chieftain, Obregon, installed in power.

These events right at our door could not fail to involve the government of the United States. In the disorders many American citizens lost their lives. American property was destroyed and land owned by Americans was confiscated. A new Mexican constitution, in effect nationalizing the natural resources of the country, struck at the rights of foreign investors. Moreover the Mexican border was in constant turmoil. Even in the last days of his administration, Mr. Taft felt compelled to issue a solemn warning to the Mexican government protesting against the violation of American rights.

President Wilson, soon after his inauguration, sent a commissioner to Mexico to inquire into the situation. Although he declared a general policy of "watchful waiting," he twice came to blows with Mexican forces. In 1914 some American sailors at Tampico were arrested by a Mexican officer; the Mexican government, although it immediately released the men, refused to make the required apology for the incident. As a result President Wilson ordered the landing of American forces at Vera Cruz and the occupation of the city. A clash of arms followed in which several Americans were killed. War seemed inevitable, but at this juncture the governments of Argentina, Brazil, and Chile tendered their good offices as mediators. After a few weeks of negotiation, during which Huerta was forced out of power, American forces were withdrawn from Vera Cruz and the incident closed.

In 1916 a second break in amicable relations occurred. In the spring of that year a band of Villa's men raided the town of Columbus, New Mexico, killing several citizens and committing robberies. A punitive expedition under the command of General Pershing was quickly sent out to capture the offenders. Against the protests of President Carranza, American forces penetrated deeply into Mexico without effecting the object of the undertaking. This operation lasted until January, 1917, when the imminence of war with Germany led to the withdrawal of the American soldiers. Friendly relations were resumed with the Mexican government and the policy of "watchful waiting" was continued.

THE UNITED STATES AND THE EUROPEAN WAR

The Outbreak of the War.—In the opening days of August, 1914, the age-long jealousies of European nations, sharpened by new imperial ambitions, broke out in another general conflict such as had shaken the world in the days of Napoleon. On June 28, the heir to the Austro-Hungarian throne was assassinated at Serajevo, the capital of Bosnia, an Austrian province occupied mainly by Serbs. With a view to stopping Serbian agitation for independence, Austria-Hungary laid the blame for this incident on the government of Serbia and made humiliating demands on that country. Germany at once proposed that the issue should be regarded as "an affair which should be settled solely between Austria-Hungary and Serbia"; meaning that the small nation should be left to the tender mercies of a great power. Russia refused to take this view. Great Britain proposed a settlement by mediation. Germany backed up Austria to the limit. To use the language of the German authorities: "We were perfectly aware that a possible warlike attitude of Austria-Hungary against Serbia might bring Russia upon the field and that it might therefore involve us in a war, in accordance with our duties as allies. We could not, however, in these vital interests of Austria-Hungary which were at stake, advise our ally to take a yielding attitude not compatible with his dignity nor deny him our assistance." That made the war inevitable.

Every day of the fateful August, 1914, was crowded with momentous events. On the 1st, Germany declared war on Russia. On the 2d, the Germans invaded the little duchy of Luxemburg and notified the King of Belgium that they were preparing to violate the neutrality of his realm on their way to Paris. On the same day, Great Britain, anxiously besought by the French government, promised the aid of the British navy if German warships made hostile demonstrations in the Channel. August 3d, the German government declared war on France. The following day, Great Britain demanded of Germany respect for Belgian neutrality and, failing to receive the guarantee, broke off diplomatic relations. On the 5th, the British prime minister announced that war had opened between England and Germany. The storm now broke in all its pitiless fury.

The State of American Opinion.—Although President Wilson promptly proclaimed the neutrality of the United States, the sympathies of a large majority of the American people were without doubt on the side of Great Britain and France. To them the invasion of the little kingdom of Belgium and the horrors that accompanied German occupation were odious in the extreme. Moreover, they regarded the German imperial government as an autocratic power wielded in the interest of an ambitious military party. The Kaiser, William II, and the Crown Prince were the symbols of royal arrogance. On the other hand, many Americans of German descent, in memory of their ties with the Fatherland, openly sympathized with the Central Powers; and many Americans of Irish descent, recalling their long and bitter struggle for home rule in Ireland, would have regarded British defeat as a merited redress of ancient grievances.

Extremely sensitive to American opinion, but ill informed about it, the German government soon began systematic efforts to present its cause to the people of the United States in the most favorable light possible. Dr. Bernhard Dernburg, the former colonial secretary of the German empire, was sent to America as a special agent. For months he filled the newspapers, magazines, and periodicals with interviews, articles, and notes on the justice of the Teutonic cause. From a press bureau in New York flowed a stream of pamphlets, leaflets, and cartoons. A magazine, "The Fatherland," was founded to secure "fair play for Germany and Austria." Several professors in American universities, who had received their training in Germany, took up the pen in defense of the Central Empires. The German language press, without exception it seems, the National German Alliance, minor German societies, and Lutheran churches came to the support of the German cause. Even the English language papers, though generally favorable to the Entente Allies, opened their columns in the interest of equal justice to the spokesmen for all the contending powers of Europe.

Before two weeks had elapsed the controversy had become so intense that President Wilson (August 18, 1914) was moved to caution his countrymen against falling into angry disputes. "Every man," he said, "who really loves America will act and speak in the true spirit of neutrality which is the spirit of impartiality and fairness and friendliness to all concerned.... We must be impartial in thought as well as in action, must put a curb upon our sentiments as well as upon every transaction that might be construed as a preference of one party to the struggle before another."

The Clash over American Trade.—As in the time of the Napoleonic wars, the conflict in Europe raised fundamental questions respecting rights of Americans trading with countries at peace as well as those at war. On this point there existed on August 1, 1914, a fairly definite body of principles by which nations were bound. Among them the following were of vital significance. In the first place, it was recognized that an enemy merchant ship caught on the high seas was a legitimate prize of war which might be seized and confiscated. In the second place, it was agreed that "contraband of war" found on an enemy or neutral ship was a lawful prize; any ship suspected of carrying it was liable to search and if caught with forbidden goods was subject to seizure. In the third place, international law prescribed that a peaceful merchant ship, whether belonging to an enemy or to a neutral country, should not be destroyed or sunk without provision for the safety of crew and passengers. In the fourth place, it was understood that a belligerent had the right, if it could, to blockade the ports of an enemy and prevent the ingress and egress of all ships; but such a blockade, to be lawful, had to be effective.

These general principles left undetermined two important matters: "What is an effective blockade?" and "What is contraband of war?" The task of answering these questions fell to Great Britain as mistress of the seas. Although the German submarines made it impossible for her battleships to maintain a continuous patrol of the waters in front of blockaded ports, she declared the blockade to be none the less "effective" because her navy was supreme. As to contraband of war Great Britain put such a broad interpretation upon the term as to include nearly every important article of commerce. Early in 1915 she declared even cargoes of grain and flour to be contraband, defending the action on the ground that the German government had recently taken possession of all domestic stocks of corn, wheat, and flour.

A new question arose in connection with American trade with the neutral countries surrounding Germany. Great Britain early began to intercept ships carrying oil, gasoline, and copper—all war materials of prime importance—on the ground that they either were destined ultimately to Germany or would release goods for sale to Germans. On November 2, 1914, the English government announced that the Germans wore sowing mines in open waters and that therefore the whole of the North Sea was a military zone. Ships bound for Denmark, Norway, and Sweden were ordered to come by the English Channel for inspection and sailing directions. In effect, Americans were now licensed by Great Britain to trade in certain commodities and in certain amounts with neutral countries.

Against these extraordinary measures, the State Department at Washington lodged pointed objections, saying: "This government is reluctantly forced to the conclusion that the present policy of His Majesty's government toward neutral ships and cargoes exceeds the manifest necessity of a belligerent and constitutes restrictions upon the rights of American citizens on the high seas, which are not justified by the rules of international law or required under the principle of self-preservation."

Germany Begins the Submarine Campaign.—Germany now announced that, on and after February 18, 1915, the whole of the English Channel and the waters around Great Britain would be deemed a war zone and that every enemy ship found therein would be destroyed. The German decree added that, as the British admiralty had ordered the use of neutral flags by English ships in time of distress, neutral vessels would be in danger of destruction if found in the forbidden area. It was clear that Germany intended to employ submarines to destroy shipping. A new factor was thus introduced into naval warfare, one not provided for in the accepted laws of war. A warship overhauling a merchant vessel could easily take its crew and passengers on board for safe keeping as prescribed by international law; but a submarine ordinarily could do nothing of the sort. Of necessity the lives and the ships of neutrals, as well as of belligerents, were put in mortal peril. This amazing conduct Germany justified on the ground that it was mere retaliation against Great Britain for her violations of international law.

The response of the United States to the ominous German order was swift and direct. On February 10, 1915, it warned Germany that if her commanders destroyed American lives and ships in obedience to that decree, the action would "be very hard indeed to reconcile with the friendly relations happily subsisting between the two governments." The American note added that the German imperial government would be held to "strict accountability" and all necessary steps would be taken to safeguard American lives and American rights. This was firm and clear language, but the only response which it evoked from Germany was a suggestion that, if Great Britain would allow food supplies to pass through the blockade, the submarine campaign would be dropped.

Violations of American Rights.—Meanwhile Germany continued to ravage shipping on the high seas. On January 28, a German raider sank the American ship, *William P. Frye*, in the South Atlantic; on March 28, a British ship, the *Falaba*, was sunk by a submarine and many on board, including an American citizen, were killed; and on April 28, a German airplane dropped bombs on the American steamer *Cushing*. On the morning of May 1, 1915, Americans were astounded to see in the newspapers an advertisement, signed by the German Imperial Embassy, warning travelers of the dangers in the war zone and notifying them that any who ventured on British ships into that area did so at their own risk. On that day, the *Lusitania*, a British steamer, sailed from New York for Liverpool. On May 7, without warning, the ship was struck by two torpedoes and in a few minutes went down by the bow, carrying to death 1153 persons including 114 American men, women, and children. A cry of horror ran through the country. The German papers in America and a few American people argued that American citizens had been duly warned of the danger and had deliberately taken their lives into their own hands; but the terrible deed was almost universally condemned by public opinion.

The *Lusitania* Notes.—On May 14, the Department of State at Washington made public the first of three famous notes on the *Lusitania* case. It solemnly informed the German government that "no warning that an unlawful and inhumane act will be committed can possibly be accepted as an excuse or palliation for that act or as an abatement of the responsibility for its commission." It called upon the German government to disavow the act, make reparation as far as possible, and take steps to prevent "the recurrence of anything so obviously subversive of the principles of warfare." The note closed with a clear caution to Germany that the government of the United States would not "omit any word or any act necessary to the performance of its sacred duty of maintaining the rights of the United States and its citizens and of safeguarding their free exercise and enjoyment." The die was cast; but Germany in reply merely temporized.

In a second note, made public on June 11, the position of the United States was again affirmed. William Jennings Bryan, the Secretary of State, had resigned because the drift of President Wilson's policy was not toward mediation but the strict maintenance of American rights, if need be, by force of arms. The German reply was still evasive and German naval commanders continued their course of sinking merchant ships. In a third and final note of July 21, 1915, President Wilson made it clear to Germany that he meant what he said when he wrote that he would maintain the rights of American citizens. Finally after much discussion and shifting about, the German ambassador on September 1, 1915, sent a brief note to the Secretary of State: "Liners will not be sunk by our submarines without warning and without safety of the lives of non-combatants, provided the liners do not try to escape or offer resistance." Editorially, the New York *Times* declared: "It is a triumph not only of diplomacy but of reason, of humanity, of justice, and of truth." The Secretary of State saw in it "a recognition of the fundamental principles for which we have contended."

The Presidential Election of 1916.—In the midst of this crisis came the presidential campaign. On the Republican side everything seemed to depend upon the action of the Progressives. If the breach created in 1912 could be closed, victory was possible; if not, defeat was certain. A promise of unity lay in the fact that the conventions of the Republicans and Progressives were held simultaneously in Chicago. The friends of Roosevelt hoped that both parties would select him as their candidate; but this hope was not realized. The Republicans chose, and the Progressives accepted, Charles E. Hughes, an associate justice of the federal Supreme Court who, as governor of New York, had won a national reputation by waging war on "machine politicians."

In the face of the clamor for expressions of sympathy with one or the other of the contending powers of Europe, the Republicans chose a middle course, declaring that they would uphold all American rights "at home and abroad, by land and by sea." This sentiment Mr. Hughes echoed in his acceptance speech. By some it was interpreted to mean a firmer policy in dealing with Great Britain; by others, a more vigorous handling of the submarine menace. The Democrats, on their side, renominated President Wilson by acclamation, reviewed with pride the legislative achievements of the party, and commended "the splendid diplomatic victories of our great President who has preserved the vital interests of our government and its citizens and kept us out of war."

In the election which ensued President Wilson's popular vote exceeded that cast for Mr. Hughes by more than half a million, while his electoral vote stood 277 to 254. The result was regarded, and not without warrant, as a great personal triumph for the President. He had received the largest vote yet cast for a presidential candidate. The Progressive party practically disappeared, and the Socialists suffered a severe set-back, falling far behind the vote of 1912.

President Wilson Urges Peace upon the Warring Nations.—Apparently convinced that his pacific policies had been profoundly approved by his countrymen, President Wilson, soon after the election, addressed "peace notes" to the European belligerents. On December 16, the German Emperor proposed to the Allied Powers that they enter into peace negotiations, a suggestion that was treated as a mere political maneuver by the opposing governments. Two days later President Wilson sent a note to the warring nations asking them to avow "the terms upon which war might be concluded." To these notes the Central Powers replied that they were ready to meet their antagonists in a peace conference; and Allied Powers answered by presenting certain conditions precedent to a satisfactory settlement. On January 22, 1917, President Wilson in an address before the Senate, declared it to be a duty of the United States to take part in the establishment of a stable peace on the basis of certain principles. These were, in short: "peace without victory"; the right of nationalities to freedom and self-government; the independence of Poland; freedom of the seas; the reduction of armaments; and the abolition of entangling alliances. The whole world was discussing the President's remarkable message, when it was dumbfounded to hear, on January 31, that the German ambassador at Washington had announced the official renewal of ruthless submarine warfare.

The United States at War

Steps toward War.—Three days after the receipt of the news that the German government intended to return to its former submarine policy, President Wilson severed diplomatic relations with the German empire. At the same time he explained to Congress that he desired no conflict with Germany and would await an "overt act" before taking further steps to preserve American rights. "God grant," he concluded, "that we may not be challenged to defend them by acts of willful injustice on the part of the government of Germany." Yet the challenge came. Between February 26 and April 2, six American merchant vessels were torpedoed, in most cases without any warning and without regard to the loss of American lives. President Wilson therefore called upon Congress to answer the German menace. The reply of Congress on April 6 was a resolution, passed with only a few dissenting votes, declaring the existence of a state of war with Germany. Austria-Hungary at once severed diplomatic relations with the United States; but it was not until December 7 that Congress, acting on the President's advice, declared war also on that "vassal of the German government."

American War Aims.—In many addresses at the beginning and during the course of the war, President Wilson stated the purposes which actuated our government in taking up arms. He first made it clear that it was a war of self-defense. "The military masters of Germany," he exclaimed, "denied us the right to be neutral." Proof of that lay on every hand. Agents of the German imperial government had destroyed American lives and American property on the high seas. They had filled our communities with spies. They had planted bombs in ships and munition works. They had fomented divisions among American citizens.

Though assailed in many ways and compelled to resort to war, the United States sought no material rewards. "The world must be made safe for democracy. Its peace must be planted upon the tested foundations of political liberty. We have no selfish ends to serve. We desire no conquest, no dominion. We seek no indemnities for ourselves."

In a very remarkable message read to Congress on January 8, 1918, President Wilson laid down his famous "fourteen points" summarizing the ideals for which we were fighting. They included open treaties of peace, openly arrived at; absolute freedom of navigation upon the seas; the removal, as far as possible, of trade barriers among nations; reduction of armaments; adjustment of colonial claims in the interest of the populations concerned; fair and friendly treatment of Russia; the restoration of Belgium; righting the wrong done to France in 1871 in the matter of Alsace-Lorraine; adjustment of Italian frontiers along the lines of nationality; more liberty for the peoples of Austria-Hungary; the restoration of Serbia and Rumania; the readjustment of the Turkish Empire; an independent Poland; and an association of nations to afford mutual guarantees to all states great and small. On a later occasion President Wilson elaborated the last point, namely, the formation of a league of nations to guarantee peace and establish justice among the powers of the world. Democracy, the right of nations to determine their own fate, a covenant of enduring peace—these were the ideals for which the American people were to pour out their blood and treasure.

The Selective Draft.—The World War became a war of nations. The powers against which we were arrayed had every able-bodied man in service and all their resources, human and material, thrown into the scale. For this reason, President Wilson summoned the whole people of the United States to make every sacrifice necessary for victory. Congress by law decreed that the national army should be chosen from all male citizens and males not enemy aliens who had declared their intention of becoming citizens. By the first act of May 18, 1917, it fixed the age limits at twenty-one to thirty-one inclusive. Later, in August, 1918, it extended them to eighteen and forty-five. From the men of the first group so enrolled were chosen by lot the soldiers for the World War who, with the regular army and the national guard, formed the American Expeditionary Force upholding the American cause on the battlefields of Europe. "The whole nation," said the President, "must be a team in which each man shall play the part for which he is best fitted."

Liberty Loans and Taxes.—In order that the military and naval forces should be stinted in no respect, the nation was called upon to place its financial resources at the service of the government. Some urged the "conscription of wealth as well as men," meaning the support of the war out of taxes upon great fortunes; but more conservative counsels prevailed. Four great Liberty Loans were floated, all the agencies of modern publicity being employed to enlist popular interest. The first loan had four and a half million subscribers; the fourth more than twenty million. Combined with loans were heavy taxes. A progressive tax was laid upon incomes beginning with four per cent on incomes in the lower ranges and rising to sixty-three per cent of that part of any income above $2,000,000. A progressive tax was levied upon inheritances. An excess profits tax was laid upon all corporations and partnerships, rising in amount to sixty per cent of the net income in excess of thirty-three per cent on the invested capital. "This," said a distinguished economist, "is the high-water mark in the history of taxation. Never before in the annals of civilization has an attempt been made to take as much as two-thirds of a man's income by taxation."

Mobilizing Material Resources.—No stone was left unturned to provide the arms, munitions, supplies, and transportation required in the gigantic undertaking. Between the declaration of war and the armistice, Congress enacted law after law relative to food supplies, raw materials, railways, mines, ships, forests, and industrial enterprises. No power over the lives and property of citizens, deemed necessary to the prosecution of the armed conflict, was withheld from the government. The farmer's wheat, the housewife's sugar, coal at the mines, labor in the factories, ships at the wharves, trade with friendly countries, the railways, banks, stores, private fortunes—all were mobilized and laid under whatever obligations the government deemed imperative. Never was a nation more completely devoted to a single cause.

A law of August 10, 1917, gave the President power to fix the prices of wheat and coal and to take almost any steps necessary to prevent monopoly and excessive prices. By a series of measures, enlarging the principles of the shipping act of 1916, ships and shipyards were brought under public control and the government was empowered to embark upon a great ship-building program. In December, 1917, the government assumed for the period of the war the operation of the railways under a presidential proclamation which was elaborated in March, 1918, by act of Congress. In the summer of 1918 the express, telephone, and telegraph business of the entire country passed under government control. By war risk insurance acts allowances were made for the families of enlisted men, compensation for injuries was provided, death benefits were instituted, and a system of national insurance was established in the interest of the men in service. Never before in the history of the country had the government taken such a wise and humane view of its obligations to those who served on the field of battle or on the seas.

The Espionage and Sedition Acts.—By the Espionage law of June 15, 1917, and the amending law, known as the Sedition act, passed in May of the following year, the government was given a drastic power over the expression of opinion. The first measure penalized those who conveyed information to a foreign country to be used to the injury of the United States; those who made false statements designed to interfere with the military or naval forces of the United States; those who attempted to stir up insubordination or disloyalty in the army and navy; and those who willfully obstructed enlistment. The Sedition act was still more severe and sweeping in its terms. It imposed heavy penalties upon any person who used "abusive language about the government or institutions of the country." It authorized the dismissal of any officer of the government who committed "disloyal acts" or uttered "disloyal language," and empowered the Postmaster General to close the mails to persons violating the law. This measure, prepared by the Department of Justice, encountered vigorous opposition in the Senate, where twenty-four Republicans and two Democrats voted against it. Senator Johnson of California denounced it as a law "to suppress the freedom of the press in the United States and to prevent any man, no matter who he is, from expressing legitimate criticism concerning the present government." The constitutionality of the acts was attacked; but they were sustained by the Supreme Court and stringently enforced.

Labor and the War.—In view of the restlessness of European labor during the war and especially the proletarian revolution in Russia in November, 1917, some anxiety was early expressed as to the stand which organized labor might take in the United States. It was, however, soon dispelled. Samuel Gompers, speaking for the American Federation of Labor, declared that "this is labor's war," and pledged the united support of all the unions. There was some dissent. The Socialist party denounced the war as a capitalist quarrel; but all the protests combined were too slight to have much effect. American labor leaders were sent to Europe to strengthen the wavering ranks of trade unionists in war-worn England, France, and Italy. Labor was given representation on the important boards and commissions dealing with industrial questions. Trade union standards were accepted by the government and generally applied in industry. The Department of Labor became one of the powerful war centers of the nation. In a memorable address to the American Federation of Labor, President Wilson assured the trade unionists that labor conditions should not be made unduly onerous by the war and received in return a pledge of loyalty from the Federation. Recognition of labor's contribution to winning the war was embodied in the treaty of peace, which provided for a permanent international organization to promote the world-wide effort of labor to improve social conditions. "The league of nations has for its object the establishment of universal peace," runs the preamble to the labor section of the treaty, "and such a peace can be established only if it is based upon social justice.... The failure of any nation to adopt humane conditions of labor is an obstacle in the way of other nations which desire to improve the conditions in their own countries."

The American Navy in the War.—As soon as Congress declared war the fleet was mobilized, American ports were thrown open to the warships of the Allies, immediate provision was made for increasing the number of men and ships, and a contingent of war vessels was sent to coöperate with the British and French in their life-and-death contest with submarines. Special effort was made to stimulate the production of "submarine chasers" and "scout cruisers" to be sent to the danger zone. Convoys were provided to accompany the transports conveying soldiers to France. Before the end of the war more than three hundred American vessels and 75,000 officers and men were operating in European waters. Though the German fleet failed to come out and challenge the sea power of the Allies, the battleships of the United States were always ready to do their full duty in such an event. As things turned out, the service of the American navy was limited mainly to helping in the campaign that wore down the submarine menace to Allied shipping.

The War in France.—Owing to the peculiar character of the warfare in France, it required a longer time for American military forces to get into action; but there was no unnecessary delay. Soon after the declaration of war, steps were taken to give military assistance to the Allies. The regular army was enlarged and the troops of the national guard were brought into national service. On June 13, General John J. Pershing, chosen head of the American Expeditionary Forces, reached Paris and began preparations for the arrival of our troops. In June, the vanguard of the army reached France. A slow and steady stream followed. As soon as the men enrolled under the draft were ready, it became a flood. During the period of the war the army was enlarged from about 190,000 men to 3,665,000, of whom more than 2,000,000 were in France when the armistice was signed.

Although American troops did not take part on a large scale until the last phase of the war in 1918, several battalions of infantry were in the trenches by October, 1917, and had their first severe encounter with the Germans early in November. In January, 1918, they took over a part of the front line as an American sector. In March, General Pershing placed our forces at the disposal of General Foch, commander-in-chief of the Allied armies. The first division, which entered the Montdidier salient in April, soon was engaged with the enemy, "taking with splendid dash the town of Cantigny and all other objectives, which were organized and held steadfastly against vicious counter attacks and galling artillery fire."

When the Germans launched their grand drives toward the Marne and Paris, in June and July, 1918, every available man was placed at General Foch's command. At Belleau Wood, at Château-Thierry, and other points along the deep salient made by the Germans into the French lines, American soldiers distinguished themselves by heroic action. They also played an important rôle in the counter attack that "smashed" the salient and drove the Germans back.

In September, American troops, with French aid, "wiped out" the German salient at St. Mihiel. By this time General Pershing was ready for the great American drive to the northeast in the Argonne forest, while he also coöperated with the British in the assault on the Hindenburg line. In the Meuse-Argonne battle, our soldiers encountered some of the most severe fighting of the war and pressed forward steadily against the most stubborn resistance from the enemy. On the 6th of November, reported General Pershing, "a division of the first corps reached a point on the Meuse opposite Sedan, twenty-five miles from our line of departure. The strategical goal which was our highest hope was gained. We had cut the enemy's main line of communications and nothing but a surrender or an armistice could save his army from complete disaster." Five days later the end came. On the morning of November 11, the order to cease firing went into effect. The German army was in rapid retreat and demoralization had begun. The Kaiser had abdicated and fled into Holland. The Hohenzollern dreams of empire were shattered. In the fifty-second month, the World War, involving nearly every civilized nation on the globe, was brought to a close. More than 75,000 American soldiers and sailors had given their lives. More than 250,000 had been wounded or were missing or in German prison camps.

The Settlement at Paris

The Peace Conference.—On January 18, 1919, a conference of the Allied and Associated Powers assembled to pronounce judgment upon the German empire and its defeated satellites: Austria-Hungary, Bulgaria, and Turkey. It was a moving spectacle. Seventy-two delegates spoke for thirty-two states. The United States, Great Britain, France, Italy, and Japan had five delegates each. Belgium, Brazil, and Serbia were each assigned three. Canada, Australia, South Africa, India, China, Greece, Hedjaz, Poland, Portugal, Rumania, Siam, and Czechoslovakia were allotted two apiece. The remaining states of New Zealand, Bolivia, Cuba, Ecuador, Guatemala, Haiti, Honduras, Liberia, Nicaragua, Panama, Peru, and Uruguay each had one delegate. President Wilson spoke in person for the United States. England, France, and Italy were represented by their premiers: David Lloyd George, Georges Clémenceau, and Vittorio Orlando.

The Supreme Council.—The real work of the settlement was first committed to a Supreme Council of ten representing the United States, Great Britain, France, Italy, and Japan. This was later reduced to five members. Then Japan dropped out and finally Italy, leaving only President Wilson and the Premiers, Lloyd George and Clémenceau, the "Big Three," who assumed the burden of mighty decisions. On May 6, their work was completed and in a secret session of the full conference the whole treaty of peace was approved, though a few of the powers made reservations or objections. The next day the treaty was presented to the Germans who, after prolonged protests, signed on the last day of grace, June 28. This German treaty was followed by agreements with Austria, Hungary, Bulgaria, and Turkey. Collectively these great documents formed the legal basis of the general European settlement.

The Terms of the Settlement.—The combined treaties make a huge volume. The German treaty alone embraces about 80,000 words. Collectively they cover an immense range of subjects which may be summarized under five heads: (1) The territorial settlement in Europe; (2) the destruction of German military power; (3) reparations for damages done by Germany and her allies; (4) the disposition of German colonies and protectorates; and (5) the League of Nations.

Germany was reduced by the cession of Alsace-Lorraine to France and the loss of several other provinces. Austria-Hungary was dissolved and dismembered. Russia was reduced by the creation of new states on the west. Bulgaria was stripped of her gains in the recent Balkan wars. Turkey was dismembered. Nine new independent states were created: Poland, Finland, Lithuania, Latvia, Esthonia, Ukraine, Czechoslovakia, Armenia, and Hedjaz. Italy, Greece, Rumania, and Serbia were enlarged by cessions of territory and Serbia was transformed into the great state of Jugoslavia.

The destruction of German military power was thorough. The entire navy, with minor exceptions, was turned over to the Allied and Associated Powers; Germany's total equipment for the future was limited to six battleships and six light cruisers, with certain small vessels but no submarines. The number of enlisted men and officers for the army was fixed at not more than 100,000; the General Staff was dissolved; and the manufacture of munitions restricted.

Germany was compelled to accept full responsibility for all damages; to pay five billion dollars in cash and goods, and to make certain other payments which might be ordered from time to time by an inter-allied reparations commission. She was also required to deliver to Belgium, France, and Italy, millions of tons of coal every year for ten years; while by way of additional compensation to France the rich coal basin of the Saar was placed under inter-allied control to be exploited under French administration for a period of at least fifteen years. Austria and the other associates of Germany were also laid under heavy obligations to the victors. Damages done to shipping by submarines and other vessels were to be paid for on the basis of ton for ton.

The disposition of the German colonies and the old Ottoman empire presented knotty problems. It was finally agreed that the German colonies and Turkish provinces which were in a backward stage of development should be placed under the tutelage of certain powers acting as "mandatories" holding them in "a sacred trust of civilization." An exception to the mandatory principle arose in the case of German rights in Shantung, all of which were transferred directly to Japan. It was this arrangement that led the Chinese delegation to withhold their signatures from the treaty.

The League of Nations.—High among the purposes which he had in mind in summoning the nation to arms, President Wilson placed the desire to put an end to war. All through the United States the people spoke of the "war to end war." No slogan called forth a deeper response from the public. The President himself repeatedly declared that a general association of nations must be formed to guard the peace and protect all against the ambitions of the few. "As I see it," he said in his address on opening the Fourth Liberty Loan campaign, "the constitution of the League of Nations and the clear definition of its objects must be a part, in a sense the most essential part, of the peace settlement itself."

Nothing was more natural, therefore, than Wilson's insistence at Paris upon the formation of an international association. Indeed he had gone to Europe in person largely to accomplish that end. Part One of the treaty with Germany, the Covenant of the League of Nations, was due to his labors more than to any other influence. Within the League thus created were to be embraced all the Allied and Associated Powers and nearly all the neutrals. By a two-thirds vote of the League Assembly the excluded nations might be admitted.

The agencies of the League of Nations were to be three in number: (1) a permanent secretariat located at Geneva; (2) an Assembly consisting of one delegate from each country, dominion, or self-governing colony (including Canada, Australia, South Africa, New Zealand, and India); (3) and a Council consisting of representatives of the United States, Great Britain, France, Italy, and Japan, and four other representatives selected by the Assembly from time to time.

The duties imposed on the League and the obligations accepted by its members were numerous and important. The Council was to take steps to formulate a scheme for the reduction of armaments and to submit a plan for the establishment of a permanent Court of International Justice. The members of the League (Article X) were to respect and preserve as against external aggression the territorial integrity and existing political independence of all the associated nations. They were to submit to arbitration or inquiry by the Council all disputes which could not be adjusted by diplomacy and in no case to resort to war until three months after the award. Should any member disregard its covenants, its action would be considered an act of war against the League, which would accordingly cut off the trade and business of the hostile member and recommend through the Council to the several associated governments the military measures to be taken. In case the decision in any arbitration of a dispute was unanimous, the members of the League affected by it were to abide by it.

Such was the settlement at Paris and such was the association of nations formed to promote the peace of the world. They were quickly approved by most of the powers, and the first Assembly of the League of Nations met at Geneva late in 1920.

The Treaty in the United States.—When the treaty was presented to the United States Senate for approval, a violent opposition appeared. In that chamber the Republicans had a slight majority and a two-thirds vote was necessary for ratification. The sentiment for and against the treaty ran mainly along party lines; but the Republicans were themselves divided. The major portion, known as "reservationists," favored ratification with certain conditions respecting American rights; while a small though active minority rejected the League of Nations in its entirety, announcing themselves to be "irreconcilables." The grounds of this Republican opposition lay partly in the terms of peace imposed on Germany and partly in the Covenant of the League of Nations. Exception was taken to the clauses which affected the rights of American citizens in property involved in the adjustment with Germany, but the burden of criticism was directed against the League. Article X guaranteeing against external aggression the political independence and territorial integrity of the members of the League was subjected to a specially heavy fire; while the treatment accorded to China and the sections affecting American internal affairs were likewise attacked as "unjust and dangerous." As an outcome of their deliberations, the Republicans proposed a long list of reservations which touched upon many of the vital parts of the treaty. These were rejected by President Wilson as amounting in effect to a "nullification of the treaty." As a deadlock ensued the treaty was definitely rejected, owing to the failure of its sponsors to secure the requisite two-thirds vote.

The League of Nations in the Campaign of 1920.—At this juncture the presidential campaign of 1920 opened. The Republicans, while condemning the terms of the proposed League, endorsed the general idea of an international agreement to prevent war. Their candidate, Senator Warren G. Harding of Ohio, maintained a similar position without saying definitely whether the League devised at Paris could be recast in such a manner as to meet his requirements. The Democrats, on the other hand, while not opposing limitations clarifying the obligations of the United States, demanded "the immediate ratification of the treaty without reservations which would impair its essential integrity." The Democratic candidate, Governor James M. Cox, of Ohio, announced his firm conviction that the United States should "go into the League," without closing the door to mild reservations; he appealed to the country largely on that issue. The election of Senator Harding, in an extraordinary "landslide," coupled with the return of a majority of Republicans to the Senate, made uncertain American participation in the League of Nations.

The United States and International Entanglements.—Whether America entered the League or not, it could not close its doors to the world and escape perplexing international complications. It had ever-increasing financial and commercial connections with all other countries. Our associates in the recent war were heavily indebted to our government. The prosperity of American industries depended to a considerable extent upon the recovery of the impoverished and battle-torn countries of Europe.

There were other complications no less specific. The United States was compelled by force of circumstances to adopt a Russian policy. The government of the Czar had been overthrown by a liberal revolution, which in turn had been succeeded by an extreme, communist "dictatorship." The Bolsheviki, or majority faction of the socialists, had obtained control of the national council of peasants, workingmen, and soldiers, called the soviet, and inaugurated a radical régime. They had made peace with Germany in March, 1918. Thereupon the United States joined England, France, and Japan in an unofficial war upon them. After the general settlement at Paris in 1919, our government, while withdrawing troops from

Siberia and Archangel, continued in its refusal to recognize the Bolshevists or to permit unhampered trade with them. President Wilson repeatedly denounced them as the enemies of civilization and undertook to lay down for all countries the principles which should govern intercourse with Russia.

Further international complications were created in connection with the World War, wholly apart from the terms of peace or the League of Nations. The United States had participated in a general European conflict which changed the boundaries of countries, called into being new nations, and reduced the power and territories of the vanquished. Accordingly, it was bound to face the problem of how far it was prepared to coöperate with the victors in any settlement of Europe's difficulties. By no conceivable process, therefore, could America be disentangled from the web of world affairs. Isolation, if desirable, had become impossible. Within three hundred years from the founding of the tiny settlements at Jamestown and Plymouth, America, by virtue of its institutions, its population, its wealth, and its commerce, had become first among the nations of the earth. By moral obligations and by practical interests its fate was thus linked with the destiny of all mankind.

SUMMARY OF DEMOCRACY AND THE WORLD WAR

The astounding industrial progress that characterized the period following the Civil War bequeathed to the new generation many perplexing problems connected with the growth of trusts and railways, the accumulation of great fortunes, the increase of poverty in the industrial cities, the exhaustion of the free land, and the acquisition of dominions in distant seas. As long as there was an abundance of land in the West any able-bodied man with initiative and industry could become an independent farmer. People from the cities and immigrants from Europe had always before them that gateway to property and prosperity. When the land was all gone, American economic conditions inevitably became more like those of Europe.

Though the new economic questions had been vigorously debated in many circles before his day, it was President Roosevelt who first discussed them continuously from the White House. The natural resources of the country were being exhausted; he advocated their conservation. Huge fortunes were being made in business creating inequalities in opportunity; he favored reducing them by income and inheritance taxes. Industries were disturbed by strikes; he pressed arbitration upon capital and labor. The free land was gone; he declared that labor was in a less favorable position to bargain with capital and therefore should organize in unions for collective bargaining. There had been wrong-doing on the part of certain great trusts; those responsible should be punished.

The spirit of reform was abroad in the land. The spoils system was attacked. It was alleged that the political parties were dominated by "rings and bosses." The United States Senate was called "a millionaires' club." Poverty and misery were observed in the cities. State legislatures and city governments were accused of corruption.

In answer to the charges, remedies were proposed and adopted. Civil service reform was approved. The Australian ballot, popular election of Senators, the initiative, referendum, and recall, commission and city manager plans for cities, public regulation of railways, compensation for those injured in industries, minimum wages for women and children, pensions for widows, the control of housing in the cities—these and a hundred other reforms were adopted and tried out. The national watchword became: "America, Improve Thyself."

The spirit of reform broke into both political parties. It appeared in many statutes enacted by Congress under President Taft's leadership. It disrupted the Republicans temporarily in 1912 when the Progressive party entered the field. It led the Democratic candidate in that year, Governor Wilson, to make a "progressive appeal" to the voters. It inspired a considerable program of national legislation under President Wilson's two administrations.

In the age of change, four important amendments to the federal constitution, the first in more than forty years, were adopted. The sixteenth empowered Congress to lay an income tax. The seventeenth assured popular election of Senators. The eighteenth made prohibition national. The nineteenth, following upon the adoption of woman suffrage in many states, enfranchised the women of the nation.

In the sphere of industry, equally great changes took place. The major portion of the nation's business passed into the hands of corporations. In all the leading industries of the country labor was organized into trade unions and federated in a national organization. The power of organized capital and organized labor loomed upon the horizon. Their struggles, their rights, and their place in the economy of the nation raised problems of the first magnitude.

While the country was engaged in a heated debate upon its domestic issues, the World War broke out in Europe in 1914. As a hundred years before, American rights upon the high seas became involved at once. They were invaded on both sides; but Germany, in addition to assailing American ships and property, ruthlessly destroyed American lives. She set at naught the rules of civilized warfare upon the sea. Warnings from President Wilson were without avail. Nothing could stay the hand of the German war party.

After long and patient negotiations, President Wilson in 1917 called upon the nation to take up arms against an assailant that had in effect declared war upon America. The answer was swift and firm. The national resources, human and material, were mobilized. The navy was enlarged, a draft army created, huge loans floated, heavy taxes laid, and the spirit of sacrifice called forth in a titanic struggle against an autocratic power that threatened to dominate Europe and the World.

In the end, American financial, naval, and military assistance counted heavily in the scale. American sailors scoured the seas searching for the terrible submarines. American soldiers took part in the last great drives that broke the might of Germany's army. Such was the nation's response to the President's summons to arms in a war "for democracy" and "to end war."

When victory crowned the arms of the powers united against Germany, President Wilson in person took part in the peace council. He sought to redeem his pledge to end wars by forming a League of Nations to keep the peace. In the treaty drawn at the close of the war the first part was a covenant binding the nations in a permanent association for the settlement of international disputes. This treaty, the President offered to the United States Senate for ratification and to his country for approval.

Once again, as in the days of the Napoleonic wars, the people seriously discussed the place of America among the powers of the earth. The Senate refused to ratify the treaty. World politics then became an issue in the campaign of 1920. Though some Americans talked as if the United States could close its doors and windows against all mankind, the victor in the election, Senator Harding, of Ohio, knew better. The election returns were hardly announced before he began to ask the advice of his countrymen on the pressing theme that would not be downed: "What part shall America—first among the nations of the earth in wealth and power—assume at the council table of the world?"

General References

Woodrow Wilson, *The New Freedom*.

C.L. Jones, *The Caribbean Interests of the United States*.

H.P. Willis, *The Federal Reserve*.

C.W. Barron, *The Mexican Problem* (critical toward Mexico).

L.J. de Bekker, *The Plot against Mexico* (against American intervention).

Theodore Roosevelt, *America and the World War*.

E.E. Robinson and V.J. West, *The Foreign Policy of Woodrow Wilson*.

J.S. Bassett, *Our War with Germany*.

Carlton J.H. Hayes, *A Brief History of the Great War*.

J.B. McMaster, *The United States in the World War*.

Research Topics

President Wilson's First Term.—Elson, *History of the United States*, pp. 925-941.

The Underwood Tariff Act.—Ogg, *National Progress* (The American Nation Series), pp. 209-226.

The Federal Reserve System.—Ogg, pp. 228-232.

Trust and Labor Legislation.—Ogg, pp. 232-236.

Legislation Respecting the Territories.—Ogg, pp. 236-245.

American Interests in the Caribbean.—Ogg, pp. 246-265.

American Interests in the Pacific.—Ogg, pp. 304-324.

Mexican Affairs.—Haworth, pp. 388-395; Ogg, pp. 284-304.

The First Phases of the European War.—Haworth, pp. 395-412; Ogg, pp. 325-343.

The Campaign of 1916.—Haworth, pp. 412-418; Ogg, pp. 364-383.

America Enters the War.—Haworth, pp. 422-440; pp. 454-475. Ogg, pp. 384-399; Elson, pp. 951-970.

Mobilizing the Nation.—Haworth, pp. 441-453.

The Peace Settlement.—Haworth, pp. 475-497; Elson, pp. 971-982.

Questions

1. Enumerate the chief financial measures of the Wilson administration. Review the history of banks and currency and give the details of the Federal reserve law.

2. What was the Wilson policy toward trusts? Toward labor?

3. Review again the theory of states' rights. How has it fared in recent years?

4. What steps were taken in colonial policies? In the Caribbean?

5. Outline American-Mexican relations under Wilson.

6. How did the World War break out in Europe?

7. Account for the divided state of opinion in America.

8. Review the events leading up to the War of 1812. Compare them with the events from 1914 to 1917.

9. State the leading principles of international law involved and show how they were violated.

10. What American rights were assailed in the submarine campaign?

11. Give Wilson's position on the *Lusitania* affair.

12. How did the World War affect the presidential campaign of 1916?

13. How did Germany finally drive the United States into war?

14. State the American war aims given by the President.

15. Enumerate the measures taken by the government to win the war.

16. Review the part of the navy in the war. The army.

17. How were the terms of peace formulated?

18. Enumerate the principal results of the war.

19. Describe the League of Nations.

20. Trace the fate of the treaty in American politics.

21. Can there be a policy of isolation for America?

APPENDIX

CONSTITUTION OF THE UNITED STATES

WE the people of the United States, in order to form a more perfect union, establish justice, insure domestic tranquillity, provide for the common defence, promote the general welfare, and secure the blessings of liberty to ourselves and our posterity, do ordain and establish this Constitution for the United States of America.

ARTICLE I

SECTION 1. All legislative powers herein granted shall be vested in a Congress of the United States, which shall consist of a Senate and House of Representatives.

SECTION 2. 1. The House of Representatives shall be composed of members chosen every second year by the people of the several States, and the electors in each State shall have the qualifications requisite for electors of the most numerous branch of the State legislature.

2. No person shall be a representative who shall not have attained to the age of twenty-five years, and been seven years a citizen of the United States, and who shall not, when elected, be an inhabitant of that State in which he shall be chosen.

3. Representatives and direct taxes[3] shall be apportioned among the several States which may be included within this Union, according to their respective numbers, which shall be determined by adding to the whole number of free persons, including those bound to service for a term of years, and excluding Indians not taxed, three-fifths of all other persons.[3] The actual enumeration shall be made within three years after the first meeting of the Congress of the United States, and within every subsequent term of ten years, in such manner as they shall by law direct. The number of representatives shall not exceed one for every thirty thousand, but each State shall have at least one representative; and until such enumeration shall be made, the State of New Hampshire shall be entitled to choose three, Massachusetts eight, Rhode Island and Providence Plantations one, Connecticut five, New York six, New Jersey four, Pennsylvania eight, Delaware one, Maryland six, Virginia ten, North Carolina five, South Carolina five, and Georgia three.

4. When vacancies happen in the representation from any State, the executive authority thereof shall issue writs of election to fill such vacancies.

5. The House of Representatives shall choose their speaker and other officers; and shall have the sole power of impeachment.

SECTION 3. 1. The Senate of the United States shall be composed of two senators from each State, chosen by the legislature thereof, for six years; and each senator shall have one vote.[4]

2. Immediately after they shall be assembled in consequence of the first election, they shall be divided as equally as may be into three classes. The seats of the senators of the first class shall be vacated at the expiration of the second year, of the second class at the expiration of the fourth year, and of the third class at the expiration of the sixth year, so that one-third may be chosen every second year; and if vacancies happen by resignation, or otherwise, during the recess of the legislature of any State, the executive thereof may make temporary appointments until the next meeting of the legislature, which shall then fill such vacancies.[5]

3. No person shall be a senator who shall not have attained to the age of thirty years, and been nine years a citizen of the United States, and who shall not, when elected, be an inhabitant of that State for which he shall be chosen.

4. The Vice-President of the United States shall be President of the Senate, but shall have no vote, unless they be equally divided.

5. The Senate shall choose their other officers, and also a President *pro tempore*, in the absence of the Vice-President, or when he shall exercise the office of President of the United States.

6. The Senate shall have the sole power to try all impeachments. When sitting for that purpose, they shall be on oath or affirmation. When the President of the United States is tried, the chief justice shall preside: And no person shall be convicted without the concurrence of two-thirds of the members present.

7. Judgment in cases of impeachment shall not extend further than to removal from office, and disqualification to hold and enjoy any office of honor, trust, or profit under the United States: but the party convicted shall nevertheless be liable and subject to indictment, trial, judgment, and punishment, according to law.

Section 4. 1. The times, places, and manner of holding elections for senators and representatives, shall be prescribed in each State by the legislature thereof; but the Congress may at any time by law make or alter such regulations, except as to the places of choosing senators.

2. The Congress shall assemble at least once in every year, and such meeting shall be on the first Monday in December, unless they shall by law appoint a different day.

Section 5. 1. Each House shall be the judge of the elections, returns and qualifications of its own members, and a majority of each shall constitute a quorum to do business; but a smaller number may adjourn from day to day, and may be authorized to compel the attendance of absent members, in such manner, and under such penalties as each House may provide.

2. Each House may determine the rules of its proceedings, punish its members for disorderly behaviour, and, with the concurrence of two-thirds, expel a member.

3. Each House shall keep a journal of its proceedings, and from time to time publish the same, excepting such parts as may in their judgment require secrecy; and the yeas and nays of the members of either House on any question shall, at the desire of one-fifth of those present, be entered on the journal.

4. Neither House, during the session of Congress, shall, without the consent of the other, adjourn for more than three days, nor to any other place than that in which the two Houses shall be sitting.

Section 6. 1. The senators and representatives shall receive a compensation for their services, to be ascertained by law, and paid out of the Treasury of the United States. They shall in all cases, except treason, felony, and breach of the peace, be privileged from arrest during their attendance at the sessions of their respective Houses, and in going to and returning from the same; and, for any speech or debate in either House, they shall not be questioned in any other place.

2. No senator or representative shall, during the time for which he was elected, be appointed to any civil office under the authority of the United States, which shall have been created, or the emoluments whereof shall have been increased during such time; and no person, holding any office under the United States, shall be a member of either House during his continuance in office.

Section 7. 1. All bills for raising revenue shall originate in the House of Representatives; but the Senate may propose or concur with amendments as on other bills.

2. Every bill, which shall have passed the House of Representatives; and the Senate, shall, before it become a law, be presented to the President of the United States; if he approve he shall sign it, but if not he shall return it with his objections to that House, in which it shall have originated, who shall enter the objections at large on their journal, and proceed to reconsider it. If after such reconsideration two-thirds of that House shall agree to pass the bill, it shall be sent, together with the objections, to the other House, by which it shall likewise be reconsidered, and if approved by two-thirds of that House, it shall become a

law. But in all such cases the votes of both Houses shall be determined by yeas and nays, and the names of the persons voting for and against the bill shall be entered on the journal of each House respectively. If any bill shall not be returned by the President within ten days (Sundays excepted) after it shall have been presented to him, the same shall be a law, in like manner as if he had signed it, unless the Congress by their adjournment prevent its return, in which case it shall not be a law.

3. Every order, resolution, or vote to which the concurrence of the Senate and House of Representatives may be necessary (except on a question of adjournment) shall be presented to the President of the United States and before the same shall take effect, shall be approved by him, or being disapproved by him, shall be repassed by two-thirds of the Senate and House of Representatives, according to the rules and limitations prescribed in the case of a bill.

SECTION 8. The Congress shall have power: 1. To lay and collect taxes, duties, imposts, and excises, to pay the debts and provide for the common defence and general welfare of the United States; but all duties, imposts, and excises shall be uniform throughout the United States;

2. To borrow money on the credit of the United States;

3. To regulate commerce with foreign nations, and among the several States, and with the Indian tribes;

4. To establish an uniform rule of naturalization, and uniform laws on the subject of bankruptcies throughout the United States;

5. To coin money, regulate the value thereof, and of foreign coin, and fix the standard of weights and measures;

6. To provide for the punishment of counterfeiting the securities and current coin of the United States;

7. To establish post offices and post roads;

8. To promote the progress of science and useful arts by securing for limited times to authors and inventors the exclusive right to their respective writings and discoveries;

9. To constitute tribunals inferior to the Supreme Court;

10. To define and punish piracies and felonies committed on the high seas, and offences against the law of nations;

11. To declare war, grant letters of marque and reprisal, and make rules concerning captures on land and water;

12. To raise and support armies, but no appropriation of money to that use shall be for a longer term than two years;

13. To provide and maintain a navy;

14. To make rules for the government and regulation of the land and naval forces;

15. To provide for calling forth the militia to execute the laws of the Union, suppress insurrections, and repel invasions;

16. To provide for organizing, arming, and disciplining the militia, and for governing such part of them as may be employed in the service of the United States, reserving to the States respectively the appointment of the officers, and the authority of training the militia according to the discipline prescribed by Congress.

17. To exercise exclusive legislation in all cases whatsoever, over such district (not exceeding ten miles square) as may, by cession of particular States and the acceptance of Congress, become the seat of the

government of the United States, and to exercise like authority over all places purchased by the consent of the legislature of the State in which the same shall be, for the erection of forts, magazines, arsenals, dock-yards, and other needful buildings;—and

18. To make all laws which shall be necessary and proper for carrying into execution the foregoing powers, and all other powers vested by this Constitution in the government of the United States, or in any department or officer thereof.

SECTION 9. 1. The migration or importation of such persons as any of the States now existing shall think proper to admit, shall not be prohibited by the Congress prior to the year one thousand eight hundred and eight, but a tax or duty may be imposed on such importation, not exceeding ten dollars for each person.

2. The privilege of the writ of *habeas corpus* shall not be suspended, unless when in cases of rebellion or invasion the public safety may require it.

3. No bill of attainder or *ex post facto* law shall be passed.

4. No capitation, or other direct, tax shall be laid, unless in proportion to the census or enumeration hereinbefore directed to be taken.[6]

5. No tax or duty shall be laid on articles exported from any State.

6. No preference shall be given by any regulation of commerce or revenue to the ports of one State over those of another: nor shall vessels bound to, or from, one State, be obliged to enter, clear, or pay duties in another.

7. No money shall be drawn from the Treasury, but in consequence of appropriations made by law; and a regular statement and account of the receipts and expenditures of all public money shall be published from time to time.

8. No title of nobility shall be granted by the United States; and no person, holding any office of profit or trust under them, shall, without the consent of the Congress, accept of any present, emolument, office, or title, of any kind whatever, from any king, prince, or foreign State.

SECTION 10. 1. No State shall enter into any treaty, alliance, or confederation; grant letters of marque and reprisal; coin money; emit bills of credit; make anything but gold and silver coin a tender in payment of debts; pass any bill of attainder, *ex post facto* law, or law impairing the obligation of contracts; or grant any title of nobility.

2. No State shall, without the consent of the Congress, lay any imposts or duties on imports or exports, except what may be absolutely necessary for executing its inspection laws: and the net produce of all duties and imposts, laid by any State on imports or exports, shall be for the use of the Treasury of the United States; and all such laws shall be subject to the revision and control of the Congress.

3. No State shall, without the consent of Congress, lay any duty of tonnage, keep troops, or ships of war in time of peace, enter into any agreement or compact with another State, or with a foreign power, or engage in war unless actually invaded, or in such imminent danger as will not admit of delay.

ARTICLE II

SECTION 1. 1. The executive power shall be vested in a President of the United States of America. He shall hold his office during the term of four years, and, together with the Vice-President, chosen for the same term, be elected, as follows:

2. Each State shall appoint, in such manner as the legislature thereof may direct, a number of electors, equal to the whole number of senators and representatives to which the State may be entitled in the

Congress; but no senator or representative, or person holding an office of trust or profit under the United States, shall be appointed an elector.[7] The electors shall meet in their respective States, and vote by ballot for two persons, of whom one at least shall not be an inhabitant of the same State with themselves. And they shall make a list of all the persons voted for, and of the number of votes for each; which list they shall sign and certify, and transmit sealed to the seat of the government of the United States, directed to the president of the Senate. The President of the Senate shall, in the presence of the Senate and House of Representatives, open all the certificates, and the votes shall then be counted. The person having the greatest number of votes shall be the President, if such number be a majority of the whole number of electors appointed; and if there be more than one who have such majority, and have an equal number of votes, then the House of Representatives shall immediately choose by ballot one of them for President; and if no person have a majority, then from the five highest on the list the said House shall in like manner choose the President. But in choosing the President, the votes shall be taken by States, the representation from each State having one vote; a quorum for this purpose shall consist of a member or members from two-thirds of the States and a majority of all the States shall be necessary to a choice. In every case, after the choice of the President, the person having the greatest number of votes of the electors shall be the Vice-President. But if there should remain two or more who have equal votes, the Senate shall choose from them by ballot the Vice-President.[8]

3. The Congress may determine the time of choosing the electors, and the day on which they shall give their votes; which day shall be the same throughout the United States.

4. No person except a natural born citizen, or a citizen of the United States, at the time of the adoption of this Constitution, shall be eligible to the office of President; neither shall any person be eligible to that office who shall not have attained to the age of thirty-five years, and been fourteen years a resident within the United States.

5. In case of the removal of the President from office, or of his death, resignation, or inability to discharge the powers and duties of the said office, the same shall devolve on the Vice-President, and the Congress may by law provide for the case of removal, death, resignation, or inability both of the President and Vice-President, declaring what officer shall then act as President, and such officer shall act accordingly, until the disability be removed, or a President shall be elected.

6. The President shall, at stated times, receive for his services a compensation, which shall neither be increased nor diminished during the period for which he shall have been elected, and he shall not receive within that period any other emolument from the United States, or any of them.

7. Before he enter on the execution of his office, he shall take the following oath or affirmation:—"I do solemnly swear (or affirm) that I will faithfully execute the office of President of the United States, and will to the best of my ability, preserve, protect, and defend the Constitution of the United States."

SECTION 2. 1. The President shall be commander-in-chief of the army and navy of the United States, and of the militia of the several States, when called into the actual service of the United States; he may require the opinion, in writing, of the principal officer in each of the executive departments, upon any subject relating to the duties of their respective offices, and he shall have power to grant reprieves and pardons for offences against the United States, except in cases of impeachment.

2. He shall have power, by and with the advice and consent of the Senate, to make treaties, provided two-thirds of the senators present concur; and he shall nominate, and by and with the advice and consent of the Senate, shall appoint ambassadors, other public ministers and consuls, judges of the Supreme Court, and all other officers of the United States, whose appointments are not herein otherwise provided for, and which shall be established by law: but the Congress may by law vest the appointment of such inferior officers, as they think proper, in the President alone, in the courts of law, or in the heads of departments.

3. The President shall have power to fill all vacancies that may happen during the recess of the Senate, by granting commissions which shall expire at the end of their next session.

SECTION 3. He shall from time to time give to the Congress information on the state of the Union, and recommend to their consideration such measures as he shall judge necessary and expedient; he may, on extraordinary occasions, convene both Houses, or either of them, and in case of disagreement between them, with respect to the time of adjournment, he may adjourn them to such time as he shall think proper; he shall receive ambassadors and other public ministers; he shall take care that the laws be faithfully executed, and shall commission all the officers of the United States.

SECTION 4. The President, Vice-President, and all civil officers of the United States shall be removed from office on impeachment for, and conviction of, treason, bribery, or other high crimes and misdemeanors.

ARTICLE III

SECTION 1. The judicial power of the United States shall be vested in one Supreme Court, and in such inferior courts as the Congress may from time to time ordain and establish. The judges, both of the Supreme and inferior courts, shall hold their offices during good behaviour, and shall, at stated times, receive for their services a compensation, which shall not be diminished during their continuance in office.

SECTION 2. 1. The judicial power shall extend to all cases, in law and equity, arising under this Constitution, the laws of the United States, and treaties made, or which shall be made, under their authority;—to all cases affecting ambassadors, other public ministers and consuls;—to all cases of admiralty and maritime jurisdiction;—to controversies to which the United States shall be a party;—to controversies between two or more States;—between a State and citizens of another State;[9]—between citizens of different States;—between citizens of the same State claiming lands under grants of different States;—and between a State, or the citizens thereof, and foreign States, citizens, or subjects.

2. In all cases affecting ambassadors, other public ministers and consuls and those in which a State shall be a party, the Supreme Court shall have original jurisdiction. In all the other cases before mentioned, the Supreme Court shall have appellate jurisdiction, both as to law and fact, with such exceptions and under such regulations as the Congress shall make.

3. The trial of all crimes, except in cases of impeachment, shall be by jury; and such trial shall be held in the State where the said crimes shall have been committed; but when not committed within any State, the trial shall be at such place or places as the Congress may by law have directed.

SECTION 3. 1. Treason against the United States shall consist only in levying war against them, or in adhering to their enemies, giving them aid and comfort. No person shall be convicted of treason unless on the testimony of two witnesses to the same overt act, or on confession in open court.

2. The Congress shall have power to declare the punishment of treason, but no attainder of treason shall work corruption of blood or forfeiture except during the life of the person attainted.

ARTICLE IV

SECTION 1. Full faith and credit shall be given in each State to the public acts, records, and judicial proceedings of every other State. And the Congress may by general laws prescribe the manner in which such acts, records, and proceedings shall be proved, and the effect thereof.

SECTION 2. 1. The citizens of each State shall be entitled to all privileges and immunities of citizens in the several States.

2. A person charged in any State with treason, felony, or other crime, who shall flee from justice, and be found in another State, shall on demand of the executive authority of the State from which he fled, be delivered up, to be removed to the State having jurisdiction of the crime.

3. No person held to service or labor in one State, under the laws thereof, escaping into another, shall, in consequence of any law or regulation therein, be discharged from such service or labor, but shall be delivered up on claim of the party to whom such service or labor may be due.

SECTION 3. 1. New States may be admitted by the Congress into this Union; but no new State shall be formed or erected within the jurisdiction of any other State; nor any State be formed by the junction of two or more States, or parts of States, without the consent of the legislatures of the States concerned as well as of the Congress.

2. The Congress shall have power to dispose of and make all needful rules and regulations respecting the territory or other property belonging to the United States; and nothing in this Constitution shall be so construed as to prejudice any claims, of the United States, or of any particular State.

SECTION 4. The United States shall guarantee to every State in this Union a republican form of government, and shall protect each of them against invasion; and on application of the legislature, or of the executive (when the legislature cannot be convened), against domestic violence.

ARTICLE V

The Congress, whenever two-thirds of both Houses shall deem it necessary, shall propose amendments to this Constitution, or, on the application of the legislatures of two-thirds of the several States, shall call a convention for proposing amendments, which, in either case, shall be valid to all intents and purposes as part of this Constitution, when ratified by the legislatures of three-fourths of the several States, or by conventions in three-fourths thereof, as the one or the other mode of ratification may be proposed by the Congress; provided that no amendment which may be made prior to the year one thousand eight hundred and eight shall in any manner affect the first and fourth clauses in the ninth Section of the first article; and that no State, without its consent, shall be deprived of its equal suffrage in the Senate.

ARTICLE VI

1. All debts contracted and engagements entered into, before the adoption of this Constitution, shall be as valid against the United States under this Constitution, as under the Confederation.

2. This Constitution and the laws of the United States which shall be made in pursuance thereof and all treaties made, or which shall be made, under the authority of the United States, shall be the supreme law of the land; and the judges in every State shall be bound thereby, anything in the Constitution or laws of any State to the contrary notwithstanding.

3. The senators and representatives before mentioned, and the members of the several State legislatures, and all executive and judicial officers, both of the United States and of the several States, shall be bound by oath or affirmation to support this Constitution; but no religious test shall ever be required as a qualification to any office or public trust under the United States.

ARTICLE VII

The ratification of the conventions of nine States shall be sufficient for the establishment of this Constitution between the States so ratifying the same.

Done in Convention by the unanimous consent of the States present the seventeenth day of September in the year of our Lord one thousand seven hundred and eighty-seven and of the independence of the United States of America the twelfth. In witness whereof we have hereunto subscribed our names,

G°. WASHINGTON—
Presidt. and Deputy from Virginia

[and thirty-eight members from all the States except Rhode Island.]

Articles in addition to, and amendment of, the Constitution of the United States of America, proposed by Congress, and ratified by the legislatures of the several States pursuant to the fifth article of the original Constitution.

ARTICLE I[10]

Congress shall make no law respecting an establishment of religion, or prohibiting the free exercise thereof; or abridging the freedom of speech, or of the press; or the right of the people peaceably to assemble, and to petition the government for a redress of grievances.

ARTICLE II

A well regulated militia, being necessary to the security of a free State, the right of the people to keep and bear arms shall not be infringed.

ARTICLE III

No soldier shall, in time of peace, be quartered in any house, without the consent of the owner, nor in time of war, but in a manner to be prescribed by law.

ARTICLE IV

The right of the people to be secure in their persons, houses, papers, and effects, against unreasonable searches and seizures, shall not be violated, and no warrants shall issue, but upon probable cause, supported by oath or affirmation, and particularly describing the place to be searched, and the persons or things to be seized.

ARTICLE V

No person shall be held to answer for a capital, or otherwise infamous crime, unless on a presentment or indictment of a grand jury, except in cases arising in the land or naval forces, or in the militia, when in actual service in time of war or public danger; nor shall any person be subject for the same offence to be twice put in jeopardy of life or limb; nor shall be compelled in any criminal case to be a witness against himself; nor be deprived of life, liberty, or property, without due process of law; nor shall private property be taken for public use, without just compensation.

ARTICLE VI

In all criminal prosecutions, the accused shall enjoy the right to a speedy and public trial, by an impartial jury of the State and district wherein the crime shall have been committed, which district shall have been previously ascertained by law, and to be informed of the nature and cause of the accusation; to be confronted with the witnesses against him; to have compulsory process for obtaining witnesses in his favor, and to have the assistance of counsel for his defence.

ARTICLE VII

In suits at common law, where the value in controversy shall exceed twenty dollars, the right of trial by jury shall be preserved, and no fact tried by a jury shall be otherwise reexamined in any court of the United States, than according to the rules of the common law.

ARTICLE VIII

Excessive bail shall not be required, nor excessive fines imposed, nor cruel and unusual punishments inflicted.

ARTICLE IX

The enumeration in the Constitution, of certain rights, shall not be construed to deny or disparage others retained by the people.

ARTICLE X

The powers not delegated to the United States by the Constitution, nor prohibited by it to the States, are reserved to the States respectively, or to the people.

ARTICLE XI[11]

The judicial power of the United States shall not be construed to extend to any suit in law or equity, commenced or prosecuted against one of the United States by citizens of another State, or by citizens or subjects of any foreign State.

ARTICLE XII[12]

The electors shall meet in their respective States, and vote by ballot for President and Vice-President, one of whom at least shall not be an inhabitant of the same State with themselves; they shall name in their ballots the person voted for as President, and in distinct ballots the person voted for as Vice-President, and they shall make distinct lists of all persons voted for as President, and of all persons voted for as Vice-President, and of the number of votes for each, which lists they shall sign and certify, and transmit sealed to the seat of the government of the United States, directed to the President of the Senate;—The President of the Senate shall, in presence of the Senate and House of Representatives, open all the certificates and the votes shall then be counted;—The person having the greatest number of votes for President, shall be the President, if such number be a majority of the whole number of electors appointed; and if no person have such majority, then from the persons having the highest numbers not exceeding three on the list of those voted for as President, the House of Representatives shall choose immediately, by ballot, the President. But in choosing the President, the votes shall be taken by States, the representation from each State having one vote; a quorum for this purpose shall consist of a member or members from two-thirds of the States, and a majority of all the States shall be necessary to a choice. And if the House of Representatives shall not choose a President whenever the right of choice shall devolve upon them, before the fourth day of March next following, then the Vice-President shall act as President, as in the case of the death or other constitutional disability of the President. The person having the greatest number of votes as Vice-President, shall be the Vice-President, if such number be a majority of the whole number of electors appointed, and if no person have a majority, then from the two highest members on the list, the Senate shall choose the Vice-President; a quorum for the purpose shall consist of two-thirds of the whole number of senators, and a majority of the whole number shall be necessary to a choice. But no person constitutionally ineligible to the office of President shall be eligible to that of Vice-President of the United States.

ARTICLE XIII[13]

Section 1. Neither slavery nor involuntary servitude, except as a punishment for crime whereof the party shall have been duly convicted, shall exist within the United States, or any place subject to their jurisdiction.

Section 2. Congress shall have power to enforce this article by appropriate legislation.

Article XIV[14]

Section 1. All persons born or naturalized in the United States, and subject to the jurisdiction thereof, are citizens of the United States and of the State wherein they reside. No State shall make or enforce any law which shall abridge the privileges or immunities of citizens of the United States; nor shall any State deprive any person of life, liberty, or property without due process of law; nor deny to any person within its jurisdiction the equal protection of the laws.

Section 2. Representatives shall be apportioned among the several States according to their respective numbers, counting the whole number of persons in each State, excluding Indians not taxed. But when the right to vote at any election for the choice of electors for President and Vice-President of the United States, representatives in Congress, the executive and judicial officers of a State, or the members of the legislature thereof, is denied to any of the male inhabitants of such State, being twenty-one years of age, and citizens of the United States, or in any way abridged, except for participation in rebellion or other crime, the basis of representation therein shall be reduced in the proportion which the number of such male citizens shall bear to the whole number of male citizens twenty-one years of age in such State.

Section 3. No person shall be a senator or representative in Congress, or elector of President and Vice-President, or hold any office, civil or military, under the United States, or under any State, who, having previously taken an oath, as a member of Congress, or as an officer of the United States, or as a member of any State legislature, or as an executive or judicial officer of any State, to support the Constitution of the United States, shall have engaged in insurrection or rebellion against the same, or given aid or comfort to the enemies thereof. But Congress may by two-thirds vote of each House, remove such disability.

Section 4. The validity of the public debt of the United States, authorized by law, including debts incurred for payment of pensions and bounties for services in suppressing insurrection or rebellion, shall not be questioned. But neither the United States nor any State shall assume or pay any debt or obligation incurred in aid of insurrection or rebellion against the United States, or any claim for the loss or emancipation of any slave; but all such debts, obligations, and claims shall be held illegal and void.

Section 5. The Congress shall have power to enforce, by appropriate legislation, the provisions of this article.

Article XV[15]

Section 1. The right of citizens of the United States to vote shall not be denied or abridged by the United States or by any State on account of race, color, or previous condition of servitude.

Section 2. The Congress shall have power to enforce this article by appropriate legislation.

Article XVI[16]

The Congress shall have power to lay and collect taxes on incomes, from whatever source derived, without apportionment among the several States, and without regard to any census or enumeration.

Article XVII[17]

The Senate of the United States shall be composed of two senators from each State, elected by the people thereof, for six years; and each senator shall have one vote. The electors in each State shall have the qualifications requisite for electors of the most numerous branch of the State legislature.

When vacancies happen in the representation of any State in the Senate, the executive authority of each State shall issue writs of election to fill such vacancies: *Provided* that the legislature of any State may empower the executive thereof to make temporary appointments until the people fill the vacancies by election as the legislature may direct.

This amendment shall not be so construed as to effect the election or term of any senator chosen before it becomes valid as part of the Constitution.

Article XVIII[18]

Section 1. After one year from the ratification of this article the manufacture, sale, or transportation of intoxicating liquors within, the importation thereof into, or the exportation thereof from the United States and all territory subject to the jurisdiction thereof for beverage purposes is hereby prohibited.

Section 2. The Congress and the several States shall have concurrent power to enforce this article by appropriate legislation.

Section 3. This article shall be inoperative unless it shall have been ratified as an amendment to the Constitution by the legislatures of the several States, as provided in the Constitution, within seven years from the date of the submission hereof to the States by the Congress.

Article XIX[19]

The right of citizens of the United States to vote shall not be denied or abridged by the United States or any State on account of sex.

The Congress shall have power to enforce this article by appropriate legislation.

POPULATION OF THE UNITED STATES, BY STATES: 1920, 1910, 1900

States	Population		
	1920	1910	1900
United States	105,708,771	91,972,266	75,994,575
Alabama	2,348,174	2,138,093	1,828,697
Arizona	333,903	204,354	122,931
Arkansas	1,752,204	1,574,449	1,311,564
California	3,426,861	2,377,549	1,485,053
Colorado	939,629	799,024	539,700
Connecticut	1,380,631	1,114,756	908,420

Delaware	223,003	202,322	184,735
District of Columbia	437,571	331,069	278,718
Florida	968,470	752,619	528,542
Georgia	2,895,832	2,609,121	2,216,331
Idaho	431,866	325,594	161,772
Illinois	6,485,280	5,638,591	4,821,550
Indiana	2,930,390	2,700,876	2,516,462
Iowa	2,404,021	2,224,771	2,231,853
Kansas	1,769,257	1,690,949	1,470,495
Kentucky	2,416,630	2,289,905	2,147,174
Louisiana	1,798,509	1,656,388	1,381,625
Maine	768,014	742,371	694,466
Maryland	1,449,661	1,295,346	1,188,044
Massachusetts	3,852,356	3,366,416	2,805,346
Michigan	3,668,412	2,810,173	2,420,982
Minnesota	2,387,125	2,075,708	1,751,394
Mississippi	1,790,618	1,797,114	1,551,270
Missouri	3,404,055	3,293,335	3,106,665
Montana	548,889	376,053	243,329
Nebraska	1,296,372	1,192,214	1,066,300
Nevada	77,407	81,875	42,335
New Hampshire	443,407	430,572	411,588
New Jersey	3,155,900	2,537,167	1,883,669
New Mexico	360,350	327,301	195,310
New York	10,384,829	9,113,614	7,268,894
North Carolina	2,559,123	2,206,287	1,893,810
North Dakota	645,680	577,056	319,146
Ohio	5,759,394	4,767,121	4,157,545
Oklahoma	2,028,283	1,657,155	790,391
Oregon	783,389	672,765	413,536
Pennsylvania	8,720,017	7,665,111	6,302,115
Rhode Island	604,397	542,610	428,556
South Carolina	1,683,724	1,515,400	1,340,316
South Dakota	636,547	583,888	401,570
Tennessee	2,337,885	2,184,789	2,020,616
Texas	4,663,228	3,896,542	3,048,710
Utah	449,396	373,351	276,749
Vermont	352,428	355,956	343,641
Virginia	2,309,187	2,061,612	1,854,184
Washington	1,356,621	1,141,990	518,103
West Virginia	1,463,701	1,221,119	958,800
Wisconsin	2,632,067	2,333,860	2,069,042
Wyoming	194,402	145,965	92,531

APPENDIX

TABLE OF PRESIDENTS

	Name	State	Party	Year in Office	Vice-President
1	George Washington	Va.	Fed.	1789-1797	John Adams
2	John Adams	Mass.	Fed.	1797-1801	Thomas Jefferson
3	Thomas Jefferson	Va.	Rep.	1801-1809	Aaron Burr George Clinton
4	James Madison	Va.	Rep.	1809-1817	George Clinton Elbridge Gerry
5	James Monroe	Va.	Rep.	1817-1825	Daniel D. Tompkins
6	John Q. Adams	Mass.	Rep.	1825-1829	John C. Calhoun
7	Andrew Jackson	Tenn.	Dem.	1829-1837	John C. Calhoun Martin Van Buren
8	Martin Van Buren	N.Y.	Dem.	1837-1841	Richard M. Johnson
9	Wm. H. Harrison	Ohio	Whig	1841-1841	John Tyler
10	John Tyler[20]	Va.	Whig	1841-1845	
11	James K. Polk	Tenn.	Dem.	1845-1849	George M. Dallas
12	Zachary Taylor	La.	Whig	1849-1850	Millard Fillmore
13	Millard Fillmore[20]	N.Y.	Whig	1850-1853	
14	Franklin Pierce	N.H.	Dem.	1853-1857	William R. King
15	James Buchanan	Pa.	Dem.	1857-1861	J.C. Breckinridge
16	Abraham Lincoln	Ill.	Rep.	1861-1865	Hannibal Hamlin Andrew Johnson
17	Andrew Johnson[20]	Tenn.	Rep.	1865-1869	
18	Ulysses S. Grant	Ill.	Rep.	1869-1877	Schuyler Colfax Henry Wilson
19	Rutherford B. Hayes	Ohio	Rep.	1877-1881	Wm. A. Wheeler
20	James A. Garfield	Ohio	Rep.	1881-1881	Chester A. Arthur
21	Chester A. Arthur[20]	N.Y.	Rep.	1881-1885	
22	Grover Cleveland	N.Y.	Dem.	1885-1889	Thomas A. Hendricks
23	Benjamin Harrison	Ind.	Rep.	1889-1893	Levi P. Morton
24	Grover Cleveland	N.Y.	Dem.	1893-1897	Adlai E. Stevenson

25	William McKinley	Ohio	Rep.	1897-1901	Garrett A. Hobart Theodore Roosevelt
26	Theodore Roosevelt[20]	N.Y.	Rep.	1901-1909	Chas. W. Fairbanks
27	William H. Taft	Ohio	Rep.	1909-1913	James S. Sherman
28	Woodrow Wilson	N.J.	Dem.	1913-1921	Thomas R. Marshall
29	Warren G. Harding	Ohio	Rep.	1921-	Calvin Coolidge

POPULATION OF THE OUTLYING POSSESSIONS: 1920 AND 1910

AREA	1920	1910
United States with outlying possessions	117,857,509	101,146,530
Continental United States	105,708,771	91,972,266
Outlying Possessions	12,148,738	9,174,264
Alaska	54,899	64,356
American Samoa	8,056	7,251[21]
Guam	13,275	11,806
Hawaii	255,912	191,909
Panama Canal Zone	22,858	62,810[21]
Porto Rico	1,299,809	1,118,012
Military and naval, etc., service abroad	117,238	55,608
Philippine Islands	10,350,640[22]	7,635,426[23]
Virgin Islands of the United States	26,051[24]	27,086[25]

FOOTNOTES:

[1] North Carolina ratified in November, 1789, and Rhode Island in May, 1790.

[2] To prevent a repetition of such an unfortunate affair, the twelfth amendment of the Constitution was adopted in 1804, changing slightly the method of electing the President.

[3] Partly superseded by the 14th Amendment, p. 639.

[4] See the 17th Amendment, p. 641.

[5] *Ibid.*, p. 641.

[6] See the 16th Amendment, p. 640.

[7] The following paragraph was in force only from 1788 to 1803.

[8] Superseded by the 12th Amendment, p. 638.

[9] See the 11th Amendment, p. 638.

[10] First ten amendments proposed by Congress, Sept. 25, 1789. Proclaimed to be in force Dec. 15, 1791.

[11] Proposed Sept. 5, 1794. Declared in force January 8, 1798.

[12] Adopted in 1804.

[13] Adopted in 1865.

[14] Adopted in 1868.

[15] Proposed February 27, 1869. Declared in force March 30, 1870.

[16] Passed July, 1909; proclaimed February 25, 1913.

[17] Passed May, 1912, in lieu of paragraph one, Section 3, Article I, of the Constitution and so much of paragraph two of the same Section as relates to the filling of vacancies; proclaimed May 31, 1913.

[18] Ratified January 16, 1919.

[19] Ratified August 26, 1920.

[20] Promoted from the vice-presidency on the death of the president.

[21] Population in 1912.

[22] Population in 1918.

[23] Population in 1903.

[24] Population in 1917.

[25] Population in 1911.

THE END

Made in the USA
Middletown, DE
22 July 2018